POETRY AND THE FATE OF THE SENSES

POETRY AND THE FATE

OF THE SENSES

SUSAN STEWART

THE UNIVERSITY OF CHICAGO PRESS
CHICAGO AND LONDON

Susan Stewart is the Regan Professor of English at the University of Pennsylvania and a MacArthur fellow. She is the author of three books of poems, most recently *The Forest*, as well as many works of literary and art criticism, including *On Longing: Narratives of the Miniature, the Gigantic, the Souvenir, the Collection* and *Crimes of Writing: Problems in the Containment of Representation.*

The University of Chicago Press, Chicago 60637
The University of Chicago Press, Ltd., London
© 2002 by The University of Chicago
All rights reserved. Published 2002
Printed in the United States of America
11 10 09 08 07 06 05 04 03 02   5 4 3 2 1

ISBN (cloth): 0-226-77413-9
ISBN (paper): 0-226-77414-7

Library of Congress Cataloging-in-Publication Data
Stewart, Susan (Susan A.), 1952–
    Poetry and the fate of the senses / Susan Stewart.
      p.   cm.
    Includes bibliographical references (p.   ) and index.
    ISBN 0-226-77413-9 — ISBN 0-226-77414-7 (pbk.)
    1. Lyric poetry—History and criticism.   2. Poetry—History and criticism.
  3. Poetics.   I. Title.
    PN1356 .S74   2002
    809.1—dc21   2001005413

In memory, H.E.S., 1926–1999

CONTENTS

This is a book about poetic making of all kinds, and particularly about such making by means of measured language. My method has been to explain to myself and to the reader a general theory of poetic forms—forms arising out of sense experience and producing, as they make sense experience intelligible to others, intersubjective meaning. I have addressed several broad developments in the history of art, but I have wanted as well to engage individual works phenomenologically as a way of sharing their intentions and furthering their reception.

My emphasis on common human experiences of the senses, facial expression, vocalization of sounds, motion, and rhythm directs the theoretical part of this argument toward, if not universality, a formalism that is meant to reach across various historical and cultural contexts. For the most part, the works I have chosen for discussion are those I have thought about over time and about which I have something to say. Like anyone who writes on poetic forms, I have been restricted as well by the availability of permissions for reproduction. Whenever possible, I have quoted poems in their entirety. There is a necessity to my choices, but it is not absolute, and the book could have been written with a different set of examples. It is my hope that other readers and writers will find this study helpful for the analysis of other bodies of work.

A project of ten years, this book evolved from work with students in poetics, aesthetics, and the history of the lyric at Temple University, the

Tyler School of Art in Rome, the Writing Seminars at the Johns Hopkins University, the University of Pennsylvania, and most recently the University of California at Berkeley. Over that period I benefited from many opportunities to present the work as lectures and conference presentations, and I particularly thank those institutions where I was able to speak of the project at length: the Poetics Program at the State University of New York–Buffalo, the Writers' Workshops at the University of Iowa, the Art History and Communications Departments of the University of Sussex, the Fine Arts Department of the University of New South Wales, and the English Department of the University of South Carolina.

I began much of my research under the auspices of a fellowship from the Getty Center for the History of Art and the Humanities, where I was fortunate to have Alexander Waintrub as my research assistant. A MacArthur Fellowship has made it possible for me to complete the project. From 1996 to 1999, a Lila Wallace Individual Writer's Award gave me funds to continue my research and also to establish a poetry program for adult literacy students in the branches of the Northwest Regional Public Library in Philadelphia. Discussing poems and poetics with these students, who often had an extensive knowledge of oral tradition and at the same time were just learning to read and write, was an invaluable experience for rethinking many of my assumptions about understanding and teaching poetry.

My work was greatly eased by the help of librarians at the University of Pennsylvania, the British Library, the Folklore Society Library at the University of London, the Vatican Library, and the University of California at Berkeley.

My deepest thanks are due to individuals. Anyone who knows Allen Grossman's work on poetics will see its imprint throughout this book, and my debt to him for his suggestions regarding the manuscript is immeasurable. Marjorie Perloff's generous and careful reading of these chapters led to significant changes in the level of detail and texture of the argument, and her enthusiasm for the project has been an ongoing gift. My editors at the University of Chicago Press, Alan Thomas and Randy Petilos, have been unstinting in their support of my work in both poetry and prose. Years of conversation and correspondence regarding literature and art with Susan Howe, Ann Hamilton, Robert Pogue Harrison, Alan Singer, and Brunella Antomarini are woven into every aspect of my thinking. Charles Baxter's engagement with, and collection of, musical nocturnes enriched my research on that genre, as did the work of my colleague at Penn, Jeffrey Kallberg. Robert Harrison's thoughtful reading of the conclusion encouraged me as I was finishing revisions. Yoonmee Chang and Sam Stewart-

Halevy helped create the book's interior images, and Bernie Rhie completed the index. Ann Hamilton deftly shaped most of the book's visual form.

This work is dedicated to the memory of my father, with love and gratitude to my immediate and extended family who carry forward the memory of his person—and it is also dedicated to his memory itself: his vast delight in, and encyclopedic knowledge of, the natural world.

Earlier and substantially different versions of portions of some chapters appeared as essays published as follows: from chapter 2: "Letter on Sound," in *Close Listening: Poetry and the Performed Word,* ed. Charles Bernstein (New York: Oxford University Press, 1998), 29–52; from chapter 3: "Lyric Possession," *Critical Inquiry* 22, no. 1 (Autumn/Winter 1995): 34–63; from chapter 4: "From the Museum of Touch," in *Material Memories,* ed. Marius Kwint (London: Berg, 1999), 17–36; from chapter 5: "Preface to a Lyric History," in *The Uses of Literary History,* ed. Marshall Brown (Durham, N.C.: Duke University Press, 1995), 199–218, and "Traherne's *Centuries,*" in *Centuries' Ends: Narrative Means,* ed. Robert Newman (Stanford, Calif.: Stanford University Press, 1996), 89–113, notes on 328–334.

Sources for chapter frontispieces are as follows. Chapter 1: J. M. W. Turner, *The Beacon Light* (detail), ca. 1835–40. Reprinted by permission of the National Museum of Wales. Chapters 2 and 3: The J. Paul Getty Museum, Malibu, California, Unknown artist, *Sculptural Group of a Seated Poet and Two Sirens* (detail). 350–300 B.C. Chapter 4: Caravaggio, *Doubting Thomas* (detail). Alinari/Art Resource, NY. Chapter 5: Gian Lorenzo Bernini, *Ecstasy of St. Teresa* (detail). S. Maria della Vittoria, Rome, Italy. Alinari/Art Resource, NY. Chapter 6: James MacNeill Whistler, *Nocturne in Black and Gold, the Falling Rocket,* ca. 1875 (detail). © The Detroit Institute of Arts 1989. Chapter 7: Unknown artist, "Execution of Rebels," The Column of Marcus Aurelius, sculpture after A.D. 173. Afterborn: *face to face (writing 2).* Copyright 2000 Ann Hamilton. Photographs courtesy Sean Kelly, New York. (The image was taken in fall 1999 in Alfred New York with Ann Hamilton and was made by placing a pinhole camera in the mouth's cavity and opening the lips to expose the film to light.)

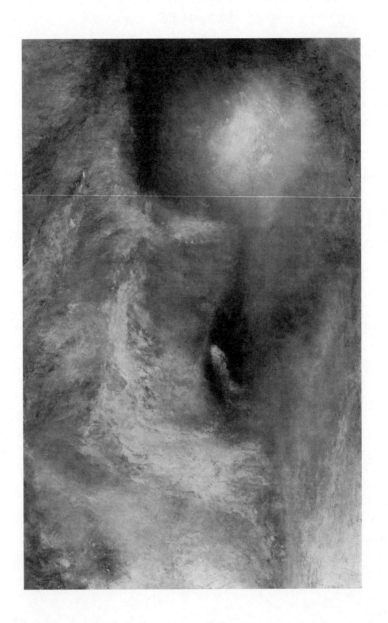

1

In the Darkness

All general privations are great, because they are terrible: *Vacuity, Darkness, Solitude, and Silence.*

—Edmund Burke

I. The Privations of Night and the Origins of *Poiēsis*

What do we fear when, in solitude, we fear absolute darkness? It is not death that we fear, for death cannot be imagined as other than the end of imagining; to fear death in the darkness is to approach the darkness as a veil between worlds and not to encounter the object of fear itself. And it is not danger that we fear, for danger would as well give a force or shape to this terrible absence of force or shape. The darkness presses against us and yet has no boundary; without edge or end, it erases and mutes the limits of our being—not as an expansion, but rather as a contraction, of whatever the mind can hold as an image of the human. It is unbearable, this loneliness of the mind working on its own to maintain the outline, the figure, of the person. Frozen, voiceless, a prisoner without sentence, the mind in the dark has no object to reflect on and no object to limit the endless racing of its reflections. In the end, the fear of the darkness is the fear that the darkness will not end.

It will be the argument of this book that the cultural, or form-giving, work of poetry is to counter the oblivion of darkness. To make such a statement may seem more fancifully "poetic" than true. But it is precisely in material ways that poetry is a force against effacement—not merely for individuals but for communities through time as well. The task of aesthetic production and reception in general is to make visible, tangible, and audible the figures of persons, whether such persons are expressing the particulars of sense impressions or the abstractions of reason or the many ways such particulars and abstractions enter into relations with one another. As metered language, language that retains and projects the force of individual sense experience and yet reaches toward intersubjective meaning, poetry sustains and transforms the threshold between individual and social existence. Poetic making is an anthropomorphic project; the poet undertakes the task of recognition in time—the unending tragic Orphic task of drawing the figure of the other—the figure of the beloved who reciprocally can recognize one's own figure—out of the darkness. To make something where and when before there was nothing. The poet's tragedy lies in the fading of the referent in time, in the impermanence of whatever is grasped. The poet's recompense is the production of a form that enters into the transforming life of language.

In thinking of poetic making as a counter to the oblivion of darkness, we continue, under aesthetic terms, an argument of long concern to Western philosophy. The interdiction against thinking *that which is not* in Plato's *Sophist* is introduced by G. W. F. Hegel in the opening to his *Phenomenology of Mind* as a specific problem of our encounter with the Night:

> Sense-certainty itself has thus to be asked: What is the This? If we take it in the two-fold form of its existence, as the *Now* and as the *Here*, the dialectic it has in it will take a form as intelligible as the This itself. To the question, What is the Now? we reply, for example, the Now is night-time. . . . The Now that is night is kept fixed, i.e. it is treated as what it is given out to be, as something which *is*; but it proves to be rather a something which is *not*. The Now itself no doubt maintains itself, but as what is *not* night; similarly in its relation to the day which the Now is at present, it maintains itself as something that is also not day, or as altogether something negative. This self-maintaining Now is therefore not something immediate but something mediated; for, *qua* something that remains and preserves itself, it is determined through and *by means of* the fact that something else, namely day and night, is *not*. . . . A simple entity of this sort, which is by and through negation, which is neither this nor that, which is *not-this*, and with equal indifference, this as well as that—a

thing of this kind we call a Universal. The Universal is therefore in point of fact the truth of sense-certainty, the true content of sense-experience.[1]

What we find here in embryo is Hegel's position on the ontology of self-consciousness. Human beings cannot know themselves in relation to an external nature that will appear as an endless presentation of particulars, each defined, as a man's being is defined under such conditions, in relation to that which it is *not*—an indefinite definition by negation. And human beings cannot leap to a self-creation by interior, subjective means, either—to declare "I am I," to claim self-coincidence as the grounds for being, is to suffer from a tautology that can only be remedied by the knowledge of its tautological status. The flux of sense impressions has a transitive and intransitive aspect. What propels us outward will also transform us, and it is only by finding means of making sense impressions intelligible to others that we are able to situate ourselves and our experiences within what is universal.

In this process, language has a particular prominence as the means of intersubjective knowledge. Language exists before our individual existence: language, a made thing made of our own nature, is at the same time our vehicle of individuation. When we express our existence in language, when we create objective linguistic forms that are intelligible to others and enduring in time, we literally bring light into the inarticulate world that is the night of preconsciousness and suffering. As we will see, *poiēsis* as figuration relies on the senses of touching, seeing, and hearing that are central to the encounter with the presence of others, the encounter of recognition between persons. These are the senses of face-to-face meetings and they are of great significance in the history of art and the hierarchy of the senses more generally because of their role in the creation of intersubjective experience and meaning. Their capacity for extension, volition, and distantiation in the end contributes to freeing us from the very burden of immediacy, of the overwhelming flux of external stimuli, sense experience in general can impose.

Aristotle had argued in *The Generation of Animals* that sense perception is what gives animals knowledge. All living beings are driven toward the reproduction of life, and sense perception in animals instantiates a movement outward:

> For plants have no other function or activity in their being except the generation of seed, so that since this is done through the coupling of male and female, nature has arranged them together by mingling them. . . . But the animal's function is not only to generate (for that is common to all

living things), but also they all participate in some sort of cognition, some
of them in more, some in less, some in very little at all. For they have perception, and perception is a sort of cognition. Its value or lack of value in
our eyes differs greatly according as we compare it with intelligence or
with the soulless kind of things. Compared with being intelligent, merely
to participate in touch and taste seems like nothing; but compared with a
plant or stone it seems wonderful. One would welcome even this share of
cognition, rather than lie dead and non-existent. It is by perception that
animals differ from things that are merely alive.[2]

The sense perception of animals is the basis of the link between their own
particularity as organisms and the life of the species through reproduction,
and it is as well the ground for their desire for an objective being, an other,
by means of which such reproduction will take place.

According to Hegel, too, only living, transforming things can strive
toward consciousness of themselves, and such striving is dependent on
what is universal in particulars and particular in universals. All beings
striving toward consciousness are motivated by a desire for an object and
are dependent on such an object for self-knowledge. In the allegory of the
master and slave that follows Hegel's discussion of sense certainty, the
master is able to wrest recognition from the slave. But the master does
not see the universal aspect of recognition. Incapable of reciprocating
such recognition, the master is dependent on a practice of destruction—
a practice of demand without transformation that will of course in the
end result in his own death. The slave, however, recognizes not just the
master but also the universal and never-ending task of consciousness;
in work that is both the transformation of nature and the means of self-
transformation and self-overcoming, the slave as *maker* creates himself in
the long path that extends from the night of sense certainty. The slave
does not die with the death of his outward form as does the master—the
slave leaves the mark of his practices in the world and forms a link with
what is universal in human culture.[3]

In *Existence and Existents*, Emmanuel Levinas also discusses the
night in phenomenological terms:

> [W]e could say that the night is the very experience of the *there is*, if the
> term experience were not inapplicable to a situation which involves the
> total exclusion of light. When the forms of things are dissolved in the
> night, the darkness of the night, which is neither an object nor the qual-
> ity of an object, invades like a presence. In the night, where we are riven
> to it, we are not dealing with anything. But this nothing is not that of

pure nothingness. There is no longer *this* or *that;* there is not "something." But this universal absence is in turn a presence, an absolutely unavoidable presence. It is not the dialectical counterpart of absence, and we do not grasp it through a thought. It is immediately there. There is no discourse. Nothing responds to us but this silence; the voice of this silence is understood and frightens like the silence of those infinite spaces Pascal speaks of.[4]

For Levinas, this experience of silence and infinity—that which Blaise Pascal spoke of in his famous pensée "Le Silence éternel de ces espaces infinis m'effraie"—always surrounds the subject as a nondialectical relation. It evokes not the fear of death but the horror of immortality, of an unending "drama of existence." As we consider the form-making capacity of *poiēsis* for the creation of intersubjectivity, Levinas reminds us of another fear, a fear that the necessity of such activity is never-ending; that it will exhaust us and outlive us if it is not met by the acknowledgment and recognition of others. Burke's "privations" were in fact taken from his reading of Virgil's images of Hell.[5]

We can find an account of the shattered human figure in the darkness in the oldest extant Western poems. In Hesiod's *Theogony,* the Night is replete with all that refuses or tears apart the relations between human beings:

Night bore hateful Doom and dark Fate and Death, she bore Sleep, she bore the tribe of Dreams. And secondly gloomy Night bore Cavil and painful Misery, bedded with none of the gods; and the Hesperides, who mind fair golden apples beyond the famed Oceanus, and the trees that bear that fruit; and the Fates she bore, and the mercilessly punishing Furies who prosecute the transgressions of men and gods—never do the goddesses cease from their terrible wrath until they have paid the sinner his due. And baleful Night gave birth to Resentment also, an affliction for mortal men; and after her she bore Deceit and Intimacy, and accursed Old Age, and she bore hard-hearted Strife.

Hateful Strife bore painful Toil,
    Neglect, Starvation, and tearful Pain,
Battles, Combats, Bloodshed and Slaughter,
Quarrels, Lies, Pretences, and Arguments,
Disorder, Disaster—neighbours to each other—
and Oath, who most harms men on earth,
when someone knowingly swears false.[6]

Hesiod creates a catalog of depletions rather than additions, an anti-catalog describing the consequences of darkest night. These consequences have a genealogical relation as each is born out of a prior consequence, and he links them by concatenation and metonymy—the devices of the insomniac's painful racing mind. The final term is the antithesis of poetic making: the oath "most harms men on earth" because it is intended from the outset as a lie; it cleaves the good faith in language by means of which all reality-making discourse proceeds. False oaths and curses are the deepest expression of human alienation; they mark the return of speaking subjects to an unintelligible autonomy—the autonomy of the figure receding back into the darkness.[7]

In the daylight battles of the *Iliad*, Trojans and Greeks are recognizable by the singularity of their individual armor; their faces are hidden and their identities, like their proper names, which the epic singer goes to such lengths to record, are yoked to the long patrimony of their origins. We see some of the consequences of this obligatory armoring of identity in the encounter between Hector and his baby son Astyanax in Book VI of the *Iliad*. As Hector reaches to embrace him, Astyanax does not recognize his father:

> the boy recoiled,
> cringing against his nurse's full breast,
> screaming out at the sight of his own father,
> terrified by the flashing bronze, the horsehair crest,
> the great ridge of the helmet nodding, bristling terror—
> so it struck his eyes. And his loving father laughed,
> his mother laughed as well, and glorious Hector,
> quickly lifting the helmet from his head,
> set it down on the ground, fiery in the sunlight,
> and raising his son he kissed him, tossed him in his arms.[8]

The audience of the epic cannot forget thereafter the human face of Hector's identity beneath his fiery sunlit armor. Whenever a victor strips another's armor, he appropriates the dignity of its symbolism and at the same time breaks into the space of the body, the intimate space of face-to-face encounter, to which, as a killer, he has no rightful claim.

The night work of Book X of the *Iliad* marks a break with the ethics of the rest of the epic action in this regard. The book begins by focusing on one sleepless Greek figure after another: the tide has seemed to turn in favor of the Trojans and Agamemnon cannot fall asleep; his mind is churning, his groans "wrenching his chest and heaving up from his heart" (ll. 10–11). Menelaus, too, cannot sleep, and the two brothers agree to go out separately to find companions to check on the steadfastness of the sentries who guard the ships against the nearby Trojans. Agamemnon awakens Nestor, who complains that typically Agamemnon is doing all the work while lazy and cowardly Menelaus hangs back. But Agamemnon assures him that, although that is a fair description of Menelaus, it is in fact his brother's idea to undertake this night-time excursion. The implication is that this action, however bold, will be more fitting of a coward's tactics than the visible declarations of the sunlit field of battle. The Greek leaders gather more men together and find, to their satisfaction, that their sentries are alert. Emboldened by the commitment of their guard, the Greeks decide to ask for a volunteer to penetrate the enemy lines and bring back intelligence of the Trojan plans. Diomedes volunteers and, as he is allowed to chose a companion, turns to Odysseus to accompany him. Significantly, the two men are then provided with the arms and armor of others; Odysseus is given a fabulous cap with a gleaming chaplet of the teeth of a white-tusked boar that in fact comes to him from his own maternal grandfather through a circuitous route; it has been stolen or borrowed by one warrior after another until this moment when Meriones donates it to him.

Master-minded by a coward, conducted by men in the guise of others' arms and armor and under the cloak of night, the events that follow are in every way *atrocious,* black with fierceness and cruelty. Diomedes and Odysseus hunt down Dolon, their Trojan victim, like an animal; rather than confront him, they conceal themselves as he leaves the safety of the Trojan lines. When he has passed, they chase him down wordlessly and relentlessly, deliberately capturing him alive so that they can press him for intelligence. Odysseus assures the terrified and talkative Dolon that "Death is [his] last worry" (l. 448). But after Dolon has told them where and how they can make the most effective raid on the Trojan forces—by attacking the sleeping Thracian contingent and murdering King Rhesus with the aim of stealing his fine horses—Diomedes reveals the truth: "if I snuff your life out in my hands, / you'll never annoy our Argive lines again" (ll. 521–522). There is no reciprocity in this language of the night. Poor Dolon then receives his second immersion in bad faith. As the Trojan reaches up for the chin of Diomedes to touch his beard in the traditional gesture of supplication, "Diomedes struck him square across the neck— / a flashing hack of the sword—both tendons snapped / and the shrieking head went tumbling in the dust" (ll. 25–27). The Greeks then immediately go about stripping off Dolon's arms and armor and steal to the Thracian camp, where they hack away at the sleeping men, killing the king and taking off his team of horses. A war inside a war, Book X of the *Iliad* illustrates the antinomy of atrocity and recognition. In the darkness all territory is without bound or name, all lines are crossed, all acts are improvisational in their means and ends, and every death is an animal death.[9]

In the Hebrew Scriptures, the opening words of Genesis, which are as well the opening words of the Pentateuch as a whole, establish a relation among light and speech and form that remains paradigmatic for much consequent Western thought about the process of creation: "In the beginning when God created the heavens and the earth, the earth was a formless void and darkness covered the face of the deep, while a wind from God swept over the face of the waters." In the Priestly source for the creation account (as opposed to the Yahwist or "J" source, which forms the other principal account), a technical verb is used to describe God's act of creation (*bara*). This verb designates an activity confined solely to the divinity. It involves no initial material out of which creation proceeds and has no human analogy.[10]

The Greeks use the term $\kappa\acute{o}\sigma\mu o\varsigma$—indicating an order, or the world or universe in its perfect arrangement—to suggest that the universe is a rationally constituted and self-sustaining structure of reality, but the Hebrew Scriptures emphasize the originary power of the Creator, who brings creation out of nothing. The personal relation between Yahweh and his creation is portrayed in the "J" account, according to which Yahweh forms man, suggesting the image of a potter molding clay. The Priestly account emphasizes that God created man by means of uttered commands alone. As in Psalm 33:9, verse 6: "He spoke, and it came to be; he commanded, and it stood forth." Creation by the Word, which is not a sound or concept but an act, event, or verbal expression of sovereignty, became the dominant expression for God's creative labor. Yet of equal importance is the idea that this creation comes out of nothing (2 Macc. 7:28; Rom. 4:17; Heb. 11:3). Forms of life were created existentially over a formless Abyss and hemmed in by indiscernible waters of chaos. Although Genesis itself is not explicit with regard to this idea, verse 2 portrays an uncreated chaos as the presupposition of God's action. God does not have the qualities of a demiurge who built the world from raw materials against which he must struggle or whose resistance he must overcome, as he does, for example, in Gnostic thought. Rather, God commands by absolute freedom, the freedom of the word as an effortless divine creation. In such commanding, an invocation is implied, for God not only brings creatures into being; he also designates their specific nature and assigns to them their specific tasks.[11]

The beginning here is only imaginable retrospectively, with reference to undisclosed dimensions: *al-penei* (upon or over) the surfaces of the heavens, the Earth, the deep. Such forms are not immanent in the void of this initial darkness. The wind as the evidence of God's agency is not formed into articulate sounds until it becomes the speech that arises in the next verse: "Then God said, 'Let there be light'; and there was light." And after the positing of light there is the differentiation of form that proceeds as a consequence of evaluation—from the immediate and formless immersion of wind to the discernment of value or particular qualities: "And God saw that the light was good and God separated the light from the darkness." Finally, the Creator calls the light Day and the darkness Night, not simply naming these states but also summoning them into a continuing existence, for calling is oriented toward future use and not simply an account of what has happened. Darkness, breath and touch, sound, speech, presentation, discernment of relation, figuration and naming: this is the sequence of emergence, the sequence of *poiēsis*, that is the pattern of divine creation in the Hebrew Scriptures; it speaks directly to the continuing experience of bringing form out of a void. The consequent passages on creation—the separation of waters into lower and higher spheres, the separation of the earth and the seas, the creation of the vegetable world and the stars, the creation of the animals and the birds, the creation of wild and domestic animals, the creation of man in the image of God, the creation of men and women—are punctuated by the repeated dicta that evening and morning continue in their cycles and God makes continuous reflective judgments, deciding that what he has made is "good."

Johann Gottfried von Herder's 1782–1783 dialogue, "The Spirit of Hebrew Poetry," comments on these themes of Genesis at some length and with great incisiveness. His two speakers, Alciphron and Euthyphron, are a study in contrasts: the naive but enthusiastic perspective of the young Alciphron continually runs against the more considered views of Euthyphron. Their discussion of the creation is framed as an account of the appearance of light in darkness. Euthyphron mentions that, unlike the Greeks, the Hebrews did not speak of a chaos. Rather, "its place was supplied by a dark gloomy sea, upon which the wind of the Almighty was hovering with an agitating effect." The dialogue continues:

A[lciphron].   The spirit, to which you allude, that brooded over the waste and fathomless abyss, is to me peculiarly striking and never fails to inspire me with awe.

E[uthyphron].   It was to the Orientals the first and most natural image of that which constitutes life, power, impulse in creation: for the idea of a spirit seems originally to have been formed from the feeling of the wind, especially at night, and combined with power, and the sound of a voice.

A.   You remind me of the appearance of an apparition in Job. There is form and yet no form; a gentle whisper, a murmuring like the voice of the wind, but with it also the power of the wind, the energy of the spirit. It raises the hair on end, and rouses all the terrors of the soul. "It harrows up the soul with fear and wonder." [12]

Given that in the classical tradition darkness is so continuously allied with bad faith and rupture in communication and that in Genesis creation follows only when the void is dispersed through the creation of intelligible forms, it is not surprising that Christianity places so much emphasis on the figure of Christ as a light in the darkness and on the appearance of a word; the voice of the wind becomes a voice, an inspirited presence, in the wind. Christ's form mediates the relation between the divine and human countenance. Yet even the light and word of Christ must be recognized by the faithful in order to be visible and audible. The Fourth Gospel begins with an echo of the opening words of Genesis, "In the beginning," and speaks of light shining in the darkness. This theme is continued in 2 Corinthians 4:6: "For it is the God who said [at the dawn of history], 'Let light shine out of darkness,' who has shown us our hearts to give the light of the knowledge of the glory of God in the face of Christ." The Johannine "word" summons presence into a world of time. This imperative of recognition is emphasized particularly in the many carols and hymns of Christmas that emphasize awakening, the star of Bethlehem, and the pun on *son* and *sun* in the darkness: a traditional Welsh carol tells the story of the wise man "Melchior": "Dark the night lay, wild and dreary / Moaned the wind by Melchior's tower, / Sad the sage, while pondering weary / O'er the doom of Judah's power: / When behold, the clouds are parted— / Westward, lo, a light gleams far!" Robert Herrick's seventeenth-century carol says in its second verse, "Dark and dull night, fly hence away, / And give the honour to this day." Richard Crashaw's carol from earlier in the same century, "Summer in Winter," begins, "Gloomy night embraced the place / Where the noble infant lay; / The babe looked up and shewed his face, / In spite of darkness it was day!" [13]

Book 3:1–15 of the Gospel of John draws a parallel between the wise men's recognition of the infant Christ in darkness and the Pharisee Nicodemus's capacity to recognize the adult Christ in darkness: "Now there was a Pharisee named Nicodemus, a leader of the Jews. He came to Jesus by night and said to him, 'Rabbi, we know that you are a teacher who has come from God and no one can do these signs that you do apart from the presence of God.' Jesus answered him, 'Very truly, I tell you, no one can see the kingdom of God without being born from above.'" In the seventeenth-century mystical poet Henry Vaughan's retelling of this encounter in his poem "The Night," a significant transformation is made in the convention of the night as the scene of the dissolution of persons, for Vaughan claims that Nicodemus was able to "know his God by night" since night is in fact a kind of "sacred veil drawn o'er thy [God's] glorious noon." [14] For Vaughan, a state of invisibility within the "deep and dazzling darkness" of God's being is far more productive of identity than the mere visibility of the sunlit world of ordinary existence. He concludes, "O for that night! where I in him / Might live invisible and dim." Vaughan's poem is more of an aubade than it is a night work: it depends on an inversion whereby this world with its "ill-guided" light is completely discounted and the son of God, the light of the world, can be summoned by faith as surely as the sun will rise each morning. Christ's figure mediates and enlightens in every sense both the blank void of the darkness and the face of the human.

Darkness remains, here by reversal, the place of error and shattered being where humans are halted from movement and knowledge. In a state of ignorance, without *gnomen* in the sense of both name and past experience, the mind must attempt to forge connections of intelligibility and recognition that will be no less than the grounds for the creation of one's own consciousness. John Milton, a blind poet counseling a blind hero, wrote powerfully in "Samson Agonistes" of the soul's light in a context of solar eclipse:

> O dark, dark, dark, amid the blaze of noon.
> Irrecoverably dark, total eclipse,
> Without all hope of day! . . .
> The sun to me is dark
> And silent is the moon,
> When she deserts the night
> Hid in her vacant interlunar cave.
> Since light so necessary is to life,
> And almost life itself, if it be true
> That light is in the soul, . . . [15]

These narratives of light in the darkness all record the emergence of the figures and forms of human making from conditions of unintelligibility; they are in this sense narratives of what has had to precede, of the emergence of, the narrative voice itself. In creating images of divine agents for such making, they set forth a space for the appearance of human culture. The Greek word ποίησις *(poiēsis)*, derived from ποιεῖν *(poiein)*, "to make," conveys two kinds of creation: the inspired creation that resembles a godlike power and the difficult material struggle, the τέχνη *(technē)*, of making forms out of the resources available. Poetry's work of creating the figure of the human proceeds by means of imagination and a material engagement with the resources of language; it takes place under a threat of overdetermination (that the Orphic creator might turn back tragically in distrust of himself, inadvertently losing the work through adherence to habit or convention) and a threat of underdetermination (that the freedom of creation could be rooted only in the particular history of the creator, or that the spontaneous and musical effects of the work might overwhelm its capacity to produce a lasting form).

What is the relation, then, of poetic making to other form-giving activities? Like all creative acts, *poiēsis* wrests form from nature without prior knowledge of ends or uses. *Poiēsis* thus exaggerates the possibilities of self-transformation available in all forms of work, for its intention cannot be fully known or totalized. The poet discovers his or her identity as a consequence of form making—the role of the maker is not predetermined by either social convention or instrumental reason. The self is objectified, but not completed, by the presentation of the form. And the form will always be both more and less than a representation of its maker.

Poetic form made of language relies on rhythm and musical effects that are known with our entire bodies, carried forward by poets working out of tradition and carried over by listeners receiving the work. In addition, poetic form relies on effects of meaning that, in their metaphorical and imaginative reach, cannot be taken up completely in any single moment of reception. The semantic dimension of poetry is an open unfolding one, stemming from both composition and reception. No poetic utterance is absorbed by its context or completed in its use; as an enduring form, transmutable and transportable across contexts, the poem is always manifold. Paradoxically, it is the close of artworks that enables the unending open task of such reception. What is this unending task? It is the task of recognition in the light of the other, for every work of *poiēsis* anticipates and is completed by practices of reception.

The poet *intends* toward another, even if the other is the poet apprehending the work in a later time and other space. Because that intention proceeds in time, the objectification of the other is also subject to transformation. Hence, in lyric poetry, especially, the presentation of face-to-face communication is always triangulated. The poet speaks to another in such a way as to make the communication intelligible to more than one person. The communication is not simply intimate: it is constitutive of the social, mutual, intersubjective ground of intimacy itself.[16] It is the kind of thing one knows that others say when they are face-to-face. The great transformation in Greek drama from the presentation of dithyrambic choruses to Aeschylus's introduction of a second actor, enabling a conflict of wills and hence inviting judgment and closure from a third position—that of the audience—grows out of the cultural work of lyric: the work of individuation under intersubjective terms.

Perhaps no one has described the historical work of *poiēsis* as a process of anthropomorphization more vividly than the great early eighteenth-century Neapolitan jurist, rhetorician, and philosopher of history Giambattista Vico. Vico's major treatise, *The New Science* (1744), is rooted in a retrospective myth about the origins of poetry that also links *poiēsis* to an originary anxiety about the absence of form. Here is the story as Vico tells it:

> [W]hen . . . at last the sky fearfully rolled with thunder and flashed with lightning, as could not but follow from the bursting upon the air for the first time of an impression so violent. Thereupon a few giants, who must have been the most robust, and who were dispersed through the forests on the mountain heights where the strongest beasts have their dens, were frightened and astonished by the great effect whose cause they did not know, and raised their eyes and became aware of the sky. And because in such a case the nature of the human mind leads it to attribute its own nature to the effect and because in that state their nature was that of men all robust bodily strength, who expressed their very violent passions by shouting and grumbling, they pictured the sky to themselves as a great animated body, which in that aspect they called Jove, the first god of the so-called greater gentes [peoples], who meant to tell them something by the hiss of his bolts and the clap of his thunder. And thus they began to exercise that natural curiosity which is the daughter of ignorance and the mother of knowledge, and which, opening the mind of man, gives birth to wonder.[17]

In this account of how the earliest humans, living naked in the forest, invented a figure by means of which they could bear their fear of the most powerful forces of nature, Vico conjectures that early peoples "created things according to their own ideas." He goes on to explain how "this [human] creation was infinitely different from that of God. For God, in his purest intelligence, knows things, and, by knowing them, creates them;

but they, in their robust ignorance, did it by virtue of a wholly corporeal imagination. And because it was quite corporeal, they did it with marvelous sublimity; a sublimity such and so great that it excessively perturbed the very persons who by imagining did the creating, for which they were called 'poet,' which is Greek for 'creators.'" [18] Vico explains that the imagination stems from the bodily or "corporeal" senses and is moved to represent itself by anthropomorphizing nature and by giving being to inanimate things. Fashioned from nature as Jove is fashioned by the first humans from their experience of lightning, these "inventions" eventually become narratives. [19] And as narratives harden into ideologies, Vico contends that authorization and legitimation give such ideologies ethical force.

In Vico's thought, poetry serves human ends in the expression of the corporeal senses, in the imaginative reconfiguration of nature through such devices as onomatopoeia, personification, and other modes of projection, and as the coordination of various modes of temporal experience necessarily *preceding* any narrative forms. Following Vico, one could claim that poetry cannot be the *subject* of history, for poetry is necessarily *prior* to history. Poetry expresses the passage from not-knowing to knowing through which we represent the world, including the perspectives of others, to ourselves and those around us. What is given birth, as "the daughter of ignorance" becomes "the mother of knowledge," is human history —the continuity of a continuously transforming human culture.

Vico's interests lie in the direction of a broad and comprehensive theory of the rise and fall of nations as social institutions: their origin, ruin, and revival—his *ricorso* under which the internal stresses of social systems compel them to processes of constant dissolution and rebirth. But for our purposes the central place of poetic thought in his theory is paramount. In Vico's own introduction to his *New Science* he explains: "We find that the principle of these origins both of languages and of letters lies in the fact that the early gentile peoples, by a demonstrated necessity of nature, were poets who spoke in poetic characters. This discovery, which is the master key of this Science, has cost us the persistent research of almost all our literary life, because with our civilized natures we [moderns] cannot at all imagine and can understand only by great toil the poetic nature of these first men. . . . Now the sources of all poetic locution are two: poverty of language and the need to explain and be understood." [20]

Language here is pressured to be in some way commensurate to sense experience and at the same time to be intelligible to others. In Vico's theory the speaking subject as the recipient of the recognition of others is not prior to language: language is the forum within which such a speaking subject emerges. Only when poetic metaphors make available to others the experience of the corporeal senses can the corporeal senses truly appear as integral experiences. The self (and here again the paradigm is the self lost in absolute darkness) is compelled to make forms—including the forms of persons striving to represent their corporeal imaginations to others. This is the situation of the person spoken by sound who becomes the person speaking—the cry of the senses coming forward beyond will is transformed into the person of volition and consequence, thus necessarily a person articulated by speaking and being spoken to. To put it another way, it is the situation of the emergence of subjectivity both ontologically—that is, in general—and historically—that is, in particular. But the reconciliation of this model as a structural problem and a historical practice is not a simple one. Like Hegel's account of the ontology of consciousness, Vico's narrative of the origins of poetry and subjectivity is a retrospective fable about our capacity for the fabular. Poetry is both the *repetition* of an ontological moment and the *ongoing process or work* of enunciation by which that moment is recursively known and carried forward.

For a later thinker such as Friedrich von Schiller, the tensions and interrelations between the senses and abstraction, or what he called the "formal" drive, achieve their most harmonious balance in art making and the capacity we have for play more generally.[21] In the twelfth of his "Letters on the Aesthetic Education of Man," Schiller suggests that through art we are able both to give reality to the necessity of sensuous experience and to bring a diversity of manifestations into harmony. The creation of form is linked to the articulation and affirmation of the individual person in his or her whole humanity: "When therefore the formal impulse holds sway and the pure object acts within us, there is the highest expansion of being, all barriers disappear, and from being the unit of magnitude to which the needy sense confined him, Man has risen to a *unit of idea* embracing the whole realm of phenomena. By this operation we are no more in time, but time, with its complete and infinite succession, is in us. We are no longer individuals, but species."[22] For Schiller, the experience of aesthetic beauty is in this way a means of renewal for individuals and for human life as a whole. Describing how man's humanity constantly is reduced by entering into determinate conditions—conditions of limit posed by our meetings with forces of nature and history—Schiller writes in his twenty-first letter of the aesthetic as a replenishing counterforce to such determinations: "he [man] possesses this humanity as a predisposition, before any definite condition into which he may come; but in actual practice he loses it with every definite condition into which he comes, and it must, if he is to be able to make the transition to an opposite condition, be newly restored to him every time by means of the aesthetic life." Schiller concludes, "It is, then, no mere poetic licence, but also philosophical truth, to call Beauty our second creator."[23]

Whereas Vico took as his task a retrospective explanation for the rise and fall of cultures and Schiller pursued the possibilities for human freedom that arise as sense experience is transformed into the forms of art, Karl Marx viewed the senses themselves as a historical accomplishment of human labor and asked what utopian potential might lie in the development of the senses once they were yoked to genuine human needs. Writing in his *Economic and Philosophic Manuscripts of 1844*, the young Marx considered the relations between sense experience and the production of individuality in more specifically historical terms. Arguing against false forms of communism that would involve the sharing of women communally as the "spoil[s] and handmaid[s] of communal lust," Marx contends that only when relations between persons are "direct and natural species-relations," relations in which what is natural and sensuous in one's existence is in the interest not merely of individual consumption but also of the ongoing articulation of what are *human* needs, can any true transcendence of private property prevail. Otherwise the "sharing" characterizing such inauthentic communism is merely a reification of property—in this case, the reification of other persons as property and the abuse of other persons to satisfy individual greed.[24]

As Immanuel Kant's argument for "purposive purposelessness" in the "Analytic of the Beautiful"[25] is the force behind much of Schiller's arguments on aesthetic experience as an avenue to intellectual freedom, so is it an influence here. For Marx suggests that only when our relation to our senses and to other persons is motivated by a desire to participate in the ongoing articulation of such human needs, and not by a desire to use our experience and our encounters with others as means to predetermined and instrumental ends, can we be fully human. In a remarkable aphorism amid these passages on the senses and human needs, Marx writes, "The *forming* of the five senses is a labour of the entire history of the world down to the present."[26] The radical innovation Marx provides here is his genuinely historical sense of the formation of the senses. He emphasizes the "forming" of the senses as a human accomplishment; in their inchoate form, sense experiences are continuous with animal life. At this level, we are caught in the dark and unending negation of night as Hegel described it. It is only in the objectification of sense experiences, the objectification that in aesthetic activity is not yoked to predetermined ends, that we acquire our humanity. Marx writes, "All history is the history of preparing and developing 'man' to become the object of *sensuous* consciousness, and turning the requirements of 'man as man' into his needs." In contrast to the inauthentic and estranged needs of mere "having" under the reign of private property and the endlessly redistributed goods of inauthentic forms of communism that remain based on a foundation of individual greed, true sense perception "exists as human sensuousness for one's self through the *other* man."[27] For Marx, the social aspect of the use of the senses is what makes it human. And, perhaps most significant, such sense experiences formed under an imperative of intelligibility to others help us form ourselves as individual persons: "it is only when the objective world becomes everywhere for man in society the world of man's essential powers—human reality, and for that reason the reality of his *own* essential powers—that all *objects* become for him the *objectification* of himself, become objects which confirm and realise his individuality, become *his* objects: that is, *man himself* becomes the object."[28]

II.   Laughter, Weeping, and the Order of the Senses

How can it be said that the senses are made by means of a historical process? Since ancient times, the senses have often been considered as a philosophical problem appearing on a boundary between what we refer to, perhaps for lack of better terms, as internal and external phenomena. The relation between external objects—that is, material forms and living organisms—and the objects of our immediate awareness of the world—color, shape, sound, smell, tactile feelings—can be both distinguished and blurred. Visual and auditory senses depend on relations to external objects and their properties, and hence propinquity and distance are central to their experience; sounds and smells are public and external; tastes are private yet external to the skin and membranes in that they require stimulation; feelings of heat, cold, warmth, and other tactile properties are partly internal and partly dependent on contact with external forms; proprioception arises from internal properties of the body in orientation to external space.

Philosophers have offered various descriptions of sense experience: John Locke, in his *Essay Concerning Human Understanding* (1690), spoke of "ideas of sense." In the early eighteenth century, Bishop George Berkeley wrote in *A Treatise Concerning the Principles of Human Knowledge* (1710, Part I) and *Three Dialogues between Hylas and Philonous* (1713) of "sensible qualities" that are not independent of the mind, and David Hume wrote in his 1739 *Treatise of Human Nature* of "impressions" inferred from empirical experience out of which all ideas are derived. Gilbert Ryle (*The Concept of Mind*, 1949) and J. L. Austin (*Sense and Sensibilia*, 1962) claimed that speaking of sense data as phenomena reified the perceived qualities of things. Such philosophical work on the senses constantly returns to a set of questions regarding the relations between sense experience and the expression of sense experience. When do sense impressions require external stimulants? What is the status of a hallucination or dream of sense experience? Are our sense impressions private or more or less public? In *talking of* an object's qualities, do we *form* an object's qualities?

Through work, play, sex, grooming, and other activities, we use our bodies to address the natural world with an ongoing mutuality. The senses cluster and work at the openings of the body; through them, we engage in an epistemology of process that is specific to parts of the body and yet evidently endlessly synesthetic and generalizable, leading to knowledge of exterior forms. Louise Vinge's important historical survey of the theme of the five senses in literature and visual art emphasizes the changing frame of this dynamic between exterior and interior, the senses on the one hand and the reason or the soul on the other. Plato argues in the "Theaetetus" that much knowledge—for example, knowledge of values—is independent of sense impressions and that sense impressions in themselves are not forms of knowledge. Philo, Cicero, and Lactantius all present, by various means, images of man that claim the head as the seat of reason; the head serves as a kind of citadel, protecting the self against the onslaught of experience. The senses in this later classical tradition sometimes appear in turn as watchmen or sentinels in relation to the external world.[29] Medieval writers such as Hugh of St. Victor in the eleventh century, Alain de Lille in the twelfth century, Jacopone da Todi in the thirteenth century, and Jean Gerson in the fourteenth century wrote allegorical and moralizing works on the theme of the five senses. These works are often directly negative in their presentation of sense impressions—impressions, according to these writers in the line of Plato's thought, inevitably hostile to reason.[30] Renaissance thinkers, particularly neo-Platonists such as Marsilio Ficino, revive a positive interest in the senses, particularly by claiming that the senses give us access to beauty. But the negative allegory of siege continues in texts like the House of Alma episode in Edmund Spenser's *The Faerie Queene*. As an embodiment of the castle of the soul, Alma is threatened by bestial attacks on her senses. Spenser borrows an iconography from emblem books like those of Cesare Ripa linking animals with certain sense impressions: owls and lynxes with sight, harts and boars with hearing; dogs, apes, and vultures with smell; ostriches, toads, and swine with taste; snails, hedgehogs, and spiders with touch. Spenser's story recounts how these animals are assembled in a menagerie dedicated to breaking down the defenses of virtue. In medieval and Renaissance topoi overall, the domain of smell, touch, and taste is properly a domain of beasts. This rhetoric of the animal and servile senses, aside from its obvious legitimating force for philosophical abstraction, establishes a subjectivity separated from nature, protected by mediation, and propelled by a desire born out of the very estranged relation thus created. As Philo is at pains to explain in his discussion of the Pentapolis, of all the monuments of the cities on the plain, only the citadel of sight was left standing.[31] Later Elizabethan and Baroque erotic poetry, as we shall see, often plays on Petrarchan idealizations of sight and hearing and at the same time makes witty, satirical use of the lower senses of taste, smell, and touch.

Something of these ascetic notions regarding the senses survived in Sigmund Freud's thought. In *Instincts and Their Vicissitudes*, for example, Freud describes the nervous system as an apparatus that has the function of getting rid of the stimuli that reach it, or at least reducing them to the lowest level.[32] But he was limited by his paradigm, derived from the experiences of adulthood, when he associated pleasure predominantly with the relief of tension. Subsequent work in psychology and the study of human development suggests that from infancy human beings find some sensory stimuli attractive and pleasant and others repellent and that such sensations are felt within the organism prior to the development of distinctions between subjects and objects. The path of development is toward more and more articulation of interior and exterior states, but that development is propelled by what seems to be an intrinsic pleasure in stimulation and articulation—all leading to the ability to be interested in objects themselves.[33]

If this argument about the role of objectification in sense perception is one of the oldest in Western thought, it is also one of the newest. Antonio R. Damasio's recent pathbreaking study of the role of body and emotion in the "making of consciousness" concludes, on the basis of his extensive neurological research, that consciousness should be seen "in terms of two players, the *organism* and the *object* and in terms of the *relationship* between the two. . . . Consciousness consists of constructing knowledge about two facts: that the organism is involved in relation to some object and that the object in the relation is causing a change in the organism."[34] Damasio's studies come directly out of the Aristotelian position: "consciousness begins as the feeling of what happens when we see or hear or touch. Phrased in slightly more precise words, it is a feeling that accompanies the making of any kind of image—visual, auditory, tactile, visceral—within our living organisms."[35] The difference between a "core" consciousness, relying simply on such sense formations, and what Damasio calls "knowledge consciousness," whose highest form is an "autobiographical consciousness," is that only the latter involves knowing one has constructed sense images. This knowledge is "autobiographical" in that it can be "stored in the memory, categorized in conceptual or linguistic terms, and retrieved in recall or recognition modes."[36]

According to Damasio, out of a "proto-self" that represents sense impressions to the organism on a moment-to-moment basis and the eventual emergence of multiple levels of the brain prior to, and without, consciousness, consciousness gradually emerges. An object modifies the proto-self, and knowledge of such modification ensues: the autobiographical self is based on implicit memories of individual experience in the past and anticipation of the future; memories can be made explicit, and when they are activated, they appear as "something to be known."[37] From proto-self to autobiographical self, there is an increase in cognitive complexity and in the reach of consciousness toward both the past and the future. In these ways, consciousness opens time beyond the moment-to-moment representation of physical states—the "here and now," the "this"-ness of the Hegelian dark, expands into the past and future of the continuous self. The philosophical problem of the senses, in that it has emphasized the status of sensory experience in relation to varying historical models of the real, has from the beginning appeared, as Damasio implies, as a moral problem—a problem of the status of human experience and human conduct, with experience and conduct forming contrasting poles of passive and active agency, as the past is known and the future anticipated.

The notion of "five senses" usually is attributed to Aristotle, although we find that, in *De Anima*, taste and seeing can be forms of touch. Here the senses are connected to the elements in a system of correspondences. The eye is associated with water, which can absorb light; hearing is associated with air; smell with fire; and touch with earth. Aristotle makes special mention of objects that are perceptible by single senses—color as the special object of sight, sound of hearing, flavor of taste.[38] This specialization and heightening of the senses plays in complex ways into later discourses on the senses: the notions of sensibility and sensitivity associated with the refining of the higher philosophical senses of seeing and hearing; the complexity of taste as a distinction ranging from coarseness to fineness—a set of terms so textural in its range that reaches back to the Aristotelian merger of taste and touch; and, correlatively, the problems of overrefined sensibilities of touch and smell—by the time of Freud linked to regression, neuroses, and even perversion.[39]

Accompanying this concern with specialized functions, Aristotle also put forward a theory of synaesthesia. "There seems to be a sort of parallelism," he notes, "between what is acute or grave to hearing and what is sharp or blunt to touch; what is sharp as it were stabs, while what is blunt pushes, the one producing its effort in a short, the other in a long time, so that one is quick, the other slow." In Aristotle's doctrine the information provided by the external senses reached the internal senses by means of a common sense of touch.[40] For Aristotle touch (and thereby taste) is found in all animals and so is the lowliest sense. He contends that this is the sense needed for being, whereas the other senses are necessary for well-being.[41] He therefore poses a hierarchical order of the senses, from most to least valuable: vision-hearing-smell-taste-touch. In the *Nicomachean Ethics*, Aristotle also develops an opposition between Heroic Virtue and sensual pleasure; the latter, when based on appetite, is "brutish" for "it attaches to us not as men but as animals."[42]

Pliny famously contends in his *Natural History* that touch and taste are superior in man to the senses of animals but that in all the other senses man is surpassed: "Eagles have clearer sight, vultures a keener sense of smell, moles acuter hearing—although they are buried in the earth, so dense and deaf an element of nature, and although moreover all sound travels upward, they can overhear people talking and it is actually said that if you speak about them they understand and run away."[43] But Pliny is an exception as he cites what traditionally have been considered animal senses (touch and taste) in humans and, in addition to smell, what traditionally have been considered human senses (seeing, hearing) in animals. More conventionally, the senses have been ranked in relation to their degree of immediacy, the hierarchy proposed by Aristotle: taste and touch, in direct contact with the world, are lowest; followed by smell, which forms a kind of mean distance to sight and hearing, which operate across distance yet can be called to mind without external stimulation. Sight and hearing, because of their link with philosophical contemplation and abstraction, hold the leading place.

The subject invented by disinterested desire presents an ideal picture of evolved, upright human being—vision and hearing directed toward the horizon and hence a spatialization of progress and self-consciousness. Taxonomy here is inextricably bound up with hierarchy: the partitioning of classes and cultures and the partitioning of the body itself. Such taxonomies assume that our human relation to the animal is a metaphorical, allegorical one and not a metonymic, contiguous one. In excess and deprivation, the economy of the senses is thereby created and regulated. Yet in thinking about the regulation of the senses, it is useful to make a rudimentary distinction between taboo and manners. We might see taboo as structural, encompassing a prohibition against the sign as well as against the referent. Hence the deep, naturalized status of taboo. We refuse to speak of the taboo and in this way keep it in the domain of the invisible. The taboos against the excrescences of the body, for example—menstrual blood, vomit, spittle, hair, dandruff, nail parings, semen, excrement, urine—appear in the West as total taboos. All five senses are closed to them, with the most animal senses, touch and taste, receiving the highest prohibition. Of course, they must not be uttered as names—and their names themselves are generalized, as are their few euphemisms. Disgust as the far register of pleasure, disgust experienced physically and not through language, however, is readily transformed into disgust as the pleasure of resistance, temptation, and fetishism: the body's system of closings and openings becomes articulated as it is exercised. Hence the residual familiarity of the tabooed substances and the private as the proper site for their management. As William James observed, we feel a slight disgust when sitting down in a chair warmed by a stranger, as well as a slight pleasure in sitting down in a chair that we ourselves have warmed.[44]

Taboo, once spoken, becomes mere manners: emergent, codified, uttered, and transformable. In his history of manners, Norbert Elias emphasizes that manners function as a way of negotiating the boundary between the animal and the human and the boundary between classes. The maintenance of these boundaries, he contends, depends on the increased tendency, from the late Middle Ages forward, of people to observe themselves and others. The notion of how to *look*, both actively and passively, is a matter of both intention and reception. Erasmus writes, for example, of the separation of the body from the animal: "some put their hands into the dishes when they are scarcely seated. Wolves and gluttons do that"; and of the separation of one class from another: "It is most refined to use only three fingers of the hands. This is one of the marks of distinction between the upper and lower classes." Such exercises of self-control, the elaborate semiotic of constraints and gestures, reshape the senses under the contingencies of the social code. They also, notes Elias, allow the state to exercise a monopoly on physical force—gestures of self-suppression are gestures of membership and self-surveillance.[45]

The pattern of manners in fifteenth-century courtesy books such as *The Babbees Book* and *The Boke of Precedence* is one of separating eating and speech. We might view the characters of Rabelais, who eat with their mouths full (Gargantua mouthing prayers when stuffed; Panurge's taste for a mass moistened with wine), as evidence of the flaunting of this rule. Lord Chesterfield's description to his son, sent in a letter in 1741, of the quintessential "awkward person" might serve as the prototype for a particularly adolescent slapstick humor regarding this theme:

> When an awkward fellow first comes into a room, it is highly probable that his sword gets between his legs, and throws him down, or makes him stumble at least; when he has recovered this accident, he goes and places himself in the very place of the whole room where he should not; there he soon lets his hat fall down; and, taking it up again, throws down his cane; in recovering his cane, his hat falls a second time; so that he is a quarter of an hour before he is in order again. If he drinks tea or coffee, he certainly scalds his mouth, and lets either the cup or the saucer fall, and spills the tea or coffee in his breeches. At dinner his awkwardness distinguishes itself particularly, as he has more to do: there he holds his knife, fork, and spoon differently from other people; eats with his knife to the great danger of his mouth, picks his teeth with his fork, and puts his spoon, which has been in his throat twenty times, into the dishes again.[46]

It is not surprising that the father next warns the boy against awkwardness in words and expression.

The prohibition against putting objects in the mouth argues for the enduring regulation of this organ of both sexual and social contact.[47] In Thomas Hardy's 1872 novel *Under the Greenwood Tree,* a work to which we will return later in a more specific discussion of Hardy's poems, there is an intriguing scene on this theme. Members of the "Mellstock quire," the local parish's male singing group, are talking about one of their oldest members, William Dewey, concluding that "he'd starve to death for music's sake now, as much as when he was a boy-chap of fifteen." But Michael Mail, another singer, replies that in fact "there's a friendly tie of some sort between music and eating." He recounts how once in an inn he was having dinner when a brass band struck up on the street outside: "Such a beautiful band as that were! I was setting eating fried liver and lights, I well can mind—ah, I was! and to save my life, I couldn't help chewing to the time. Band played six-eight time; six-eight chews I, willy-nilly. Band plays common: common time went my teeth among the liver and lights." Mrs. Dewey responds that she doesn't like "Michael's tuneful stories. They are quite coarse to a person of decent taste."[48]

Consider, as well, the neoclassical anxiety regarding laughter. Although traces of this prejudice appear in Torquato Tasso's description of the Fountain of Laughter associated with Armida and in the Acrasia episode of Edmund Spenser's *The Faerie Queene*, it is the neoclassical prohibition against excess that results in a number of works specifically designed to inhibit laughter.[49] Anthony, earl of Shaftesbury, who otherwise was an important advocate of the comic as a correction to pedantry, quotes Ecclesiastes 21:20 with approval in his *Regimen* (1698–1712): "A fool lifteth up his voice with laughter, but a wise man doth scarce smile a little."[50] He contends that outright laughter is much more frequent among "porters, carmen, and clowns" than among well-bred people.[51] William Hogarth's *Analysis of Beauty* (1753) similarly states that "the expression of excessive laughter more often than any other, gives a sensible face a silly or disagreeable look, as it is apt to form regular plain lines about the mouth, like a parenthesis, which sometimes appears like crying."[52]

Indeed, weeping comes under similar rules of prohibition. The interdiction is not against laughter or weeping per se so much as the excessive and unmeasured flow of expression out of the face: unbidden tears and explosive laughter involve a loss of volition. A striking account of this fear of the lability between laughter and liquidity is T. S. Eliot's prose poem "Hysteria," from his 1917 volume *Prufrock and Other Observations*. Eliot begins the poem by describing a woman's mouth as a kind of entrance to hell: "As she laughed I was aware of becoming involved in her laughter and being part of it, until her teeth were only accidental stars with a talent for squad-drill. I was drawn in by short gasps, inhaled at each momentary recovery, lost finally in the dark caverns of her throat bruised by the ripple of unseen muscles."[53]

This poem gives us a far clearer notion of the perils of laughter than any courtesy book interdiction might provide. The speaker fears being actually engulfed, inhaled by this open laughing mouth with its animated teeth. As the poem continues, an elderly waiter's nervous repetitions give the speaker an objective correlative for his fear. But it is the elderly waiter who shows the primary symptom of hysteria—his insistent repetitions thwarting all sense of purpose or direction. The waiter wants to displace the laughter to the garden where its effects might be less concentrated. The speaker will cure the problem by removing the source, what feeds the hysteria now that it is exposed to view is described as "the shaking of her breasts"—a shaking the speaker resolves to stop. Laughter, like weeping and other unintended flows of liquidity from the body, is particularly dangerous when it is expressed idiosyncratically, when it is not taken up socially and yet threatens to contaminate whatever lies within its range.

Weeping or crying conventions also are often, as is "Hysteria" the poem, specifically gendered. George Puttenham writes in a chapter of his 1589 *The Arte of English Poesie:*

[G]enerally to weepe for any sorrow (as one may doe for pitie) is not so decent in a man: and therefore all high minded persons, when they cannot
chuse but shed teares, wil turne away their face as a countenance unde-
cent for a man to shew, and so will the standers by till they have supprest
such passion, thinking it nothing decent to behold such an uncomely
countenance. But for Ladies and women to weepe and shed teares at every
little greefe, it is nothing uncomely, but rather a signe of much good nature and meeknes of minde, a most decent propertie for that sexe; and
therefore they be for the more part more devout and charitable, and
greater gevers of almes than men, and zealous relievers of prisoners, and
beseechers of pardons, and such like parts of commiseration. Yea they be
more than so too: for by the common proverbe, a woman will weepe for
pitie to see a gosling goe barefoote.[54]

Despite Puttenham's light tone, women's weeping has a long Western
cultural history embedded in mourning practices, and it is their weeping
that moves the inarticulate cries of the grieving into intersubjective
speech, placing the dead in memory as the body is buried in the earth. In
Ireland, for example, women deliver first the death wail, the *ullagone*, and
then the keen that describes the life and achievements of the dead figure.
There is, in their death work, a recapitulation or representation of the
birth work that moves from crying into achieved form: the mother's cries
in labor end in song and speech to the newborn baby; the baby's own first
cry marks its entry into the world and the socialization language will
bring.

Steven Feld's studies, beginning in the 1970s, of Kaluli weeping and
song present a subtle analysis of the gendering of weeping within one cultural system. In Kaluli society, women are given the "task" of weeping,
and men are given the task of creating songs that move others to burst
into wailing or tears. Feld explains: "The western ethnopsychological
link between women, emotion, and irrationality is clearly not shared by
Kaluli. . . . For Kaluli, men are far more typically and stereotypically culturally constructed as the emotional gender, the more unpredictable, po-
tentially irrational, the more moody, prone to burst out in tears at any moment, or become flamboyantly seized with tantrums of rage or sadness.
Kaluli men seem to have more trouble controlling anger and upset than do
Kaluli women . . . women's crying is more melodic, texted, controlled, reflective and sustained."[55] Although in this passage Feld is drawing a distinction between Western and Kaluli ways of expressing emotion, it is
clear that there is also a parallel structure: it is women who are given the
license of socially structured, what might be called "formal," weeping. If,

as Puttenham suggests, men are not to weep at all, as a consequence men's weeping is likely to appear as the return of the repressed—as unexpected, unlawful outburst.

I have taken this rather long detour on the regulation of the senses to provide a context for poetry's appearance in culture: the transformation of sense experience into words, the mark of the human, is implicit in the admonition we constantly give to overwrought children: "Use *words.*" As emotional expression, poetry is subject to social rules in complex ways. Erotic and rhetorical at once, replete with irrational rhythms and compulsions to repeat, emerging through the mouth in face-to-face encounters that are also imitations and re-creations of others' speech and gestures, poetry is embedded in cultural systems of decorum and sensual regulation and at the same time has its own sphere of constraints, expectations, and permissions. Puttenham's *Arte* devotes an entire chapter to "Of decencie in behaviour which also belongs to the consideration of the Poet or maker":

> And there is a decency to be observed in every mans action and behaviour aswell as in his speach and writing which some peradventure would thinke impertinent to be treated of in this booke, where we do but informe the commendable fashions of language and stile: but that is otherwise, for the good maker or poet who is in decent speach and good termes to desscribe all things and with prayse or dispraise to report every mans behaviour, ought to know the comelinesse of an action aswell as of a word and thereby to direct himselfe both in praise and perswasion or any other point that perteines to the Oratours arte.[56]

Puttenham prescribes acceptable behaviors between rich and poor persons and between wise and foolish ones, discourses at table and in public assembly and in private, forms of decent apparel and grooming, balance in gift giving, proper carriage and movement, and, as we have seen, the proper expression of the passions, weeping, and laughter. He concludes that "all your figures Poeticall or Rhethoricall, are but observations of strange speeches, and such as without any arte at al we should use, and commonly do, even by very nature without discipline. But more or lesse aptly and decently, or scarcely, or aboundantly, or of this or that kind of figure, and one of us more then another, according to the disposition of our nature, constitution of the heart, and facilitie of each mans utterance: so as we may conclude, that nature her selfe suggesteth the figure in this or that forme; but arte aydeth the judgement of his use and application."[57] The regulation of the senses, of mouth and speech, is completely bound up with processes of social decorum: with who may do and say what in the presence or absence of whom on what occasions. The notion of poetic *kinds* is tied to the specificity of their use and occasion: the epithalamion, the elegy, the aubade are at once works of art independent of their particular contexts of production and use and social acts tied to specific rules of decorum. Poems are in this sense acts of social intent and consequence and not things in a world of things.

If we look at some of the relatively rare poems in the English tradition that focus on the "lower" senses of taste and smell, we find in fact that they continually play on the absent situation of writing and the conceit of the speaker's presence in a scene to which the reader has no access. Such poems therefore make a special use of lyric's triangulation of speaker, addressee, and reader; in this case, the inherent voyeurism of the reader's position is all the more emphasized by the focus on these nonvisual senses so embedded in proximity. And not surprisingly, such poems almost always are erotic—even when they express what might be called an erotic sense of repulsion. They often display the irreverent attitude sixteenth-century and later poets came to hold toward Petrarchan conventions.[58] Yet while such poems may mock the conventions of sonnet comparisons, they also contribute to our understanding of the sensual realism of erotic forces of attraction and aversion. Compare, for example, the bland sweetness of these lines from Sonnet 64 of Edmund Spenser's "Amoretti":

> Her lips did smell lyke unto Gillyflowers,
>> her ruddy cheekes lyke unto Roses red:
>> her snowy browes lyke budded Bellamoures,
>> her lovely eyes lyke Pincks but newly spred.
> Her goodly bosome lyke a Strawberry bed,
>> her neck lyke to a bounch of Cullambynes;
>> her brest lyke lillyes, ere theyr leaves be shed,
>> her nipples lyke yong blossomd Jessemynes.
> Such fragrant flowres doe give most odorous smell,
>> but her sweet odour did them all excell.[59]

to these lines out of the relentlessly negative structure of John Donne's Elegy 8, "The Comparison":

> As the sweet sweat of roses in a still,
> As that which from chafed musk cat's pores doth trill,
> As the almighty balm of th'early east,
> Such as the sweat drops of my mistress' breast.

And on her neck her skin such lustre sets,
They seem no sweat drops, but pearl carcanets.
Rank sweaty froth thy mistress' brow defiles,
Like spermatic issue of ripe menstruous boils,
Or like that scum, which, by need's lawless law
Enforced, Sanserra's starved men did draw
From parboiled shoes, and boots, and all the rest
Where were with any sovereign fatness blessed,
And like vile lying stones in saffroned tin,
Or warts, or weals, they hang upon her skin. . . .
. . . Thine's [thy breast] like worm-eaten trunks, clothed in seal's skin,
Or grave, that's dust without, and stink within. . . .
And like a bunch of ragged carrots stand
The short swoll'n fingers of thy gouty hand. . . .
Are not your kisses then as filthy, and more,
As a worm sucking an envenomed sore?
Doth not thy fearful hand in feeling quake,
As one which gathering flowers, still fears a snake?
Is not your last act harsh, and violent,
As when a plough a stony ground doth rent?

Donne's poem ends, "She, and comparisons are odious." [60] Like the complex discourses on odor in William Shakespeare's Sonnets 54 ("O, how much more doth beauty beauteous seem") and 69 ("Those parts of thee that the world's eye doth view"),[61] Donne's elegies go beyond the simple formulas of comparison as a model of positive attraction and negative repulsion. Here repulsion, in its elaborate detail, borders on fascination. A kind of trompe l'oeil effect is created wherein what seem to be fixed visual images melt into decay, releasing their odors before our very eyes if not our very noses. Such an effect is a verbal analogue for the vanitas motif of the insistent skull that plays such an important role in works like Hans Holbein's anamorphic "The Ambassadors" and indeed throughout Renaissance painting. The fleeting lives of flowers, the fleetingness of smells and tastes, are resources for driving home the ephemerality of life's pleasures and the inevitability of death.[62]

Donne's Elegy 4, "The Perfume," is a kind of bawdy detective story that ends darkly with this vanitas theme. In this elegy the lovers make elaborate precautions to keep their meetings secret from the rest of the household, but the man is given away to the woman's father by his perfume: "Had it been some bad smell, he would have thought / that his own feet, or breath, that smell had wrought." The elegy closes with an apostrophe to perfume itself:

Only, thou bitter sweet, whom I had laid
Next me, me traitorously hast betrayed,
And unsuspected hast invisibly
At once fled unto him, and stayed with me.
Base excrement of earth, which dost confound
Sense, from distinguishing the sick from sound;
By thee the silly amorous sucks his death
by drawing in a leprous harlot's breath;
By thee, the greatest stain to man's estate
Falls on us, to be called effeminate;
Though you be much loved in the prince's hall,
There, things that seem, exceed substantial.
Gods, when ye fumed on altars, were pleased well,
Because you were burnt not that they liked your smell; . . .
All my perfumes, I give most willingly
To embalm thy father's corse; What? will he die?[63]

Donne's erotic poems are often brilliant plays on the voyeuristic inclinations and absent presence of his readers. In the elaborate striptease of Elegy 19, "To His Mistress Going to Bed," the speaker imploringly and systematically asks his mistress to take off her clothes and then tricks the reader by revealing in the last two lines that he, too, by now is naked—reminding us quite vividly that we have only been in the scene through his control of the perspective all along:

. . . cast all, yea, this white linen hence,
Here is no penance, much less innocence.
To teach thee, I am naked first, why then,
What needst thou have more covering than a man.[64]

It is not surprising that the satirical poetry of the "lower senses" thrives in the period when scribal publication is still flourishing, a viable alternative even as the resources of printing are being fully developed. Donne is, according to the foremost authority on scribal publication, Harold Love, "committed to manuscript." Love draws an insightful comparison between Spenser, whose didactic Puritanism and nationalistic fervor are readily displayed by the march of regular printed columns of verse,

and Donne, whose meandering catachrestic poetry "follows the requirements of the thought," without consideration for visual effect. Donne's
use of erotic triangulation is well served by the palpability of scribal
texts—they bear the presence of a human hand tracing a human voice
and can be read by a third party in an atmosphere of intimate proximity. When Donne emphatically begins "The Canonization," "For God's
sake hold your tongue, and let me love," the convention of immediacy in
scribal publication enables his address cleverly to command both the
racket of third persons occupying his "private" erotic space and the
protesting words of the lover being implored to "let him love," the unob-
servable and inaudible accompaniment to the rest of the poem. Love discusses John Dryden, born in the year of Donne's death, as another poet
who used scribal publication for certain effects: "Dryden took a holiday
from print to write *MacFlecknoe,* which, withheld from the press, circu-
lated alongside Rochester's verse in scribally published miscellanies. . . .
Mackflecknoe differs from every other known poem written by Dryden to
that date [1678] in being vituperative, scatological and riddlingly allusive.
But in this Dryden was simply accepting the decorum of the alternative
medium."[65]

Jonathan Swift, as a Scriblerian and coterie poet, also wrote for scribal
publication and continued the tradition of anti-Petrarchanism that lam-
pooned the kinds of love poems found in print anthologies. Love notes that
"the scribal phase of the circulation of Swift's writing is undocumented"
but adds that even in print publication Swift continued the satirical tradition of scribalism.[66] In "The Lady's Dressing Room," by means of the conventions of material realism more often found in the novel, Swift creates
an extravaganza of the lower senses, drawing along the reader with tanta-
lizingly sensual details, mixing metaphors of smell and taste, and in the
end fooling the reader by turning attraction into another example of fasci-
nated disgust. The poem narrates how Strephon sneaks into Celia's dressing room after she has spent five hours getting ready to go out. His path
through the cluttered space is guided by smell:

> And first a dirty Smock appear'd,
> Beneath the Arm-pits well besmear'd. . . .

> But oh! it turn'd poor *Strephon*'s Bowels,
> When he beheld and smellt the Towels,
> Begumm'd, bematter'd, and beslim'd
> With Dirt, and Sweat, and Ear-Wax grim'd. . . .

The Stockings, why shou'd I expose,
Stain'd with the Marks of stinking Toes;
Or greasy Coifs and Pinners reeking,
Which *Celia* slept at least a week in?

Most of the poem focuses on his discovery of "the chest" or chamber pot:

For *Strephon* ventur'd to look in,
Resolv'd to go thro' thick and thin;
He lifts the Lid, there needs no more,
He smelt it all the Time before.
As from within *Pandora*'s Box,
When *Epimetheus* op'd the locks . . .
As Mutton Cutlets, Prime of Meat,
Which tho' with Art you salt and beat,
As Laws of Cookery require,
And toast them at the clearest Fire;
If from adown the hopeful Chops
The Fat upon a Cinder drops,
To stinking Smoak it turns the Flame
Pois'ning the Flesh from whence it came,
And up exhales a greasy Stench,
For which you curse the careless Wench;
So Things, which must not be exprest,
When plumpt into the reeking Chest,
Send up an excremental Smell
To taint the Parts from whence they fell.
The Petticoats and Gown perfume,
Which waft a Stink round every Room.
Thus finishing his grand Survey,
Disgusted *Strephon* stole away
Repeating in his amorous Fits,
Oh! *Celia, Celia, Celia* shits!
    But Vengeance, Goddess never sleeping
Soon punish'd *Strephon* for his peeping;
His foul Imagination links
Each Dame he sees with all her Stinks;
And, if unsavory Odours fly,
Conceives a Lady standing by.[67]

Such poems are "distasteful," as Hardy's Mrs. Dewey would say, precisely because they are so evocative of smell and taste. Donne and Swift make extensive use of the directional aspect of smell; the sensation of smell becomes stronger and stronger as one approaches its origin, and the person following an olfactory sense in this way becomes more and more enveloped by the power of that force until the point where it is impossible to hold it at a distance. Even in those poems that tend to emphasize smell over taste, taste as incorporation, and the idea of reciprocally being incorporated is implied. Taste involves the touch and feel of the object in the mouth and results in the liquification of its object. The melting words of the lover, the manipulation of words in the mouth as an extension of erotic manipulation through hands and limbs—all can be resources for the poet of erotic poems, especially in manuscript form. Comparison, with its implication of a distanced view, is in fact a terminus for the sensual work of the erotic poet in a voyeuristic culture of written texts. Hence, the erotic poet has a strong interest in keeping the lover "beyond compare"; beyond compare is the place where the lover has immediate access to the object of his or her desire, and the reader is stranded just beyond the scene.

Works of art representing the lower senses thereby often do so in the interest of the lower genre of satire. Like all grotesque works of art, many of these poems of smell and taste rely on the exaggeration of parts for their effects: we never view the figure of Celia; we only find the detritus she leaves behind. Donne's lovers are represented metonymically through their smells and articles of clothing—we find our voyeuristic desires blocked; in the place of views, fetishistic images with meanings interior to the world of the poem are presented before us. Even in the serious and didactically religious poems of George Herbert, the smells and tastes of this world are like will-o'-the-wisps that we would be fools to chase, especially if we forget we are in fact running toward death.

Yet just as representations of experiences of smell and taste are common to the "lower" genres of poetry, so are representations of experiences of pure visuality often called on when poetry seeks to objectify its referents or to free itself of past practices. Tasting and smelling are associated with animal life and with experiences of intense intimacy and sexuality. Correlatively, experiences of distanced viewing are associated with objectification. To treat a person like a thing, to look without reciprocity, is to seek a form of language that is purely material. There is a long tradition in Western thought about language that seeks such an intransitive model: a view of language as antirhetorical and sufficient in and of itself as it approximates the abstraction and self-sufficient terms of musical and visual patterns.

Puttenham discusses pattern poems as "ocular representations" in Book II, Chapter XI, of his *Arte*. Here he writes, "Your last proportion is that of figure, so called for that it yelds an ocular representation, your meeters being by good symmetrie reduced into certaine Geometricall figures, whereby the maker is restrained to keepe him within his bounds, and sheweth not onely more art, but serveth also much better for briefenesse and subtiltie of device." He mentions the lozenge, the spindle, the triangle, the square, the pillaster, the piramis, the rondel, and the egge, explaining that he learned of them by

> being in Italie conversant with a certaine gentleman, who had long travailed the Orientall parts of the world, and seene the Courts of the great Princes of China and Tartarie. I being very inquisitive to know of the subtillities of those countreyes, and especially in matter of learning and of their vulgar Poesie, he told me that they are in all the inventions most wittie, and have the use of Poesie or riming, but do not delight so much as we do in long tedious descriptions, and therefore when they will utter any pretie conceit, they reduce it into metricall feet, and put it in forme of a *Lozange* or square, or such other figure and so engraven in gold, silver, or ivorie, and sometimes with letters of ametist, rubie, emeralde or topas curiousely cemented and peeced together, they sende them in chaines, bracelets, collars and girdles to their mistresses to weare for a remembrance.[68]

These "poem gems" are as two-dimensional as written inscriptions and as three-dimensional as artifacts. Like all glimmering and glittering things, they appeal to the eye first of all and then to the hand that reaches toward them. As C. A. Patrides notes in his standard edition of *The English Poems of George Herbert*, pattern poetry was so popular in the Renaissance that Gabriel Harvey was driven to protest against poems that "represente the form and figure of an egg, an ape, a winge, and sutche ridiculous and madd gergawes and crockchettes."[69] Such poems became the rage especially after the last decades of the sixteenth century when Petrarchan conventions wore thin and poets turned against the available rhetorical devices.

Puttenham often takes the names for his figures from geometry and heraldry as he claims an "Orientall" source for the forms. There are indeed resemblances between the poems Puttenham presents and the Turkish and Persian pattern poem tradition that goes beyond the presentation of word sequences shaped as overall forms into a full art of calligraphy and manuscript ornamentation. Ernst Robert Curtius contends in *European Literature and the Latin Middle Ages* that Persian pattern poems may share with Western medieval and Renaissance examples of the genre a common Hellenistic source. Such "figure poems," τεχνοπαίγνια (*technopaignia*), he writes "have come down to us in the corpus of the Greek bucolic poets and in the Greek anthology."[70] Puttenham probably received his own knowledge of "pattern poems" by oral transmission, and Western poems of this type compel us to read lines from left to right just as any conventional poem would. Such English poems are quite different from the mazes, labyrinths, medallions, and endlessly decipherable inscriptions of the ghazals of Persia.

Practices of pattern and concrete poetry remove the poetic from its attachment to particular voices and bodies to create a poetry that is objectlike or artifactual. Such poems—in the Hellenistic age, in the Renaissance, and revived under Modernism—are the most visual and objectifying of all poetic forms. It is indeed not surprising that the final "glimpse" of the experience of imagery such a poem produces is a geometrical abstraction, a pure Platonic form that overrides the fallen materiality of the words. A poem such as George Herbert's "The Altar" uses an extended conceit comparing the speaker's heart to an altar on which the consequent poems in the section called "The Church" of Herbert's volume *The Temple* will be placed as offerings:

> A broken ALTAR, Lord, thy servant rears,
> Made of a heart, and cemented with tears:
>   Whose parts are as thy hand did frame;
>   No workman's tool hath touched the same.
>   A   HEART   alone
>   Is   such   a   stone,
>   As   nothing   but
>   Thy power doth cut.
>   Wherefore each part
>   Of   my   hard   heart
>   Meets in this frame,
>   To praise thy Name:
>   That, if I chance to hold my peace,
>   These stones to praise thee may not cease.
> Oh let thy blessed SACRIFICE be mine,
> And sanctify this ALTAR to be thine.[71]

The "pedestal" of "The Altar" is built first from a transposition of Scripture from Luke 19:10—"I tell you that, if these should hold their peace, the stones would immediately cry out"—and second from the transposition of positions between the sacrificed and the recipient of sacrifice. The speaker asks that *"thy* sacrifice" (i.e., Christ's sacrifice) be "mine" so that the altar of his own heart, as yet "uncut" stone like that described in Exodus 20:25 and Deuteronomy 27:5–8, be sanctified. Herbert's poem is one of his "sacred parodies": a poem that substitutes a sacred theme within the form of an existing secular poem. In this case he has borrowed the shape of an altar from an anonymous work, "An Altare and Sacrifice to Disdaine, for freeing him from love," which appeared in a 1602 anthology, *A Poetical Rhapsody.* In Herbert's poetry visual resolution helps abstract language from its ordinary contexts of usage, sanctifying it and teaching the reader to look beyond the immediate world of sensual impressions.

Three hundred years later, Stéphane Mallarmé's analogous fin de siècle search for a "poésie pur" and his interest in arabesques, typography, and opacity are another important contribution to the tradition of an antirhetorical and visual poetics. The tradition continues throughout the twentieth century in the avant-garde interest in a poetics of experiment and materiality.[72] The aims of the Imagist movement in the early years of the century were to employ the "exact word" with no rhetorical decoration; to forgo conventional (i.e., metrical) form; to write on any subject; to present an image; to produce a "hard and clear" poetry without blurring or indefiniteness; to promote "concentration" as the "essence" of poetry. This position, which not only promotes the visual but also refutes the aural dimension of poetry, is relentlessly antirhetorical. Its objectlike hardness and clearness were not meant to touch or move the reader beyond whatever emotion can arise from visual clarity. T. E. Hulme, the movement's foremost theorist, as Ezra Pound was its most prominent literary practitioner, wrote, "This new verse appeals to the eye rather than to the ear. It has to mould images, a kind of spiritual clay, into definite shapes. The material . . . is image and not sound. It builds up a plastic image which it hands over to the reader, whereas the old art endeavored always to influence him."[73] "Sea Violet," a 1916 poem in three stanzas by "H.D." (Hilda Dolittle), is a well-known example of the work of the Imagist school. Here are the two opening stanzas:

The white violet
is scented on its stalk,
the sea-violet

fragile as agate,
lies fronting all the wind
among the torn shells
on the sand-bank.

The greater blue violets
flutter on the hill,
but who would change for these
who would change for these
one root of the white sort? [74]

"Sea Violet" introduces one positive visual image at a time: the white violet, the sea violet, the torn shells, the sand bank, the greater blue violets, the hill, the violet, the sand hill, the light, frost, star, and fire. An image like "one root of the white sort" is used as an absent image; it resembles the role of the wind, which we cannot see but know from resistance to it (the sea violet lies fronting it) and from the fluttering of the greater blue violets. As is often the case with Imagist poetry, verbs of being do most of the work. There is no motion brought about by human intention. Color and location are the individuating qualities of types of things here. As specific kinds of violets (white and sea and greater blue) become *the* violet, "the sand-bank" and "the hill" quite beautifully seem to erode into the conglomerate form: the "sand-hill." And what can H.D. mean by "fragile as agate"? Agate is a stone, the variegated chalcedony whose colored bands and markings are known to most of us through its use in playing marbles. It is no more fragile than any other kind of quartz, but its coloring might be described as fragile: its milky whiteness or grayness is marked with delicate striations and streams of other hues. The sea violet is as fragile as the stone in the register of visual appearance only— the comparison cannot work if the flower and stone themselves are juxtaposed. And all those things that follow—light and frost and star and fire— are mutable in ways that negotiate the place between things as firm as agate and things as fleeting as the wind. H.D.'s use of visual comparison also depends on an abstract sense of smell ("is scented") and an abstract sense of touch (the "torn shells," "fluttering blue violets," and the "grasp" doing the catching in the last stanza). "Sea Violet" only broadly follows the dictates of the Imagist manifesti, but perhaps what makes it a good poem is what does not make it a reverently Imagist poem. When she repeats "who would change for these," she lets the rhetorical reenter, creating an effect of awakening the reader from a dream of images into a world made of words.

Dylan Thomas, too, with his unsurpassed genius for sound, uses dia-mond and wing forms in his "Vision and Prayer" in such a way as to un-dermine the visual resolution of the work: the poem is an unusual in-stance of the possibility of putting sound into tension with image in a pattern poem. The sequence of geometrical forms is the first thing we no-tice in reading the poem, but once we enter the left-to-right progression of lines with their complex tension between exact rhymes, slant rhymes, and true "eye" rhymes at the line endings, and his cacophonous use of internal rhymes, assonance, and consonance, we are thrown into a kind of lurching, dancing imbalance. While such movement unsettles us, we travel horizontally across the lines and vertically down the page. Thomas uses these shapes, which are visual "opposites," to produce a pulsating tension between the externality of vision and the internality of prayer—or, because such reversals are truly the aim of the sequence, the inter-nality of vision and the externality of prayer.[75] What is outside in the realm of appearances and sounds is taken within the self, and what is in-side as image and thought is projected out into the world in this beseech-ing form. The beginning and end of the sequence as a whole indicate the bringing forward of the form and its gradual dissolution. The "midwife" of the opening "diamond" stanzas breaches internal and external space. Yet the final "wing" announces at its visual center, the place where a body would yoke the "wings" themselves, "I am found." And then the close of the same piece announces, "Now I am lost." The visual resolution of the poem thereby literally is undermined by the temporal, sequential order of the sounds.

In his classic study of the theory of perception, *Metamorphosis*, Er-nest G. Schachtel distinguishes between the lower senses of smell and taste and some forms of touch as "autocentric" and other forms of touch, sight, and hearing as "allocentric." The erotic satires we have been read-ing would be strongly autocentric, and the Imagist and concrete poems would be strongly allocentric in this sense. However, by these terms Schachtel does not intend an ascetic rejection of the animal senses but rather attempts to distinguish between senses resulting in feelings of plea-sure and pain and physically localized on or in the body (the lower senses) and senses transmitting knowledge about reality needed to orient the self (the higher senses).[76] The possibility that touch can be both autocentric and allocentric—it can be passively located in the body and limited to pleasure and pain as well as extending from the body and resulting in the externalization of its object—is an indication that there is not an absolute division between the function of the senses and that any given sense can be used for various ends. Visual experience, for example, can be autocentric or partial, when it involves the simple pleasure of enjoying a pure color or form, and it can be allocentric, or objectifying, when it grasps an object in the totality of its otherness. Pattern poems are of the group of phenomena we think of as having "outlines"—objects that have definable and recognizable spatial boundaries clarifying what they are from what they are not. When we apprehend another person allocentrically, in such an objectifying or outlining way, we also think of subjectivity as bound or delimited, and we ignore the temporal aspect of existence, thinking of other persons as fixed identities and viewing them from a fixed perspective.

Autocentric sense perception, Schachtel writes, "remains through life so much closer to the state of fused perceptions in which there is no clear distinction between subject and object and between sensory quality, pleasure, or unpleasure; they are particularly apt to reactivate complex, global sensorimotor-affective states, and, conversely, eidetic experiences in the autocentric senses are apt to arise when such a complex is activated by a need, a wish, a longing, or mood."[77] In other words, the autocentric senses of smell and taste merge the subject with the object of sense impression and thereby are strongly evocative of feelings and memories of past experiences with such objects: autocentric senses are particularly Proustian in this way. They are also, in their continuity and partialness, often surprising—although they involve elements of volition, they do not hold the object at a distance. Hence, smell and taste lend themselves readily to an aesthetic of surprise and involuntary evocation. In the poems quoted earlier, wit is often consequent to these autocentric qualities to the extent that wit involves both surprise and aggression. Surprise is the result of an unexpected proximity and aggression is linked to repulsion. On the scent of the closure of the poem, we can open the lid to find a place where "sweets compacted lie" or a Pandora's box that is in reality a brimming chamber pot.

III. THE LYRIC *EIDOS*

It is obvious that we could construct a history of the senses by tracing the functions of "lower" and "higher" sense experiences. That is, we could consider the history of the senses as the history of an economy that ranks the senses and regulates the body's relation to the social world. When we read a history of the theme of the five senses such as Vinge's *The Five Senses*, we become vividly aware of the role of anthropomorphic and allegorical representations of the senses in legislating human conduct. Even today we see evidence of the importance of this paradigm: the foregrounding of the senses of sight and hearing in electronic technology; transitory forms of asceticism in gastronomy and body building and the idea of being in training for one's own sexuality; the hyperadvertising of perfume and burgeoning popularity of aromatherapy made possible by the wafting away of their referents; the insertion of spectacle into new social spheres in the surveillance technology of the workplace and the photo opportunities of the political domain; the narrative of dissipation and conversion of television talk shows with their simultaneous ecstasy and denigration of the senses.

When works of art take on the theme of the five senses, an atmosphere of prurience and regulation is often created, regardless of the attitude of the creator. In Richard Brathwaite's early seventeenth-century *Essay upon the Five Senses*, the influence of Ignatius of Loyola's *Spiritual Exercises* of the 1520s, with their instructions for deploying the senses to spiritual ends, is readily evident. Brathwaite writes in "An advertisement to the devout Reader, upon the use of the five Senses" in the second edition of 1620: "Lend here thine *eare* of Zealous attention, fixe here thine *eye* of inward contemplation, that following the *savour* of thy Saviours oyntments, and *tasting* how Sweet he is in godness, thou may unfainedly be *touched* with remorse of conscience. Farewell." This lineage of the regulation of the senses can also be found in the humanist imperatives of these lines from W. H. Auden's well-known poem on the senses of 1950, "Precious Five":

Be patient, solemn nose,
Serve in a world of prose
The present moment well, . . .

Be modest, lively ears,
Spoiled darlings of a stage
Where any caper cheers
The paranoic mind
Of this undisciplined
And concert-going age, . . .

Be civil, hands; on you
Although you cannot read
is written what you do . . .

Look, naked eyes, look straight
At all eyes but your own . . .

Look outward, eyes, and love
Those eyes you cannot be.

Praise, tongue, the Earthly Muse
By number and by name
In any style you choose, . . .

Be happy, precious five, . . . [78]

Ignatius's exercises, here in felicitous form, are nevertheless the source of Stephen Dedalus's terror of the sermon on hell recorded in *A Portrait of the Artist as a Young Man*, and we will encounter them again as the foundation for Gerard Manley Hopkins's "desolate sonnets" of 1885.

This concern with regulating the senses, although of paramount importance in constructing a history of the senses, nevertheless tends to increase our alienation from the senses and takes us farther and farther away from an understanding of the broader place of the senses in aesthetic activity. Aesthetic activity viewed in the light of the history of ideological ends is no longer aesthetic; it erases the free activity of pleasure and knowledge that the aesthetic brings to human life. When Marx wrote that "the forming of the five senses is a labour of the entire history of the world down to the present," he was not beginning with an assumption of the senses as natural or given processes to be restricted and controlled by cultural and social activity. Rather, he considered the senses to be both shaped and shaping forces, productive of forms, influenced by and influencing historical developments in the species beyond the agency of individual subjects. Writing of vision, he says, "The eye has become a *human* eye, just as its *object* has become a social, *human* object—an object made by man for man. The senses have therefore become directly in their practice theoreticians." He goes on to propose, "Not only the five senses" but what he calls the "mental" or "practical" senses (will, love, etc.) come to be "by virtue of their object, by virtue of humanized nature." [79] The relation of a person to his or her senses is imagined by Marx as of increasing importance. The ongoing formation, even cultivation, of the senses is for Marx a recovery of that power of the body lost to the alienating effects of private property. "The transcendence of private property," he writes, "is therefore the complete *emancipation* of all human senses and quantities, but it is this emancipation precisely because these senses and attributes have become, subjectively and objectively human." Humanized nature is contrasted to elemental need: "for the starving man it is not the human form of food that exists, but only its abstract being as food . . . the dealer in minerals sees only the commercial values, but not the beauty and unique nature of the mineral: he has no *mineralogical* sense."[80]

Who knows, even more than a hundred years after that sentence was written, what such a pure "mineralogical sense" might be? Marx imagines the history of sense impression as a labor of emancipation that would only be finished in a moment of Hegelian fulfillment, a point of replete consciousness, where the senses, free of the contingency of nature and the political economy, were wholly determined and determining in accordance with human ends. Marx's version of the history of the senses might be seen as compensatory to the ways of looking at the senses we have emphasized thus far—the history of taxonomies, hierarchies, and other models of the senses. For taxonomies and hierarchies of the senses tend both to overestimate the role of human will and overgeneralize the senses. In contrast, the history of the senses can be enriched and made more particular by an analysis of aesthetic acts and their consequences.

If we want to examine the senses as a historical, human formation, the place to begin is not only in the philosophical debates on the status of the senses in relation to reality, or in the history of courtesy books and other documentary records of first-person experience, but also in the history of art as the history of human making in accordance with human ends of expression. Poetic metaphor is at the center of form-giving activity in any aesthetic practice; it enables us to mediate and entertain at once our capacities for sense impressions and abstraction and to imagine, through both memory and projection, forms beyond the contingent circumstances of our immediate experience. The various arts of sculpture, painting, music, drama, dance, and poetry—regardless of genre or theme—all call on the senses used in our meetings with other persons by foregrounding certain experiences of touch, seeing, hearing, or kinesthesia or by presenting them in synesthetic combination. Lyric poetry in particular as the expression and record of the image of the first-person speaker across and through historical and cultural contexts provides us with a form on the boundary among sense impressions, somatic memory, individuation of agency, and social context.

In many ways the genre of lyric has as its task the crossing of thresholds among persons, positions, and social groups. Whenever traditions have first-person expression in song or otherwise metrically organized language and distinguish such expression from choral forms, prose forms, and other genres, lyric takes on this function. Although clearly there are myriad particular genres and finer distinctions one might make culturally and historically in studying lyric, it is also possible to argue the case for a transcultural study of lyric and for lyric to be considered specifically as a genre of cultural transformation.

Of course, we remember that Herder, Hegel, and others held that, in distinction to the musical, visual, and plastic arts with their respective reliance on hearing, seeing, and touch, poetry works by no sense at all, through an immediacy of the soul or an energy emanating from a shaping spirit. But we can also find in lyric a repository of synaesthesia, an archive of the history of how the form has served as a means for working through the body's ongoing mutuality of relations between nature and exterior objects and the ego's necessary articulation of itself as both separate from the world and transformed by the world. Kant's discussion of time in his *Critique of Pure Reason* is of particular relevance here as we think about the relations between interiority and external objects. For Kant, time is a pure form of sensuous intuition and a necessary representation within which all phenomena appear, including our sense of our inner consciousness. Kant argues that "time is nothing but the form of our own internal intuition," our primary means of representing ourselves to ourselves."[81] As first-person expression in measured language, lyric poetry lends significant —that is, shared and memorable—form to the inner consciousness that is time itself. The most obvious facts of lyric practice—lyric as first-person expression and lyric as the most musical of literary forms—are the most interesting here. In lyric synaesthesia figuration is accomplished by sound, and spatial interval makes sound intelligible and subject to measure.

In "On Lyric Poetry and Society," first delivered as a radio address to the German public, Theodor Adorno argues that the bourgeois ideology of lyric—that lyric works are opposed to society, fragile, and removed from historical and political concerns—conceals the genuine cultural work of lyric. For Adorno, lyric's task is to mediate between particularity and totality in the representation of persons. His concern is with the status of lyric in late capitalist society, but it echoes aspects of Romantic philosophies of lyric that in turn drew on Aristotle's account in the *Poetics* of poetry's situation between the particulars of history and the abstractions of philosophy. Samuel Taylor Coleridge writes in the *Biographia Literaria*, "I adopt with full faith the principle of Aristotle that poetry as poetry, is essentially *ideal*, that it avoids and excludes all *accident*, that its apparent individualities of rank, character, or occupation, must be *representative* of a class; and that the *persons* of poetry must be clothed with *generic* attributes, with the *common* attributes of the class: not with such as one gifted individual might *possibly* possess, but such as from his situation it is most probably before-hand that he *would* possess."[82] William Wordsworth also follows Aristotle in "Preface to *Lyrical Ballads*," in viewing poetry's universality as rooted in the specificity of emotion and formal effects:

> In spite of difference of soil and climate, of language and manners, of laws and customs, in spite of things silently gone out of mind and things violently destroyed, the Poet binds together by passion and knowledge the vast empire of human society, as it is spread over the whole earth, and over all time. The objects of the Poet's thoughts are everywhere; though the eyes and senses of man are, it is true, his favorite guides, yet he will follow wheresoever he can find an atmosphere of sensation in which to move his wings. Poetry is the first and last of all knowledge—it is as immortal as the heart of man.[83]

In line with these pronouncements and the aesthetics of Schiller, Adorno writes that "the substance of a poem is not merely an expression of individual impulses and experiences. Those become a matter of art only when they come to participate in something universal by virtue of the specificity they acquire in being given aesthetic form."[84] He advocates a particular kind of formalist method that moves inductively from an account of the features of the work outward to social forms. He rejects the idea that the poem can be a symptom of a preconceived ideology. Like Marx, he contends that the "I" of the artwork, especially in lyric work, attempts to restore, through animation and figuration, the subject alienated from nature. Lyric poems are always in this sense occasions for the emergence of subjectivity out of alienation:

> Even lyric works in which no trace of conventional and concrete existence, no crude materiality remains, the greatest lyric works in our language, owe their quality to the force with which the "I" creates the illusion of nature emerging from alienation. Their pure subjectivity, the aspect of them that appears seamless and harmonious, bears witness to its opposite, to suffering in an existence alien to the subject and to love for it as well—indeed, their harmoniousness is actually nothing but the mutual accord of this suffering and this love.[85]

Adorno's argument concludes that the temporal enunciation of the subject counters both a reification of the subject and any finite determination of subjective lack.

We might remember that in Vico's argument about the origins of metaphor in the experience of terror and fear of nature, metaphor bridges the

relations between individual human experiences: metaphor's aim is not—
like that of sacrifice, for example—to establish a determined relation between human beings and gods. In this sense, Vico's ideas about intersubjectivity and metaphor intersect in interesting ways with the work of the
pioneering semiotician Charles Morris. Writing on "the interpersonality
of the language sign," Morris notes that "only if an organism can react to
its own activity (or its products) with an interpretation similar to that
made to this activity (or its products) by another organism can a sign pro-
ducible by one organism have to that organism a signification in common
with that of other interpreting organisms." Organisms must, in this sense,
be able to "stand in each other's shoes" in order to represent experiences
to themselves. Morris especially emphasizes the importance of response:
"most responses of an organism do not affect the receptors of an organism
making the response as they do the receptors of other organisms—the organism, for instance, does not see its facial movements as do other organisms." [86] Just as language is necessary to our sense that objects are enduring, so is the reception of facial movement necessary for our sense of our
own reality. This is the basis of recognition, the emergence of the person
that begins in the intersubjective interpretation of metaphor and continues in the cultural work of all poetic forms.

The punctuation of the temporal flow of inner consciousness, the
organization of memory, the determination of feeling, the articulation of
point of view in space and time—these qualities of lyric are not the eruption of the body in an already-determined framework of perception.
Rather, these qualities characterize our transition toward subjectivity,
just as reflection on them transforms the terms of subjectivity and consequently transforms the terms of objectivity so that neither can provide the
"context" for the other. Adorno writes:

> The paradox specific to the lyric work, a subjectivity that turns into ob-
> jectivity, is tied to the priority of linguistic form in the lyric; it is that pri-
> ority from which the primacy of language in literature in general (even in
> prose forms) is derived. . . . Hence the highest lyric works are those in
> which the subject, with no remaining trace of mere matter, sounds forth
> in language until language itself acquires a voice. . . . This is why the
> lyric reveals itself to be most deeply grounded in society when it does not
> chime in with society, when it communicates nothing, when, instead, the
> subject whose expression is successful reaches an accord with language
> itself, with the inherent tendency of language.[87]

Adorno's argument here is that subjectivity articulates itself as a singular
voice when it is most objective, when it takes itself to the limit of what

linguistic experience might be able to produce and at that limit is expressed in its fullest particularity.

This transition from an inarticulate subjectivity toward an articulate one via objective form is familiar to us by now from Vico's discussion of the "extremely disturbed passions" at the root of the production of metaphor and Jean-Jacques Rousseau's theory of the origins of language in emotion.[88] A similar approach can be found in Coleridge's position on metric as an act of will. In a passage in the *Biographia Literaria*, Coleridge explains that meter arises as an act of mastery or pleasure in the face of an onslaught of passion (i.e., pain): "This [meter] I would trace to the balance in the mind effected by that spontaneous effort which strives to hold in check the workings of passion. It might be easily explained likewise in what manner this salutary antagonism is assisted by the very state which it counteracts; and how this balance of antagonists became organized into meter . . . by a supervening act of the will and judgement, consciously and for the foreseen purpose of pleasure . . . [there must be] an interpenetration of passion and of will."[89]

Indeed, there is a long tradition linking pain and mastery. This idea stems from Anaxagoras's argument that perception involves pain or, alternatively, Plotinus's gloss on Anaxagoras, that suffering is likened to unknowing and knowledge is likened to mastering. Anaxagoras's argument is helpful as a theory of metaphor, for he contended that the effect of "unlike upon unlike" was particularly difficult to bear when it was excessive in duration or intensity. Confronted with the cognitive dissonance of unintelligible relations, we find relief in comparisons of likeness and similitude.[90] Vico and Friedrich Nietzsche, too, argue that pain necessitates the invention of metaphor. Such arguments rest on the assumption that lack motivates the desire for the production of form and that a trajectory from pain to pleasure is created through such production.

Such ontological arguments should not be confused with themes of pleasure or pain in works of art. That producing a thematic of pain might be a cure for pain and consequent form of pleasure is discussed early on in Aristotle's *Poetics* with its comments on the pleasure we might take in viewing an exact representation of a corpse. Another key text would be Wordsworth's "Preface to *Lyrical Ballads*" for its complex presentation of the interrelations of pain and pleasure in poetic composition.[91] Wordsworth writes:

> The end of Poetry is to produce excitement in co-existence with an overbalance of pleasure; but, by the supposition, excitement is an unusual and irregular state of the mind; ideas and feelings do not, in that state,

succeed each other in accustomed order. If the words, however, by which this excitement is produced be in themselves powerful, or the images and feelings have an undue proportion of pain connected with them, there is some danger that the excitement may be carried beyond its proper bounds. Now the co-presence of something regular, something to which the mind has been accustomed in various moods and in a less excited state, cannot but have great efficacy in tempering and restraining the passion by an intertexture of ordinary feeling. . . . [T]here can be little doubt but that more pathetic situations and sentiments, that is, those which have a greater proportion of pain connected with them, may be endured in metrical composition, especially in rhyme, than in prose.

In theories of lyric from Vico forward, the enunciation of pain at the origin of lyric must appear before the emergence of a self-conscious sense of one's own subjectivity—what Damasio called the "autobiographical self." To equate pain with subjectivity is to equate the body with subjectivity and so to confuse the most collective with the most individual. Pain has no memory; its expression depends on the intersubjective invention of association and metaphor. The situation of the person resides in the genesis of the memory of action and experience in intersubjective terms— that is, in the articulation and mastery of the originating pain. Coleridge explains that in the "frequency of forms and figures of speech," we find "offsprings of passion" who are as well "adopted children of power."[92] Yet the mastery of pain through measures and figures is not merely repressive; it is as well a matter of coming to knowledge and expression. Coleridge's explanation shows a subject coming into activity out of a passive relation to sense experience, memory and expectation. Here the figures and forms created are those of a subjectivity enunciating itself.

Divergence in lyric is thus not between language and music but between a subject transforming him- or herself from the somatic both toward and against the social. The history of lyric is thereby the history of a relation between pronouns, the genesis of *ego-tu* and *ego-vos* in the reciprocity of an imagination posing and composing itself and its audience via the work of time. Lyric conventions of addresser and addressee are the working through on the level of literary *genre* of the function of linguistic shifters. As Roman Jakobson, following the pioneering work of Emile Benveniste, explains in his classic essay on "Shifters, Verbal Categories, and the Russian Verb," shifters are both *symbols*, associated with represented objects by conventional rules, and *indices*, terms in existential relation to those objects they represent. Shifters are "indexical symbols." The pronoun *I*, explains Jakobson, means the person uttering *I*. "Thus, on one hand, the sign *I* cannot represent its object without being associated with the latter by a conventional rule [the conventional aspect is that *I* always means the addresser and *you* the addressee of the message to which it belongs] and in different codes the same meaning is assigned to different sequences such as *I, ego, ich, ja*, etc.: consequently *I* is a symbol. On the other hand, the sign *I* cannot represent its object without being in existential relation with this object: the word *I* designating the utterer is existentially related to his utterance, and hence functions as an index."[93]

First-person expression in lyric is related existentially to the context of the poem as a whole; it is the poem that makes first-person expression emerge in its individuality as it engages the reader in the eidetic task of the appearance of the "you." The doubled "I" (authorial intention, the expression of first-person voice in the text) encounters a doubled "you" (the reader's intention toward reception, the implied addressee in the text). The contemporary philosopher Giorgio Agamben emphasizes that "before designating real objects, pronouns and other indices of enunciation indicate precisely that *language is taking place*; in this sense, they refer to the very *event* of *language* before referring to a world of signifieds."[94] We are reminded of Adorno's point that in the most sublime lyric works, the first-person expression evolves into the voice of language itself. Lyric brings forward, as the necessary precondition of its creation of a world of "I's" and "you's" in mutual recognition, this place of language as the foundation of intersubjectivity and intersubjectivity as the foundation for the recognition of persons.

A poem such as the closing work of Eliot's *Collected Poems*, "A Dedication to My Wife," summarizes these aspects of poetic intersubjectivity with an uneasy sense of lyric as an intimacy overheard: "But this dedication is for others to read: / These are private words addressed to you in public."[95] The poem contends that sensual pleasure is replete in itself and has no need for articulation; speech between lovers needs only proximity—the call for meaning arises as a consequence of distance. Eliot addresses the public from the start—indeed, from the instantiating moment of his desire to write a poem. But he also addresses the public with his use of the possessive "ours and ours only," placing all others beyond the space he thereby dedicates to his wife. The poem begins in pleasure, but somehow, for some unarticulated reason, pleasure does not suffice and the poet feels compelled toward meaning, that meaning that only comes into being in its encounter with the third position—the listener who introduces the social realm of intersubjectivity.

Bruno Snell makes a sweeping historical argument for this role of lyric in culture in his book on *The Discovery of Mind* in Greek thought. His influential theory regarding the rise of the concept of the individual in early Greek lyric is based on his studies of the "personal lyrics" of Sappho, Archilochus, and Anacreon. For the Greeks, the lyric is a sung poem and "they did not list 'personal' poetry as a separate genre." Such personal lyrics could be sung to a lyre or, in another form, sung to a flute. Snell argues that in talking of themselves in such lyrics, poets came to be conscious of what was particular or distinctive about their persons. Sentiments such as Archilochus's "each man has his heart cheered in his own way" may universalize the emotion of being cheered, yet they also single out the experience of individual persons. In Anacreon's and Archilochus's poems, individualism is tied to individual choice and values often at odds with the values of society as a whole. A separation between internal and external values thus arises. Sappho may have been familiar with the poems of Archilochus, and Snell argues that what comes to fruition in her work is this distinction between "what others prize and what one's own judgment declares to be essential." The particular innovation she creates is "a new distinction between Being and appearance . . . since it is understood that love is not a private whim, not a subjective affectation, but an experience of the supra-personal of divine dimensions. The lover cannot but find his way to some reality through the agency of his individual passion."[96]

Snell's is a dramatic and controversial statement, contending nothing less than that the practice of the art form evokes a change in consciousness. Yet he builds his case very carefully, and his critics have often missed the subtlety of his discussion. For Snell has singled out the formal features of lyric—the musical accompaniment that makes the creation of form out of rhythm an analogue for emotional compulsion; the first-person expression evolving under a restriction of intelligibility toward others; the mutual articulation of, and tension between, "interior consciousness" and "external decorum"—and argues that the process of artistic choice, orientation, closure, and reception created such changes in consciousness incrementally. Choice is the means of poetic making and the very substance of the dawning self. Snell reminds us especially that such a "self" only emerges in a context of reception, a context both anticipated and realized: "Emotion never relaxes into uncertainty, but always maintains a steady course towards a concrete goal dictated by desire or ambition. This also explains why the archaic poets, as has long been recognized, never express themselves. . . . They always address themselves to a partner, either a deity—especially in prayer—or an individual or an entire group of men. Though the individual who detaches himself from his environment severs many old bonds, his discovery of the dimension of the soul once more joins him in company with those who have fought their way to the same insight. The isolation of the individual is, by the same token, the forging of new bonds."[97]

What Snell does not discuss is that historically such classical lyrics have become for us emblems of a fragmented, yet perfected, subjectivity, just as the Apollo Belvedere or the Venus de Milo represent bodily ideals through their very partiality. W. R. Johnson writes in *The Idea of Lyric,* "No experience in reading, perhaps, is more depressing and more frustrating than to open a volume to Sappho's fragments and to recognize, yet again—for one always hopes that somehow this time will be different— that this poetry is all but lost to us. . . . Even though we know that Greek lyric is mere fragments, indeed, *because* we know that Greek lyric is mere fragments, we act, speak, and write as if the unthinkable had not happened, as if pious bishops, careless monks, and hungry mice had not consigned Sappho and her lyrical colleagues to irremediable oblivion."[98] Here is Sappho's *phainetai moi,* "peer of the gods," in a recent translation by Jim Powell:

In my eyes he matches the gods, that man who
sits there facing you—any man whatever—
listening from closeby to the sweetness of your
voice as you talk, the

sweetness of your laughter: yes, that—I swear it—
sets the heart to shaking inside my breast, since
once I look at you for a moment, I can't
speak any longer,

but my tongue breaks down, and then all at once a
subtle fire races inside my skin, my
eyes can't see a thing and a whirring whistle
thrums at my hearing,

cold sweat covers me and a trembling takes
ahold of me all over: I'm greener than the
grass is and appear to myself to be little
short of dying.
But all must be endured, since even a poor [[99]

In this fragment the speaker describes her reaction to her own merely voyeuristic position as one of hushed voice, broken tongue, fire beneath the flesh, tremors, pains, sweat and blanched limbs. Powell includes the final fragmented line, usually omitted by translators: "But all must be endured, since even a poor [." At least since Longinus, who preserved in his treatise on the sublime the only existing early record of the lyric, it has been this fragment, without the final line, that has come to exemplify the sublime unity of classical lyric: "Do you not marvel," Longinus writes, "how she seeks to make her mind, body, ears, tongue, eyes, and complexion, as if they were scattered elements strange to her, join together in the same moment of experience? In contradictory phrases she describes herself as hot and cold at once, rational and irrational, at the same time terrified and almost dead." Longinus praises "her selection of the most vital details and her working them into one whole which produce the outstanding quality of the poem."[100] In Longinus's account, it is the third-person viewpoint—what we might see as both the "natural" viewpoint of the poem and its viewpoint on the level of representation—that unifies the poem. But Powell, following Snell's work on the relation between lyric and first-person consciousness, points to what is perhaps a more profound aspect of this poem and of Sappho's lyrics more generally: Sappho has visualized her sensations from "the vantage afforded by the spectacle of their repetition."[101]

In Sappho's lyric the sensations presented might be more accurately described as experiences of pain. By staging the scene of her sensation of suffering, Sappho acquires an intersubjective position from which to speak. If Eliot's "Dedication" acknowledges the necessity of the third person as the excluded listener, Sappho's lyric compels an identification *between* the listener and the speaker as excluded listener. Although the space described is open to view, the poem might be considered as an instance of the genre παρακλαυσίθυρον *(paraclausithyron)*, the "excluded lover's complaint," or complaint at the door, for it describes the progress of the lover from one blockage to another, the senses constantly turned back from the object of the speaker's desire. The path of sensation in the poem moves from the objectivity of sight to the interior, tactile sensation of trembling. At the outset sight blocks hearing—in torment, the speaker can hear *sound* but not actual words and phrases. And this sensation of a kind of broken synesthesia, in which sight is accompanied by an intricate blockage in hearing, results in the shaking, first of the heart and eventually of the whole body, that breaks down the speech by which the poem itself is being constructed. As seeing entirely gives way and hearing even of sounds gives way, the speaker's trembling takes her to the "green" state of near-death. She moves, as do all lyric speakers, from being spoken to *speaking,* from pain to articulation, from private sensation to intersubjectivity. "Peer of the gods" serves as Longinus's example of sublimity because he contends the representation of sublimity in art is the repetition and mastery of physical or cognitive pain. Emotion recollected in tranquility[102] is emotion under the rule of either the understanding or the reason, shaped into form in accordance with human ends.

To what extent this paradigm of the repetition of pain under conditions of mastery might be a transcultural account of lyric origins is yet another question. Let us look at some metrically organized first-person expressions from a quite different linguistic tradition: the Tlingit people of Alaska. In his 1908 report to the Bureau of American Ethnology, "Tlingit Myths and Texts," John R. Swanton records a variety of examples of Tlingit genres, including myths, speeches for ceremonial occasions, and songs, which he had collected in Sitka and Wrangell, Alaska, in the winter and early spring of 1904. Franz Boas noted ten years later, in his own studies of Northwest Coast art, that like other forms, verbal art was marked by "simplicity of style . . . where poems consist sometimes of the introduction of a single word into a musical line, the music being carried by a burden, sometimes of a purely formal enumeration of the powers of supernatural beings."[103] Of the songs he collected, Swanton wrote, "The language of these songs is so highly metaphorical that they are often difficult to understand even in the light of the native explanations, and in some cases the author's informants were themselves uncertain with regard to the meaning. Several songs refer to myths and are explained by them, and there are a few shamans' songs, but by far the larger number were composed for feasts or in song contests between men who were at enmity with each other."[104] Among the latter is number 64, a song "composed by Among-the-brant (Qênxo') of the KîksA'dî, about Sāxa', when his wife had been taken from him, and he felt very sad. The last words are said to be in Tsimshian":

Xāq! łidzī' yaAxtuwu'. Wudjkē't xoyā'îtc yāt Axtuwu'.
[To me is very this my [Around I were to my mind]
hard mind] carrying this
Hayu' wAłgā'k cînda'?
[In Tsimshian: What is the matter with you?]

Swanton translates as follows: "My own mind is very hard to me. It is just as if I were carrying my mind around. What is the matter with you?"

This song is linked to several other texts in the Swanton anthology. First, it bears some reference through the composer's proper name "Qênxo'" (the prefix *qên* meaning "brant"—in English, "Among-the-brant"), to myths Swanton records as numbers 24 and 54. These two myths recount stories of brant brides, who alternate between their bird and human forms and who marry human men. In both these stories, the human husbands leave their own moieties to act to help the brant, and specifically their fathers-in-law, in situations of war and distress. Tlingit marriage is exogamous and matrilineal, so when a man makes an exogamous marriage to a brant woman, his progeny will be members of the brant, just as the future actions of the mythic exogamous husbands demonstrate newly assumed brant filiations. The historical actions lying behind this mourning song reverse the situation of a man making an exogamous marriage, for here the wife is the one who is removed from her family group as she is taken away by force.

These myths can be said to bear a relation to the first-person present experience of the song in a fashion analogous to the role allusions to the *Iliad* play in many of Sappho's present-centered lyrics. Among-the-brant is allying himself with Sāxa' in a situation of distress as the mythic husbands ally themselves with their brant relatives. The lyric singer seems spoken through by a pain comparable to that of the injured Sāxa' himself: he is alienated from his own mind, a condition that is very "hard" to him and that recapitulates the situation of incommensurable identification with the pain of another. The last line, in Tsimshian, moves away from the deep interiority of this painful state into a situation of overly extended exteriority—"What is the matter with you?" is a question that can be answered only through a process of intersubjective translation, whether it is addressed from the closest interior identification or the most extended boundary-crossing communication between Tlingit and Tsimshian speakers. Remarkably, the lyric compels any Tlingit listener to move toward a less intelligible, or unintelligible, language at closure and any Tsimshian listener to begin in a situation of less intelligibility, or unintelligibility, toward the closure as a revelation. The singer, Among-the-brant, is speaking out of the pain of empathy and being spoken through by the utterance of Sāxa': there is no place in the song where we can tell whether the convention at work is direct first-person expression or dramatic monologue.

The problem is already anticipated in Aristotle's *Poetics*, Section III, where he writes "given the same medium and the same object, one can imitate partly by narration and partly by dramatic dialogue (as Homer does); or one can speak invariably in one's own person; or one can use actors to imitate the whole thing as though they were living in it themselves." [105] A work is narrative if the poet him- or herself is the agent of the presentation in the work, whereas it is dramatic if the work involves a presentation by his agent or actor. In Among-the-brant's song we find the same ambiguity between the first person and the representation of first person that we might encounter in any textual fragment from any tradition. Yet inevitably there is a figuration of one person by means of another's expression through retrospection.

Of even more immediate relevance to Among-the-brant's song is a second textual analogue: the next song Swanton records, number 65, which is on the same subject of the kidnapping of Sáxa''s wife. In this case the song was composed by Sáxa' himself and Swanton provides further information in a note, explaining that a man named K!ułt!e'-īc, belonging to the Chilkat Ká'gwAntān, ran away with Sáxa''s wife. Then Sáxa''s wife was afterward killed by the kidnapper's first wife, whom he had abandoned:

Dēsgwʌ'tc	gî gêsîtī'n	ke	yAgAdîda'	yʌ'diyēł.
[Already	you have seen	up	going to the spirit world	this Raven.]

Acdayī'n	āyʌ'x	uwagu't	doqōdjî'.	NA'na	yîs	aositī'n	dogodjî'.
[To see her	out to her	has come	her Wolf (phratry)	Death	for	she has seen	her Wolf (phratry).]

Swanton's translation of this song is "You have already seen this Raven going up to the ghost country. Her Wolf phratry has come out to see her. She has seen her Wolf phratry for death."

The Ká'gwAntān clan is part of the Eagle moiety, and the Chilkat River is predominantly the territory of Raven (KîksAdî) moiety clans, according to a recent essay on Swanton's work by the foremost contemporary authorities on Tlingit, Dick and Nora Dauenhauer.[106] The Dauenhauers have both praised Swanton's care in his transcription and criticized his neglect of details of the kinship terms that they contend lie at the heart of the motivation for Tlingit songs, including mourning songs such as these. Nevertheless, following their work on another Swanton song, number 80, we might note that Sáxa''s wife, kidnapped by a man whose name reflects a territorial ambiguity between the Eagle and Raven moieties, is mourned by Sáxa' in such a way as to restore her identity to her Wolf moiety, the moiety that would have been the locus for his relationship with her and for their progeny, now cruelly thwarted by her murder. Her dislocation as a Raven is ended by the greeting of the wolves.

Too much is missing for any reading of such a poem to be confident of explanation. Johnson's lament about the material disappearance of Sappho's lyrics is readily transposed to the problem of Native American songs recorded by textual means and now often our only evidence of languages that have either disappeared or are threatened with disappearance. But even through such fragments of songs, we can see that lyric expression differs significantly from myth and discursive speech by its immediacy, its expression of pain through sung means, and its ability to cross the threshold between subjects in the interest of the figuration of a human countenance. I would argue that we do not have to know, nor indeed could we know, cultural contexts in all of their particularity before we follow the movement of available lyric fragments—such a totality of contextualization is impossible. Nor must we root every detail of such works in specific historical and cultural precedents, for it is one of the cultural tasks of lyric to create the specificity of such contexts—to manifest individual experience in such a way that particulars are intelligible. There is not a boilerplate for understanding Sāxa''s emotion; Sāxa''s expression of emotion and Among-the-brant's expression of Sāxa''s emotion are the beginning of a possibility of understanding what is Tlingit and what is universal about the situation of mourning.

In the transference of emotion in these lyrics, we find the work of lyric form to be the constitution of the image or *eidos* of persons.[107] There is a profound connection between the person and the *persona* or figured mask here. Pound's 1952 assemblage of his shorter poems under the title *Personae* call attention to the relation between representing the self and representing others in two poems that we can read as a progression. The first dates to his 1908–1910 collection:

> *On His Own Face in a Glass*
>
> O strange face there in the glass!
> O ribald company, O saintly host,
> O sorrow-swept my fool,
> What answer? O ye myriad
> That strive and play and pass,
> Jest, challenge, counterlie!
> I? I? I?
>   And ye?

The second is from the "Lustra" collection of 1912:

> *Coda*
>
> O My songs,
> Why do you look so eagerly and so curiously into people's faces,
> Will you find your lost dead among them? [108]

Whereas the first poem displays the face of the self in the mirror's mask, in which myriad are the face's expressions and myriad are the responses of others until the multiplication of "I's" is only resolved in the second-person plural view of "ye,"[109] the second poem shows the self turning away from its own image in the desire to recover what is truly its own and what it truly has lost—its own dead, its own beloved faces in the faces of others.

Rather than think of the mask as a device of concealment under which the true identity, the irreducibility of material flesh, will lie, we might think of the mask as the representation of intelligible expressions of emotion. Human beings are unique in the complexity of form and range of semantic interpretations of their facial expressions—expressions that we have seen, in our mention of Charles Morris's work in semiotics, are dependent on the recognition of others, for we cannot see our own faces. Recent work on animal calls as antecedent to the evolution of human linguistic behavior has linked several features of such calls to human facial expressions. Most significant, these features indicate that many animal calls are volitional and not merely, as eighteenth- and nineteenth-century writers had often contended, unbidden responses to pain, alarm, or other forms of stimulation. Correlatively, many animal calls are context-dependent, often involving an "audience effect," whereby the presence of a "listener" or recipient for the call stimulates calling behavior. Even more dramatically, such calls can be fictional, as when the food calls of cocks to hens are given deceptively; the male holds something inedible in his bill as he calls from a distance to the female. Such calls can show signs of individual idiosyncrasy, and the successful functioning of a social group might depend in fact on the overlapping functions of such individual markers. Human facial expressions are analogously used in a paralinguistic way to modulate the meaning of spoken words, to indicate emphasis, and to stimulate turn taking in conversation.[110] Furthermore, human facial displays are most likely to be expressive *to* another person, rather than expressive of underlying states of emotion. They are far more likely to be expressed when there is a receiver present.[111]

This research suggestively recalls R. G. Collingwood's important distinction in his *Principles of Art* between arousing and expressing emotions: "'Expressing' emotions is certainly not the same thing as arousing them. There is emotion there before we express it. But as we express it, we confer upon it a different kind of emotional colouring; in one way, therefore, expression creates what it expresses, for exactly this emotion, colouring and all, only exists so far as it is expressed. Finally, we cannot say

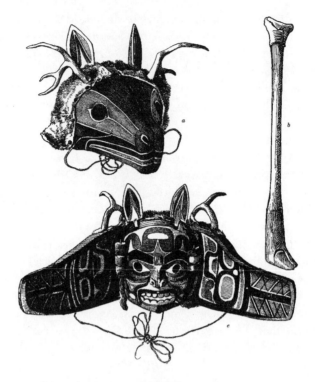

Laŏ'laxa Mask Representing the Deer
(a) Mask closed; (b) bone of the foreleg of the deer, carried in the
hands of the dancer; (c) mask opened, showing the figure of a
human face. (From Boas 1895)

what 'emotion' is, except that we mean by it the kind of thing which, on
the kind of occasion we are talking about, is expressed." Simply arousing
emotion is something Collingwood associates with craft and the generalization or typification of response: it is clear that by "craft" he has something in mind like mere rhetoric. Art proper was the expression of emotion in a highly individuated sense. Collingwood feels that art enlarges
and clarifies consciousness as it involves more and more complex forms
of emotional expression.[112]

Masks can be seen as devices for extending further the possible range
of emotional expression. As D. W. Lucas explains in his history of the
Greek tragic poets, "It is probably no accident that Dionysus, the god of
tragedy, was one of the two Greek gods who thought to enter into possession of human beings, and that the mask is associated with his worship."[113] In his classic essay on the origins of the self, Marcel Mauss discusses how the entire dramatic system of a culture can be more than

aesthetic: "it is religious, cosmic, mythological, social and personal." At stake in such a system is every aspect of the social hierarchy and its articulation of individuals as well as the very existence of "the ancestors who are reincarnated in those who have a claim to them, who return to life in the bodies of those who bear their names—to which perpetuity is guaranteed by the ritual in all its phases." He particularly cites "an institution and object common from the Nootka to the Tlingit of Northern Alaska; this is the use of remarkable masks with double and even triple shutters, which open to reveal the two and three beings (superimposed totems) personified by the creator of the mask."[114] If we look at the text Mauss used as evidence for this point, Franz Boas's 1895 compilation of the field notes of George Hunt (the son of a Scottish father and a Native American mother who was trained as an ethnographer by Boas), we find that it is often the case that the last shutter opens to reveal a human face. In figure 192 of this text, reproduced here on p. 56, a deer mask opens to a human face; in figure 195, a killer whale mask opens to a human face; and in figure 194, a collection of masks is displayed which represents a range of human speakers.[115]

I would suggest that it is exactly this sort of shuttering effect that is created when Among-the-brant expresses in Tlingit Sāxa''s emotion and then asks his question of the audience in Tsimshian. Sappho, in the spectacle of the repetition of her experience of shattering, similarly gives aesthetic boundaries—the Sapphic that is her very namesake—to an experience that cannot be totalized or visualized because it takes place deep within her own body and consciousness. In Sappho's lyric the speaking subject triumphs over the subject of mere being. Lyric poems and masks arrest the flux of facial expression. As forms of art with closure and repeatability, they enable a complex and overdetermined response in the realm of face-to-face experience—experience to hand and within the sphere of individual gesture and individual reception.

2

SOUND

I. DYNAMICS OF POETIC SOUND

At dawn as the bird songs come to the surface of the light, I hear the call and then the spill of songs—like pages flying from a musical copying machine—of the mockingbird. Does the mockingbird express not only a compulsion to sound in his own song but also, in his mimicking songs, another form of will—a compulsion to individuate sound? Is this then his song: "I am the mockingbird, the one who sounds *like* a cardinal, like a wren, like an oriole, as I please"? And in what ways are the mockingbird's songs continuous with the human uses of sound, for the mockingbird, *mimus polyglottos*, not only sings his own songs, which are wonders of improvisation and special effects; he also can imitate the songs of others.

The mockingbird's mocking songs are imitations without reciprocity. Properly, they are forms of echo. Though his songs arise from their songs, and although they are occasionally fooled, the cardinal, the wren, and the oriole do not respond to what he sings. Herder once said of parrots and starlings, they "have learned enough human sounds; but have they ever thought a human word?"[1] The mockingbird is not thinking a cardinal word, a wren word, an oriole word. Human songs can be carried over time and space, and they will be met with response and acted on. When they are reported and repeated in this way, they acquire both fixed form and a capacity to change. We humans speak in conditions of reciprocity, but also, like mockingbirds, we speak in conditions of imitation—and when we practice the arts of fiction, we are imitating, and responding to, our own conditions of reciprocity. Yet when the human voice is singing, no birds sing.

Mauss suggests that it was only retrospectively that etymologists constructed the source of the Latin term *persona* in *per-sonare*, the mask through which the voice of the actor or agent will sound.[2] Nevertheless, throughout his history of the development of the concept of a person—the relation of masks to the rights of name and family in ancient Rome; the attachment of the cognomen to the *imago* or wax death mask of the face; the dual sense of the person as a role and inner, intimate conscience that arose under Stoic philosophy; the Christian concept of the soul; and the modern concept of the psychological self—a paradigm of inner feeling and outward expression develops wherein the individuality of the inner self is the ground of all rights and receptivity regarding expression. As Mauss himself summarizes such a history, "From a mere masquerade to the mask, from a role to a person, to a name, to an individual, from the last to a being with metaphysical and ethical values, from the latter to a fundamental form of thought and action—that is the route we have covered."[3] This is thereby the history of the modern notion of the person, one who is the subject of experience and maker of choices, one whose existence is in and for itself.

Thus far we have spoken in general terms about the origins of subjectivity in the drive toward figuration or representation of persons and of the ongoing work of *poiēsis* as the articulation and preservation of such images as we encounter them in face-to-face situations. Yet poetry is a form of verbal representation, and, even in its written form, it evokes aspects of aurality in production and reception. In this chapter and the next I will focus on this aural dimension of poetry, placing it within a phenomenology of hearing and voicing. To speak of the aural aspect of poetry is to begin to speak necessarily of its linguistic dimension, but we will also need to consider the prelinguistic and extralinguistic dimensions of sound embedded in the language of poetry. Here the semantic and discursive aspects of poetry emerge from, but do not entirely displace, such nonsemantic features.

Earlier we saw in the discourses on the hierarchies of the senses that eating and speech were necessarily regulated, that the mouth as a site of introjection and extrajection came under a certain economy. The separation of animal and human functions is key to that economy and one that marks the division between the expression of nonmeaningful and meaningful sounds. Ovid, for example, turns many of his transformations upon this boundary. Io is changed into a heifer by Jupiter, and when she tries to complain, she is "terrified by her own voice," a lowing sound from her lips. Phaethon's sisters are turned into trees, able to move only their lips: they call to their mother until the bark closes over their last words. Juno turns Callisto into a bear and "deprives her of the power of speech." Ocyrhoe, the daughter of the centaur Chiron and the nymph Chariclo, loses her sense of prophecy and more when she is changed into a horse: first she speaks, then she sounds like a person trying to imitate a horse, and then she "gives vent to shrill whinnyings." Ovid reminds us that animals are not "dumb" and in fact have their own methods of communication, including communication with humans, but animals do not speak; they do not produce individual expressions of meaning designed to be intelligible and at the same time uniquely expressive of their own being. The mortals become "a" heifer, "a" bear, "a" horse. Perhaps worst of all, the terrible grief of Hecuba is expressed by her barking like a dog. For these characters, losing a capacity for speech is yoked not just to the loss of their human form but also to the loss of the form of their persons or proper names— that name by which they are called or summoned into the reciprocity of living human speech.

Yet no story in the *Metamorphoses* is more indicative of the relations between animal sounds, human cries, human calls, and naming than that of the destruction of Actaeon, whom Diana turned into a stag as a punishment for entering her sacred grove and seeing her bathing. As he describes Actaeon's transformation, Ovid lists, over many lines, all the particular names by which he calls his hounds. Actaeon utters "a groan . . . a sound which, though not human, was yet such as no stag could produce." When the stag Actaeon falls into a posture of prayer, his friends urge on the dogs and at the same time call out for "Actaeon," who, from their perspective, is now missing. Actaeon turns his stag's head at the sound of his name (he is now an animal who recognizes his "call"), but no one reciprocally can recognize him, and his own dogs tear him to pieces. It is hard to imagine a more carefully plotted and graphic description of the total breakdown of communicability between persons, between persons and animals, and between animals and other animals.[4]

In a paradigmatic essay on "Conditions of Personhood," Daniel Dennett lists six necessary conditions for personhood that are the very qualities broken down in these legends. These are (1) that persons are *rational beings*; (2) that persons are beings to which states of consciousness are attributed, or to which psychological or mental or *intentional predicates* are ascribed; (3) that a person is the recipient of a certain attitude or stance adopted with respect to him- or herself in regard to such personhood;

(4) that persons are capable of reciprocating in relation to this stance taken toward them; (5) that persons are capable of verbal communication; and (6) that persons are distinguishable from other entities by being *conscious* in some special way.[5] If we read back Dennett's conditions into Ovid's characters' losses, we see that the loss of a facility for verbal communication involves the loss of those attitudes or stances that will be adopted with respect to figures who speak their consciousness and rationality— and hence the loss of both the attribution of intention and the attribution of consciousness. It is verbal communication that exists on the periphery of internal consciousness and external expression and reception. The bark closing over the lips of Phaethon's sisters is like a stone sealing up the cave of their personhood. The "special" consciousness of human agents is dependent on our facility for forming our interior thoughts into syntactical units, units that articulate relations of causality and consequence, giving closure to material in such a way as to produce aggregations of meaning, or repeating to ourselves, and projecting into time and space, models of experience. All of their expressions of form, and expressions of mastery of form, go beyond mere utterance—the kind of utterance we would associate with an unbidden response to pain or surprise. We saw in the previous chapter that many animal calls, too, go beyond such unbidden responses: such capacities for volition, for sensitivity to context and the receptivity of given audiences, and for individuation can be said to flower in the evolution of human gesture, facial articulation, and language.

Producing and receiving sounds in order to form intelligible meanings involves mastery over relations of proximity and distance and presence and absence. In this is the profound relation we began to speak of in the first chapter between the cultural work of poetry and the ontology of persons. Young children play with absence and presence in a game Freud termed "fort [gone]/da [here]." There are many ways to play this game. A father might put his hands over his face or over a rattle and say, "Where's Daddy?" or "Where is the rattle?" and then, unveiling the face or rattle, exclaim, "Here I am!" or "Here it is!" Soon, a child will do the same with her own face and her own objects. And then the child will be able to play both roles, hiding and finding from her and for her own self, feigning puzzlement during the hiding and both feigning and expressing delight in the finding. Freud explained that the game supplants an absence (the absence, ultimately, of the nurturer) with a rhythm. The child masters desire and produces pleasure under conditions no longer external to his or her agency: "the child may, after all, only have been able to repeat his unpleasant experience in play because the repetition carried along with it a yield of pleasure of another sort but none the less a direct one."[6] This rhythm suffuses the production of speech in general, yet it is heightened in the many forms of repetition we find in poems. In later work on this topic, Jacques Lacan discusses the importance of the presence and absence of sound and figuration as part of what he calls the *invocatory* drive, the propulsion to make one's self heard and seen in general. He describes an outward and return movement as part of all drives: the oral as the urge to incorporate, the anal as the urge to retain, the scopic as the urge to organize the visual field.[7] Through the invocatory drive, the infant's need for nurturance becomes expressed as well as a desire—the call or summons becomes vocalization for its own sake, the sake of the pleasure of mastery and expression over the pulsion or rhythm between sounding and interval.

Allen Grossman's *Summa Lyrica* argues for the continuity between such early experiences of the world and specific features of sound and rhyme in poetry:

> The mother is present wherever in the poem language is specialized toward sound, as in rhyme which arrests the word in the ear, requiring that it lay in the realm of the body, before passing to sensory extinction as mere notation in the brain. Rhyme, like all phonic or merely structural repetition (as in grammatical rhyme) summons to common membership at the level of the species, tending to extinguish difference as transcendence and establish difference at the level of substance. The difference/no difference ambiguity in rhyme functions as the repetition of the sufficient conditions of sensing (the rule of texture), and as the substantiation of the parallel ambiguity at the level of meaning. Sound as silence (rhyme as sensation) articulates silence as sound (the meaning of words and sentences).[8]

Contrast Grossman's position in this regard with that of Julia Kristeva on the significance for poetic theory of the idea of a *chora*—a retrospectively posited prelinguistic condition out of which linguistic form (i.e., one's socialization into linguistic form) emerges:

> The *chora* is not yet a position that represents something for someone (i.e. not a sign); nor is it a *position* that represents someone for another position (i.e. not yet a signifier either); it is, however, generated in order to attain to this signifying position. Neither model nor copy, the *chora* precedes and underlies figuration and thus specularization, and is analogous only to vocal or kinetic rhythm. We must restore this motility's

gestural and vocal play (to mention only the aspect relevant to language) on the level of the socialized body in order to remove motility from ontology and amorphousness where Plato confines it in an apparent attempt to conceal it from Democritean rhythm. The theory of the subject proposed by the theory of the unconscious will allow us to read in this rhythmic space, which has no thesis and no position, the process by which significance is constituted. Plato himself leads us to such a process when he calls this receptacle or *chora* nourishing and maternal.[9]

Grossman's thinking follows Kristeva's only to a certain point. Whereas for Kristeva there is a "theoretical imperative" to the positing of a "semiotic" (i.e., nonsymbolic, or prelinguistic) sphere of the *chora*—a relation prior to language, between motility and amorphousness that would necessarily be a precondition to the intelligibility and naming of forms —'for Grossman the maternal rhythm is never superseded by language; rather, it remains within language as the surprise of difference/nondifference and the recurring substantial bodily sensitivity to sound. Sound making is always in tension with sense making, yet is also the precondition for sense making. Grossman thus also separates the "measure" or "counting" of articulated rhythms in poetry from the sensual immersion of sound. "At the level of prosodic order the vehicle of care in the poem is meter, which masters the tendency of speech to disappear . . . syllable count, and linear order in general, represent the care which keeps world in being."[10] Measurement in prosody is literally a counter to the sensual amorphousness of sound articulation.

If meter is the evidence of intended care and so evidence of human countenance, then what are we to make of the sense of human intervention that arises when the line is either halted or spilled, as we find in caesura and enjambment, respectively? This "pausing" and "running on" is, like catachresis in metaphor, even deeper evidence of the individuation of sound production in the poem. We could argue that it was not always so, as many nursery rhymes still demonstrate. In Old English verse the medial caesura was automatically used to separate each line into two isochronous hemistichs and to emphasize the regularity of the structure. Counting-out rhymes, for example, often depend on such pounding hemistichs to effect their final, determining emphasis—the word that "counts out" the player:

One-erzoll, two-erzoll, // zick-erzoll zan,
Bobtail vinegar, // little tall tan;

Harum, squarum, // Virgin Marum
Zinctum, zanctum, // buck![11]

By 1599, the date of George Peele's lovely "Bethsabe's Song" from his drama "David and Fair Bethsabe," the transformation of expectations between the predictable hesitations of medial caesuras and the mimetic spontaneity and emotional force of enjambment can be, indeed, the focus of the poem:

> Hot sun, cool fire, tempered with sweet air,
> Black shade, fair nurse, shadow my white hair;
> Shine, sun; burn, fire; breath, air, and ease me;
> Black shade, fair nurse; shroud me and please me:
> Shadow, my sweet nurse, keep me from burning,
> Make not my glad cause cause of mourning.
>   Let not my beauty's fire
>   Inflame unstaid desire,
>   Nor pierce any bright eye
>   That wandereth lightly.[12]

The pattern of oxymorons and antinomies (hot sun/cool fire, black/fair, shadow/white, glad/mourning) brought forward by the medial breaks and relations between paired lines beautifully is brought to a climax by the necessary pause between *cause* and *cause*—a pause that is both retrospectively known as a reversal and proleptically anticipating a complete turn in perspective: the speaker asks in the final "run-on" lines that no other be inflamed or pierced by her own beauty's radiance. By means of this type of anticipated caesura, regularity of effect slows the pacing of speech and silence in conformity to expected patterns and norms.

Yet when irregularity is presented by the sudden or idiosyncratic use of caesura or when enjambment is used, the speaking voice is counter to the rhythm. Lacan's discussion of the invocatory drive suggestively claims that, alone among the drives, it "has . . . the privilege of not being able to close."[13] Rather than thematize this as a tension between uniformity and singularity, however, we can see that such caesuras bring pulse and breath to the poem itself—they are animating features that add to the *embodiment* of voice in the poem. In two intriguing passages amid his theoretical speculations on classical drama, the Romantic German poet Friedrich Hölderlin in fact considers caesura as a far-reaching device of individuation. He writes that "in the rhythmic sequence of the representations wherein *transport* presents itself, there becomes necessary *what in poetic meter is called cesura,* the pure word, the counter-rhythmic rupture; namely, in order to meet the onrushing change of representations at its highest point in such a manner that very soon there does not appear the change of representation but the representation itself." The caesura "calls up" and breaks through the transport of rhythmic propulsion. Although we can read these remarks as a useful account of the work of caesura in the individual line, Hölderlin's thoughts on such breaks extend to the structure of the entire drama. He writes that in the Oedipus cycle "the speeches of Tiresias form the caesura. He enters the course of fate as the custodian of the natural power which, in a tragic manner, removes man from his own life-sphere, the center of his inner life into another world and into the excentric sphere of the dead." And in his discussion of *Andromache* he draws an analogy between the "calculable law" of rhythm and the play's concern with the rents and breaks in that coherence.[14]

Hölderlin shows that the unanticipated caesura is not simply an alternation of a rhythmic pattern, but is as well a gesture of breaking or hesitating that opens the text to the excentric positions of unintelligibility and death. Milton's lines on his blindness in Book III (ll. 40–48) of *Paradise Lost* present an array of uses of the caesura as they mark his severing from the world of nature and other men. The passage is a moving and extreme example of the kind of lyric of individual preference and circumstance Snell described in his account of the origins of Greek lyric:

> . . . Thus with the Year
> Seasons return, but not to me returns
> Day, or the Sweet approach of even or morn,
> Or sight of vernal bloom, or summer's rose,
> Or flocks, or herds, or human face divine;
> But cloud instead, and ever-during dark
> Surrounds me, from the cheerful ways of men
> Cut off, and for the book of knowledge fair
> Presented with a universal blank.

We cannot anticipate where the caesura will fall in these pentameter lines and so are ourselves going forward in blindness without knowledge of how the pattern will proceed. Those lines with initial caesuras—"Day," "Surrounds me," and "Cut off"—create an incremental progression of meaning, as if they were themselves a kind of sentence. Those with medial caesuras inevitably pair "vernal bloom" with "cloud instead" and "summer's rose" with "ever-during dark." The return to "blank verse" in the final line I have transcribed here presents its own dark pun: "a universal blank."[15]

The invocatory act creates a dynamic between the emergent and the unlimited in the pattern of rhythm's repetitions. Rhythm involves volition toward mastery, yet it also involves, in the ways it comes to inhabit us, a compromise between volition's expression and the demand for repetition of the form. Poetry imitates the invocatory drive, but not simply in terms of the articulation of the speaker. Rather, as imitation, poetry presents an image of the speaker in relation to a listener and begins the social work of making that relation intelligible through its own projected conditions of reception. Poems are not a matter of producing discursive sentences, although they often involve the imitation of the production of discursive sentences. At the core of invocatory activity is repetition evolving into rhythm. Hegel's *Philosophy of Fine Art* explicitly connects rhythm to our capacity for self-identity in this regard. Relying on a notion of single-point perspective, Hegel says that in space everything exists in juxtaposition and can be taken in at a glance. Yet, following Kant's thoughts on time as the continuity of internal intition, he says, in time one moment vanishes into another in an unending flow. When we use musical time or beats to give shape, to *inform*, this flow, we often find our own selves caught up in "keeping time"—even unconsciously. Hegel makes a point of saying that rhythm should be differentiated in this regard from both tones as musical sounds per se and time measurements regarded abstractly, for neither tones nor a general sense of time are involved in the keeping of uniform divisions and repetitions. He concludes:

> Musical time is consequently something wholly created by the human
> mind; and indeed there is more than a suggestion of this in the fact that
> in listening to musical time we are at once impressed with the convic-
> tion, that we have, in this control of time according to fixed rule, nothing
> less than a real reflection of our spiritual nature, or rather that of the fun-
> damental truth of self-identity, an illustration absolutely precise of the
> way in which the subject of consciousness applies this very principle
> of uniformity, unity with itself, that is to say, in constant recurrence,
> throughout all the variety and most intricate multiplicity of experience.
> And it is for this reason that the beat of musical time meets with such
> a startling response in the very depths of our being, gripping hold, as it
> does, of that self-identity, which is the fundamental abstract principle

of our inmost life. . . . And the same remarks apply to the measure and rhyme of poetry. The sensuous medium is here, too, in the same way carried out of the sphere of that which is external to ourselves.[16]

Poems compel attention to aspects of rhythm, rhyme, consonance, assonance, onomatopoeia, and other forms and patterns of sound to which attention is not necessarily given in the ongoing flow of prose and conversation.[17] This attention to sound is defined against, and helps establish, the various intelligible units or parts of poems, all of which are put into mutual relation or tension: individual words, the pauses and breaks between words, lines, and sentences; line beginnings and endings, features internal to individual lines, such as internal rhyming, the structure of stanzas and relations between stanzas, between stanzas and choruses, burdens and refrains, and, finally, of course, closure as the overall temporal dimension, or drive toward ending, of the poem and closure as the overall spatial dimension or "taking place" of the poem—the latter the drive toward integrity and singularity in the work as a whole.[18]

In classical practice, and classical criticism, the bond between music and lyric is paramount—nonnarrative and nondramatic poetic genres were intended to be sung, chanted, or recited to musical accompaniment.[19] *Lyra*, a musical instrument; *mele*, air or melody. These are commonplaces of the history of lyric poetry, and when we read a poem, regardless of the language in which it is composed, we speak of such features as counterpoint, harmony, syncopation, stress, duration, and timbre as if the ways in which sound is measured in music and lyric were analogous. But lyric is not music—it bears a history of a relation to music—and, as a practice of writing, it has no sound; that is, unless we are listening to a spontaneous composition of lyric, we are always *recalling* sound with only some regard to an originating auditory experience.[20]

The sound recalled in poetry is not abstract, not a succession of tones without prior referents; rather, the sound recalled is the sound of human speech. What is the nature of this recalling? It is not like reading a score or script with an orientation toward performance, for we are absorbed in the temporality of the poem's form and have no need to prepare ourselves for, or orient ourselves toward, a replication of the poem—in fact, to produce such a replica would not necessarily require reading the poem at all.[21] It is not like viewing a representation of an utterance, as in looking at a painting of sound—Edvard Munch's screaming figure or the "mouthing" of *The Oath of the Horatii*—for the poem itself is an utterance, an expression of a person that we apprehend in turn as the expression of a person. And it is not like an exercise in historical linguistics in which we try to reconstitute a context of original utterance, for we are interested in attending to both *what* the poem says and *how* the poem says as part of a semantic orientation in reception. Because we cannot reconstitute these auditory conditions of the poem's production, our recalling will always have a dimension of imagination. Such remembering in fact requires neither auditory prompting nor the presence of a text at all. Just as we have the capacity to compose or remember a visual field or sequence of musical phrases without external stimuli, so can we "hear" a poem when a text is present by calling it to mind. In turn, we will bring to a text our memories of speech experience, including what we may know of the intended speaker's speech experience, but such "voicing" will be in the service of, provide the vehicle for, the apprehension of the poem as a whole.[22]

A whole range of sensual associations can come to mind with particular sounds and sound clusters. Consider the powerful synesthesia that is often at work between sound and color in poems. The classic instance of such a poem is Arthur Rimbaud's "Voyelles" of 1871:

A noir, E blanc, I rouge, U vert, O bleu: voyelles,
Je dirai quelque jour vos naissances latentes:
A, noir corset velu des mouches éclatantes
Qui bombinent autour des puanteurs cruelles,

Golfes d'ombre; E, candeurs des vapeurs et des tentes,
Lances des glaciers fiers, rois blancs, frissons d'ombelles;
I, pourpres, sang craché, rire des lèvres belles
Dans la colère ou les ivresses pénitentes;

U, cycles, vibrements divins des mers virides,
Paix des pâtis semés d'animaux, paix des rides
Que l'alchimie imprime aux grands fronts studieux;

O, suprême Clairon plein des strideurs étranges,
Silences traversés des Mondes et des Anges:
—O l'Oméga, rayon violet de Ses Yeux![23]

Reuven Tsur's intriguing analysis of this poem points to the work's underlying analogy between the open and ranging "acoustic energy" of vowels and the open and ranging "visual energy" of colors. Throughout Tsur finds that vowels of indeterminate range, such as the French *e*, are associated with the mediating place of white on the color scale or with the "pastoral calm" of green and blue, which are nearer the short-wave end of the spectrum, whereas intense and extreme vowel sounds, such as the high *i* in Romance languages, are associated with red, the color with the longest wave on the spectrum. Tsur also considers how associations with the meaning of words (e.g., *clairon* with the clear blue sky) and effects of clusters of nouns *(blanc/bleu* and *rouge/jour)* all contribute to the synesthesia of color and sound as well.[24]

If we look briefly at some other poems fusing sound and color, we see the continuity of these conventions of increased and diminished intensification. Federico García Lorca's "Romance Sonámbulo," with its hypnotic opening line—"Verde que te quiero verde"—derives a beautiful set of variations from the increasing intensity of these initial vowel sounds: *e* to *a* to *i*, proclaiming "Green how much I want you green." The vowels mount in intensity and then return to *e* as the color name is repeated. But of course the poem also acquires its resonant "greenness" from the juxtaposition of the sweeping natural landscape, all spread with green, and the "painted" figure of the dreaming gypsy: "verde carne, pelo verde / con ojos de fría plata." These cold silver eyes put the green into relief. By juxtaposition with the reflection of silver, the absorbing, world-devouring power of green becomes clearer: "las cosas la están mirando / y ella no puede mirarlas" (all things look at her / but she cannot see them).[25]

Something of the same absorption and reflection contrast is present at the beginning of Rafael Alberti's "Rojo," one of his early color poems from the series "A la Pintura" of 1948:

1
Lucho en el verde de la fruta y venzo
2
Pleno rubor redondo en la manzana.

Here as well a repetition of the *o* sounds of *rojo,* spaced at the beginning and end of the first line and then clustered at the front of the second, adds to the effect of meaning or discovery of the fruit, that concentration of redness in the midst of the green leaves.[26]

In a final example, taken from a poet who was primarily a painter, we can see a brilliant use of parallels of intensity between the vowel and color spectrums once again. The Scuola Romana painter Gino Bonichi, who used the name "Scipione" for his artistic endeavors, wrote only ten poems during his brief life, but these have an extraordinary sense of color imagery. One of them, "Sento gli strilli degli angioli," provides further evidence of the association between the high *i* and the color red:

Sento gli strilli degli angioli
che vogliono la mia salvezza
ma la saliva è dolce
e il sangue corre a peccare

l'aria è ferma
tutto è rosa come la carne
se pervade è beatitudine
bisogna rompere e cadere

Il sole entra nel mio petto
come in una canestra
    e io mi sento voto,

la mano si stacca da terra
tocca l'aria, la luce, la carne.
. . . .
. . . .
la lancia si sprofonda nelle reni
della cavalla che corre—e urla
con la testa sul cielo.[27]

Whenever a poetic values metaphor, or the supersensible dimension of poetry more generally, sound as the material manifestation of the work will be less emphasized; often sound will be held in diminished estimation as a mere "prop" or frame for poetic thought. Consider Kant's elevation of poetry over music in the "Analytic of the Sublime":

Among all the arts *poetry* holds the highest rank. (It owes its origin almost entirely to genius and is least open to guidance by precept or examples.) It expands the mind: for it sets the imagination free, and offers us, from among the unlimited variety of possible forms that harmonize with a given concept, though within that concept's limits, that form which links the exhibition of the concept with a wealth of thought to which no linguistic expression is completely adequate, and so poetry rises aesthetically to ideas. Poetry fortifies the mind: for it lets the mind feel its ability—free, spontaneous, and independent of natural determination—to contemplate and judge phenomenal nature as having aspects that nature does not on its own offer in experience either to sense or to the understanding, and hence poetry lets the mind feel its ability to use nature on behalf of and, as it were, as a schema of the supersensible.

In contrast, music, as an art of tone, "speaks through nothing but sensations without concepts, so that unlike poetry it leaves us with nothing to meditate about." Kant does emphasize, however, that the transience of music makes it "agitate the mind more diversely and intensely."[28] Hegel's *The Philosophy of Fine Art* promotes a similar view of the relation between the sensible and the thought in poetry:

> Mind, in short, here determines this content for its own sake and apart from all else into the content of idea; to express such idea it no doubt avails itself of sound, but employs it merely as a sign without independent worth or substance. Thus viewed, the sound here may be just as well reproduced by the mere letter, for the audible, like the visible, is here reduced to a mere indication of mind. For this reason, the true medium of poetical representation is the poetical imagination and the intellectual presentation itself; and inasmuch as this element is common to all types of art it follows that poetry is a common thread through them all, and is developed independently in each. Poetry is, in short, the universal art of the mind, which has become essentially free, and which is not fettered in its realization to an externally sensuous material.[29]

Yet as Kant's position gives us a clue that the intensity of affect in music might lend something of its emotional force to the sonorous dimension of the poetic, so does Hegel's position stray so far from the reception of particular instances of the poetic that poetry threatens to disappear entirely as it makes its way toward the universal.

Neoclassical theories considering sound as a mode of ornament can make meaning seem ornamental as well: "When Alexander strives some rock's vast weight to throw / The line too labors, and the words move slow." Is Alexander, then, the example of the sound or the sound the example of Alexander? Although Pope has complained only a few lines earlier about the "sure returns of still expected rhymes," there is such ease to his own perfect rhymes that we wonder whether self-parody is really the point.[30] Conversely, avant-garde materialism in twentieth-century poetics (the Symbolist ideal of fusing meaning and sound as expressed in Verlaine's "Art Poetique," F. T. Marinetti's "bruitisme," or Dada sound poems) with its pursuit of pure sound finds itself readily encapsulated into prior generic conventions—either "nonsense" discourse or experimental music. A "sound poem" such as Hugo Ball's

> gadji beri bimba
> glandridi lauli lonni cadori
> gadjama bim beri glassala
> glandridi glassala tuffm i zimbrabim
> blassa galassasa tuffm i zimbrabim . . .

reverses the conventional priority of meaning over sound. Ball wrote in his autobiography, *Flight Out of Time*, "I have invented a new genre of poems, 'Verse ohne Worte' [poems without words], or Lautgedichte [sound poems], in which the balance of the vowels is weighed and distributed solely according to the values of the beginning sequence . . . we must give up writing secondhand: that is, accepting words (to say nothing of sentences) that are not newly invented for our own use."[31] Significantly, the improvisatory aspect of such a poem makes it a challenge to memory; memory relies on the "placing" or contextualization of language in relation to other language, and "pure" sounds are indeed pure of such context. They are harder to call to mind than musical sequences, for musical sequences are themselves coded in relation to expectations of musical sequence. Ball's demand that language be "newly invented" depends on the novelty and surprise produced by the unpredictability of the sequence. A claim is made for the "pure" incantatory experience of the sound poem, but the theory nevertheless is used as a frame for the sound.

Furthermore, since we have prior speech experience of these sounds as discernible phones, if not as discernible words, we "hear" them phonetically. The few repetitions in Ball's poem and the sequence of sounds in time compel us to hear aural connections, as in the sequence of first "words" of the "lines"—gad*ji*, gad*jama*—which are heard as deploying suffix variations, or the way *bl*assa and *ga*lassasa appear as prefix variations, or the repetitions of gla*ndridi*, gla*ssala*, and the "phrase" *tuffm i zimbrabim*, or the variations in "a" and "i" endings, which seem to echo Latinate noun and pronoun endings for gender and number. In other words, we produce phonemes whenever we can, even if the lexical level remains opaque, here defined only by the intervals between clusters of syllables rather than by prior reference. A student of historical linguistics coming upon this poem would know that it is closer to Italian, French, and Japanese than to English because of its emphasis on syllabics. The mind is a grammar-making device, and it is difficult to turn it off, even though Ball has not provided a syntactical framework of the kind maintained in Lewis

Carroll's "Jabberwocky," where the connective words remain in the standard lexicon. The first (which is again the last) "Jabberwocky" stanza will be enough to show this technique:

> 'Twas brillig, and the slithy toves
>> Did gyre and gimble in the wabe:
> All mimsy were the borogoves,
>> And the mome raths outgrabe.

We could conclude that Ball is performing a poem because he has framed his performance, he has spoken in "lines," and "the work" has a beginning—if it does not have closure, it nevertheless does *stop*. Sounds follow other sounds and so appear in a *relation* to those sounds preceding and following them. Play within the determinations of such a relation will always be in tension with any "pure" arbitrariness.

There are, then, a number of complex conditions under which we can say that "sound" is and is not an aspect of poetry. When poetry is disseminated through written form, speech is represented through alphabetical letters and diacritical marks and symbols; as systems of differentiated marks, these forms of representation stand for the differentiation of phones in sound production. Most features of spoken intonation, pitch, stress, and intensity must be supplied by the reader. There is no reason to emphasize the idiolectal quality of speech in this regard—phonetic patterns are learned at an early age for one's own primary language and can be discerned for other languages whether or not one actually "knows" the language.[32] This is why a parrot will repeat phrases without what we might call a "parrot" accent, for the parrot is producing a string of phones, but human beings who learn languages after puberty will bring the inflection of that language or those languages they have first learned.[33] John Skelton's clever macaronic poem, "Speak, Parrot," written in 1519–1524 and published in 1554, makes a witty play on this feature of bird language from the "parrot's" point of view. Here is one of the parrot's speeches from the opening stanzas:

> My lady mistress, Dame Philology,
>> Gave me a gift, in my nest when I lay,
> To learn all language, and it to speak aptly.
>> Now *pandez mory*, wax frantic, some men say,
>> Phroneses for Freneses may not hold her way.
> An almond now for Parrot, delicately drest:
> In *Salve festa dies, toto* there doth best.[34]

As a reader of poems takes up the sequence of written symbols, he or she thereby supplies the rhythm that characterizes his or her experience of the language. For English speakers the linguistic principle of isochronism, which breaks utterances into segments correlated to the pulses of breathing, will not be based on the syllable (as it is in French, Japanese, and "gadji beri"); rather, the unit of utterance generally will include a stressed syllable and a number of unstressed syllables. This interval, from stress to stress rather than from syllable to syllable, has of course had a profound effect on English metrics. Because the stress generally falls on form words, rather than grammatical and structural elements, stress will underscore the structure of the grammar.[35]

In speech, stress can determine emphasis in ways that remain indeterminate to writing without the addition of supplemental discourse or diacritical marks: Did Isolt say hello to *Tristan?* Did Isolt say *hello* to Tristan? In a poem the acoustical "space," the context wherein the stress is reconstructed, becomes the work itself—the consequent phrase or sentence or stanza or the entire form from title or first line to closure. Writing in his *Summa Lyrica,* Grossman takes the consequences of stress even further and emphasizes the tension in English metrics between stress and syllabics: "Where there is dispute about stress the reader need only accept as an obligation the semantic consequences of any given stressing. . . . Stress is the inscription of the subjective or meaning-intending volition of the speaker (this is for the reader). We may dispute about stress. Syllable count, by contrast, is by its nature at the other extreme of intersubjectivity. It has the character of the 'objective' and we do not dispute about it, only correct one another with the understanding that the solution to the counting problem will be univocal. Stress is the point of presence of the hermeneutic issue in the substance of the hermeneutic object itself."[36] This process from sound production to inscription to reading to sound reception is pocked with anachronisms that in themselves are productive of historical meaning. Spelling, for example, always lags behind pronunciation;[37] off-rhyming can be taken as exact rhyming and vice versa; poetry itself is often cited as an index to past pronunciation of the language. The sounds of a poem are not heard within the room of the poem, but they are heard within a memory of hearing that is the total auditory experience of the listener in response to what knowledge of the poem is extant at a given moment.

Paul Fussell's majesterial study of the theory of prosody in eighteenth-century England argues that there was a gradual shift in rhythmical taste "from the Restoration to the nineteenth century, in all the arts based on repetition in time instead of space: the process . . . in the field of metrical theory could be paralleled by similar developments in the theory of music and dancing. In poetry and metrics, the shift is one from an attention to many minor units of time to a concern with only a few major units: from all syllables, that is, to only accented syllables as the marked and perceived units of temporal measurement." Trisyllabic substitution called attention to major syllables and allowed variety in the numbers of minor syllables to such a degree that accentualism could return to dominate English poetry, here under what is often confusedly called the "accentual-syllabic" system that would continue through the nineteenth century until the Modernist innovation of free verse.[38]

Musical conventions proper have been applied to our sense of poetry's "musicality" yet do not overlap with poetry's meter even within the domain of spoken poems. It is not that some speech is organized rhythmically and other speech is not. Victor Zuckerkandl has suggested that "whereas melody and harmony are essentially musical phenomena, native to the world of tone and not to be found elsewhere (the adjectives derived from these terms can be applied only metaphorically outside the realm of music), rhythm is a truly universal phenomenon . . . rhythm is one manifestation of the reign of law throughout the universe."[39] Speech arrives in rhythmical form, and our experience of it cannot be separated from our knowledge of its rhythmical structure.

Zuckerkandl's writings on music provide a number of valuable insights regarding these issues. He points to the important distinction between rhythm and meter. Rhythm is described after the fact as the particular structure or order of tones in time. Although Zuckerkandl does not explicitly define rhythm as a historical and actual phenomenon, his emphasis on rhythm as the "living" dimension of music helps us see the tension between the organic and experiential unfolding of rhythm and the "time" of meter—that fixed and ideal measurement by which we say we are "keeping time."

Zuckerkandl in fact uses poetry as his example of an art form that uses both rhythm and meter and nevertheless constantly asserts the priority of rhythm over meter: "A poem is a rhythmic construction. . . . We could beat time to a poem if the syllables in it were all of equal length or departed from a basic unit in accordance with simple numerical proportions. . . . 'Time' and rhythm here appear even to exclude each other: rhythm resists regular time: 'time' appears to suffocate rhythm." He points out that

> except for the special case of dance music, which is obliged to conform to the bodily movement it supports, musical rhythm in general is of the nature of the poetic rhythm; free rhythm in the sense that it is not con-

strained to keep time. There is one notable exception, Western music of
the second millennium of our era—our music. It alone has imposed the
shackles of time, of meter, upon itself, and indeed at the same moment
when it was preparing to take the momentous step into polyphony. So
long as only a single voice is involved, it is free to give each of its steps
whatever duration it pleases. But if several voices, voices saying different
things, are to proceed side by side and together, their motions must, for
better or worse, be regulated by some time standard.[40]

In lyric, then, especially, we find the continuance of a prepolyphonic
emphasis on the individual voice and the tension between rhythm and
meter. A key dimension of this tension is its productivity: "musical meter is not born in the beats at all, but in the empty intervals between the
beats, in the places where 'time merely elapses,'" writes Zuckerkandl.
"The mere lapse of time here effects something; it is felt as an event,
strictly speaking as a wave. In the macroscopic picture something else
happens; to the wave, intensification is added. As wave and intensification
the lapse of time sustains and nourishes the rhythmic life of music. The
function of time here is, then, no longer that of the empty vessel, which
contains the tones, or the bowling alley down which the tones roll; on the
contrary, time intervenes, is directly active, in the musical context."[41]
Meter augments, extends, and organizes our hearing of speech rhythm in
such a way as to intensify our experience—we hear the sound of sound
and become aware of the meaning of sound in consequence. "Meter . . .
draws boundary lines, interrupts, and separates. Rhythm is the unbroken
continuity of a flux, such a continuity as the wave most graphically represents. . . . Meter is the repetition of the identical; rhythm is return of the
similar."[42] The sound of the poem emerges from this dynamic tension between the unfolding temporality of the utterance and the recursive temporality of the fixed aspects of the form. There is something of this in the
multiple senses of the word itself—for sound as the most material and
"superficial" dimension of speech is also sound as the measure, the depth,
the "sounding" of the material, as when we ask whether something
"sounds good"—that is, good enough to act upon, bearing the integrity of
a completed form. Because lyric maintains the convention of the individual speaking voice, a convention under which rhythm continues to have
priority over the mechanical imposition of meter no matter how strongly
organized the metrical dimension of the poem, it will not, in the Western
tradition, be synonymous with music.

Another complexity of the relation between poetry and musicality is
that the dynamic tension between sound and semantic can at once both

extend and diminish meaning. David I. Masson's comprehensive entry on "sound" in *The Princeton Encyclopedia of Poetry and Poetics*, for example, delineates fifteen forms of "sound manipulation" that affirm the relation between sound and meaning in individual poems: structural emphasis (rhetorical addition to the formally required sound structure); underpinning (subtle reinforcement of the verse structure through features like Milton's use of line-end consonance and assonance in blank verse); counterpoising (sounds employed in opposition to the verse structure, as in imperfect rhymes used in line endings in combination with internal rhymes); rubricating emphasis or words or images (his examples come from Tudor echo effects, as in Henry Howard, earl of Surrey's "The turtle to her make hath tolde her tale" where *turtle, to, told,* and *tale* are in effect underlined by the sound); tagging (punctuation of syntax by words or sounds); correlation (indirect support of argument by related echoes); implication (interconnection of sound, meaning and feeling); diagramming (abstract pattern symbolizing sense—as in the relation between "leaping" syllables and "leaping" fire in Dryden's "He wades the Streets, and streight he reaches cross"); sound representation (onomatopoeia); illustrative mime (mouth movements recall motion or shape); illustrative painting (articulations, sounds and patterns correspond synesthetically to appearances and nonacoustic sensations); passionate emphasis (emotional outburst); mood evocation (choice of tone colors resembling the usual sounds expressed in a given emotion); expressive mime (mouth movements ape the expression of emotion, as in the spitting effects necessary for pronouncing Adam's expulsion of the serpent in these lines from Milton: "Out of my sight, thou Serpent, that name best / Befits thee with him leagu'd, thy self as false / And hateful"); expressive painting (sounds, articulations correspond to feelings or impressions, as in George Crabbe's "And the dull wheel hums doleful through the day"); ebullience (pure exuberance or pleasure in sound); embellishment (superficial musicality, as in Howard's application of a rubricating emphasis noted earlier); and incantation (musical or magical use of sound).[43] Such a taxonomy is helpful for understanding the effects of particular sounds in individual poems. Yet who is to say that W. B. Yeats's "That dolphin-torn, that gong-tormented sea" is an example of incantation, as it is for Masson, rather than embellishment or ebullience? Surely the most effective alignments of sound and meaning will use a number of these techniques.

Furthermore, the relation between sound and meaning "created" by such lines depends on a prior expectation of a connection between sound and meaning, an expectation brought to the reading of poetry more generally. When Laura Riding and Robert Graves wittily suggest there is an arbitrary, rather than onomatopocic, rclation between sound and meaning in Alfred, Lord Tennyson's

> The moan of doves in immemorial elms
> And murmuring of innumerable bees

by pointing to how the sounds produced in a line of different meaning ("More ordure never will renew our midden's pure manure")[44] hardly produce a similar onomatopoeic effect, they miss the point. Sounds in poems are never heard outside an expectation of meaning, and sounds in nature will be framed for human listeners by human expectations. Robert Frost, in "The Oven Bird," reminds us vividly that we hear even bird songs in terms of human phonemes—the robin's "cheer, cheer, cheer"; the nighthawk's "sp-e-e-d"; the nuthatch's "yank, yank"; or Henry David Thoreau's suggestion that the song sparrow sings "Maids, maids, maids, hang up your teakettle—ettle—ettle." When Frost writes of this bird who "knows in singing not to sing" but rather to frame questions, we silently "hear" the song of the oven bird: "teacher teacher."

Such features of sound manipulation in poetry as counterpoising, tagging, echo effects, diagramming, and the "ornamental" devices of rubrication and embellishment can, as David Masson emphasizes, make the relation between sound and meaning particularly textured and complex. Yet they also point to the possibilities of severing the relation between sound and meaning. Such a severing is possible because of the ineluctable fact of the arbitrary nature of language forms. Long before the insights of Saussurean linguistics, folk forms often pointed to this dilemma. Think of the legends of Tom Tit Tot and Rumpelstiltsken: human beings will not be able to reproduce themselves (to name or claim their own offspring) until they use their intelligence to tease out a completely arbitrary name for the source of their suffering; only language can reveal to them the hidden term.

Ballads, too, often stage the separation of sound and meaning to create anticipation in the progress of narrative. For example, nonsensical sounds are used both to arrest and move forward the incremental repetitions of this version of the "Wife Wrapt in Wethers Skin," collected in North Carolina in 1962:[45]

> (chant) There was an old man who lived in the West
> (sung) Dandoo
> (chant) There was an old man who lived in the West
> (sung) To my clash a-my klingo

(chant) There was an old man who lived in the West
(chant) He married him a wife which he thought the best
(sung) Lingarum, lingorum smikaroarum, kerrymingorum
(sung) To my clash a-my klingo

This is a particularly rich example, for the ballad tetrameter is followed exactly in the first three chanted narrative lines, but the narrative development is halted until the fourth narrative line where the meter is abandoned. In the fourth line the only way to get a four-beat measure is to switch from ballad meter into pure accentual verse. In this the song merges ballad form and the particular pattern of repeated lines common to blues form. Meanwhile, the nonsense syllables, which, because they are sung, would be expected to be in the more regular meter, are not in any particular meter at all until the final sung line "to my clash a-my klingo." The listener hears three chanted lines before the narrative starts and three sung lines before the meter starts.

Few poets have been as engaged with song as Thomas Hardy was throughout his writing life. Consider, for example, how he uses song techniques in "During Wind and Rain":

> They sing their dearest songs—
> He, she, all of them—yea,
> Treble and tenor and bass,
>   And one to play;
> With the candles mooning each face. . . .
>   Ah, no; the years O!
> How the sick leaves reel down in throngs!
>
> They clear the creeping moss—
> Elders and juniors—aye,
> Making the pathways neat
>   And the garden gay;
> And they build a shady seat. . . .
>   Ah, no; the years, the years;
> See, the white storm-birds wing across!
>
> They are blithely breakfasting all—
> Men and maidens—yea,
> Under the summer tree,
>   With a glimpse of the bay,

> While pet fowl come to the knee . . .
>   Ah, no; the years O!
> And the rotten rose is ript from the wall.
>
> They change to a high new house,
> He, she, all of them—aye,
> Clocks and carpets and chairs
>   On the lawn all day,
> And brightest things that are theirs . . .
>   Ah, no; the years, the years;
> Down their carved names the rain-drop ploughs.[46]

Hardy uses the purely "emotional" refrain "Ah, no; the years O!" (changed in the last stanza to "Ah, no; the years, the years") to lend particular weight to the slowly building drama of the exclamatory last lines of each stanza: "How the sick leaves reel down in throngs!"; "See, the white storm-birds wing across!"; "And the rotten rose is ript from the wall"; "Down their carved names the rain-drop ploughs." In this way the last lines of the stanzas, which seem to be as well "mere" ejaculations of feeling, create a kind of trellis to support the emerging meaning of the poem, showing the deep dimension of time emerging out of what might be called the "ordinary" or everyday narratives described in the lines preceding the refrain lines.[47]

Such juxtaposition of song and speech is typical of other forms as well, such as the cante-fable. In the cante-fable, song sections often include set pieces, riddles, dialogue, sayings, imitations of animal sounds, or magical utterances; the speech sections will stage the scene and explain the narrative. In ballad and song burdens, mood and place may as well be set by an incantatory, evocative repetition: "Down by the greenwood side" or "Down by the green, by the burnie-o."[48] In the rubato-parlando style of dramatic recitative found in much of Eastern European and Anglo-American balladry in which the last words of the song are uttered as speech, speech marks the return to the threshold of reality; in consequence, singing is associated with the incantatory, the sacred, and the imaginary.

The trajectories of speech and song are both opposed and complementary in such forms. The sounds of speech rhythmically proceed forward in time according to conventions of articulation and interval. The sounds of song are organized both melodically and harmonically—that is, in both linear and recursive fashion—and use fixed repetitive patterns of stress, tone, and duration. Speech disappears into the function of its situation; it

can be repeated as fixed text or reported in an approximation. Song, by virtue of its measure, is fixed and repeatable, although it is, like all utterances, subject to transformation.[49] Of course, the sweet new measures of
the relations between verse and discursive prose in Dante's *Vita Nuova*,
which itself follows this device in Boethius's *Consolation of Philosophy*, remain the prototype for Western poetry that foregrounds the tensions between singing and speaking. Much of the later Romantic arti-
factualization of poetry within poetic forms, such as the juxtaposition of
tetrameter song and pentameter speech in poems like Coleridge's "Kubla
Khan" and Charlotte Turner Smith's "Beachy Head," is a legacy of Dante's
innovations.

Yet the simultaneous appearance of the unfolding semantic pressure of
speech and the asemantic pulse of measure may also be said to define the
possibilities of poetic art more broadly. W. K. Wimsatt wrote of this tension between meaning and arbitrariness in *The Verbal Icon*, "Verse in general, and more particularly rhyme, make their special contribution to poetic structure in virtue of a studiously and accurately semantic character.
They impose upon the logical pattern of expressed argument a kind of
fixative counterpattern of alogical implication."[50] Telling as telling slant
makes lyric capable of evoking not only meaning but also the conditions
under which meaning is formed by human speakers.

There is an axiological consequence to this account of poetry. Poetry
that mechanically emphasizes the fulfillment of metrical expectations
will result in mere "tub-thumping," as Robert Lowell described the fourteeners of Arthur Golding's 1567 translation of Ovid's *Metamorphoses:*
"Even if one is careful not to tub-thump, as one reads Golding's huge,
looping 'fourteeners,' for 'sense and syntax' as Pound advises, even then
one trips, often the form seems like some arbitrary and wayward hurdle,
rather than the very backbone of what is being said."[51] John Thompson,
in a discussion of this passage in his work on *The Founding of English
Meter*, suggests that the early Elizabethans may not have had the same
difficulty in keeping poulter's measure from overwhelming the grammatical and logical structure of the language. But he also explains that whenever there are balanced contours in evenly spaced rhythm units that dominate the grammatical units of the language, "singsong" will result.[52] If
such a reification of meter results in an overwhelmed semantic level, similarly a semantic level organized without consideration of metrical coun-
terpatterning will be absorbed into mere rhetoric. Any poetry produced
under conditions that suppress the recursive and patterned dimensions of
form cannot hope to move the reader or listener beyond the expectations
of speech absorbed into the time of everyday life.

When Wimsatt mentions "a counterpattern of alogical implication," we might well ask what it is to which the metrical pattern is counter and what is so alogical about meter's implications. The pattern of *logical* implication in speech will be oriented toward the future; given a set of conditions and elements, a certain consequence will follow. Speech in a poem, like speech in the face-to-face communication of everyday life, is articulated in time. But unlike speech oriented toward conversational purposes, speech in a poem is not absorbed in time. Essentialist arguments that negate any purported differences between "ordinary" and "poetic" language always already cheat in this regard, for attending to ordinary language in order to emphasize its inherently "poetic" qualities is synonymous with *poiēsis* in the first place and imagining "ordinary" functions for poetic utterances ("I'd like to go out tonight, but I'm feeling half in love with easeful death") is inseparable from the fabrication of fictive contexts. Once one is involved in such self-conscious making, there is no return to the contingencies of mere "function," let alone nature.

Attention to the material elements of form in both its production and reception moves counter to that temporal absorption; indeed, attention to the material elements of form threatens to halt reception and to dominate the semantic dimension. This threat demands a certain complex kind of apprehension wherein the logical implication, the implication of the reason, is put into play with the recursive and repetitive trajectory of the meter. Here is the *compulsion* of meter to return, to reenact, to transform and imitate. A tension ensues between the intentional and volitional dimensions of both sound production and listening and the involuntary dimension of hearing—the unregulated openness of the ear to the world and the infinite nuance of the unsaid. Meter, and song as its vehicle, is the repository of emotion as *compositio* is the repository of the reason. Meter disrupts the absorptive dominance of time and makes time manifest as the dimension of interval.[53] In poems, interval loses its "natural stance"; just as the phonemic dimension of sound only comes into existence as a system of differences, so the rests and caesuras, the line and stanza breaks of poems are "sounded" or measured. Through poems the human voice reenacts the conditions of its emergence from silence and wrests that silence into the intersubjective domain of made and shaped things.

"Keeping time" in poetry, unlike keeping time in postpolyphonal Western music, does not involve a reduction of sound to the interstices of a metrical grid. Keeping time in poetry is exercised through the single voice manipulating duration in such a way as to produce both expectation and surprise. The posture of reception is that of listening—an orientation of hearing within a finite auditory space. When Lacan describes the invocatory drive as one of going out and coming back, he is careful to specify that this movement is not a matter of "a reciprocity," for the pure activity of the drive is not "balanced" by the narcissistic field of love;[54] what goes out overwhelms what comes back—what goes out is constant and inescapable, whereas what comes back is contingent and determined. Here we find the incommensurable relation between production and reception as a "nonreciprocal" production in its own right. This incommensurability is not a barrier to some recuperable originary meaning; it is in itself the "mishearing" or "misrecognition" under which the material element of the sign acquires an untotalizable semantic dimension. Poets who have worried the relation between sound and sense—the slant and off-rhymes of Emily Dickinson and Wilfred Owen, the use of "noise" in Hart Crane, the coining of neologisms in Paul Celan and César Vallejo—have provided a vivid commentary on the alienation that can arise between speakers on the one hand and between human beings and nature on the other. It is significant that these are also poets for whom the stance of the "natural person," or any enthusiasm in the presentation of the self, is unbearable.

Let us look at two well-known poems by Wallace Stevens, one that primarily *is* sound and one that primarily is *about* sound. The first is "Ploughing on Sunday" from *Harmonium:*

> The white cock's tail
> Tosses in the wind.
> The turkey-cock's tail
> Glitters in the sun.
>
> Water in the fields.
> The wind pours down.
> The feathers flare
> And bluster in the wind.
>
> Remus, blow your horn!
> I'm ploughing on Sunday,
> Ploughing North America
> Blow your horn!
>
> Tum-ti-tum,
> Ti-tum-tum-tum!
> The turkey-cock's tail
> Spreads to the sun.

The white cock's tail
Streams to the moon.
Water in the fields.
The wind pours down.[55]

How can we begin to account for all that is happening in the sound of this poem? *Harmonium* as a whole is a panoply of joyful noises, a fabulous excursus on the relations between sounds in nature, human vocalization, and music. Its harmony is built from a cacophony of claviers, pianos, oboes, mandolins, guitars, bird songs, glossolalia, and cries. "Peter Quince at the Clavier" realizes that "music is feeling, then, not sound." And the very last poem of the 1922 *Harmonium*, "To the Roaring Wind," is a condensed ode to the Romantic invocation of the wind itself as inspiriting spirit of sound:

What syllable are you seeking
Vocalissimus
In the distances of sleep?
Speak it.

The title of "Ploughing on Sunday" might be read in the other direction—against the very first poem of the volume, "Earthy Anecdote," where the bucks clattering over Oklahoma constantly swerve to the right and then to the left in "swift circular lines."[56] Swerving to the right, then the left, evokes the long-standing Western relation between poetry and plowing. The Greek adverb βουστροφηδόν (*boustrophēdon*) describes both the turning of oxen in ploughing and writing from left to right and right to left in alternation. This deep analogy between the turning that opens the earth to the sky and the turning that inscribes the page with a record of human movement is carried forward in the notion of verse as a series of turns and in the circling recursivity of all lyric forms. Here, too, the nystagmus, or back-and-forth motion of the eyes, is emphasized as a process of reading and hearing at once. Reversals of direction of many kinds are relevant here. For example, we might recall "the sun came up upon the left" and "the sun came up upon the right"—lines 29 and 81, respectively, of Coleridge's "Rime of the Ancient Mariner." Stevens, the weekend poet, often "ploughed on Sunday." The interdiction against working on the Sabbath that we might hear from "A High-Toned Old Christian Woman" is violated by Stevens, who contends, "Poetry is the supreme fiction, Madame. / Take the moral law and make a nave of it /

And from the nave build haunted heaven. Thus / the conscience is converted into palms, / Like windy citherns hankering for hymns."[57]

On its spindle of meaning, "Ploughing on Sunday" places just a few threads. The scene evokes a period after a storm—water is in the fields, making the labor of plowing all the more difficult; the wind is still "pouring down," implying that, in taking on what we would expect to be the function of the rain, wind is now doing the work of water. The white cock and the turkey cock are out in this weather, as they would not be in a storm, and the sun is now shining. What is the relation between a white cock (which would be some variety of a white leghorn rooster, given its coloration and the fact that it has a tail that can be tossed and streamed—perhaps a Rhode Island White) and a turkey cock (which glitters because its spreading fan-shaped tail feathers have hints of gold and bronze—perhaps a Narragansett Black)? The wind pouring down is paralleled by another wind—the blustering human breath "Remus" must gather to play his horn, announcing that the speaker is "ploughing on Sunday / Ploughing North America." And who is Remus? The wolf-suckled Abel figure of Roman legend? The "Uncle Remus" of Joel Chandler Harris's stories that also are structured by the relations between animal and human life and often involve other "characters" we find in Stevens's poem: "Mr. Sun," "Sister Moon," and "Uncle Wind"? The final stanza reverses the order of precedence between the white cock and the turkey cock. The turkey cock remains, spreading his glittering tail in the sunlight, while the white cock streams to the moon and the plowing has gone on into the night. The poem's closure rests on the meaning of the close of day and, contiguously, the rooster's association with the threshold between night and daybreak.

Describing the poem in conventional metrical terms does not get us very far. The pure stress tetrameter quatrains make some use of a play between rising and falling meters. Such meters alternate in the first stanza; there is a repetition of two trochees and a spondee between the last line of the first stanza and the first line of the second stanza; and an inversion appears (three iambs into two trochees and a spondee) between the last line of the second stanza and the first line of the third stanza. These "turns" between rising and falling meters add to the charming effect of plowing—albeit under serious conditions of weather.[58] The speaker is working on steadily, and everything is being transformed: the water evaporates into wind and the wind pours down. There is no exact rhyming, but there are important instances of mirroring and inversion of sound and meter. "SPreaDs to the SuN" and "STreaMs to the MooN" are lines with the same meter, but they also play complexly with parallel sounds. The bilabial *p* is to the alveolar *d* as the alveolar *t* is to the bilabial *m*. We could say that "sun and moon" already appear as an off-rhyme in experience and that in the course of time the moon always follows the sun. Yet as well, the bilabial *m* appears then as the resolving turn after the alveolar *s*. Simple acrostic changes of sound patterns are at work in the turn between "DoWN" and "WiND" and the slanted use of the cognates *t* and *l* in the change from "FeaTheRs" to "FLaRe."

Coleridge wrote in his "Table-talk" of 20 August 1833, "Brute animals have vowel sounds; man only can utter consonants. It is natural, therefore, that the consonants should be marked first, as being the framework of the word; and no doubt a very simple living language might be written quite intelligibly to the natives without any vowel sounds marked at all. The words would be traditionally and conventionally recognized, as in short-hand, thus: Gd crtd th hvn nd th rth."[59] But our anthropomorphization of animal sounds frequently attributes to animals the articulation of consonants. We know, for example, from another poem in *Harmonium*, "Depression before Spring," that Wallace Stevens's roosters can sing the syllables "Ki ki ro ki." Following a pioneering essay on "Musicality in Verse" by Kenneth Burke and further recent work by Tsur on sound patterns and expression, we might look more closely in this vein at the sound patterns in the poem.[60] The first stanza literally bristles with an inverted play upon the "ki ki ro ki" (here ko ko ri ko) of the white cock:

The white CO-CKs tail
tOsses in the wind
the tuR(K)EY COCK's tail
GLitters in the sun.

The turkey cock's "gobble" makes an appearance in the hard *g* and *l*, but the *b* does not appear; the stanza's consonants remain entirely in the alveolar, velar, and back-velar region. There is not a simple bilabial or labiodental sound in the entire stanza. But the bilabials return dramatically as plosives in the third stanza with the *bl* and *pl* sounds indicating Remus's blowing of his horn:

Remus BLow your horn
I'm PLoughing on Sunday
PLoughing North America
BLow your horn.

Blowing and plowing are parallel activities here. And when, in the poem's climactic moment, the horn plays its news—"Tum-ti-tum / Ti-tum-tum-

tum"—all the instruments, the alveolars and the bilabials, are brought to the fore. In his choice of *b* and *p* as contrasting phonemes, Stevens returns to a common, but by no means invariable, primitive structure of early sound production. Infants align random sounds into fundamental groups that contrast with one another in terms of articulating mechanisms, and the difference between voiced *b* bilabials and unvoiced *p* bilabials is frequently the alignment of choice.[61]

If *Harmonium* is Stevens's exploration of the emergence of human sounds from nature, many of the poems in *Transport to Summer* address the cultural meanings of sounds and the relations among naming, calling, and speech. The poem "Certain Phenomena of Sound" begins with forms of sound play based on the phonemes of the "Ploughing on Sunday" type —that is, mostly alveolars (*tnsl*) and velars (*kg*):

> THe CriCKeT oN THe TeLePHoNe iS STiLL
> A GeRaNiuM WiTHeRS oN THe WiNDoW SiLL

But the last stanza emphasizes the invocatory relation between naming and being: "you were created of your name, the word / Is that of which you were the personage / There is no life except in the word of it."[62]

One of Stevens's most rigorous and complete statements on the relation between sound and poetry can be found in a consequent poem in *Transport to Summer*, "The Creations of Sound." The poem takes up the idea of the relation between persons and language in a complex way that acknowledges the necessary separation between speaking in poems and speaking to represent ourselves. The poem is a powerful critique of the "Poet X" who claims a connection between the spontaneity of his poetic art and the intrinsic nature of his person. This simple idea of Romantic expressivity is an anathema to Stevens, who is far more interested in the way poetic expression frees us from the bonds of lived experience and reified personality. The close of the poem gives instructions for correcting such a Romantic error:

> Tell X that speech is not dirty silence
> Clarified. It is silence made still dirtier.
> It is more than an imitation for the ear.

> He lacks this venerable complication.
> His poems are not of the second part of life.
> They do not make the visible a little hard

To see nor, reverberating, eke out the mind
On peculiar horns, themselves eked out
By the spontaneous particulars of sound.

We do not say ourselves like that in poems.
We say ourselves in syllables that rise
From the floor, rising in speech we do not speak.[63]

In a number of ways, this poem is the theory of which "Ploughing on Sunday" and the peculiar horn of Remus is the practice. But the poem is not a work of prose discourse. It is itself a poem and its structure is *built*, as if it had descended from Herbert's *The Temple* as an architectural conceit. The close of the poem completes the extended metaphor: poems are made from the syllables that rise from the floor and not from the music of the walls and the ceiling. The Poet X makes the solipsistic error of confusing the expression of his feelings (which we know in Stevens's register are synonymous with music) with the work of the poet. The poet works from the received foundation of speech—out of this inheritance, the poet makes another self, an eidetic self estranged from mere authorship. We do not "speak" from speech; rather, it is already waiting to speak us, both to enunciate our being and to enable us to remake and extend ourselves. In poems we "eke out the mind" on "peculiar horns," and spontaneity belongs to the particulars of sounds, not to the intended gestures of human beings.

Such a theory of sound returns us to Adorno's point that in the greatest lyric works it is language itself that is speaking and changing. And it also returns us to our earlier discussion of the assumption of persona as the assumption of poetic voice. In a general survey of North American mythology, written in 1914, Franz Boas describes the use of changes in speech as a means of representing characters who are neither the narrator or speaker: "Another artistic device that is used by many tribes to assist in the characterization of the actors [in verbal art forms] is the use of artificial changes in speech. Thus among the Kwakiutl the Mink cannot pronounce the sound *ts*, among the Kutenai Coyote cannot pronounce *s*, among the Chinook the animals speak different dialects. Dr. Sapir has called attention to the development of this feature among the Shoshoni and Nootka."[64] Lest we think that such a technique is only used in the representation of animal characters, we might remember that Charles Dickens invented what seem to be genuinely idiolectal features of speech as a device of characterization throughout his novels.[65] No one would ever accuse Dickens of forgetting to eke out the mind on the most peculiar horns.

II. HOPKINS: INVOCATION AND LISTENING

Stevens's meditations on sound have every confidence in the ability of poetry to sound its way into significance. But now I want to go back to the late nineteenth century to a poet who made sounding a much more problematic activity, returning us to the very origin of the appearance of the invocatory drive and linking the sounds of suffering to the sounds of poetic making in profound ways. My focus will be Gerard Manley Hopkins's "desolate sonnets" of 1885.

Hopkins's writings on poetics, informed by his deep knowledge of classical literature and his skills as a musician and draftsman, constantly return to the relation among sound, meter, and emotion. In his lecture notes on "Rhythm and the Other Structural Parts of Rhetoric—Verse," Hopkins defines verse as a "figure of spoken sound": "verse is speech having a marked figure, order/ of sounds independent of meaning and such as can be shifted from one word or words to others without changing."[66] He creates a taxonomy of possible kinds of verse by "the kinds of resemblance possible between syllables: musical pitch or tonic accent; length or time or quantity so called; stress or emphatic accent; likeness or sameness of letters, vowels or consonants initial or final [alliteration]; holding, break and circumflexion, slurs, glides, slides etc." He contrasts quantification of syllables (as in classical verse) with lettering (early English alliteration) the first "running" and the second "intermittent," explaining that stress is between these two, with English verse characterized by a strong stress and weak pitch.[67] In further notes, he explains that "all poetry is not verse but all poetry is either verse or falls under this or some still further development of what verse is, speech wholly or partially repeating some kind of figure which is over and above meaning, at least the grammatical, historical and logical meaning."[68]

Yet here what seems to be a technical definition of the relation between syllabification and metrical systems, and a separation of the material and semantic aspects of poetry, is for Hopkins part of a complex metaphysic he has borrowed from Parmenides and combined with Christian, particularly Ignatian, theology. In Hopkins's notes on Parmenides, he particularly singles out the ways "the phenomenal world (and the distinction between men or subjects and the things without them) is unimportant in Parmenides: the contrast is between the one and the many is the brink, limbus, lapping, run-and-mingle or two principles which meet in the scape of everything—probably Being, under its modification or siding of particular oneness or Being, and Not-being, under its siding of the Many. The two may be called two degrees of siding in the scale of Being. Foreshortening and equivalency will explain all possible difference. The inscape will be the proportion of the mixture."[69]

It is in these notes on Parmenides that we find the earliest evidence of Hopkins's use of what were to become key terms in his work: "inscape" and "instress." Although he uses these words almost colloquially and does not provide a clear definition of them, he usually implies by *inscape* the characteristic shape or pattern of a phenomenon; he describes in his journal the ways in which fine "stems" of a cloud can change into images of ribs or coral: "Unless you refresh the mind from time to time you cannot always remember or believe how deep the inscape of things is."[70] *Instress* is the identifying impression a thing can communicate and is associated with emotion; as a "stress within," it is a force binding something or a person into a unit.[71] Being and not-being, the one and the many, the constantly changing aspect of things—"the brink, limbus, lapping, run-and-mingle," which induces in the perceiver an emotional response.[72] This way of seeing the phenomenal world cannot be separated in Hopkins's thought and practice from the running and intermittent aspects of English speech as they are used in the poem; by torquing the relation between stress and pitch, deploying sprung rhythm as the reawakened tension between pure accentual and accentual syllabic traditions, Hopkins is able to invent a mode of poetic utterance that will serve his philosophy of perception and representation.

Consider, for example, two uses of the term *siding* that appears first in the Parmenides discussion quoted earlier. In a journal entry of 13 June 1871, he writes, "A beautiful instance of inscape sided on the slide, that is / successive sidings of one inscape, is seen in the behaviour of the flag flower from the shut bud to the full blowing: each term you can distinguish is beautiful in itself and of course if the whole 'behaviour' were gathered up and so stalled it would have a beauty of all the higher degree."[73] A second example comes from the discussion of the definition of verse in the lecture notes on rhythm: "[the figure of spoken sound] must be repeated at least once, that is / the figure must occur at least twice, so that it may be defined/ Spoken sound having a repeated figure. (It is not necessary that any whole should be repeated bodily; it may be *sided off* [Hopkins's emphasis], as in the metres of a chorus, but then *some* common measure, namely the length or strength of a beat etc., recurs)."[74]

In addition to the "siding" of the metrical scheme, caesura can break up the rhythm into "sense-words of different lengths from sound-words; alliteration and *skothending* (the Icelandic practice of ending with the same consonant, but after a different vowel) can break up the run of the sense with intermittent sound; open sounds can be transformed by *vowelling on* (assonance) or *vowelling off* (changing the vowel down some 'scale or strain or keeping')." Hopkins made lists of words of similar sound, listening for semantic connections between them, as in "drill, trill, thrill, nostril nese-thirl." "Common idea piercing. To *drill*, in sense of discipline, is to wear down, work upon. Cf. to *bore* in slang sense, wear, grind. So *tire* connected with *tero.*"[75] In the end there is little difference between "sense" and "sound" words as words "tone up" or vary the implications of sound and meaning. Hopkins pointedly remarks that "these various means of breaking the sameness of rhythm and especially caesura do not break the unity of the verse but the contrary; they make it organic and what is organic is one."[76]

As a figure of *spoken* sound, the poem produces effects of transformation in sound; it does not fix the terms of utterance; it becomes in itself a living, breathing, phenomenon. The technique works by lending emotional stress to the otherwise inherent qualities of speech: "Emotional intonation," he notes, "especially when not closely bound to the particular words will sometimes light up notes on unemphatic syllables and not follow the verbal stresses and pitches."[77] In a New Year's Day letter to Robert Bridges in 1885, Hopkins describes the alexandrine: "there is according to my experience, an insuperable tendency to the Alexandrine, so far, I mean, as this, that there is a break after the third foot cutting the line into equal halves. . . . I have found that this metre is smooth, natural and easy to work in broken dialogue. . . . In passionate passages I employ sprung rhythm in it with good effect."[78] In April he suggested that in regard to alexandrines, "as the feeling rises the rhythm becomes freer and more sprung."[79]

The emotional resources of meter are paramount for Hopkins; he is able to use the rhythms of speech as a kind of backdrop against which the emotions play their changes in stress and emphasis. In his lecture notes on rhythm, he explained how the syllabic, lexical, and "emotional" levels of the poem could be in dynamic tension:

> We may think of words as heavy bodies, as indoor or out of door objects of nature or man's art. Now every visible palpable body has a centre of gravity round which it is in balance and a centre of illumination or *highspot* or *quickspot* up to which it is lighted and down from which it is shaded.

The centre of gravity is like the accent of stress, the highspot like the accent of pitch, for pitch is like light and colour stress like weight and as in some things as air and water the centre of gravity is either unnoticeable or changeable so there may be languages in a fluid state in which there is light difference of weight or stress between syllables or what there is changes and again as it is only glazed bodies that shew the highspot well so there may be languages in which the pitch is unnoticeable. English is of this kind, the accent of stress strong, that of pitch weak. . . . Emotional intonation, especially when not closely bound to particular words, will sometimes light up notes on unemphatic syllables and not follow the verbal stresses and pitches.[80]

Stress is like the weight or volume of water and air here; pitch like the glancing play of light or color on the surface of water and other "glazed" objects.

Against this general theory of stress and pitch, Hopkins created effects particular to the emotional valences of individual lines. Consider the tension between the standard reading of the stress at the closure of "Spelt from Sibyl's Leaves," Hopkins's meditation on doomsday: "*thoughts against thoughts in groans grind*" is heard against the mounted stress Hopkins marks for the line—"*thoúghts agáinst* thoughts *ín* groans *grínd.*"[81] It is as if, at the end of this sonnet, Hopkins were stripping the gears of sound. By putting the emphasis on the *in*, Hopkins makes us push down the emphasis on the second *thoughts* and *groans*, forcing down our voices and foregrounding the carrying over of sound from *in* to *grind*. It is not so much that there is a slight change of semantic emphasis, which of course there is, but that we must go against our inclinations, against ourselves— everything in speech is made hard or difficult.

"Spelt from Sibyl's Leaves," begun at the end of 1884 and completed in 1886, is a transitional poem, produced in a period of pessimism that would result in Hopkins's "desolate" or "terrible" sonnets of 1885: "To seem the stranger," "I wake and feel the fell of dark, not day," "No worst there is none," "Carrion Comfort," "Patience, hard thing," and "My own heart." Because these poems existed only in manuscript at the time of Hopkins's death and were never dated or prepared for publication by Hopkins, we do not know the order in which he wrote them. They seem to have been composed between January and August of that year.[82] A great deal has been written about these sonnets. They mark the end of Hopkins's intense involvement with describing external nature; they appear during a period of despair regarding his situation as a teacher and examiner in classics at the Royal University, an English Catholic posted in Ireland. His health was poor, and his eyesight was failing him. He wrote in his journal, "being unwell I was quite downcast: nature in all her parcels and faculties gaped and fell apart, *fatiscebat*, like a clod cleaving and holding only by strings of root."[83]

The 1885 sonnets and "Spelt from Sibyl's Leaves" follow Hopkins's reading of Ignatius's instructions for meditating on sin and hell in his *Spiritual Exercises of 1541.* The role of sound here becomes foregrounded in such a way as to obviate any distinction between the form and theme of the poetry. The poems obey the Ignatian mandate of "imitatio Christi"— the imitation of Christ's suffering, a serious mimicry that is a form of incarnation as Christ himself incarnated, or was inhabited by, both divine and human being. As an "experiment"—although such a word hardly begins to approach the stakes involved for Hopkins—these poems make a formidable contribution to our understanding of the possibilities of sound in lyric.[84]

Yet Hopkins's 1885 poems also, and foremost, work through the capacity of sound in the sonnet—the "son" taking place in a confined room —to express mental despair. Norman White's biography of Hopkins quotes a 1953 book by Denis Meadows, *Obedient Men,* which describes the Jesuit novitiate's exercise on hell, a composition of place required by the 1541 *Exercises:* "We must take each of the senses in turn. First, says St. Ignatius, you see the fire, and the souls as though in bodies of fire. With your ears you hear the wailing, howling, and blasphemy of the lost ones. You smell the sulphur, smoke and putrescence of hell. Then you taste in imagination the bitterness of tears, sadness, and conscience ever remorseful, ever unabsolved, yet ever in rebellion. Last of all, you feel the fire touching and burning even an immaterial entity like the soul."[85] The use of the term *exercise* indicates, then, a method of self-transformation, or unmaking and remaking of the self. In Hopkins's own commentary on Ignatius's prescription, he wrote, "Sight does not shock like hearing, sounds cannot so disgust as smell, smell is not so bitter as proper bitterness, which is in taste . . . still bitterness of taste is not so cruel as the pain that can be touched and felt. Seeing is believing but touch is the truth the saying goes."[86] The function of the "exercise" was not to distance one's self and so acquire an encompassing view of hell but rather to experience, and engage, the sufferings of the damned.

After the "lonely began" of "To seem the stranger," "I wake and feel the fell of dark, not day" introduces the onset of hell's night—where light, the instrument of reason, should be, touch discovers the fall of the night and the animal pelt of the darkness:

I wake and feel the fell of dark, not day.
What hours, O what black hours we have spent
This night! what sights you, heart, saw, ways you went!
And more must, in yet longer light's delay.

With witness I speak this. But where I say
Hours I mean years, mean life. And my lament
Is cries countless, cries like dead letters sent
To dearest him that lives alas! away.

I am gall, I am heartburn. God's most deep decree
Bitter would have me taste: my taste was me;
Bones built in me, flesh filled, blood brimmed the curse.

Selfyeast of spirit a dull dough sours. I see
The lost are like this, and their scourge to be
As I am mine, their sweating selves, but worse.[87]

Because *fell* also means "a blow," it is symptomatic of originary suffering and sin: Adam's curse, the murder of Abel, the "long night" "full of tossing until dawn" of Job 7:4. Hopkins continues to link bitterness and orality in "Bitter would have me taste: my taste was me; Bones built in me, flesh filled, blood brimmed the curse." When in the last stanza Hopkins ends the first line "I see," he again interrupts the continuity of sight—the line break turns into a kind of trick, for the line continues, "I see / the lost are like this." In his sermons, Hopkins associated sight with continuous apprehension and hearing with intermittent apprehension.[88] Sight is, however, intermittent in hell and linked to the invisibility of sin. In his commentary on the exercise, Hopkins writes of the sinner's "imprisonment in darkness . . . for darkness is the phenomenon of foiled action in the sense of sight. . . . But this constraint and this blindness or darkness will be most painful when it is the main stress or energy of the whole being that is thus balked."[89]

Hence, this thwarted, balked stress or energy of being is expressed in a continuous, and continuously painful, form of utterance that is the sonnet itself. "I wake and feel" uses sound pairs—"feel the fell," "sights saw," "ways went," "longer light," "cries countless," "alas away," "gall heartburn," "deep decree," "bitter taste," "bones built," "flesh filled," "blood brimmed," "selfyeast of spirit," "a dull dough," "lost like," and "sweating selves"—that are also semantic pairs: nouns are often followed or preceded by adverbs functioning as adjectives. In this way, a quality of an object is put into a dynamic relation with it, transforming it as that quality adheres to, or becomes part of, its structure and so continuing the "siding" process Hopkins pursued since his early studies of Parmenides. But here this "siding" is not a joyful insight into the transformative dimensions of nature. Indeed, the poem is literally "wracked" on the level of sound. What Kenneth Burke had described as "musical effects" in Coleridge's poetry are here a form of physical torture. *Compression*, as in "NighT" to "weNT"; *inversion*, as in "muST" to "lighT'S" and "SaW" to WayS"; *augmentation*, as in "iN yeT loNger lighT," are not expressive of musical sensations so much as symptoms of a dire tension, a "failed action," that seems to be punctuated by human cries. These cries move concertedly from an emphasis on the "bright vowels" *i* and *e* at the start of the poem to the dark vowels *u* and *o*, which become more emphasized in the final two stanzas.[90]

The singularity and futility ("cries like dead letters sent") of mortal entities are brought to an abrupt halt, a final judgment: "but worse." What does it mean for Hopkins to say that his "cries" are "like dead letters sent / To dearest him that lives alas! away"? Whether "dearest him" is God, or Christ, or Robert Bridges, or some other interlocutor, he is not present—neither within the range of the speaker's cries nor available as the recipient of a letter. There is no "delivery" from torment; here the tautological consequences of sin are expressed as a tautology of the poet speaking to and for himself: "my taste was me"; "selfyeast of spirit a dull dough sours."

Hopkins wrote to Bridges in May 1885, "I have after long silence written two sonnets, which I am touching; if ever anything was written in blood one of these was."[91] Bridges himself later concluded that the poem "written in blood" might have been "Carrion Comfort," but what also is emphasized here is that Hopkins is "touching" two sonnets. Although we have no way of knowing which two sonnets or which sonnet "written in blood" Hopkins had in mind, "I wake and feel" and "No worst there is none" may be the "two," for "No worst" can be read as a complex "response" or echo to "I wake and feel."

> No worst, there is none. Pitched past pitch of grief,
> More pangs will, schooled at forepangs, wilder wring.
> Comforter, where, where is your comforting?
> Mary, mother of us, where is your relief?
> My cries heave, herds-long; huddled in a main, a chief-
> Woe, wórld-sorrow; on an áge-old ánvil wínce and síng—
> Then lull, then leave off. Fury had shrieked 'No ling-

Ering! Let me be fell: force I must be brief.'
O the mind, mind has mountains; cliffs of fall
Frightful, sheer, no-man-fathomed. Hold them cheap
May who ne'er hung there. Nor does long our small
Durance deal with that steep or deep. Here! creep,
Wretch, under a comfort serves in a whirlwind: all
Life death does end and each day dies with sleep.[92]

The last words of "I wake and feel the fell of dark, not day," "but worse,"
are answered "No worst, there is none." Issues of sequence are complicated in auditory ways, for if we here have an "answer" or echo, "no
worst" will return to the earliest sounds of speech, like pains experienced
retrospectively once the knowledge of pain has begun. In the opening lines
of "No worst," we find that word pairs are set up not via a truncated echoing effect but rather in a reverse fashion, so that the first instance is extended: no/none, pangs/forepangs, comforter/comforting, lull/lingering.
These balked phrases, interspersed with repetitions (pitched past pitch of
grief) and clotted spondees ("my cries heave, herds-long"; "huddled in a
main, a chief- / woe, wórld-sorrow"; "on an áge-old ánvil wínce and síng—
/ then lull, then leave off"), produce an effect of *stuttering*. The involuntary hesitations, rapid repetitions of speech elements, sputtering, and violent explosions of breath following a halt characteristic of that speech disorder are all here.

Look at the distribution of stops (*d, p, k, g, b*, and *t* sounds) and nasal
stops (*m, n*, and closing *g* sounds):

No worsT, there is NoNe, PitcheD PasT Pitch of Grief,
More PaNGs will, sCHooleD aT forePaNGs, wilDer wriNG.
CoMforTer, where, where, is your CoMforTiNG?
Mary, Mother of us, where is your relief?
My Cries heave, herDs-loNG, huDDleD in a Main, a chief-
Woe, worlD-sorrow; oN aN age-olD aNvil wiNce aND siNG—
TheN lull, theN leave off. Fury haD shrieKed 'No liNG-
EriNG! LeT Me Be fell: force I MusT Be Brief.
O the MiND, MiND has MouNTaiNs; Cliffs of fall
FrighTful, sheer, No-MaN-fathoMeD. HolD theM cheaP
May who Ne'er huNG there. Nor Does loNG our sMall
DuraNce Deal with thaT sTeeP or DeeP. Here! CreeP,
Wretch, uNDer a coMforTer serves in a whirlwiND; all
Life Death Does eND aND each Day Dies with sleeP.

The stops are most intense at the beginning and end of the sonnet. In the phrases "Mary, mother of us, where is your relief?" and "Then lull, then leave off," relief and lulling are palpably present as the stops briefly decline. But after Fury reenters, the anvil of torment is vividly rung: "liN-GeriNG" echoes against all the other NG sounds: *pangs, wring, comforting, sing, hung, long*. We could draw a different map of the pattern of bilabials that would include the recurring *m* sounds used at the starts of words and phrases like an incessant murmuring or prayer, creating the sequence "more; Mary; mother; my; main; me; must; mind; mountains; man; may." And the sure-footed *m*, associated with these words of comfort and stability, is undermined by its opposite, the unbalanced *w*, appearing in the sequence "worst, wilder, wring, where, where, where, woe, world-sorrow, wince, wretch, whirlwind." An effect of pathos is also produced by the tension between the fricative *(f)* sounds at the ends of all unstopped lines until they gradually add the liquids *(l)*. Tsur's study of sound implication argues that this sequence—vowels, liquids, nasals, voiced fricatives, voiced stops, voiceless fricatives, and voiceless stops—produces a decreasing periodicity or sonority of sounds. The sequence also might be read as moving like the grieving Hecuba from tones to noises or from harmonious to unharmonious sounds. Vowels, nasals, and liquids are all acoustically periodical. In poems that are incantatory or hypnotic, the marked regularity of rhyme is brought forward by the emphasis on such vowels, liquids, and nasals. In Hopkins's "No worst, there is none," the stops startle the reader in patterns that work against the meter as the fricatives recede into a closing use of liquids.[93]

The stutterings diminish by the close of the octave, another *f–l* sequence: "Let me be fell." At this moment the stuttering is overcome and the speaker *is* "the fell"—the animal pelt and mantle of darkness, the blow of awakened consciousness from which the rhetorical grandeur of the sestet next proceeds with its admonition regarding the scale of our "small durance" "under a comfort serves in a whirlwind." The body as a hollow instrument nevertheless can barely breathe as it struggles into speech. In this sonnet, Hopkins does not assume the invocatory drive but rather expresses the conditions under which that drive is externalized. To read this sonnet is to listen to sound unborn being born. Nevertheless, the final line, with its deliberate and theologically bankrupt oversimplification "Life death does end and each day dies with sleep," marks the closure of abstract human time—the closure is like a false bottom; it will offer no consolation; hell itself gives testament to the incapacity of death to end life.

"Carrion Comfort" can be read as a transition to "Patience, Hard

thing," the most consoling and resolved sonnet of the group. It is likely to
have been based on Ignatius's spiritual exercise (VIII) on patience. In "Carrion Comfort" the exact repetition of "not" ("Not, I'll not carrion comfort,
Despair, not feast on thee; Not untwist . . . not choose not to be") produces
a pattern of negatives and positives ensuing from double negatives—
"turns of tempest."

Carrion Comfort

Not, I'll not, carrion comfort, Despair, not feast on thee;
Not untwist—slack they may be—these last strands of man
In me—ór, most weary, cry *I can no more.* I can;
Can something, hope, wish day come, not choose not to be.

But ah, but O thou terrible, why wouldst thou rude on me
Thy wring-earth right foot rock? lay a lionlimb against me? scan
With darksome devouring eyes my bruisèd bones? and fan,
O in turns of tempest, me heaped there; me frantic to avoid thee and flee?

Why? That my chaff might fly; my grain lie, sheer and clear.
Nay in all that toil, that coil, since (seems) I kissed the rod,
Hand rather, my heart lo! lapped strength, stole joy, would laugh, cheer.

Cheer whóm though? The héro whose héaven-handling flúng me, fóot
    tród
Me? or mé that fóught him? O whích one? is it eách one? That níght,
    that year
Of now done darkness I wretch lay wrestling with (my God!) my God.[94]

Hopkins brilliantly uses stops to evoke hesitation and struggle within this
poem as well, yet here he concentrates on the "primitive" relation between *p* and *b* sounds that we discussed earlier in Stevens's "Ploughing on
Sunday." In Hopkins this plosive pair is often mediated by an *m* stop. The
first eight lines show the following distribution of repetitions and inversions: (1) *m p*; (2) *m b*; (3) *m m m*; (4) *m p m b*; (5) *b b b m*; (6) *m b m*;
(7) *m m b b*; (8) *mp m p m*.

Yet in "Carrion Comfort" we encounter more than a problem of stuttering—it is stuttering's problem of thwarted beginnings that is raised.
In keeping with the theme of "carrion" or predation, the endings or closings are as well made problematic through the use of echo effects. Echoes,
which are themselves parasitical in their structure, are found not only in
the rhyming words but also in consonant repetitions and inversions be-

tween many of the stanza sections: "MaN" to "iN Me" to "oN Me" between the end of line two, the beginning of line 3 and the end of line 5, for
example. The final echo—"(my God!) / my God"—implies not an an-
swering reciprocity but the terrible hollow return of the speaker's voice in
a void. This is the only kind of comfort he receives—the carrion comfort
of self-reifying repetition.

The poem has a great deal of the hysterical mixture of sounds one finds
in extreme situations—"cry"; "wish"; "fan"; "frantic"; "coil"; "laugh";
"cheer." Utterances are spoken and quoted at once: "cry *I can no more
I can*" and, again, "(my God!) my God." The God who is both the addressee
of the exclamation and the object of the verb ("I wretch lay wrestling with
my God") appears then in the second person and the third person and so
throws light (itself described negatively as "now done darkness") back
upon the question "cheer whóm though? . . . Me? or mé that fóught
him?" Here Hopkins uses interpolated utterance (as he had in the famous
"fancy, come faster" of "The Wreck of the Deutschland") to express an
agonized self-consciousness. The self who acts is part of the mortal fallen
world, and the self who speaks carries a painful knowledge of the conditions under which he speaks, a knowledge that is inherently tautological:
"we hear our hearts grate on themselves; it kills / To bruise them dearer,"
Hopkins writes in "Patience, hard thing," thus echoing the "thoúghts
agáinst thoughts ín groans grínd" of "Spelt from Sibyl's Leaves." Hopkins had written in his *Sermons* of how "nothing else in nature comes
near this unspeakable stress of pitch, distinctiveness, and selving, this
self-being of my own,"[95] but the signs of pitch and stress that mark the individuality of being are now, in a negative analogy to poetic expression,
the material cries of a material being condemned to suffering by insight as
well as experience.[96]

Hopkins's 1885 sonnets return us to the origins of the invocatory
drive, but in doing so they underscore the relation of sound production to
a heightened consciousness of reception in aurality. Like the reception of
visual phenomena, the reception of sound might be framed as a *feeling*;
we receive light and sound waves as we receive a touch, a pressure. They
touch not only our ear membrane but also the entire outer surface of the
skin.[97] Yet when we hear, we hear the sound *of something*; the continuity
of sight does not provide an analogue to this attribution of source or cause
in sound reception. And we do not pinpoint sound in space. We see properly only what is before us, but sound can envelop us; we might, as we
move or change, have varying experiences of sound's intensity, but it will
not readily "fit" an epistemology of spatiality, horizon, or location.[98] As
Herder writes, "Most visible things move. Many sound while moving. If

not, they lie close to the eye in its early state, directly on it as it were and can be felt. The sense of feeling is close to that of hearing. Its epithets— such as hard, rough, soft, woolly, velvety, hairy, rigid, smooth, prickly, etc. which all concern only surfaces and do not penetrate—all sound as though one could feel them."[99] For Herder, the capacity of hearing to bring the full stretch of vision nearer and to open up the narrow range of touch impressions is key to its role in communicability. Hearing is a "middle" sense, according to Herder, for other reasons as well: it mediates the vagueness of touch and the cold brightness of vision; it negotiates the partiality of the immediacy of touch and the objectified "all at onceness" of vision; and it stands between those objects of touch that are as mute as the fell of dark and those objects of vision that are endlessly describable.[100] Whereas vision and touch refer to stationary objects, hearing indicates movement and change and so hearing is especially conducive to the transformation and unfolding of language. Tsur describes how "while in the visual mode we are inclined to *attend away from* the signifier to the object signified, in the auditory mode we are inclined to *attend to* the ever-changing labile signifier so as to be able to detect any minute change in our environment."[101]

There is an incommensurability between the production of sound and the reception involved in listening. Listening has no limit, no articulation, but waits in the silence that fills the future lying all about the utterance. The silence of listening permeates the poem—it exists in the silences between sounds and stanzas and the turning of the page. This is not the silence of the medial caesura, whether expected or producing surprise, for the caesura's silence is properly an interval—a delimited pause between marks of rhythm. The silence all about and through the poem is outside the marked time of its meter and rhythm; it is not yet awakened.[102] Every "dead" letter still dreams of animation in this sense. Herder writes about this issue at the very beginning of his "Essay on the Origin of Language":

> While still an animal, man already has language. All violent sensations
> of his body, and among the violent the most violent, those which cause
> him pain, and all strong passions of his soul express themselves directly
> in screams, in sounds, in inarticulate tones. A suffering animal, no less
> than the hero Philoctetus, will whine, will moan when pain befalls it,
> even though it be abandoned on a desert island, without sight or trace or
> hope of a helpful fellow creature. It is as though it could breathe more
> freely as it vents its burning, frightened spirit. It is as though it could sigh
> out part of its pain and at least draw in from the empty airspace new
> strength of endurance as it fills the unhearing winds with its moans. So

little did nature create us as severed blocks of rocks as egotistical monads! Even the most delicate chords of animal feeling . . . even the chords whose sound and strain do not arise from choice and slow deliberation, whose very nature the probing of reason has not as yet been able to fathom, even they—though there be no awareness of sympathy from outside—are aligned in their entire performance for a going out toward other creatures.[103]

Yet when we turn to Homer's lines on "Philoctetus"'s (Philoctetes') suffering, we find in fact that Herder has underestimated the human capacity to internalize the recognition of others:

> Philoctetes the master archer had led them on
> in seven ships with fifty oarsmen aboard each.
> Superbly skilled with the bow in lethal combat.
> But their captain lay on an island, racked with pain,
> on Lemnos's holy shores where the armies had marooned him,
> agonized by his wound, the bite of the deadly water-viper.
> There he writhed in pain but soon, encamped by the ships,
> the Argives would recall Philoctetes, their great king.[104]

This situation, which we might call the "Philoctetes problem" or "the dead letter problem," is far more complex than Herder's presentation of it as an example of animal expression indicates. How can the poet know —how can anyone know—what sounds, what cries, were uttered, how agony was expressed, by Philoctetes in his abandonment? It is only because of a consequent reception, one that followed the "recalling" of Philoctetes by his men after his command had been replaced by others, that such suffering can be given voice. Philoctetes may call forever to the wind; it is only this recalling that can bring back the repetition of his utterance—the repetition that also enables the poet to create the image of his suffering.

Let us consider one other complex example of the Philoctetes problem here: Shakespeare's striking use of the representation of reported suffering in *Hamlet*, act 4, scene 7. Here Gertrude tells Laertes that his sister has drowned, explaining:

> There is a willow grows aslant a brook,
> That shows his hoar leaves in the glassy stream.
> There with fantastic garlands did she come
> Of crowflowers, nettles, daisies, and long purples,

That liberal shepherds give a grosser name.
But our cold maids do dead men's fingers call them.
There on the pendent boughs her coronet weeds
Clamb'ring to hang, an envious sliver broke
When down her weedy trophies and herself
Fell in the weeping brook. Her clothes spread wide
And, mermaid-like, awhile they bore her up;
Which time she chaunted snatches of old tunes,
As one incapable of her own distress,
Or like a creature native and indued
Unto that element; but long it could not be
Till that her garments, heavy with their drink,
Pull'd the poor wretch from her melodious lay
To muddy death.

This passage is suffused with the sensibility of the obscene. Who has seen the specific flowers that adorned Ophelia as she fell? How does Gertrude know the grosser names that shepherds call them, and who has seen Ophelia's clothes spread wide before they pulled her down? Who has heard the "chaunted snatches of old tunes" she sang? The situation is the opposite of the recalling of Philoctetes. There is no survivor to report Ophelia's cries of distress, though there must be witnesses to these details—witnesses who heard and did not intervene. No one drew Ophelia back to life; whoever heard her heard as one would hear a sound of nature—without reciprocity, without listening. Ophelia therefore dies like a part of nature into nature, a creature "native and indued / Unto that element."

In Hopkins's 1885 sonnets, the tormented "groans" and heaving "cries within cries" resound in a claustrophobic space yet are locationless. The "something" to which we attribute these sounds is a self "pitched past pitch" by the anxiety of his own capacity for self-reference. The poems are a radically vivid expression of the "silence" of lyric sound. Rather than assuming the presence of speech and reception, they struggle with our presumptions of speech and reception; their theological matrix only heightens the torment of Hopkins's insights into the human ends of *poiēsis*. What saved Hopkins, or at least saved the poetry of Hopkins from the Philoctetes problem and rescued it for the future, was that there *was* a recipient to the "dead letter": Bridges, who so patiently brought the work into history. For Hopkins, in the midst of a theological crisis regarding the reality of his perceptions and the impossibility of ascribing a divine source to mortal apprehension, there was ultimately little salvation in poetry itself.

But Bridges's commitment to Hopkins's letters is significant for the analogy I want to make, in closing this chapter, between the silence of the poem and the recalled aurality of its reception. There is a limit to the metaphor of presence in lyric. When we attend a poetry reading or hear a poem read aloud by its author in a recording or some other context, we may confuse the speech in the poem with the speech of the person, and we may confuse the person who speaks with either the person who speaks in the poem or the person who speaks at the reading. It is not that such information is not useful and interesting; however, it will be information that will be both too particular (specific to an occasion) and too general (theatrical and repeatable in its exaggeration of "significant" features). As a consequence, the "poet" him- or herself runs the risk of becoming an artifact of the poem, and the poem itself becomes an artifact of performance.

I propose that the sound of poetry is heard in the way a promise is heard. A promise is an action made in speech, in the sense not of something scripted or repeatable but of something that "happens," that "occurs" as an event and can be continually called on, called to mind, in the unfolding present. When I promise, I create an expectation, an obligation, and a necessary condition for closure. Whether we are in the presence of each other or not, the promise exists. Whether you, the one who receives the promise, continue to exist or not, the promise exists. Others may discontinue making and fulfilling promises, the word *promise* might disappear, you or others may no longer remember, or deserve, or make sense of that promise—nevertheless, the promise exists.

As J. L. Austin wrote in *How to Do Things with Words*, promises and other "commissives" are not intentions, although intending itself is a commissive—"declarations of intention differ from undertakings" especially if they are framed by the expression "I intend." [105] The promise can be, must be, fulfilled in time; a "broken promise" cannot be mended—it can only be regretted or used to establish new grounds of demand or indifference. When we consider the historical path of lyric poetry, we find an ongoing process of exploration of the dynamic we have already mentioned between an "I" (the speaker) and a "you" (the addressee). Poetry can, it is true, involve a speaker speaking to him- or herself as another, and it can involve an apostrophe to the wind or to a crowd. But personification is *voiced* in poetry—that is, voice takes place not merely as a presence but as the condition under which the person appears. The realization of expression depends on the *bind*, the implicit tie of intelligibility between speaker and listener that links their efforts toward closure. Through lyric we return literally to the breath and pulse of speech rhythm in tension with those formal structures we have available to us for making time manifest. In this way, lyric, no matter how joyous or comic, expresses that seriousness, the good faith in intelligibility, under which language proceeds and by means of which we recognize each other as speaking persons. The object of that recognition is a sound that becomes a human voice.

3

VOICE AND POSSESSION

I. THE BELOVED'S VOICE

L et's say I am thinking about my love for your voice—not the sources of my love for your voice, but what it is I love when I love your voice. What is the "object" of this love? I could not love the voice of an animal or the voice of a god. I would not be able truly to *listen* to the voice of an animal, and I could not bear to listen, on the scale of human history where we live, to the voice of a god. Yet it is not really the anticipation of reciprocity that fuels my love for your voice. Nor is it simply that the voice is metonymic to the body as a whole. We love voices as we love eyes—as vessels of that presence we call the soul: to love the voice and the eyes is far different from loving the color of someone's hair or even someone's way of walking. The individuation of the voice is not synonymous with the individuation of the body as the site of experience: the body is too general an entity, too material a substance, to account for the individuality of the voice. After death, when the voice is silent and the light in the eyes is gone, the body—the shell that is the body—remains.[1]

Marcel Proust, in his account of Marcel's first experience with a telephone in *The Guermantes Way*, writes with great subtlety on the love for a voice and the love expressed in a voice. In this passage, Marcel awaits a call from his grandmother. He is at Doncières and she is in Paris. And when the call comes, he hears her voice for the first time: "seen without the mask of her face, I noticed in it for the first time the sorrows that had cracked it in the course of a lifetime." He hears her voice as *her* voice, not as the instrument of language and expression but in its particularity as the reservoir of her life's experiences.[2] In complex ways this scene will bear upon a later situation of involuntary memory as Marcel puts on his boots in the hotel room in Balbec where previously he and his grandmother had communicated by means of a private language of knocks on the party wall between them. Marcel will for the first time acknowledge to himself the reality of her death. Yet already in the discussion of this first experience of the telephone, the narrator realizes that to hear the individuality, the idiosyncratic "grain" of the voice, is both to encounter and to defer the encounter with the death of the beloved:

> [A]t what a distance we may be from the persons we love at the moment when it seems that we have only to stretch out our hands to seize and hold them. A real presence, perhaps, that voice that seemed so near—in actual separation! But a premonition also of an eternal separation! Many are the times, as I listened thus without seeing her who spoke to me from so far away, when it has seemed to me that the voice was crying to me from the depths out of which one does not rise again, and I have felt the anxiety that was one day to wring my heart when a voice would thus return (alone and attached no longer to a body which I was never to see again), to murmur in my ear words I longed to kiss as they issued from lips forever turned to dust.[3]

The beloved's voice is untouchable. It is that which touches me and which I cannot touch. Yet the one who "owns" it—that is, the one who belongs to it—cannot touch it either. I cannot see my eyes when I see; they are invisible to me.[4] And I cannot hear my own voice when I speak: I hear only its echo or resonance and when it comes to me on a recording it comes as a stranger's voice, as horrid and uncanny as a glimpse of my own corpse. The voice and the eyes take part in the more general truth that I cannot witness my own motion as a whole: I cannot see what is alive about myself and so depend on the view of others. It is the viewpoint of the beloved that gives witness to what is alive in our being.

What Proust brings forward is that what is irreducible in one's voice is the irreducibility of one's death. Yet as the individual voice contains within it the seed of its own disappearance, its fragility and impermanence, so, in its fleetingness, does it bear a kind of aural imprint of its history, its ancestry—in the voice is the voice of all first voices. The dead are the source of the continuing seed of death in the voice. And when we love voices, we love beyond language, beyond articulation. All love may be, as Freud contends in *Civilization and Its Discontents,* counter to socialization;[5] but the love for the voice alone is the most asocial of all—not because it returns us to an animal connection, for in this sense animal voices are preeminently social, but rather because the love of a voice in its individuality draws us toward all that resists the law, including that death which has dominion over law.

Voice in poetry is a further development of a path toward volition that Hegel describes in his *Philosophy of Fine Art:* "Motion, however, is not the only expression of animated life. The free tones of the voices of animals, which are unknown in the inorganic world, where bodies merely roar and clatter through the blow of objects external to them, then already present to us in the higher expression of animated subjectivity."[6] But because poetic voice is informed by, often indeed formed by, the imperatives of rhythm and repetition, its volition is problematic—more problematic than, say, the production of discursive sentences in prose such as these. We will see that this doubled movement in poetic production, toward mastery on the one hand and toward being mastered on the other, has made poetry suspect as a force against reason and valued as a means of ecstasis. It is suggestive that in his late nineteenth-century history of Greek poetic forms, Gilbert Murray mentions the Socratic tradition that "string instruments allow you to be master of yourself, while flute, pipe, or clarionette or whatever corresponds to various kinds of 'aulos' puts you beside yourself, obscures reason and is more fit for barbarians."[7] Tactility, manipulation, and externalization remain the "touchstones" of reality here and the wind as a force of possession the vehicle of transport and self-transformation.

In our discussion of sound, I have emphasized the broadest aspects of sound production and reception in poetry: such aspects are continuous with our reception of sound in nature, in manmade environments and conversation, with animal cries, and utterances of pain and fear. But I have underemphasized the made and intended production of sound—the ways in which sound is *formed* for pleasurable, beautiful, and ultimately social ends. Specifically, sound production and reception in poetry always carry an image of the particularity of human voices. It is not just sound that we hear; it is the sound of an individual person speaking sounds. The diffuseness of sound, the problem of invocation and the specific consequences invocation bears regarding the impossibility of closure, our need to attribute source or causality to sounds when we hear them—in the production of lyric all of these amorphous qualities of sound production are traced to the situation of the speaking person. Such sounds might be imitations of sounds in nature, of animal cries, or of the most elaborately inflected nuances of human conversation, but in every case sound is here known as a *voice.*

What do we mean when we speak of "voice" in poetry? To indulge in such creative writing workshop clichés as that of "the poet finding his or her own voice" is to substitute a reifying and mystifying version of subjectivity for what is in fact most profound and engaging about poetic voice—that is, the plays of transformation it evokes beyond the irreducibility of its own grain, its own potential for silence.[8] The "object" of my love for your voice emerges in the relation between my history and the uniqueness of your existence, the particular timbre, tone, hesitations, and features of articulation by which all the voices subject to your own history have shaped your voice's instrument. In listening, I am listening to the material history of your connection to all the dead and the living who have been impressed upon you. The voice, with the eyes, holds within itself the life of the self—it cannot be another's.

The individual voice is in these ways demonic, mediating, traversing, in Diotima's sense of the δαίμων *(daimōn)* of love in her discourse to Socrates in the *Symposium.* Diotima explains that the *daimōn* is a spirit, intermediate between the divine and mortal—the power that interprets and conveys to the gods the prayers and sacrifices of men and to men the commands and rewards of the gods; and "this power spans the chasm which divides them and in this all is bound together, and through this the arts of the prophet and the priest, their sacrifices and mysteries and charms and all prophecy and incantation find their way."[9] In an elaborate development of metaphors and analogies, Diotima explains that poetry as the creation or passage of being out of nonbeing is an apt description of all forms of making or *poiēsis*, but it is most truly the art of music and meter. Analogously, the lover seeks the passage or creation of nonbeing into being through the immortality of human reproduction—whether through biology or through cultural forms that outlast their makers. But in either case love is not something that one has. Love is set in motion instead as a lack, and love is not a form of being; "no man can want that which he has and no man can want that which he is." Love is a process of bringing to birth the beautiful and the good—what exists "without diminution and without increase."[10]

In the *Symposium* the inspiriting and inspired creation of poetry is thus analogous to the creation of love. Nevertheless, Diotima speaks with particular favor of those creators who use not merely their bodies as their means of production: "creative souls—for there are men who are more creative in their souls than in their bodies—conceive that which is proper for the soul to conceive or retain. And what are these conceptions?—wisdom and virtue in general. And such creators are all poets and other artists who may be said to have invention." She asks, "Who, when he thinks of Homer and Hesiod and other great poets, would not rather have their children than any ordinary human ones? Who would not emulate them in the creation of children such as theirs, which have preserved their memory and given them everlasting glory?"[11] This model of *poiēsis* shows the poet as a master of form, seeking models in what is truly good and beautiful and thereby ensuring his immortality in the future, his intelligibility across generations. While the context of the banquet gives comic instances of a loss of mastery—the flute girls; the wine; the hiccups of Aristophanes—Diotima describes the purposeful path of "that life above all others which man should live, in the contemplation of beauty absolute." Here "the true order of going or being led by another to the things of love, is to use the beauties of earth as steps along which he mounts upwards for the sake of that other [absolute] beauty."[12]

Regardless of this purposeful trajectory, the tension we have described between mastery and surrender in processes of *poiēsis* is deeply inscribed in Plato's texts when we consider them as a whole. The model of poetic mastery in the *Symposium* is countered by the account of poetic inspiration presented in more complex and even negative terms in the *Republic* and several of the Platonic dialogues. In these texts a recurring anxiety accompanies the idea of poetic will, and this anxiety centers constantly on the question of whose agency is speaking in the poetic voice—what is the source or cause of the sound that is heard in poetry? It is an anxiety that affects poet and reader alike; indeed, it is often expressed as an anxiety about the contamination that might arise between these two positions.

For all of those reasons we have discussed—the ways in which rhythms inhabit the body beyond volition; the ways in which others, including the dead, are manifested in the voice of the poet as an individual speaking person; the ways in which sound tends to escape the confines of closure—poetry becomes a suspect source of thought. When actors become the recipients of actions, when speakers speak from the position of listeners, when thought is unattributable and intention wayward, the situation of poetry is evoked. In *Phaedrus,* Plato explains, "There is . . . a third kind of madness, which is a possession of the Muses; this enters into a delicate and virgin soul, and there inspiring frenzy, awakens lyric and all other numbers . . . he who, not being inspired and having no touch of madness in his soul, comes to the door and thinks that he will get into the temple by the help of art—he, I say, and his poetry are not admitted; the sane man is nowhere at all when he enters into rivalry with the madman."[13] Poets who work by means of *technē* alone (that "art" that he has in mind) will remain outside the door of artistic success.

Yet in the *Republic* Plato also has another kind of exclusion in store for successful poets because of his deep suspicion of the consequences and effects of their work. Although he is willing to accept certain forms of epideictic poetry celebrating heroism or the gods, at the heart of his objection is the derivative nature of poetic imitation. Slippages between poetry and the ideal/real make poetry a fertile ground for corruption: poetry can provide false prophecies (Book II, 383c); variations in poetic form can produce licentiousness (Book III, 404e), and lawlessness in poetic form can result in changing the laws of the city (Book IV, 424c). Poetry can corrupt the concept of beauty by promoting what is merely crowd pleasing (Book VI, 493d), and it can corrupt the crowd by providing a substitute for thought (Book X, 595b/c). Correlatively, poetry is easy to compose without knowledge of the truth (Book X, 598e), and poetry appeals to the excited and variable in character (Book X, 605a).[14] Throughout these well-known arguments of the *Republic,* the corrupting power of poetry resides in its charm, and the most dangerous aspect of this charm is that it is *unthought.* Here the threat to the citizenry arises from the qualities of poetry and the definition of knowledge that are outlined respectively in *Ion* and *Theaetetus.*

Socrates explains to Ion that "the spectator is the last of the rings which, as I am saying, receive the power of the original magnet from one another. The rhapsodist and the actor are intermediate links, and the poet himself is the first of them. Through all these God sways the souls of men in any direction which he pleases, causing each link to communicate the power to the next. . . . And every poet has some Muse from whom he is suspended, and by whom he is said to be possessed, which is nearly the same thing, for he is taken hold of."[15] Socrates is interested in critiquing the claims to knowledge of rhapsodists such as Ion, but he relegates the poet to a similar position by viewing the poet as a conduit to the power of the muse or God. The meaning of possession here does not reside simply in the idea that the poet's utterances are not *original* or *reasoned.* Rather, such utterances pass through the speaker by means of an external force. One is "beside one's self," and the distinction the *Theaetetus* draws between having and possessing knowledge has thereby complex implications for both the situation of the muse who *possesses* the poet and the situation of the poet who merely *has* what the muse has endowed to him.

In his image of the aviary, Socrates explains that one must distinguish between *possessing* and *having* knowledge: "Well, may not a man 'possess' and yet not 'have' knowledge in the sense in which I am speaking? As you may suppose a man to have caught wild birds—doves or any other birds—and to be keeping them in an aviary which he has constructed at home; we might say of him in one sense, that he always has them because he possesses them, might we not? . . . And yet, in another sense, he has none of them."[16] The distinction between possessing and having knowledge arises during Socrates' analysis and refutation of the Pythagorean equation of knowledge and sense perception. Furthermore, the metaphor that most systematically suffuses his rhetorical strategies, that of the active/passive reciprocity between the midwife and the laboring woman, forms an analogy to what is productive, but limited, in sense perception—that one is both the agent and vessel of sense perception.

The rhapsodist and the poet *possess* knowledge—it is present or at hand—but they do not have it; they are not in control of it or able to transform it. Rather, they are themselves possessed by the power of the muse who inhabits them. In picturing this situation, forms of play that might be termed ventriloquistic come to mind. Ventriloquism per se is characterized by speaking from the belly or trunk of the body rather than from the head, projecting a voice from or across a *distance* spatially (and in the metaphor of possession, temporally as well). This voice is distinguished by its origin in *another place*. We might also recall the children's game in which one person stands behind another with the person in front keeping his arms behind the back with elbows protruding; the person behind puts her arms through the crooks of the partner's elbows and moves his limbs in coordination with the facing partner's speech. A dissociation of voice and gesture, and gesture from the body, results. Such forms of play, and expressions such as being "out of one's head," "out of one's mind," or, as cited earlier, "beside one's self," provide a sample of ways in which we make possession manifest through qualities of distantiation and disassociation. It is not coincidental that these instances are alterations or reversals of the standard reality-making situation of reciprocal face-to-face communication.

Friedrich Schiller writes analogously of the loss of self in aesthetic experience in which "man is an occupied moment of time": "Everyday language has for this condition of absence-of-self under the domination of sense-perception the very appropriate expression *to be beside oneself*—that is, to be outside one's ego."[17] Standing behind, standing before, standing beside—all send the voice into a difficult trajectory; it is the trajectory of writer and reader who can only project and approximate one another's presence, and it is the trajectory of generations, of the many-branched temporal path between the dead and the living. As the *daimōn* of the *Symposium* bore messages by means of incantation and prophecy through the space between gods and men, the voice as sound is resolved in the meeting between persons that moves or touches those who are in its presence —those touched, Diotima explains, "whether awake or asleep."[18] Plato is making a broad claim that poetic making is in fact the *performance* of something scripted in another context. Paradoxically, these examples of play as possession are *willed* by the players. The possibility of willed disassociation thereby reintroduces the issue of sincerity in regard to the paradigm of possession. The point for Plato is that one cannot intend to be possessed; one is helpless before the power of the magnet and one's helplessness is contagious. Yet this very complaint reintroduces poetic images into the thought of Plato himself and makes his thought all the more readily taken up by others.[19] Such paradoxes of willed possession run from Plato to Romantic inspiration to the trope of sleep in Surrealism and the trope of chance in Modernism.

In contrast, Monroe Beardsley and W. K. Wimsatt's classic examination of intention in "The Intentional Fallacy"[20] links the notion of a mastering and original poetic will to Romantic genius theory. "It is not so much a historical statement as a definition to say that the intentional fallacy is a romantic one," they write, citing Longinus as their first example of a Romantic before the period and continuing on to the affinities between Johann Wolfgang von Goethe and the aesthetics of Benedetto Croce.[21] Yet the argument of "The Intentional Fallacy" reintroduced the Platonic critique by claiming that following such a will would lead one astray from doing the serious public work of reception. By asserting that poets could not know or anticipate the effects of their work and by idealizing the rationality of the public in receiving poetic compositions, Wimsatt and Beardsley continued the project of the *Republic*.

When we remember that both the positive arguments about creativity in the *Symposium* and the negative arguments about inspiration in the *Republic* and other texts involve accounts of *poiēsis* that imply processes that are passive and active at once, we can, however, begin to consider a more complex model of poetic subjectivity and agency. For poets, like all humans, are creatures who both strive toward mastery and seek the release or end of stimulation. The creative, beauty-pursuing artists of the *Symposium* will hear the messages of the gods whether they are awake or asleep, and they will seek out the absolute whether it is attainable or not. The poets described in "Phaedrus," "Ion," "Theaetetus," and the *Republic* will seek an inspiration that can only descend unbidden—there is no *technē* to help the poet's desire for habitation by the muse, and any poet who proceeds by rules alone, we have learned, is doomed to failure, the failure of the merely sane.

Therefore, the relations between seeing and hearing, or image and metrical structure, and the reciprocating relations of presence and absence between speaker and listener might be explored more usefully in terms of concepts of language and poetic convention as they are historically constructed: in relation to a conflicted—rather than unified—subjectivity and in relation to a differentially organized community of reception. Here another theoretical discussion of possession is relevant: Nicolas Abraham's study of transgenerational haunting and the permeability of voice and person outlined in his psychoanalytic study "L'Ecorce et le noyeau." Abraham's work focuses on patients who engage in compulsive and repetitive actions that seem to have no obvious referent yet turn out to be the continuation of conflicts dating to previous generations. For example, one of Abraham's patients, an amateur geologist, spends his weekends breaking rocks. In doing so, Abraham writes, "he is acting out the fate of his mother's beloved. The loved one had been denounced by the grandmother (an unspeakable and secret fact) and having been sent to 'break rocks' (*casser les cailloux* = do forced labor), he died in the gas chamber . . . a lover of geology, he [the patient] 'breaks rocks,' then catches butterflies which he proceeds to kill in a can of cyanide." Abraham sees the patient as inhabited by a *foreign body*. The "staging of a word" by the patient constitutes "an attempt at exorcism, that is, an attempt to relieve the unconscious by placing the effects of the phantom in the social realm."[22] Abraham uses the image of ventriloquism to describe the phantom's effect: "The phantom is a formation of the unconscious that has never been conscious—for good reason. It passes—in a way yet to be determined—from the parent's unconscious into the child's. . . . The phantom's periodic and compulsive return lies beyond the scope of symptom-formation in the sense of a return of the repressed; it works like a ventriloquist, like a stranger within the subject's own mental topography."[23]

Abraham is concerned with those cases in which a powerful trauma has initiated the repetition of gestures through generations. Such a singular cause provides a useful explanation within the therapy of individual patients. Although poems are more often the outcome of many forces, rather than such a singular event, this notion of a haunting under terms that have outlived their referents is an account of poetic possession of tremendous power and usefulness. It introduces into the concept of poetic action a temporal dimension that significantly complicates issues of semantics. And it is exactly the phenomenon of which Plato warns us—that a subject possessed by an unfathomable and external agency will place words into the social realm where they will continue their profoundly "irresponsible" effects or consequences. Yet what is this irresponsibility other than the inevitability of mediation in the construction of meaning—those very forms of mediated reception Wimsatt and Beardsley describe as superseding the intentions of the maker? Even given the vast disparities between the cultural and historical contexts of the classical and psychoanalytic arguments, we can find here an account of the way poetry involves being spoken through as well as speaking. And the music and meter of poetry can be seen as not simply the application of the rules of art—which Plato, of course, so strenuously recommends as a kind of cure here. Rather, music and meter have an overdetermined semantic reference, a *meaning*, that they bear forward in time regardless of whether at any given moment the poet or reader can explain or refer to such a meaning. Indeed, recent work on aphasia suggests a separation between propositional speech—the deliberate production of context-bound and comprehensible utterances—and nondeliberate, or "automatic," utterances. In patients with global aphasia, propositional speech is lost, but the ability to hum previously learned melodies and sing their lyrics, as well as the ability to count or recite the days of the week, is maintained.[24] I am not claiming, as Plato did, that all poetic utterance comes from elsewhere in this sense, but rather that *poiēsis* involves a dynamic between propositional will on the one hand and somatic meaning on the other.[25]

Abraham has worked more directly on the relations between poetry and the body in other works, particularly in his 1985 book *Rythmes*,[26] and in his "Notes on the Phantom," he mentions poetry once. He says that the gestures of the phantom, "by their gratuitousness in relation to the subject, create the impression of surrealistic flights of fancy or of *oulipo*-like verbal feats,"[27] referring to the workshops in experimental writing run by Raymond Queneau and others from the 1960s into the present. Yet if we return to the paradox of willed possession, it is clear that this type of intentional scrambling of meaning is exactly *not* like the effects of the phantom. To set out to alter or displace reference in a poem is to attempt, by mastering contingency itself, to master completely the situation of writing. What is more relevant to the situation of the phantom are the ways in which return to certain types of music and rhythmic form in one's writing signal the possibility of a recovered somatic meaning. In other words, we might read the symptoms of meter just as the painter, or other maker of visual images, can attend to the obsessional image or the rebus structure of certain scenes. In the accumulation or accrual of returns to certain meters, the poet can come to learn *in time* and in an ongoing practice the deeper structures of his or her own thought and emotion in relation to the world. Hence, the picture of mastery in a ready experimentalism is self-deluding. But one can also argue intention the other way—that one cannot set out to know the reference of one's forms.

The poet needs a continuing reader—both the social and historical context in which the poem is on a continuum with other poems, making it intelligible, and the poet himself or herself as changing reader of his or her own practice over time. As knowledge of reference necessarily withers, the poem does not lose fullness or complexity but rather acquires a residue of accrued meanings that expand the possibilities for poetry's significance. The particularity of a poem, its occasional quality, falls away as its form comes forward.

Although we could find this process of residual meanings at work in any poem's meter, it seems that particular poems acquire particular force in this regard. Nevertheless, we should not discount the idea that the force of some lines or works depends on what we might think of as almost purely formal features tied to physiology or the structure of the language itself rather than to the particulars of generation or an individual poet's psychology. For example, we might wonder why a line such as the opening of Thomas Gray's elegy, "The curfew tolls the knell of parting day," is both memorable and enduringly familiar. We might note its perfect iambic pentameter that washes against the trochaic pull of the words of compound syllables *(curfew* and *parting)* and the elision of "tolls the" and "knell of." It is a line that sounds like what it is about, and it uses the range of vowel sounds in English, making a pattern in a single line of gathering and receding echoes *e/u/e/o/e/e/o/a/i/a*—an effect that contributes to the growing sense of ringing loudness we have as it progresses.

In other cases, an individual word, gradually accumulating a veneer of the archaic, comes to signify allusion to the history of poetry as much as to any available reference. I have in mind the recurrence of *guerdon* in Geoffrey Chaucer's translations of Boethius and the *Romaunt of the Rose,* in Tennyson's "The Princess" and "Enid," in William Carlos Williams's "Asphodel," and in Ashbery's "Finnish Rhapsody."[28] Or we become aware of rhyme and rhythm signifying the surrender of the will to compulsory form in poems such as Sylvia Plath's "Lady Lazarus" with its exact rhymes, slant rhymes, and repeated terms, evident, for example, in the following stanzas from the middle of the poem:

Dying
Is an art, like everything else.
I do it exceptionally well.

I do it so it feels like hell.
I do it so it feels real.
I guess you could say I've a call.

It's easy enough to do it in a cell.
It's easy enough to do it and stay put.
It's the theatrical

Comeback in broad day
To the same place, the same face, the same brute
Amused shout:

"A miracle!"
That knocks me out.
There is a charge

For the eyeing of my scars, there is a charge
For the hearing of my heart—
It really goes.

In these central lines, the too-slant and too-exact rhymes *well, hell, real, call, cell,* and *theatrical* all lead to *miracle*—mirror/call, the problem of the repetitive call, the calling and calling that was needed to bring Plath back from an earlier second suicide attempt; the call to death mirrors the call to life. The poem's final emphasis on images of resurrection hardly solves this problem of repetition.

Gwendolyn Brooks's "Anniad," a poem to which we will return at length later, follows a strict tetrameter and equally relentless use of exact rhymes in an infinitely varying pattern over its forty-three seven-line stanzas. In lines such as these from the opening stanzas, Brooks uses exact end rhymes and internal consonant pairs *(folly, tatters, berries, littering, little)* to create a Spenserian effect, a kind of confettied milieu, for the appearance of her heroine, who is associated with "sweet and chocolate" and at the same time "left to folly or to fate." "Fancying on the featherbed / what was never and is not," Annie dreams:

What is ever and is not.
Pretty tatters blue and red,
Buxom berries beyond rot,
Western clouds and quarter-stars,
Fairy-sweet of old guitars
Littering the little head
Light upon the featherbed.

Both Plath and Brooks employ redundant word choice and exact rhyming as a means of representing the transport or compulsive way-laying of subjective intention. To this extent, they demonstrate that we cannot necessary conclude that strict form signifies authorial mastery or control; it as readily can signify the submersion of will within convention.

When we listen to a meter with a specific function and history, we find that the choice of meter is not simply a matter of dipping into a repertoire of simultaneously available, and determined-by-occasion, metrical varieties. Meter has its own internal history, its own evolution, and along that temporal path it accrues a weight of allusion.[29] The history of meter is tied to the specific development of national languages and at the same time to what might be called the creolization of forms as languages merge and are distinguished in political and historical contexts.[30] The consequences of translation, and error in translation, are relevant in this regard. Jean-Michel Rabaté writes of Mallarmé's translations of Edgar Allan Poe's poems: "[Mallarmé's translations into prose] can seem absurd in the case of purely musical poems, such as 'The Bells,' which plays an alliterative music based on echoes, internal rhymes, and tintinnabulation effects of pure sound. Mallarmé realizes that this poem is untranslatable but nonetheless strives to render it in French—that is, in the language that can absorb it (and not on the page) as a signifying dissemination. . . . Error becomes productive and positive since it assaults the language and fashions a new sort of French, halfway between a misunderstood original and an excessively faithful paraphrase."[31] Implicit in such a translation from sound effects into a discursive semantic is the idea that the absence of reason will continue to haunt the sentences of the prose text and pull against the sense of its meaning in "French."

Consider as well the forms we know as short meter (trimeter quatrain with one tetrameter line), common meter (alternating trimeter, tetrameter quatrains), and long meter (tetrameter quatrains). Ballad, hymn, and other song forms using this structure are meters with a particularly rich legacy of accrued meanings. To use these forms means that one carries over into writing an enormous weight of social and cultural resonance. The phrase *common meter* joins with the terms from music, *common measure* and *common time*, to signify the two beats to a measure, 4/4 rhythm, under which the entire musical system is coordinated and out of which variations proceed. Common meter presents itself as the most suitable form for group singing—the coordination of song and the coordination of social life under a common temporal framework emphasizes integration and solidarity.

Beneath these meters lies the four-beat line of early English accentual verse. At the same time, the reliance on iambic places them between the spoken "naturalness" of iambic pentameter as it developed in English and the rhythmic thumping of the Germanic forms—either dipodic or four-beat.[32] If, as the *Princeton Encyclopedia of Poetry and Poetics* claims, iambic pentameter has "been fashionable in English primarily during periods marked by an interest in classical rhetoric and by a commitment to the maintenance of a sense of order and limitation, for of all English metrical systems, it is the one most hostile by nature to impulse, irregularity, and unrestrained grandiosity,"[33] the pentameter only developed out of a long process of the loss and recovery of Chaucer's iambics, the increasing consciousness of the parallels and tensions it evoked in relation to English spoken syntax, and the residual echo of the pure stress and syllabic conventions between which it was negotiated.[34]

When Emily Dickinson uses hymn meters, she radically disrupts the possibility of social integration by her breaks and interruptions within the lines and the slanting of rhyme—like a person breaking off the smooth flow of received language or emphatically singing off-key in a crowded church. Moreover, her use of hymn meters makes us hear the individuality of her voice and the specificity of her words because of their dissonance from the habits of tradition.

Here is one of the most famous of her poems on "religious" subjects, a poem that can be seen readily as a critique of religion, the 1859 version of #216:

Safe in their Alabaster Chambers—
Untouched by Morning
And untouched by Noon—
Sleep the meek members of the Resurrection—
Rafter of satin,
And Roof of stone.

Light laughs the breeze
In her Castle above them—
Babbles the Bee in a stolid Ear,
Pipe the Sweet Birds in ignorant cadence—
Ah, what sagacity perished here![35]

The pure stress tetrameter lines in this poem—"Safe in their Alabaster Chambers / Sleep the meek members of the Resurrection / Babbles the Bee in a stolid Ear / Pipe the Sweet Birds in ignorant cadence— / Ah, what sagacity perished here"—present a clear narrative order: the meek dead lying in their tombs, despite the babbles of the bee and the piping of the birds, will not awaken. Their "sagacity" has perished, but the sagacity of the dead is more than a little ironized. No one would read this poem and choose the sagacity of the dead over the ignorant cadence of the sweet birds. Nor would we ever be willing to give up the breeze's castle for the safety of the satin rafters and stone roofs of an alabaster chamber. The dimeter lines—"Untouched by Morning / And untouched by Noon— / Rafter of satin, / And Roof of stone. / Light laughs the breeze / In her Castle above them"—give qualifying information, functioning like asides to the audience. The poem could readily be put back into hymn meter by joining the dimeter lines and thus producing two quatrains, but the point is that Dickinson pulls out these lines and thereby individuates her voice. By doubling the consciousness of the narrative in this way, she establishes the basis for our ability to read a double meaning into "what sagacity perished here!" at the close. This is hymn meter transformed by sotto voce effects of dissonance.

Ballad form can also present complex possibilities for deepening the texture of common meter. The traditional Anglo-Scots ballad builds a narrative structure on a repeating pattern of quatrains. Thus, narrative movement, the propulsion forward, is conducted against a current of alternating repetitions in beat and rhyme. And this narrative movement, unlike that in other narrative forms, is presented in a relatively unusual way. A solo singer performs as if spoken through—he or she voices, with no signal in the voice itself, shifting points of view through dialogue or other conversational means. If we return to the model of ventriloquism, the ballad singer performs all the parts of a play as if inhabited by the characters, yet within a presentation of physical person that remains constant throughout. Of all the singers of Western lyric, the ballad singer is the one most radically haunted by others—for he or she presents the gestures, the symptoms, of a range of social actors, and he or she presents those gestures as surviving symptoms of a previous action.[36]

If you can imagine what it would be like to sing a ballad such as the well-known Child Ballad "Edward,"[37] keeping your body contained and your voice constant, you will see how powerfully the starkness of ballad form emerges. Here is the first stanza as it is written in Child (No. 13B):

"Why dois your brand sae drap wi bluid,
    Edward, Edward,
Why dois your brand sae drap wi bluid,
    And why sae sad gang yee O?"
"O I hae killed my hauke sae guid,
    Mither, mither,
O I hae killed my hawk sae guid,
    And I had nae mair bot hee, O . . . ."[38]

In "Edward," it is clear that the repeating lines of dialogue with their tags of apostrophe ("Edward, Edward"; "Mither, mither") produce an effect in time that is not adequately represented by print. Ballad criticism refers to this effect as "leaping and lingering." Even though this term is usually applied to the narrative movement of the ballad, it is also a way around the problem of the impossibility of a definitive quantitative verse in English— that is, a way to get something like a musical, rather than a spoken, sense of duration into the sound. In "Edward" the lingering happens through repeated questions, repeated answers, the redundancy in the mother's speech, and the apostrophes that destabilize the meter. The "leaping" happens at the close of sections where Edward's answers acquire their definitive and elaborated meaning. The asymmetry between Edward's speech and his mother's speech exaggerates the discontinuous relation between their utterances. And the pattern of closure on the level of the stanza prepares us for an overall effect of incremental repetition across stanzas—an effect culminating in the powerful information delivered in Edward's last words in stanza 7:

> "And what wul ye leive to your ain mither deir,
>> Edward, Edward?
> And what wul ye leive to your ain mither deir,
>> My deir son, now tell me, O?"
> "The curse of hell frae me sall ye beir,
>> Mither, mither,
> The curse of hell frae me sall ye beir,
>> Sic counseils ye gave to me, O."

Stanzas 5, 6, and 7 make up the ballad testament, the pronouncement of judgment that is often found at ballad closure. Before Edward delivers the final pronouncement of the testament, giving "the curse of hell" to his mother, he tells her, in answers to her questions about his property, that he will let his "towers and ha'" "stand tul they down fa'" and that he will leave to his "bairns and . . . wife" "the warlde's room" where they will go begging. In the ballad's testament, goods are dispersed, the boundary between life and death is breached, and the audience is guided toward a moral or judgment.

In "Edward" the ventriloquism works through shifts in voice staged in tension with a movement toward dramatic resolution. In other ballads, such as "The Three Ravens," the voice is haunted by means of a shadow effect of etymology. "Edward" is probably a later ballad than "The Three

Ravens" (Child No. 26A) or its variant, "Twa Corbies" (Child No. 26B), the latter beginning, "As I was walking all alane, I heard twa corbies making a mane." "The Three Ravens" tells a story of the fidelity of "hawks, hounds and leman" to a stricken knight; "The Twa Corbies" tells of a knight abandoned by his hawk, his hound, and his "lady fair."[39] Dialogue, narrative movement across repetition, testament, and judgment are all present here as they are in "Edward." The narrative frame in "The Three Ravens"—"There were three ravens sat on a tree"—is necessary so that the speakers can be designated as animals. Once that is established in stanza 2, the three ravens can take turns speaking. Their threefold position as predators is inversely mirrored in the threefold helpers—the hounds, hawks, and fallow deer "as great with young as she might go," transposed in the end to hounds, hawks, and leman. This transposition comes to reside in the extraordinarily complex etymology of the Old English *fallow*—the color of the deer is the color of unplowed earth. Yet the barrenness of this earth, left unplanted so that weeds might grow and die on it as "bastard fallow," is key to the fertility of the crops that will later be planted there. At the same time, a *fallow*, from the late sixteenth century forward, is "a substitute or supplement" in mechanics and, in physiology, a spurious conception—one in which "a shapeless mass is produced instead of a foetus" (*Oxford English Dictionary*). As profound as any change between the animal and human world in Ovid, or as any Freudian slip, the transposition from pregnant deer to leman links the ballad to the antique world of the moral fable and to the symbolism of feudal allegory.

I have chosen these examples to indicate the extraordinary richness of issues of "readability" underlying our use of traditional forms. Although one could construct a genealogy of these issues around other forms, such as the tension I have indicated between the Germanic four-stressed line and iambic pentameter, I want to emphasize here the tensions between spoken and sung discourse, and so propositional and what might be called somatic utterance, in poems by Keats, Hardy, and Elizabeth Bishop. Although it is not coincidental that these are three poets with especially complex relations to issues of genealogy and tradition as *themes* in their works, I am interested primarily in the ways in which our readings of certain of their poems recapitulate the ambivalence between will and possession that seems to mark the process of each poem's creation.

II. THREE CASES OF LYRIC POSSESSION

KEATS

In a letter of 22 November 1817 to Benjamin Bailey, Keats wrote, "[H]ave you never by being surprised with an old melody—in a delicious place— by a delicious voice, felt over again your very speculations and surmises at the time it first operated on your soul—do you not remember forming to yourself the singer's face more beautiful than it was possible and yet with the elevation of the moment you did not think so—even then you were mounted on the wings of imagination so high. . . . What a time! I am continually running away from the subject."[40] This passage forms part of one of Keats's early statements on poetics and goes on to emphasize sensation and somatic memory as key to imaginative work. At this point in his progress as a poet, Keats contrasts such a state of mind with complex thought and consecutive reasoning. His description of his own imaginative process is consonant with contemporary accounts of his chanting mode of recitation.[41] Keats's emphasis on the disassociation of poetic feeling and conscious thought is best exemplified by the "gothic" poems predating the great odes. Keeping the structure of the traditional ballad in mind, we might turn to the earliest manuscript of "La Belle Dame sans Merci." This is the version of Keats's poem recorded in a journal letter of 1819 to his brother George and his wife Georgiana, who had emigrated to America at the time of Keats's writing:

La belle dame sans merci—

O what can ail thee Knight at arms
    Alone and palely loitering?
The sedge has withered from the Lake
    And no birds sing!

O what can ail thee Knight at arms
    So haggard, and so woe begone?
The Squirrel's granary is full
    And the harvest's done.

I see ~~death's~~ a lilly on thy brow
    With anguish moist and fever dew,
And on thy cheeks death's a fading rose
    [FAST]Withereth too—

I met a Lady in the ~~Wilds~~ Meads
  Full beautiful, a faery's child
Her hair was long, her foot was light
  And her eyes were wild—

I made a Garland for her head,
  And bracelets too, and fragrant Zone
She look'd at me as she did love
  And made sweet moan—

I set her on my pacing steed
  And nothing else saw all day long
For sidelong would she bend and sing
  A faery's song—

She found me roots of relish sweet
  And honey wild and honey manna dew
And sure in language strange she said
  I love thee true—

She took me to her elfin grot
  And there she wept { and sigh'd full sore,
                      { ~~and there she sighed~~
And there I shut her wild wild eyes
  With Kisses four—

And there she lulled me asleep
  And there I dream'd Ah Woe betide!
The latest dream I ever dreamt
  On the cold hill side.

I saw pale Kings and Princes too
  Pale warriors death pale were they all
Who cried La belle dame sans merci
  Thee hath in thrall.

I saw their starv'd lips in the gloam
  ~~All tremble~~
  With horrid warning { gaped wide
                      { ~~wide agape~~

And I awoke, and found me here
   On the cold hill's side
And this is why I ~~wither~~ sojourn here
   Alone and palely loitering;
Though the sedge is withered from the Lake
   And no birds sing—. . . . .[42]

The commonly acknowledged sources for "La Belle Dame" are what was once thought to be Chaucer's pentameter translation and adaptation of Alain Chartier's dialogue "La Belle Dame sans Mercy"; the Paolo and Francesca episode from the fifth canto of Dante's *Inferno*; the Cymochles and Phaedria episode and the Rock of Vile Reproach in Book II and the adventure of Britomartis in the Castle of Busirane in Book III of *The Faerie Queene*; a passage in Shakespeare's *Pericles*; and Keats's rereading of his own poems *Endymion* and *The Eve of St. Agnes*, where the song Porphyro sings to Madeline in stanza 33 is "La belle dame sans mercy." There is a great deal of argument regarding which of the many sources might be dominant—some references are particular, such as the "pacing steed" that is linked to Chartier's language, and others are structural, as in the outlines of *Endymion*.[43]

Sometimes mentioned, but without specific evidence of Keats's coming into contact with the source, is the link between "La Belle Dame" and the ballad and legend of Thomas Rymer or True Thomas, a ballad whose narrative maps closely on that of "La Belle Dame" and which Keats could have known through reading Robert Jamieson's *Popular Ballads and Songs* or Sir Walter Scott's *Minstrelsy of the Scottish Border*.[44] Thomas is a thirteenth-century Faust figure who is taken away by the Queen of Elfland and forced to serve her in her kingdom for seven years. Thomas is a "rymer" because he has written a romance in which he tells of his visit to Elfland and of his gift of prophecy from the queen.[45]

The Scott and Jamieson volumes contained, in addition to versions of the traditional ballad, copies of manuscript editions of this metrical romance written in long-meter quatrains rhyming a/b/a/b. The thematic connections of the ballad and romance to Keats's poem are obvious, but the structure of the Thomas ballads is characterized by an immediate plunge into the scene of meeting between Thomas and the Queen of Elfland and "he said/she said" bracketing of the dialogue. The power of Keats's poem comes not only from the thematic borrowings he has made and from his use of ballad clichés such as the rose and the lily, the light foot, pacing steed, and fairy song but also from the ways he has taken up the most dominant formal features of the traditional ballad and used or adapted them.

To speak or sing Keats's "La Belle Dame" would be to engage in the experience of disassociated ventriloquism characteristic of ballads such as
"Edward"—to plunge one's self immediately into the urgent context of
speech. "La Belle Dame" is not a ballad with a frame narrative. Rather, the
interlocutor begins with his question, "Oh what can ail thee, knight-at-
arms," and the switch to the knight's voice, which will narrate his cap-
tivity and awakening, begins without marking or frame in stanza four. Although the rest of the ballad, stanzas 4 through 12, is in the knight's voice,
the knight's long "answer" does address the interlocutor's question—
"what can ail thee?" The question requests a diagnosis; the answer provides a narrative of experience, and it is only in the dream's reported
speech, the pale kings' announcement, that the knight himself has come
to consciousness of his condition. It would be, therefore, misleading to
claim that the ballad is in "dialogue" form.[46] Rather, there is a systematic
displacement of voice from the interlocutor to the knight to the fairy
queen to the kings until at the end the knight takes up the very language
of the interlocutor: "And this is why I sojourn here / Alone and palely loitering; / Though the sedge is withered from the Lake / And no birds sing"
—he is *repeating* the interlocutor's language as a sleepwalker would; the
language speaks through him. Although it often has been noted that the
knight's figure seems dissipated, drained of its energy by the intensity of
the sexual encounter, it should also be obvious that *in his speech*, the
knight appears at the end *without will*. Keats emphasizes this in the manuscript by adding ellipses to the final stanza.

A disassociation and merger of voices and persons is evident in the
relation between the two names of the ballad—"True Thomas" and
"Thomas Rymer"—and the relation between the two brothers Thomas
and John Keats that provides the historical context for the poem's composition in the journal letter to George and Georgiana Keats.[47] This long
letter was begun on Valentine's Day of 1819 and completed on 3 May of
that year. On 15 April, Keats had found a set of letters that were part of a
hoax perpetrated on his brother Tom by their mutual friend George Wells
during Tom's fatal illness.[48] Wells had forged letters to Tom from a fictional French girl named Amena, and John Keats was convinced that his
brother's suffering had been worsened by the effect of the letters. In the
journal letter, he mentions his discovery of the letters to George and Georgiana and moves on to other topics, including a fantasy in "extempore"
couplets: "When they were come unto the Faery's Court."[49] Three characters are presented in this fantasy—an Ape, a Dwarf, and a Fool, all in the
service of a "fretful" princess. When the princess turns on the three with
a switch, the Dwarf distracts her with rhymes. In this fanciful allegory,
George is the Ape, John is the Dwarf, and Tom is the sleeping Fool.[50]

Although the letter goes on in a lighter vein, with a parody of Spenser making fun of Keats's friend Charles Brown and gossip about Keats's circle, the mistaken obsession of Tom with the "false Amena" continues to be on Keats's mind. He writes on 16 April, "I have been looking over the correspondence of the pretended Amena and Wells this evening—I now see the whole cruel deception. I think Wells must have had an accomplice in it—Amena's letters are in a Man's language, and in a Man's hand imitating a woman's. . . . It was no thoughtless hoax—but a cruel deception on a sanguine Temperament, with every show of friendship." Keats continues his judgment with language of unremitting violence, language quite untypical of his tone in his correspondence: "I do not think death too bad for the villain. . . . I consider it my duty to be prudently revengeful. I will hang over his head like a sword by a hair. . . . I will harm him all I possibly can—-I have no doubt I shall be able to do so."[51] A true Thomas who is also a Thomas Rymer collapses the identities of the two brothers and presents a scenario in which they are simultaneously elected and made to suffer by an unearthly lover. The third position Keats is able to attain is that of the interlocutor—the ballad figure who questions the knight and is able to cross the threshold into knowledge of death. He is bound to silence, and the reward is prophecy. Furthermore, by miming the violent distantiation of Wells's hoax, Keats is able to master it.

Keats's "La Belle Dame" displays many parallels to the metrical romance of *Thomas Rymer* as recorded by Jamieson and Scott.[52] In both versions of the romance, the beginning of Thomas's journey is distinguished by the singing of birds. This is the beginning of the Jamieson text:

> As I me went this Andyrs day,
>> Ffast on my way makyng my mone,
> In a mery mornyng of May,
>> Be Huntley Bankis my self alone;
>
> I herde the jay and the throstell,
>> The mavis menyd in hir song,
> The wodewale farde as a bell,
>> That the wode aboute me rong.[53]

And this is the Scott version:

> In a lande as I was lent,
> In the gryking of the day,
> Ay alone as I went,

In Huntle bankys me for to play;
I saw the throstyl, and the jay,
Ye mawes movyde of her song,
Ye wodwale sange notes gay.[54]

Although the connection of "and no birds sing" to William Browne's refrain, "Let no birds sing," has often been noted,[55] Keats also has taken the singing birds of the start of the romance and made their silence the dominant feature of the nature portrayed in "La Belle Dame." In a similar inversion, the sexual encounter of the romance leaves the fairy queen wasted. In the Jamieson text, the fairy queen warns Thomas that if he has her, "fore alle my bewte thu wille spille." After he "lies with her," the following consequences ensue:

And all hir clothis were away
    That he before saw in that stede;
Hir een semyd out that were so gray,
    And alle hyr body like the lede.

Thomas seid, "alas! alas!
    In feith this is a doleful sight,
That thu art so fadut in the face,
    That be fore schone as sunne bright!"[56]

In the Scott version, Thomas complains, "Allas / Me thynke this is a dull-full syght / That thou art fadyd in the face."[57] This transformation turns in the ballad, romance, and "La Belle Dame sans Merci" on the ambiguity of the word *moan/mone*, which can mean both a complaint or expression of grief and sexual intercourse. Keats's belle dame makes sweet moan as she loves, sings a fairy's song, says "I love thee true" in "language strange," weeps, sighs, and lulls the knight to sleep. In the romance it is the knight who is "making mone" at his being alone. The reversibility between male and female positions echoes the inversion of the "language strange" of Amena, who seems a woman but is "really" a man and who seems a person but is really a fiction. And it replays the reversibility of writer and subject—the grieving John Keats as Thomas Rymer and the fading Tom Keats as knight.

One of the most intriguing aspects of the problem of the relation between Keats's poem and the traditional ballad of "Thomas Rymer" (or "Rhymer") as one of its historical sources is that both the poem and ballad thematize the problem of archaic, or dead, forms of expression. Here is the opening to Mrs. Brown of Falkland's (born 1747) version:

> True Thomas lay oer yond grassy bank
> And he beheld a ladie gay,
> A ladie that was brisk and bold,
> Come riding oer the fernie brae
>
> Her skirt was of the grass-green silk;
> Her mantle of the velvet fine,
> At ilka tett of her horse's mane
> Hung fifty silver bells and nine.
>
> True Thomas he took off his hat
> And bowed him low down till his knee:
> "All hail, thou mighty Queen of Heaven!
> For your peer on earth I never did see."
>
> "O no, o no, True Thomas," she says,
> "that name does not belong to me;
> I am but the queen of fair Elfland,
> And I'm come here for to visit thee."

In this initial encounter between Thomas and the queen, we find a constant splitting of perspectives. Thomas is lying on the bank, and the queen comes riding on her horse. As we are given descriptions of her skirt, her mantle, and the bells on her horse's mane, our eyes follow those of Thomas as he rises to meet her. But his greeting is mistaken: this is not the Virgin Mary, the Queen of Heaven. This is an emissary from an archaic and pagan world, a dead world that is animated here and will make the world Thomas knows fall away. The term *knight-at-arms* introduces a similar problem of identification, for it is a catachretic expression of "man-at-arms"—by making Tom a "knight," the poet places him in the same fictional realm as the Amena and fairy queen figures. The *Indicator* version of the poem, published in 1820, may seem at first glance more antiquated in its use of a term like "wight." This term, meaning "a corpse," is also brutally realistic.[58] But even in the revisions of the letter version of the manuscript, copied earlier, we see that in the encounter between the interlocutor and the knight, Keats has twice crossed out "death's" as an attribute of the Knight's countenance, and the withering of the sedge at the close of the poem has been transposed from the draft that had the knight saying "I wither here" rather than "I sojourn here." Speaking to fairies, according to British folklore, can be deadly. As Falstaff says in *The Merry Wives of Windsor*, act 5, scene 5, "They are fairies; he that speaks to them shall die." Latin could be used when it was necessary to speak to a fairy, and perhaps Thomas's greeting is therefore not so much an error as a precaution that matches a dead Christian language to an encounter with the pagan world.[59]

Keats has used the trimeter line to break the common meter, making these lines also bear the weight of deepening meaning just as do Edward's reply lines. The trimeter lines introduce the theme of silence: the silence of the birds and the silence of the missing beat. This break in the meter is often noticed and has been juxtaposed to the poem's continuing iambic structure. But in fact we could also see these fourth lines as doing what the first stanza signals; that is, they can be heard as making a break with song into raw speech. In this reading, one can hear the tetrameter continuing, but here as spondees. This effect seems most pronounced when it is underlain by the awkward inversion of the possessive pronoun and verb in the kings' pronouncement: "Who cried La belle dame sans merci / Thee hath in thrall." The tension between singing and speech suffuses the ballad, just as it underlies the two qualities of Thomas as "rymer" and as prophet, as shown in his traditional nickname, "Tammy-tell-the-truth."

In addition, the ballad form refigures the context of the meeting of the knight and the interlocutor as an account of causality. The knight is giving testimony, and, as in the case of Edward's mother, the interlocutor comes to a realization of his or her own peril in this dead world to which the knight has awakened. A great deal of our reading of "La Belle Dame" rests in the meaning of the word *latest* in "latest" dream—the term refers to both the most recent event in the situation—the dream of the pale kings' warning—and to the idea of last things implied by that situation. The warning finally gives a *name* to the phenomenon that has occurred to the knight. Keats's pale kings are linked to the prophecies ascribed to Thomas in the latter parts of the romance—prophecies that predict the death of Alexander III, the Battle of Bannockburn, the accession of James VI to English rule, and other struggles between Scotland and England.[60] The problematic name of the fairy queen also links the poem to the tradition of deathbed conversation that runs throughout Anglo-Scots balladry, conversations in which true names and true identities are at last revealed. In all of these ways, the choice of ballad form enables Keats to reenact the betrayal of his brother by an unreal lover, to provide testimony, and to provide himself with a testament.

HARDY

My second example of a poem haunted by the structure of a preexisting work is "The Voice," from Hardy's 1912–1913 sequence published as part of his collection *Satires of Circumstance*.[61] The 1912–1913 series consists of poems that also take up the theme of a conversation at a graveside. The first four poems of this series—"The Going," "Your Last Drive," "The Walk," and "Rain on a Grave"—deal with the sudden and unexpected death of Emma, Hardy's first wife, in November 1912. The next three—"I Found Her Out There," "Without Ceremony," and "Lament"—return to the period thirty years before, the early 1870s, when Hardy met Emma Gifford in the west near Cornwall and reprise the history of their courtship. "The Haunter" and "The Voice" then introduce the separation that had occurred in the Hardys' marriage in more recent years and the separation that has been brought about by Emma's death.

The next group of poems describes earlier years of the marriage. "His Visitor" and "A Circular" provide details of the Hardys' house and their domestic life. "The Phantom Horsewoman" is written in the third person and pictures the bereft Hardy looking out toward the sand and sea of Cornwall for Emma as "a ghost girl-rider."[62] "The Spell of the Rose," imagined as uttered in Emma's voice, projects Hardy's regret when he will see, after Emma's death, the rose bush she planted as an expression of her hope of symbolically mending their marriage. Others—"A Dream or No," "After a Journey," "A Death-Day Recalled," "Beeny Cliff," "At Castle Boterel," "Places," "St. Launce's Revisited," and "Where the Picnic Was"—narrate various locations connected to the Hardys' life together—scenes that Hardy would go on actually to revisit after his completion of the series. To an extent, the series instantiates Hardy's own voyage as a haunter of haunted places. One way of reading the shifting dialogue between deceased and mourner here is to see that Hardy has dispersed the ballad conversation across poems, so that the individual pieces are linked in a pattern of call and response—a pattern that in fact materially severs the relation between call and response just as the lack of reply and introduction of repetition in "La Belle Dame" emphasize the discontinuous relation between interlocutor and knight. Hardy's poems address each other repeatedly from incommensurable places and times.

One of the most striking aspects of this series is its variation in form. Each of the poems in the series has a different stanza form. Eighteen of the forms appear for the first time in the sequence, and Hardy never used fourteen of these again. Yet Hardy was a poet who returned to certain permutations of forms. As in his taste in music, he preferred the most traditional forms, especially relying on common meter with alternating abcb rhyming in his work. As we saw in the example of "During Wind and Rain" in the previous chapter, he often was influenced by the prosody of folk song and hymns: in addition to common meter, the forms he most frequently used were long meter and ballad meter. Hardy's family had been involved in vernacular music traditions—both sacred choral song and secular dance and game music—for generations.[63] His grandfather, father, and uncle were all string players; as part of the Stinsford church band they, like the Mellstock quire described in several of the poems ("The Rash Bride," "Seen by the Waits," and "The Paphian Bull") and *Under the Greenwood Tree*, played the "waits" traditional to Christmas. Hardy's 1897 poem on the Mellstock quire, "The Dead Quire," is of particular biographical interest for it takes up the theme of generations in relation to music. The poem tells of a Christmas Eve when the current young people of Mellstock are carousing in a tavern, singing "songs on subjects not divine." At the stroke of midnight they hear singing outside, "The ancient quire of voice and string / Seemed singing words of prayer and praise / As they had used to sing." Hardy describes the dead quire's singing as being itself replete with the voices of the dead:

> The sons defined their fathers' tones,
> The widow his whom she had wed,
> And others in the minor moan
> The viols of the dead.[64]

The roisterers silently file after the sound of the voices until they reach the headstones of the quire members in the cemetery. In this poem contrasting ghostly singing and silence, it is worth noting that Hardy uses the stanza structure of Keats's "La Belle Dame"—long meter with a trimeter line concluding each quatrain.

In later life, Hardy arranged for a local pianist to accompany his own playing of fiddle tunes he had known by heart since childhood. He kept books of dance tunes and their steps and wrote in his copy of Hullah's *The Song Book* the names of people he associated with various songs. Twenty-five of his poems simply say "song" beneath their titles. He has a group of poems called "A Set of Country Songs," and he frequently attaches to his titles such phrases as "written to an old folk tune," "echo of an old song," "a new theme on an old folk measure," "to an old air," and "with an old Wessex refrain." Significantly, he associated "fiddle playing" with obsession, referring in *Under the Greenwood Tree*, for example, to fiddlers who "saw madly at the strings with legs firmly spread and eyes closed, regardless of the visible world."[65] In *The Life and Work of Thomas Hardy*, initially compiled by his second wife, Florence, mention is made of Hardy's obsessive performances of dance tunes only brought to an end by the anxious intervention of the hostess of the dance "clutching his bow-arm at the end of a three-quarter-hour's unbroken footing to his notes by twelve tireless couples."[66] Florence Hardy also records that at the age of four, Hardy would be moved to tears by his father's playing and would dance "to conceal his weeping."[67] "Bowing higher," obsessive speed and repetition, weeping, and catharsis are some of the psychological and physiological qualities Hardy associates with traditional music and dance, and this is the context traditional metrics provides in his poetry.

"The Voice" is a kind of hinge in the 1912–1913 sequence. It underlines the dramatic divergence between past and present, between received and invented form, and, in terms of the overdetermined and ambivalent grief expressed throughout the sequence, between convention and truth. The poem follows "The Haunter," one of only two poems of the series (the other is "The Spell of the Rose") put into Emma's voice. It thereby, in its account of the dispossessed, disassociated relation between the dead and the living, foregrounds its incapacity to "answer" Emma's "calling."[68]

The Voice

Woman much missed, how you call to me, call to me,
Saying that now you are not as you were
When you had changed from the one who was all to me,
But as at first, when our day was fair.

Can it be you that I hear? Let me view you, then,
Standing as when I drew near to the town
Where you would wait for me: yes, as I knew you then,
Even to the original air-blue gown!

Or is it only the breeze, in its listlessness
Travelling across the wet mead to me here,
You being ever dissolved to wan wistlessness,
Heard no more again far or near?

Thus I; faltering forward,
Leaves around me falling,
Wind oozing thin through the thorn from norward,
And the woman calling.[69]

The poem has dramatic metrical shifts. The first two stanzas have the triple-time dactylic meter that Hardy used in at least sixteen other poems in his oeuvre. But the third stanza has a pattern that only appears in this work. The opening's triple dance rhythm and galloping effect bring forward many allusions to the dancing and horseback riding of his courtship—effects evident as well in the early poems of the sequence. When after "Can it be you that I hear?" a caesura is introduced, the spell of that rhythm is broken, but only gradually as "Standing as when I drew near to the town" reintroduces the dominance of the rest of the stanza. Breaking the dactylic and then reintroducing it creates an effect of fading echo, and the reimposition of the consonance between the earlier rhythm and the secondary rhythm, the past and the present, is reinforced by the central visual image in the poem—the original air blue gown whose authenticity is proclaimed and lost at the very instant of its mention; the gown appears as a literally evaporating image. When the rhythm strikes up a third time in the third stanza, Hardy uses spondees to break it—the emphatic "heard no more again far or near." And the echo of these spondees becomes "Thus I"—the stark realization of his singularity and loneliness as falling meters become quite literally falling meters: faltering forward. "Leaves around me falling" changes the direction toward a trochaic meter before one last imposition of the dactylic associated with Emma "Wind oozing thin through the thorn from norward" and the break again through spondees.

This poem has a rather startling amount of tension between metrical organization and metrical noise. It is a poem full of emotion worked through on the level of sound and is about as close as poetry can come to the condition of music and still maintain its meaning as poetry. Hardy put into this poem an entire world of metrical allusion. For example, the poem borrows its triple rhythm from what is often described as a "song," "Haste to the Wedding." But "Haste to the Wedding" is in fact the melody to a traditional dance tune involving two couples alternately casting, swinging, and advancing to a gallop step and another triple time step. Like many such dance tunes, the work ends on a dominant in the expectation that it will continue, like a round. The version collected by Cecil J. Sharp in 1909 is reproduced here (p. 136).[70]

Furthermore, critics have often noted that "the original air blue gown" is a reference to a blue gown Emma wore when Hardy first met her. Even when her age made such clothing inappropriate, Emma wore muslin dresses with blue ribbons.[71] But this image also conflates two other related song and dance texts, "Jan O Jan" and "The Blue Muslin Gown." "Jan O

HASTE TO THE WEDDING (First Version).

Triple Minor-Set.

MUSIC.	MOVEMENTS.
A1. and A2.	The first woman moves down and back, and casts down and back; while the first man casts down and back, and moves down and back. Fig. 31 (p. 44).
B1.	First couple leads down the middle and back again. Fig. 4 (p. 29).
B2.	First and second couples swing and cast one (progressive). Fig. 8 (p. 29).

"Leading back again" is danced to the galop step, and the "swing" to the following :—

L   R L   R   L R   L   R L

HASTE TO THE WEDDING (Second Version).

Duple Minor-Set.

MUSIC.	MOVEMENTS.
A1.	First woman and second man advance, bow, turn round and swing. Fig. 13 (p. 35).
A2.	First man and second woman advance, bow, turn round and swing. Fig. 14 (p. 35).
B1.	First couple leads down the middle and back again. Fig. 4 (p. 29).
B2.	First and second couples swing and cast one (progressive). Fig. 8 (p. 29).

The "swing" and "leading back again" are danced to the same steps as in the first version.

"Haste to the Wedding"
From *The Country Dance Book* (1909).

Jan" is probably the older work. Hardy writes that it was "played in his childhood at his father's house, around 1844." Hardy wrote an operetta in 1923 based on the piece; the operetta was performed by the local Dorchester players and directed by Hardy in his old age. The work is a courtship dance in which the men advance, offering the women various forms of wealth: "O madam I will give you a fine silken gown / With four-and-twenty flounces a-hanging on the ground, / If you will be my joy, and my only only dear / And if you will walk along with me everywhere!" But the women respond with emphatically negative replies: "O I will not accept of your fine silken gown / With four-and-twenty flounces a-hanging to the groun' / And I'll not be your joy, or your only only dear, / And I'll not walk along with you, anywhere."[72] The stakes grow higher, until the final verse, where the man's offer of "true love" is greeted with assent.

"The Blue Muslin Gown" is a popular song contemporary to Hardy that has the same structure based on courtship. It begins:

"O will you accept of the mus-e-lin so blue,
    To wear all in the morning, and to dabble in the dew?"
"No, I will not accept of the mus-e-lin so blue,
    To wear all in the morning and to dabble in the dew;
        Nor I'll walk, nor I'll talk—with you."

But the ending of this version is more applicable to the Hardys' in many respects failed romance:

"O will you accept of a kiss from loving heart;
    That we may join together and never more may part?"
"Yes, I will accept of a kiss from loving heart,
    That we may join together and never more may part,
       And I'll walk and I'll talk with you."
"When you might you would not;
Now you will you shall not,
    So fare you well, my dark eyed Sue."

The directions for the song and dance say that "it then turns back in reverse order, going from the grandest to the smallest offers of wealth and ends with 'When you could you would not.'"[73]

These songs obviously seem overdetermined in relation to "The Voice." "The Blue Muslin Gown" with its familiar dress, dabbling in dew, and rather bitter mutual refrain "When you might you would not / now you will you shall not" echoes the conditions of tragically delayed expression and regret running throughout the sequence. Furthermore, if we turn to the 1858 edition of *Psalms and Hymns*, one of Hardy's own hymnals, we find that he has also picked up on the conventional Christian hymns of parting—hymns that contend that life is parting and eternity the end of parting.[74] Hymn 891 with its falling meter and emphatic language seems particularly relevant to the form Hardy has worked through and by means of which he has achieved this extraordinary nexus of emotion and sound:

When shall we meet again,
Meet ne-er to sever;
When shall peace wreathe her chain
Round us for ever?
Our hearts will ne-er repose,
Safe from each blast that blows,
In this dark vale of woes,
Never, no, never!

When shall love freely flow,
Pure as life's river?
When shall sweet friendship glow,
Changeless for ever?
Where joys celestial thrill,
Where bliss each heart shall fill,
And fears of parting chill
Never, no, never!

The hymn goes on in the remaining two verses to turn to heaven as the place where "soon shall we meet again." That these songs are complexly interrelated is even more exaggerated by the fact that versions of the "Jan O Jan" and "Blue Muslin Gown" song-dances were sometimes referred to as "The Keys of Heaven."[75]

Underlying "The Voice" and the 1912–1913 series as a whole is the expression of grief as inaudibility. Hardy has used the printed poem to emphasize the incommensurability between life and death, past and present. The frantic survey of alternative sites of life and activity returns as inevitably as the Mellstock quire members to the site of the silent tomb. The structure of the series does not lead toward resolution; rather, it presents us, like the separations and rejoinings of "Haste to the Wedding" and the reversible emotions of the "Blue Muslin Gown," with an infinitely creating and negating activity. The end of "The Voice" emphasizes the tension induced by the multiple referents of silence—the certainty of the opening of the poem, "Woman much missed, how you call to me, call to me," is, by the end of the poem, the certainty that the sound is the wind with the wind in fact taking up again the lost dactylic music of the opening: "Wind oozing thin through the thorn from norward." At the greatest emotional distance from the ease of the dactylic are the harsh, metrically clumsy, falling lines directly preceding these: "Thus I; faltering forward, / Leaves around me falling," lines that obsessively mime their thematic of the fall from grace. The reader feels he or she has stumbled into the reality principle—the wind now taking the place of the ghostly voice, until the last line, when we turn back inevitably into reversal: "And the woman calling."

The staging of grief here, like the staging of grief throughout the sequence, raises issues of authenticity that acquire their own tragic cast, for the authenticity of the speaker's emotion can be created only in a context of dialogue and third-person viewpoint. The single lyric singer here has summoned a literal choir of witnesses to his grief, yet Hardy with his characteristic tragic sense comes to repeat and enact the bleak prospect of unintelligibility as the only means for bringing "peace thereto."

BISHOP

In concluding, I want to consider briefly a third example of metrical haunting, Bishop's meditative poem "At the Fishhouses."[76] Bishop is a poet who often used traditional hymn, ballad, and blues meters in her work. In such pieces as "Visits to St. Elizabeths," which uses the cumulative structure of "This is the House That Jack Built" to re-create the aura of Ezra Pound's confinement in a madhouse; "The Burglar of Baby-lon," which displays variations on ballad meter simulating the quality of a broadside sheet; and "The Riverman," with its underlying samba rhythms, Bishop shows the extraordinary facility with which she could use metrical allusion. The opening line of "Arrival at Santos," "Here is a coast; here is a harbor," echoes the children's finger play, "Here is the church; here is the steeple." In this poem, as Bishop moves into the ornate diction of the next three lines—"meager diet of horizon"; "self-pitying mountains"; "frivolous greenery"—she even further exaggerates the sim-ple dichotomy of the opening echo.

"At the Fishhouses" is a poem that at first does not strike us as having a musical structure. It begins:

> Although it is a cold evening,
> down by one of the fishhouses
> an old man sits netting,
> his net, in the gloaming almost invisible,
> a dark purple-brown,
> and his shuttle worn and polished.
> The air smells so strong of codfish
> it makes one's nose run and one's eyes water.
> The five fishhouses have steeply peaked roofs
> and narrow, cleated gangplanks slant up
> to storerooms in the gables
> for the wheelbarrows to be pushed up and down on.

Nevertheless, the poem moves brilliantly between speech and song; the initial tetrameter and the immediate discursive sense of speaking evoked in the beginning connective, "Although," establish an initial rhythm against which variations will arise. The first variation comes after the opening quatrain. The two lines "a dark purple-brown / and his shuttle worn and polished" evoke a digression from the meter that is an intensi-fication of attention to the subject—they note closely and thereby lose the exactness of the form. When the tetrameter is reintroduced in "The air smells so strong of codfish," it is quickly extended by a line of pentame-ter, miming the excess of the body's response to codfish: "it makes one's nose run and one's eyes water." The playful movement between form and content continues as the next line introduces a number that the change in meter has already brought forward: "The five fishhouses have steeply peaked roofs." Here the shift between the tetrameter and pentameter is es-tablished as the baseline of the poem. In other words, the poem's lines are, as it explains in a self-referential pun in lines 43 to 46, like "thin silver trunks laid horizontally across the gray stones, down and down, at intervals of four or five feet."

Throughout the poem much of the metric is exemplary to the meaning: the stressed tetrameter/pentameter baseline is broken for the first time in line 14 describing the spilling over of the sea. The sea functions as a mnemonic in the poem, its rhythm and generality sending the speaker into a sequence of reveries that will in each case evoke a particular. The tetrameter quatrain and theme of the herring signaled by abcb rhyme in lines 21 to 24 introduce a metrical allusion from Eugene Field's children's poem, "Wynken, Blynken, and Nod." Under Bishop's lines: "The big fish tubs are completely lined / with layers of beautiful herring scales / And the wheelbarrows are similarly plastered / with creamy iridescent coats of mail," we can hear and see those of Field: "Where are you going and what do you wish / The old moon asked the three / We have come to fish for the herring fish / That swim in this beautiful sea / Nets of silver and gold have we/ Said Wynken, Blynken, and Nod."[77] Bishop breaks the spell of this allusion with the introduction of the flies and the prosaic, and death-ridden, language of "crawling on them" in line 25.

Despite the extensive manipulation of sound and music being worked by these metrical puns and allusions, the poem up until the moment of the speaker's offer of a Lucky Strike to the old man is constructed almost entirely (the exception is the smell of codfish) of visual references. And even the visual references can pun on this silence, for the "ancient wooden capstan / cracked with two long bleached handles / and some melancholy stains, like dried blood," brings to mind the Romance words for "a halter or muzzle" derived from the Latin *capistrum* and including the Portuguese *cabresto*. Similarly, the introduction of the "black old knife" that scrapes the fish from its scales, or "principal beauty," marks the first stanza break in the poem.

There are, in fact, three stanzas in "At the Fishhouses"—irregularly shaped and fitting loosely into the ode divisions of strophe (here the introduction of the scene and animation of the figure in the landscape); antistrophe (the turn away from the land to the shore and the metacommentary on the metric); and epode (the final trajectory of immersion first with sight, then sound, then touch, then taste). The initial triple spondees of the refrain introducing the epode, "Cold dark deep and absolutely clear," are also presented with a reference to their source—the three hammering chords that open each of the first two periods of "A Mighty Fortress Is Our God." Luther's hymn, which Bishop shares a knowledge of with the seal, may be read as a reference to the part of her childhood spent with the Bulmer (alternatively spelled "Boomer") branch of her family, the hymn-singing Baptist relatives of her mother, in Great Village, Nova Scotia. This thereby is the site of the poem, the referent of both sense impression and memory.

In lines 60 to 62, that rock against the flood is transmuted into another prior part of this conversation whose response has begun "Although"— Marianne Moore's 1924 poem "A Grave," which begins:

> Man looking into the sea,
> taking the view from those who have as much right to it as you have to
>   it yourself,
> it is human nature to stand in the middle of a thing,
> but you cannot stand in the middle of this;
> the sea has nothing to give but a well excavated grave.
> The firs stand in a procession, each with an emerald turkey-foot at the top,
> reserved as their contours, saying nothing;
> repression, however, is not the most obvious characteristic of the sea; . . . [78]

Moore's poem—with its bleak materialism, its emphasis on the human denial of death, and its final lines "the ocean, under the pulsation of lighthouses and noise of bell-buoys, / advances as usual, looking as if it were not that ocean in which dropped things are bound to sink— / in which if they turn and twist, it is neither with volition nor consciousness"—can be seen to be the prior discourse to which Bishop's "Although" is a response.[79] In counterpoint to the sea as a site of repression, Bishop gradually arrives at the possibility of the sea as a site of knowledge—the music evoked by its presence has reawakened the sound of a tragic childhood. At its close the poem returns to the origins of sense impressions under the frame of experience in a dialectic between the senses and abstraction that is powerfully evocative of Wordsworth's "Intimations" ode:

> If you should dip your hand in,
> your wrist would ache immediately,
> your bones would begin to ache and your hand would burn
> as if the water were a transmutation of fire
> that feeds on stones and burns with a dark gray flame.
> If you tasted it, it would first taste bitter,
> then briny, then surely burn your tongue.
> It is like what we imagine knowledge to be:
> dark, salt, clear, moving, utterly free,

drawn from the cold hard mouth
of the world, derived from the rocky breasts
forever, flowing and drawn, and since
our knowledge is historical, flowing, and flown.

This transposition from the most abstract senses of sound and sight to the immediate physicality of touch and taste is a historical journey to the sources of Bishop's early loss of her father and mother. Indeed, in her well-known masterpiece, the villanelle "One Art," Bishop proclaims herself, in full mastery, as an artist of loss.

Bishop's short story "In the Village" tells of the onset of her mother's madness after her father's death. It begins, "A scream, the echo of a scream, hangs over that Nova Scotia Village."[80] The scream, her mother's scream, recurs through her memory, yet it is juxtaposed by another sound—that of Nate the blacksmith, whose shop is at the end of the garden. As a child, Bishop cries, "Make me a ring! Make me a ring, Nate!" and the blacksmith complies by making a horseshoe nail into a ring for her finger. But her request is also to make the hammer ring, and the work ends, "Nate! Oh, beautiful sound, strike again." The blacksmith's ring, like the transmutation of fire at the end of "At the Fishhouses," promises the Pythagorean dream of a harmony of sound and number, and a harmony of the world. It is a harmony also imagined out of the intervals of the blacksmith's hammer. Here Bishop marks the transition from an unattributable, almost animal, scream to a form of volitional sound—the sound of her own art's mastery of suffering. This is one dimension of "At the Fishhouses"'s deeply serious pun on the idea of "sounding"—the sounding of a voice and the sounding of the depths of the sea as means to knowledge. Many of the poem's early lines have to do with the glancing and glittering light that falls on earthly things—those flashes of beauty to which we are given access and which provide us with reflections or mirrors of reality. These sparkling images find their resolution and opposition in the poem's final emphasis on "total immersion"—the plunging beyond the surface of things, the abandonment of light in pursuit of depth. The conclusion to "At the Fishhouses" establishes the viability of being mothered by a grave, just as the poem as a whole works through the process by which music is refined from pain.

Readings of voice and possession necessarily run the risk of an undue emphasis on coincidence, an amorphous notion of influence, and an unsatisfactory explanation of intention. There is perhaps no more considered thinking about these possibilities of poetic voice than Walt Whitman's "Vocalism." Beginning with a definition, "Vocalism, measure, concentration, determination, and the divine power to speak words," Whitman describes voice as a willed aspect of the body: it is the volition to speak that is at the core of vocalism, a volition that he describes as arising from extensive experience in the world. Such experience—"armies, ships, antiquities, libraries, paintings, machines, cities, hate, despair, amity, pain, theft, murder, aspiration"—throngs at the mouth, ready to emerge. And then the poet reverses perspectives and asks, "O what is it in me that makes me tremble so at voices?" The answer lies in the final lines:

> I see brains and lips closed, tympans and temples unstruck,
> Until that comes which has the quality to strike and to unclose,
> Until that comes which has the quality to bring forth what lies slumber-
> ing forever ready in all words.[81]

"What lies slumbering in all words" is beyond the simple model of volition offered at the start of the poem. "What lies slumbering" is the long history of the use of words, the legacy of generations of the dead and the somatic memory of living speakers. By taking the notion of lyric possession as a description rather than a problem to be overcome or refuted, we attend to the many springs of a poem's generation. By acknowledging the ways in which our voices are spoken through, we are bound to hear more than we meant to say.

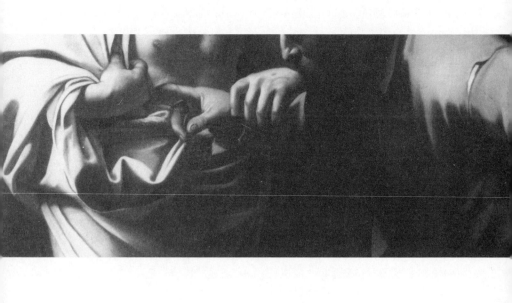

4

FACING, TOUCH, AND VERTIGO

I. THE EXPERIENCE OF BEHOLDING

"Clat-thump-clat-thump-clat-thump-ping. . . ." Looking out, I can see
a boy with a stick, trailing it along a wrought-iron fence. The
"clats" are the posts, the "thumps" are the fall of the stick into the spaces
between, the "ping" the sound of arrival at the gate. What is this pleasure
or obsession that makes us want to touch a pattern? The pleasure of trailing a stick along a fence, running a finger along a wall of rough bricks and
smooth pointing, drawing a splayed hand across a swath of corduroy?

Movement and time are part of the phenomenology of touch, part of
its experience, as they are also preconditions for transitive touch to take
place. As touch moves and takes time, pattern becomes apparent,[1] just as
following sound, we trace a path for it: we hear and feel sound emerge, discerning its form. Even as it surrounds us, sound pulls our attention to its
source as, simultaneously, we wait for its ending. As surely as we trace the
sound of water to a spring and imagine its dispersal in the sea, we seek out
the origins of sounds and anticipate their disappearance into an engulfing
silence. When we invoke or call for sound, we bring ourselves, too, into a
certain path: we take our place in time. And when we attribute sound to a
voice, we wonder what figure will be made, who speaks and from where—
when the voice arrives, we learn something, too, about where we stand.
Sound and voice in lyric, as we have seen, take part in these common as-

pects of aurality and the reception of aurality. Yet lyric also is made from silence, from the pull of sound against sense, and from places where voices are at the brink of their individuality. Such voices are filled with the voices of others who have been brought to bear on the speaking or singing person. The person is the vessel of the particular meeting of these particular voices.

In the previous two chapters I have emphasized many features of aurality, and now I want to turn to the experience of beholding in poetry, but to do so will involve discussing as well other face-to-face forms—those forms of art that involve experiences of individual presence, including sculpture and painting. The power these forms have for changing or moving us has a great deal to do with their propinquity to us and the reciprocity such close conditions imply. We do not separate ourselves from what they present as we might separate ourselves from monumental and spectacular works of art. Of course, the very ideas of the monumental and spectacular are determined in many ways through culture and through works of art themselves. But it may be that the profound intimacy and affect of face-to-face works of art stem from our biological experiences. In human evolution, the development of breasts led to an association among nurturing, sexuality, and conversation. And a human predilection for frontal sex led to notions of uniqueness in sexual encounters and to the development of the idea of the personal lover.[2] These vital experiences of our own nature contribute to the expectations we bring to all face-to-face meetings, including those encounters we have with objects.

The moment of beholding resolves what Lacan had described as the problem of closure characteristic of the invocatory drive—it establishes the outline or figure and so "ends" the echoing diffuseness characteristic of sound. When sound turns back to silence, beyond pattern, it returns to nothingness: its condition of invisibility again makes its claim, and we are no longer able to figure the line of its form. This relation between invisibility and visibility—between infinite silence and darkness on the one hand and beholding on the other—is the relation with which we began our study, and here I return to it as the most profound aspect of poetry's relation to vision. The cliché of the blind poet is one we must take seriously—for the poet beholds the other and at the same time creates the conditions for beholding, seeing without needing to see. The poet is summoned by another and in turn summons another into presence. The reader or hearer of the poem recalls these forms of summoning when she attributes intention to the poem as a made form.

The oldest extant poem in English, "Cædmon's Hymn," composed at some point between 658 and 686, is in fact accompanied by a legend about the summoning of the poet in darkness. The Venerable Bede records the story of how Cædmon, an illiterate stable boy and cowherd, was divinely endowed with the powers of the poet:

> [H]e did not learn that art of singing from men, nor taught by men, but he received freely by divine aid the gift of singing . . . he had lived in the secular habit until he was well advanced in years, and had never learnt anything of versifying; and for this reason sometimes at an entertainment, when it was resolved for the sake of merriment that all should sing in turn, if he saw the harp approaching him, he would rise from the feast and go out and return home. When he did this on one occasion, and having left the house where the entertainment was, had gone to the stable of the cattle which had been committed to his charge that night and there appeared to him someone in his sleep, and greeting him and calling him by his name, he said: "Cædmon sing me something." But he replied: "I cannot sing: and for this reason I left the entertainment and came away here, because I could not sing." Then he who was speaking to him replied: "Nevertheless you must sing to me." "What," he said, "must I sing?" And the other said, "Sing me of the beginning of creation." On receiving this answer he at once began to sing in praise of God the Creator, verses which he had never heard.[3]

Bede tells how Cædmon went the next morning before the local abbess and proved to her his newly found powers of composition by turning passages of Scripture into verse: "And remembering all that he could learn by listening, and like, as it were, a clean animal chewing the cud, he turned it into most harmonious song." This, in the Northumbrian version at Cambridge, is the hymn that Cædmon sang in the night to his mysterious interlocutor:

Nu scylun hergan	hefaenricaes uard,
metudæs maecti	end his modgidanc,
uerc uuldurfadur,	sue he uundra gihuaes,
eci dryctin,	or astelidæ.
He aerist scop	aelda barnum
heben til hrofe,	haleg scepen;
tha middungeard	moncynnæs uard,
eci dryctin,	æfter tiadæ
firum foldu,	frea allmectig.[4]

Here is a literal translation: "Now let us praise the Keeper of the Heavenly Kingdom, the Might of the Creator and His Thought, the Work of the glorious Father, how He each of wonders, Eternal Lord, established the beginning. He first created for the sons of men heaven as a roof, the Holy Shaper; then middle-earth the Keeper of Mankind, Eternal Lord, afterwards made for men, [made] earth, the Lord Almighty."[5]

It is a commonplace of the criticism to note that Cædmon's hymn resembles many of the psalms in their praise of the Lord's accomplishments.[6] Yet we might also note that the legend of Cædmon's calling in fact reverses a situation described in Psalm 137:

> By the rivers of Babylon—
> there we sat down and there we wept
> when we remembered Zion.
> On the willows there
> we hung our harps.
> For there our captors
> asked us for songs,
> and our tormentors asked for mirth, saying,
> "Sing us one of the songs of Zion!"

If Cædmon's hymn in fact does date to some time around 670, then he, too, could have been composing for an audience with knowledge of more than one tradition. Only a hundred years after Augustine's missionaries landed in England and fifty years after the Northumbrian king Edwin at York converted to Christianity, Cædmon is following the pagan pattern of the four-beat alliterative line in a Judeo-Christian context: in his dream vision, he receives a demand to convert the traditional poetic formulas to Judeo-Christian ends. Cædmon says he cannot sing—that is, he cannot sing when asked to perform in the hall for the entertainment. But the interlocutor changes the conditions of performance entirely: "Nevertheless you must sing *to me.*" Cædmon immediately understands the necessity of this demand, using the imperative in his reply—what *must* I sing?—and he sings what is requested: the story of God's own *poiēsis* out of nothingness and darkness. The hymn's *poiēsis* is a recalling of the divine *poiēsis* of the Scriptures. The demand comes to Cædmon out of the darkness. Awakened, he cannot discern the figure who is the source of the voice that commands him. But it is the call from another that summons his voice nevertheless. And later, as his singing is legitimized by Hild, the abbess of the monastery at Whitby, he goes on to take the role of a poet summoned more broadly by social sanction.[7]

The legend of Cædmon is an important counter to the anxieties around poetic intention we followed in many of the texts of Plato. Cædmon is inspired by a force outside himself, just as the rhapsodes Plato describes are "spoken through." But Cædmon's inspiration brings him to himself, to something hidden or latent inside himself—inspiration is a summons to the face-to-face encounter with another who makes a demand on the poet. Here the poet's praise work is closer to the *daimōn* of Diotima's discourse on love than to the crowd-corrupting words of the rhapsode. Cædmon's legend gives an account of poetic suasion that is reciprocal—the demand precedes the composition and is not an artifact of composition. The poet begins by readying a space for reception and beholding: *Nu scylun hergan,* "*Now* let us praise"—this space and this time, this creator and this creation. When poet and listener are engaged in this scene, they turn to the intersubjective task of making significance, of pointing to meaning.

Praise poetry of the type Cædmon sings—the type of "hymn to the gods or praises of virtuous men" that was, as we noted earlier, the only poetry Plato would allow to be practiced in the *Republic*—is exemplary; it quite literally leads to significance. Like Schiller's beauty as our "second creator," Cædmon's praise re-calls and re-creates the *poiēsis* of the world. Sir Philip Sidney argued specifically for this role for poetry in his *Apology for Poetry,* composed between 1581 and 1583, arguing that "of all those who study the works of nature—astronomers, mathematicians, musicians, natural and moral philosophers, lawyers, historians, grammarians, rhetoricians, physicians and metaphysicians, only the poet disdaining to be tied to any such subjection [to mere universals and abstractions] lifted up with the vigor of his own invention, doth grow in effect another nature, in making things either better than nature bringeth forth, or quite anew, forms such as never were in nature . . . so as he goeth hand in hand with nature, not enclosed within the narrow warrant of her gifts, but freely ranging only within the zodiac of his own wit."[8] The reflexivity, or tendency toward self-reference, of this tradition of praise poetry illuminates the situation of both speaker and audience, establishing "a local habitation and a name," yoking the airy abstractions of philosophy to the immediacy of sense impressions and moving persons to identification through valediction or, in other cases, to repulsion through blaming or making "odious comparisons" of the type we saw in our discussion of some of Donne's erotic poems.

The pointing or designating, the giving frame, that such poetry completes is derived from the face-to-face situation of the poet and his or her listener. The frontality of face-to-face communication bears with it concepts of the behind as the past and the beyond and between as spheres of anticipation and heightened expectation. The rhetorical term *deixis*, signifying "to point out" or "pointing," is of great use to us in thinking through such issues. In this chapter we will consider its implications for proximity in poetic forms; in the next chapter we will consider its implications for the temporality of poems. Liddell and Scott's Greek lexicon gives the following as translations of *deixis:* "to show forth, point, display, bring to light, hail, exhibit, reveal, to greet by means of words or form." The word *deixis* connotes the appearance of form in more than its visual dimensions and implies apprehension by touch or motion. Emphasizing the bringing forth of form over notions of imitation and representation per se, deixis yokes rhetoric—that is, an intention to move and a reciprocal receptivity to be moved—to visual and aural appearances. In lyric, painting, sculpture, and other arts, the stored activity of the maker is simultaneous to an implicit and reciprocal capacity for animation in the receiver.

Deixis is indeed a more general term for those shifters, such as the pronouns *I* and *you* that we discussed earlier. All such terms—indexical signs and demonstratives—are of relevance to speakers and to relations of proximity and propinquity between speakers and persons, and speakers and things. There is a somewhat paradoxical quality to indexical signs and demonstratives as the specifications of coordinates of time and space. Whenever we use the terms *now* or *here* or *I* or *you*, we find ourselves immersed in the "now" of articulation, the "here" of the space in which speech is spoken, the "I" of the speaker, the "you" of the listener. It is, as we saw with pronominal shifters alone, not just that such terms are context-dependent: they themselves define and create the circumstances of specific contexts.

Yet we also understand such terms across contexts—we carry over their meaning, but not their particular referents. And this is another way in which face-to-face genres recapitulate and continue the work of shifters in making specificity intelligible. In the following sonnet, for example, Petrarch uses the *or* (now) and *qui* (here) both to make the past immediate as a continuing state of affairs and to show the rapid changes in emotion the speaker is expressing to his friend and fellow poet Sennuccio del Bene regarding his feelings for his love Laura, signified in the pun at the beginning of the fourth line, "L'aura":

112

Sennuccio, i' vo' che sapi in qual manera
trattato sono et qual vita è la mia:
ardomi et struggo ancor com'io solia,
l'aura mi volve et son pur quel ch'i' m'era.

Qui tutta umile et qui la vidi altera,
or aspra or piana, or dispietata or pia,
or vestirsi onestate or leggiadria,
or mansueta, or disdegnosa et fera.

Qui cantò dolcemente, et qui s'assise,
qui si rivolse, et qui rattenne il passo,
qui co'begli occhi mi trafisse il core,

qui disse una parola, et qui sorrise,
qui cangiò il viso. In questi pensier, lasso,
notte et dì tiemmi il signor nostro Amore.

This is Robert Durling's translation:

Sennuccio, I wish you to know how I am treated and what my
life is like: I am burning up and suffering still just as I used to,
the breeze turns me about, and I'm still just what I was.

Here I saw her all humble and there haughty, now harsh, now
gentle, now cruel, now merciful; now clothed in virtue, now in
gaiety, now tame, now disdainful and fierce.

Here she sang sweetly and here sat down; here she turned about
and here held back her step; here with her lovely eyes she transfixed
my heart;

here she said a word, here she smiled, here she frowned. In these
thoughts, alas! our Lord Love keeps me night and day.[9]

The poem begins (i' vo' che sapi in qual manera / trattato sono) in the present progressive tense that Petrarch frequently employs. As Robert Pogue
Harrison has written of this tense, mentioning as well its appearance in
"I' vo gridando" (128), "I' vo pensando" (264), "I' vo piangendo" (365), this
tense "is only a version or instantiation of the ideal present tense that
keeps the voice present to itself throughout the duration of its speech. The
tense is unusually appropriate for Petrarch, for it prolongs the presence of
the temporal 'I' as that same 'I' drags the here and now with it through
time."[10] The overall effect instantiates or, in the case of 128, closes the
poem as a setting forth, followed by a relentless pointing to changes that

lead all the more to a binding or constraining in place—the place to which Laura has pinned him as her eyes have transfixed his heart.[11]

Over time, poetry figures the human as those meanings carried over from the context-dependent, contingent situations of individual speakers. As we saw in Damasio's account of the progress from a "proto-self" to an autobiographical self, the particularity of context-dependent existence is transported by consciousness to establish what is in fact context-independent in individual persons. Grossman has written that *"poetry means, to put it crudely, the context-independence of the person, whose right of presence is not a contingency of history alone, and is in many respects inimical to life itself."* [12] Poetry is inimical to life in this sense because it frees us from life's transient dependence on context-bound meaning and because it takes a stance against death—against death's contingent, and monumental, claim to the significance of our individuality.

Yet the particular means of poetry's role in carrying over context dependence into the figuration of context independence has to do as well with a transfer of sense impressions. Bertrand Russell thought that all deictic terms took their reference from sense data—any shifter could be translated as "this"—this sensation at this time to this speaker. Therefore, just as the meanings of shifters were both bound to their situation of utterance and intelligible across utterances, so was each sense datum described both private to the speaker (what Russell called an "egocentric particular") and intelligible to other speakers and other listeners at other times. We are again in the worlds of Sappho's shattering, of Among-the-brant's mourning song, and Sonnet 112's complaint to Sennuccio, worlds where private sense impressions are made intelligible beyond their context dependence.[13] As poetry establishes rhythms into measures, as it forms the coincidence of rhymes into patterns of expectation and surprise, sensations internal to individual persons are carried over into context-independent forms of tension and release. This is not simply a making public of private sensations: it also gives form to the chaos, and even pain, of such private sensations for those persons who bear them. And it emphasizes the ways in which all perceptions, all impressions of sense data, are already involved in previous experiences of perception—whether our "own" or "others." As Henri Bergson wrote in his 1908 treatise *Matter and Memory*, "there is no perception which is not full of memories. With the immediate and present data of our senses, we mingle a thousand details out of our past experience." [14]

Consider the mixture of metrical and cultural allusion on the one hand and immediacy of presentation on the other in William Cowper's unusual adaptation of the Sapphic form for his poem beginning "Hatred and vengeance, my eternal portion":

> Hatred and vengeance, my eternal portion,
> Scarce can endure delay of execution:—
> Wait, with impatient readiness, to seize my
>   Soul in a moment.

> Damn'd below Judas; more abhorr'd than he was,
> Who, for a few pence, sold his holy master.
> Twice betray'd, Jesus me, the last delinquent,
>   Deems the profanest.

> Man disavows, and Deity disowns me.
> Hell might afford my miseries a shelter;
> Therefore hell keeps her everhungry mouths all
>   Bolted against me.

> Hard lot! Encompass'd with a thousand dangers,
> Weary, faint, trembling with a thousand terrors,
> Fall'n, and if vanquish'd, to receive a sentence
>   Worse than Abiram's:

> Him, the vindictive rod of angry justice
> Sent, quick and howling, to the centre headlong;
> I, fed with judgments, in a fleshly tomb, am
>   Buried above ground.

Written in 1774 after his mental crisis of 1773 (this particular breakdown one of many in his life), the poem expresses a despair precipitated over the sin of despair, a kind of theological tautology that produced its own circle of torment. As the poem opens with a fear of the ever-hungry mouths of hell that will seize his soul in a moment, Cowper finds that unlike Abiram, whose rebellion against the authority of Moses and Aaron, recounted in Numbers 16, was met with the earth opening her mouth and swallowing him, he greets Hell's mouths as portals bolted against him. Cowper's hell is the tomb of his own flesh as the source of his despair is his own despair.[15]

In a passage from his study of speech genres, Mikhail Bakhtin writes that every dialogue "takes place as if against the background of the responsive understanding of an invisibly present third party who stands above all the participants in the dialogue (partners) (cf. the understanding of the Fascist torture chamber or hell in Thomas Mann as absolute *lack of being heard,* as the absolute absence of a *third party).*"[16] Cowper's voice echoes alone: "Man disavows, and Deity disowns me." The poem at first seems horrifying because of its enumeration of conventional punishments for damnation, but at this point we realize that higher stakes are involved: what if there are *no* punishments, no hell? What if the void is everything and the only certainty is the fleshly tomb of one's own pain in a universe where no one is listening?[17]

Weary, faint, trembling with a thousand terrors—the problem of emotion recollected in tranquility hardly does justice to the situation of the here and now in this poem. Cowper borrows not only the form of the Sapphic but also an urgent sense of time, as if he were on a temporal precipice. It is the sense we find in the Greek adverb δηῦτε *(dēute)* occasionally found in classical lyric signifying that something is actually taking place at a given moment ("hither," explain Liddell and Scott) and also happening again. *Dēute* strikes, as Anne Carson has explained, "a note of powerful, alert emotion," especially in love poetry.[18] Here Cowper has used the same kind of "now" to emphasize the crouching inevitable threat of damnation: "wait with impatient readiness to seize my / Soul in a moment." This temporal suspension is yoked to a spatial suspension—even Hell, which might offer his misery a form, is bolted against the speaker. He is "buried above ground"—that is, blocked from action in a form of torment that is the prison of his mortal, yet still living, body.

Deictic terms always raise issues of intention and reception. When we attend to the "thisness" of an artwork, we give priority to the emergence of the artwork in time (this time "counts") and the nontacit situation of the artwork in space (the space of the work begins where the space around it ends). In his classic lectures on linguistic aspects of deixis, Charles Fillmore—like Benveniste, Jakobson, Russell, and the pragmatist C. S. Peirce—defines *deixis* as those aspects of utterances anchoring sentences in space and time, including features indexical to cultural and social allusion.[19] Yet Fillmore's work is of specific use to us in considering face-to-face situations because of what he says about frontality. Writing on frontality as a deictic aspect, Fillmore says:

> Many of the expressions by which we locate one object with respect to some other object impute to that second or reference object some sort of horizontal orientation. One of the surfaces of many animals and artifacts is regarded as having a special orientational priority. The word in English

for what I have in mind is "a front." For animate beings having a certain degree of complexity, the front is that portion of it which contains its main organs of perception and which arrives first whenever it moves in its most characteristic manner. . . . This double criterion for frontness in animate beings may lead to some uncertainties. I assume that for animals the location of the main organs of perception outweighs the direction of movement criterion, since we speak of crabs as moving sideways, not as having heads on one side of their bodies; and since if we found a race of people who typically get around in the way we see people move in reverse motion pictures, I believe we would say of these that they walk backwards rather than that they have faces on the backs of their heads.[20]

Fillmore describes how issues of frontality are transferred from persons to objects and how deixis describes orientation along up/down axes. Left/right orientation is possible for objects only if that object has both a vertical or up/down orientation and a front/back orientation. Positions shift between objects and persons in a process of mutuality like that of deictic pronoun shifts as Jakobson and Benveniste described them.[21] We therefore speak of places as having a point of view—sinister and dexter portions of an escutcheon, for example, are defined in heraldry as right or left sides from the point of view of the bearer—the implied being residing behind the frontality of the object. Expressions such as *stage right* and *stage left* are similarly from the point of view of performers whether performers are present or not.[22]

The study of deixis compels us to identify the relations between objects and persons as relational and mutual, but not in indeterminate ways. The articulation of proximity, of edges and interiors, and the use of prepositions such as *at, on,* and *in* thrust us toward the presence or absence of dimensionality, bounded or unbounded space, and surface. Fillmore especially emphasizes how deixis aids the manipulation of objects in everyday life via the manipulation of position: one can be in front of something or in back of it, or an object can be in front of, or in back of, one's self, not just in reverse perspective but also because persons and things can turn around and over. In contrast, the conventional time system lacks this flexibility—the earlier and later orientation is permanently set.[23] Although Fillmore's interests remain exclusively linguistic, works of art, in their articulation of alternative models of time and space, and as they compel a suspension of the performative, pragmatic, and instrumental functions of discourse and gesture, counter the rigidity of this time system and enable reflection, recursiveness, and the utopian possibilities of repetition and simultaneity.

Deixis fuses form, expression, and theme as one event in place and time—the inseparability of frame and context in deictic forms is evident in the impossibility of paraphrasing or abstracting them. We therefore could not speak of the specificity of the deictic as translatable or transportable to other locations, for it is its own location. Yet we can understand its meaning or significance independent of its reference to the here and now of apprehension. The form creates or defines its location and the listener, viewer, or apprehender finds his or her position established in relation to the concrete determinants of the form—everything "matters" as an aspect of the manifestation. In this way the artwork's very specificity, its "finality of form," enables its context independence. The theory of deixis in linguistics has implications for presentational forms more generally, helping us consider framing the time and space of apprehension, the mutuality, reciprocity or nonreciprocity, of relations between positions and perspectives, the reversibility of things amid the unidirectionality of everyday time, and assumptions of intention and reception.

Of all poetic conventions, one that makes particularly strong use of deictic gestures of immediacy and specificity of context is the *carpe diem* tradition. A carpe diem poem such as Ben Jonson's "Song: To Celia (I)" makes a great deal out of the specificity of the scene of poetic utterance, effectively shutting out all that is not relevant to the immediacy of the lover's imploring words:

Come, my Celia, let us prove,
While we can, the sports of love;
Time will not be ours forever;
He at length our good will sever.
Spend not then his gifts in vain.
Suns that set may rise again;
But if once we lose this light,
'Tis with us perpetual night.
Why should we defer our joys?
Fame and rumor are but toys.
Cannot we delude the eyes
Of a few poor household spies,
Or his easier ears beguile,
So removèd by our wile?
'Tis no sin love's fruit to steal;
But the sweet thefts to reveal,
To be taken, to be seen,
These have crimes accounted been.[24]

In Jonson's plea and similar poems such as Robert Herrick's well-known "To the Virgins, to Make Much of Time," a subtle appeal to the senses is staged: the smell of rosebuds; the suffusion of sunlight; the feeling of warmth that comes from within.[25] The poems of John Wilmot, earl of Rochester, are particularly skillful in taking advantage of such expressions of "thisness" in erotic terms. In "Love and Life" (1667), for example, he makes wry use of the immediacy of the poem's moment of revelation, erasing the past in the first stanza and the future in the second stanza:

All my past life is mine no more;
The flying hours are gone,
Like transitory dreams given o'er
Whose images are kept in store
By memory alone.

Whatever is to come is not:
How can it then be mine?
The present moment's all my lot,
And that, as fast as it is got,
Phyllis, is wholly thine.

Then talk not of inconstancy
False hearts, and broken vows;
If I, by miracle, can be
This livelong minute true to thee,
'Tis all that heaven allows.[26]

The close of the poem, the fulfilled "minute," is also the point of departure or escape from the poem's conditions of fidelity of attention.

Such issues of the here and now in poetic works can be usefully framed by the more abstract speculations of Martin Heidegger on nearness and being to hand and the contributions of Heinrich Wölfflin and José Ortega y Gassett on empathy and proximity in aesthetic experience in general. Heidegger suggests in his thoughts on "the thing" that "To discover the nature of nearness we give thought to the jug nearby. We also catch sight of the nature of nearness. The thing things . . . the thing is not 'in' nearness, in proximity as if nearness were a container. Nearness is at work in bringing near, as the thinging of the thing."[27] Wölfflin's theory of empathy also emphasizes proximity: "We always project a corporeal state conforming to our own onto the object of interpretation."[28] Here inanimate objects are endowed with a sense of body posture and mood. And Ortega y Gassett argues specifically that "proximate vision has a tactile quality. What mysterious resonance of touch is preserved by sight when it converges on a nearby object? We shall not now attempt to violate this mystery. It is enough that we recognize this quasi-tactile density possessed by the ocular ray, and which permits it, in effect, to embrace, to touch the earthen jar. As the object is withdrawn, sight loses its tactile power and gradually becomes pure vision. . . . An age-old habit, founded in vital necessity, causes men to consider as 'things,' in the strict sense, only such objects solid enough to offer resistance to their hands. So in passing from proximate to distant vision, an object becomes illusory."[29]

But Ortega y Gassett's exploration of proximate and distant vision also argues that "seeing requires distance. Each art operates a magic lantern that removes and transfigures its objects. On its screen they stand aloof, inmates of an inaccessible world, in an absolute distance. When this derealization is lacking, an awkward perplexity arises: we do not know whether to 'live' the things or observe them."[30] Obviously, these are somewhat incommensurable positions, but they also pose the very kinds of pleasurable tensions the lover experiences when invited to move forward to seize the day. What Ortega y Gassett finds to be an awkward perplexity is exactly what Wölfflin finds a source of power and pleasure in apprehension. For Heidegger the constant play among nearness, thingness, and farness is essential to our apprehension of our being in the world. Nevertheless, Heidegger does not specify the sensual apparatus at work in this play.

Dickinson's 1869 poem beginning "Split the Lark—and you'll find the Music—" is a powerful commentary on the tensions between "living" and "observing" the things of the world:

> Split the Lark—and you'll find the Music—
> Bulb after Bulb, in Silver rolled—
> Scantily dealt to the Summer Morning
> Saved for your Ear when Lutes be old.
>
> Loose the Flood—you shall find it patent—
> Gush after Gush, reserved for you—
> Scarlet Experiment! Sceptic Thomas!
> Now, do you doubt that your Bird was true?[31]

The tragic equivalence between murder and dissection that Wordsworth wrote of in "The Tables Turned" (l. 28)[32] is brought out powerfully by the use of medial caesuras. Taking apart something in order to understand it inevitably raises the possibility of killing the whole. The music is a manifestation of the lark's entire being and to try to find it through dissection would be to discover the hidden affinity between the bird's music and its blood; to spill it by artificial means would be to drain the body of its life. The poem shows the danger of touch that goes over into destruction and of sight without empathy. The poem is a profound comment on the interdependence of immanence and transcendence in any artwork: the life of the work is embodied and must precede transcendence, but transcendence is able to rise from these very conditions of immanence: the "music" of organic wholes in nature and in art cannot be traced to any particular and cannot be accounted for by a knowledge of its merely material source.

The skepticism of Thomas, his "scarlet experiment," is a central legend of touch in the Christian West. The allusion is to John 20:24–29:

> One of the Twelve, Thomas the Twin, was not with the rest when Jesus
> came. So the others kept telling him, "We have seen the Lord." But he
> said, "Unless I see the mark of the nails on his hands, unless I put my
> finger into the place where the nails were, and my hand into his side,
> I will never believe it." A week later his disciples were once again in the
> room, and Thomas was with them. Although the doors were locked, Jesus
> came and stood among them, saying "Peace be with you!" Then he said
> to Thomas, "Reach your finger here; look at my hands. Reach your hand
> here and put it into my side. Be unbelieving no longer, but believe."
> Thomas said, "My Lord and my God!" Jesus said to him, "Because you
> have seen me you have found faith. Happy are they who find faith with-
> out seeing me."

This passage is not merely a remarkable gloss on empiricism and a consequent critique of empiricism, as Dickinson indicates; it also sets up a complex irony of faith in which the reader notes that Christ, though not "present" materially, overhears the specific tests Thomas demands to justify belief. Christ gives Thomas tangible evidence of his wounds consequent to a completely immaterial appearance—his walking through the doors and walls to stand in the midst of the disciples.

In his *Doubting Thomas* of 1602 or 1603, Michelangelo Merisi da Caravaggio, the great practitioner of painting as immediate touch and gesture, plays with the dynamic between the surface of the skin and the surface of the paint. Through touch he represents a touch that penetrates the reality of the representation itself. We could in fact only discover that this wound, like all painted wounds, is a trompe l'oeil effect on the skin of the painting by placing our finger where Thomas has placed his. What does Thomas doubt? He doubts the resurrection of the body; he doubts that what was dead can now be alive, that the presentation can contradict the inevitable unidirectionality of time as it is known through the inevitable death of the subject. Caravaggio's composition provides a subtle gloss on the transitivity and intransitivity of touch as well. The four heads are clustered in a central diamond and three pairs of eyes are directed to the wound, while Thomas is depicted as being either oblivious to the visual dimensions of the wound or in fact literally blind. There is also a complication of agency in the depiction of the hands. Is it Christ's left hand that supports and directs the crooked index finger of Thomas? And is Thomas's splayed left hand, as it parallels the open position of Christ's supporting hand, somehow continuous as well with the arm of the disciple behind him? How are we to read the blank shallow tear in Thomas's cloak in relation to the replete and profound tear in the flesh of Christ? The visual geometry of such a work, the overall organization of the visual field, cannot be readily abstracted from the relation between the painter's work of hand and eye and the viewer's engagement with the multiple depictions of eyes and hands.

Ortega y Gassett's emphasis on the proximate and distant finds its source in the most elemental painterly gestures of production. The deictic gesture, the *monstans*, sets aside just as in the representations of traced hands making up some of the earliest Western paintings presentation itself is presented. The prehensile hand represents its own opened state.[33] There is something of this in the complex confusion of subject and object that ensues from the simple exercise of touching one of our hands with the other.[34] And it continues in such issues of art history as Wölfflin's account of the progress from linear to painterly style as a movement from the tactile apprehension of things in space to a mode of visual contemplation. Yet the work of the hand—the smooth, cold sculptural effects of Michelangelo's paintings; the enameled surfaces of Mannerism; the relief effects of painted detail in prequattrocento Italian and seventeenth-century Dutch painting; the visible brushwork of Titian and Tintoretto—is so often present, even if its appearance is repressed by the illusions of surface it has created or by a mandate of distanced viewing.

II. TOUCH IN AESTHETIC FORMS

Keats's "This Living Hand" is a work found written on a manuscript page of his unfinished satire "The Cap and Bells" (begun in 1819) after his death in 1821:

This living hand, now warm and capable
Of earnest grasping, would, if it were cold
And in the icy silence of the tomb,
So haunt thy days and chill thy dreaming nights
That thou wouldst wish thine own heart dry of blood
So in my veins red life might stream again,
And thou be conscience-calmed—see here it is—
I hold it toward you.[35]

The poem makes bold use of the motility of touch, crossing the threshold between death and life, tomb and flesh, the inanimate and the animate, proleptically anticipating its reception and the retrospective consequences that will be evoked by that moment. If this living hand were dead, it would so haunt the living addressee that he or she would wish his or her own life to pass back into the hand and revive it and so assuage the troubled conscience the maker anticipates. The poem itself bears a frame connoting warmth (the first two lines and last two lines) that surrounds an icy center: it demonstrates the seed of death in all living things by means of a showing forth left as evidence after the speaker himself is gone. The poem's many shifts—temperature changes, from warmth to ice; the transition from dryness to fluidity, from icy silence to red streaming life—are worked within an envelope structure that emphasizes all the more the relation between the opening gesture and the closing one—the latter made slow and emphatic by the spondees necessary to complete the pentameter pattern, a device we saw Keats using as well in "La Belle Dame sans Merci." Severed from the living Keats, the poem, in his hand and representing his hand, seems to animate metonymically his living spirit.

Face-to-face forms, regardless of their media, bring forward a desire to touch, a compulsion to be in proximity to the material of the work of art even as they require the receiver to orbit between absorption and withdrawal.[36] Keats's poem particularly is evocative of the play between looking and touching, opening and closing, at work in any art taking the form of a box or container. Horace wrote in his *De Arte poetica* 268: "vos exemplaria Graeca nocturna versate manu, versate diurna" (For yourselves, handle the Greek models by night, handle them by day). Horace held that "with fingers and ear [poets] can catch the lawful rhythm."[37] Once poetry is a written form, it can be opened or closed, hidden or revealed, as a physical object. We recognize the handwriting of the person as we hear the grain in the voice. In a manuscript, as the name indicates, the work has been touched or shaped by an intending hand. Analogously, the earliest publications of poems in English were often presented with titles conferred by copyists, editors, commentators, translators, printers, publishers, or booksellers indicating both the completed thinglike aspect of the work and its conferral on the reader as recipient, as we can see, for example, in the titles of Sir Thomas Wyatt's poems in *Tottel's Miscellany* of 1557, such as "The lover sheweth how he is forsaken of such as he sometime enjoyed" or "Of his love called Anna."[38]

We recorded earlier Hopkins's tentative and fearful touching of his sonnets of desolation. Dickinson's manuscripts are similarly complex records of the speed and patience by which she created her poems, later gathering and sewing them into fascicles that she would store away like cherished objects in a chest of drawers.[39] The word *fascicle* extends from such small written or printed pamphlets to its botanical uses, indicating a tight cluster or bundle of flowers or leaves. And from the myriad miscellanies called "bouquets" to Whitman's *Leaves of Grass*, the poet's assembled work is envisioned as an offering of this type.

John Clare, the early nineteenth-century English rural poet, left in his journals and other autobiographical writings many accounts of his tactile relation to his own poems and those of others: he often would write his verses inside the crown of his hat, or carry slips of paper covered with lines in his pockets until they fell apart from wear, or paste broadsides up as Christmas decorations: "the cottage windows and the picture ballads on the wall all stuck with Ivy Holly Box & Yew."[40] Clare made a collection of his poems and called it "The Midsummer Cushion," explaining it was "a very old custom among villagers in summertime to stick a piece of greensward full of field flowers and place it as an ornament in their cottages which ornaments are called Midsummer Cushions."[41] In handicrafts that are two-sided, such as embroidery and rug making, there is often a front for viewing and a back that shows evidence of touching and making. Whether we are thinking of paintings on canvas or the reliefs on sarcophagi, all visual forms, including the visual forms of poetry, have as well a tactile dimension that comes into play even if it is repressed.

Of all the senses, touch is most linked to emotion and feeling. To be "touched" or "moved" by words or things implies the process of identification and separation by which we apprehend the world aesthetically. I have noted that we do not see our eyes when we see or hear our ears when we hear, but tactile perception involves perception of our own bodily state as we take in what is outside that state. The pressure involved in touch is a pressure on ourselves as well as on objects.[42] Although the hand is paramount, no particular organ is exclusively associated with touch; rather, the entire surface of the body is touch's instrument. The early mutuality of the mother's nipple and the child's mouth is the paradigm for the reciprocity found in all tactile experiences and for the triangulation between gaze, utterance, and touch.[43]

Merleau-Ponty draws, in his *Phenomenology of Perception*, a parallel between passivity and activity in touch and vision:

> It is true that the visible object is in front of us and not on our eye, but we have seen that in the last resort the visible position, size or shape are determined by the direction, scope and hold which our gaze has upon them. It is true that passive touch (for example, touch inside the ear or nose and generally in all parts of the body ordinarily covered) tells us hardly anything but the state of our own body and almost nothing about the object. Even on the most sensitive parts of our tactile surface, pressure without movement produces a scarcely identifiable phenomenon. But there is also passive vision, with no gaze specifically directed, as in the case of a dazzling light, which does not unfold an objective space before us, and in which the light ceases to be light and becomes something painful which invades our eye itself. And like the exploratory gaze of true vision, the "knowing touch" projects us outside our own body through movement. When one of my hands touches the other, the hand that moves functions as subject and the other as object. . . . Movement and time are not only an objective condition of knowing touch, but a phenomenal component of tactile data.[44]

Tactual perception gives us information about our own bodily states. We can distinguish between transitive acts of touch, involving clear patterns of causality and intention and various intransitive situations of touch, in which bodily feeling is affected in a complex way and may even involve hallucinatory tactility, instances of referred pain, and tactual afterimages. In reality the situation is quite mutual, with distinctions between intransitive and transitive states easily blurred.[45] As happens when we touch one hand with another, we can move between feelings of subjectivity and objectivity, between sensations that are localizable and those that are dispersed; we experience a confirmation of our state of being and alienation from it at once.

Touching by means of the skin is often mediated by an appendage: follicles of hairs and roots of nails. In animals, claws, horns, and hooves are wrapped in nerve fibers. The skin itself is in fact a three-dimensional object. What can this object register in contact with other objects? As color is only visible, temperature is only tangible. Qualities of roughness and smoothness; sticky things that remain in contact with the skin and slippery things that move readily across it; qualities of wetness and dampness and dryness in relation to each other; heaviness and lightness, hardness and softness; clues as to position and state of motion.[46] When we list such qualities, they come to mind as the names of sensations particular to tactility. But just as we saw the synaesthesia linking sound and color, so can these tactile qualities be taken up in forms of presentation that we often think of as dominantly visual. The sculptural approximation and use of effects of wind and water or the wetness, dampness, dryness, hardness, and softness of paint itself are obvious examples. We have only to think of the use of these possibilities in the work of Willem de Kooning[47] or of Emil Nolde's 1909 account of painting as a going over into the erasure of painting: "I was no longer satisfied with the way I drew and painted during the last few years, imitating nature and creating form all done preferably with the first stroke, the first brushful of paint. I rubbed and scratched the paper until I tore holes in it, trying to reach something else, something more profound, to grasp the very essence of things."[48]

There are, it is true, a few forms that can be considered to be purely visual objects. But even holographs, rainbows, and images in dreams are consequent to certain physical processes in the world. To be in contact with an object means to be moved by it—to have the pressure of its existence brought into a relation with the pressure of our own bodily existence. And this pressure perceived by touch involves an actual change; we are changed and so is the object. As we noted in chapter 1, Aristotle had suggested in *De Anima* that seeing and tasting could also be forms of touch; touch thus mediated the relation between the higher external senses and the lower incorporative senses.[49] Touch thereby continues its dual trajectory of going out and bringing in; in the "shuttle" of visual perception, we have a gestural enactment of the coming and going of deixis, motions that articulate the point of contact.

Whereas Hegel described the human gestures stored in the made object, Heidegger took this in a certain metaphysical and ethical direction, arguing that the things we handle will always reciprocate the treatment we administer to them. When our gestures are caring, the Heideggerean contends, they receive back a deeper disclosure of their ontological truth, and the same result follows from gestural involvements with others.[50] Hence, a key difference between the temporal immediacy of visual perception under the grid of single-point perspective and the spatial immediacy of tactile impressions is the latter's motility. To experience the roughness or smoothness of an object, to examine its physical position or come to understand its relative temperature or moistness, we must move, turn, take time. Visual perception can immediately organize a field; tactile perception requires temporal comparison. We may say in fact that visual perception becomes a mode of touching when comparisons are made and the eye is "placed upon" or "falls upon" relations between phenomena.

This temporal aspect of touching also implicitly bears a notion of causality. The pressure we feel when touching a material thing—a pressure toward and against the thing and toward and against ourselves—brings about an idea of causality, of something having happened or made another thing to happen. Only touch yields immediate perception of pressure. We sometimes perform actions tactfully—by "touch" or "feel"; to this extent touching is also doing in a way unique to touch as a sense. Indeed, some of our distinction between seeing and doing relies on this difference between vision and touch.

The transitivity and motility of touch are key to all legends and myths of animation. Because immediate tactual perception involves contact between a sensitive portion of the body and the things perceived, it also involves perception of this contact itself. There is a carrying over from experience to experience of the experience, a kind of doubling that finds its illustration in the image of a living thing bringing a dead thing to life through the transitivity of touch. We might consider here the complex relation the four elements have to our capacity for touching. Wind and water press against us and move us, but they cannot be grasped. By flying and floating we can have some sense of mastery over our contact with these elements, but we cannot contain them in our hands for more than a moment. Fire's contagion, radiating from a central point or source, is the opposite of such fleetingness—when we play with fire we are threatened with our own dissolution. Fire purifies and so resolves the danger of touching taboo substances, but its purification is at best transformation and at worst destruction—a destruction worked on particular objects in particular times and places. Wind and water, in contrast, constantly erode the world: they are mutability itself producing mutability.

But it is earth that grounds us, ready to be traced by our footsteps and marked by our impressions. In his pairing of individual senses with particular elements, Aristotle, we remember, wrote that touch corresponded to earth. In its hardest form, as stony flint, earth is the touchstone used for fire; in its softest form, as mud, it is as mutable as water and at the same time, in its formlessness, ready to be shaped by our hands.[51] Wind and water disappear and erase all evidence of our existence: earth is shaped and shapes us and takes our form into itself after death. Wind comes to us, we search for water, we must make or escape fire, yet earth is always waiting. Herman Melville's powerful poem of 1891, "Fragments of a Lost Gnostic Poem of the Twelfth Century," is meant, as a fragment, to represent the irreducibility of matter and at the same time speaks about the irreducibility of matter. Human activity, whether expressed through reproduction (the first stanza) or moral action or inaction (the second stanza) has no consequence on matter's "ancient brutal claim":

> Found a family, build a state,
> The pledged event is still the same.
> Matter in end will never abate
> His ancient brutal claim.
>
> Indolence is heaven's ally here.
> And hungry the child of hell:
> The good man pouring from his pitcher clear
> But brims the poisoned well.[52]

The poem's aphoristic form lends it the authority of inscription, but at the same time its stasis as a fragment undermines the integrity of its pronouncements. Given the futility of human attempts to alter the "ancient brutal claims" of this world's facticity, Melville, with considerable bitterness, prescribes indolence and restraint.

Inscriptions are meant to resist weather, yet at the same time, of course, they are being worn away by wind and water. And stone is stone uniformly through its substance. A shell has an exterior—and what seem to be sound and hidden life lie inside. When the shell is broken open, the life is vulnerable and exposed, the "sound" dispersed. When we write on stone, we try to open a space for our voices in that "never abating" hardness. Near the close of Andrew Marvell's "The Nymph Complaining for the Death of Her Faun," the nymph predicts:

> For I so truly thee bemoane,
> That I shall weep though I be Stone:
> Until my Tears, still dropping, wear
> My breast, themselves engraving there.[53]

Where the statue weeps her own inscription, a transposition of interior and exterior occurs: The tears will *wear* the breast; as the breast displays the tears, the tears break down the exterior shell of the body and unfreeze its deadly fixity.

An intriguing and related problem is posed by the depiction of rain and snow and wind in poems and paintings. Rain and snow and wind cannot be represented in sculpture except as the representation of effects of abrasion, ruin, and fragmentation. But in poems and paintings these phenomena present particular foreground–background conundrums. Wind is sound in three-dimensional space, yet it cannot be represented in two dimensions. In a poem, wind is often the background, the source, from which the poet literally draws inspiration. We have only to think of the powerful role the wind plays in poems of the British Romantic tradition, such as Shelley's "Ode to the West Wind" or Keats's "Ode to Autumn." Rain can serve in a poem as an unorganized rhythm, a nonpattern in which the pattern of the poem is immersed and from which it arises in relief. In Robert Creeley's beautiful lyric, "The Rain," the closing line dissolves the threshold between inner feeling and sense impression: "Be wet with a decent happiness." Verlaine's classic poem of identification between rain and tears, "Il pleut doucement sur la ville," the third of his "Romances sans Paroles," addresses directly the sympathy between mood and rain that is perhaps our physical response to the changing ionization of the air—an explanation that does not "explain" the emotions that rain evokes so much as it deepens the mystery of that connection:

III. Il pleut doucement sur la ville
     —Arthur Rimbaud

    Il pleure dans mon coeur
    Comme il pleut sur la ville.
    Quelle est cette langueur
    Qui pénètre mon coeur?

    O bruit doux de la pluie
    Par terre et sur les toits!
    Pour un coeur qui c'ennuie,
    O le chant de la pluie!

    Il pleure sans raison
    Dans ce coeur qui s'écoeure
    Quoi! nulle trahison?
    Ce deuil est sans raison.

    C'est bien la pire peine
    De ne savoir pourquoi,
    Sans amour et sans haine,
    Mon coeur a tant de peine![54]

In a painting such as Van Gogh's *Enclosed Field in the Rain*, in which horizontal slashing lines of blue-green move across the surface of the painting like a screen, or those Japanese wood-cuts in which white dots flood the foreground as images of snow, the natural elements restrict the frame of artifice of the work. Representations of rain and snow erase the fixity of outline: they promote the recession of the integrity of the form as they heighten the effect of the foreground through which seeing is finally noticed as seeing. Yet rain is to tears as snow is to silence. When rain increases and diminishes in density, it increases and diminishes in sound. As tears can themselves produce tears, the sound of rain seems to produce more sound incrementally when it echoes and bounces off wet and resonating surfaces. But snow gathers and disappears in silence. As Dickinson wrote of snow in "It sifts from leaden sieves" (1892), snow "stills its Artisans like Ghosts / —Denying they have been." [55]

Shifts between activity and passivity, subjective agency and objective matter, are the physiological equivalent of the shift between subject and object positions in deixis. It is not simply an issue of the simultaneous appearance and dependent relation of the two positions—it is always also a matter of the shift itself, of the capacity for reciprocity that is the foundation for the intersubjective experience of communicability or intelligibility. One hand or the other can be subject or object; one "I" or the other can take the position of the "you"; one speaker or the other can become the listener—indeed, each is in waiting upon the other, anticipating the other. The capacity for movement and temporality is intrinsically bound to the capacity for touching and transformation.

This emphasis on process led Levinas to emphasize touch as the central device of ritual. Touch is nonteleological; it begins and goes forward without anticipating any particular point of arrival. For Levinas, the caress is the ultimate example of such nonteleological touching: "the seeking of the caress constitutes its essence by the fact that the caress does not know what it seeks." [56] Touch is the paradigm for the reciprocal open-endedness of all art forms involving the representation of persons. As in the identification and separation necessary to any form of catharsis, the hand touching its companion must know the connection in order to know the separation. Being is spoken through the words of the other: when one is loved, one is "spoken for." [57]

Rilke captures a great deal of the endlessly open and endlessly wandering capability of touch in his poem "Handinneres," which begins:

Innres der Hand. Sohle, die nicht mehr geht
als auf Gefühl. Die sich nach oben hält
und im Spiegel
himmlische Straßen empfängt, die selber

wandelnden.
Die gelernt hat, auf Wasser zu gehn,
wenn sie schöpft,
die auf den Brunnen geht,
aller Wege Verwandlerin.

Here are these lines in Stephen Mitchell's translation, "Palm":

Interior of the hand. Sole that has come to walk
only on feelings. That faces upward
and in its mirror
receives heavenly roads, which travel
along themselves.
That has learned to walk upon water
when it scoops,
that walks upon wells,
transfiguring every path.[58]

The English version cannot really capture the ways in which Rilke has orchestrated the falls, pauses, and echoes of the sound of the poem in such clusters as *geht, Gefühl, hält, gehn, geht* and *selber, wandelnden, Verwandlerin, wandert.* Rilke—secretary to Rodin; poet of things, who wrote of music as the "breathing of statues"—describes the hand as if it were as mutable as those elements it encounters—its interior and surface, its capacity for extension, enclosure, and traversal, and, most of all, the dynamic between transitivity and intransitivity in the hand's movements.

The ontology of myths of animation may lie in the absolute fact that only material substances can provide us with adequate sustenance—only material substances can be the fuel for our own animation as living beings. Our living bodies require contact with living bodies in order to survive and grow. Part of the power of Keats's "This Living Hand" is its implicit premise that even if death might be contagious, the power of love might bring red life back to another, a narrative we also know through the story of Sleeping Beauty. In the narrative of Doubting Thomas, we find a temporal recasting of an earlier scene in which Christ had met Mary Magdalene at a moment between his death and his ascension, telling her "Noli me tangere."[59] Caravaggio shows us the living Christ after the Resurrection; in this meeting, it is Christ who is animating Thomas. Statues may bleed or weep like Marvell's nymph, and such liquification is often preparatory to, or follows upon, their emergence as *speakers.* In this sense, the animation of stone is a projection of an extreme version of the renovation that occurs whenever we voice prior voices. Paul Ricoeur describes this process precisely as a matter of calling on the resources of language in order to fill and awaken a void in ourselves: "speech is itself the reanimation of a certain linguistic knowledge which comes from the previous words of other men, words which are deposited, 'sedimented,' 'instituted,' so as to become the available *credit* by which I can now endow with verbal flesh this oriented void in me (which is signifying intention) when I want to speak." [60]

In Ovid's version of the Pygmalion legend, touch and impression are key elements of the scene of awakening: "She seemed warm; he laid his lips on hers again, and touched her breast with his hands—at his touch the ivory lost its hardness, and grew soft; his fingers made an imprint on the yielding surface, just as wax of Hymettus melts in the sun and, worked by men's fingers, is fashioned into many different shapes, and made fit for us by being used. . . . The veins throbbed as he pressed them with his thumb. . . . At long last, he pressed his lips upon living lips, and the girl felt the kisses he gave her, and blushed." [61] In granting Pygmalion's prayers to give him a lover like the ivory statue, Venus does not present him with a fait accompli; Pygmalion must touch in order to be touched, must move in order to be moved. A blush is an involuntary physical response, but it is a response that is an index to consciousness. Ovid typically does not let too much happen too quickly.

In his enlightening book on "the dream of the moving statue," Kenneth Gross points out that in the tradition of associating touch with the bestowal of life, "it is the illusions and self-alienations of touch, rather than its apparent claim to subjective certainty, that many of the stories dwell on." He cites, among other examples, the case of Jean-Jacques Rousseau's *Scène lyrique pygmalion*. Galatea, the statue, awakens and touches herself: "C'est moi," she says, and turning to the block of marble, "Ce n'est plus moi." But when she touches her creator she finds only more of herself: "Ah, encore moi!" [62]

Condillac seeks in his treatise on sensation to show how modifications of the mind, or impressions received through the senses, can give rise to all mental ideas. He suggests that a marble statue, first closed and then opened to the external world, will acquire intellectual life and will by being endowed with the senses one at a time. First, he would give the statue odor so that it would not confuse the external world with the mind's modification of it—olfactory sensation would involve first perception, then attention, or focused sensation, and then memory, as well as judgment as to agreeableness or disagreeableness. Second, he would give the statue touch. By touch Condillac has in mind both kinesthesia (our internal sensations of the body) and the felt pressure of the body on an outward object. Through touch the statue would come to know itself as subject and object and to an awareness of the external world. Condillac holds that touch is the "teaching" sense; in exploring the world through touch, the statue would come to associate seeing, hearing, and tasting with relations of proximity and distance.[63] In Condillac's thought, as in the legend of Galatea, touch and the reciprocal motility of touch are the beginning of agency. The sense of attachment, touch is in Condillac's model the most important vehicle for our access to reality.

It is a cliché of contemporary culture to consider our lives as increasingly dominated by visuality. Yet if we review the history of our relation to the muses, we can in fact see that whereas a great shift seems to have taken place from the tactile to the visual, at the same time a residual desire to empathize with, and animate, the visual through tactile means is everywhere apparent. There is a distinct tradition of valorizing the directness of touch over the distance of visual perception. David Summers, in his study of Renaissance naturalism and aesthetics, *The Judgment of Sense*, explains that Aristotle had written that sight can correct the errors caused by other senses but that touch was the most exact of human senses. Juan Luis Vives, in his *Opera Omnia* of 1782, argues that touch may verify the falsity of illusion of relief in painting, for example.[64] Robert Mandrou gives a complementary account of the priority of touch in his history of early modern France, arguing that "Until at least the eighteenth century touch remained one of the master senses; it checked and confirmed what sight could only bring to one's notice. It unified perception, giving solidity to the impressions provided by other senses, which were not as reliable."[65] And in claiming that "the sense of touch, when trained, can become more delicate than sight," Diderot writes in his 1749 "Letter on the Blind for the Use of Those Who See" that "a blind people might have sculptors and put statues to the same use as among us to perpetuate the memory of great deeds, and of persons dear to them: and in my opinion feeling such statutes would give them a keener pleasure than we have in seeing them. What a delight to a passionate lover to draw his hand over beauties which he would know again, when illusion, which would act more potently on the blind than on those who see, should come to reanimate them! But perhaps, as he would take a deeper pleasure in the memory, his grief would be the keener for the loss of the original."[66]

Museums are designated as sanctified and inspiring places. The showing forth that takes place, literally, in the museum space is a consequence of a series of gestures and actions, and these in turn evoke a set of gestural responses on the part of the viewer. There is, of course, a sense in which

museums are institutions organized around an elaborately ritualized practice of refraining from touch. Children early on learn this rule that they
must not touch works of art unless they are themselves the makers or
have been granted an exceptional permission—that what in fact distinguishes the architecture of a museum from its holdings is the taxonomy
of what can and cannot be touched. Also, museums are guarded against all
practices of touching, ranging from breathing on the artwork to stealing it.
The museum's customary velvet ropes may be seen as compensatory in
this sense. Yet in the ways in which the museum organizes seeing into
looking and so organizes a passive into an active relation—one capable of
transforming the motion of the spectator into emotional response—the
museum retains a vestigial relation to touch as the primary sense for the
apprehension of powerful matter or material.

The prehistory and early history of the institution of the museum often provide accounts of touch. Gregory of Nyssa, for example, wrote in his
fourth-century account of the reverence of saints' relics in his "In Praise
of Theodore the Great Martyr":

> These spectacles strike the senses and delight the eye by drawing us near
> to [the martyr's] tomb which we believe to be both a sanctification and
> blessing. If anyone takes dust from the martyr's resting place, it is a gift
> and a deserving treasure. Should a person have both the good fortune and
> permission to touch the relics, this experience is a highly valued prize
> and seems like a dream both to those who were cured and whose wish
> was fulfilled. The body appears as if it were alive and healthy: the eyes,
> mouth, ears, as well as the other sensations are a cause for pouring out
> tears of reverence and emotion. In this way one implores the martyr who
> intercedes on our behalf and is an attendant of God for imparting those
> favors and blessings which people seek.[67]

The later role of display and touch with regard to the shrines holding relics
of saints and other cultic objects in the pre-Renaissance culture of Europe
has been described by Stephen Bann. He quotes Erasmus's *Peregrinatio
Religionis Ergo* as to how the prior at the shrine of Becket in Canterbury
Cathedral, which Erasmus would have visited between 1512 and 1514,
would point out the jewels of the reliquary by touching them with a white
rod, adding each jewel's French name, its worth, and the name of the do-
nor. Bann emphasizes how this gesture survives in the discursive narrative attached to the objects in any display or collection.[68]

By the time of the Council of Trent (1545–1563), a practice for the worship of relics is set forward by the church in an effort to revive the relation

of believers to church doctrine and the rhetorical power of these practices is carried over into the paintings, sculptures, and architectural forms of the Counter-Reformation more generally. At the twenty-fifth session of the council, on 4 December 1563, a decree was issued "On the Invocation, Veneration, and Relics of Saints and on Sacred Images." The decree stated that "images of Christ, of the virgin Mother of God, and of the other saints are to be placed and retained especially in the churches, and that due honor and veneration is to be given them; not, however, that any divinity or virtue is believed to be in them by reason of which they are to be venerated, or that something is to be asked of them, or that trust is to be placed in images, as was done of old by the Gentiles who placed their hope in idols; but because they represent, so that by means of the images which we kiss and before which we uncover the head and prostrate ourselves, we adore Christ and venerate the saints whose likeness they bear."

The church immediately recognizes that the boundary between likeness and referent might slip away and the observer will confuse the image with the subject of adoration. Those untutored observers the church was particularly eager to reach through its art commissions were at the same time the source of this worry:

> And if at times it happens, when this is beneficial to the illiterate, that the stories and narratives of the Holy Scriptures are portrayed or exhibited, the people should be instructed that not for that reason is the divinity represented in pictures as if it can be seen with bodily eyes or expressed in colors or figures. Furthermore, in the invocation of the saints, the veneration of relics and the sacred use of images, all superstition shall be removed, all filthy quest for gain eliminated, and all lasciviousness avoided, so that the images shall not be painted or adorned with a seductive charm, or the celebration of saints and the visitation of relics be perverted by the people into boisterous festivities and drunkenness, as if the festivals in honor of the saints are to be celebrated with revelry and with no sense of decency.[69]

Yet sacred aesthetic objects are not the only recipients of immediate tactile responses. In a recent essay, Richard Wrigley describes the emphasis on close physical engagement with sculptures in eighteenth-century French salons. He mentions drawings by Gabriel de St. Aubin that "celebrate such contact in the way that they show spectators being closely intertwined with the works, turning them almost into extensions of their own bodies. This has the effect of emphasizing the sculpture's sensual presence, and also the physical engagement involved in viewing small sculptures displayed on the same level as the standing spectators, heightened by the nudity of sculptural forms." He concludes that touching sculptures was evidently not unusual before the 1780s when practices developed to protect works within arm's reach from public spectators.[70]

In Sophie von la Roche's 1786 *Diary* of her travels in London, she speaks at length of her delight in exploring William Hamilton's collection of Roman and Etrurian antiquities in the British Museum, writing:

> With what sensations one handles a Carthaginian helmet excavated near Capua, household utensils from Herculaneum . . . lachrymary vessels from the graves of Magna Graeca. . . . There are mirrors, too, belonging to Roman matrons, golden earrings, necklaces, and bracelets. With one of these mirrors in my hand I looked amongst the urns, thinking meanwhile "Maybe chance has preserved amongst these remains some part of the dust from the fine eyes of a Greek or Roman lady, who so many centuries ago surveyed herself in the mirror, trying to discover whether the earrings and necklet before me suited her or not." Nor could I restrain my desire to touch the ashes of an urn on which a female figure was being mourned. I felt it gently, with great feeling, between my fingers, but found much earth mixed with it. The thought "Thou divided, I integral dust am still," moved me greatly, and in the end I thought it must be sympathy which had caused me to pick this one from so many urns to whose ashes a good, sensitive soul had once given life. This idea affected me, and again I pressed the grain of dust between my fingers tenderly, just as her best friend might once have grasped her hand, complaining that she had but ill reward for her kindness, or that her best intentions were misread. And gently I returned the particle I had taken to the rest of the dust, murmuring to myself, "Forgive Hamilton and me for breaking in on your peace." I had become quite attached to that ash and would have liked to bury it somewhere, so as to prevent its being shaken up and fingered again; but how was I to shield that which had been taken from its mother's womb one thousand years ago?[71]

In museums today, when we turn quickly from the untouchable artwork to the written account or explanation placed beside it, we pursue a connection no longer available to us: the opportunity to press against the work of art or valued object. As public museums and forms of collective memory supersede devotion and private manipulation, the contagious magic of touch is replaced by the sympathetic magic of visual representation. There is a paradox of materiality here: the precious metals and materials of art objects are precious precisely because of their durability and because they are divisible without loss of value. Nevertheless, materials also become precious because they must be conserved or maintained with care in order to exist; they store our labor and our maintenance of them is a stay against the erosion of time. Those works of art that we cannot touch are repositories of touch and care—the touch and care of their makers and conservators. Our engagement through looking is a ritualized practice of restraint and attention. Rather than assume the historical triumph of distantiated vision in the apprehension of artworks, as so many theories of modernity and postmodernity do, we might instead continue to consider the constant play among deixis, tact, proximity, and negation that is at work in the sensual creation and apprehension of all aesthetic forms. Henri Focillon has written on "the touch" in this regard with particular elegance, suggesting "the touch . . . represents a single moment in which the tool awakens form in the substance, and it represents permanence, since because of it form has structure and durability. The touch does, to be sure, conceal what it has done: it becomes hidden and quiescent. But underneath any hard and fast continuity, as for example, a glaze in painting, we must and we can always detect it. Then it is that a work of art regains its precious living quality."[72]

Focillon may have taken this idea from an earlier text by an artist who knew well the dynamic between concealment and awakening in poetry and sculpture. In the first stanza of his celebrated sonnet "Non ha l'ottimo artista," Michelangelo writes that every conceit and concept the sculptor might have already lies hidden in the block:

Non ha l'ottimo artista alcun concetto
ch'un marmo solo in sé non circoscriva
col suo soverchio, e solo a quello arriva
la man che obbedisce all'intelletto.

(The greatest artist does not have any concept that a single piece of marble does not itself contain within its excess, though only a hand that obeys the intellect can discover it.)[73] Here Michelangelo's speculations regarding the life within stones follow Dante's "Rime petrose" and the story of the second creation, after the flood, in Ovid's *Metamorphoses*. In Ovid's account, Deucalion and Pyrrha follow Themis's allegorical advice to repair the destruction of man by "throw[ing] behind you the bones of your great mother." When they realize the "bones of their great mother" are the stones in the body of the earth, "they went down the hillside, veiled their heads, loosened their tunics, and threw the stones behind them, as they had been bidden. . . . The stones began to lose their hardness and rigidity, and after a little while, grew soft. Then, once softened they acquired a definite shape. When they had grown in size, and developed a tenderer nature, a certain likeness to a human form could be seen, though it was still not clear; they were like marble images, begun but not yet properly chiselled out, or like unfinished statues."[74]

One of the most remarkable poetic meditations on the relations between the stillness of objects and the capacity of art for animation is Goethe's "Roman Elegy," usually numbered "VII." This work is one of a series of erotic poems stemming from the poet's Roman sojourn in early 1788; the series was completed in Weimar in 1790. The elegies as a whole break with the acceptable conventions for love poems of Goethe's day and return to the Roman conventions of "quinque lineae amoris"—the five stages of erotic encounter: *visus* (seeing); *allocutio* (addressing); *tactus* (touching); *basium* (kissing); *coitus* (union). Goethe's guides in this regard are the Latin erotic poets Catullus (84–54 B.C.), Tibullus (48–19 B.C.) and Sextus Propertius (48–15 B.C.), those the Renaissance aesthetician Julius Caesar Scaliger called the "triumviri amoris" and whom Goethe cites particularly at the end of the elegy.[75]

Elegy VII is a marvel of animation. The speaker himself begins in the deictic "now" as a kind of speaking statue in the initial line: "Froh empfind ich mich nun auf klassischem Boden begeistert." Then, charmed and enchanted by the apparition of the past within his present circumstances, he follows the Horatian mandate to hold the works of the ancients in his hands—here by a displacement of one step: as Horace held the Greeks, Goethe holds the Romans:

> Vor- und Mitwelt spricht lauter und reizender mir.
> Hier befolg ich den Rat, durchblättre die Werke der Alten
> Mit geschäftiger Hand, täglich mit neuem Genuß.

What that gesture reveals is the relation between dead stone, the marble of statues, and the living animate flesh of his lover. While she lies suspended in sleep, his love can be watched over without reciprocity, as one observes a statue. She is the perfect metaphor for his engagement with the past as a living entity and indeed, her back is the tabula upon which he taps out his classical hexameters. She is at the same time a silent "thing" of erotic contemplation to be presented or exchanged between the speaker and his precursors in the tribe of male poets. Nevertheless, her breathing is a sign of life, and the immateriality of her breath pierces the depths of the speaker's heart, serving as the source of his literally inspired ability to "sehe mit fühlendem Aug, fühle mit sehenden Hand." The poem's eroticism, like the figure of Eros himself here trimming the lamp, is in the service of awakening the past to a living connection to the dead and enabling the speaker to move his verse making into the grace of a truly felt, and not merely observed, relation.

Indeed, Goethe may be taking a device directly from Propertius, who frequently wrote of inanimate things coming alive into speech. For example, Propertius's Elegy I.16 is spoken from the point of view of, and in the voice of, "ianua Patriciae vota Pudicitiae" (a door vowed to Patrician chastity). This elegy is another instance of *paraclausithyron*—like Sappho's "phainetai moi" and Cowper's cries at the bolted door to hell, an "excluded lover's complaint." But here Propertius cleverly has the door itself complain about the racket sent up by the excluded lover, who cries, "O that a word of mine might pass through an open crack, and reach and strike upon my sweetheart's ears! Though she be more impassive even than Sicilian lava, though she be harder even than iron and steel, yet she will not be able to control her eyes, and sobs will arise amid involuntary tears. Now she lies cradled in the happy arms of another, while my words fall unheeded in the night wind."[76]

In Elegy IV.7, Cynthia's ghost comes to the poet: "I dreamt that Cynthia, who had lately been buried to the drone of the funeral trumpet, was leaning over my bed when after my love's interment sleep hovered over me and I bemoaned the cold empire of my bed. Her hair, her eyes, were the same as when she was borne to the grave: her dress was charred at the side, and the fire had gnawed at the familiar beryl on her finger, and Lethe's water had withered her lips. But it was a living voice and spirit that emerged as her brittle fingers cracked with a snap of her thumb." Cynthia lashes into a bitter speech against Propertius for his neglect at the time of her death and funeral, and delivers a testament to him. In another elegy (IV.11), Cornelia addresses her husband Paullus from the grave, delivering a similar, if far less furious, testament, though all she is "now can be gathered with the fingers of one hand."

As these dead figures come to life and speech, Propertius also frames their words within a convention that declares that the speech itself could then be turned into inert materiality by being engraved on a funeral stone.[77] In this continuing tradition from the Roman triumvirs of love to Goethe's Roman elegies, we see lyric poets using tactility to move their audiences and at the same time to animate the artwork beyond its status as a mere artifact. Yet we might also remember that Goethe was contemporaneously writing his *Faust* (as he was, indeed, through most of his life), and he names his mysterious Roman mistress Faustina. Most likely a young widow with a child, she represents a living link with both the past and the future. The exhaustion Faust suffers as a consequence of his pursuit of empty technology and instrumental knowledge, the wasteful spirit with which he trades his intellectual gifts for endless jokes and tricks, is remedied here by poetry as a state of temporal grace, where the dead come to life and the living are connected organically to the past.

III. Vertigo: The Legacy of Baroque Ecstasy

All touch traverses the boundary between interiority and externality and reciprocally returns to the agent of touching. Touch, like dizziness, is a threshold activity—subjectivity and objectivity come quite close to each other. Just as we have a repertoire of legends of animation in which things come to life and volition is a consequence of touch, so do we have a recurring topoi of imagining the self as a thing. In the remainder of this chapter, I want to suggest that dizziness, and vertigo in particular, is the ever-present shadow of touch—the sign of the absence of grounding or anchoring and the physical manifestation of the desire to be free of internal pressure and contingency. Vertigo can be experienced whether the body is actually engaged in gross-motor movement or not—whether one apprehends the object only through eye motion or, in the end, only imagines a vertiginous motion. Vertigo can be induced by a poem or painting or moving image. To this extent, as a sense experience, it returns us dramatically to the philosophical problem of the often-disjunctive relation between sense impressions and their referents.

The three semicircular canals of the inner ear are oriented at perpendicular axes to each other, approximating the planes of three-dimensional space. This vestibular system maintains our equilibrium with relationship to movement and to the Earth's gravity. Vertigo is often defined as the sensation of spinning. A standard textbook on vertigo explains:

> [T]he fact that the vestibular sense of balance is as much one of the special senses as the traditional five of smell, touch, taste, vision and hearing is not always appreciated. Moreover, like these other senses, the balancing sense consists of sensory receptors housed in the vestibular part of the inner ear. . . . Impulses aroused in the sensory end organs of the labyrinth by movements or alternation of the position of the head are conveyed to the eyes, trunk, and limbs, and also by some as yet not clearly defined route to the posterior part of the temporal lobe, where these sensations will reach the conscious level. Throughout most of our waking and all of our walking life this sense of balance is constantly at work receiving im-

pressions and passing them on to influence the posture of the body and the movement of the limbs and eyes.[78]

In patients with psychosomatic vertigo, dizziness appears in circumstances in which an exit from the scene seems blocked; a panic reaction sets in.

Thus, vertigo is a common feature of diseases involving loss of distance judgment, such as agoraphobia and claustrophobia. Whether Dickinson's reclusiveness was a matter of agoraphobia strictly defined or not, her poems constantly refer to situations of ecstasy: the ek-stasis, or being "beside the body," that is characterized by vertiginous symptoms and that we discussed earlier in relation to poetic voice and possession with particular reference to Schiller's aesthetics. Consider, for example, her 1862 poem beginning "I would not paint—a picture—":

I would not paint—a picture—
I'd rather be the One
It's bright impossibility
To dwell—delicious—on
And wonder how the fingers feel
Whose rare—celestial—stir—
Evokes so sweet a Torment—
Such sumptuous—Despair—

I would not talk, like Cornets—
I'd rather be the One
Raised softly to the Ceilings—
And out, and easy on—
Through Villages of Ether—
Myself endued Balloon
By but a lip of Metal—
The pier to my Pontoon—

Nor would I be a Poet—
It's finer—own the Ear—
Enamored—impotent—content—
The License to revere,
A privilege so awful
What would the Dower be,
Had I the Art to stun myself
With Bolts of Melody![79]

Dickinson creates the ecstatic thinking of the poem by first, in the opening stanza, imagining herself as a thing—the picture of a being whose "rare celestial stir" is a sweet torment or sumptuous despair. By being such a picture, she could know literally and figuratively "how the fingers feel." We can see that a kind of reverse animation is taking place: the poet is not awakening inanimate matter to life but is turning Medusa's reifying gaze on herself as she projects herself into the space of the inanimate on the threshold of animation. In the second stanza, she would rather not be "like" cornets but be "the one," the sound of the cornet itself as it is raised softly to the ceiling like a balloon or pontoon—a boat of the air or a bubble of the sea, a rhyme between sounds and objects at once. She would be "out" and "on"—and so not "in" and "off." And at the close of the poem she emphasizes the "one" she would truly like to be: not the poet whose (poetic) "license" places herself within a closed sphere of obligations and privileges, an economy of reverence paid for by a currency of impotence, but the maker of an "awe-full" art that will stun or surprise her own self into transformation—an art with bolts of melody. The lightning bolt illuminates and freezes its target. Dickinson's various modes of ecstasy often imagine this carrying over of the self, this halting of haptic motion, whether she is writing of "Wild nights" where she might "moor" in another[80] or, at the end of "I felt a funeral in my brain," of how "a Plank in Reason, broke, / And I dropped down, and down— / And hit a World, at every plunge, / And Finished knowing—then—."[81] Stasis and the vertiginous are yoked in a paralysis that is in fact transporting or illuminating.

Vertigo as a phenomenon of the balance system of the inner ear in conflict with the eye, a conflict bringing about a reaction of expulsion or disgust, can be described in physiological terms as a struggle between the senses, as an aberration of the senses, and as the obverse of synesthesia or its analogue in that a presumed relation between the senses refuses coordination. Yet Dickinson's ecstasies follow a much longer tradition of Christian levitation and conversion around vertiginous experiences of "ungroundedness." Another staging of sensation might be helpful here:

Beside me, on the left hand, appeared an angel in bodily form such as I am not in the habit of seeing except very rarely. Though I often have visions of angels, I do not see them. But it was our Lord's will that I should see this angel in the following way. He was not tall but short, and very beautiful; and his face was so aflame that he appeared to be one of the highest rank of angels, who seem to be all on fire. They must be of the kind called cherubim, but they do not tell me their names. I know very well that there is a great difference between some angels and others, and between these and others still, but I could not possibly explain it. In his hands I saw a great golden spear and at the iron tip there appeared to be a point of fire. This he plunged into my heart several times so that it penetrated to my entrails. When he pulled it out, I felt that he took them with it, and left me utterly consumed by the great love of God. The pain was so severe that it made me utter several moans. The sweetness caused by this intense pain is so extreme that one cannot possibly wish it to cease, nor is one's soul then content with anything but God. This is not a physical, but a spiritual pain, though the body has some share in it—even a considerable share. So gentle is this wooing which takes place between God and the soul that if anyone thinks I am lying, I pray God in His goodness, to grant him some experience of it.[82]

This is the well-known account of the ecstasy of the sixteenth-century Spanish mystic Teresa of Avila, founder of the Order of Discalced Carmelites. It is the rhetorical account of the transmission of faith presented in such immediate sensual, even sexual, terms, despite its stated claim to spirituality, that it serves as a paradigm for the evocation of the senses made by many Counter-Reformation artworks of the next century—most specifically, Richard Crashaw's three poems on the subject, "A Hymn to the Name and Honor of the Admirable Sancte Teresa," "An Apologie for the Fore-going Hymn," and "The Flaming Heart,"[83] and Gianlorenzo Bernini's great sculpture group of *The Ecstasy of St. Teresa* in the Cornaro Chapel of Santa Maria della Vittoria in Rome. In Teresa's autobiographical writings, the Counter-Reformation has a brilliant example of the power of visual images to induce sensations of touch and the power of rhetoric to stimulate visual images of great immediacy. The reader or hearer is, in fact, so struck by the sensational aspect of the image that he or she might not at first notice its most obvious feature: that Teresa has been touched through the mediation of a single arrow—the iron arrow with a burning golden tip that converts the internal to the external and compels the saint to utter sounds. These are sounds of pain and pleasure at once and are the prelude to the spoken teachings by means of which the saint will found her order. Although Teresa has taken in the fiery arrow, it is she who has been consumed as she has been directed toward God.

In Bernini's theatrical sculpture group, the suspension of the figure, the vast portfolio of possible treatments of the surface of the stone, the transposition of left and right figures in terms of agency and reception, the immediacy of penetration and the lack of observation or the absence of rhetorical touch on the part of the cardinals of the Cornaro family, who are busy in the side boxes *not* observing the ecstasy and who are in fact an assemblage of the dead, make this work an example of deixis reflecting on its own untotalizable conditions of showing forth.

In full Baroque fashion, Crashaw's poems on Teresa follow many of the scene's potential reversals: the healing wound, the joyful pain, and the living death. Crashaw's own biography (1612 or 1613–1649) is a study in political and religious turmoil. The son of a prominent and vehemently anti–Roman Catholic Puritan clergyman, Crashaw became a friend of the poet Abraham Cowley during his undergraduate years at Pembroke College, Cambridge. Later he stood as a fellow of Peterhouse, following the High Anglican theology of Archbishop William Laud, which, though rejecting of Calvinism, was also strongly anti–Roman Catholic. While Crashaw was at Peterhouse, he gradually became attached as well to the religious community led by Nicholas Ferrar at Little Gidding, with which George Herbert was also affiliated. In the spring of 1643, Cromwell's soldiers seized Cambridge and dismantled most of the High Church embellishments at the chapel at Peterhouse. Crashaw then began a period of exile and retreat, first going to Little Gidding, then to Leyden, then, after a brief period in England again, to Paris, where he stayed in the court of the exiled Queen Henrietta Maria, whose secretary Abraham Cowley had become. While Cowley remained an Anglican, Crashaw converted to Roman Catholicism at some point in 1645. His Royalist attachments, his conversion, and his devotion to the cult of St. Teresa all made him a protégé of the queen and a favorite of her lady-in-waiting Susan Villiers, the countess of Denbigh, to whom Crashaw would later dedicate the final edition of his poems, the Carmen deo Nostro, which appeared posthumously in 1652.

In 1646, Henrietta Maria wrote to the pope, Innocent X, asking for a position for Crashaw. The poet went on to Italy but apparently spent a year fruitlessly waiting for help before another letter from the queen prompted Innocent to action. In 1646–1647, the English cleric John Bargrave discovered Crashaw in Rome in the retinue of Cardinal Pallotta. Among his benefices, the cardinal claimed that of the "Santa Casa" or Holy House of Mary at Loreto, and he gave Crashaw the holding of this benefice. The shrine was what remained of the Virgin's house that legend said had sailed through the air from the Holy Land to the Italian village of Tersato in 1291 and then sailed again several times in the ensuing years until it arrived through the air to Loreto. It was a popular pilgrim's destination in Crashaw's time, as it is today. A church was built around the small, foundationless (all the better to fly) building in 1350, and a great brachia was built around it in 1468. Crashaw was inducted into his position as "beneficiatus" of Loreto in April 1649. By August, he was dead; his contemporaries claimed that the ardor of his soul had overheated his body with a fever from which he never recovered.

Crashaw's "A Hymn to the Name and Honor of the Admirable Sancte Teresa, Foundresse of the Reformation of the Discalced Carmelites, both men and Women: A Woman for Angelicall hig[ht] of speculation, for Masculine courage of performance, more then a woman, who Yet a child, out ran maturity, and durst plott a Martyrdome," was written in fact before his conversion, as explained by his accompanying "An Apologie for the Foregoing Hymne as having been writt when the author was yet among the Protestantes." Yet the "Apologie" as a retrospective gesture of framing in fact contributes to Crashaw's ongoing efforts at conversion as reversal. The hymn does not reflect on a conversion that preceded it; rather, it has *effected* the conversion. Teresa, in teaching Crashaw that "love is eloquence," made her words "transfuse" like a flame to inspire his words.

"The Flaming Heart" is constructed of tetrameter couplets with some pentameter variations, such as those in the first lines:

> Well meaning readers! you that come as freinds
> And catch the pretious name this peice pretends;
> Make not too much hast to'admire
> That fair-cheek't fallacy of fire.
> That is a SERAPHIM, they say
> And this the great TERESIA.
> Readers, be rul'd by me & make
> Here a well-plac't & wise mistake
> You must transpose the picture quite,
> And spell it wrong to read it right;
> Read HIM for her, & her for him;
> And call the SAINT the SERAPHIM.

The opening of "The Flaming Heart" constructs its rhetoric of transposition in three arguments, each twelve lines in length. After the mandate to the reader that he or she must "spell it wrong to read it right," an address to the painter accuses him of erring in his presentation of Teresa: if only his "cold pencil" had "kist her PEN" (her dart). "Thou couldst not so unkindly err / To show us This faint shade for HER. / Why man, this speakes pure mortall frame; / And mockes with female FROST love's manly flame." The next twelve lines develop this accusation until the command expressed in line 37:

> Doe then as equall right requires,
> Since HIS the blushes be, & her's the fires,

Resume & rectify thy rude design;
Undresse thy Seraphim into MINE.
Redeem this injury of thy art;
Give HIM the vail, give her the dart.

Crashaw is demanding a complex transvestitism of power that is completely in line with Counter-Reformation dictates about the reception of holy images. Nothing leaves the realm of representation here—the argument is that the painter has made a mistake, and the "well-meaning" reader is invited to identify with the verbal artist who is making the poem, whose words will produce and reproduce an image of Teresa as her own words and teachings produced and reproduced "the saint." Crashaw moves us not merely in a back-and-forth motion between the seraphim and the saint but also in a forward-and-return motion between the image and the speaker and ourselves—supposedly behind him. This "squaring" and turning is a kind of circulation of meanings that puts every turn into transformation and as well materially approximates the experience of the Cornaro Chapel with its theatrical staging of Teresa's vision. Although Crashaw could never have seen the completed sculpture group, it is likely that he did see drawings and plans for it during his period in the retinue of Cardinal Pallotta.

At line 59 the "Flaming Heart" turns away from the "Give HIM the vail"/"Give her the Dart" reversals to another level of reversal. If "all's praescription" and the painter cannot change his convention, then the speaker says "Give me the suff[r]ing SERAPHIM. . . . Leave HER alone THE FLAMING HEART." Now the speaker moves beyond the two-dimensional world of the pictorial image to metaphor, explaining that the Flaming Heart is "love's whole quiver." Then, just as quickly, he explains the paradox: "For in love's feild was never found / A nobler weapon then a WOUND / Love's passives are his activ'st part / The wounded is the wounding heart." Like all visual representations of wounds, including the one which we saw Thomas examining, Teresa's wound opens up the space of representation into the real. Whereas trompe l'oeil reveals to touch its impermeability, these miraculous wounds open mere surface to meaning.

The remainder of the poem, from line 75 to line 108, is an apostrophe to the heart. But the heart is immediately—swollen as it is with "wound and darts"—compared to a book—"these conquering leaves"—and the image is then developed with more refinement into the heart as a "sweet incendiary" that sends its shafts of light "that play / Among the leaves of thy larg Books of day." These lines focus on the command that the heart "live here"—"here" is in the speaker's own heart: the speaker implores that the particulars of Teresa's autobiography become those of his own:

> Leave nothing of my SELF in me.
> Let me so read thy life, that I
> Unto all life of mine may dy.

Once this final transposition, the identification of the speaker with the saint, takes place, the well-meaning readers who have been following along can complete their own identification with the Flaming Heart.

We cannot overestimate the importance of rhetorical gestures of being moved, moving, reversing, and transposing in these poems on Teresa. Crashaw's work may superficially seem to be imitative of the visual forms of Baroque art, including its many images of flaming and wounded hearts, but it is far more accurate to say that the words *are* the event or expression; they twist, torque, and turn the reader about and summon the mind to heavenly aspirations in the ways bodies careen through Baroque architectural spaces. As Gilles Deleuze has suggested in his study of Leibniz and the Baroque:

> It might be claimed that physical gravity and religious elevation are quite different and do not pertain to the same world. However, these are two vectors that are allotted as such in the distinction of the two levels or floors of a single and same world, or of the single and same house. It is because the body and the soul have no point in being inseparable, for they are not in the least really distinct. . . . From this moment on any localization of the soul in an area of the body, no matter how tiny it may be, amounts rather to a *projection* from the top to the bottom, a projection of the soul focalizing on a "point" of the body . . . that develops from a Baroque perspective. In short, the primary reason for an upper floor is the following: there are souls on the lower floor, some of whom are chosen to become reasonable, thus to change their levels. Movement, then, cannot be stopped.[84]

Crashaw's "Hymn" to Teresa is particularly remarkable in this regard because the narrative of her autobiography is prepared as a kind of haptic journey for the reader, capitulating her into the space of the poem, inviting her to follow in the footsteps of the speaker, who follows in the footsteps of the saint, who follows in the footsteps of the Virgin (in the tradition of the "figlia del suo figlio"), who follows in the footsteps of Christ.

The hymn begins with an address to Christ as the "Absolute sole lord OF LIFE & DEATH." To prove the "word," the speaker will not turn to the "old soldiers" and "martyrs" of Christ but rather to a child. Reversal is again the initial rhetorical gesture; as in the title, which declared Teresa to be a woman "for Masculine courage of performance more than a woman," so is the child more than a child. Among the many devices of reversal at work, Crashaw often uses the reversed foot to great effect:

> Such as could with lusty breath
> Speak lowd into the face of death.

Lines such as "Making his mansion in the mild / And milky soul of a soft child" might be described as metrical palindromes. The first four syllables of the first line and the last four syllables of the second line mirror each other, and the second four syllables of the first line and the first four syllables of the second line are also mirrored. Of course, the chiastic effect is another allusion to Christ's "sacrifice"—the proof of the "word" with which the poem begins.[85]

A sacred paradox is introduced: Teresa, though she has hardly any blood, has a heart that can show that death is not as strong as love. The narrator goes on to tell the story from the autobiography of how Teresa tried to join the Crusades at the age of nine. At this point in the narrative, Crashaw builds a set of vivid metrical changes:

> FAREWEL then, all the world! Adieu.
> TERESA is no more for you.
> Farewell, all pleasures, sports, & joyes,
> (Never till now esteemed toyes)
> [Farewell what ever deare may bee,]
> MOTHER's armes or FATHER's knee.
> Farewell house, & farewell home!
> SHE's for the Moores, & MARTYRDOM.

The rising, almost skipping, tetrameter of the first three lines is slowed by the hesitation and falling meter of "Never till now." The next line returns to the ease of the iambics and then falls again with "Mother's armes or father's knees." "Farewell house and Farewell home!" reintroduces the trochaic and is reversed by "She's for the Moores and Martyrdom." Crashaw wittily shows the back-and-forth movement of the child's motion and resolve, ending in the forward and rising iambic. And then he addresses Teresa directly for the first time, ending the forward propulsion of narrative: "SWEET, not so fast!"

The speaker moves to the present tense, recounting the story of Teresa's visitation and piercing by the seraphim and reintroduces the paradoxes of that event:

> How kindly will thy gentle HEART
> Kisse the swee[t]ly-killing DART!
> And close in his embraces keep
> Those delicious Wounds, that weep
> Balsom to heal themselves with.

The remainder of the poem, which stretches to seventy-three lines, describes the apotheosis of Teresa to heaven as all her mystical deaths "at last dy into one." This ascent "into perfuming clouds" is described quite magically and economically as a "sigh" that exhales Teresa to heaven. There

> the MOON of maiden starrs, thy white
> MISTRESSE, attended by such bright
> Soules as thy shining self, shall come
> And in her first rankes make thee room;
> Where 'mongst her snowy family
> Immortall wellcomes wait for thee.

As Teresa takes her place in the Virgin Mary's "snowy family" she will be greeted by "reveal'd LI[FE]," and the Virgin Mary will "dart / Her mild rayes through thy melting heart." Angels and her own "good WORKES" will attend her there and "weave a constellation / OF CROWNS" and all her old woes and sufferings will be smiling and divine, her "TEARES" will turn to "gemms," and "WRONGS" will "repent to Diademms." Death itself will live and "dress the soul," and her wounds will "blush to such bright scarres." Her works will continue to feed and clothe souls on Earth. As she looks about her, she will see thousands of "crown'd Soules" who "throng to be / Themselves thy crown." These are the souls of those she has converted or "kindled to stars," and she will wear them like sparkling and sacred flames:

> Thou with the LAMB, thy lord, shalt goe;
> And whereso'ere he setts his white

Stepps, walk with HIM those wayes of light
Which who in death would live to see
Must learn in life to dy like thee.

Crashaw's "Hymn" thus ends in this great crowded scene culminating in a walk among the stars in Christ's footsteps.

In paraphrasing the work, I have not done justice to the careful sequence of epithets and euphemisms Crashaw uses. No member of the Council of Trent could accuse him of allowing his audience to confuse the artwork with experienced reality. The hymn constantly appeals to all of the senses: the smell of perfumed divinity; the taste of the fruits of Teresa's works; the touch of Christ on the lips of the saint; kisses and seizures and penetrations; fire and snow at once; the sparkling of flames and gems and stars; the haptic progress of "those wayes of light." At the same time, its elaborate metaphors, paradoxes, and inversions depend on an allegorical interpretation the reader herself must supply. This allegory is the final transposition of all the reversals and inversions Crashaw makes in his poems on Teresa as a whole: the transposition of this world into heaven, of dying into eternal life. The allegory is the motif of "meeting again in glory," and we might notice that Crashaw calls on what Marx had tentatively, and in a deferred utopian way, called a "mineralogical sense" —a sparkling, starry, gleaming world in the darkness of the heavens.

From where does this imagery come? Crashaw's "moon of maiden stars" clearly resembles Dante's "donna che qui regge" (*Inferno* X:80) with her crown of stars, and the theme of the Milky Way, or "via lactea," had earlier appeared as well in the poems of Giambattista Marino on "La Strage degli Innocenti," which Crashaw translated in 1637.[86] Such images seem to have had a particular appeal to Crashaw: milk, the milk of the Virgin's breasts, the milky souls of children, the eyes as nests of milky doves, the "milky streame that pours from the christall globe of heaven"—these are just a few of the many ways Crashaw uses milk imagery.[87] He is a poet of liquification and stone: the tears, blood, and milk that flow from his sacred figures have sometimes been condemned as the most far-fetched of all metaphysical conceits. In 1883, Edmund Gosse wrote that the description of Mary Magdalene's eyes as "Two walking baths; two weeping motions; / Portable, & compendious oceans" in Crashaw's poem "The Weeper" were "perhaps the worst lines in all English poetry."[88] As late as 1943 Yvor Winters was still ranting about this "foolish poem."[89]

Yet the hymn's starry depictions are typical of Counter-Reformation imagery more generally. Crashaw's use of techniques of figuration and liquification is part of the much longer tradition we have traced of legends of animation with their bleeding and weeping statues, and it no doubt has an even deeper resonance in the phenomenology of our relations to stone and water. But the poem's particular terms of light and darkness and its final scenes of crowds in motion might be compared to another form of Crashaw's period: the religious procession. Lorenzo Cardella's late eighteenth-century *Memorie storiche de' cardinali della santa romana chiesa* includes a record of a nocturnal procession led by Crashaw's patron Cardinal Pallotta in honor of "la Chiesa della Madonna di Loreto" annually on 10 December that bears a striking resemblance to the imagery of the Teresa poems.

Accompanied by drums and trumpets, the torch-lit procession, led by the cardinal and other ambassadors of the church, wound through the city, down the Corso and through the other major streets of Rome, past palaces and cafes. Hundreds of men lifted a "macchina" of the Santa Casa into the air, thus simulating its "flight" to Loreto. The four corners of the macchina were decorated by large angels depicted in relief, and above it all stood a statue of the Virgin Mary with an infant Christ in her arms. The entire effect was crowned by a wide framing band of artificially lighted "stars." The macchina moved like a cloud, at times behind a diaphanous screen of smoke and at other times "solidly material." A great number of young boys dressed in angels' robes and singing accompanied the spectacle. A barrel of oil was carried along to keep the lights illuminated. Cardella records that in the end there was "no more beautiful, noble and splendid sacred ceremony." Most admired of all, he claims, was Cardinal Pallotta, accompanied by the officials of the confraternity of the Santa Casa, who assisted with "inexplicable fervor."[90]

Clearly many of what have often been viewed as Crashaw's idiosyncratic and fanciful images were already embedded in the religious culture that surrounded him.[91] In the flying Santa Casa, the gyrations of the Virgin's crown of stars, the bleeding and weeping of statues, and the sharp turns and reversals of rhetorical paradoxes and oxymorons, this art constantly unsettles the stance of the receiver, providing experiences that are analogues of ecstasy. If the selflessness of a saint is aptly demonstrated in this figure who is being turned inside out, the observer is similarly required to abandon the conventions of frontality and left–right reception and torque his or her consciousness into communication with the image. An ecstasy is not something we have, in our usual model of sense impression; rather, an ecstasy has us. The ecstasy is profoundly detached from the reality of this world yet provides the particular terms of an ungrounded state. Christian levitation promises the end of weight, the "weight of the world" borne by our physical selves, just as it threatens the loss of grounding and orientation.

Consider more closely the importance of Teresa's unanchored, ungrounded foot. As is the case with many of the analogous spiritual exercises of the Baroque, like those Ignatian exercises Hopkins practiced, the senses are directed or aimed in a certain syntactical progression toward elevation. When we look at a standard concordance to Crashaw's poems, we find that among his most frequently used words are *flying* and *falling*.[92] And when we look at Bernini's depiction of the ecstasy, we see that he, too, has joined flying and falling in a visual oxymoron. Teresa's unanchored—and, of course, discalced—foot beside the wildly billowing textures of her coarse dress and the frail cloud juxtaposed to the polished flesh of the angel all seem to be both kept from falling and simultaneously made to float upward to the source of the rays of golden light and the real light source that was above and behind the group in the seventeenth century and recently restored.[93] Stone and light present antinomies of the relation touch can have to external mass. That most resistant to pressure and that least resistant to pressure are yoked in Bernini's spectacle. If stone is made weightless and light given material form, then the earth might be swept from beneath us and we might aim through space toward heaven.

I bring up these expressions of what might be called Baroque vertigo to emphasize the consequences of the deictic representation of sensation. Such vertigo dramatically enacts for social ends the nervous system's stimulation by, and flight from, sense impression. The spiraling verticality of Baroque art becomes a device of conversion engaged in a powerful disorientation of the relation between seeing, touch, and hearing. I am thinking as well of Francesco Borromini's accomplishment at Sant'Ivo, the stretched metaphors of Donne and Marino, or Andrea dal Pozzo's ceiling painting of the Apotheosis of Sant'Ignazio, and, indeed, ceiling painting in general.

One poet who claimed a direct relation to Crashaw's work is Coleridge. In his *Table Talk*, amid the undated "Additional" sections, he writes on Crashaw, citing "his lines on St. Theresa" as "the finest" and especially quoting lines 4 to 64 discussed earlier: "Where he does combine richness of thought and diction nothing can excel." He notes that "these verses were ever present to my mind whilst writing the second part of Christabel: if, indeed, by some subtle process of the mind they did not suggest the first thought of the whole poem."[94] It is not difficult to discern the influence of Crashaw's hymn on "Christabel," a poem Coleridge describes as taking him out of a state of "suspended animation into the wholeness, the liveliness, of vision."[95] Formally, Coleridge has, as he states in the preface to the poem, used a pure stress line to explore syllabic substitution "in correspondence with some transition, in the nature of the imagery or passion." These shifts in the number of syllables add to an array of effects of hesitation, necessity, and ease, as in lines 58 to 70 describing Christabel's first view of Geraldine:

> There she sees a damsel bright,
> Drest in a silken robe of white,
> That shadowy in the moonlight shone:
> The neck that made that white robe wan,
> Her stately neck, and arms were bare;
> Her blue-veined feet unsandal'd were,
> And wildly glittered here and there
> The gems entangled in her hair.
> I guess, 'twas frightful there to see
> A lady so richly clad as she—
> Beautiful exceedingly!
>
> Mary mother, save me now!
> (Said Christabel) And who art thou?[96]

With the shift in line 60, what is seen is also obscured by shadows, but it is in lines 67 to 70 that the meaning of "I guess 'twas frightful" is explicated through irregular lines—rich and beautiful as the lady is, her appearance spurs Christabel to call upon the Virgin Mary. The white robes, the blue-veined bare feet, and the wildly glittering gems are all evocative of Counter-Reformation imagery and particularly of representations of the ecstasy of Teresa, but why does Coleridge speak first of the inspiration of Crashaw for the second part of his poem, which describes the encounter of Geraldine and Christabel the next morning with the Baron in the presence of Bracy the Bard?

One reason might be that the second part of "Christabel" is a veritable festival of transposed identifications: the Baron sees in the face of Geraldine the face of her father, who had been his childhood friend. Bracy the Bard sees Geraldine in the dove destroyed by a snake that appears in his dreams. Geraldine meanwhile, with her serpent's eyes shrinking in her head, glances at Christabel, who begins to shudder and hiss, taking on a snakelike appearance as she views Geraldine's own serpentine image. Geraldine takes her place as the most beloved of the Baron as he concludes he has been disgraced by Christabel and leads Geraldine in honor from the hall. The conclusion to Part II explains that the father "must needs express his love's excess / with words of unmeant bitterness / Perhaps 'tis pretty to force together / Thoughts so unlike each other."

Here, too, you "must transpose the picture quite / and read it wrong to read it right." This is not the place to undertake an extensive reading of Coleridge's long and complex poem. Nevertheless, Coleridge took from Crashaw a rhetoric for writing "visions" that disorients and transforms the reader. As these barefoot girls cross the vast halls of the castle, Christabel must carry Geraldine across those thresholds that would constrain her evil influence. But in the hysterical environs of the poem, thresholds break down, pain becomes pleasure, one figure becomes another, histories turn to dreams, and the carved figures in the woodwork acquire an uncanny life.

As is often the case with Coleridge's borrowings, and at times his virtual plagiarisms, the "direct" influence perhaps is not the most direct at all. "Kubla Khan," first published in a pamphlet with "Christabel" and "The Pains of Sleep," is even closer to the disorientations of Crashaw's Teresa poems. The space of "Kubla Khan" is like a great labyrinthine ear. Here, too, is an unenclosed architecture:

> The shadow of the dome of pleasure
> Floated midway on the waves;
> Where was heard the mingled measure
> From the fountain and the caves.
> It was a miracle of rare device,
> A sunny pleasure-dome with caves of ice![97]

Generations of undergraduates have tried to draw representative maps or landscapes of the pleasure dome of Kubla Khan and its environs. But it is impossible to follow the path of the sacred River Alph, through measureless caverns to the sunless sea; to circle the ten miles of enclosed fertile ground, to link the gardens to the forests, to follow the "deep romantic chasm which / slanted down the green hill athwart a cedarn cover." Once we arrive in this chasm, we find a fountain bursting huge fragments in the other direction. And what is the source of that fountain but the sacred river with which we began? We are back in wood and dale and caverns measureless to man by that point. Coleridge moves constantly from plural terms to particular ones, sunken scenes to sunny ones—measurements that seem incommensurable, weights impossibly suspended, a green world juxtaposed to an icy one.

The haptic progress of the reader is alternately propelled and blocked. Yet what is constantly present is a panoply of unattributed, imaginary, sounds: "as e'er beneath a waning moon was haunted / By woman wailing for her demon-lover!"; "with ceaseless turmoil seething / As if this earth in fast thick pants were breathing"; "And 'mid this tumult Kubla heard from far / Ancestral voices prophesying war"; "the mingled measure / From the fountain and the caves."

The solution to the reader's inability to draw a total picture of the scene is then suddenly released in an act of beholding that is based in memory:

> A damsel with a dulcimer
> In a vision once I saw:
> It was an Abyssinian maid
> And on her dulcimer she played,
> Singing of Mount Abora
> Could I revive within me
> Her symphony and song,
> To such a deep delight 'twould win me
> That with music loud and long
> I would build that dome in air,
> That sunny dome! those caves of ice!
> And all who heard should see them there,
> And all should cry, Beware! Beware!
> His flashing eyes, his floating hair!
> Weave a circle around him twice,
> And close your eyes with holy dread.
> For he on honey-dew hath fed.
> And drunk the milk of Paradise.

Of course, the untotalizability of the scene is one definition of the sublime—when the imagination is blocked and the understanding cannot make a phenomenon intelligible through our existing categories of things, we are overwhelmed with feelings of power and grandeur. The extraordinary ending of "Kubla Khan" works through this problem in a number of ways. The figure of the damsel was *once* seen, but now it escapes the speaker's powers of "revival." However, it is not simply her figure that he wishes to revive; it is also her symphony and song, the music that, with the immateriality of all music, is gone forever. It cannot win or touch him, although he knows that, if it *could* touch him, he would find his poetic power restored. As surely as "this living hand," if it came back from the grave, would make the listener wish she were dead, so, inversely, would the song of the Abyssinian maid fill this speaker with new form-giving powers. A lesser poet might have ended the work with that dream of self-renewal. But Coleridge, whose own visions were a source of considerable pain to those around him, recognizes that poetic inspiration can also be lawless and dangerous—the sublimity of the world of "Kubla Khan" is not something others desire in human subjects. All who "heard should see them there," and they would issue a warning and undertake a spell of binding such a subject—weaving a circle round him thrice and warning others to close their eyes "with holy dread."

I have emphasized the physical reality of presentation consequent to the use of touch, but deixis, or showing forth, in the absence of touch, as in Christ's interdiction to the Magdalene and the final response to the figure of the subject in "Kubla Khan," results in effects of sublimity, magnitude, and ungraspability. As we know from Kant's account of the sublime, such effects exaggerate the visual at the same time as they prohibit the organizing functions of the imagination and the understanding. Here the presentation, confronting the beholder, far outstrips the possibilities of comprehension and reference. Yet because the receiver is at a sufficient distance to avoid harm, and thus is not distracted by fear, he or she is able to reach a condition of suspended judgment. The artwork embedded in contexts of decorum and ritual is available to touch; the relic and icon taken up by lip and hand would be the obvious example. When a painting is apprehended through the grid of single-point perspective, the field of representation is put into a dynamic relation with the visual evidence of tangible surface. Similarly, when sculpture is apprehended at a distance, either from a fixed position or via a determined path of reception, qualities of relief, abrasion, polish, and chiaroscuro are in play with a total impression of integrated position and movement.

Yet the sublime offers the possibility of deixis without orientation. Baroque art indicates the ways in which vertigo might be more broadly connected to aesthetic devices such as wit, trompe l'oeil, or perceptual surprise in general. Its appearance as an effect in works of art calls on an array of aesthetic problems that I have been pursuing: the ways vertigo compels dread, anxiety, anticipation, and repetition once it has been experienced; the ways an aberration or failure in hearing creates a problem of unfathomable distance; the ways the internal labyrinth of the ear can be projected into models of space in works of art; the ways vertigo is characterized by a loss of, or absence of, the anchoring capabilities of touch. Hence, the dynamic between falling and being caught might stem from infantile experience.

In the experience of sound, we noted the coming forward of the invocatory drive—the drive to be seen and heard. In the experience of falling
and being caught, the "catch" must precede the "toss." In this is the sanctity of the sanction given Cædmon. The poet does not merely sing out of
a welling up of a need for expression; the need for expression comes from
the grounding sphere of those who wait and listen, those who have made
their way in the darkness toward the poet, bearing their irrevocable demand that he or she sing. The toss may seem to prompt the catch, but in
fact the toss is what the catch both presumes and demands.

5

The Forms and Numbers
of Time

I. The Deictic Now

Keeping time, the work of intended care in meter, is a counter to the ceaselessness of all ceaseless things, including the unending silence and darkness with which we began. Yet waves of sound, like waves of the sea, arrive amorphously, without a graspable limit or edge; their reception is both the end of their insignificance and the beginning of their return to formlessness. It is unbearable to be left on the scale of human life without the scale of human time with which to measure this encounter. We have seen how poetic making creates an *eidos* of the human figure, a presence in space that begins to define the significance of space. Whereas the immediacy of mere sense certainty overwhelms us with its "here and now," *poiēsis* creates, by means of the senses, other versions of the "here and now" under conditions of human ends and needs. Keeping time makes infinity bearable; in the face-to-face world of the poem, we enter into human history by encountering the traces of predecessors unknown to us, by realizing our contemporaries, and by anticipating the responses of those who follow. Ten years for the Trojan War, dactylic hexameter applied to immeasurable suffering, no more no less; otherwise, the beating of waves on the shore takes place on a scale so far beyond our intelligibility that even a concept of divinity cannot encompass it.

We often note that lyric poetry, in particular, extends from the present. But what does this extension from the present involve, and what are its consequences? In the last chapter we considered some issues of deixis in space: relations of proximity in poetry and other face-to-face art forms; shifts in pronouns, uses of demonstratives, the "here" of the lyric speaker. Fillmore's work on frontality demonstrated how deixis aids in the manipulation of position, reversals of perspective, and shifts in the status of objects themselves in contrast to the conventional time system with its permanent orientation of "earlier" and "later." In this chapter I want to turn more fully to the poetic uses of temporal deixis—the deictic "now" —within larger considerations of how poetry takes place within, speaks to, and often transforms concepts of time.

We have considered how lyric's first-person, subjective, and emotional rendition of time is built through processes of incremental repetition, progression, and return. In this sense, lyric can both oppose, and go beyond, other models of sequential and chronological time—particularly, as we shall see, the teleology of narrative plot and including the plot of history. Yet what is true of the forms of time made in lyric practice is in fact true of the poetic more generally—the poetic in its two modes, first as sudden inspired creation and second as *technē*, the laborious considered making that proceeds from the interaction of mind and hand. Inspiration and *technē* already imply two different "speeds" within which *poiēsis* emerges. But inspiration does not always precede *technē*, and *technē* can itself provide a source of inspiration as aspects of the material only come forward within the process of *poiēsis* itself.

Much of what we have thought about regarding touch and animation in the last chapter stems from this possibility. Poetic making is sustained by leaps of association and metaphorical connection. What are such leaps leaping? They collapse and fuse and fragment the usual separations posed by time and space and bring the actual and imagined, the constraints of form and the abstractions of idea, into new configurations. Owen Barfield has written succinctly, "Poetry differs from all her sisters in this one important respect, that (excluding the sound values) consciousness is also the actual *material* in which she works." "Excluding the sound values" is of course an important qualification, as we saw in our discussion of the nonsemantic pull of rhythm in chapter 2 on sound and in the somatic memory of metrical form in chapter 3 on voice and possession. But Barfield reminds us that the work of the poem in transforming consciousness precedes temporality, so that the material is emergent in the form: "it is a peculiar mark of this poetic cognition (inspiration) that it commonly has a counter-effect (recognition) in the very *observation* through which it has

been generated in the first instance."[1] There is not an instantaneous synthesis that results in poetic knowledge; rather, the forces of inspiration
unfolding temporally in the form provide retrospective and recursive insight into the originating terms of the inspiration itself. Writing is reading
and reading is rewriting or revising in this sense of unfolding—there is no
"all at onceness" under which a revelation appears.

Time itself is a made or given feature of consciousness. Time is not nature but rather is one of the aspects of mind by which we are able to know
nature. This problem of time as a derived order of being has been a continuous theme of the philosophy of time in Western culture. Plato, for example, argued in the *Timaeus* that time is not an aspect of eternity or a
dimension of space and matter, but is rather a product of our sensations
working in combination with our beliefs. He held that time is something
that becomes and changes rather than something belonging to the un-
changing realm of reality.[2]

An early poem by Milton, "On Time" (the date is uncertain, but it was
probably written before 1631), expresses quite clearly this division: the
first ten lines address experienced time, lines 11 and 12 effect a turn, and
lines 13 through 22 expand into eternity. A manuscript subtitle indicates
that Milton intended the poem to be "set on a clock-case."

On Time

Fly envious Time, till thou run out thy race,
Call on the lazy leaden-stepping hours,
Whose speed is but the heavy plummet's pace;
And glut thyself with what thy womb devours,
Which is no more than what is false and vain,
And merely mortal dross;
So little is our loss,
So little is thy gain.
For whenas each thing bad thou hast entombed,
And last of all, thy greedy self consumed,
Then long eternity shall greet our bliss
With an individual kiss;
And joy shall overtake us as a flood,
When everything that is sincerely good
And perfectly divine,
With truth, and peace, and love shall ever shine
About the supreme throne
Of him, t'whose happy-making sight alone,
When once our heavenly-guided soul shall climb,

> Then all this earthy grossness quit,
> Attired with stars, we shall for ever sit,
>   Triumphing over Death, and Chance, and thee O Time.[3]

The first ten lines follow the present-tense motion of time as it greedily swallows everything in its path, including itself. The brief lines "So little is our loss" and "So little is thy gain" exemplify a reciprocal economy: what we lose in time and what time gains from our loss is in perfect balance, yet insignificant. Gain follows loss as line 8 follows line 7, but anyone can see that the measures of these two lines are exactly the same, and so where is the loss and where is the gain?

After the "last of all" of self-consumption, time is used up and eternity begins. Here Milton turns to the future tense, but he relies on a theology of the individual consciousness at the core of cosmic eternity, a microcosm in a macrocosm, that we will take up later in this chapter. Like the two halves of an hourglass, the two halves of the poem meet in this "kiss" between the vastness of Eternity and the individual, between the most universal and the most particular models of time. We notice that Eternity now comes *before* the object of its kissing. Time is turned upside down as an hourglass turned upside down is the small-scale beginning of a new era. The poem's symmetrical structure is all the more emphasized by the way the second half catalogs eternal values against the sweeping ephemerality of all that is listed in the first half. The final apostrophe to time counters the opening apostrophe, claiming Time's endurance only in the transcendence that the first line cannot imagine. This symmetry, however, remains asymmetrical, for it is time itself that must run the race to eternity: ordinary life must consume and then entomb itself before eternity can take precedence. The hourglass in this instance can be turned only once, for death, and chance, and time are defeated in the poem's final triumph of eternity. After that turn, there is no more need for calculating time or for the measures of the poem to continue.

From Plato forward, the theory of time in the West is dominated by this hypothesis of multiple realms of time: time ontologically derived from eternity, time as experienced by human beings differing from the time of nature, and more recently these experiential and cultural forms of time as differing from the time not only of natural "history" but also of physics. The philosopher of science Rudolf Carnap recorded that Albert Einstein worried about the special meaning the "now" had for human beings, finding that such a "now" had no relevance for physics and so marked an aspect of the universe that physics could not grasp. Bergson's distinction between subjective time and time in nature was another contribution to this split between existential and objective forms of temporality.[4]

Yet Aristotle had dissented from Plato's view, arguing that time was not so much created out of a timeless eternity as that eternity is an endless series of moments and time is a measure applied to motion. In Aristotle the continuity of our awareness of our own being is necessary for our recognition of moments constituting the time continuum. When we measure time, we are as well taking time.[5] Combining something of both the Platonic and Aristotelian positions, the dominant metaphor for time as movement within an unspecified eternity is time as a river or flow. This liquification of time aptly indicates the notion of water's eroding power, the force of time in wearing down and, as Milton imagines, consuming material things. All inscription is abraded back into the earth; the contrary possibility, that inscription will transcend or overcome the earth, brings forward Milton's image of eternity as a flood in which all things are encompassed and suspended forever.

One of the most comprehensive surveys of the metaphor of time as a flow of water is Ovid's discussion of time near the close of the *Metamorphoses.* "Time itself flows on with constant motion," he writes, "just like a river, for no more than a river can the fleeting hour stand still. As wave is driven on by wave, and, itself pursued, pursues the one before, so the moments of time at once flee and follow, and are ever new." He describes how every minute gives place to another, how night passes into day, morning into night, the sky passes through its colors from red at sunrise to red at sunset, the moon waxes and wanes, the seasons change, human bodies pass from infancy to youth to middle and old age, earth and water are heavy and sink down, fire and air are light and rise up, the earth becomes liquid, water becomes air and wind, air flashes into the fiery atmosphere of the heavens, fire condenses and thickens into air, air into water, and water, under pressure, turns into earth. Rivers appear and disappear; marshes become deserts and deserts marshes; seashells lie far from the ocean; volcanoes become extinct; bees are born in the rotting carcasses of bulls, hornets in the carcasses of war horses; within the silence of the tomb, the rotting marrow forms into a snake. As these images accrue, Ovid realizes that his own account is taking place in time and that, as he has seemed to embrace time within his writing, so will time eventually overcome that inscription: "The day will end, and Phoebus sink his panting horses in the deep, before I recount all the things that have been altered to a different shape. So we see times change, and some nations gain strength, while others sink into obscurity."[6]

In one of the earliest English lyrics on Christ's passion, the anonymous poem, or perhaps fragment of a longer work, beginning "Nou goþ sonne vnder wod,—" the possibilities of parallel times occurring within a deictic "now" that is itself taking time truly structure the entire work:

> Nou goþ sonne vnder wod,—
> me reweþ, marie þi faire Rode.
> Nou goþ sonne vnder tre,—
> me reweþ, marie, þi sone and þe.[7]

The poem is in the pure stress four-beat meter we last read in Cædmon's "Hymn," but it is also in couplets. Spoken from the perspective of the first person, the poem proceeds in a remarkable way through time and space. It begins in the "now" and links the expression of that first person present to two events taking place on other scales: the first, the setting of the sun on the visible landscape; the second, the crucifixion of Christ. The "sonne" that "goþ vnder wod" is both the sun setting behind a wood on the horizon and the son, Christ, going under the wood of the cross. The next line, as we say in film analysis, "cuts" to the interior of the speaker: "Me reweþ, Marie, þi faire rode." And that interior expression in turn breaks into two referents: "I pity Marie, þi faire rod (or rosy complexion, the color evoking the sunset's reflection)" and "I pity þy fair rood" or cross, as well as "scion" or "offspring." The next line moves back to the external view by means of an incremental repetition: "Nou goþ sonne vnder tre." The sun is still setting, but it has fallen behind the wood and the view is now both more advanced and more particular—the sun is now seen behind a specific tree, farther down upon the horizon. The eye individuates as the mind multiplies: the "tre" is both the wood of the rood and the place of Christ in the Trinity. The speaker cuts to the interior again with another incremental repetition. As the referent of external movement shifts from the general to the singular, so does the referent of internal movement—the movement of pity—become individualized. Third person becomes second person "þi sonne and þe," and the speaker completes a metaphorical identification with the position of Mary herself as she watches the crucifixion (John 9:25) amid another group of three—with Mary the wife of Clopas and Mary Magdalene.

How long does pity take? As long as a sunset? Do we measure a sunset from the moment the base of the sun's sphere touches the horizon to the moment of its final disappearance? Or is the sunset teleologically present from the very moment of the sunrise, as Christ's death was implicit in his birth? And does the sunset promise the sunrise, as Christ's fall reversed time into the promise of his rise? Does pity take as long as the flashlike insight of metaphorical connection, where descent is transformed in ascent? In Christian theology the god's pity for another's suffering is reversed in perspective, for his suffering, too, is an expression of pity. Such ideas are, of course, at the center of the Christian mandate to "imitate the passion." What unifies the most interior view and the most extended view here in time and space is the "measure of motion"—those sixteen beats and slight shifts (wod to rode, tre to þe) that turn these four sentences into an eternity through its incremental "nows."

The most important early source of our sense of the relation between poetry and present-centeredness is the meditation on subjectivity and time in Augustine's *Confessions*. The *Confessions*, written in 397–398 and addressing the circumstances of the saint's life and conversion between his birth in 354 and his mother's death in 387, is a book that substitutes one "now" (the now of sense impressions) for another (the now of eternal life). Augustine creates this transformation by narrating through the past tense his early life of sinfulness and then expressing in the present tense all his thoughts and prayers after his conversion. This profound change in tense is the great break effected between Book VIII and Book X: Augustine's conversion, his mother's death, and his turn to eternity. After Book X, the past appears in the frame of a discourse on memory: memory is *willed* and is a device for distancing the senses, making them objects of contemplation: "I recognize that I like honey better than wine and smooth things better than rough ones, although at the moment I neither taste nor touch anything. All this goes on inside me, in the vast cloisters of my memory. In it are the sky, the earth, and the sea, ready at my summons, together with everything that I have ever perceived in them by my senses, except the things which I have forgotten. In it I meet myself as well."

Poetic forms play a key role in a series of scenes in which Augustine's turn from narrative is effected. First, in Book VIII in the climactic moment of despair when Augustine has flung himself beneath a fig tree and poured out his tears in "sacrifice," following Psalm 51:17, "The sacrifice acceptable to God is a broken spirit; a broken and contrite heart, O God, you will not despise," he asks why he continually defers his conversion to "tomorrow": "Why not now . . . at this moment?" he asks. At that moment he hears the "sing-song voice" of a child, repeating the refrain, "Take it and read, take it and read." What he then hurries home to read, through the pagan practice of *sortes virgilianae* applied to the Bible, is a passage from Paul's epistles directing him to turn against "nature's appetites." What is this sing-song voice, and from where has it come? Augustine thinks "hard whether there was any kind of game in which children used to chant words like these, but I could not remember ever hearing them before."[8] Like Cædmon's interlocutor, the voice invoking the call to self-transformation directly commands *this* subject at *this* moment and memory begins at the point where forgetting takes place.

In Book IX, in the period after his mother's death, Augustine describes a scene in which the relation between tears and sing-song is reversed. Here he awakens after a sleep that has brought him some relief from his sorrow, and he remembers Ambrose's "Evening Hymn":

> Deus, Creator omnium,
> polique Rector, vestiens
> diem decoro lumine,
> noctem sopora gratia;
>
> Artus solutos ut quies
> reddat laboris usui,
> mentesque fessas allevet,
> luctusque solvat anxios.

The hymn evokes memories of Augustine's mother, and he is able to release his emotions: "the tears which I had been holding back streamed down and I let them flow as freely as they would, making of them a pillow for my heart."[9] Then, in Book XI, this relation among sing-song, weeping, and reversal becomes a sustained theory of time. Poetic forms are no longer eruptions in the flow of secular time: they now provide a model for the subjective consciousness of time as an eternal present. Realizing that time is "an extension of the mind itself," Augustine writes, "Suppose that we hear a noise emitted by some material body. The sound begins and we continue to hear it. It goes on until finally it ceases. Then there is silence. The sound has passed and it is no longer sound. Before it began it was future and could not be measured, because it did not yet exist. Now that it has ceased it cannot be measured, because it no longer exists. It could only be measured while it lasted, because then it existed and could be measured. But even then it was not static, because it was transient, moving continuously toward the point where it would no longer exist." He concludes that "what we measure is the interval between a beginning and an end," yet he realizes that "we cannot measure it [time] if it is not yet in being, or if it is no longer in being, or if it has no duration, or if it has no beginning or end." He returns once more to the beginning of Ambrose's "Evening Hymn," with its eight syllables alternately short and long. As "far as" he "can trust" his practiced ear he can measure these syllables: "It is in my own mind then, that I measure time. I must not allow my mind to insist that time is something objective." Poetry is the paradigm for this internal consciousness of time. He writes:

> When we measure silences and say that a given period of silence has lasted as long as a given period of sound, we measure the sound mentally, as though we could actually hear it, and this enables us to estimate the duration of the periods of silence. Even without opening our mouths or speaking at all we can go over poems and verses and speech of any sort in our minds, and we can do the same with measurable movement of any kind. . . . Suppose that I am going to recite a psalm that I know. Before I begin, my faculty of expectation is engaged by the whole of it. But once I have begun, as much of the psalm as I have removed from the province of expectation and relegated to the past now engages my memory and the scope of the action which I am performing is divided between the two faculties of memory and expectation. . . . What is true of the whole psalm is also true of all its parts and of each syllable. It is true of any longer action in which I may be engaged and of which the recitation of the psalm may only be a small part. It is true of a man's whole life, of which all his actions are parts. It is true of the whole history of mankind, of which each man's life is a part.[10]

At the heart of the capacity art has for the transformation and mediation of time is the dual work of memory and imagination. Indeed, the very "thingness" of art, which I have referred to earlier using Kant's term, the "finality of form," depends on the work of memory. When we discern the thingness of a phenomenon, we sense its continuous aspect in time. It is not fleeting or ephemeral or indiscernible, and even these qualities imply a thingness of nondurability of which we can have some intuition—a factor that contributes in significant ways to the category of the sublime.

Replicability, closure, meaning, uniqueness, reportability—these attributes and devices for articulating thingness are consequent to the closure afforded by memory. As Augustine's discussion of the hymn form demonstrates, the musicality of poetic form affords an ideal paradigm for this process precisely because of the fleetingness of its material aspect. Like thinking, the discernment of metrical form requires an effort. In the same way that visual art compels us to see and not merely look, sound patterns teach us to listen and not merely hear. A volition that is intersubjective and active is required. Indeed, patterns or orders in time differ from randomness and disorder in part because they *are* memorizable. Experiments in memory show that of all the information borne by a melody, the temporal relationships internal to the work are the most central to our capacity to retain it. Variations in pitch, loudness, and timbre can all be completely changed and the melody is still recognizable, but if the internal temporal relationships are changed, even without any other changes, the melody is unintelligible.[11] And when we know a poem or melody in its thingness, either through the repetition of performances in time or the relation between individual performances and a text or score, we are able to convey in our imagination, by means of the continuity of our memory, a sense of the work that puts the material qualities of any individual performance in high relief.

Augustine replaces temporal description in terms of inalterable before and after sequences with an account of the moving experiential perspective of past, present, and future. In his account, the atomicity of separate perceptual moments disappears into the continuity of the past, present, and future in the desiring self. The relation between anticipation and the time sense is an intersubjective one. The person experiencing time is called to attention, whether by the sing-song voice of the child or the memory into which the work itself will eventually be submerged. It is significant that Augustine links the experience of measured forms not just to poetry but as well to experiences of weeping and sleeping. The weeper has no measure and is in fact the vessel of the agency of his or her tears. The sleeper must hear, awaken, listen, and stop the immeasurable flow in order to attend to the duration of silences and sounds that will produce form.

Poetry organizes weeping into intelligible expression. Similarly, as René Descartes was to write in his *Meditations on First Philosophy*, memory organizes perception into intelligible continuities, and this is how we can discern the differences between sleeping and waking: "I find a very noticeable difference between the two [the sleeping and the waking state], inasmuch as our memory can never connect our dreams one with the other or with the whole course of our lives, as it unites events which happen to us while we are awake." Thus, he concludes that if he can connect perceptions to "the whole course of his life" through the senses, memory, and the understanding, then he will know he is awake.[12]

In "A Slumber Did My Spirit Seal," a work from 1800 and the finest of what are known as his "Lucy" poems, Wordsworth moves backward in time, from consequence to cause, out of sleep and into the waking mind:

A slumber did my spirit seal;
I had no human fears:
She seemed a thing that could not feel
The touch of earthly years.

No motion has she now, no force;
She neither hears nor sees;
Rolled round in earth's diurnal course,
With rocks, and stones, and trees.[13]

In the shift from first to third person, this poem truly seems to be upside down—the opening lines centering on the "I" seem to be the consequence of all the other information of the poem, and so we would expect them to appear as the logical close. But here they are the instantiating terms of the account of another.[14] The course of the work moves from a subjective viewpoint to an objective viewpoint to an eternal time closer to that of the pre-Socratics than to any conventional Judeo-Christian belief system. The "she" of this poem is like Condillac's statue, but here stripped of the senses once more: shorn of her volition and capacity for abstraction, she moves but cannot move by will. She cannot "feel the touch of earthly years" and so can only be thus an object of touch, an intransitive locus for forces of nature. Consequently, the speaker has no "human fears," and his own spirit is sealed by slumber in a sympathetic parallel, a kind of *couvade* of death. Dorothy Wordsworth wrote in her journal that she and William would often think of death as being like lying awake in a grave.[15] Human lives are measured in "earthly years" and not scrutinized within the flux of Earth's "diurnal" course, but the latter is here much closer to a cosmic time beyond even the eternity of death.

The simplicity of this poem belies the ways that the world can resist integration into consciousness. Indeed, the poem itself, in narrating the problem and then bringing it into immediate pressure on the reader in the shift to the present tense, demonstrates such resistance.[16] The point where consciousness has no inside, where it is overwhelmed by the world but not in fear of it, is the point of sublimity where time, in the sense of conventional instrumental and socially integrated form, is halted or placed in abeyance and existence takes place in a series of powerful "nows" inseparable from one another. Of course, our subjective time sense enters this state whenever we are enveloped in reverie, dreams, or meditation— imaginative or memorializing states continuous with the states of apprehending various art forms.[17] The fiction of single-point perspective theory may be an all-at-onceness of perception, but to be moved by an art work, even one that resists most strenuously the identifications of catharsis, is to be engaged with it haptically and tactically. "A Slumber Did My Spirit Seal" is in this way a reworking of Ovidean characters like Aretusa and Daphne who retreat from consciousness: moving figures frozen at the threshold of their reentry into nature's flux.

II. TRACES OF HUMAN MOTION: THE *UBI SUNT* TRADITION

Is there a way to construct an art history that could provide a genealogy of any given work and address the long duration of its genesis in thousands of years of human making? And is there a way to create and apprehend any given work that assumes an unending future of reception that would include trajectories of ruin and restoration? The artwork is the occasion for tracing specific intentions and specific responses indicative of the subjective experiences of the maker and receiver. We think of such intentions and the responses they evoke as part of an economy of exchanged meanings that follow from the work's finitude. Yet the finality of form manifested in the artwork is important to us precisely because it creates a space and time for the apprehension of a manifold of causes and consequences. Hence, the finality of form always leaks out into the environment and is broken open by the pressures of what precedes, surrounds, and follows it. The indeterminacy of "A Slumber Did My Spirit Seal" is certainly an example of this problem that is also a resource, for it demonstrates how closure in works of art is precisely the aspect that gives us a perspective on the limits of closure.

The universe, though spatially symmetrical, displays a temporal asymmetry: galaxies appear to be distributed evenly in all directions, but rather than approaching each other, they are all receding from each other in time, and so time appears as a *direction*. In our everyday experience of time, we similarly think of both the past and the future as commensurable infinities. But we have traces of the past, memories and records, and no traces of the future. The concept of "trace formation" is key to understanding how, in a given universe, entropy can proceed at different rates. While one part of a universe may be increasing in entropy, other parts may be decreasing. J. J. C. Smart explains in an essay on "Time" in a standard reference book of philosophy that

> the formation of a trace is the formation of a subsystem of temporarily lower entropy than that of its surroundings and the trace is blotted out when the entropy curve of the subsystem rejoins that of the larger system. A footprint in sand is a temporarily highly ordered state of the sand: this orderliness is bought at the expense of an increased disorderliness (metabolic depletion) of the pedestrian who made it, and this extra orderliness eventually disappears as a result of wind and weather. . . . [S]uch systems of temporarily lower entropy . . . nearly all (in practice, quite all) go in the same direction. This direction defines a temporal direction for the universe or at least for our cosmic era of it. On investigation it will be

seen that all sorts of traces, whether footprints in sand, photography, fossil bones, or the like, can be understood as traces in this sense. Indeed, so are written records.[18]

Recall, then, two traces of human presence in the earth: one greeted with dread, the other with longing. The first, closer to us in chronological time, is viewed by a famous descendant of Philoctetes, Robinson Crusoe:

> It happen'd one Day about Noon going towards my Boat, I was exceedingly surpriz'd with the Print of a Man's naked Foot on the Shore, which was very plain to be seen in the Sand: I stood like one Thunder-struck, or as if I had seen an Apparition: I listen'd, I look'd round me, I could hear nothing, nor see any Thing; I went up to a rising Ground to look further; I went up the Shore and down the Shore, but it was all one, I could see no other Impression but that one, I went to it again to see if there were any more, and to observe if it might not be my Fancy; but there was no room for that, for there was exactly the very print of a Foot, Toes, Heel, and every Part of a Foot; how it came thither, I knew not, nor could in the least imagine. But after innumerable fluttering Thoughts, like a Man perfectly confus'd and out of my self, I came Home to my Fortification, not feeling, as we say, the Ground I went over.[19]

We humans are tracking animals who can read the signs of animal tracks: when Crusoe sees the single footprint on the beach, he also "sees" and "hears" what is not there—not simply the missing body whose gravity, weight, and significance is cast in the earth itself as the print, but as well those missing prints—the other foot, the steps preceding and following—which in their absence speak powerfully to the obliteration of all that gives human beings their bearing: "What marks were there of any other Footsteps?" he asks. Before Crusoe arrives on the scene, the weather has completed this portion of its unending work of eroding all three-dimensional forms in time. Crusoe literally looks at the signature of change. This print that terrifies him has nothing to do with him and in that is the source of its horrifying potential. Like Cowper longing for the finite architecture of hell, Crusoe says he almost hopes that Satan has left the print, for then it would have an intention or "purpose." But the footprint erupts within his Paradise, where all things are to hand and have their reasons, as the sign of his own disappearance. Here nature and time take place on that scale where he is bound to oblivion. As he delineates the specificity of the print—toes, heel, and every part in evidence—he flies out of himself, "not feeling . . . the Ground" he walks over.

What Crusoe does not want to see, Petrarch longs for: the footprint as a sign of habitation on earth, of mutual ground, of writing as indelible human presence. In early lines (7–10) of number 125 of the *Rime sparse*, the speaker says:

> men solitarie l'orme
> foran de' miei pie' lassi
> per campagne et per colli,
> men gli occhi ad ogn'or molli, . . .

([If only Laura were aflame with love,] less solitary would be the prints of my weary feet through fields and across hills, my eyes less wet always: . . .) At the end of this long poem, which addresses the landscape since Laura herself is absent from it, the speaker finds through an act of the imagination some evidence of his beloved's presence (lines 53–65):

> Ben sai che sì bel piede
> non toccò terra unquanco
> come quel dì che già segnata fosti,
>   onde 'l cor lasso riede
> col tormentoso fianco
> a partir teco i lor pensier nascosti
>   Così avestu riposti
> de' be' vestigi sparsi
> ancor tra'fiori et l'erba
> che la mia vita acerba
> lagrimando trovasse ove acquetarsi!
> ma come po s'appaga
> l'alma dubbiosa et vaga.

(You know well that so beautiful a foot never touched the Earth as on that day when you were marked by hers, wherefore my weary heart comes back with my tormented flanks to share with you their hidden cares. Would that you had hidden away some lovely footprints still among the flowers and grass, that my bitter life might weeping find a place to become calm! but my fearful yearning soul satisfies itself as best it can.)

That act of imagination is obviously an analogue between the *vestigi sparsi* and the *rime sparsi* themselves. There is a great change in perspective from the prints of his weary feet "per campagne et per colli," so abstractly and vaguely left in such vast spaces, and "knowing well" the Earth might hold Laura's footprints among the flowers and grass. Footprints

among flowers and grass are fleeting impressions: the poet is free to confuse the work of the wind with those flowers and blades of grass that
Laura's weight might have bent in passing. Between the underdetermination of his own marks on Earth and the overdetermination of his tracing
of Laura's, the poet finds the paradigm for his scattered rhymes—incomplete forms of completely devoted attention. As Robert Durling, translator of these passages, has written of Petrarch's title *Rerum vulgarium frag-
menta* (*Rime sparse* in Italian), it "expresses the intensely self-critical
awareness that all integration of selves and texts is relative, temporary,
threatened. They flow into multiplicity at the touch of time, their incon-
sistencies juxtaposed as the successive traces of a subject who dissolves
and leaves only words behind."[20]

To claim for art powers of restoration and significance is also, however,
to underline the tragedy of the inevitability of its material loss and disappearance. This is not only a matter of ecological disasters, nuclear catas-
trophes, or the eventual inevitable disappearance of our sun. It is an aspect
of every material thing that it will decay and disappear. As we have seen,
wind and water are the great forces of wearing away and wearing down, but
as they are eroding elements they are also inspiring elements. The passage
of time is greeted with emotions of regret and elation at once. The very
idea of a "trace" betrays its fragility. Each material thing contains within
its future the inevitability of the loss of the past. As Merleau-Ponty wrote
in his study of the phenomenology of time, "no preservation no physiological or psychic 'trace' of the past can make consciousness of the past
understandable. . . . A preserved fragment of the lived-through past can be
at most no more than an occasion for thinking of the past, but it is not the
past which is compelling recognition; recognition, when we try to derive
it from any content whatever, always precedes itself. Reproduction presupposes re-cognition and cannot be understood as such unless I have in
the first place a sort of direct contact with the past in its own domain."[21]

Footprints show the purposiveness of haptic movement, but they are
not intentional marks like those prehensile hands left on the walls of
caves. They are the vestiges of our movement as writing is the vestige of
our thought. They display a trajectory that may have passed readily from
our minds in our eagerness to arrive. This is why dancing, which does not
arrive but ends, is an art and walking is not. And why dancing, which is
repeatable, can endure beyond the dancer. Paul Valéry has left us with a
considered account of walking as an activity without volition: "I had left
my house to relax from some tedious piece of work by walking and by a
consequent change of scene. As I went along the street where I live, I was
suddenly *gripped* by a rhythm which took possession of me and soon gave

me the impression of some force outside myself. It was as though someone else were making use of my *living-machine*. Then another rhythm
overtook and combined with the first, and certain strange *transverse* relations were set up between these two principles (I am explaining myself as
best I can). They combined the movement of my walking legs and some
kind of song I was murmuring, or rather which was being murmured
through me."[22] Here is the capacity of rhythm to occupy the body and to
produce unconscious effects of poetic form that we discussed earlier in relation to both poetic sound and poetic possession. But Valéry's description
of the "transverse" relation of two rhythms is particularly useful in its
suggestion of a contrast between two kinds of poetic "feet." Consider the
rhyming superstition children often recite when walking along the blocks
of a sidewalk:

> Step on a crack,
> you'll break your mother's back.

We would have to describe the first line as the spondees "step" and
"crack" separated by a pyrrhic ("on a"), and, of course, the second line is
in a perfectly regular iambic trimeter. The first line is static and symmetrical and compels a halting caution; the second gives license to move forward in a predictably rhythmic way.

Poems on walking often juxtapose two meters and produce just this
sort of tension between moving and stopping. Hölderlin's "Der Spaziergang" ("The Walk") is written in *abab* quatrains that alternate feminine
amphibrachic line endings and mostly anapestic masculine line endings,
using enjambment to give a sense of propulsion forward, as is evident from
the opening lines:

> Ihr Wälder schön an der Seite,
> Am grünen Abhang gemahlt,
> Wo ich umher mich leite,
> Durch süße Ruhe bezahlt

And Auden's "As I walked out one evening" uses the same effect of alternating amphibrachic feminine and cretic, iambic, or other masculine endings in trimeter quatrains:

> As I walked out one evening,
> Walking down Bristol Street,
> The crowds upon the pavement
> Were fields of harvest wheat.

In the 1805 *Prelude,* Book XIII, lines 399–403, in a passage addressed to Coleridge and recalling to him the circumstances of the spring and early summer of 1798 when the two wrote the *Lyrical Ballads,* Wordsworth leaves a record of his process of composing while walking. In this case he was composing "The Thorn":

And I, associate in such labour, walked
murmuring of him, who—joyous hap—was found,
After the perils of his moonlight ride,
Near the loud waterfall, or her who sate
In misery near the miserable thorn.

He speaks a few lines later (414) of how he and Coleridge "Together wandered in wild poesy."[23] Their contemporaries have left other records of the simultaneity of their walking and composing. Dorothy Wordsworth's Grasmere Journal records on 28 August 1800, "William went into the wood & altered his poems"; on 29 August, "We walked through the wood over the stepping stones. . . . John & I left Wm to compose an Inscription."[24] And William Hazlitt wrote, "There is a *chaunt* in the recitation both of Coleridge and Wordsworth, which acts as a spell upon the hearer and disarms the judgment. . . . Coleridge has told me that he himself liked to compose in walking over uneven ground, or breaking through the struggling branches of a copse-wood; whereas Wordsworth always wrote (if he could) walking up and down a straight gravel-walk, or on some spot where the continuity of his verse met with no collateral interruption."[25]

Straight on the gravel path or not, Wordsworth associated walking with the stirring of the senses and awakening, as he writes in both the 1805 (Book XI, ll. 126–145) and 1850 (Book XII, ll. 127–144) versions of the *Prelude* in passages contrasting the dominion of the "bodily eye" with a summoning of the other senses for the purposes of contrasting them and using them to correct each other in an effort at "liberty and power." As a consequence, he writes, "vivid the transport, vivid though not profound; / I roamed from hill to hill, from rock to rock" (1850; Book XII, ll. 142–143). Wordsworth's habitual use of the rhythm of back-and-forth movement recapitulates the nystagmus of the reading eye we followed earlier in Stevens. Dorothy Wordsworth recorded on 15 June 1802, "we walked backwards and forwards a little."[26] The pacing of walking, thinking, writing the turns of the verse line, and reading are all parallel courses or traces running through the practices of his life and art.[27]

Our efforts to preserve our traces on the earth are more often than not in vain. Petrarch's rueful legacy of scattered forms not only can be found in Defoe but is of course also a staple of Renaissance sonnet tradition. The consciousness of the devastation nature can work upon inscription that we saw earlier in Melville's "Fragments" is turned into a form of wishful thinking, for example, in Sonnet 75 of Spenser's "Amoretti":

> One day I wrote her name upon the strand,
>   but came the waves and washed it away:
>   agayne I wrote it with a second hand,
>   but came the tyde, and made my paynes his pray.
> Vayne man, sayd she, that doest in vaine assay,
>   a mortall thing so to immortalize,
>   for I my selve shall lyke to this decay,
>   and eek my name bee wyped out lykewize.
> Not so, (quod I) let baser things devize
>   to dy in dust, but you shall live by fame:
>   my verse your vertues rare shall eternize,
>   and in the hevens wryte your glorious name.
> Where whenas death shall all the world subdew,
>   our love shall live, and later life renew.[28]

or in Shakespeare's Sonnet 55: "Not marble, nor the gilded monuments / Of princes, shall outlive this powerful rhyme."[29] But marble is among the softest of stones and gilding, if it resists piracy, is readily vulnerable to erosion.

By the time Shakespeare was writing Sonnet 55, Petrarchism itself had become a kind of fossil. The endurance of form over time can of course be another version of death—a disappearance into the rigidity of reification or idealization, a kind of petrified portraiture. Later, from the rise of the topographical poem at the end of the seventeenth century to the full flowering of the Romantic concept of organic form, artists who want to create a living work thus identify with the forces of nature themselves. The great example of the latter is, of course, Shelley animating himself in these famous lines from the close of "Ode to the West Wind," written in 1819:

> Make me thy lyre, even as the forest is:
> What if my leaves are falling like its own!
> The tumult of thy mighty harmonies
>
> Will take from both a deep, autumnal tone,
> Sweet though in sadness. Be thou, Spirit fierce,
> My spirit! Be thou me, impetuous one!

Drive my dead thoughts over the universe
Like withered leaves to quicken a new birth!
And, by the incantation of this verse,

Scatter, as from an unextinguished hearth
Ashes and sparks, my words among mankind!
Be through my lips to unawakened Earth

The trumpet of a prophecy! O Wind,
If Winter comes, can Spring be far behind? [30]

No contemporary poet has pursued the consequences of entropy and natural forces of decay and regeneration more rigorously and sustainedly than A. R. Ammons. His early poem, "The Pieces of My Voice," might be seen as a twentieth-century "cast" of Petrarch's 125: the theme of disappearance finds its ultimately appropriate formal task: to "build the whole silence back," rather than to try to create something along the lines of a gilded monument. These are the first two stanzas of the poem:

The pieces of my voice have been thrown
away I said turning to the hedgerows
and hidden ditches
Where do the pieces of
my voice lie scattered
The cedarcone said you have been ground
down into and whirled

Tomorrow I must go look under the clumps of
marshgrass in wet deserts
and in dry deserts
when the wind falls from the mountain
inquire of the chuckwalla what he saw go by
and what the salamander found
rising in the changing sand
I must run down all the pieces
and build the whole silence back. . . . [31]

The future tense proper is so infrequently found in poems that we are inevitably invited to compare the wild nature here to the domestic nature in the "I will arise and go now" frame of Yeats's "The Lake Isle of Innisfree." [32] But Ammons ingeniously anticipates both the speaker's resolve and its impossibility. He will look for signs of his voice in the desert where the sand's changes will inevitably have erased their traces. In the third stanza, which returns to the immediacy of the present, the fields and hills, just as in Petrarch, appear as abstract terrains that might yield some trace. Yet Ammons emphasizes these natural forms as blockage: the sun big in the eyes blackens the view, rather than illuminating it, for through that lens, he sees the "black unwasting silence" of the hills. That knowledge of the nonreciprocity or asymmetry of the relation between nature's agenda and our own compels the speaker to imagine going beyond the hills. The end of the poem anticipates the impending sacrifice of the body to death, a sacrifice whose meaning can only be found beyond nature, beyond the hills, and the broken vestiges of human marks on Earth is the condition of the poem's reception by a reader. In all of his work, Ammons continually spoke of those great natural forces that make our efforts at building lasting forms pitiful and the equally tragic error of identifying our own subjectivity with the power of natural forces. His work has sought the interface between his voice and nature, where meaning in time might counter the decay of particulars into a universal entropy. It is lived experience that has counted in Ammons's poetics, an Emersonianism that presciently has anticipated the "leave no traces" ethic of contemporary ecological thought.[33]

We have seen the powerful effects of the experience of succession and generation in our earlier discussion of voice and possession. But just as the carpe diem tradition addresses the possibilities of deictic immediacy, so does the tradition of *ubi sunt qui ante nos fuerunt?* (Where now are those who lived before us?) take up the problem of the vanished dead. As the dead pass away, the living come forward to speak of their disappearance in wondering, if general, terms. As Henry Vaughan's marveling poem beginning "They are all gone into the world of light! / And I alone sit ling'ring here" (1655) suggests:

> He that hath found some fledged bird's nest, may know
> At first sight, if the bird be flown;
> But what fair well, or grove he sings in now,
> That is to him unknown.[34]

The carpe diem tradition, like the gesture of animation in all its forms, took us to the point where proximity was near merger. The *ubi sunt* tradition addresses the farthest reaches of sensual apprehension, the point where such apprehension trails into unintelligibility and disappearance and so where memory turns to imagination. Consider, for example, this fragment of elegiacs by Venantius Fortunatas (530–603), a troubadour who later became bishop of Poitiers. He is here writing to Iovinus, the governor of Provence:

Tempora lapsa volant, fugitivis fallimur horis . . .
sic quoque dissimiles ad finem tendimus omnes,
   nemo pedem retrahit quo sibi limes erit.
. . . .
quid, rogo, cantus agit? modulis blanditus acutis
   Orpheus et citharae vox animata iacet. . . .
quidve poema potest? Maro Naso Menander Homerus,
   quorum nuda tabo membra sepulchra tegunt?
cum venit extremum, neque Musis carmina prosunt,
   nec iuvat eloquio detinuisse melos.
sic, dum puncta cadunt, fugiunt praesentia rerum,
   et vitae tabulam tessera rapta levat. . . .

Time that is fallen is flying, we are fooled by the passing hours . . .
Likeness is none between us, but we go to the selfsame end.
The foot that hath crossed that threshold shall no man withdraw again.
. . . .
And where are the songs of the singers? Silent for all their sweetness.
Orpheus and the voice of the lute that he wakened are still.
Yea, but the poets, Virgil, Ovid, Menander, and Homer?
Their naked bones are laid in the damps of the grave.
Come to the end, small aid is there in the songs of the Muses.
Small joy to be won in prolonging the notes of the song.
Even as the moments are dying, the present is flying,
The dice are snatched from our hands and the game is done. . . .[35]

The best-known English *ubi sunt* poem (an anonymous work of the thirteenth century preserved in whole and sometimes in attached stanzas in various manuscripts, the most intact in the Digby Manuscript and most of the stanzas as well in the Auchinleck manuscript, c. 1320) begins:

Uuere beþ þey biforen vs weren,
Houndes ladden and hauekes beren
And hadden feld and wode?
þe riche leuedies in hoere bour,
þat wereden golden in hoere tressour
Wiþ hoere briȝtte rode;[36]

Describing the life of pleasure, sport, and wealth led by such ladies and their male companions—a paradise on Earth—the speaker recounts that this world was completely lost: "forloren." This poem, unlike Fortunatas's "Tempora lapsa," emphasizes that the pleasure-loving dead have gone to hell. The listener is urged to forgo sensual temptations, sent by the "Fiend," Satan. The poem sends out a plea to the Virgin Mary for help in that endeavor. The poem's turn from rich description to theological abstraction is like the turn of Augustine's *Confessions* from sense impression to prayer. Such a turn undermines the pleasure in song itself and we see that the sentiments of "quid, rogo, cantus agit" are much closer to that of the Renaissance sonneteer or modern poet who holds that while forms may pass away into the earth, some memory of content might be transmitted in time. In an elegy such as Robert Hayden's "Elegies for Paradise Valley," published in his *American Journal* (1978, 1982), the names of the dead are summoned as a catalog of remembrance. This is from the opening of Part V of that poem:

> Where's fast Iola, who so loved to dance
> she left her sickbed one last time to whirl
> in silver at The Palace till she fell?
>> Where's mad Miss Alice, who ate from garbage cans?
>> Where's snuffdipping Lucy, who played us 'chunes'
> on her guitar? Where's Hattie? Where's Melissabelle?
> Let vanished rooms, let dead streets tell.[37]

Here the elegy and the votive inscription are yoked in function; "vanished rooms" and "dead streets" have a doubled silence: the silence of inanimate spaces that have themselves disappeared. Only the name-bestowing speech of the poet can serve as the monument to Iola, Alice, Lucy, Hattie, Melissabelle, and the others memorialized in this sequence.

The *ubi sunt* topos often incorporates the theme of the invocation of the elements. The disintegration of the mourned beloved and the disintegration of the poet's voice take place as the poet summons nature to take up the lament. Curtius explains that these forms of prosopopoeia applied to nature are "at the poet's service when he wishes to heighten the effect of the lament for the dead." He particularly cites Bion's "Lament for Adonis" in which streams, cliffs, rocks, beasts, and the wind might continue the poet's lamentation. The conventions of the disturbances of Nature during Christ's crucifixion (earthquakes and rocks are rent in Matthew 27:51; darkness rises in Mark 15:33 and Luke 23:44–45) show a similar interruption and eruption of natural time.[38]

In "A Slumber Did My Spirit Seal," we saw the emphasis on the restoration of the pattern of the "diurnal" course as effecting the elegy's
close. A complex use of this idea of "dailiness" as what anneals the rupture death makes in time can be found, too, in Frank O'Hara's remarkable
and well-known elegy for Billie Holiday, "The Day Lady Died." As the
opening indicates, the poem retraces the speaker's steps in an exact re-
construction of events from 12:20 forward:

> It is 12:20 in New York a Friday
> three days after Bastille Day, yes
> it is 1959 and I go get a shoeshine
> because I will get off the 4:19 in Easthamptom
> at 7:15 and go straight to dinner
> and I don't know the people who will feed me

The poem is based on a complicated series of alterations of temporality,
all in the service of pointing to what is not in the "now" of its unfolding
present. The title effects the first reversal: Holiday's honorific "Lady Day"
appears in mirror form, and the specificity of the definite article is negated
by the final "died." That completed past action will not be found again until the final stanza of the poem.

But meanwhile we enter into a lyric present, the present of "emotion
recollected in tranquility"—or is it? O'Hara has taken the temporal convention of the poem not just from the present-centeredness of lyric; he has
also specifically borrowed a temporal structure from everyday experience:
the structure of recollection we employ when we have lost something. We
might call it the genre of "Where did I put my keys?" O'Hara brilliantly
plays on the *ubi sunt* convention as well: "Where is Billie Holiday?" He is
remembering the "day" Lady Day died and remembering what he didn't
know—or *did* he know in some uncanny way? For as he retraces his steps,
steps that truly are not even *vestigi sparsi* on the concrete sidewalks of
New York, he traces a journey full of subtle and not so subtle allusions to
history and mourning. He makes an unthinking journey retrospectively
into a kind of pilgrimage—one appropriate to a "holy day." The steps
themselves proceed by means of a choice foreign to most of O'Hara's poetic practice; they are in a fairly regular hexameter, the French heroic
form. Furthermore, by means of such typographical devices as the capi-
talized place names and titles and the abbreviations "trans." and "6th,," he
reminds us that this is *not* present-centered speech but rather an inscription, a record of what he remembers.

The person the speaker has lost is never named by name, but she is immediately named by allusion. It is three days after "Bastille Day," the great "holiday" of emancipation; a shoeshine man is evocative of the demeaning occupations that continued for African Americans even after slavery ended; journals from Africa evoke as well the relation between the old world and the New World: Verlaine and Bonnard, most elegiac of poets and painters; Hesiod's night; the "Black Irish" Behan, Genet's discourses on blackness, and then again, the return to France, the Gauloises and Picayunes evocative of creolization, and then what he has been seeing and not seeing: the votive inscription and portrait on the "post." This is a journey out of the underworld, but why has the speaker gone there? Like Orpheus, he is not able to turn and see the truth until he is face-to-face with the figure behind his consciousness: and at that moment she vanishes. The poem could end at this point, but it doesn't, for O'Hara completes the work of facing death, the work of death's realization, by means of another dimension of temporal specificity—the deep time of involuntary memory:

> and I am sweating a lot by now and thinking of
> leaning on the john door in the 5 SPOT
> while she whispered a song along the keyboard
> to Mal Waldron and everyone and I stopped breathing.[39]

In the merely real world, persons are types or references—a Patsy or Mike—but here Holiday's last accompanist Mal Waldron is given his full name, and Holiday herself is like a deity defying figuration: all the others are merely "everyone." The speaker is "leaning on the john door"—a place of threshold and expulsion for the speaker who is "propped" by memory at the moment of staggering truth. The speaker's symptoms are those of the shattering we saw in Sappho's *phainetai moi*—he is sweating; he can just hear her whispering, he feels he has "stopped breathing." He has literally stopped breathing the form of the poem, and he as well finds himself, his very being, the consequence of the end of inspiration.

Wordsworth famously said that the "poet makes absent things present," for surely *poiēsis* bears magical powers of representation and restoration of emotion. But in this particular tradition of elegy, the poet also makes the brutal absence of absent things present. A prototype for "The Day Lady Died" readily can be found in Wordsworth's own "Surprised by joy—impatient as the Wind":

> Surprised by joy—impatient as the Wind
> I turned to share the transport—Oh! with whom

But Thee, deep buried in the silent tomb,
That spot which no vicissitude can find?
Love, faithful love, recalled thee to my mind—
But how could I forget thee? Through what power,
Even for the least division of an hour,
Have I been so beguiled as to be blind
To my most grievous loss!—That thought's return
Was the worst pang that sorrow ever bore,
Save one, one only, when I stood forlorn,
Knowing my heart's best treasure was no more;
That neither present time, nor years unborn
Could to my sight that heavenly face restore.[40]

The "volta" or turn at the heart of all emotion or knowledge expressed in sonnet form is in "Surprised by Joy" effectively split and multiplied. The syntax of the opening lines is mimetic of the action: the initial clauses establish a mood with no referent; the interpolation *is* and speaks of impatience; the turn results in the surprise of beholding—a beholding of utter, irrevocable absence: "that spot which no vicissitude can find." The next line on "love" and recollection is the conventional, rationalizing answer to the problem: in the place where the dead are not, love can recall their presence. However, Wordsworth has more stringent standards of emotional truth: "But how could I forget thee?" What is the agent of forgetting, even in "the least division of an hour"? What possibly could make him unable to recognize that joy is a blinding of loss? The very possibility of that forgetting, expressed in "that thought's return," the repetition of the grief in the dynamic between forgetting and remembering, is the worst "save one" of all his losses—the one that was the death itself. No better example could be found of the principle that trauma "exists" in its repetitions. A trauma cannot be known at the moment of its experience, for such an experience is untotalizable and unintelligible phenomenologically. Analogously, the overly intelligible knowledge that arrives through rationalization and euphemism—"Love, faithful love, recalled thee to my mind"—is equally stripped of emotion and cognition. It is in its repetition, the repetition of loss worked through involuntary experiences of memory, here given shape through the replete recollection of the sonnet form, that Orphic trauma can be recognized and "faced" as the disappearance of the beloved's face.

Among the most remarkable aspects of this poem is its use of deixis to anchor a spinning subject. The poem brings us, in this regard, to the central role of deixis not just in the expression but as well in the determination of subjectivity. As Ludwig Wittgenstein wrote in *The Philosophical Investigations*, "The demonstrative 'this' can never be without a bearer." [41] The linguist John Lyons similarly contends that the idea that "language is, essentially, if not solely, an instrument of propositional thought fails to do justice to the phenomenon of subjectivity. One cannot reduce the speaker's expression of himself in his utterance to the assertion of a set of propositions." [42] What Lyons says about deixis and subjectivity in this discussion helps us understand how the deictic can involve complex uses of all tenses within its shifts and articulations. Hence, the deictic "now," as we have employed it thus far as a device of immediacy and making present, can also function as a set of temporal frames for subjectivity. Although Lyons's argument is rather technical, it promises a number of insights into the working of lyric forms and in the end gives us a way of talking about the incorporation of narrative into lyric forms.

In a poem like "The Day Lady Died," a series of "nows" unfolds into a final past-tense recollection—a recollection that, in coming to the fore, "recesses" the opening "nows" into their proper place as ground or context: the photograph of Billie Holiday on the cover of the *New York Post* comes into focus as the real photograph might have emerged from its bath of developer. And in "Nou goþ sonne vnder wod," there is a binary shift between narration and commentary. Lyons points out that linguistic and literary theories frequently have developed various categories in order to explore the differences between aspect and tense: between narration and discourse, between narrative and statement, or between narrative and commentary. In each instance, such approaches have a category of narrative that is opposed by some nonnarrative category that is considered to be more "subjective." But Lyons argues that "discourse can contain both narrative and commentary, or statement" and proposes that a distinction be made instead between "historical" and "experiential" discourses, the former is more objective, the second addresses the "greater subjectivity that is associated with the description of personal experience." Although he is concerned more with everyday spoken discourse than with forms of literature, Lyons emphasizes how "the speaker can project himself, in memory or imagination, to a power of reference different than that of the situation of utterance and, from that point of reference, describe situations in the experiential mode as if they were currently taking place. This experiential mode is more subjective in that it describes what the speaker is, or could be, currently perceiving or feeling." [43]

Many of the enduring cruxes of defining poetic genres, should we be inclined to such definitions, are "solved" by Lyons's insight. First, poetry is not merely the imitation of an utterance—it also *is* an utterance, and whatever speech might be imitated in dramatic poetry is continuous with the imitation of speech more generally in the experiential mode. Furthermore, the speaker is accounting for perceptions and feelings that may be hypothetical, fictional, or involuntary. The fictive status of poetic utterance is only relevant if we assume that propositional content and external reference are the standard of truth for poetic sentences. Wordsworth's recollections in "Surprised by Joy" give us the immediate experiential account of being surprised by joy and its aftermath: the poem is in the past tense, the feeling is not. This is a matter of the "here and now" implicit in the sudden expression of the first word, "Surprised," just as Bishop's "At the Fishhouses" had begun with an "Although" that indicated complete immersion in the immediacy of speech.

A small gloss by Merleau-Ponty on "here" is of particular relevance "here": "The word 'here' applied to my body does not refer to a determinate position in relation to other positions or to external co-ordinates, but the laying down of the first co-ordinates, the anchoring of the active body in an object, the situation of the body in face of its tasks."[44] If we follow Lyons's distinction, we also see that what seems to be a problem in Augustine's model of time—that the present is constantly in a flux of emergence and disappearance, including that present under which "the present" is articulated—is in fact the condition of the present perfect tense, the imperfect, by means of which all "experiential" discourse proceeds, regardless of the tenses used within it.[45]

Contemporary philosophers of time have continued to struggle with the relation between time consciousness and subjectivity. Merleau-Ponty's phenomenology of perception argues in Kant's shadow that the experience of time presupposes a view of time. But Merleau-Ponty also suggests that the subject has the capacity to introduce nonbeing into time experience: subjects have awareness of the past that is no longer lived and of a future not yet lived. By introducing nonbeing into the plenitude of being, subjects clarify perspectives and bring to the present those phenomena that are not there. Like Augustine, Merleau-Ponty opens up our sense of our relation to objects of nature and made things—objects that we animate in accordance with our memories and our expectations of the future.[46]

All theories of time confront two inevitabilities: first, the inevitability of sequentiality and the impossibility of true repetition and, second, the inevitability of death and forgetting as symptoms not just of loss of the past but of the decay of the self. Indeed, social conventions structuring time consciousness are in the end the secular equivalents of Platonic eternity: by submitting ourselves to the constraints of the social order of time, we enter into a grid of temporal order that continues regardless of the interruptions posed by death. Such a grid, with its increasing distance from the uneven fluctuations of the natural bases of temporal change, truly evades human intention and consequence. In the end the perpetuity of the mechanical clock becomes a second, more perfect nature. Yet, in the absence of differentiating marks or periods, the hum of its repetitions signifies nothing at all.

In his essay on *Time*, an unfinished work published posthumously, Norbert Elias writes, "That time takes on the character of a universal dimension is nothing other than a symbolic expression of the experience that everything which exists is part of an incessant sequence of events. Time is an expression of the fact that people try to define positions, the duration of materials, the speed of changes, and such like in this flow for the purpose of orientation."[47] The sun, moon, stars, and irregular movements of nature as sources of measure are replaced by a mesh of human inventions that then in turn appear as mysterious components of their own nature. This drift toward an eternalization of time, the imagination of a permanent form for time, Elias writes, is no doubt necessary in light of our fear of transience and death.[48]

Yet one of the most significant aspects of Elias's theory of time is his discussion of how the social integration of time permits the organization of violence—in the sense not simply that the state can more readily summon forces of control and manipulation, but also that violence is less able to erupt from individuals when they have submitted their agency to the time system and committed themselves to its reproduction through their everyday lives.[49] Therefore, we might contend that the most powerful works of art will go against the grain of this submission by offering an alternative to the grid of temporality driven by instrumental reason. In light of this grid, the local and small-scale reception of any work of art, no matter how monumental, returns us to that opening where our own lived experience of time intersects with that of individual others, acquiring a social horizon where collective history is not yet alienated from the experience of individual subjects.

Shelley's "England in 1819" is founded on the possibility of such an intersection:

England in 1819

An old, mad, blind, despised and dying King;
Princes, the dregs of their dull race, who flow
Through public scorn,—mud from a muddy spring;
Rulers who neither see nor feel nor know,

But leechlike to their fainting country cling
Till they drop, blind in blood, without a blow.
A people starved and stabbed in th' untilled field;
An army, whom liberticide and prey
Makes as a two-edged sword to all who wield;
Golden and sanguine laws which tempt and slay;
Religion Christless, Godless—a book sealed;
A Senate, Time's worst statute, unrepealed—
Are graves, from which a glorious Phantom may
Burst, to illumine our tempestuous day.[50]

The poem is a response to the Peterloo Massacre, the attack on an assembly demanding annual Parliaments and universal suffrage at St. Peter's Field in Manchester on 16 August 1819 by members of the Manchester Yeomanry, a militia group, and members of the Fifteenth Regiment of British Hussars, veterans of Waterloo.[51] Shelley has turned the sonnet form backward—the octave follows the sestet, with the first volta at "A people starved and stabbed in an untilled field": the men, women, and children trapped between the "rulers," those who promulgate injustice, and "the army," those who enforce it.

Shelley uses objective discourse, the assertion of propositional sentences, to create a catalog by means of plural groups and indefinite articles (*an* old, mad, blind, despised, and dying king; princes; public scorn; rulers; *a* people; *an* army; laws; *a* book; *a* senate). What is this list of thinglike names, this unheroic catalog, accumulating? The answer is *graves*. They are all destined for burial and disappearance, if not in revolt, then in time. The culminating lines turn at the grave as history will turn at the glorious moment of the rise of the Phantom of Liberty from their burial. As Shelley reverses the sonnet form, so does he reverse the temporality of the deictic present: what all these objective present truths are is revealed in their immanent deaths, their incipient *pastness,* and what the poem proclaims is the future that will truly illumine "our tempestuous day." "Time's worst statute" may be the 1801 Act of Union between Ireland and England that excluded Roman Catholics from civil rights, or it may be an appositive for the Senate itself, continuing to function without a populist sanction.[52] Yet in the end, Time's worst statute, its inexorable law, is death. Shelley proclaims in that death—the death consequent to enduring injustices—the promise of the ghostly return of revolutionary Liberty from its own youthful death. The hypothetical "may" here—both projected and given permission, echoes with great resonance to the poem's predecessor, Milton's "On the Late Massacre in Piedmont," which implores God to construct a similar catalog of sufferings ("in thy book record their groans"). "Their martyred blood and ashes sow / O'er all th'Italian fields where still doth sway / The triple tyrant: that from these may grow / A hundredfold."

The great moral depth of both poems stems from the use of a traditionally "personal" form within a public and historical frame. Shelley's reversals point to the ironies of history inherent in Milton's situation of writing and his own: Milton writes from England about a martyrdom of Protestants in Italy; Shelley writes from Italy about a massacre and intolerance toward Roman Catholics in England. Milton implores God; Shelley the atheist blasts religious hypocrisy. Yet Shelley's poem bears as well the bitter truth of its own inadequacy to provoke social change: he is much too far from the massacre to do anything about it. In fact, the poem itself never was published as a public outcry but remained unpublished for twenty years. Shelley included the sonnet in a letter to Leigh Hunt on 23 December 1819.[53] Although he urged Hunt to write on the contemporary crisis in England, he also said of the sonnet, "I do not expect you to publish it, but you may show it to whom you please." And although his sonnet displays much of Milton's powerful use of enjambment as an expression of violence in response to violence, the Phantom that may "burst" may not only shed its liberating light but also disperse in form— that form constantly deferred by our present hopelessness.

"England in 1819" moves from the most specific instance of social time in Elias's terms. Shelley had initially attached the title "England in 1820" to the poem in his fair copy, but Mary Shelley changed the title to "England in 1819" when she published it in the 1839 posthumous edition of his poems. Here any specific date is transformed via the particulars of the massacre to more and more abstraction until this final image of a bursting Phantom. This is an instance of how the assumption that every term of a poem must be anchored in its historical particularity can undermine the simultaneous aesthetic and political intentions of its author. Shelley has deliberated with great care on what is particular or incidental in the event, on what is subject to the "rhyme" of history that links his situation to Milton's and the massacre in Piedmont to the massacre in Peterloo, and on what is universal. The last is the Phantom of Liberty, that utopian project which for Shelley stands in the place of Milton's God. Once we insist that history is made of events that only happen once, it is far easier to break away from their significance and not to include ourselves among the members of Shelley's (and Milton's) closing utopian pronoun, "*our* tempestuous day."

III.   MEDITATION AND NUMBER: TRAHERNE'S *CENTURIES*

Anyone who reads "England in 1819" will notice the final bursting is already incipient in the spondees and overruns of the opening lines. Shelley
lets his measures spill; he is fed up with moderation and evenness of temper. This resource for expressing exasperation is in fact possible because
of the available metrical repertoire of sonnet and song tradition. A Renaissance poet musician such as Thomas Campion wrote of "that smoothe
toong whose musicke hell can move" ("When Thou Must Home"), of how
"lovely formes do flowe / From concent devinely framed" ("Rose-cheeked
Laura") and of "well-tun'd words" that "amaze / With harmonie divine"
("Now winter nights enlarge").[54] When Renaissance poets write of their
"numbers" and "measures," they remind us of the connection between
poetry and music we spoke of earlier, but they also recall the ways in
which poems are constructed models of time. Such temporality unfolds
on many levels at once. As the future becomes past, many other aspects of
time are revealed: the tension—or as Hopkins practiced it, the counterpoint—between metrical structure and the shifting progress of the individual line; the lexical transformation implicit in rhyme with its simultaneous link across time and denial of repetition; the tension between
pronounced speech and fixed inscription; the reversal and reorganization
of syntax and the disjunctions between syntax and rhythm; the fluctuat-
ing stability of stanzaic structure and the spatial and temporal breaks
effected by such forms as the caesura, the volta, refrains, choruses and burdens; and the historical accretions, borrowings, and metaphorical approx-
imations of "metrical structure" itself in practices such as contrafacta,
parody, and other modes of metrical allusion.

"Being in number" is thus a concept that is central to the place where
theories of time and practices of *poiēsis* meet. In Plato's *Timaeus* the
demiurge creates, after the World Soul, time as "a moving likeness of
eternity":

> When the father who had begotten it saw it set in motion and alone, a
> shrine brought into being for the everlasting gods, he rejoiced and being
> well pleased he took thought to make it yet more like its pattern. So
> as that pattern is the Living Being that is forever existent, he sought to
> make this universe also like it, so far as might be, in that respect. Now
> the nature of that living being was eternal, and this character it was
> impossible to confer in full completeness on the generated thing. But he
> took thought to make, as it were, a moving likeness of eternity; and, at

the same time, he ordered the Heaven, be made of eternity that abides in unity, an everlasting likeness moving according to number—that to which we have given the name Time.

The movement of days and nights, months and years, the "was" and "is" and "shall be" all are the parts or divisions of a Time that as motion confirms eternity as its image, that become and resolve "according to number." Number is the multeity that confirms the unity of Time.[55] The *Timaeus* proposes the Great Year as the cycle in which the heavenly bodies go through all their possible courses and return to their original positions.

Aristotle wrote of "being in number" specifically in his *Physics* in the passages after his discussion of "time [as] a measure of motion and of being moved." He writes "to be in time" means that something's "being should be measured by time." "'To be in time' is one of two things: (1) to exist when time exists, (2) as we say of some things that they are 'in number.'" He continues, "Since time is number, the 'now' and the 'before' and the like are in time, just as 'unit' and 'odd' and 'even' are in number. . . . But things are in time as they are in number. If this is so, they are contained by time as things in place are contained by place." Aristotle further specifies that things that *always* are are not in time, "for time is by its nature the cause rather of decay, since it is the number of change, and change removes what is." To be numbered, as our days on Earth are numbered, means that they count in time and also that they are subject to an eroding change.[56]

When poetic works are constructed by number, they are themselves moving models of time, as Time is for Plato a moving image of Eternity and as place becomes replete with being in Aristotle. But such number practices have their own history of emergence and disappearance.[57] Often linked to a mysticism that would replace the "now" of existential time with the infinity of the number system or the perfection of other structures of categorization (frequently, as we will see, the alphabet), numbers and measures come to the forefront of poetic practice when poets want to make a claim for transcending the immediacy of the world and return us to some of the ecstatic reasoning that characterized the Baroque engagement with eternity. The Counter-Reformation strategy was to make a direct appeal to the senses and thus, by means of a careful staging of forms of visual and aural rhetoric, to move the viewer or listener to transcendence. Yet many practices of numerical composition sidestep such an initial sensual appeal apparent in the form. And when such works are in prose, they forego the somatic pull of rhythm and song patterns, moving directly to the arithmetical and geometrical patterning of the allomorphic.

I now want to turn to a particular seventeenth-century practice of poetic meditation based on numerical composition in order to consider further the relations between the senses and temporal abstraction—and as well to consider the continuity of Platonic and neo-Platonic values in poems and the appearance and, as we will see, the disappearance of particular poetic forms. In this case, we will focus on the *century*, or composition made from units of one hundred. This concept in fact structures what is often considered to be the first sonnet sequence in English, Thomas Watson's *The Hekatompathia, or Passionate Centurie of Love*, registered in 1582. Watson's collection of one hundred poems was divided into two parts: "the first expresseth the Authors sufferance in Love; the latter, his long farewell to Love and all his tyrannie" and thus yokes its individual lyrics, which Watson called "passions" (each composed of eighteen lines in iambic pentameter), into the overall unit of one hundred and gives ample evidence of a will to form shaping emotion—in fact, taking emotion far over into the sphere of convention.

But Watson's volume, being a scrapbook of experiments in dialogue poems, echo poems, acrostics, aphorisms, quasi-sestinas, Latin hexameters, and a pillar verse stretching beyond the eighteen-line limit, connects not so much to the idea of one hundred as a perfect number as it does to the Italian *cento*—a composition made from pieces—coming from the Greek, Sanskrit, and Latin terms for a ragged or patched garment. And the form appears to be relatively simple given the complexity of number symbolism in other medieval and Renaissance texts.[58] In *The Hekatompathia*, a hundred poems serves as a description of the volume more than as a principle of composition.

As a mode of lyric composition, the century is relatively rare and generally limited in English to the seventeenth century—or what we call the seventeenth century in our habit of counting from the birth of Christ. It is this paradox—the rarity of the century form in the history of poetry and the prevalence of it in our organization of historical thought—that interests me. Calculation by units of one hundred has become so commonplace as to seem to be given by nature. Beyond the centennial, centurion, or Roman century as a count of eligible voters or our measurements for perfect test scores and the honeymoon period of the U.S. presidency, we can think as well of the Greek hecaton in hectare, hectograph, and hectometer.

The century form can be linked to other forms that appear in the intersection of linguistic and arithmetical systems. In any culture a principle of order governs the use and understanding of time, coordinating aspects of social life and integrating internal time consciousness into a social system.[59] Russell emphasizes in his *Introduction to Mathematical Philosophy* (1920) that order will be a property of the members of any set in which there is a recognized relation of precedence and succession. In the measurement of time linguistic and arithmetical concepts are both employed. The conjoined systems of ordinal and cardinal numbers provide the link between them.

The linguistic system is used to name different, and possibly recurrent, points in time, whereas the arithmetical system measures the lapse of time according to an end in view. The former is consistent with "traditional" time—that is, time as calculated by cultures tied to the cyclic aspects of nature such as slaughter, harvest, and planting. Arithmetical time or abstracted time begins with modernism and the use of measuring instruments tied to distance, money, and other noncyclical features of culture. Traditional time, as we saw in Ovid's *Metamorphoses*, is Pythagorean, part of a numerical cosmology based on nonmathematical associations of numbers. Pythagoras said all things are numbers, but by this he meant as well that all numbers are things. Numbers are significant for meanings that have been established extrinsically. The history of the computation of time therefore tends in both its particular and larger aspects toward abstraction and the eventual severing of any intrinsic relation between numbers and things. In other words, just as the use of natural numbers in the West depends on categorizing in a perfectly abstract way, in order that the system of numbers can operate in relation only to itself, so in the history of the use of numbers does calculation according to increasingly large units of time result in an abstraction of the order of time from the experiencing of events on the level of the individual body—even if the body is nevertheless the basis for such calculation.[60]

Numbers, arising from the bodily experience of time, provide in systems of divination and mysticism an extension out of experiential time. And in the case of numbers beyond ten, written notation and means of calculation such as an abacus can admit of increasing abstraction and complexity in their use or application. In the West, the scriptural basis for the relation of numbers to divine order is provided in Solomon 11:20: "Thou hast ordered all things in measure, number, and weight." In the Middle Ages, this order is divine. Augustine argues, for example, that the inherent beauty of music results from measure and number as successive repetitions of unity.[61]

In Renaissance aesthetics, the concept *ratio* gets linked to *concinnitas*—the concordance between nature and reason. Leon Battista Alberti

calculates the ideal proportion of the human body to an architectural column as a mean of eight and links this to the role of the octave in musical
harmony.[62] But, given the intrinsic relation of ten to the body, not all numerical composition is tied to bodily proportion or theories of cosmology.
When a number results from squaring or cubing, going one beyond the
number will have significance as a transgression of the bounds of a system.
For example, Scheherazade survives one night longer than the cube of
ten—that is, when she steps beyond the system of counting she escapes
mortality.[63] The same is true of thirty-three, the number of Christ's years
on Earth, as one beyond the fifth power of two. As the cube of a bodily proportion and as the marginal number to the Trinity times Christ's number,
one hundred is a particularly rich instance of the merging of linguistic and
arithmetical meanings.

But the boundary between the logic of number and cultural symbolism
is itself the source of cognitive pleasure as static contemplation of order is
juxtaposed to the movement of experienced time.[64] Poetry and music as
the enunciation of this tension between rhythm (or the somatic apprehension of interval) and meter (the abstract system of numerical order
governing a given composition) are the aesthetic forms most deeply engaged with this integration. Curtius notes that by the twelfth century the
concept of *saeculum*, or lifetime, found in Tacitus and Amobius was combined with the modern reckoning by centuries, *centennium*.[65] But even in
antiquity, the numbers 10 and 100 and their multiples were considered to
be aesthetically satisfying. We have already mentioned that in Plato's
Timaeus, the Great Year links the circuit of the heavenly bodies to 360
times one hundred days, to the ideal human life of one hundred years in
such a way that the microcosm of one human life mirrors the macrocosm
of the great year. The early sixteenth-century occult philosopher Henry
Cornelius Agrippa had similarly suggested "simple numbers signify Divine things; numbers of ten, Celestiall; numbers of one hundred terres-
tiall; numbers of a thousand, those things of a future age."[66]

Under the number symbolism and number mysticism taken from
Pythagoras and joined to Christian number symbols, ten is *plenitudo sa-
pientiae* since seven means the creation and three the Trinity.[67] In the
cabalistic hierarchy, as it was adapted by the Florentine neo-Platonists,
the soul and inner life of the hidden God were expressed in the *sefirot*, or
ten primordial numbers. There are three spheres: the angelic, the celestial, and the corruptible. The angelic world is the root of unity, or ten; the
celestial sphere is "unity squared" or one hundred, and the corruptible
sphere is unity cubed, or one thousand.[68] Marsilio Ficino links the square
of ten to the life of man and the cube of ten to the number of the firma-

ment of fixed stars.[69] From the enneads of the *Vita Nuova*, Dante proceeded to the structure of the *Commedia*—1 + 33 + 33 + 33 = 100 cantos designed to conduct the reader through three realms, the last of which contains ten heavens.

It is not so much that we might pursue a genealogy of our current use of the term *century* by looking at these practices. But rather, by following a particular practice, we might be able to imagine the time consciousness of another time and shed some light on our own sense of context and chronology. In the spiritual exercises of the Baroque, the general pattern of the Christian progress of the soul from innocence to fall to redemption acquires a numerical significance. There are four conventional stages of medieval Christian mysticism: preparation, purification, illumination, and perfection. Ignatian exercises such as those Hopkins practiced often have five steps that lead to quickened experience: composition of place, premeditation, memory, understanding, and will. Bonaventure followed Augustine's precepts and suggested three stages—we should look for traces of God in the external world, the self, and God's attributes. These methods influenced in turn Baroque practices of devotional and meditative writing using numerical composition.[70]

Joseph Hall (1574–1656) recommended in his 1606 treatise, *The Art of Divine Meditation*, a practice of writing devotional paragraphs of various lengths into units of one hundred.[71] Hall's earlier *Centuries of Meditations and Vows: Divine and Moral* (1605–1606) explicitly links his devotional writings to the Psalms of David. Both are described as extemporal meditations produced by the free play of the mind over what it sees. Hall's *Centuries* thus have a seemingly spontaneous lyricism that distinguishes them from catechisms such as Martin Zeiler's collections, *Centuria Variarum Quaestionum, Oder Ein Hundert Fragen* of 1658 and *Centuria II* of 1659, and Alexander Ross's 1646 work, *A Centurie of Divine Meditations upon Predestination and Its Adjuncts*. Ross's work consists of prose paragraphs of about 150 words, each divided into two parts, a general observation and a prayer.[72]

Nevertheless, the most well-known use of the century form appears in the writings of Thomas Traherne.[73] This body of work itself bears a dramatic and unusual relation to time because of its belated discovery. In 1895, two manuscripts were found in a London bookstall by W. T. Brooke —a folio volume containing thirty-seven poems and a commonplace book made of extracts from other texts; the second volume contained prose works now entitled "Centuries of Meditation," for the works were organized into units of one hundred and labeled "first century," "second century," up to an incomplete fifth century that stopped at its tenth paragraph or strophe. Neither volume was signed or attributed. The works were purchased by the editor and bibliophile Alexander Grosart, who thought, as Brooke did, that the poems might belong to Henry Vaughan. After Grosart's death in 1899, Bertram Dobell bought the manuscripts. Dobell traced the authorship definitively to Traherne, a shoemaker's son from Hereford who had received a B.A. and M.A. from Oxford, had been rector of the small Anglican parish of Credenhill just outside Hereford, and had served as chaplain at the end of his life to Sir Orlando Bridgeman, Lord Keeper of the Great Seal. Traherne died at the age of thirty-seven in 1674.

Dobell published the poems in 1903 and the centuries in 1908. In 1910, another manuscript of Traherne's poems was found in the British Library. It was entitled *Divine Reflections on the Native Objects of an Infant's Ey;* this work had been copied and edited by Traherne's brother Philip. In 1964, an additional manuscript of meditations, entitled *Select Meditations,* was discovered by James Osborn. This manuscript is also organized into centuries, although it is incomplete, for the first forty-three leaves are missing and other pages are damaged or missing as well—there are 376 of 468 meditations remaining, grouped into four centuries. In 1967, Traherne's massive draft of the beginning of an encyclopedia, his *Commentaries of Heaven,* a work of nearly four hundred pages of minute double-columned writing, was pulled from a burning rubbish heap in Lancashire.[74]

This story raises obvious problems of authenticity and textual authority for anyone working with these manuscripts and printed volumes. Traherne readily belongs to the professionalization of literary scholarship and the revival of metaphysical poetry under Modernism, just as he belongs to the world of seventeenth-century devotional writers. The only work of his published during his lifetime was his *Roman Forgeries* of 1673, a polemical work of scholarship dedicated to his patron and designed as an attack on the papacy. His *Christian Ethics,* another work composed under Bridgeman's patronage, was designed as a handbook of practical morality for educated laymen and was published in 1675, a year after Traherne's death. In 1699, his *Thanksgivings* was published anonymously under a different title *(A Serious and Pathetical Contemplation of the Mercies of God);* in 1717, his *Meditation on the Six Days of Creation* was published as part of a collection of meditations and devotions under the name of his friend and spiritual associate, Susanna Hopton.[75]

In addition to these works, Traherne kept a book of devotions on the principal days of the church calendar from Easter to All Saint's Day. A notebook of 396 pages, now in the Bodleian Library, contains undergraduate notes on ethics, geometry, and history and later notes on the writings of Francis Bacon.[76] Yet another notebook is now in the British Library: it is made up of the comments of Ficino affixed to Ficino's translations of Plato and Hermes Trismegistus, notes made by an amanuensis from Theophilus Gale's *Court of the Gentiles*, and notes from a work called "Stoicismus Christianus."[77]

When we consider these extant texts, Traherne can be seen to be taking up a conversation influenced by the concepts of continuous creation found in Plato's *Timaeus* and in the writings of Hermes Trismegistus, Agrippa, Augustine, Ficino, Pico della Mirandola, and the Cambridge Platonists. Traherne's writing practices, ranging from public tracts to writings by his amanuensis, to lyrics and notes constructed in solitude, encompass a variety of possible audiences. He at times has dictated the terms of writing to his amanuensis and at other times has left pages blank—a practice tied to the invitation he offers in his inscription on the first leaf of the Dobell manuscript of the *Centuries:* "This book unto the friend of my best friend / As of the wisest Love a mark I send, / That she may write my Makr's prais therin / And make her self therby a Cherubin." Traherne's writing practices in fact fulfill the mandate of the enormously popular anonymous work of 1658, *The Whole Duty of Man*, a mandate commanding that one serve one's self, one's neighbor, and one's God.

Traherne himself gives an interesting gloss on his method of composition in the *Select Meditations*, perhaps giving evidence of a more eclectic plan. In Meditation 15 of the "Forth Century," he adds a small lyric that begins, "O Sing, O Soar, O faint, O pant of Breath! / O Saint Rejoyce." Meditations 16 and 17 are blanks, but at 18 Traherne writes, "Here Aphorism and there a Song: here a supplication and there a Thanksgiving. Thus do we bespangle our way to Heaven." The presence of blanks is intriguing. We also find in the second century of the *Centuries of Meditation* that Meditation 88 is blank. Because the *Select Meditations* seem to be a fair copy, there is a conscious use of the blank. In other words, the careful marking of space in the text makes it unlikely that a simple error in numbering is being noted. Although a conjecture, we might deduce that this blank represents the reality of some other measurement, such as a day, and that perhaps the centuries were written over hundred-day time spans.

In the entry under "Author" in his *Commentaries of Heaven*, Traherne writes, "An author is a living person, or a free and intelligent Agent that works to voluntarily produce his work of himself and design an End for which he produceth it. He is distinct from his Work and from the Instrument by which he worketh. . . . God alone is the author of all good. . . . Rational persons are God's instrument." The writer is thus the instrument of God's creation, miming that creation by his free activity. The two texts that will be my focus here—the *Centuries of Meditation* and *The Commentaries of Heaven*—continue this emphasis on the microcosmic and macrocosmic orders of creation. Here the influence of the Augustinian theme of mirroring the creation of God is combined with the numerical and taxonomic basis of creativity found in the *Timaeus* and in the temporal plan of Genesis, in cabala, and in devotional exercises.[78] The five centuries of the manuscript found by Brooke by now have often been reprinted, whereas the *Select Meditations* and *Commentaries of Heaven* exist only in manuscript—the Select Meditations at Yale and the Commentaries at the British Library.

Much has been made of the plan of the five centuries in the Dobell manuscript. The text is composed in heavily stressed prose paragraphs, usually made up of seven sentences or more and characterized by an aphoristic style making frequent use of incremental repetition, exclamation, and shifting modes of direct address. The first century attends to the importance of what Traherne calls "enjoyment," a term that he uses to intersect concepts of pleasure and apprehension. "Enjoyment" is rooted in desire yet achieves its positive effects only in the communion of all souls in God. The century discusses Christ and the cross as mediating the relation between the wants of men and the wants of God.

The second century continues with the theme of the union of souls— man as the image and son of God, the enjoyment of Christ as the son of God, and love as the expression of the Trinity. The third century shows the soul's movement toward the attainment of enjoyment; this century has a stronger narrative direction than the other four centuries, for it moves from "infant vision"; to the fading of early vision; to the discovery of the Bible as a compensation for such loss; to a discussion of the value of formal education, solitude, and contemplation; to a concluding meditation on the Psalms of David. The third century also is distinguished by having seven poems serve as units of the whole and function as lyric eruptions on themes introduced in the preceding prose paragraphs: these poems appear at 4, 19, 21, 26, 47, 49, and 69. The fourth century presents an outline of the principles of enjoyment and their practice; a discussion of the relation between contemplative and active happiness, of the necessities of poverty, free will, and self-love; and a proclamation of God's love of man's creaturely nature. The fifth century, which breaks off after the tenth paragraph, emphasizes infinity, eternity, and God's omnipresence.

We now know that there were probably more centuries written by Traherne and that these were most likely completed before the writing of the Dobell manuscript. The *Select Meditations* contain references to the king and Parliament that seem to date them as being consequent to the Restoration.[79] Furthermore, the fragmented state of the fifth century only emphasizes Traherne's habit of beginning his numbering again after each unit of one hundred. Traherne gives several significant clues as to how we are to read the incomplete condition of his manuscript. In paragraph 5 he says, "Infinity of space is like a painter's table, prepared for the ground and field of those colours that are to be laid thereon. Look how great he [God] intends the picture, so great doth he make the table—It would be an absurdity to leave it unfinished or not to fill it. To have any part of it naked and bare, and void of beauty, would render the whole ungrateful to the eye, and argue a defect of time or materials, or wit in the limner." In paragraph 6 he continues with an idea from Augustine and Plotinus regarding the split between earthly and heavenly duration: "This moment exhibits infinite space, but there is a space also wherein all moments are infinitely exhibited, and the everlasting duration of infinite space is another region and room of joys. Wherein all ages appear together, all occurrences stand up at once, and the innumerable and endless myriads of years that were before the creation and will be after the world is ended, are objected as a clear and stable object, whose several parts extended out at length, give an inward infinity to this moment and compose an eternity that is seen by all comprehensors and enjoyers." He concludes in paragraph 10 that God is busied in all parts and places of his dominion, perfecting and completing humankind's bliss and happiness. There cannot be any fragmentation or stray unit for Traherne because all human activity is embraced and completed by God's work in the nexus of infinity and eternity.[80]

If we look closely at such passages in the centuries and turn as well to the *Commentaries of Heaven*, it becomes evident that the century is not so much a heuristic as a theology of time. The full title of the *Commentaries* is *Commentaries of Heaven wherein the Mysteries of Felicitie are Opened and ALL THINGS Discovered to be Objects of Happiness Every Being Created and Increated being Alphabetically Represented (as it will appear) in the Light of Glory Wherein also for the Satisfaction of atheists and the Consolation of Christians, as well as the assistance and Encouragement of Divines; the Transcendent Verities of the Holy Scriptures and the Highest Objects of the Christian faith are in a clear mirror Exhibited to the Ey of Reason in their Realities and Glory.* Designed to be comprehensive, the Commentaries are organized by alphabetical entries, extending from "Abhorrence" to "Bastard." There are ninety completed articles, eighty-two under the letter *A* and eight under *B*. Each entry discusses a concept and concludes with a poem, usually in couplets and summarizing the points that have been made. Unlike the poems functioning as units of the third century, which seem to erupt out of the restrictions of the prose form, these works, following the carefully stressed and orchestrated prose passages, emphasize a rhyming didactic ease. The incremental repetitions of the prose work by halting turns and digressions. They show a mind struggling toward definition. But the lyric sections flow with neat precision as if the meaning of the concept now suffused or overwhelmed the speaker.

Because of the frequent cross-references at the end of entries (e.g., under "Baseness," Traherne writes, "vid. Redemption, Incarnation, Passion, Christ," etc.), it is generally thought that his writing of the manuscript, begun in the 1670s, was cut short by his death. The longest entry, extending to thirty-eight columns, addresses the topic of "Ages" and provides an understanding of the meaning of the century form.

Traherne had mentioned the notion of ages several times in the five centuries. In the first century, paragraph 78, in a passage of direct address to God, he says, "since the World is sprinkled with Thy blood, and adorned with all Kingdoms and Ages for me: which are Heavenly Treasure and vastly greater than Heaven and Earth, let me see Thy glory in the preparation of them, and Thy goodness in their government." Furthermore, in the third century there is much discussion of the boundaries or limits of the world and its temporal ends. In paragraph 24 Traherne says:

> When the Bible was read, my spirit was present in other ages. I saw the light and splendour of them: the land of Canaan, the Israelites entering into it, the ancient glory of the Amorites, their peace and riches, their cities, houses, vines, and fig-trees, the long prosperity of their kings, their milk and honey, their slaughter and destruction, with the joys and triumphs of God's people. . . . I saw and felt all in such a lively manner, as if there had been no other way to those places, but in spirit only. This showed me the liveliness of interior presence, and that all ages were for most glorious ends, accessible to my understanding, yea with it, yea within it. . . . Anything when it was proposed, though it was ten thousand ages ago, being always before me.

As Traherne begins his description of the "nature" of ages in the *Commentaries of Heaven,* he emphasizes the ratio between human life and the concept of an age:

> An age is a part of Time measured by the Life of Man who being the best and most Noble of the Creatures, as he is the Lord of the World, is a Lord of Ages, which is said concerning one and is said concerning all. A Crow may live 300 years and a Raven 900, an Oake perhaps 1000 yet are not

Ages adopted to their Lives but accommodated to ours as Empires are measured and distinguished by the Lives and Periods of their Emperors, not of meaner Vassals and inferior Subjects. The Duration of Mans Life being Various and uncertain it is something difficult to find the standard by which an Age is computed but general Custom and Authority has prevailed to define an Age within the Limit and Measure of an Hundred years. Duration is their Matter, to which such a Relation and Quantity gives the forme. (f. 57r)

Traherne goes on to explain that at first, because there was no sin, there were no Ages:

No Man's Death had distinguished one Generation and another. Since therefore the Form of one Generation was counted an Age, in Eden certainly there had been no Ages. . . . From the Creation to the Deluge man generally lived 8 or 900 years and sometimes they wanted but little of 1000. During that time, because any round number is perfect and no broken number [respondeth or agreeth as] a whole with the Soul of Man, an Age was reckoned 1000 years. In after times the Life of man was shortened to 120 years and he that lived more upon Earth was esteemed a very Aged person as by man Sin came into the World, and Death by Sin, so by the Multiplication of Sin, Death were multiplied and by the Continuance of Increase in Sin Life was shortened. Much to the Benefit of the World, and man, that Labor and vanity might be a little lessened and Eternity filled perhaps with more persons and Greater Wonders. (f. 57r)

Hence, Traherne moves toward his explanation of the discrepancy between the length of life he finds in his contemporary world and the Platonic contention that one hundred years is the life of man:

Since threescore years and ten is the Life of Man in these days and by reason and strength it be fourscore years, it is full of Labor and Sorrow, an Age would be accounted 70 years and the other ten but unprofitable vanitie did not some men yet live to an hundred and Twenty, which gives occasion to Nature always ambitious of Perfection to lay hold on the full Time of an hundred years. Otherwise because the Life of some men even now exceedeth it, an Age would be more were it ever measured by the Longest Life. . . . [I]t is tacitly agreed upon by Mankind [that their] years should be reduced to a certain Number since therefore Space of an Hundred Years is the neerest round and perfect Number to the Length of Life, in these days and for many Generations past. Time by the learned is mea-

sured by *Centuries* and he that liveth 300 years, as Nestor of Old and
Joannos Temporibus of late did, is said to have exceeded his own age and
to have continued three. (f. 57r)

Traherne separated the formal device of measurement by century from
the content or matter of ages, claiming the latter for God alone (f.57r). In
this choice we find him following the neo-Platonic use of number and
cosmology to reach beyond experiential time. And his emphasis on the duration of the life of the individual person adapts Augustine's philosophy
of history from *The City of God* to such a numerical scheme. Augustine
had argued against the cyclical theories of time in Platonism by refusing
any chronological continuity between the finite dimensions of subjective
time and the infinity of God's creation. By encompassing ages in eternity,
Traherne maintains such a separation but does not resolve the issues of
whether the world was created in time, whether it would end in a specific
time known to God (as Augustine contended), or whether time was synonymous with eternity and infinity. Augustine had refused to link the
"progress" of Christianity to the progress of the Roman state or any other
secular institution; he continually framed history in terms of the individual's relation to revelation: "Like the correct knowledge of an individual
man, the correct knowledge of that part of mankind which belongs to the
people of God, had advanced by approaches through certain epochs of
time, or, as it were ages, so that it might be lifted from the temporal to the
perception of the eternal and from the visible to that of the invisible."[81]
By measuring ages according to an ideal span of human life, Traherne as
well ties ages to individual salvation and the perspective of individual
agents.

Within Traherne's ecstatic reasoning, ages become the vehicle of man's
apprehension of eternity:

> [T]he duration before the Beginning of the World and after its End are
> measured by Ages, Eternity itself wherein there is no succession of part,
> being represented and conceived under the Notion of a space including
> innumerable Ages, ever continuing, neither beginning nor ending. . . .
> Hence it appeareth that man gave the Denomination and Measure to an
> Age, tho God to Duration. The Matter of an Age being purely his, but the
> Form or Manor of its Being ours for its Limits are derived from our Hu-
> man Conception, without which as there had been no zones and thoughts
> in the Heavens, so neither had there been any set Periods or Distinctions
> of Time which are like to Lines in the Zodiack, imaginary all, but fit and
> serviceable for our calculation. In every Thousand years there are ten

ages, as in every Age there are an Hundred Years. The World therefore
having lasted 5600 years, hath contained 56 Ages. But where they are is
a material and doubtfull question. (f. 57r)

This calculation is most likely borrowed from the *Chronographia* of
Julius Africanus. Julius took from Hebrew tradition the idea of the millennium, or thousand-year-long kingdom of the Messiah; the end of that
kingdom would be the end of the world. The whole of history would equal
a cosmic week, with each day constituting a thousand years. As Psalm 90,
verse 4, had declared, "A thousand years in thy sight are but as yesterday."
The first six days covered a period beginning with creation. This order
would end at the millennium, or final day, with the second coming of
Christ. Julius claimed that five and one half cosmic days had lapsed between the creation and the birth of Christ, or 5,500 years. By this reasoning, in the year 500 the second coming could be expected. Even though
that year came and went, a time scheme of six thousand years more or less
lasted well into the period of the Reformation.[82] Traherne explains that it
is up to the learned men of every period to define and measure the limits
of ages, and he presents a sample of etymological reasoning: "Ages are limited and defined by the Sages. Wise and venerable men being therefore
called Sages because they see into Ages" (f. 57v.).

As Traherne goes on to elaborate a general theory of "ages," the concept of the century reaches a maximal point of mystical imagination. He
writes, "[T]he utmost Bounds of the Everlasting Hills being the same as it
is in a Mirror, so it is here. The Highest in the Hemisphere is the lowest
in the Glass. The Skies above are the pavement beneath, and East is the
West, the Remotest thing without, the deepest within" (f. 61r). The initial
determination of an age as a hundred years on the basis of the span of a human life becomes, through the transformations of God's grace manifested
within eternity and infinity, a purely formal determination. Simply put,
the triumph over mortality promised by Christian teleology obviates the
necessity of history.

In Traherne's lyric practice, neo-Platonism becomes a formal operation. Reference to the world is constantly altered and extended into reference to the ideal. When Traherne turns to the issue of the contents of the
ages, he looks to the Bible, giving a list of events that, because they occur
after the Fall from Eden, enter into the rubric of ages: early Rites of offering Sacrifice, Abel and Cain, Translation of Enoch, the Righteousness of
Noah, the Renewal of the Covenant, the Rebellion and Dispersion at Ba-
bel, the confusion of Languages and Genealogies of Nations, the Calling
of Abraham, and so on, through the Old Testament until he reaches "The

Incarnation of God and Miracles of his Nativity, his Life Doctrine, Parables, Miracles and Virtues, His Cross and Passion his / Love the extent of it and of his merits. Like the Rays of the Sun they reaching all Ages" (f. 64v, f. 65r, and f. 65v). Traherne goes on to list elements of the New Testament and extends his history to include the conversion of Constantine, "Councils, Fathers, Martyrs, Universities, Temples created throughout the World. Governments, Kingdoms . . . the long-suffering of God and the continuance of the Gospel until our Days. Therefore, are the Joys of Ages in a direct line from the beginning to our Time" (f. 65v).[83] Just as the birth of Christ reverses time, turning back death and carrying forward the vatic promises of the Old Testament at once, so does a textual history become its own fulfillment.[84] The history that comes from the Bible is the Bible as the manifestation of history. One can look near or far, forward or backward, upside down or right side up and in every difference will find the glory of the world displayed for the enjoyment of the individual soul. In Traherne we find the triumph of a textual practice at odds with death.

All of this might be, as Traherne himself would say, interesting because it is enjoyable. It is obvious that Traherne's poetic practices grow out of and develop a model of time attempting to rewrite the world in celestial terms. And it does not take any fineness of discrimination to conclude that the impulse toward mysticism and an encompassing synthesis of positions here comes out of the most painful personal and social circumstances of religious strife.[85] Furthermore, we might conclude with the clear lesson that our sense of periodization by centuries has much to do with the mystical operations of alphabetical and numerical symbolism[86] stretching from Plato, to cabalism, to Florentine neo-Platonism, to the Cambridge Platonists, to Traherne and beyond. But we also find here a genealogy of poetic subjectivity and its relation to the determinations of narrative history. Traherne wrote under his entry on "Ancestor": "so many true and real Worlds salute mine Ey as there are generations some one or other of My Ancestors lived in them all. The Sun gave him Light and Moon refreshment and Earth nourishment the Sea moisture, the Air Breath, the Fire warmth and all those assisted him that he might live and beget me. The influences of all the Stars and of all other things in that Age descend upon me, extend to me and rest in me and that perhaps 10,000 ways exciting my praise."

In this passage is the explanation for the third, autobiographical century's conclusion in the merging of Traherne's language with that of the Psalms of David.[87] The progress of the writer is to write him- or herself deeper and deeper into the past, so that the unfolding of the text, the realization of time, is the simultaneous encompassing and uncovering of what has come before—a writing practice virtually synonymous with Augustine's terms as we addressed them earlier: "as the past increases, the future is diminished." The techniques used in the Psalms—the interchangeability of alphabet and number and their use as modes of composition, the use of semantic parallelism to generate phrase and temporal sequence, the shifts from subject to object within epideictic form, and the orchestration of shifts of pronouns[88]—are taken up by Traherne as a spiritual practice enabling him to articulate the self and revert it, in Platonic terms, to the One. Arbitrariness in alphabetical, numerical, and metrical systems is thereby a way of mastering contingency of reference and extending the freedom of thought.

But the movement of reversion and reincorporation in Traherne is a narrative turn, a turn of reinscription back into the Christian plot. Here Traherne shows us the synonymity of aspects of seventeenth-century lyric with aspects of the medieval—the particularity of the subject is emergent, but ultimately collapsed back into the generalizations of Christian redemption. In this regard, there can be no Christian tragedy, and it is therefore exemplary that Traherne uses in the third century the first person when he speaks of universal experience and the third person when he turns to spiritual autobiography.[89]

IV. THE PROBLEM OF POETIC HISTORY

If we look at poetry's history in formal terms, the particularity continued by Aristotelianism, the revival of classical lyric via archaeology, and Modernism's diremption of seventeenth-century lyric from its religious context all push us toward a necessary misreading of such work as Traherne's—a reading that would emphasize the extension of mind in lyric as the subject's struggle toward articulation, individuation, and agency. This misreading enables both the threshold of historical recognition and the jubilation of the necessarily mistaken historical imagination. Practices of numerical composition are just one of many ways a poet might create a moving model of eternity. Once we read a sonnet sequence as a numerical progression, the turns between poems, the aggregation and dispersal of themes, the changes in point of view and addressee all move toward more and more occasions for the transformation of subjectivity. William Blake's "Songs of Experience" necessarily follow his "Songs of Innocence" in their composition and in the experience of the reader, but Blake also expects that the capacity for "willed innocence" he wants to promote arises from a return to the earlier poems under changed conditions of knowledge.

Poems in sequences and in bound books are both constrained in time and opened to new relations by their fixed orders. A poet such as Whitman, who wrote his *Leaves of Grass* by means of a long process of expansion and revision, is able to manifest in the sequence of editions certain principles of inclusion that underlie his practice of composition and his politics. And the *Cantos* of Pound, with their record of "fifty years of the growth of the poet's mind," including sites of dogma, unwarranted self-righteousness, and rigidity, nevertheless continue a seventeenth-century practice of meditation on the relations between diurnal time and the grander scale of history or cosmological thought. In Pound's case, his *Cantos* provide a record of his anguished attempt to figure the political and economic history of poetic powers of representation.[90]

Nevertheless, eternity and infinity are for Traherne terms for a universe replete with temporal experiences—experiences without boundary or limit. To think such a universe was to invite ecstasy. It is the residue of that theology that confers the aesthetic pleasure in our use of the century form and that as well reminds us we might proceed from practices rather than taxonomy in thinking about history. There is a clear and vastly syncretic line of continuity in the use of numerical symbolism. Pythagorean theory, the compositional modes of the Hebrew Scriptures, the symbolism of cabalism, neo-Platonism and Spenserian allegory, the "number-tumbling" of Louis Zukofsky and the contemporary artist Jonathan Borofsky, the numerical rules of the "Oulipo" group of experimental writers[91]—all pose numeration as a model of temporality in tension with the temporality of the social grid. Time is *thought* and therefore *made* in such forms. The practice of numerical form becomes a means of exploring the significance of seriality and chroniclism beyond the teleology of narrative's ends—just as the deictic situation of poetic speakers enables an imperfect and continuing relation to narrated experiences.

To imagine the relations between poetry and history is to bring forth immediately the problem of genre as fixed form and the problem of history as a discourse of reference. *Genre* is a problematic term because it implies fixed categories of the literary that, if they do not transcend, at least endure temporal change. It is quite easy to call immediately into question all of the essentialism, or nominalism, or idealism regarding cultural forms implied by such a stance.[92] And *history* as we commonly use the term to refer to a narrative of event or events raises questions of rhetorical convention and, ultimately, ideology as conditioning the possibility of historical perceptions from the outset.[93] If we think dialectically regarding the relations between poetry and history by paying attention to poetry as a structure of thought mediating the particular and the general, then we find the very terms of generality and specificity that appear in the tensions between genre and history are those poetry takes as its task to determine. It may be the case that the mediation of the particular and the general characterizes the production and apprehension of *any* art form and, indeed, that the aesthetic and the historical have shared this task of determination since the very emergence of "the aesthetic" in the eighteenth century.

Even privileging the aesthetic as the encompassing term here, we can say that the history of poetry "has" a history. That is, it is possible to find accounts of these problems regarding poetry and history, the universal and the particular, as stemming from quite opposed philosophical traditions. In what might be placed as the first of these traditions, Aristotle in the famous passage in Chapter IX of *The Poetics* mentioned in chapter 1 contends that "the poet's function is to describe, not the thing that has happened, but a kind of thing that might happen . . . [the distinction] consists really in this, that the one describes the thing that has been, and the other a kind of thing that might be. Hence poetry [and here Aristotle has in mind both narrative and lyric verse] is something more philosophic and of graver importance than history, since its statements are of the nature rather of universals, whereas those of history are singulars."[94] In this emphasis on events that, once reflected on, turn out to be generalizable, we find, of course, the continuing bias of a Platonism wherein poetry acquires status over history because it is universal but ultimately loses status to philosophy because it is hypothetical and fictional.

Throughout this tradition of thought—which extends, if somewhat ironically, from Aristotle to Augustine's division between perception and conception to seventeenth-century empiricism and its consequences— a split between subject and object, between "inner" and "external" phenomena, is maintained regardless of the varying values placed on either term. Perhaps its most delicate balance is effected in the mixture of neo-Platonism and Aristotelianism of Sidney's *Apology*, in which poetry is poised as the middle term between the overparticularity of history and the overgenerality of philosophy.[95] Even in Hegel's dialectic, aspects of Platonism appear in the rendering of art as the ideal in sensual particulars. As we noted in our discussion of his attitudes toward sound, Hegel finds art to be a more primitive form on the path to *Geist* than the forms of religious and philosophical thought respectively. Poetry remains "the universal art of the mind, which has become essentially free," but that "essentially" is of great import: because of poetry's stronger tie to the sensuous materiality of language it is still in Hegel's system an *adequation*, rather than an expression, of the ideal.[96]

But there is, of course, another, nonmimetic tradition of thought, which we have already glimpsed in our earlier discussion of Hegel on sense certainty. This tradition imagines the subject/object dichotomy as a false problem, claiming that expression is prior to subjectivity, that ideology is a consequence of form, and that thought is productive of culture, including its concepts of nature, rather than a mere reflection on it. This tradition is perhaps most vividly articulated by Vico in those passages on the origins of social life in metaphor that we discussed in our opening chapter. But it can be linked to a more general view of historiography if we see it as a facet of the break with medieval thought enabling the establishment of modernity. In broad terms, as classical aesthetics emphasizes imitation, morality, and the analysis of rhetorical effects, modern aesthetics emphasizes expression, the imagination, and autonomy of production.

We remember that Vico argued that poetry cannot be the *subject* of history, for poetry is necessarily *prior* to history, serving as the metaphorical process through which we represent the world to ourselves. As mentioned in chapter 1, Vico merges his account of the ontology of poetry and culture with an agenda of ideology critique because, he claims, ideologies develop out of the "hardening" of those narratives we initially drew from our metaphorical explanations of the universe. All "wisdom" arises from such needs for explanation. He writes:

> All that has been so far said here upsets all the theories of the origin of poetry from Plato and Aristotle down to Patrizzi, Scaliger, and Castelvetro. For it has been shown that it was a deficiency of human reasoning power that gave rise to poetry so sublime that the philosophies which came afterward, the arts of poetry and of criticism, have produced none equal or better, and have even prevented its production. . . . This discovery of the origins of poetry does away with the opinion of the matchless wisdom of the ancients so ardently sought after from Plato to Bacon's *De sapientia veterum*. For the wisdom of the ancients was the vulgar wisdom of the lawgivers who founded the human race, not the esoteric wisdom of great and rare philosophers.[97]

Such wisdom is "vulgar" in that it is a social accomplishment. Vico continues with the claim that the origins of poetry precede the origins of languages and letters, including histories. He contends that humankind developed from muteness to the articulation of vowel sounds by singing, then to stammering out the first consonants. Ludovico Castelvetro's neo-Aristotelian claim that history must have come first and then poetry, for history addresses the true and poetry is an imitation, is refuted by Vico: "inasmuch as the poets came certainly before the vulgar historians, the first history must have been poetic." Sidney makes a similar argument in his *Apology*, but in mythological terms, rather than textual ones. He claims that the legends of poets precede any histories: "And even historiographers (although their lips sound of things done, and verity be written in their foreheads) have been glad to borrow both fashion and perchance weight of poets. So that truly, neither philosopher nor historiographer could at the first have entered into the gates of popular judgments if they had not taken a great passport of poetry."[98]

Vico arrives at the rather stunning conclusion that memory "is the same as imagination. Imagination is likewise taken for ingenuity or invention. . . . Memory thus has three different aspects: memory when it remembers things, imagination when it alters or imitates them, and invention when it gives them a new turn or puts them into proper arrangement and relationship."[99] In this account of the place of memory, we find the dual relation of memory to historical and poetic thought. Memory is the method of history, but it is only intelligible through the imagination's determination and organization of its elements. And that determination and organization pose a theme, the particularization of parts in accordance with a totality or end, of both forms: poetry's own history is internalized and displayed in its perfected form. Moreover, history, shaped by processes of memory informed by imagination, becomes a consequence of poetic activity.

Vico's thoughts on poetry therefore foreground for us the nexus of aesthetics and a critical historiography we have come to associate with later thinkers. We find here an idea of the redemptive, future-oriented account of the past hoped for in Walter Benjamin's "Theses on History." This emphasis is particularly found in Thesis XVIII (A): "Historicism contents itself with establishing a causal connection between various moments in history. But no fact that is a cause is for that very reason historical. It became historical posthumously, as it were, through events that may be separated from it by thousands of years. A historian who takes this as his point of departure stops telling the sequence of events like the beads of a rosary. Instead, he grasps the constellation which his own era has formed with a definite earlier one. Thus he establishes a conception of the present as the 'time of the now' which is shot through with chips of Messianic time."[100]

Yet an earlier and more direct connection can be drawn to Croce,

Vico's most prominent modern follower, who related this way of thinking more particularly to issues in historiography. Contending that there are no "non-historical facts" but only "unthought facts,"[101] Croce draws, within a discussion of issues of chronicle and period in history, an analogy to metrical form that recalls Augustine's thoughts mentioned earlier on the parallels among the progress of a hymn, of an individual's life, and "the whole history of mankind":

> It has sometimes been said that every periodization has a "relative" value. But we must say "both relative and absolute," like all thought, it being understood that periodization is intrinsic to thought and determined by the determination of thought. However, the practical needs of chroniclism and of learning make themselves felt here also. Just as in metrical treatises the internal rhythm of a poem is resolved into external rhythm and divided into syllables and feet, into long and short vowels, tonic and rhythmic accents, into strophes and series of strophes, and so on, so the internal time of historical thought (that time which is thought itself) is derived from chroniclism converted into external time or temporal series, of which the elements are spatially separated from one another.[102]

Croce's statement includes a number of key insights into poetry's relation to history. First, his emphasis on the *relative* value of periodization brings forward the intersubjective ground on which historical judgments are made, their orientation toward an intelligible version of both the present and the future. But the *absolute* value of periodization stems from the problem articulated in Augustine's theory of time more generally. In returning to Augustine's concept of the coincidence of divine knowing and making, we properly remember, in fact, an important antecedent to Vico's thinking on this subject. Croce's discussion of interval in history has a profound connection to a much older formulation arguing that the experience of duration relies upon an internal time consciousness that itself is contiguous to the experience of language. Following Augustine and Vico, he defines history as that which is *thought* and therefore *made* so that the measurement of time is not dependent on some external Nature. Croce draws from a dialectical analysis of the relations between "general" history and "special" histories (between "History" as a narrative of the past and the particular histories of phenomena and discrete "moments"). He concludes that "nothing exists but general history." Not surprisingly, the formulation is both an homage to and a critique of Hegelian teleology, for Croce writes that "all doctrines that represent the history of nations as proceeding according to the stages of development of the individual, of his psychological development, of the categories of the Spirit, or of anything else, are due to the same error, which is that of rendering periodization external and natural." [103]

In Croce's critique of periodization and his claim that a general history must be constructed from a constant dialectic moving between particulars and abstractions, including that of a "general history," we find certain resources for considering poetry within the general history of our anthropomorphization of the human. Any theory of literary history that celebrates the so-called marginal status of poetry, that posits poetry as deviation, or that imagines poetic consciousness only within hackneyed terms of free expression and spontaneity is necessarily a functional theory incapable of addressing the complexity of poetry's relation to subjectivity and narrative. It has been a frequent claim of both cognitive anthropology and comparative poetics that poetry exists in tension with speech on the one hand and song on the other. But the fixed terms of such a model of genre can hardly accommodate the temporal nature of poetic experience. Nor can a static model acknowledge the complexity of the subject's passage from reception to expression in the *work* of poetry as it moves between aspects of received tradition such as metrical convention, aspects of sense impression such as rhythm and interval, and individuation of utterance.

Hence the impasse at which any current history of poetry finds itself: first, the contradiction of a constantly varying and multiple "form" that emerges from the classical aesthetic view; second, the hardly disinterested formulations of historical context posed as "surrounds" of various lyric practices that emerge from the modern aesthetic view. In any formalist account of poetry's history, poetry will be the subject of a larger "framework," but one that resists any encroachments that would threaten an intelligibility of form. We have only to think of how the very binding of the *Norton Anthology of Poetry* can make its contents seem equally alike and equally different. Yet in our considerations of deixis we have seen that the experiential stance of lyric can readily enclose or incorporate the "objectivity" of narrative and the ventriloquism of dramatic forms. It would be a mistake to reduce poetry to its propositional content, just as it would be a mistake to overlook its propositional content as it appears within a subjective framework of the "here" and "now."

From fragments such as *phainetai moi*, which explain the most intense contexts of feeling and perception within the abstraction of an addressee who is both herself and the third-person viewpoint, to the voyeurism implicit in Donne's and Eliot's overheard forms and Herbert's pedagogy in the guise of abstracted prayer, the triangulation of desire in

lyric structure is characteristic of a process of reversal and recognition between subject and object. The ideology of the "natural" subject—the subject who speaks from feeling, from the heart, from disinterestedness—is
a consequence as much as a source of lyric history.[104] How noncoinci-
dental, then, that innovations in discursive lyric (Pindar's reinvention of
the vatic and Jonson's reinvention of the Pindaric, eighteenth-century
"minor" poetry's striving after oral effects, aspects of such a syncretism
between the oral, the written, the archaic and the "modern" in Spenser,
Dryden, Gray, Burns, Keats, Yeats, Hughes, Dunbar, Heaney, Brooks, and
others) have typically been accompanied by accusations of a certain failure to gain or to hold an audience.[105] We have already mentioned Donne's
innovations as tied to his practice of scribal publication. In Hölderlin's
lyrics there is a tension set up between the ancient model of the poet's divinely prompted vocation, the Romantic aesthetic ideal of poetry as the
expression of genius, and the social fact of the contemporary diremption
of the poet from the organic community. Hölderlin's "Heimkunft" or
"Homecoming" elegy says in its final stanza:

> Aber ein Saitenspiel leiht jeder Stunde die Töne
> Und erfreuet vieleicht Himmlische, welche sich nahn.

As translated by Michael Hamburger: "Yet a lyre to each hour lends the
right mode, the right music, / And it may be, delights heavenly ones who
draw near."[106] The fit of poetic decorum with the world of the "ver-
wandten," those "relatives" to whom the poem is dedicated, is the basis
for the poem's ability to summon the gods; the poet declares in line after
line his affinity with the canny world to which he has returned, but the
reader notices that such affinity must be declared and that the poem itself
is not a song from the repertoire of such modes and musics but rather a
reflection on them addressed to a more distant, and broader, audience. In
"Dichterberuf" ("The Poet's Vocation"), Hölderlin writes:

> Doch nicht behält er es leicht allein,
> Und gern gesellt, damit verstehen sie
> Helfen, zu anderen sich ein Dichter.

"Yet never gladly the poet keeps / His lore unshared, but likes to join with
/ Others who help him to understand it."[107] These breaks in practices signify the recomposition of audience and are not merely instances of authorial innovation. Hölderlin reminds us that poetry, even poetry bringing
news from the gods, relies on and contributes to an intersubjective ground
of meaning between human beings.

It is something of a commonplace in aesthetic theory to argue that single-point perspective determined, in its initial appearance in the classical period and in its rediscovery in fifteenth-century Florence, the individual subject as rational observer and nature as "scene" or pictorial space.[108] This commonplace has been enabling of formalism in all the plastic arts and has made such terms as *property, landscape, viewpoint, work,* and *field* the "natural" vocabulary of the critic. But despite the superficial coherence between single-point perspective and the solo singer, only a weak analogy can be made with lyric. As lyric has come forward in language, it has necessarily come forward in processes of cultural catachresis and transformation. Virgil, Horace, and the Latin elegists faced enormous technical problems in reviving Greek meters and themes in Latin. In relying on *hyperbata*, they emphasized the violent mastery of time implicit in any metrical revival. By transforming syntax, such poetry necessarily affects our concepts of causality and temporality.[109] As we noted in chapter 3 on voice, English meter broke with pure-accentual forms and turned to accentual-syllabics as poets were influenced by continental examples, by the revival of classicism, and by the loss and rediscovery of Chaucer's use of the iambic line. The choice of "quantitative meter" (always a fiction of approximation) or iambics or any other system becomes ideologically laden—a matter of an attitude toward the past, toward nation, toward authorship.

Milton's prefatory discourse on "Verse" framing "Paradise Lost," explains: "The measure is English heroic verse without rhyme, as that of Homer in Greek and of Virgil in Latin; rhyme being no necessary adjunct or true ornament of poem or good verse, in longer works especially, but the invention of a barbarous age, to set off wretched matter and lame metre; graced indeed since by the use of some famous modern poets, carried away by custom, but much to their own vexation, hindrance, and constraint to express many things otherwise, and for the most part worse than else they would have expressed them." In these few sentences, he explains that his own formal aim is to assure "the sense [is] variously drawn out from one verse to another, not in the jingling sound of like endings." Enjambment and iambics are in the service of the continuity of the rhetoric, and when Milton does in fact use end rhyme at irregularly spaced intervals as early in Book I as these lines, 146 to 151, it has all the ease and natural appeal of coincidence:

> Have left us this our spirit and strength entire
> Strongly to suffer and support our pains,
> That we may so suffice his vengeful ire,

Or do him mightier service as his thralls
By right of war, whate'er his business be
Here in the heart of hell to work in fire, . . .[110]

Yet he also distinguishes himself from Christian writers of the fifth and sixth centuries who would have written hymns of such "wretched matter and lame metre"; his topic of man's disobedience requires heroic *English* measures, and he finds his compatriots not in those of his contemporaries who don't seem to know what they are saying but in a few "Italian and Spanish poets of prime note."[111] When in the early part of the twentieth century Pound, with a similar attitude toward convention, sought to break the "heave of the pentameter," he, too, looked for both ancient and European traditions that might serve as vehicles for his monumental themes.

The revival of forms has meant by definition the imposition of inappropriate context—either generally, in the sense that revival is always accompanied by an accretion of nostalgia, or specifically, as is the case when the ancient system of decorum (classical iambics for conversation; heroic hexameter for epic and pastoral eclogue; the couplet for inscription, epigram, satire, and epistle) is altered by the application of old meters to new situations (stressed decasyllabics for the stage, iambic pentameter adapted for high and low forms, and couplets for heroic verse in Renaissance practices).[112] The important break with song and narrative effected in Baroque poetry is not simply a consequence of new forms of conversion, spiritual discipline, and meditative practices; it is as well a matter of an attention to the *duration* of perception, a formal change coincident with transformed and transforming concepts of subjectivity.[113] If musicality is not only an abstract quality of lyric but also a specific historical practice whereby even the concept of musicality appears as ideologically laden, this is just one aspect of the temporally bound nature of lyric "timelessness." Lyric by definition appears in the unfolding web of memory, perception, and expectation so continually described in poetic theory from Augustine forward. The much-noted spatiality of poetry after the advent of print is only, in fact, an exaggeration of this position of ephemeral yet significant enunciation. The poignant anxiety regarding the material status of poetic utterance that we have found so often in the Renaissance sonnet tradition and later works, for example, both foregrounds and undermines this newly found spatial stability, this uncertain fixity.

The temporal impossibility of any pure repetition is emphasized in poetry by the creation of redundancy on the level of the somatic where sensual information offered to sight and sound appears to be the same. As I mentioned in chapter 1, synaesthesia in poetry produces *figuration* in sound while spatial interval makes sound intelligible and subject to mea-sure. And because that measure does not fade as the semantic burden in-creases, any semantic transformation remains inseparable from the so-matic. In the chapter on sound I discussed how a tension between sound and sense worked through off-rhymes and neologisms can indicate an alienation from the habits of both everyday speech and conventional po-etic form. We here return to a number of examples explored earlier: the emotional and literal "burden" of Dickinson's recurring slant rhymes such as *port* and *chart* (in "Wild nights—Wild nights!") or *spar* and *de-spair* (in "It was not Death, for I stood up") or *grace* and *price* (in "Publi-cation is the Auction"); the deadening and deadly insistent exact rhymes we found in Plath's "Lady Lazarus"; and the refusal of rhyme and breaking of pattern in the final lines of many stanzas in Wilfred Owen's work. In this process of objectification of what is most individual, what is brought forward is the subjective view of the social; what is felt is brought to the light of what can be known via the intersubjective work of speaking and listening in time. Lyric here departs from the narrative tradition in its break with teleology and closure. It departs from dramatic tradition in its resistance to the typification of subjectivity. Whatever catharsis lyric ef-fects resists abstraction and calls for a recognition of the other and the temporal reformulation of judgment.

Every formal feature of poetry is thereby a social-historical feature and at the same time makes possible links and adaptations between and across social and historical contexts. Forms are a legacy from the dead and to the future. They make us intelligible to others by providing limits. Truisms such as the natural "lightness" of trochaic meters or the comic resonance of triple rhymes depend on the stability of conventions produced by re-current historical practices of speech and writing in general and not just lyric in particular. Lyric timelessness may be promised by sight and hear-ing as those senses most capable of being mobilized in a project of over-coming *distance.* But as the media of poetry, sight and hearing also *define* distance. Unheard melodies, things not yet imagined, selves unsullied by the world, appear only by means of their negation, only in a relation that is both historical and material. However, they also draw us back from any paradoxical idealism regarding the status of the historical and the material. When accounts of lyric have forgotten the practice's cognitive and spiritual dimensions and capacity for cultural transformation, the result has been a distorting artifactualism of the kind we find in attempts to unify classical lyric fragments or to read such poets as Traherne, Ed-ward Taylor, or Christopher Smart as products merely of their belated reception.

As we survey the current methods for imagining poetry's history, at least among English-speaking critics, positions ranging from formalism to contextually based historicism yet fall within the range of what Croce would call "special histories" and are not dialectically sufficient to bring forward as practices of a general history. Contextual historicism has made the error of assuming the coincidence of subjectivity and the somatic and hence has confounded its own basis in sensation for a universal interest. If the body is the least common denominator of human history, it has been the task of lyric to move the subjective forward toward more complex structures of agency and engagement. In addition, functional models are fixed on the attribution of simple cause and so have little cognitive utility. The merit of a general history is its capacity for a critique of ideology and a refusal of reification regarding language and subjectivity. This point might sound like a hidden agenda of emancipation. But I would suggest that emancipation is precisely what is promised falsely by the formalist method in its claim of literary transcendence and by any historicist method claiming contextual explanation. The special history of literary transcendence is ultimately unintelligible and idiosyncratic; its meticulous particularity, a refusal of judgment. And the dioramas of context offered by a narrow historicism are the projection of a model of history necessarily aestheticized in the first place by its drive toward closure of explanation.[114]

In the next two chapters, I will consider the effects of poetry in two historical developments. The first may be seen as placing poetry and the poetic as a bridge between human thought and nature: this is the development of the nocturne form, the story of the gradual human habitation of the night in aesthetic terms. Through the nocturne, the darkness was restored to the continuity of human experience—that ancient darkness, full of atrocity, with which we began our study, came under human ends: the ends of producing an enduring form pursued as the expression of the fleeting phenomenal experience of the night. The second development describes the emergence of first-person expression of the senses in lyric forms as a counter to the abstraction of epic form. In this story, the particular first-person experiences of soldier poets and civilian bystanders played a role in wresting the language of intersubjectivity from a context of identification through sacrifice and ritualized violence into a context of individual mortality—hence into the recognition of tragedy on the level of the person.

OUT OF THE DARKNESS: NOCTURNES

I. FINCH'S TRANSFORMATION OF THE NIGHT WORK

Orpheus went into the darkness of the Underworld, turning against reason and time. There his plea for the release of Eurydice moved even the "bloodless ghosts" to weep. Ovid says that "Ixion's wheel stood still in wonder, the vultures ceased to gnaw Tityus' liver, the daughters of Danaus rested from their pitchers, and Sisyphus sat idle on his rock." Never before had the cheeks of the Furies been wet with tears. Orpheus's imploring words, accompanied by his lyre, were a great success, but his task was a failure. The god of death had put him under an interdiction: all ocular acknowledgment was forbidden, the face-to-face relation was to be held in abeyance until the lovers emerged from the Valley of Avernus. When he turned too early to Eurydice, he undid all direction: the face-to-face relation was shattered and reversed. She receded into death and he reverted alone to the world. Eurydice died twice; Ovid calls this her "second death," and it is in this repetition that the trauma of her first death by the serpent's sting is confirmed. After this second death, the outcome of his own neglect of the law, Orpheus wandered in the Thracian wilderness; when he rested, the trees moved themselves to shade him and savage animals were charmed by his songs. He sought homosexual lovers exclusively, and so the frenzied Thracian women, driven wild by his refusals,

tore him apart. But his severed head continued to deliver its poetry to humankind.[1]

In disobeying the interdiction against the face-to-face, Orpheus encounters the disappearance of his beloved and must attempt to fill her absence with compensatory song. Orpheus was the son of a Muse's union
with a human father—in various versions of the myth the father was the
poet Linus or a river god or Oeagrus, a Thracian king. He is sung *through*;
his parentage reflects his muse-given inspiration and the human *technē*
underlying his *poiēsis*. Rather than following the teleology of purpose or
goal, he moves by means of wandering. His singing survives the sacrifice
of his body, reaching into the future only as a consequence of this very
sacrifice. At Orpheus's death, nature herself learns the lament with which
the poet had previously charmed all savage things. His son or disciple
Musaeus is associated with composition and imitation, those poetic arts
that are the human continuance of what in Orpheus were divine powers.[2]

The story of Orpheus underlies every poem. The poet risks the dangers
of silence and darkness, bringing the message of human emotion to the
gods and carrying back news of the gods to men. In this chapter, I want to
think about the ways the Orphic journey into darkness is a prototype for
the claims poetry makes against mortality. The poet's nocturnal wandering is a mythic archetype found throughout a number of cultural traditions.[3] But we can also trace the particular story of the development of the
nocturne form in Western poetry, painting, and music as part of the general history of artistic making. I would suggest that a dialectic between
sense impression and abstraction characterizes the production of all artistic forms and is analogous to the immediacy of *technē* and the imaginative reach of inspiration as two complementary means of *poiēsis*. In visual
experience, this dialectic puts the sense impressions of vision as stimulation and response in tension with the abstractions of the memory and
imagination. We see what is before us as well as what is in the mind's eye
—and what is before us is organized by our memories and expectations
just as what is in the mind's eye arises from particular visual experiences
in the world.

This problem of seeing in the darkness extends from the accounts of
darkness in the earliest Western poems, with which we began our study,
to the break Modernist abstraction makes with the conventions of realism. The assumption of sensory realism in painting is based on Cartesianism: Descartes associates the self-identity of human reason with sunlight
and rejects temporality in favor of instant certitude.[4] In Cartesianism, resemblance and difference are the grounds for authority and error. Hence,
this Cartesian realist tradition—one might say anachronistically even

before Descartes—is analogous to the stable monocular conventions of single-point perspective. Under the light of reason, gesture is stopped and reveals in the stable conditions of the view the truth of the material category.

Consider, however, an alternative history whereby we might pursue not the sunlit progression of perspectivalism but rather the ways in which such perspectivalism is compensatory to our awareness of blocked perception and the deprivations of seeing brought on by temporal contingency. Correlatively, consider that the inability of perspectivalism to account for the perceptual fields of memory and imagination has led to alternative accounts of visual space—accounts that would not emphasize the readiness of the world to hand so much as the capacity of visual experience to engage in perpetual and unresolved activity. The nocturne conventions of Western art present one of our most sustained meditations on this problem: the problem of going beyond the confines of material experience and the necessity to express in visual terms the endless play between the senses and abstraction.

As organisms of diminished vision, human beings in the night rely on kinesthesia, touch, and imagination in order to proceed. An absence of clarity and distinctness of phenomena, an inability to organize the visual field, and a problematic relation to depth perception are managed by means of heightened senses of tactility and hearing. In the night we rely on connotation, we gather information in time, we tolerate ambiguity, and we proceed by means of subjective judgment. The nocturne in all its artistic forms is an alternative to the sunlit world of perspectival realism. In the visual arts, nocturnal works pose possibilities for synaesthesia and synesthetic allusion; they bring forward the potentials for seeing beyond single-point perspective's present-centered conditions.

Donne had been the first English poet to use the term *nocturnal (Oxford English Dictionary)* as a genre designation in his "A Nocturnal upon S. Lucy's Day, being the shortest day," first published in 1633 but perhaps written as early as 1612. Here he was borrowing from the night offices of the Roman Catholic canonical hours to create an elegy on the winter solstice, a "study" in "absence, darkness, death; things that are not. "Yet since the neo-Platonists, night is also associated with the spiritual contemplation that is part of the Orphic nox—a world of cosmic, Pythagorean, harmony, and the lively creativity of the tradition of Saturnian melancholy. The neo-Platonic Orphic hymns, a group of texts that are first mentioned in a scholium on Hesiod's *Theogony* in the first half of the twelfth century and that most likely date to the second part of the third century A.D., mark a significant change in the approach to nocturnal experience, envisioning the night as a scene of transformation and wonder rather than as a site of the atrocious or sublime. Here is a translation of the Orphic hymn to Νυκτός *(nuktos)* by Apostolos Athanassakis:

> I shall sing of Night, mother of gods and men.
> (Night—and let us call her Kypris—gave birth to all.)
> Hearken, O blessed goddess, jet-black and star-lit,
> Whose delight is in quiet and slumber-filled serenity.
> Cheerful and delightsome, O mother of dreams, you love the nightlong
>   revel,
> and your gentleness rids of cares, and offers respite from toil.
> Giver of sleep, beloved of all you are as you drive your steeds and gleam
>   in darkness.
> Ever incomplete, now terrestrial and now again celestial,
> you circle around in pursuit of sprightly phantoms,
> you force light into the nether world, and again you flee
> into Hades. Dreadful Necessity governs all things.
> But now, O blessed one—yea beatific and desired by all—I call on you
> to grant a kind ear to my voice of supplication
> and, benevolent, come to disperse fears that glisten in the night.[5]

Here Night herself bears the resources to remedy those fears that arise in the night—the cares of the day, the cares of Necessity. The hymn associates her with the fertile powers of Kypris, Aphrodite, "giver of birth and of life," the "scheming mother of necessity" in the Orphic "Hymn to Aphrodite," but she is also the one who presides over "maidenly whispers and smiles and tricks and sweet delight and honey-like love," as described in the *Theogony*, lines 205 to 206.[6]

The sensibility of the Orphic hymn to the Night—Night as the soother of cares and Night as a place of trickster-like delight and change—extends to a night poem that was written fifteen hundred years later by an English noblewoman exiled in the countryside of Kent: Anne Finch's "A Nocturnal Reverie." It is this poem that will be my focus for most of this chapter. Here I want to view the work as fully as possible as an outcome of the poet's intention. But I also want to read the poem closely—so closely, in fact, that I seek to hear the poems that lie beneath it. I assume that the poem is a product of the relation between the poet's knowledge and the poet's experience. Thus, I also consider the premises of the work in relation to this long tradition of night poetry. I contend that those premises arise from conditions of nature as well as culture. Under her particular circumstances, Finch takes up certain conventions of the nocturne tradition and at the same time departs from them. Yet this tradition itself might be more fully examined in phenomenological, even physiological, terms that link the aesthetic of the nocturne in poetry to its appearance as well in music and painting. "A Nocturnal Reverie" has an internal textual history that goes far deeper than any "period" reading, however rich, can provide and has an external history as extensive as the human relation to the night. The history of the poem begins in all the poet knew or thought and ends when there is no longer a reader. This chapter is a study of influences, but not in the traditional literary historical sense; it is a study of a practice of *poiēsis* that involves transposing the sense experiences of the night into a number of forms. Through this practice, the artistic equivalent of the long path of lighting the night by means of various technologies, human makers came to inhabit night experience and to take from it new ways of thinking about perception and abstraction.

Written at some point between 1709 and 1713, "A Nocturnal Reverie" has been cited continuously as a work outside its own historical moment. Here is the poem in its entirety, as it appeared in Finch's 1713 *Miscellany Poems on Several Occasions:*[7]

A Nocturnal Reverie

In such a *Night,* when every louder Wind
Is to its distant Cavern safe confin'd;
And only gentle *Zephyr* fans his Wings,
And lonely *Philomel,* still waking, sings;
Or from some Tree, fam'd for the *Owl's* delight,
She, hollowing clear, directs the Wand'rer right;
In such a *Night,* when passing Clouds give place,
Or thinly vail the Heav'ns mysterious Face;
When in some River, overhung with Green,
The waving Moon and trembling Leaves are seen;
When freshen'd Grass now bears it self upright,
And makes cool Banks to pleasing Rest invite,
Whence springs the *Woodbind,* and the *Bramble*-Rose,
And where the sleepy *Cowslip* shelter'd grows;
Whilst now a paler Hue the *Foxglove* takes,
Yet checquers still with Red the dusky brakes:
When scatter'd *Glow-worms,* but in Twilight fine,
Shew trivial Beauties watch their Hour to shine;
Whilst *Salisb'ry* stands the Test of every Light,
In perfect Charms, and perfect Virtue bright:
When Odours, which declin'd repelling Day,

Thro' temp'rate Air uninterrupted stray;
When darken'd Groves their softest Shadows wear,
And falling Waters we distinctly hear;
When thro' the Gloom more venerable shows
Some ancient Fabrick, awful in Repose,
While Sunburnt Hills their swarthy Looks conceal,
And swelling Haycocks thicken up the Vale:
When the loos'd *Horse* now, as his Pasture leads,
Comes slowly grazing thro' th' adjoining Meads,
Whose stealing Pace, and lengthen'd Shade we fear,
Till torn up Forage in his Teeth we hear:
When nibbling *Sheep* at large pursue their Food,
and unmolested Kine rechew the Cud;
When *Curlews* cry beneath the Village-walls,
And to her straggling Brood the *Partridge* calls;
Their shortliv'd Jubilee the Creatures keep,
Which but endures, whilst Tyrant-*Man* do's sleep:
When a sedate Content the Spirit feels,
And no fierce Light disturbs, whilst it reveals;
But silent Musings urge the Mind to seek
Something, too high for Syllables to speak;
Till the free Soul to a compos'dness charm'd,
Finding the Elements of Rage disarm'd,
O'er all below a solemn Quiet grown,
Joys in th'inferiour World, and thinks it like her Own:
In such a *Night* let Me abroad remain,
Till Morning breaks, and All's confus'd again;
Our cares, our Toils, our Clamours are renew'd,
Or Pleasures, seldom reach'd, again pursu'd.

"A Nocturnal Reverie" became a paradigmatic example of what anachronistically is known as "pre-Romanticism" after it was praised by Wordsworth in his "Essay, Supplementary to the Preface" of 1815 and several of his letters to Alexander Dyce. Wordsworth admired the poem for its contribution to a view of "external nature." For Wordsworth, "A Nocturnal Reverie" and some passages in Pope's "Windsor Forest" were the only such contributions of any value made between *Paradise Lost* and James Thomson's *The Seasons*.[8] More recent critics have looked at the poem within the context of Augustan period verse and in terms of Finch's status as a nonjuror and intellectual woman.[9]

Born in 1661, Anne Kingsmill was by 1683 a maid of honor to Mary of

Modena, wife of the duke of York, in the court of Charles II. At court Kingsmill was part of a circle of literary women, including Sarah Churchill and Anne Killegrew, who acted in masques and plays, exchanged poems, and read books aloud to one another. In 1684 she married Heneage Finch, who was captain of the Halberdiers and gentleman of the bedchamber to the duke. After marriage, she left her position as a maid of honor, although Heneage continued to serve the court, his duties increasing with the accession of the duke as James II in 1685. With the deposition of James in 1689, the Finches refused to swear allegiance to William and Mary and took refuge in various houses of friends. At one point, Heneage Finch was arrested as he tried to join the exiled Stuart court. In 1689 or 1690, amid this turmoil, Heneage's nephew, the earl of Winchelsea, invited the couple to live at his estate at Eastwell. The Finches stayed at the estate for twenty-five years, following literary and scholarly pursuits. When the young earl died prematurely and without heir, Heneage inherited the title, and Anne became countess of Winchelsea. Although life at Eastwell was a kind of retirement, Anne Finch maintained links to a wider literary and social world through correspondence and visits with her former friends at court, through friendship with the Thynnes of Longleat and her Kent neighbor, Catherine Cavendish, countess of Thanet, as well as Thanet's daughters, and through literary exchanges with Pope, Swift, John Gay, and Nicholas Rowe. Finch's *Miscellany Poems* of 1713 was published under her supervision, and at the time of her death in 1720 she left several manuscripts, arranged for publication, but these works in manuscript did not appear until 1903.[10]

In the opening lines to "A Nocturnal Reverie," the senses' immediate relation to the phenomenal world is described both empirically and ecstatically:

In such a *Night*, when every louder Wind
Is to its distant Cavern safe confin'd;
And only gentle *Zephyr* fans his Wings,
And lonely *Philomel*, still waking, sings; . . .

Yet these opening lines give us further insight into the poem's cultural and historical context. The insistent rhetoric of the long sentence making up the body of the poem is framed by the opening phrase, repeated here at line 7 and later at line 47, "In such a night." Although we are struck by the immediacy of the opening, the first phrase is in fact a direct quotation, citing the antiphonal musical theme of the final act of *The Merchant of Venice:* "In such a night."[11]

The final, fifth act of *The Merchant of Venice* brings together, in sequential arrivals, three pairs of lovers—Lorenzo and Jessica; Bassanio and Portia; Gratiano and Nerissa. Their return to Belmont presents the completion of a circle, the restoration of rings—all this happens in the hours before dawn, and Gratiano has the last speech, which echoes Ovid's (and Marlowe's) "Lente currite noctis equi." Gratiano explains, "But were the day come, I should wish it dark / Till I were couching with the doctor's clerk. / Well, while I live, I'll fear no other thing / So sore, as keeping safe Nerissa's ring" (act 5, scene 1: 304–307).[12] The fifth act is a nocturne surveying the features of night, and night's return, as a scene of reestablished order and soothed fears. Lorenzo and Jessica's teasing antiphon in the moonlit grove traverses time and space to give an overview of all those who have worried in the night: Troilus, sighing on the walls of Troy; Thisbe, frightened by the lion's shadow; Dido, holding a willow on the wild sea banks; Medea gathering herbs in the full moon's light. The antiphon then turns to a lover's verbal duel (act 5, scene 1: 4–13). They are interrupted by Stephano, the messenger, but once he has left, Lorenzo returns to the nocturnal theme. He draws Jessica's attention to the moonlight, to the harmony of music and the stars, and tells her that "immortal souls" have such harmony, "but whilst this muddy vesture of decay / Doth grossly close it in, we cannot hear it" (act 5, scene 1: 64–65). He calls on musicians to "wake Diana with a hymn / With sweetest touches pierce your mistress' ear, / And draw her home with music," noting the power of music to tame a "wild and wanton herd / or race of youthful and unhandled colts" and describing Orpheus's capacity to charm the forces and things of nature, including human emotions, by means of his music.

In this speech, two kinds of night are contrasted: the sweet moonlit context of Orphic enchantment in which wildness is tamed and the Hellish dark of "treasons, stratagems, and spoils." George Chapman's *The Shadow of Night,* a poem that must be seen as contemporaneous in that its date of 1594 matches the earliest possible date for *The Merchant of Venice,*[13] borrows from the same stock of Orphic imagery, as in these lines from the first part, the "Hymnus in Noctem":

So when ye heare, the sweetest Muses sonne,
With heavenly rapture of his Musicke, wonne
Rockes, forrests, floods, and winds to leave their course
In his attendance; it bewrayes the force
His wisedome had, to draw men growne so rude
To civill love of Art, and Fortitude.[14]

In an apostrophe to Night, Chapman writes, "We basely make retrait, and are no lesse / Then huge impolisht heapes of filthinesse. / Mens faces glitter, and their hearts are blacke, / But thou (great Mistresse of heavens gloomie racke) / Art blacke in face, and glitterst in thy heart. / There is thy glorie, riches, force, and Art; / Opposed earth, beates blacke and blewe thy face, / And often doth thy heart it selfe deface."[15] Chapman's reversals are poised between the medieval view of Melancholy's swarthy face and an emerging consciousness of Night's charms and powers, a glittering heart within nocturnal experience. Night is no longer simply made of what is indistinguishable and invisible—it is an emblem of something transcendent that mere earth might "deface," its purity contrasted with human sinfulness.

The figure of Diana as chaste huntress is conflated as well with that other nocturnal huntress, Hekatē. In the Orphic hymn to Ἑκάτη, the first hymn after Orpheus's invocation to the muses in extant manuscripts, the goddess is described:

> tomb spirit reveling in the souls of the dead,
> daughter of Perses, haunting deserted places, delighting in deer,
> nocturnal, dog-loving, monstrous queen,
> devouring wild beasts, ungirt, of repelling countenance.
> You, herder of bulls, queen and mistress of the whole world,
> leader, nymph, mountain-roaming nurturer of youth.[16]

A contrast is drawn between the work of the hunting goddesses, destroyers of wild beasts, and the taming, enchanting music of Orpheus. These two forces, one toward disorder and destruction and the other toward charm and resolution, come to characterize the particular transitions in nocturnal experience.[17]

"A Nocturnal Reverie" marks both a continuity and a break in this Renaissance notion of melancholy with which Finch's poetry more generally was deeply engaged.[18] Finch could have been familiar with this concept not only from Chapman and Shakespeare but also from Albrecht Dürer, Vaughan, Milton, and Robert Burton, for although no edition was published of the *Anatomy* between 1677 and 1799, Burton's work never disappeared.[19] In "The Spleen," the poem for which Finch was most well known during her lifetime, she addresses the melancholy illness itself, describing how "Trembling sometimes thou dost appear, / Dissolv'd into a Panick Fear; / On Sleep intruding dost thy Shadows spread, / Thy gloomy Terrours round the silent Bed, / And crowd with boading Dreams the

Melancholy Head."[20] Throughout her several poems of melancholy, Finch writes of sleeplessness, care, and sorrow keeping her awake at night and of her poems as forged within that mood. For example, "Ardelia to Melancholy," a poem written in the voice of "Ardelia," Finch's poetic alter-ego, recounts how she has sought a cure for melancholy:

> I have apply'd
> Sweet mirth, and musick, and have try'd
> A thousand other arts beside
> To drive thee from my darken'd breast,
> Thou, who hast banish'd all my rest.[21]

In a dedication "To the Right Honorable the Countess of Hartford with her Volume of Poems," Finch describes her work as the "fruits" "Of sleepless nights, and days with cares o'ercast."[22] Although her lyrics on melancholy are also written in couplets, they do not have the discursive structure of "A Nocturnal Reverie." Addressing melancholy or sleeplessness, they describe the effects produced in the speaker by such states and end in resignation or surrender; the structure is one of diminishment rather than extension into the world.

This is the negating side of melancholy; it is the choleric and insomniac sadness of the thinker at the end of thought rather than Saturnian melancholy—the latter linked to memory, and ultimately reconstructive and compensatory. The opening to Milton's "L'Allegro," for example, gives what remains a most sublime evocation of negating melancholy—perhaps because its rhetorical aim is to disperse it:

> Hence loathed Melancholy
>   Of Cerberus, and blackest Midnight born,
> In Stygian cave forlorn
>   'Mongst horrid shapes, and shrieks, and sights unholy
> Find out some uncouth cell,
>   Where brooding Darkness spreads his jealous wings,
> And the night-raven sings;
>   There under ebon shades, and low-browed rocks,
> As ragged as thy locks
>   In dark Cimmerian desert ever dwell.[23]

It is obvious that Finch's initial claim that every louder wind is to its cave self-confined repeats Milton's rhetoric and adds to the joyful effect of the turn toward nature taken after the initial lines. Zephyrus, the sweet-breathed wind who inspires in every "holt and heeth" organic growth, will surround the wanderer as she turns to the landscape. But one can also see that this turn is itself anticipated by the structure of "L'Allegro"'s companion poem, "Il Penseroso." "L'Allegro"'s catalog of daylit pleasures, delivered often in end-stopped lines, poses a problem of paternity and authenticity. "Il Penseroso" begins with what might be called a hidden, semantic, rhyme—"Hence vain deluding Joys / The brood of Folly without father bred, / How little you bestead"—that is, between an unuttered, but inferred, "bastard" and "bestead." Sensation bereft of thought and meditation yields only fleeting, unanchored, pleasure. Hence, the wandering through a physical landscape in "L'Allegro" is transformed into wandering through a mental landscape, a path of obsessive association that any insomniac knows well as the phenomenon of "the mind racing."

In "Il Penseroso," Milton uses a set of "or" clauses to emphasize the switch from topic to topic and scene to scene; their increasing frequency after line 77 speeds the pace of mental turning. The poem early on establishes an incestuous paternity for Melancholy, claiming she is the daughter of Saturn by his daughter Vesta. Milton relies on the Orphic connections and iconography of Melancholy we have been considering.[24] As the speaker calls on Philomel, who sings while Cynthia drives a team of dragons above an oak tree, he explains, "And missing thee, I walk unseen / On the dry smooth-shaven green, / To behold the wandering moon, / Riding near her highest noon, / Like one that had been led astray / Through the Heaven's wide pathless way; . . ." If wandering in this landscape is not possible because of the "air," the speaker will seek out a solitary interior space "where glowing embers through the room / Teach light to counterfeit a gloom, . . ." This space then turns to a high lonely tower where his lamp will be seen. He asks that when daylight comes he be brought "to archèd walks of twilight groves" where he might be hid "from day's garish eye." Yet this scene changes, too, as he then asks that as he wakes he will ". . . never fail / To walk the studious cloister's pale," where "all heaven" might be brought before his eyes. Finally, in one more scene change, he asks that he be brought to "the peaceful hermitage, / the hairy gown and mossy cell" in his old age. In this context, he asks Melancholy to give him the "pleasure" of "prophetic strain."

"Il Penseroso" is a consummate representation of a mind wandering. It is not a dream poem, for the thoughts have a clear source in the desire of the speaker. The speaker is journeying through a simultaneously mental and physical landscape, and the boundary between exterior and interior experience is continually muted. The solitude of the imagination and the baroque complexity of the imagery risk unintelligibility. The reader follows the speaker through the poem as the watcher follows the sleep-walker—unaware of what direction will be taken, what motive is pro-pelling the movement. The poem is entirely in interior space, yet when the speaker goes outside into the "smooth-shaven green," we are struck by the specificity of that image. As Aristotle contended, sight can some-times be a form of touch, especially when considered from the viewpoint of the recipient of the gaze. Here touch obviates the need for sight; in fol-lowing the wandering moon, the speaker risks encountering obstacles and loss. He is, after all, following a moon that itself has been "led astray through the Heaven's wide pathless way," but he is kept safe by this regu-larity in the landscape.

With the next four lines, "A Nocturnal Reverie" has made three allu-sions to external nature—the owl, the tree (famed for the owl's delight), and the passing clouds that, at the end of the octave, veil the face of the heavens:

> Or from some Tree, fam'd for the *Owl*'s delight,
> She, hollowing clear, directs the Wand'rer right:
> In such a *Night,* when passing Clouds give place,
> Or thinly vail the Heav'ns mysterious Face; . . .

The poem begins in mythic time: the wind is Zephyr; the nightin-gale is Philomel. But the song of Philomel is joined or replaced by the "hol-lowing clear" of the owl—who is a female. Owls can see both ahead and behind as they turn their heads on a 180-degree axis. The owl appears here on the boundary between the natural and cultural worlds; this is a typi-cal owl in a typical hollow tree, but she is also the symbol of Minerva and will set a wanderer "right." Although a wanderer by definition does not have a prechosen path, the owl forms a fixed point of reference, for she will stay in the same spot throughout the night and so enable the wanderer to determine bearings within an amorphous landscape and under a chang-ing sky.

Wandering in "A Nocturnal Reverie" is linked at every point with the facts of firsthand experience. Like other animals who journey in the night, human beings must make the best use of diminished vision and align themselves by kinesthetic sense, following in familiar territory their own motor movements. This is the sense by which we steer ourselves to-ward a keyhole in a dark room or balance our steps by aligning our spines along a trajectory we keep in mind even without visual clues.[25] The night marks a great shift in animal movement: birds of the open fields come into the forests to be sheltered; deer, red foxes, striped skunks, banded raccoons, porcupines, otters, beavers, bears, weasels, and muskrats are night drinkers; searching for roots, hunting, or building dams, such animals are active in the dark.[26] Significantly, these are not the animals Finch considers; her nocturnal world is a domestic and Orphic one where wild beasts have been tamed. And the absence of such animal life gives us another indication that the opening of the poem takes place in the park at Eastwell.

Yet "being set" into a path of nocturnal wandering is also a quality we find in the relatively rare Greek term for "causing to wander by night, or rousing from a bed," νυκτίπλαγκτος (nuktiplanktos), which Aeschylus uses in the Oresteia to describe the groping night thoughts of the watchman at the opening of the Agamemnon and the creeping terror of Clytemnestra in The Libation Bearers. Although there are many Greek terms for nightly roaming to and fro, strolling in the darkness, and prowling by night, it is the particularly involuntary quality of this wandering that is compelling. A more purposive night wandering is often linked to the figure of Cynthia the Huntress. In the "Hymnus in Cynthiam,"[27] the second part of Chapman's The Shadow of Night, the muse is asked to

> Sing then withall, her Pallace brightnesse bright,
> The dasle-sunne perfections of her light,
> Circkling her face with glories, sing the walkes,
> Where in her heavenly Magicke mood she stalkes,
> Her arbours, thickets, and her wondrous game,
> (A huntresse, being never matcht in fame).[28]

Agrippa wrote that because the moon is associated with Earth and water, the places particularly under its influence are "wildernesses, woods, rocks, hills, mountains, forests, fountains, waters, rivers, seas, seashores, ships, high-ways, groves, and granaries for Corn and such like." As Cynthia presides over these landscapes of wild and open territory, she has a magical sympathy with animal life: "Swine, hinds, goats and all animals whatsoever that observe and imitate the motions of the moon; panther is said to have a spot upon her shoulder like the Moon, increasing into a roundness, and having horns that bend inwards."[29] All of this imagery can be found in the Orphic hymn to Σελήνη (Selēnē), the Moon:

> Hearken, O divine queen, light-bringing and splendid Selēnē,
> bull-horned Moon traversing the air in a race with night.
> Nocturnal, torch-bearing, maiden of fair stars, Moon
> waxing and waning, feminine and masculine,
> glittering lover of horses, mother of time, bearer of fruit,

amber-colored, brooding, shining in the night,
all-seeing, vigilant, surrounded by beautiful stars,
you delight in quiet and in the richness of the night.
Shining in the night, like a jewel, you grant fulfillment and favor;
long-cloaked marshal of the stars, wise maiden whose motion is circular,
come! Blessed and gentle lady of the stars, in three ways
shine your redeeming light upon your new initiates.[30]

The moon's "motion is circular" and is as well marked by changes in form: the "three ways" are waxing, waning, and full.[31]

Although water is an implied referent throughout the poem because of Finch's emphasis on plants and birds that inhabit wetlands, two distinct allusions to water are made: the first is this set of lines with their emphasis on reflective vision:

When in some River, overhung with Green,
The waving Moon and trembling Leaves are seen;

The second (l. 24) will emphasize hearing. Our attention in this first instance is quickly drawn to the mediated relation the speaker has to the image. The nocturne tradition, from Ovid to Claude Monet, constantly involves a relation among night, light, and bodies of water. Finch does not introduce us to the pleasures, and at times dangers, of water at night, as do the Narcissus story and Thoreau's essay on night fishing. Rather, Finch gives us the distant prospect that will be so important to later eighteenth-century poetry and painting: "some river," not a particular river; "trembling Leaves" in general. What is emphasized is the wavering and transitory quality of the seeing—the night equivalent of clouds and other effects of weather in which temporal fleetingness is what one sees rather than a thing in itself. Furthermore, there is the important issue of the conflation of surface and depth. Objects reflected in the water imply infinity in their bridging of indiscernible distances; by diminishing or magnifying images, they transform the relation between foreground and background and make depth perception problematic. In motion and mediated by reflection, phenomena appear, as Wordsworth would have been pleased to note, as the consequence of our sensual apprehension of them and not as they might be in nature.[32] When the eye follows the path the moonlight makes on the water, the night wanderer reaches a kind of epiphany in which it is the mind that takes over the progression of movement. In a moving visual conundrum, the moon as the source of images is here seen as its own consequence, as if we had come on a goddess inventing the mirror in which her own face first appears.[33]

In the following lines, too, sight and touch are linked:

> When freshen'd Grass now bears it self upright,
> And makes cool Banks to pleasing Rest invite,
> Whence springs the *Woodbind*, and the *Bramble*-Rose, . . .

The sight of the cool upright grass is an invitation to recline on it. As the change of light from day to night determines the differing sap pressure in the cells where leaflets join their petioles, some plants—such as wisteria, bean, clover, and wood sorrel—will droop and others—such as rhododendron and grape leaves, water lilies, evening primrose, and honeysuckle—will turn upward or open.[34] Just as the freshened grass invites our touch, Finch's choice of plants that seem to touch reciprocally in their springing growth is significant: the woodbind climbs and tangles by means of its tendrils with their small adhesive disks; the bramble-rose by its thorns.

The next lines, justly famous for their specificity, might be admired as well for their accuracy:

> And where the sleepy *Cowslip* shelter'd grows;
> Whilst now a paler Hue the *Foxglove* takes,
> Yet checquers still with Red the dusky brakes:
> When scatter'd *Glow-worms*, but in Twilight fine,
> Shew trivial Beauties watch their Hour to shine; . . .

Humans can see at night as well as an owl and better than a rabbit or whippoorwill.[35] For vertebrates to be able to use the natural light at night as illumination, they must have a certain number of rod cells in the retina; but rod cells are not useful for discerning color—human beings are color-blind at night. When a full moon provides maximum light in the night, the cells that do provide for color discrimination—the cone cells—can operate on a minimal level. Human beings can begin to see red and yellow and blue and green as differences.[36] Finch attentively paces her detail here, showing us aspects of nature in a flickering, particular, and intermittent way. She notes the grisaille effect of the night light but also gives us a clue as to the intensity of the moonlight by her discernment of the foxglove's red. The cowslip, foxglove, and brake all indicate the proximity of water. It is perfectly believable that these are all real plants in the real park at Eastwell; in fact, a twentieth-century account notes the presence of ancient and imposing stands of brakes: "We pass through hills, slopes, undulations, and levels, which, with their ancient timber and high fern, form the very ideal of an ancestral park of the ancient noblesse."[37] In "An Invitation to Dafnis," Finch had proclaimed the superiority of Nature to its representations: "Reading the softest Poetry, refuse / To view the subjects of each rural muse; / Nor lett the busy compasses go round, / When faery Cercles better mark the ground."[38] Yet once more, Finch plays between realism and allusion: we might remember that the "oxlips," "Luscious woodbine" and "sweet musk-roses" are the flowers on which Titania sleeps (*A Midsummer Night's Dream*, act 2, scene 1), and foxglove was so named because it was the glove of the fairy fox or folk.[39]

The mating signals of the glow-worms with their cold and flickering light provide a little allegory of the fleeting charms of trivial beauties. The glow-worms are among a number of gendered natural figures in the poem. Beetles, rather than worms, male glow-worms are winged and possess only a few small spots of light at the end of the abdomen. But the wingless female is a long, dark gray, grublike creature with six legs and the power to produce an "exquisite pale green light" at the end of the body. The three last segments are illuminated: there are two circular spots of light at the end of the last segment and broad bars of light on the second and third posterior segments. These lights apparently can be extinguished and expressed volitionally.[40] Robert Herrick had asked the glow-worm to lend her "eyes" or lights to his lover in his "The Night-piece: To Julia," first published in 1648 with the rest of his poems. This work urges a woman to make her way directly in the night to the speaker, a nocturnal version of his "carpe diem" motif, and mentions those dangers that might mislead her: a "will-o'-the-wisp," a biting snake or slow-worm, a ghost. Herrick imagines darkness as an encumbrance, whereas for Finch it is, in the end, a condition of mobility and emancipation.

The consequent lines on "Salisb'ry" have posed a continual problem for critics:

> Whilst *Salisb'ry* stands the Test of every Light,
> In perfect Charms, and perfect Virtue bright: . . .

Wordsworth suggested they be taken out, and as recently as 1994, the critic Charles Hinnant has agreed with him.[41] But like any lacunae, the lines that seem accessory can be as readily seen as central to the poem. Why do readers have such difficulty absorbing these lines? The problem is that the reader's pleasure in the flow of detail is interrupted; we are speeded through one sensual image to another until we are halted by "Salisb'ry." The poem reaches a kind of crisis regarding the threshold of nature and culture at this point; its universality as a nature poem is undermined by its specificity as an occasional poem.

As early as Myra Reynolds's 1903 edition of Finch's work, it has been assumed that the reference is to Anne Tufton, countess of Salisbury, the daughter of Finch's dearest friend, Lady Thanet. Between her marriage in 1708–1709 and the latest possible date of the poem's composition in 1713, Salisbury would have been between fifteen and twenty years old.[42] There are several clues to the early years of Salisbury's marriage as the context for the poem. As noted earlier, the wind that blows at the beginning of the poem is Zephyrus, the West Wind, and in a few lines we will find a reference to a landscape and an "awful ruin" that seem to be Stonehenge. Finch was not given to using proper names in her poetry; instead, she preferred literary names like her own "Ardelia" or her husband's "Dafnis." The special emphasis given to Salisbury makes us see a conflation between the person of the young bride and the city over which she rules. In the preceding lines the choice of the verb *chequers,* aside from its evident accuracy and frequent appearance in eighteenth-century verse, might also give a clue, for this is the particular word used in Salisbury for its squares. Salisbury, first established as the Roman fortress Old Sarum before its relocation in the thirteenth century, even today continues its tradition of being at night a locked city. Here we find that Finch has compressed a remarkable range of meanings and symbols into her reference, for the chastity of the bride is linked to the locked city in a tradition that goes back to Orphic imagery and its revival under Elizabeth I. Chapman, for example, asks of the "Elisian Ladies," "Build Cynthiaes Temple in your vertuous parts, / Let everie jewell be a vertues glasse: And no Herostratus shall ever race, / Those holy monuments: but pillers stand, / Where every Grace, and Muse shall hang her garland." In a note he explains that a woman's genitals are called "the girdle of Cynthia"; when Athenian women lost their virginity, they "put of[f] their girdles."[43]

But Salisbury stands the test of every light in another sense. Her steadiness reminds us of the initial fixity of the "owl" who will set the wanderer right. At this point we learn why and how the wanderer can be led to virtue. Here Finch is drawing on an older juxtaposition of the owl and the nightingale. The opening of Finch's "Nocturnal Reverie" in fact compares Philomel and the owl. I have already mentioned the ways in which this is a comparison of classical myth and observed nature. But for a writer as familiar with the fabular tradition as Finch, the choice of the nightingale and the owl would also follow the medieval debate between the owl and the nightingale and, perhaps, its written version in the twelfth-century poem variously ascribed to John or Nicholas of Guildford, or a writer under patronage to one of them.[44] This poem presents an extensive and rambling quarrel regarding the various qualities ascribed to the two birds. The poem has some basis in natural history, yet it pursues an anthropomorphic agenda. The Owl's song is "zozelinge," according to the Nightingale; the Nightingale's song is "writelinge," according to the Owl. The Owl sings her woeful song in winter; the Nightingale pours forth its song in summer. Each customarily bears a relation to the sexuality of women: in a tradition that dates to Pliny, the Nightingale sings until its lust is fulfilled and urges maidens to love, although, according to the Owl, she also gives encouragement to adulteresses. The Owl is the confidante of wives, cheering those loyal wives whose husbands are away and praying for the death of cruel husbands.[45] It is evident that the debate between the Nightingale and the Owl already anticipates the conflict between joyful and somber moods and their consequences worked through in "L'Allegro" and "Il Penseroso." On the western wind, on a summer night, Finch sends to the young bride a message full of pleasure and rectitude at once.

If the poem arrives at its most abstract point of allegorical rhetoric after the reference to Salisbury, Finch returns us to the immediate world through the most immediate and animal of the senses—that of smell:

When Odours, which declin'd repelling Day,
Thro' temp'rate Air uninterrupted stray;
When darken'd Groves their softest Shadows wear. . . .

Several features of the natural world are closely accounted for here. First, as temperatures drop with the onset of night, humidity increases, and the lack of upward air currents makes odors more static in just the way in which Finch describes them.[46] Second, Finch notes here a quality of the night often described via a mistaken metaphor. Darkness rises; it does not fall. It spreads from woodland floors to thickets to valleys. The day lasts longest in open pastures and mountain peaks; there is a vast north/south transition from day to night.[47] By linking vision to smell, Finch materializes the air and light; the air has its own qualities and is not simply the medium through which we pursue other referents. She produces an innovation in the representation of light and, more generally, nature. Her attention to qualities of air as not just a vehicle but also a material of perception is an innovation that presages the specific development of the nocturne as a form in visual art into the nineteenth century.

"And falling Waters we distinctly hear; . . ." As mentioned in our discussion of aurality, we can choose to see or not to see by turning our head or closing our eyes. But we cannot as readily choose not to hear. The involuntary aspect of hearing links sound to emotion and movement just as the willed aspect of sight links seeing to rationality and volition.[48]

In the night, hearing is given special precedence. As Hermia explains in act 3, scene 2 of *A Midsummer Night's Dream:* "Dark night, that from the eye his function takes, / The ear more quick of apprehension makes, / Wherein it doth impair the seeing sense, / It pays the hearing double recompense." Thus far in the poem, we have heard Zephyr, Philomel, and the Owl—and these sounds appear before the shift to visual imagery and wandering. Whereas Philomel and the Owl produce distinctive sounds of fixed intelligible form, wind and water are as amorphous to the ear as light is to the eye—wind surrounding the hearer with its element, water signifying the emergence of a threshold or boundary. Finch cleverly uses this reintroduction of sound as water to signal a change in landscape—for falling water is a clue to the night wanderer that the topography is about to change in level.

The pictorial imagery of the poem undergoes a tremendous shift at this point:

> When thro' the Gloom more venerable shows
> Some ancient Fabrick, awful in Repose,
> While Sunburnt hills their swarthy Looks conceal,
> And swelling Haycocks thicken up the Vale: . . .

Across the threshold of the heard water and "thro' the Gloom," which by definition is not clearly defined, we see an "ancient Fabrick, awful in Repose." The "gloom" is "more venerable" in that it extends through both time and space. Our attention is drawn to two types of manmade forms that nevertheless stand in the elements like the consequences of acts of nature: the ruins and the haycocks. By making the "sunburnt hills their swarthy Looks conceal," Finch imaginatively blurs the outer edges of this open landscape and banishes once more the "swarthy Look" that characterizes the black face of Melancholy, the hidden outer edge of the poem. Coincidentally, the haycocks would resemble the rounded structures that also "thicken up" the plain of Salisbury: the barrows or burial mounds that make the view, as William Gilpin was to write later in the eighteenth century, both an "ocean" and a "cemetery." By resolving the scene with the image of the haycocks, the terror and sublimity that might be evoked by the ancient fabric have receded into an image of plenty and domesticity.

It is surprising that it has not been frequently noted that this "awful" and "ancient" "fabric" is likely to be Stonehenge, or perhaps nearby Old Sarum: the image is hardly as concrete as Keats's description in *Hyperion* of "a dismal cirque of Druid stones, upon a forlorn moor," yet the poem's occasion and topography give every indication that we are in Wiltshire at this point.[49] In either case, the Wiltshire ruins present another connection to the poem's occasion and an image resonant to the poem's concern with pleasure and meditation. The publication of Camden's *Britannia* in 1586 had included some engravings of Stonehenge apparently based on Dutch originals. In 1695, Edmund Gibson produced a new edition of Camden. He augmented Camden's texts with extracts from John Aubrey's *Monumenta Britannica*, especially from the "Templa Druidum" section, and he included extensive topographical and antiquarian notes. His book was especially popular with members of the country gentry, clergy, and rural doctors, those amateur antiquarians who would by 1740 virtually invent the beginnings of field archaeology as a discipline.[50] Inigo Jones, stage designer and architect to the king, had conducted a study of Stonehenge, including the making of sketches, in 1655. He proclaimed, "Roma quanta fuit, ipsa ruina docet."[51] As Gilpin later wrote, "the celebrated Inigo Jones, on his return from Italy, having nothing but Italian architecture in his head, . . . found out that Stonehenge was a Roman ruin."[52] Other works of the time linked the ruin to the Druids, including Walter Charleton's of 1663 and John Webb's of 1655 and 1665. All of these works were summarized in Gibson's edition of Camden. Furthermore, Johann Georg Keysler in 1720 cites a 1659 book, *Brittaniae in Wiltonia*, for its mention of Stonehenge.[53]

It would be unlikely for the Winchelseas not to have known any, if not all, of the contemporary works on Stonehenge. Their publication coincides precisely with the period of retirement during which Heneage Finch had devoted himself to antiquarian research. And the Finches' friendship with the Salisbury family would have made them well acquainted with the ruins. In 1723, three years after Anne Finch's death, William Stukeley (who also was an expert on the medical history of "the spleen") was taking the first scientific measurements of Stonehenge and recorded in a letter how he had been helped by Heneage Finch and others, his fellow members of the "Society of Roman Knights,"[54] the forerunner of the Society of Antiquities: "[Lord Winchelsea and others] took I believe among us 2000 measures. . . . Lord Winchelsea has workt very hard, and was ravisht with Stonehenge, it was a great strife between us, which should talk of leaving it first."[55]

Our interest here should not be simply a matter of identification, however. In Finch's time, Stonehenge was known as "the circles," and at the heart of speculation about its origins and that of other monuments of prehistory lay controversies regarding religion: Was the center stone really an altar stone, used for human sacrifice? Did the open sky and expansive site facilitate the communication of prayer? Were the many barrows on the plains of Salisbury surrounding the monument connected to it? How were the stones placed in relation to the diurnal and seasonal paths of the sun and the moon? The *ubi sunt* tradition of meditation in medieval and Renaissance poetry that we examined in the previous chapter has a particular resonance to the meaning of ruins—it is a theme that will continue with various permutations in the "graveyard school" poetry of the eighteenth century. Here a stark contrast is drawn between "Salisbury," which "stands the test of every light" as an enduring symbol of the Finchs' church, and the "awful fabric" of a ruined religion. J. M. W. Turner was to draw the same contrast one hundred years later in his paintings of Stonehenge and Salisbury: whereas the Stonehenge picture shows a shepherd killed by lightning, the Salisbury piece puts the cathedral squarely in the middle of the painting, with a shepherd and his contented flock in the foreground making the allegory complete. "A Nocturnal Reverie"'s opening invocation of "In such a night" as the antiphon that completes the ring, the consequent turn of the poem toward "something too high for syllables to speak," and the profound political-historical significance of a religious site in ruin would have affected Finch's choice of terms. Finally, we should remember that in the "Invitation to Dafnis" passage quoted earlier, Finch had suggested to Heneage "Nor lett the busy compasses go round, / When faery Cercles better mark the ground."

If the lines on Salisbury are the key to the allegorical focus of the poem, the next lines clarify the link between the Orphic theme and the direct apprehension of the senses:

> When the loos'd *Horse* now, as his Pasture leads,
> Comes slowly grazing thro' th'adjoining Meads,
> Whose stealing Pace, and lengthen'd Shade we fear,
> Till torn up Forage in his Teeth we hear:
> When nibbling *Sheep* at large pursue their Food,
> And unmolested Kine rechew the Cud; . . .

We remember that in the Orphic hymn to the Moon, the moon was the "glittering lover of horses, mother of time, bearer of fruit."[56] Finch's choice of the horse brings to mind once again Lorenzo's soliloquy of the "race of youthful and unhandled colts, their savage eyes turn'd to a modest gaze, by the sweet power of music." A similar, but more comically mundane, magical image appears in act 2 of *A Midsummer Night's Dream*, where Robin Goodfellow responds to the fairy who has asked if he is not the one who likes to "mislead night-wanderers, laughing at their harm," saying, "Thou speakest aright; / I am that merry wanderer of the night. / I jest to Oberon, and make him smile / When I a fat and bean-fed horse beguile, / Neighing in likeness of a filly foal." Yet most importantly in Finch's poem the horse's transformation, from "stealing Pace and lengthen'd Shade we fear" into a completely ordinary horse chewing up forage in a completely ordinary way, wonderfully reproduces in the reader the speaker's sensation of fear assuaged.

The wandering sheep and the unmolested cattle represent a world where boundaries are fluid and open, where no harm is given or taken— the world of charmed nature produced by Orpheus's lyre. Orpheus had sworn, after he left the cult of Dionysus and went into retreat in the forest to live among the wild beasts, *phonôn t'apechesthai*, or "refrain from killing."[57] There is a clever pun in the image of the sheep that translates the Orphic interdiction into eighteenth-century terms, for the English term *owling* was used since the Middle Ages for the raiding of sheep out of the kingdom. *Owling* was the referent because it was usually done at night. At the time of Finch's writing of the poem, a debate regarding the penalty had emerged. The penalty originally had been the cutting off of the thief's left hand, which was then nailed in a public place; in 1717, the penalty was changed to transportation for seven years.[58] These domestic animals are unmolested not just because they are not being consumed but because they are not being disturbed or moved; they signify the tranquility of the territorial aspect of the landscape and the end of a medieval association among night walking, poaching, and criminality.

In the next lines, Finch continues her emphasis on the coexistence of cultural and natural spheres:

> When *Curlews* cry beneath the Village-walls,
> And to her straggling Brood the *Partridge* calls;
> Their shortliv'd Jubilee the Creatures keep,
> Which but endures, whilst Tyrant-*Man* do's sleep: . . .

The presence of the curlew by the village walls gives us another indication that this is a summer night: during its summer sojourn in moorlands, the curlew feeds at night. But the curlew is also a bird with an elaborate folkloric tradition attached to her cry and appearance. The curlew calls at night while feeding. In the north of England, a flock of curlews calling out in their "eerie musical voices" presages a death; such a flock is often referred to as "The Seven Whistlers" who search, calling for a lost one— when they reunite, the end of the world will come. The Seven Whistlers, and the term "Gabriel Hounds," given to calling geese, are related to the nocturnal tradition of "The Wild Hunt." In this tradition, ghostly hunters, the souls of the restless dead, ride through the sky, presaging bad news. Dogs on Earth, the acolytes of Hekatē, howl when these hunters pass by.[59] By putting her curlew on the ground and safely outside of the village walls, Finch minimizes the terror of such legends, just as at the opening of the poem she had followed Milton in keeping louder winds to distant caverns safe-confined. But we can also detect that this is another reference to the topography of Salisbury, for curlews often spend their summers in chalk country—the day in the open barren turf above the chalk deposits and the night in more moist and fertile places nearby. The partridge is also chosen with a careful sense of detail. Partridges more often run than fly; they have a raspy sawlike voice, and many varieties often make two nests and lay two clutches, the cock bringing up one brood and the female the other, hence the "straggling brood."[60]

A jubilee implies a period of emancipation and remission for penalty, as well as a season or time for rejoicing. The jubilee of the birds is short-lived because it is limited to the night when humans are sleeping; the night wanderer can hear them; at this moment of the night they are as safe as the sheep and cows, for she has no intention of putting them to her own material use. Furthermore, by comparing a bird with a plaintive human-like voice and rich traditional associations to another who comically runs along rasping and sawing, Finch is perhaps referring to Portia's characteristically even-handed approach to judgment: "The crow doth sing as sweetly as the lark / When neither is attended; and I think / The nightingale, if she should sing by day / When every goose is cackling, would be thought / No better a musician than the wren. / How many things by season seasoned are / To their right praise and true perfection! / Peace, ho! The moon sleeps with Endymion, / And would not be awak'd." These closing lines of *The Merchant of Venice* bring us full circle from the opening "In such a night." At this point, Finch's poem leaves the immediate sensual world and moves toward abstraction and closure.

The introduction of the religious and civil concept of a "jubilee" marks a turn from external nature back to the meditative tradition. Just as "every louder Wind" was prohibited at the beginning of the poem, now "no fierce Light disturbs":

When a sedate Content the Spirit feels,
And no fierce Light disturbs, whilst it reveals;
But silent Musings urge the Mind to seek
Something, too high for Syllables to speak;
Till the free Soul to a compos'dness charm'd,

Finding the Elements of Rage disarm'd,
O'er all below a solemn Quiet grown,
Joys in th'inferiour World, and thinks it like her Own: . . .

The concept of revelation and transcendence as accompanying the night goes back to the biblical story of Nicodemus we spoke of in our first chapter; indeed, in contrasting this light of Christ with the fierce light of day, Finch was likely to have known Vaughan's "The Night."[61] Like Vaughan, Finch draws on both the imagery of Cynthia and a picture of external nature. That pure "Virgin-shrine" is the Virgin Mary in Vaughan and "Cynthia" in Finch's neoclassical imagination. But the "Glow-worms" are, as we have seen, "real" glow-worms.[62]

Of course, Wordsworth was exactly wrong when he thought that Finch was interested in external nature for its own sake. We see that the overall structure of the poem pulls the reader through the lived present time of experienced nature and poetic occasion; the historical time of myth, tradition, and landscape; and the eternal time of religious meditation. As we read the last lines of this section, we find that the Orphic charm has in fact been worked on the speaker herself; the transition from rage to joy addresses the many sources of the poem at once. Significantly, it reverses the consequences described near the end of Chapman's "Hymnus in Cynthiam":

Thus nights, faire dayes: thus griefs do joyes supplant:
Thus glories graven in steele and Adamant
Never supposd to wast, but grow by wasting,
(Like snow in rivers falne) consume by lasting.
O then thou great Elixer of all treasures,
From whom we multiplie our world of pleasures,
Discend againe, ah never leave the earth
But as thy plenteous humors gave us birth,
So let them drowne the world in night, and death
Before this ayre, leave breaking with thy breath.[63]

In contrast, it echoes the completion of the plots of *The Merchant of Venice* and *A Midsummer Night's Dream*. The comic pastoral has triumphed over melancholy.

In neo-Platonic Orphic cosmology, Night is a primeval black-winged bird that gave birth to Eros. The halves of the shell became Sky (Uranus) and Earth (Ge). The "inferior world" in these terms is the sensible domain of Earth itself. Once Finch stops the description of night wandering, she organizes the poem within the vertical axis common to prayer and the meditative tradition. "Something too high for syllables to speak," the ineffable, is at the upper limit of this axis; the sensual world is the lower. But the speaker is careful to make "her own" world *like* the lower world. There is an obvious political pun being made here as Finch implies that her "retreat" from the high world of the court has made her world like a "lower" world. And at the same time the poem has itself descended, traveling westward in the imagination, from the dense woodland of the park, presumably at Eastwell, into the open landscape of Salisbury plain; the trajectory of night wandering follows the path of darkness itself from forest shadows to open fields. Finch thereby joins her world with Tufton's world and aligns herself with the goddess Nyx who has power over tyrant men—and even over Zeus—as she wanders the Earth like the star-crowned "donna che qui regge" of Dante's *Inferno* and Crashaw's "moon of maiden stars" who rules the sky.

This is the lesson of the Orphic hymn to the Moon's claim that night "grants fulfillment and favor." Thomas Taylor's later eighteenth-century translation of that hymn gives these lines as "Fair lamp of Night, its ornament and friend, Who giv'st to Nature's works their destin'd end."[64] Birds and insects go to the same place to sleep each night. A bumblebee may choose the same hollyhock; butterflies return to the same swatch of bark; birds return to the same roosting spot.[65] The language of the closure is direct:

> In such a *Night* let Me abroad remain,
> Till Morning breaks, and All's confus'd again;
> Our Cares, our Toils, our Clamours are renew'd,
> Or Pleasures, seldom reach'd, again pursu'd.

The antiphonal "In such a Night" completes the circle. The breaking of morning reinstates the everyday narrative of desire, where pleasure will not be immediate but something we pursue. The flat realism of these lines breaks the enchantment of Orphic magic. The clarity of Finch's rural morning is reminiscent in outward form of a poem by one of her acquaintances that is exactly contemporary to "A Nocturnal Reverie"—Swift's "Description of a City Morning." The brisk clauses and the final couplet, which doesn't stop but rather ends on "renewed," underline the reimposition of clock time and the shift from wandering to conscious direction.[66] Yet the closure exaggerates the paradox of clarity as confusion. "Cares, toils, clamours, pleasures seldom reached" are what the daylight shines upon—what should be particular nouns, given the light source, are in fact murky abstractions, just as in the darkness we were able paradoxically to attend to the particular features of nature. The speaker's overriding desire here, "let me abroad remain," emphasizes the inversion of daylight's clamours and cares; it is night that has given the speaker access to, and has enabled her to produce, both music and pleasure.

II. THE EMERGENCE OF A NOCTURNE TRADITION

"A Nocturnal Reverie" is one of those singular artworks in which one can see the emergence of a change in consciousness. It makes maximal use of the Ovidian, Orphic, and neo-Platonic traditions; it is at the same time immersed in the new positivism and attentive to theological convention. It is a poem of sensual expression for its own sake and an occasional poem deeply reliant on allegorical imagery.[67] If it has represented a model of aesthetic freedom for nature poets and contemporary feminists alike, that freedom arises from its complex use of varying paradigms of thought and action. When we look at the consequent tradition of night poetry in English, it is, nevertheless, not surprising that Finch's poem had little influence—even in Wordsworth's mention of the poem, he drew more attention to her affinity with later Romantic poetics than to her actual themes or techniques. In fact, although it serves different ends at different historical moments, night poetry dominantly continues to be in the Orphic and meditative vein with few exceptions. In the "Triumph of Dulness" section of Book IV of the *Dunciad* (1742), Pope was readily able to rattle off a parody of the sable throne of Night primeval and Chaos old where even Lord Chesterfield makes a cameo appearance with tears in his eyes.[68] And Young's "Night Thoughts" (1742–1745) is far more concerned with the relation between night and death than with any account of external nature. Although Young refers to the "midnight raven," night remains allegorical; the use of night imagery is designed to supplement the tone:

> Thou darkness aiding intellectual light
> My song the midnight raven has outwing'd
> And shot, ambitions of unbounded scenes
> Beyond the flaming limits of the world,
> Her gloomy flight. . . .[69]

The poem conducts a complaint regarding the authenticity of grief within a theology of immortality; skulls, bones, and instruments of death are among the ornaments in the speaker's study. The speaker is in a position previously occupied by St. Jerome and Melancholy herself.

In contrast, Joseph Warton's "The Pleasures of Melancholy" of 1747 is an apostrophe to Melancholy worked through a kind of weaving of all the conventions of the form. The poem is written in blank verse and makes quite explicit its aim as an homage to Spenser, Shakespeare, and Milton; no one could mistake this work for anything but a British poem and, if they did, the raising of infant Melancholy by a Druid at the end would set them "right." Warton sings of a hail storm, "Pale Cynthia [in] her silver-axled car," "ruin'd Abbey's moss-grown piles," "the lone Screech-owl," "cloisters," "Arabian wastes," and "gloomy battlements and ivied tow'rs": "a blended scene . . . Where, with his brother horror, ruin sits." Such conventions are joined by rhetorical connectives: "Hail," "O wrap me," "O tell"—the wandering here is mental wandering. Contrast, for example, the details of nature we have found in Finch with Warton's presentation: "O wrap me then in shades of darksom pine, / Bear me to caves by desolation brown, / To dusky vales, and hermit-haunted rocks! / And hark, methinks resounding from the gloom / The voice of Melancholy strikes mine ear."[70]

Coleridge's "Frost at Midnight," first published in 1798, takes up and transforms an image of sleeplessness from Genesis 31:40. In these lines Jacob makes complaint to Laban: "Thus I was: in the day the drought consumed me and the frost by night; and my sleep departed from my eyes." Coleridge is not suffering physically; yet he cannot *think* because of the silence around him: "so calm, that it disturbs and vexes meditation." The great innovation, and central theme, of Coleridge's poem is that the night speaker is not entirely alone: his infant son Hartley is sleeping in a cradle by his side. Coleridge brilliantly puts forward the problem of the vatic in this poem as he makes the child the vehicle of the move toward the future. Even the poem's reminiscence—which is itself a reminiscence of a childhood daydream—is linked not so much to the past as to the continuity of the idea of *anticipation*. The "stranger" whom Coleridge awaited as a boy in the schoolroom and could only imagine at that time as someone familiar from infancy becomes his own infant. Coleridge has the poem take an ecstatic turn as his passive childhood relation to the world (a world of the pent cloister of the great city) becomes his active shaping of his own child's experience (a world of sublime nature where God will be the "Great Universal Teacher" who replaces the "stern preceptor"). The "secret ministery" of the night frost is to make what was amorphous tangible, a task synonymous with the realization of time. Coleridge takes up many of the conventions of the night soliloquy here: attention to the wind, the cry of the owl, discursive thought, the neo-Platonic conflict between the *vita activa* and the *vita contemplativa,* and the return to the initial theme. However, the poem is a complete reversal of the *ubi sunt* tradition. It takes the silence and vacancy of the present darkness as an opportunity to project a replete future moment.[71]

Keats's "Ode on Melancholy" (1819–1820) also draws on the imagery of Renaissance melancholy: the choleric's turn to poison; the ruby grape of Proserpine; the yew, the beetle, death-moth, and owl; and the figure of Psyche, who was loved in the darkness and by the nineteenth century had become a synonym for the soul that leaves the body at death. But the "Ode on Melancholy" suggests, like "L'Allegro," that the vividness of daylight imagery is an antidote for dark melancholy: the morning rose, the rainbow of the salt sand-wave, the globed peonies, or the lover's "peerless eyes"—sight is the antithesis of melancholy, although it cannot completely disperse her since she lies ever-present in the fleeting temporal nature of all beauty.

The contemporaneous "Ode to a Nightingale" begins, however, not with sense impression from which inference is then drawn but with the aching and drowsy poet's response to the nightingale's song. Keats begins with a mood and proceeds only in the last line of the first stanza to give its cause: the nightingale singing of summer in full-throated ease. The first half of the poem is the written expression of the poet's longing. Only at the end of strophe 4—where the imaginary portrait of the "Queen-Moon on her throne / Clustered around by all her starry Fays" draws the poet's attention to what might be described as the "shadow" of her light, the faint moonlight with "the breezes blown / Through verdurous glooms and windy mossy ways"—does the poet return to the immediate scene. Strophe 5 has many resonances to *A Midsummer Night's Dream* as well as to Finch's consequent inventory of night phenomena: Keats skillfully emphasizes that he *cannot see* and so from the "embalmed darkness" will guess each "sweet": grass, thicket, fruit tree wild, white hawthorn and the pastoral eglantine, fast-fading violets and the coming musk rose, the "murmurous haunt of flies on summer eves."

The last line of each strophe produces an echo effect generating the next strophe: the nightingale's "full-throated ease" of 1 leads to the "O, for a draught of vintage" in 2; the "fade away into the forest dim" of the nightingale in 2 turns into the "fade far away, dissolve" of 3's speculation on death; the thought of new love "beyond tomorrow" in 3 leads to the projected "away! away! for I will fly to thee" claim of 4; the windy mossy ways of 4 lead to the inability to see the flowers at the start of 5; the flies' murmur in 5 turn to "Darkling I listen" in 6; the poet who is "a sod" to the nightingale's "high requiem" in 6 turns to the rhetorical apostrophe countering the thought that opens 7: "Thou wast not born for death." And at the end of 7 and beginning of 8 the whole technique is directly described as "faery lands forlorn" lead to "Forlorn! the very word is like a bell / To toll me back from thee to my sole self."[72] Keats has taken the standard nocturne convention of the dueling birds and made himself the counter to the nightingale. The night wandering of the sleepless melancholic is carefully worked through the meandering of *sound* through the darkness. This effect is brought to stunning closure by the final flight of the nightingale away through more and more distant regions—past the near meadows, over the still stream, up the hill side: "and now 'tis buried deep in the next valley-glades." If Finch's owl "set the wanderer right," Keats's nightingale in contrast is the phantom of consciousness itself; once the music is gone, the thresholds between life and death and waking and sleeping have disappeared.

James Thomson's *The City of Dreadful Night,* written between 1870 and 1874, is today little read and little known, but it is a remarkable and fantastic evocation of the experience of night drawn with a deep knowledge of the tradition of night poetry.[73] From the many references to Dante to Thomson's sometime pseudonym, "B.V." ("Bysshe Vanolis"), with its allusions to both Shelley and Novalis, the poet creates a complex amalgam of nocturne images and structures. This is not the sweet moonlit night of rural wandering; rather, it is the lamplit night—half fantasy, half social realism—of the city: a night for suicides, drunks, transients, and others who are existentially lost. It is an account of urban night wandering situated between the cursed and blighted "midnight streets" of Blake's "London" and many of the images of Eliot's poetry.[74]

The City of Dreadful Night is structured in an elaborate pattern; it has twenty-one cantos of iambic pentameter. By making all the even-numbered cantos further the action and all the odd-numbered cantos provide a commentary, Thomson shapes the whole poem around the vita activa/vita contemplativa distinction. The commentary sections are usually written in seven-line stanzas rhyming ababccb; the narrative sections are most often in six-line stanzas rhyming ababcc. Therefore, there is a base rhyming structure from which variations are played. The cantos vary from three to fifteen stanzas; the commentary cantos have from three to five stanzas; the narrative sections vary from eight to nineteen stanzas. By making occasional use of triplets, quatrains, and a range of rhyme variations, Thomson is able to create a complex sense of tone and texture.

The first-person narrator moves through the City and beyond during a single night. He seems to be traveling northward, toward wastelands and trackless marshes, and away from the river that girds the city on the south and west. But as he follows a ghostly figure, he turns right three times, and the reader begins to lose any sense of direction as the trajectory becomes more amorphous and as Thomson moves between sweeping and particular details. Consider, for example, how much the following stanza resembles the empty, yet haunted, spaces of de Chirico:

> Although lamps burn along the silent streets;
>> Even when moonlight silvers empty squares
> The dark holds countless lanes and close retreats;
>> But when the night its sphereless mantle wears
> The open spaces yawn with gloom abysmal,
> The sombre mansions loom immense and dismal
>> The lanes are black as subterranean lairs.[75]

The speaker wanders in the outer regions of the City and eventually arrives on a plateau overlooking the urban landscape where he encounters the image of Dürer's *Melencolia, I*—Thomson had in fact picked up a print of the engraving in the early 1860s.[76] The concluding image of "Melencolia" here appears like a monumental statue: "Titanic from her high throne in the north, / That City's sombre Patroness and Queen, / In bronze sublimity she gazes forth."[77] Dürer's *Melancolia* links the Saturnian to memory and is ultimately reconstructive and compensatory. Ever since the pioneering iconological studies of this image by Raymond Klibansky, Erwin Panofsky, and Fritz Saxl, we have come to see Dürer's work as a portrayal of the tragic relation between creative desire and measurement. The shadowed, exhausted anthropomorphic figure as an emblem of human striving and failure; the famished sleeping dog as an emblem of the insatiability of animal appetite; the purse and keys as signs of worldly ambition; the drooping head on the clenched fist as an illustration of both the fatigue of creative thought and the grasping nature of human intelligence; the compasses, hammer, molding plane, set square, and writing implements as tools of a geometrically defined optics—these elements of the picture build to an allegory of human creativity wherein the particularity of animal desire and the universality of measure must somehow be mediated.

Thomson had taken this image of Melancholy not only from Dürer but also from the description of the brass city in *The Thousand Nights and One Night*.[78] This strange image of the cold stone figure whom one encounters in the night like a form of psychological blockage or arrested life echoes to the figure of the castrating father, the Commandant, in Mozart's *Don Giovanni* and to the figure of the patriarch, the Colossus, in Sylvia Plath's poetry as well. The protagonists in the work of Thomson, Mozart, and Plath resemble the wandering flaneurs of Baudelaire, yet we also can see that their overwhelming sense of dread arises from the anticipation of this encounter with stone. Water and stone—as we have discussed them in previous chapters as elements of mutability and intractability—form two boundaries for the night wanderer who is constantly negotiating his or her way between them.

In 1814, a generation before Chopin, the Irish composer John Field published the first piano works he called "Nocturnes." Although previous works throughout the Baroque and eighteenth century had been called *notturni* or *nachtmusiken* because they were designed to be played in salons in the evening, Field was to develop a particular method of composition and performance that would establish the initial sense of the genre. As a form, the nocturne returns to the Renaissance conflation of "mode" and "mood." Relatively brief, the nocturne approximates the fluid melodic line of bel canto, emphasizes decoration over development, and uses special pedaling effects such as shifting harmonies over a sustained tonic.

In his study of Field's nocturnes, Patrick Piggott explains that the first six nocturnes all had "the same basic idea: a *cantilena* for the right hand accompanied by left-hand figurations which depend for their effect on subtle pedalling."[79] In later nocturnes Field developed melodic features for the left hand. It is obvious that his innovations played an important role in the development of piano virtuosity through the nineteenth century. Jeffrey Kallberg, the foremost theorist of the musical nocturne, has noted features in the nocturne as a genre that seem to stem from Field's early works: floridly ornamented tunes, widely spanned broken chords, downbeat accents, harmonically static beginnings, subdominant related keys, and return to the opening theme at closure.[80] In more recent work, Kallberg has explored the ways in which the nocturne is bound to a cultural thematic of the feminine through nineteenth-century readings of such features as "feeling" and "detail"—as an 1844 reviewer of Schumann's piano music put it: "the rapturous, tender, lyrical, almost womanly character of the Fieldian 'cantilena.'"[81]

The piano nocturne has many features in common with the literary nocturne. The role of the melodic line in the piano nocturne is far more reminiscent of the picaresque detail of the night wanderer than it is like any narrative or dramatic form of progression. Field's piano works, in particular, express a sense of the pianist finding his or her way, meandering through the tune until finding him- or herself returned to the initial theme. The use of pedal work to represent depth and resonance and of trills and triplets to signify quick fleeting motion each add to the pictorial quality of the piano nocturne—its ability to represent effects of light and water, as well as birdsong.

Consider the bird call as piano trill at the conclusion to Schubert's "Notturno" for trio or the lively junglelike night of Colin McPhee's symphonic "Nocturne." Bird effects are sometimes far from nature as in the anachronistic larks in Richard Strauss's "Im Abendrot." Ralph Vaughan Williams's "Symphony #2" was specifically designed to be the musical equivalent to the Thames nocturnes of James Whistler in its largo section; the third movement, the "Nocturne" proper, dramatizes the theme of the return by using a Cockney worker's song to signify the laborers going out to work at dawn. This use of the "nocturne" is very much like the return to care and toil in Finch's reverie and as well the use of the theme of early morning workers in Thomson's night poems.[82] Furthermore, the piano virtuoso's gradual and stunning development of a balance between both sides of the body in playing recapitulates quite elegantly the whole concept of kinesthetic sense in the darkness. It is as if the pianist is making his or her way through darkness by the act of playing itself.

We could make the case for a genealogy that would extend between Finch's "Nocturnal Reverie" and the specific features of the piano nocturne. But what is perhaps more interesting is to note, following Kallberg, that the "feminine" aura of the piano nocturne that developed in the nineteenth century would also have led to a particular retrospective reading of Finch's poem. The poem's qualities as a sensual poem of external nature, a meditation on the condition of women's freedom, and a mood piece come forward as its connection to the Orphic hymns and its implicit religious and specific historical aspects fade from the culture.

Nocturnal works in painting before the eighteenth century are usually interior scenes. Yet there are a number of conventions that are exceptions to this rule. In the iconography of saints, Saint George fights the dragon in the evenings—in this way the hero can soon go to sleep and experience thereby the magical healing of his wounds that can only occur in the darkness. Uccello makes brilliant use of this tradition in his 1455–1460 version as he has St. George's lance proceed in perspective directly toward the dragon's eye—putting it out for the night. As we can also see in Uccello's *Hunt* (1465–1470), the diminishment of vision gives the painter an opportunity to emphasize other senses—the dogs' keen sense of smell; the noise and cries of the men and animals.[83] Dutch and English landscape painting of the seventeenth century as well often created effects of moonlight.

But many paintings, including landscape paintings on biblical themes, display a tradition of light as an emission of the sacred, a sign of redemption in standard Christian iconology and a sign of transcendence in neo-Platonism. Following biblical precedent, they often focus on scenes of adoration, contemplation, and recognition—all gestures that depend heavily on light and so emphasize all the more the miraculous qualities of light in the darkness: the Nativity; the Calling of Matthew; Nicodemus recognizing Christ; Saint Jerome in his study. The nocturnal paintings of Caravaggio and Salvado, for example, with their emphasis on realism within a context of unspecified light source, yoke the real into the service of the holy. It is the radiance of the holy that animates the scene from within. Perhaps nowhere is this more evident than in the *L'Adorazione de'Pastori* of Gerritt van Honthorst (Gherardo delle Notti) destroyed in the Uffizi bombing in 1993. In this painting the shepherds must shield their eyes with their hands because of the strength of the radiant light coming from the Christ child; the putti flying high above are also illuminated by the infant's light. In his 1952 survey of Caravaggio's work, Roger Hinks suggests that Caravaggio's use of a concentrated light source focused on foreground figures against a neutral field of darkness in fact had many antecedents: Antonello, Bellini, Corregio, Lotto, Savoldo, Bassano, and Tintoretto especially, as well as Caravaggio's immediate masters, Peterzano and the Campi, had all worked in what Hinks calls a "nocturne" form. Even so, he notes that hardly any of Caravaggio's pictures do in fact represent lamplight or torchlight scenes: "the 'Seven Works of Mercy' forming almost the solitary exception before the latest works, where the lighting is, of course, magical rather than rational."[84]

Caravaggio's emphasis on nocturnal experience gives us further insight into why so many of his paintings focus on varieties of sound: music, a moment of significant speech, or a cry. Consider, for example, his early paintings on the theme of music such as *Una Musica, The Rest on the Flight to Egypt, The Lute Player,* and *Amore Vincitore;* the emphasis on moments of revelation by speech such as the supper at Emmaus and the betrayal of Saint Peter; as well as the open mouths of Isaac, Holofernes, Narcissus, St. Matthew, Goliath, and, of course, the Medusa—and the boy bitten by a lizard, the Christ child bitten by a serpent, the weepers at the Deposition, the screaming acolyte who witnesses the martyrdom of Saint Matthew, and the anguished, truncated portrait of John the Evangelist caught while crying out in the recently discovered *Taking of Christ.*[85]

As the nocturne develops in music and the visual arts in the eighteenth, nineteenth, and early twentieth centuries, the emphasis shifts to the experience of hearing and seeing rather than toward their referents or consequences. This is perhaps why the aesthetic form of the nocturne, in whatever medium it appears, is not a dreamscape. The nocturne develops on a trajectory of sensory realism that finds its logical end point in abstraction. Finch's poem, in its overall form—its careful attention to what night perception is truly like, joined to its complex use of history, myth, and occasion—remarkably anticipates the development of the nineteenth-century visual nocturne.

In Turner's *Liber Studiorum* mezzotints with their views of Paestum, Catania, Shields Lighthouse, and *The Evening Gun* and his 1835 painting *Keelmen Heaving in Coals by Moonlight*, moonlit night is a time of stasis and peacefulness. In contrast, the anachronistic night brought on by the effects of storms in his paintings is often the site of human catastrophe—and the idea of an unnatural night extends to concepts of eclipse and overweening power. Perhaps most dramatic among his works addressing the night brought on by weather is his monumental *Shade and Darkness—The Evening of the Deluge* of 1843 in which, according to a caption he provided from his lectures on "The Fallacies of Hope," Turner wanted to restate the sublimity of darkness, representing "negative disobedience" and using color to symbolize the "awful gloom of approaching horror."[86] Within Turner's complex iconography, as in the legend of Regulus and Coleridge's story of the Ancient Mariner, the sun is so intense that it blackens vision. Yet the sun also creates a vortex out of which all visual experience struggles. In Turner's work the moonlit night is often the medium of more contemplative seeing and the place where seeing and hearing are more closely aligned.[87] In some verses of 1808, Turner wrote these central stanzas:

> With [word illegible] tones at Evening's hour
> Sweet Philomel resumes her power
> The echoing woods, the moonlight gleam
> With silver radiance gilds the stream.
>
> The darkened heath once gay with Green
> The feathered songsters hail their Queen
> Impassioned spread their spotted wings
> And love with Music's influence sings.

The poem ends in an appeal that the "sweet inspiring power" of night will shine on him and lull him "with harmonious meledy to rest."[88]

Andrew Wilton has provided a particularly intriguing discussion of a Turner watercolor study from 1830 known as *A Mountain Pass: Night:* "The contrast between the tunnel of darkness on the left and the area of light at the right is typical of Turner's compositional organization in the 1830's, but it is impossible to be sure precisely what is intended here: are we among the wilds of a bleak mountain pass, or is the scene a more familiar one, with streets and houses, and perhaps a torchlight procession?" The amorphousness of the painting comes from the status of the swirling circular area of light, which throws into darkness the rest of the painting. There is an uncanny resemblance between viewing this painting and the experience of listening to Charles Ives's "Calcium Light Night": in Ives's little piece, a raucous procession of Yale undergraduates carrying calcium lights comes toward us in the night; the silence fills gradually, starting with a few faint notes that sound like flutes or kazoos, until it reaches an almost unbearable cacophony; it then recedes as the procession moves away and we hear again only silence, which is now synonymous with darkness.

In contrasting the stillness of moonlit night with the terror of night when associated with storms or other natural disasters, Turner is following Burke's mandate on the nocturnal sublime: although darkness is more productive of sublime ideas than light, Burke also notes that darkness will only evoke the sublime if it is painful or terrible.[89] He also mentions the phenomenon of the sun's production of blackness: "Extreme light, by overcoming the organs of sight, obliterates all objects, so as in its effect exactly to resemble darkness. After looking for some time at the sun, two black spots, the impression which it leaves, seem to dance before our eyes . . . [two ideas of] opposite nature [are] brought to concur in producing the sublime."[90] Coleridge presents what could be considered to be a textbook case of this distinction between kinds of nocturnes when we compare the stasis of "Frost at Midnight" with its "silent icicles, / Quietly shining to the quiet moon" to the violent sublimity of the agitated weather effects in his later "Dejection: An Ode."

Coleridge had come to identify moonlight with the "modifying powers of the imagination" characteristic of poetry itself.[91] In his "Ten O'clock" lecture of 1885, Whistler similarly asserted a particular affinity between night (where nature sings "in tune") and artistic consciousness: "And when the evening mist clothes the riverside with poetry, as with a veil, and the poor buildings lose themselves in the dim sky, and the tall chimneys become campanili, and the warehouses are palaces in the night, and the whole city hangs in the heavens, and fairy-land is before us—then the wayfarer hastens home; the working man and the cultured one, the wise man and the one of pleasure, cease to understand, as they have ceased to see, and Nature, who, for once, has sung in tune, sings her exquisite song to the artist alone."[92] By now the figure of Melancholy awake in his den or cell in the night and contemplating mysteries not available to others is both continued and transformed in the image of the artist who wanders and sees in the night. For Whistler, moonlit walks along the Thames were the source of a new harmonic technique that would culminate in his famous nocturnes: *Nocturne in Blue and Silver* of 1872–1875 (later titled *Nocturne: Blue and Gold—Old Battersea Bridge*); *Nocturne in Blue and Silver* of 1871; *Nocturne in Blue and Gold* of 1871; *Nocturne in Black and Gold: The Falling Rocket* of 1875. By 1872, he was calling his "moonlight" pictures "nocturnes"—a term, he contended, "poetically" said "all I want to say and *no more* than I wish."[93] Whistler's nocturnes were, in fact, constructed by a particular process of impressing the night scene on the mind with the aid of language. His pupils, Elizabeth and John Pennell, wrote in their biography that Whistler would go out in the night and stand before the scene he wanted to paint; then turn his back on it and review to a companion "the arrangement, the scheme of colour, and as much of the detail as he wanted. The listener corrected errors when they occurred, and, after Whistler had looked long enough, he went to bed with nothing in his head but his subject. The next morning, if he could see on the untouched canvas the completed picture, he painted it; if not, he passed another night looking at the subject."[94]

Whistler developed special methods of using color and "wetness" of paint in the nocturnes. In the *Nocturne in Blue and Silver: Cremorne Lights*, he used a pale blue scumble over a dark ground initially to cool and soften his image, then defined the dark passages, and then scumbled almost the entire surface with a uniform color. In the *Nocturne in Blue-Green* he used the same technique, but the initial ground of lead white and ivory black is exposed for the dark passages.[95]

In 1877, after seeing Whistler's nocturnes at the Grosvenor Gallery, Ruskin complained in a published series of letters titled *Fors Clavigera*, "I have seen, and heard, much of Cockney impudence before now; but never expected to hear a coxcomb ask two hundred guineas for flinging a pot of paint in the public's face." Whistler decided, in turn, to sue Ruskin for libel. In testimony on his own behalf, Whistler stated, "By using the word 'nocturne' I wish to indicate an artistic interest alone, divesting the picture of any outside anecdotal interest which might have been otherwise attached to it. A nocturne is an arrangement of line, form, and color first. The picture is throughout a problem that I attempt to solve. I make use of any means, any incident or object in nature, that will bring about this symmetrical result."[96] Throughout his testimony he insisted that he was painting harmonic arrangements of color and not more particular referents.[97]

Although Ruskin was, of course, the great champion of Turner, making him the touchstone for his arguments in *Modern Painters*, he was as well continuing and furthering a long tradition of criticizing abstraction.

Hazlitt had derisively referred to Turner's pictures as "pictures of nothing," writing, "The artist delights to go back to the first chaos of the world, or to that state of things when the waters were separated from the dry land, and light from darkness, but as yet no living thing nor tree bearing fruit was seen upon the face of the earth. All is 'without form and void.' Some one said of his landscapes that they were *pictures of nothing, and very like.*"[98] In fact, this is precisely the case; they are pictures of light and its atmospheric effects. Ruskin understood this quality in Turner as an aspect of exactness and fidelity to nature. But for an artist like Whistler, the painting of the medium of seeing brought the act of seeing and the act of painting into a continuous process.

The structural elements of Finch's "A Nocturnal Reverie"—melancholic and Orphic conventions; reflection, vision, touch, and hearing, wandering and return as bodily responses to the physical world; water and stone as metaphysical and emotionally charged images—are found in the time and space of other nocturne forms as well. Finch's poem is contemporary to the development of the novel, and we can readily find in Gothic and Romantic fictions such as *The Monk* and *Frankenstein* the continuation of the theme of Faustian melancholy. And in the urban night of *A Tale of Two Cities* and the night on the marsh in *Great Expectations*, in the night journeys of Celine, and Joyce, and Barnes, in the truncated light of forests and the mist and storm-wrapped ships of Conrad, and in countless other novels, the phenomenology of the night is set forward as it is in night poems, musical nocturnes, and paintings. But it is significant that we consider these elements of such novels to add to their lyric and poetic qualities—that night scenes are used to interrupt the teleology of narrative, to heighten symbolism, to lend musical structures of return and repetition, and to signify movement toward the interior, or solitary delight or fear in the nocturnal encounter with nature.

When we think of the history of poetry, we find that the relation between the senses and their imaginative representation is both particular and continuous to prior tradition. Here, too, we discover a vague transposition of "the poetic" to other genres of literature and to modes of visual art and music. It was "the evening mist," Whistler contended, that "clothed the riverside with poetry." The history of the nocturne itself has a lyric, and not merely a narrative, dimension. As representations of our experience of the night accrue, it is sense impression itself that evolves: new modes of moving and attending, of using touch, sight, smell, and hearing, are the consequences as well as the source of these forms that are created to express all that is not day.

7

LYRIC COUNTER EPIC

I. WAR AND THE ALIENATION OF THE SENSES

When Marx wrote, "The forming of the five senses is a labour of the entire history of the world down to the present,"[1] he emphasized that the senses as we know them are a human accomplishment. Yet he also was expressing a utopian hope that the senses would be, in time, free to serve whatever might be those human needs that could be articulated beyond mere necessity. He argued passionately that thinking of our lives as a form of economic, rather than sensual, being is a travesty of all that human history might be, and that the consequence of such a travesty is a despairing alienation. "If you live only as an economic being," he wrote,

> you must not only stint the gratification of your immediate senses, as by
> stinting yourself on food, etc.: you must also spare yourself all sharing of
> general interest, all sympathy, all trust, etc. if you want to be economical,
> if you do not want to be ruined by illusions. You must make everything
> that is yours *saleable*, i.e. useful. . . . Do I obey economic laws if I extract
> money by offering my body for sale, by surrendering it to another's lust?
> (The factory workers in France call the prostitution of their wives and
> daughters the Xth working hour, which is literally correct.)—Or am I not

acting in keeping with political economy if I sell my friend to the Moroc-
cans? (And the direct sale of men in the form of a trade in conscripts, etc.,
takes place in all civilized countries.)[2]

Prostitution and conscription are here linked as the ultimate examples of
the degradation of the senses brought about by the alienation of labor.
Such economic exploitation of the body is negatively compared to a projected utopian existence within which, Marx proposes, sensual being is an
end in itself and social relations are formed out of a recognition of the individual sensuous existence of others. For Marx, our humanity depends
therefore on an unalienated relation to sense experience itself. His negative account of prostitution and conscription may seem almost a moral
commonplace to us. Yet his argument is an enduring critique of certain
idealizations of what might be called trade in bodies. Prostitution and conscription still flourish, and marriages and wars that are primarily economic transactions come veiled in layers of romantic, or nationalist, ideology. When the body is exchanged as an economic abstraction, or when
the senses of others are used for ends at odds with the sensuous existence
of those others, "all general interest, all sympathy, all trust" are eroded.

Marx's story of the senses differs significantly from empirical and Enlightenment accounts of the senses. In arguing that the senses are a historical, rather than a natural, development, Marx considers the senses as
instruments and consequences of human action. Compare his position,
for example, to this passage published fifty-four years earlier in Kant's
third *Critique:* "Even war has something sublime about it if it is carried
on in an orderly way and with respect for the sanctity of the citizen's
rights. At the same time it makes the way of thinking of a people that carries it on in this way all the more sublime in proportion to the number of
dangers in the face of which it courageously stood its ground. A prolonged
peace, on the other hand, tends to make prevalent a merely commercial
spirit, and along with it base selfishness, cowardice, and softness, and to
debase the way of thinking in that people."[3] These reflections might be
said to undermine the moral force of Kant's arguments regarding intellectual freedom in aesthetic judgment, for they conflate the willed actions of
war with the unattributable sources of the sublime. The passage in fact
follows that part of the discussion of the sublime in which Kant carefully
argues that "we cannot pass judgment at all on the sublime in nature if we
are afraid. For we flee from the sight of an object that scares us, and it is
impossible to like terror that we take seriously. That is why the agreeableness that arises from the cessation of a hardship is *gladness.*"[4] From

a position of safety, the viewer admires, on aesthetic grounds, the soldier's lack of fear.

The problems of generalization in the apprehension of suffering, and the conflicting solutions of a Kantian transcendentalism and a Marxist humanism, continue in contemporary culture with particular vividness. In arguing against Kant's emphasis on "rational respect," Richard Rorty has recently contended "there is such a thing as moral progress, and that this progress is indeed in the direction of greater human solidarity. But that solidarity is not thought of as recognition of a core self, the human essence, in all human beings. Rather, it is thought of as the ability to see more and more traditional differences (of tribe, religion, race, customs, and the like) as unimportant when compared with similarities with respect to pain and humiliation."[5] Rorty proceeds toward a human universal, not in a deductive fashion as does Kant and not in a deferred utopian discourse of self-realization as does Marx, but rather by means of a clarification of particulars.

It is in the accrual of particular knowledges made under a rubric of inclusiveness without ready identification or typification that Rorty constructs such a universal. He posits this universal as synonymous with an ongoing and *made* moral sphere. It is perhaps impossible to avoid the irony of juxtaposing the "moral progress" Rorty hopes for with the brute reality of current stages of war: tribal genocide; the drumming up of local, virulently typifying, ethnic hatreds; and forms of technological warfare where large-scale systematic killing is conducted on a level of abstraction that refuses even to account for enemy deaths.[6] The old equation between love and hate that reminded us that we cannot love another at a distance as we cannot destroy another at a distance is set askew by technologies with unfathomable powers of destruction.

George Eliot suggested in an 1856 essay that "[t]he greatest benefit we owe to the artist, whether painter, poet, or novelist, is the extension of our sympathies. Appeals founded on generalizations and statistics require a sympathy ready-made, a moral sentiment already in activity; but a picture of human life such as a great artist can give, surprises even the trivial and the selfish into that attention to what is apart from themselves, which may be called the raw material of moral sentiment."[7] Rorty similarly valorizes the particularity of novelistic and ethnographic accounts as vehicles for the expression of individual suffering and, therefore, claims that such genres promote an intolerance for cruelty: "In particular, novels and ethnographies which sensitize one to the pain of those who do not speak our language must do the job which demonstrations of a common human nature were supposed to do."[8] I would like to take seriously his suggestion that literature is a vehicle of moral progress if by such progress we mean an increasing recognition of individual persons and a reciprocal attention to the consequences of actions in relation to intentions. But I would argue that we can as readily find an analogue to the contrast between the abstracted and sublime view of human suffering and the immediacy of first-person experience in the contrast between two poetic modes: the first associated with public representations of war and the expression of tribalism and nationalism—the epic—and the second associated with the expression of the senses and emotions out of first-person experience—the lyric.

Criticism at least since Hegel commonly assumes that the rise and fall of literary genres is in concert with the domination and recession of modes of consciousness. To this end, epic is the genre characterizing an archaic social order, an order organized hierarchically and maintained through warfare against what was barbaric, or outside its boundaries. Here the unitary worldview promoted by the epic is in fact synonymous with hegemonic models of consciousness. Classical epic theory, stemming from Aristotle's *Poetics*, emphasizes this modeling function of epic action; epic imitates men as they are and as they ought to be, their actions depend on good moral choices with the consequences of moral failings and errors shown as well. The "outstanding and noble" characters of the epic are admired for their deeds and suffering.

Epic appears in the dignified form of dactylic hexameter and is narrated by epic bards who themselves, because of their special inspiration and ability to transcend the limits of mere sense—hence the bard's characteristic blindness—have remarkable skills in preserving the past and moving their listeners to pity and fear. When, in Book XII, the narrator of the *Iliad* says, "It were too much toil for me, as if I were a god, to tell all this, for all about the stone wall the inhuman strength of the fire was rising, and the Argives fought unhappily, yet they must fight on, to defend their ships. And all the gods who were helpers of the Danaans in the fighting were dejected in spirit,"[9] the audience immediately understands that the narrator's articulation of a limit to his capacities is undermined by the passage itself—a passage that simultaneously grasps a range of spatial coordinates and at once breaches the gaps between both internal consciousness and external action and human and divine will. Epic narrative is expressed in *segments* that should not be confused with the partiality of fragments; the epic segment functions as a mnemonic for bard and audience. Bakhtin has described how in the epic "it is possible to take any part and offer it as the whole . . . the structure of the whole is repeated in each part, and each part is complete and circular like the whole."[10] There is no emphasis on novelty; rather, the audience is compelled to draw connections and extend narrative elements. Vico said of "The True Homer," "Peoples who have first created heroic characters for themselves afterward apprehend human customs only in terms of characters made famous by luminous examples."[11] By the time of Virgil's *Aeneid*, this kind of ideological work enables the epic to serve as the record of, and reify, the destiny of a people.

As authority marks the context of epic narration, and opening *in medias res* and segmentation mark its form, a particular cluster of themes is associated with the heroic protagonist. C. M. Bowra explained in *From Virgil to Milton*, the hero of oral epic "is the superman, the leader who inspires and commands others in the work of war which precedes the establishment of a new order. The claim of this heroic ideal is that after all it is an ideal and that its adherents are ready to make any sacrifice for it."[12] The dynamic between will and sacrifice—the will of the hero and the sacrifice of his followers—is a mirror of the situation of bard and audience, for it is by force of will that the bard reconvenes the great amalgam of information and events that take form in the epic. And it is by means of submission to its contents that the audience directs its energy and thought toward the reification of the group. There is no emphasis on self-interest or individual person in the theme or reception of the epic. The brooding of Achilles comes into relief here as a problem that can only be addressed through sacrifice—what Max Horkheimer and Adorno have critiqued as the "archaic principle of blood and sacrifice, bad conscience and deceit of domination."[13] As the *Iliad* unfolds, the individual claims of Achilles and Agamemnon are not put into play with one another; each figure must abandon his individual desires for the general good. "The epic past," writes Bakhtin, "walled off from all subsequent times by an impenetrable boundary, is preserved and revealed only in the form of national tradition. The epic relies entirely on this tradition—by its very nature the epic world of the absolute past is inaccessible to personal experience."[14] We see in the dynamic between sacred and secular sacrifice a tension as absolute sacrifice (the offering of hecatombs to the gods) gives way to barter (the offering of mutual gifts). In its secular form, sacrifice requires the surrender of particular and individual needs to the abstraction of an exchange economy.[15]

In a well-known argument, Bakhtin has contended that the epic is "transposed into novelistic material, into precisely that zone of contact that passes through the intermediate stages of familiarization and laughter."[16] But the secularization of the epic has in fact a more complex trajectory. After *Paradise Lost*, the principal epics of the late seventeenth and eighteenth centuries—for example, Richard Blackmore's *Prince Arthur* (1695), *King Arthur* (1697), *Eliza* (1705), and *Alfred* (1723); Richard Glover's *Leonidas* (1737); William Wilkie's *The Epigoniad* (1757); James Ogden's *The Revolution* (1790); and John Ogilvie's *Britannia* (1801)— adapt an abstracted classicism to historical subjects for nationalistic and religious ends.[17] Stuart Curran has traced the ways in which such epics were in fact countered by the antiwar and anti-imperialistic ethos of Southey's *Joan of Arc* (1796) and the epic invocation of Joel Barlow's *The Columbiad* (1807), which condemns the corrupting influence of Homer and Virgil. For Barlow, the harnessing of epic discourse to ideological ends was a disaster; he wanted his work "to discountenance the deleterious passion for violence and war."[18] Here the high seriousness of the epic is maintained, even beyond the development of the novel, but a fissure develops between state and individual; a state dedicated to the pursuit of individual liberty will require an epic that is a kind of contradiction in terms.

Writers in the eighteenth century produced a number of mock epics that completely overturned the "high seriousness" of epic works. Employing much of the standard formal paraphernalia of the epic such as invocations, dedications, celestial interventions, epic similes, canto divisions, and battles, mock epics like Pope's *Rape of the Lock* and *Dunciad* and Dryden's *MacFlecknoe* critically address social, moral, and literary issues. Richmond P. Bond's classic study, *English Burlesque Poetry, 1700– 1750*, distinguishes between various types of burlesque, explaining that parody and mock heroic elevate a trifling subject to a higher style, whereas travesty and hudibrastic degrade a serious subject in a lower style. Like any reversal, the mock epic in the end negatively emphasizes the qualities of epic. To write from the viewpoint of the servant rather than the master, the domestic rather than the martial, the female rather than the male, ends in the reification of the master, the martial, and the male as the "high forms." But as is the case also with any reversal, such works of transformation will have unintended consequences. By turning to particular experiences outside the sphere of epic discourse, mock epic and other forms of burlesque widen the domain of knowledge and the potential of literary representation.

Bond cites, for example, two important prefaces that indicate the expansion of epic content in burlesque forms: Dryden's preface to *Annus Mirabilis* of 1667 "[the descriptions or images, well wrought] of heroick

Poesie, beget admiration, which is its proper object; as the images of the Burlesque, which is contrary to this, by the same reason beget laughter; for the one shows Nature beautified, as in the picture of a fair Woman, which we all admire; the other shows her deformed, as in that of a Lazar, or of a fool with distorted face and antique gestures, at which we cannot forbear to laugh, because it is a deviation from Nature"; and the "Advertisement" to the anonymous hudibrastic, *Pendragon: or, the Carpet Knight* of 1698: "As true Heroick may be compar'd to a Beautiful Well-dress'd Lady, who, ... advances with an even and graceful Motion; so *Burlesque* may be likened to her wanton Chambermaid, with her Petticoats tuck'd up, in her Masque and Pattens, who walks, runs, shambles, stops, looks about, and laughs."[19] The burlesque, with its travesty of style, produces a split between the identities of narrator and protagonist. In a work such as *The Rape of the Lock*, a meaningless sacrifice becomes the lever for a sardonic view of war. If war is not able to legitimate its losses, if deaths are in vain, the ideology of epic is destroyed.

After the eighteenth century's adaptations of epic to serious, yet novel, ends and transforming reversals, the form appears under the rubric of occasional poetry. In periods of war or national crisis, epic conventions are summoned for ideological ends. But parodies commend themselves, once heard, forever to the ear, and the reified form can no longer readily be adapted to a changed consciousness regarding violence and sacrifice. Something of the ambivalent status of late epic is captured in much of Tennyson's work.[20] His "Ulysses," written in 1833, repeats the Dantean prototype—beached, at rest, as in this final set of lines that fall weakly from the waning voice of the figure:

Though much is taken, much abides; and though
We are not now that strength which in old days
Moved earth and heaven; that which we are, we are,
One equal temper of heroic hearts,
Made weak by time and fate, but strong in will
To strive, to seek, to find, and not to yield.[21]

Tennyson's "The Epic," probably written between 1837 and 1838 and later becoming the frame poem for the "Morte d'Arthur," shows the classical form requiring considerable hedging in order to proceed. "The Epic" begins with friends at a Christmas Eve party, talking about developments in geology and (a consequent) loss of faith, when the conversation turns to how the poet Everard Hall has written a poem in twelve books on the Morte d'Arthur, but then "burnt it":

"Why take the style of those heroic times?
For nature brings not back the Mastodon,
Nor we those times; and why should any man
Remodel models? these twelve books of mine
Were faint Homeric echoes, nothing-worth
Mere chaff and draff, much better burnt."

Nevertheless, the burning of his epic poem provides an occasion for Francis Allen to tell how he "pick'd the eleventh [epic book] from this hearth." Hall reads the poem into the dawn when Christmas morning church bells ring, solemnly declaring, "Arthur will come again." [22]

In 1855, Tennyson was capable of glorifying unthinking sacrifice in the short lyric form of "The Charge of the Light Brigade. " Yet in that year he also invents the hysterical maelstrom of perspective displayed in *Maud*. Here he was able to show the consequences of following "a martial song like a trumpet's call." When the poem's narrator, whose sanity is made suspect by a head wound, concludes that he has "awaked . . . to the better mind," the reader is left to judge the merits of entering a light of "splendid names" that is synonymous with death. Significantly, *Maud* turns on an act of fratricide, or at least what the speaker believes to be an act of fratricide. Once the enemy is imagined as a kind of brother, the epic-heroic code of conduct and its dependence on the manufacture of abstractions are blocked. [23]

Whitman's *Drum-taps*, first published in 1865 and later integrated into the structure of the 1871–1872 edition of *Leaves of Grass*, also shows how fratricide blocks the enthusiasm of epic. [24] The drumming up of support for war's "red business" is broken down in Whitman's poem sequence via a complex relation of perspectives: the child's naive identification with the bright pennant of war; the veteran's testimony (within which the general is depicted watching, with sickened heart, the youngest soldiers, whom he knows individually, sacrificed); the father, mother, and sister receiving news of a brother's death; the comrade; the wound dresser; the old general and the artilleryman; the slave woman greeting Sherman's troops in the Carolinas; the enemy in his coffin, whose face the poet lightly kisses. The sequence is a profound meditation on the ideal of union or connection in the context of a nation sundered, but Whitman refuses the ideology of nationalism as the remedy for such sundering. As perspectives are rendered typical, they are also, through minute attention to individuality of emotion and expression, drawn beyond their typicality.

We see this gesture of individuation particularly powerfully in the lines describing the mother of the dead soldier reading the falsely consoling letter in "Come Up from the Fields Father." Up until this point, the poem's perspective is structured by a dynamic between dramatic monologue, expressed as the voice of the daughter, sister of the soldier "our Pete," and the epic sweep of the poet's voice describing both broad vistas of sky and field and particular sense impressions—the smell of the grape and the buckwheat; the sound of the bees buzzing around. The narrator moves urgently to the letter and stands within the mother's consciousness as she reads the actual words on the page. At this moment there is a conflation of the situation of the poet, the situation of the mother, and the situation of the reader of the poem. Suddenly, the voice of the poet is stripped of its anonymous omniscience:

> Ah now the single figure to me,
> Amid all teeming and wealthy Ohio with its cities and farms,
> Sickly white in the face and dull in the head, very faint,
> By the jamb of a door leans.[25]

In these lines the view extends beyond the landscape into the supersensible realm of the state, a territory existing only in abstraction, and at the same time the speaker reaches deep into the physical feelings of the mother herself—her white face taking on the mask of the many white faces of the dying and dead in the sequence as a whole. "Ah *now* the single figure to me" returns us to the deictic immediacy of the situation of the utterance of pain in the presence of another, the *to me* as compelling as the *to me* uttered by Cædmon's interlocutor.

As "Reconciliation" marks the final recognition of the enemy—"For my enemy is dead a man divine as myself is dead, / I look where he lies white-faced and still in the coffin—I draw near, / Bend down and touch lightly with my lips the white face in the coffin"—so does the end of the war signify the breakdown of the mass of troops into singular figures once more:

How Solemn as One by One

> How solemn as one by one,
> As the ranks returning worn and sweaty, as the men file by where I stand,
> As the faces the masks appear, as I glance at the faces studying the masks,
> (As I glance upward out of this page studying you, dear friend, whoever
>   you are,)
> How solemn the thought of my whispering soul to each in the ranks, and
>   to you,
> I see behind each mask that wonder a kindred soul,

> O the bullet could never kill what you really are, dear friend,
> Nor the bayonet stab what you really are;
> The soul! yourself I see, great as any, good as the best,
> Waiting secure and content, which the bullet could never kill,
> Nor the bayonet stab O friend.[26]

The relation between face and mask becomes once more a matter of preservation and disclosure accomplished through the word, the recognition of the suffering of others and the eidetic work of lyric "facing." As the beginning of "Reconciliation" resolutely claims, the mark of the word endures beyond all violence and mortality: "Word over all, beautiful as the sky, / Beautiful that war and all its deeds of carnage must in time be utterly lost." This is an idea we have encountered in many forms—the hope of the sonnet writer that his work will outlast "the gilded monuments" or withstand the force of the sea. But in Whitman there is a deliberate effort to recognize the face of the other within a context of unlimited human will—that context of organized human violence on a level of abstraction where the tragedy of the individual is discounted.

The mass deaths of the Civil War and the brutality of its internecine nature made Whitman's task of recognition all the more impossible and all the more moving. World War I, of course, was in every way a continuance and even larger-scale context for the deployment of an abstract technology of mass death. An aestheticized enthusiasm for battle preceded the war, was contemporaneous with it in the work of Wyndham Lewis, Pound, and others and followed in the work of the Futurists. But there is no greater critique of this enthusiasm than the leveling effects produced by the lyrics rooted in the first-person experience of soldier poets. When we think of poetry and war, we turn to this work where theme and life are one, to the achievement of the World War I soldier-poets—Wilfred Owen, Isaac Rosenberg, Siegfried Sassoon, Rupert Brooke, Edmund Blunden, and others—who wrote of their experience of the trenches in traditional lyric forms altered into dissonance. The dimensions of that war, a war conducted on a scale hitherto unknown, are focused—and thereby amplified in significance—to the domain of the first person. War is apprehended within the experience of that person and the face-to-face world of his life in the war. At this historical moment, the soldier-poet has ready access in memory to forms of beauty and tradition that he finds now must be bent to circumstance. In these lyrics he returns his body to its subjectivity; to read the trench lyric is to disregard the generalizations of sublimity in favor of the particular apprehension of the voice of the person.

A poem like Owen's "Conscious" is defiantly made of pure sense impressions; it is a poem of the minimally alive, those who return to life after a kind of death and as quickly will slide back into the dark again. The poem will make no further concessions to the intersubjectivity of meaning than that the reader understand that state of being:

Conscious

His fingers wake, and flutter; up the bed.
His eyes come open with a pull of will,
Helped by the yellow may-flowers by his head.
The blind-cord drawls across the window-sill. . . .
What a smooth floor the ward has! What a rug!
Who is that talking somewhere out of sight?
Why are they laughing? What's inside that jug?
"Nurse! Doctor!"—"Yes; all right, all right."

But sudden evening muddles all the air—
There seems no time to want a drink of water,
Nurse looks so far away. And here and there
Music and roses burst through crimson slaughter.
He can't remember where he saw blue sky.
More blankets. Cold. He's cold. And yet so hot.
And there's no light to see the voices by;
There is no time to ask—he knows not what.[27]

Owen's well-known use of dissonance in his closing lines is particularly evident in the false hope of rhyming *hot* and *what*. The poem ends as the soldier's mind breaks down into the inchoate once more.

Yet the critique offered by first-person soldier poetry goes even deeper, for the soldier's immediate sensual knowledge of war, a knowledge consequent to his willingness to sacrifice his senses to the effort of war, is given as an authentic moral discourse to be pitted against the unknowing rhetoric of warmongering. Rosenberg's *Trench Poems of 1916–1918* talk specifically of the thirst of the dying soldier, the feel of a rat against the hand, the search for lice, and the shut mouths and sprawled limbs of the dead. In "In War" he tells how while the priest prays, "Our ears half heard, / And half we thought / Of alien things, irrelevant; / And the heat and thirst were great."[28] Sassoon writes in "The Fathers" of two fathers, "snug at the club," "gross, goggle-eyed, and full of chat," who gossip about their sons' war experience before they "toddle through the door." In his "Suicide in Trenches" he juxtaposes starkly the immediacy of the soldier's sensual life with the abstractions of rhetoric:

I knew a simple soldier boy
Who grinned at life in empty joy,
Slept soundly through the lonesome dark,
And whistled early with the lark.

In winter trenches, cowed and glum,
With crumps and lice and lack of rum,
He put a bullet through his brain.
No one spoke of him again. . . .

You smug-faced crowds with kindling eye
Who cheer when soldier lads march by,
Sneak home and pray you'll never know
The hell where youth and laughter go.[29]

The authenticity of the soldier-poet is an attack on the rhetoric of the ideology of war. But another factor in the dynamic affecting the tension between experience and rhetoric in modern war poetry is the place of the civilian during wartime. Civilian life necessarily is bound up with the pastoral and domestic worlds to which war is counter.[30] E. M. W. Tillyard has suggested that the tension between the martial and the domestic is already apparent in the differing agendas of the *Iliad* and the *Odyssey:* "The *Iliad* is primarily warlike and political, and its men are heroic fighters or statesmen. Such problems as what good it is to fight and how political unity may be achieved are paramount. The *Odyssey* is primarily peaceful and domestic; its politics are local. Odysseus strives for an ordered and settled home life, which he not only re-establishes in Ithaca but witnesses in Phaeacia, his son too having witnessed it in Pylos and Sparta." Tillyard notes how these dominant emphases also enable the *Iliad* to make poignant allusions to the domestic even in descriptions of war, as when Achilles hounds Hector around the Trojan walls and a picture of the Trojan wives and girls washing in days of peace is inserted. Conversely, in the world of the *Odyssey*, the Trojan war is never forgotten, and Odysseus must exercise consummate political skills to regain his position of power.[31] Nevertheless, the epic poet does not question his ability to represent the heroic point of view; there is no expression of anxiety or inauthenticity regarding the poet's relation to the past or the immediate experience of war.

By the end of World War II, the tenuous authority of the civilian poet as bystander is particularly and rigorously brought forward in the responses of Marianne Moore and Wallace Stevens to the war. Moore's war poetry appears primarily in two books, *What Are Years!* of 1941 and *Nevertheless* of 1944.[32] "What Are Years" is the first poem of the 1941 volume. Like her earlier poem, "The Hero," from *Selected Poems* of 1935 ("He's not out / seeing a sight but the rock / crystal thing to see—the startling El Greco / brimming with inner light—that / covets nothing that it has let go"),[33] "What Are Years" is both hopeful and abstract as it asks:

> What is our innocence,
> what is our guilt? All are
>   naked, none is safe. And whence
> is courage; the unanswered question, . . .

> . . . He
> sees deep and is glad, who
>   accedes to mortality
> and in his imprisonment rises
> upon himself as
> the sea in a chasm, . . .

Moore ends the poem by claiming that ". . . The very bird, / grown taller as he sings, steels / his form straight up . . ." and that "his mighty singing / says, satisfaction is a lowly / thing, how pure a thing is joy."[34] "What Are Years" presents a kind of optimism regarding heroism, even as it questions whether gladness and joy might result from sacrifice. The poem is suffused with a sense of tentativeness. It paradoxically asserts the impossibility of closure, the emptiness of aphorisms, and the poverty of those lessons from nature that are the bedrock of Moore's usual poetics.

"Nevertheless," the first poem of her 1944 volume of the same name, also ends with an assertion of optimism, here consequent to Moore's belief in the ability of the weak to overcome the strong: "The weak overcomes its / menace, the strong over- / comes itself. What is there / like fortitude!"[35] But all the examples of particulars in the poem come from nature, far beyond the sphere of human volition, and the reader is left with the impression of a wish rather than a statement of fact. In "The Mind Is an Enchanting Thing," also from *Nevertheless*, as elsewhere in Moore's poetry, the experience of war is linked to blindness:

> the mind
> feeling its way as though blind,
> walks along with its eyes on the ground. . . .

> Unconfusion submits
> its confusion to proof; it's
> not a Herod's oath that cannot change.[36]

A Herod's oath: a resolution to slaughter. Moore writes that "the moral of this poem [is] that there is something more important than outward rightness. One doesn't get through with the fact that Herod beheaded John the Baptist, 'for his oath's sake'; as one doesn't, I feel, get through with the injustice of the deaths died in the war, and in the first world war."[37]

Of her most famous and celebrated poem in response to the war, "In Distrust of Merits," Moore writes, "It is sincere, but I wouldn't call it a poem. It's truthful; it is testimony—to the fact that war is intolerable and unjust. . . . Haphazard as a form, what has it? It is just a protest—disjointed, exclamatory. Emotion overpowered me."[38] "In Distrust of Merits" specifically associates the "blind man" with the enemy:

> They're fighting, fighting, fighting the blind
> man who thinks he sees,—

and the speaker associates herself with illness:

> they're fighting that I
> may yet recover from the disease.

Parts of the poem read like war propaganda posters: "As contagion / of sickness makes sickness / contagion of trust can make trust." Yet underlying the poem is the sense of the "contagious" quality of war—both a contagion between public opinion and the actions of warriors ("My/Self; some have it lightly; some will die. 'Man's / wolf to man'—and we devour / ourselves") and a contagion between the enemy's hatreds and the home front's:

> We
> vow, we make this promise
>
> to the fighting—it's a promise—"We'll
> never hate black, white, red, yellow, Jew,
> Gentile, Untouchable." "We are
> not competent to
> make our vows."

Moore concludes:

> There never was a war that was
>   not inward; I must
> fight till I have conquered in myself what
> causes war, but I would not believe it.
>   I inwardly did nothing.
>   O Iscariot-like crime!
>   Beauty is everlasting
>   and dust is for a time.[39]

Moore rests only on the laurels of her own self-examining. Her language in this poem is completely riddled with skepticism—distrust of merits leads once again to distrust of her own aphorisms, and the closure of the poem hardly resolves the problem. The act of vowing ends in a disavowal of the very grounds making a promise possible. Instead, the reader is left with war's horrific frame of mind—that beauty is for a time and dust is everlasting. In contrast to the disinterested contemplation typical of her usual approach to observation and description, this poem constantly falls out of focus and is interrupted by outbursts of emotion. The breakdown of form *is* the consequence of war in the poem and in the culture. It is the question Moore asked in reviewing Pound's *Cantos:* "Why cannot money and life go for beauty instead of for war and intellectual oppression. Books and arms. Under the head of arms, as you will have noticed, come daggers."[40]

Issued in the *Collected Later Poems* of 1951, her last published work on the war, "'Keeping Their World Large,'" was based on a comment that had been printed in the *New York Times* on 7 June 1944: "All too literally, their flesh and their spirit are our shield." She again contrasts the "illness" at home with the soldiers' efforts: "They fought the enemy, we fight / fat living and self-pity. Shine, O shine / unfalsifying sun, on this sick scene." Although often considered to be a "war poem," the poem is careful to distance itself from the immediate experience of war. The exact date of the *Times* quote is provided; the speaker is speaking "this Christmas Day / this Christmas year." The speaker's eyes "won't close to" the "forest of white crosses" of the war dead and the poem steadily moves into the past tense only to show that it is imperfect: "all too literally were our shield, are still our shield."[41] The emphasis on the shield necessarily alludes to the great ekphrastic image of the shield of Achilles; in fact, the first words of the poem are "I should like to see." But the speaker cannot see the beauty of the Italian landscape because it is blocked by the blinding spectacle of the sacrifice. Read in sequence, the poem continues the problem of "In Distrust of Merits"—perhaps those who were defended by the soldiers are not worthy of them. "Sick" and unable to keep a vow, the public is not enobled, or even changed, by the war. The seamless relation among poet, warrior, and national audience, first separated by the horror of civil war and the gap between home front rhetoric and battlefield experience in the poetry of World War I, is now even further torn open.[42]

Stevens's *Parts of a World* is similarly informed by a tormented relation to the "war effort."[43] "Examination of the Hero in a Time of War" contrasts the reality of "each man's" experience—

> Force is my lot and not pink-clustered
> Roma ni Avignon ni Leyden,
> And cold, my element. Death is my
> Master and, without light, I dwell.

—with the representation of the hero: "the hero is not a person." The following lines recall the anonymity of the night raids of the *Iliad*, the *Aeneid*, and *Orlando Furioso*:

> Say that the hero is his nation,
> In him made one, and in that saying
> Destroy all references. This actor
> Is anonymous and cannot help it.[44]

In the "Prose statement on the poetry of war," which he published on the last page of *Parts of a World* in 1942 (and later omitted in the *Collected Poems*),[45] Stevens begins by claiming that "the immense poetry of war and the poetry of a work of the imagination are two different things. In the presence of the violent reality of war, consciousness takes the place of the imagination." But in the second paragraph he explains that "we leave fact and come back to it, come back to what we wanted fact to be, not to what it was, not to what it has too often remained. The poetry of a work of the imagination constantly illustrates the fundamental and endless struggle with fact . . . in war, the desire to move in the direction of fact as we want it to be and to move quickly is overwhelming. Nothing will ever appease this desire except a consciousness of fact as everyone is at least satisfied to have it be." The immense ideological pressures of the war effort are here contrasted to the work of imagination, which must necessarily take on "the fundamental and endless struggle with fact" and hence strive to take up fact as what it is: force, cold, death and not, as "The Examination of the Hero" describes the "profane parade" in support of war, "Hip, hip, hurrah. Eternal morning."[46]

II.   TWO LYRIC CRITIQUES OF EPIC: BROOKS AND WALCOTT

In contrasting the rhetoric of warmongering—or broadly, in Stevens, the rhetoric of the reality-building activity of language in everyday life—with the exact and creative powers of poetry, the poet assumes that the immediacy of lyric will counter the abstraction of rhetoric and propaganda. But it is in the aftermath of war that we find lyric poetry especially at odds with epic ambitions. In the remainder of this chapter, I will focus on two examples, perhaps ironically *monumental* examples, of lyric transformations of epic ends: Gwendolyn Brooks's "Anniad,"[47] a long poem that is part of her 1949 Pulitzer Prize–winning volume *Annie Allen*, and Derek Walcott's *Omeros*, a book-length poem published in 1990.[48] Both works use lyric as a first-person critique of the epic. Both are concerned with the role of ideology in creating and sustaining certain models of the self. But Brooks's "Anniad" addresses the limits of wartime hegemony in a racist and sexist culture, attacking Romantic myths of female sacrifice. And Walcott, who describes a world in transition from colonialism to postcolonialism, critiques notions of heroic destiny, originary myth, and national identity.

Both works raise again for us the "Philoctetes" or "dead letter" problem we discussed in relation to Hopkins's desolate sonnets of 1885: how can anyone know the agony of Philoctetes in his abandonment? Brooks will focus on the character of Annie Allen, a young woman married to a soldier, who constantly seeks intelligible forms for her suffering in her efforts to express herself in history. Walcott will make a modern-day namesake of Philoctetes himself the center of a communal quest to find a cure for Philoctetes' wound—the sore on his ankle that is a vestigial survival of the chafe of the chain of slavery. In Walcott's poem, the traumas of slavery and colonial oppression are repeated in postmodern forms of tourism and sacrifice to a brutal economic system. Through such repetitions, history is at once disclosed and necessarily distorted and transformed.

Born in 1917 in Topeka, Kansas, Gwendolyn Brooks grew up in Chicago, attended Wilson Junior College, and after graduation worked for a quack "spiritual adviser" in the Mecca Building on South State Street, writing letters to the adviser's prospective patients. She later studied art and poetry with Inez Stark Cunningham and others at the South Side

Community Center. In her twenties during World War II, she published *A Street in Bronzeville*, her first book, in 1945. *Annie Allen* was her second book. Despite winning the Pulitzer, *Annie Allen* has, as well, been studiously attacked or neglected from its first reception forward. The early reviews of the work are deadening in their racism and condescension. For example, an anonymous reviewer in *Kirkus* wrote of the poem's "warm animal vitality." Rolphe Humphries found the poem weak wherever "awkwardness and naiveté when the big word or spectacular rhyme carries her away," gratuitously conceding "she is capable of more than one tone." [49] The 1973 *Norton Anthology of Modern Poetry* assures its readers, "She knows her people and her themes, and though she writes in irregular lines, she keeps close control on manner and matter alike. . . . She is for gumption, not compromise"—indicating that the editors have in fact not even read *Annie Allen*, a poem in strict tetrameter, and perhaps have not read any of the rest of Brooks's formal verse. The biographical sketch in the 1996 fourth edition of the *Norton Anthology of Poetry* mentions only the 1945 *A Street in Bronzeville* but says that "her work has grown more militant and political." As recently as 1986, R. Baxter Miller announced, "Brooks tried to write a Black epic in the title poem of *Annie Allen* but failed. Because the style was too lofty for the theme, an unintentional mock epic resulted. She had heeded the critics too carefully; their requests had led her to substitute Germanic mythology for the Black folk life that she knew. If Latin and Greek Diction replaced the Black vernacular, the folk voice would not be evident." [50] And in his preface to Brooks's autobiography, *Report from Part I*, Don L. Lee continues the attack from a reverse, but equally racist, angle: "Annie Allen (1949) important? Yes. Read by blacks? No. Annie Allen more so than *A Street in Bronzeville* seems to have been written for whites. For instance, 'The Anniad' requires unusual concentrated study. She invents the sonnet-ballad in part 3 of the poem 'Appendix to the Anniad, leaves from a loose-leaf war diary.' This poem is probably earth-shaking to some, but leaves me completely dry. The poem is characterized by fourteen lines with a three part alternating rhyme scheme and couplet at the last two lines. Only when she talks of 'The children of the poor' do we begin to sense the feel of home again." [51]

All of *Annie Allen* is dedicated to Edward Bland, a fellow member of the South Side community poetry workshop before the war who was killed in action in Germany on 20 March 1945. The work's dedication to a black soldier continues Brooks's enduring concern with the meaning of African American patriotic sacrifice. In her poem "Negro Hero," published in *A Street in Bronzeville*, Brooks writes, as she inscribed the poem, "to suggest Dorie Miller," an African American hero of Pearl Harbor.

Miller had been a navy messman at the time of the attack on Pearl Harbor. At that moment the forces were rigidly segregated by race, and blacks were forbidden to man guns. As the attack began, Miller ran to a machine gun and shot down four enemy planes. He later received the Navy Cross for his courage under fire, but racist critics continued to argue that black soldiers were incapable of participating in armed positions. The poem addresses not only white responses to Miller but also imagines Miller's own sense of the contradictions between democratic ideals and the reality of "the law": "I had to kick their law into their teeth in order to save them" he says, angrily asking, "Still—am I good enough to die for them, is my blood bright enough to be spilled?"[52]

A Street in Bronzeville's sonnet sequence "Gay Chaps at the Bar" also addresses the tensions felt by African American men and women during World War II and its aftermath. Individual sonnets such as "piano after war" and "the white troops had their orders but the Negroes looked like men" shift perspectives to show the catastrophic and yet at times redemptive social changes the war evoked. In the paired "love note" sections, the narrator alternates the voices of parted lovers—the first voice argues, "Surely you stay my certain own, you stay," and concludes, "This morning men deliver wounds and death. / They will deliver death and wounds tomorrow. / And I doubt all. You. Or a violet." The second voice declares, "Still, it is dear defiance now to carry / Fair flags of you above my indignation, / Top, with a pretty glory and a merry / Softness, the scattered pound of my cold passion." The final sonnet of the group, "the progress," shows the resolve of those who wear their uniforms and "applaud the President's voice and face" but inwardly feel "a deepening hollow through the cold. . . . The step of iron feet again. And again wild." Memories of the underlying legacy of slavery and racism are "put aside" by these figures for the sake of patriotism, but the poems reason that if the war does not overcome that legacy, such patriotism is by definition misguided. During the war, this paradox in fact led to such major race riots as the 1943 uprising in Detroit. In this now largely forgotten battle over the status of black citizenship, twenty-five blacks and nine whites were killed, and much property destroyed.[53]

In the "love notes," Brooks foregrounds the figure of the civilian, the wife or sweetheart who stays behind during the war, who will become in "The Anniad" merged with the betrayed figure of Dido. Just as in *A Street in Bronzeville* Brooks has used the traditional associations of the sonnet with Renaissance love conventions and Romantic political expression, so in "The Anniad" does she use the conventions of epic genre to build her theme. The title refers at once to the *Iliad*, which Brooks claimed as a direct allusion,[54] the *Aeneid,* and Pope's *Dunciad.* The suffix *-ad,* meaning a descent from an epoch of time, brings a Greek root to what will be a courtly love theme. Originally Brooks had in mind the name "Hester Allen" for her character and had named the work "The Hesteriad" when she first sent it to her publisher.[55] Under this title, the protagonist's function as keeper of the hearth in wartime is even more fully emphasized. In early negotiations with the publisher, she changed the book's title to the more sonorous *Annie Allen* and so changed as well "The Hesteriad" to "The Anniad."

Like the *Iliad,* "The Anniad" begins with the brooding of a protagonist. As segmentation, grandeur, hegemony, and sacrifice characterize the classical epic, so, too, do they emerge here as themes. Yet "The Anniad" owes as much to the serious social criticisms of the mock epic tradition as it owes to high epic tradition. Segmentation in the poem is linked to erratic romantic thought, grandeur to rhetoric and empty dreams, hegemony to claustrophobia, and sacrifice to meaningless loss. We are reminded of John Crowne's 1692 exercise in mock heroic, his *Episode* "to that called the Daeneids; as that of Dido is to the Aeneids," for that poem also addressed the theme of desertion and, despite Crowne's intentions, was both too reversing of classical values to be a "high epic" and too serious to succeed as a mock epic.[56]

Each of "The Anniad"'s forty-three septets is like an instance of ottava rima that has come up short. Brooks herself called the form a "version of rhyme royal." Although trochaic tetrameter is employed throughout the poem, the extraordinarily complex rhyme scheme varies from stanza to stanza, with occasional use of closing couplets. The effect produced by this trotting meter is mesmerizing and adds to the hypnotically romantic atmosphere around Annie herself, as in the Spenserian lines "Pretty tatters blue and red, / Buxom berries beyond rot, / Western clouds and quarter-stars, / Fairy-sweet of old guitars" mentioned earlier in our discussion of meter. From her boudoir, Annie broods, "Waiting for the paladin. . . . Who shall rub her secrets out / And behold the hinted bride." The opening stanza uses the traditional evocation of the gods, but Annie is a girl "Whom the higher gods forgot, / Whom the lower gods berate." She is left to "folly" [her own] "or to fate" [the chance of history].

"The Anniad" might be said to have a "plot," but it has no single moment of peripety. At the start of the poem, as Annie waits for her "paladin," she is a "thaumaturgic lass / Looking in her looking glass" and "Taming all that anger down" in her "black and boisterous hair." When the paladin comes, he is a "man of tan," and his arrival is presented through images of consumption (he "eats the green by easy stages" and "nibbles . . . with intimidating teeth") and romantic idealization: "and the godhead glitters now / Cavalierly on his brow."[57] Annie is awed by a "hot theopathy," but the path "his pocket chooses. / Leads her to a lowly room." She is quick to make a "chapel" of the room, decorating it with silver flowers. Into this scene of impoverished, but papered-over, domestic "bliss," a "Doomer" comes prophesying "hecatombs." Here Brooks uses an Anglo-Saxon kenning, as she has used alliterative technique elsewhere in the poem, to show an external interruption in Annie's domestic dream. If Annie's bower is as overornamented as Belinda's toilet, Brooks here turns to realism, for the hecatombs required truly will be large-scale public sacrifices. Doomer sweeps up "tan man" and "Names him. Tames him. Takes him off / Throws to columns row on row. . . . Then to know / The hunched hells across the sea."

Following epic conventions of amplification and segmentation, Brooks brings the soldier home, irreparably damaged, within just a few lines. Yet here the amplification again emphasizes the domestic; there are no battle scenes, no details about the soldiers' experience before he is "tossed to [Annie's] lap entire," a twitching, aching, wreck who still hears the "eerie stutter" of the guns and retches and wheels from tuberculosis. As the soldier "lifts his power off," he searches for some recompense to his suffering and turns to an affair with a "gorgeous and gold shriek . . . a maple banshee . . . a sleek slit-eyed gypsy moan." At this point the poem goes back to its opening invocation, "Think of sweet and chocolate," to negate all of the gains Annie has made: she is now "minus passing-magistrate / minus passing-lofty light" and "minus passing-stars for night." Brooks thereby inverts the epic catalog, with its accrual of prizes, spoils, and knowledges; Annie is depleted. She now begins to wander in snow, in springtime green, in summer "gourmet fare," running to parks, and deluding herself by claiming she is "bedecked with love" and swearing "I am philanthropist."

The poem has circled often around glimmering images of color (blue and red, half-blue, springtime green, apple green, ruby, flamingo, fuchsia, gilt, crimson, silver, white, tan, yellow, and maple skin), taste (berries, candy, confections, and vinaigrettes), and smell (chocolate, warm candles, sirocco wafts, and perfumes). Yet in the end, Annie's Bovaryesque accoutrements, her imaginary jewels and romantic dreams, are shown to be "copies of all her bright copies. Glass begets glass" and her "demi-god"'s tastes tend to dill pickles and beer. At this point in the poem, the narrator "twists to Plato, Aeschylus, / Seneca and Mimnermus, / Pliny and Dionysius"—experts on the very themes of idealization, tragedy, aging, and history that are structuring Annie's destiny. Like gods looking down on the pathetic struggles of human combatants, the classical sages here "lean and laugh at one who looks / To find kisses pressed in books."

Annie is advised to "incline to children." Eventually the soldier returns to Annie. He is wracked by "rust and cough," but he sits propped in his tavern chair. In the consequent lines of densely layered meanings, Annie seems to be pregnant: she bears the "weight of passing" and the "telephone hoists her stomach to the air." With understandable ambiguity, Brooks next presents a vivid sense impression of a suction dilation and curettage or abortion:

> In the indignant dark there ride
> Roughnesses and spiny things
> On infallible hundred heels.
> And a bodiless bee stings.
> Cyclone concentration reels.
> Harried sods dilate, divide,
> Suck her sorrowfully inside.

The reader is left with a picture of Annie "tweaked and twenty-four." No longer "sweet and chocolate," she is "derelict and dim and done," left in her kitchenette "kissing . . . The minuets of memory."

"The Anniad" is followed immediately by an "Appendix to the Anniad." The appendix's tripartite structure, labeled "leaves from a loose-leaf war diary," brilliantly uses techniques of documentation and at the same time alludes to the Sibyl's leaves. The first section, "thousands-killed in action," addresses the problem of response to war death, asking "why nothing exhausts you like this sympathy." The second nine-line untitled section speaks to the desire for life in the absence of belief in an afterlife: "The certainty we two shall meet by God / . . . is no ointment now." The poem translates that "now" into the final emphatic "Now," which represents "nights of vague adventure, lips lax wet and warm"—the sensual pleasures of immediate existence. The final "sonnet-ballad" with its opening and closing question "Oh mother, mother, where is happiness?" summarizes the plot of the "The Anniad" with immediacy and poignancy. Annie here serves as her own Greek chorus wherein the role of protagonist and helpless, commenting, bystander are now one: "They took my lover's tallness off to war. / Left me lamenting. Now I cannot guess / What I can use an empty heart-cup for."

"The Anniad" reverses conventions of epic significance throughout, focusing on the empty and disappointed experience of the woman who waits for a "knight" or "warrior" and is met with the disease, ravage, and infertility that are more often than not the true consequences of war. There is thereby, as in many mock epics, a typical inversion of attention from master to servant and from the hero to the abandoned supplicant, Dido. But here such inversions—an emphasis on meaningless sacrifice, compulsive ritual, and helplessness rather than willful action—are used by Brooks for critical ends, presenting a devastating attack on the glorification of war.

Derek Walcott's *Omeros* also both uses and overturns epic conventions, but Walcott does not focus on epic issues of war so much as upon epic issues of cultural origin and sacrifice. The poem, made of eight thousand lines, is put together in seven books, yet it is also divided into sixty-four continuously numbered "chapters," each of which have three parts. Song, speech, and text are thereby put into a complex relation, and the reader's pursuit of "plot" across chapters is both augmented and interrupted by the myriad dimensions of the form. The stanzas are generally terza rima, continuing the poem's many allusions to Dante and placing it in explicit opposition to Milton's "English heroic" rejection of rhyme. Like "The Anniad," *Omeros* displays an encyclopedic variety of rhymes and rhyme schemes: feminine, masculine, visual, pararhyme, rim rhyme, anagrammatic rhyme, apocopated rhyme, macaronic, rime rich, and various slant rhymes.[58] Rhyme as a historical issue, the issue of resonance across time and transformation through repetition, becomes in fact the major structural and philosophical principle of the work's reformation of epic conventions: "Because Rhyme remains the parentheses of palms / shielding a candle's tongue, it is the language's / desire to enclosed the loved world in its arms" (75), explains the poem's narrator.

The action itself is inflected with previous "plots" to which it does and does not adhere. Although there are more than twenty-five "characters" in the work, the action focuses in epic fashion on a number of decentralized segments or threads: the picaresque journey of the narrator, a thinly veiled portrait of Walcott himself, as he pursues the figure of the sage-poet Omeros throughout the Americas and the British Empire; the competition between Achille and Hector, two St. Lucian fishermen, for the love of Helen, who is literally a "maid"—Hector abandons his vocation to become a taxi driver, and in the end Helen has become a waitress dressed in native costume working in the Halcyon, a tourist restaurant—; the pursuit by the shaman and café owner Ma Kilman for a cure to the deadly wound suffered by the fisherman Philoctete; the quest for identity, through a historical search for origins and lament over lost progeny, conducted by the retired British major, Dennis Plunkett, who has settled on St. Lucia with his wife Maud to farm and raise pigs.

Omeros uses a number of epic devices in a relatively straightforward way: invocations to the muse ("O open this day with the conch's moan, Omeros" [12] and "O was the conch-shell's invocation, *mer* was / both mother and sea in our Antillean patois, / *os*, a grey bone and the white surf as it crashes" [14]); statement of theme ("This wound I have stitched into Plunkett's character. / He has to be wounded, affliction is one theme / of this work, this fiction, since every 'I' is a / fiction finally" [28]); *in medias res* (here exaggerated as film technique, as in "Cut to a leopard galloping on a dry plain / across Serengeti. Cut to the spraying fans / drummed by a riderless stallion, its wild mane / scaring the Scamander" [230]); catalogs; visits to the underworld (Achille returns underwater to Africa where he meets his own history and the narrator, led by Omeros, follows the goat track into the volcano of La Soufrière); and communication with the dead (Plunkett and Achille both meet, by various means, their ancestors, and the narrator Walcott converses with both his father, Warwick, who died before he and his twin brother Rodney were born, and, later, with his dead mother).

Other epic devices used include set speeches, set descriptions, and a number of epic similes or symbols—Helen's yellow dress, the sea swift who leads Achille to Africa, an encrusted wine bottle in the island museum that is a souvenir that has survived its possessors and so lost its discernible origin. It may have come from the shadowy galleon, the *Ville de Paris*, below the water that only Achille has seen in a fortune-hunting diving expedition.[59] Whereas such conventions serve to unify nationalist sentiment in traditional epic, they here present a complex, kaleidoscopic picture of the manifold cultural sources of the action. Erzulie, Ogun, and Damballa are among the gods. They live in the sky above the chapel of the narrator's boyhood and create a cyclone's havoc—although later he finds "their outlines fading, thinner / as belief in them thinned" (242). Their power is in the end concentrated in the healing plant sought by Ma Kilman.

The poem is in many respects an epic of place, and the center of its universe is the hunched island of St. Lucia—known by both its Arawak name, "Iounalao," or "Where the iguana is found," and its European name, "Helen." St. Lucia was discovered, probably by the Spanish, between the late fifteenth and early sixteenth centuries. The indigenous Caribs or Arawaks were eventually destroyed; in 1650, the French made the first successful attempt at settlement. From 1657 forward, the French and the

British struggled to gain the island as a military stronghold. Control over the island passed fourteen times between them. The crucial Battle of the Saints in which the British admiral Rodney defeated the French in 1782 off Dominica led eventually to British dominance in the early nineteenth century. Nevertheless, the island remained culturally French, with a common French patois and Roman Catholicism as the most popular religion. Walcott, child of Methodists, grew up at a time when the population of the island was eighty thousand and a meager sugar industry and dying coal works provided the major means of employment in the capital of Castries.[60]

The action in the poem, however, follows a far-ranging journey undertaken by the narrator and his "characters": from a grove of bay laurels in the shadow of volcanoes where Philoctete shows tourists how he builds canoes ("and then went down to the ships," now a commercial metadiscourse); to Castries; to Boston, where the narrator learns the Greek word for "Homer," *Omeros,* from a homesick young Greek woman; back to Castries and its environs, with memories of the Trojan war, Walcott's early marriage and childhood home, and the Plunketts' history intertwined; to the eighteenth-century site of Dutch settlement in the Antilles and the Battle of the Saints, in which Plunkett's first ancestor spies on the Dutch for Admiral Rodney and Achille's ancestor Afolabe is a slave renamed "Achilles"; to Achille's dreaming flight to Africa and back to Castries; to the narrator's memories of his mother; to New England and Boston; to the far western plains in the late nineteenth century at the time of the Ghost Dance uprising; then back to Boston, to Portugal, London, to Glen-da-Lough in western Ireland, birthplace of Maud, and then Dublin; to Odysseus's ships off the Aegean coast; to Istanbul, Venice, Philadelphia, Concord, Boston, Toronto, and then Boston again; back to the Ghost Dance uprising, in which Omeros utters the speeches of Sitting Bull; then back to Boston in search of the Greek girl; then to St. Lucia where the threads of the narrative are drawn together: "I followed a sea-swift to both sides of this text," says the narrator, ". . . its meridian / was not North and South but East and West. One, the New / World, made exactly like the Old, halves of one brain, / or the beat of both hands rowing that bear the two / vessels of the heart with balance, weight, and design . . . no other laurel but the *laurier-cannelle's*" (319).

What is the meaning of this journey if it is not conducted as part of the epic's traditional task of nation building? When Walcott suggests at the end of the poem that "the place held all I needed of Paradise," he has in mind the conditions under which expulsion is a mandate to work. In a well-known essay that, like much of his writing, critiques the idea of mimicry and the state sponsorship of carnival and other cultural forms, Walcott declares:

> History, taught as morality, is religion. History, taught as action, is art. Those are the only uses to which we, mocked as a people without history, can put it. Because we have no choice but to view history as fiction or as religion, then our use of it will be idiosyncratic, personal, and therefore creative. All of this is beyond the sociological, even beyond the "civilized" assessment of our endeavor, beyond mimicry. The stripped and naked man, however abused, however disabused of old beliefs, instinctually, even desperately begins again as a craftsman. In the indication of the slightest necessary gesture of ordering the world around him, of losing his old name and rechristening himself, in the arduous enunciation of a dimmed alphabet, in the shaping of tools, pen or spade, is the whole profound sigh of human optimism, of what we in the archipelago still believe in: work and hope.[61]

The Western history of St. Lucia is built from the erasure of the native population and the labor of African slaves. Here the story of his native place becomes for Walcott the story underlying all of Western narrative. But that story is also one of complex transposition and syncretism and what he called "the amnesia of the races," where "what has mattered is the loss of history" that necessitates imagination.[62]

Walcott's distinguished body of work before *Omeros* continually returns to these issues. In *Another Life* he had presented portraits of local figures, "stars of his mythology," which found for each local person a parallel among the Greek epic heroes. Janie, the "town's one clear-complexioned whore," for example, is nicknamed "Helen." In chapter 7 of that book, Walcott writes:

> Provincialism loves the pseudo-epic,
> so if these heroes have been given a stature
> disproportionate to their cramped lives,
> remember I beheld them at knee-height,
> and that their thunderous exchanges
> rumbled like gods about another life.[63]

The transposition of epic stature to everyday figures is countered in the New World by a diminution of tradition in the shadow of an overwhelming nature—a nature that undermines any simple reembodiment of old names in new forms. The long poem "The Sea Is History" in *The Star-Apple Kingdom* asks:

> Where are your monuments, your battles, martyrs?
> Where is your tribal memory? Sirs,
> in that gray vault. The sea. The sea
> has locked them up. The sea is History . . .
> and in the salt chuckle of rocks
> with their sea pools, there was the sound
> like a rumor without any echo . . .
> of History, really beginning.[64]

The whole poem contrasts categories of European knowledge with the unforeseen nature of the New World. Distrusting rhetoric, Walcott places all of the work's emphasis on the first-person experience of sense impression.

If such early work now seems like a series of sinopie for the great fresco of *Omeros*, it is also the case that Walcott has set forward a deliberately contradictory set of terms for the apprehension of his "epic." In his 1970 introduction to *Dream on Monkey Mountain and Other Plays*, he writes, "We knew the literature of Empires, Greek, Roman, British, through their essential classics; and both the patois of the street and the language of the classroom hid the elation of discovery." In his poem "Homecoming: Anse la Raye" in *The Gulf*, he says:

> Whatever else we learned
> at school like solemn Afro-Greeks eager for grades,
> of Helen and the shades
> of borrowed ancestors,
> there are no rites
> for those who have returned.[65]

During his constructive quarrel with the "black aesthetic" position of Kamau Brathwaite in "The Muse of History," Walcott urges a recognition of the centrality of Western literature for the Caribbean writer. In *Omeros* we find "on their varnished rack, *The World's Great Classics* read backwards" in the mirror of the corner barber, the town anarchist. And that backward view becomes associated with the progress of forgetting. Around the time of the publication of *Omeros*, Walcott began to claim little knowledge of the classics for which he had earlier argued so strenuously. In a 1990 interview he said, "As a narrative thing, the poem is not like a rewrite of the *Aeneid*. I don't know the *Aeneid* and I don't know the *Odyssey*. I've never read them. The only thing I know about those passages has to do with weather." In the same interview he suggested that Shakespeare's *Tempest* had taught him that "the work of the world revolves backwards, as it does in Paradiso, with Sybil's leaves reeling backward, all memory gone. . . . I wouldn't say all this if I was an American or British poet, but I'm from the Caribbean." [66] He had earlier claimed in a conversation with D. J. R. Bruckner, "One reason I don't like talking about an epic is that I think it is wrong to try to ennoble people. And just to write history is wrong. History makes similes of people, but these people are their own nouns." [67] As the narrator follows Omeros to La Soufrière, the old man says "you get my drift, a drifter / is the hero of my book." The narrator replies, "'I never read it,' I said, 'Not all the way through'" (282–283).

Creating a dialectic between memory and forgetting, between the accrual of history and the revisionist agendas of literary art on the one hand and tourism on the other, becomes the work of *Omeros* itself. Thus, we find here a layered and difficult process by means of which characters are more than characters—they are "their own nouns." However, these nouns are not sui generis—memory will place them in a context that both defines and eludes them. As in so much of Walcott's work, naming is more than cataloging or creating categories and types. In its use of nouns, *Omeros* confronts the generalizations of epic with the specificity of the novel. Yet, by unveiling the specific consciousness of history's "minor" characters within a rigorously particular historical frame, Walcott continually uses lyric's first-person consciousness and recursive structures of time to "unpack" the narrative of Western history.

Consider the use of proper names. Achille's name has come to him across generations as a consequence of a whimsical act by Admiral Rodney. When Walcott recounts how Afolabe "to keep things simple," lets "himself be called" Achilles (83), we are given an instance of the ignorant yoking of classical ideals with the reality of slavery: "the Jeffersonian ideal in / plantations with its Hectors and Achilleses, / its foam in the dogwood's spray, past towns named Helen, / Athens, Sparta, Troy" (177). But Achille (A-sheel), although we see him, too, dress like a girl (273) on Boxing Day and dreaming of a wound to his heel (148), is not Achilles; and his canoe says "In God We Troust," not "In God We Trust." The language is made anew with each utterance, just as each bearer of a name transforms the name. Rarely has a poem resisted allegory as strenuously as *Omeros* does. Hector is Hector, but in his taxi, *The Comet*, he is also Phaeton; Philoctete has a wound like the character abandoned on an island in the *Odyssey*, but here Philoctete is also linked to Achilles because he has a wound to his heel; he is cured by a "Machaon"—Ma Kilman, but this is the Ma Kilman of the St. Lucian *conte*, "heard on the back of an open truck travelling to Vieuxfort, some years ago," as Walcott had recorded it in "Iona: Mabouya Valley," in *Sea Grapes:*

> Ma Kilman, Bon Dieu kai punir'ous,
> Pour qui raison parcequ'ous entrer trop religion.
> Oui, l'autre coté, Bon Dieu kai benir'ous,
> Bon Dieu kai benir'ous parcequi'ous faire charité l'argent.

> (Ma Kilman, God will punish you,
> for the reason that you've got too much religion.
> On the other hand, God will bless you,
> God will bless you because of your charity.)[68]

Helen is the island and the person—Plunkett will try, via history, to make her a metaphor and the narrator, in "opposing stratagems," will try, via literature, to make her a reality (270–271); Troy is evoked by Castries, which was half-destroyed by a fire in Walcott's boyhood; Circe is reincarnated in a pig farm and in a swinish scene of lovemaking; the Cyclops is Joyce with his eye patch, the "gliding glass" of a telescope, the lighthouse at La Toc, and a tourist with a camera; Charon is a "charred ferryman"; Omeros is both a white marble bust of Homer and the ebony bust of the blind seer of the island, Seven Seas, and a Virgil to the narrator's Dante; Penelope appears as Maud, who is patiently weaving a tapestry, but Maud is also Tennyson's Maud of birds and flowers who inspires men to epic-heroic conduct; her native Glen-da-Lough is Yeats's world of sun and shadow. As Maud embroiders her silk tapestry of the birds with their names attached as tags, she is remarkably reminiscent of a woman artist whose work was also done in silk embroidery whom Valéry once described: "Artistic observation can attain an almost mystical depth. The objects on which it falls lose their names. Light and shade form very particular systems, present very individual questions which depend upon no knowledge and are derived from no practice, but get their existence and value exclusively from a certain accord of the soul, the eye, and the hand of someone who was born to perceive them and evoke them in his own inner self."[69] Yet whereas Maud's art begins in the sun-lit color of the living birds and the inscription of their names, it ends when the tapestry becomes in truth her shroud: Maud "preferred gardens to empires," the given to the manmade. The birds continue while the names are buried. Walcott, in his own voice as the narrator, says "what I preferred / was not statues but the bird in the statue's hair" (240).

The layered and contingent history of nouns in their particular occasions of use is indicative of the layered and contingent history of culture once it is imagined beyond the confines of nationalism. There are only islands here, yet each island is inflected by the sweep of every historical agent and force that touches it, including the agency and force of nature. Walcott brings us to the moment when history itself is commodified; the reification or fossilizing of culture under tourism becomes another device by means of which the poet might examine contradictions between surface and depth of meaning. As tourists watch Achille explain how the cedars are felled to make canoes, the idea of the "local" place is embedded in frames within frames of allusion; the tourist's camera is of small scope compared to the broad tradition of men going down to ships and alphabets constructed from trees. Later, Walcott will rework the traditional rhyme mapping, and interweaving, London's neighborhoods through its bells into an allegory of commodification. The traditional rhyme is as follows:

"You owe me five shillings,"
Say the bells of St. Helen's.
"When will you pay me?"
Say the bells of Old Bailey.
"When I grow rich,"
Say the bells of Shoreditch.
"When will that be?"
Say the bells of Stepney.
"I do not know,"
Says the great Bell of Bow.
"Two sticks in an apple,"
Ring the bells of Whitechapel.
"Halfpence and farthings,"
Say the bells of St. Martin's.
"Kettles and pans,"
Say the bells of St. Ann's.
"Brickbats and tiles,"
Say the bells of St. Giles.
"Old shoes and slippers,"
Say the bells of St. Peter's
"Pokers and tongs,"
Say the bells of St. John's.

During a sojourn in London where he sees the figure of the blind poet on the steps of St. Martin-in-the-Fields, the narrator of *Omeros* asks and answers:

Who decrees a great epoch? The meridian of Greenwich. . . .
Who screams out our price? The crows of the Corn Exchange.
Where are the pleasant pastures? A green baize-table.
Who invests in our happiness? The Chartered Tour.
Who will teach us a history of which we too are capable?
The red double-decker's view of the Bloody Tower. (196)

Walcott's panorama, with its tremendous scope and false bottoms, serves as an example of, and antidote to, the epic function of cultural allusion. No aspect of culture can be yoked in his epic to nationalist terms. The great cultural myth of the West—the cure for the wound of the father—is here broken down into a vast number of permutations that are by their very process antihierarchical and antipatriarchal. Philoctete's wound is slavery itself: "the hacked yams, the hold / closing over their eyes, the bolt-closing iron / over eyes that never saw the light of this world" (277). The pregnant Helen (both person and island) will give birth to a child of indeterminate and multiple lineage—Plunkett believes "he had given her a son" (103); Ma Kilman says, "Achille want to give it, even is Hector's, an African name" (318). Philo will be the godfather. Plunkett, like the unreliable narrator of "Maud," who thinks he has "awaked, as it seems, to the better mind," has a head wound from his stint with Montgomery (whose craftiness and mobility rivaled that of Odysseus) under the full moon at El Alamein. As in the reunion of Aeneas and Anchises in the underworld, the narrator meets his dead father, and Achille meets his ancestor Afolabe. Plunkett discovers an ancestor who becomes his missing son by the same logic under which Ma Kilman knows that a cure must precede a wound.

Just as allegory is undermined by the transformation of apparent depth into surface, so do connections that seem arbitrary and almost superficial turn out to be deeply coherent. The many references to, and passages about, the early Native American rights activist Catherine Weldon's witnessing of the Ghost Dance uprising provide an obvious parallel between the oppression of native peoples in the Caribbean and the oppression of native peoples in North America. Furthermore, the Ghost Dance analogue foregrounds the theme of redemptive ancestors. But when we look at the particulars of Weldon's life, we find that after she was exiled to Parkin Farm because of her unrelenting support of Sitting Bull, she was joined by her young son Christie. During the violence of 1890, "Christie stepped on a rusty nail which pierced shoe leather to lacerate and infect his right foot. The wound stubbornly refused to heal and the boy died of lockjaw poisoning."[70]

Whereas traditional epic emphasizes intention and teleology through its rhetoric of sacrifice, Walcott's work asks us to consider the labor of meaning from multiple perspectives within a universe of accident and co-incidence. Like Brooks, he draws our attention to the suppressed point of view of Dido—not so much to *who* Dido is as to what she knows, for we should remember that, because of Aeneas's preoccupation with action and destined glory, Dido is aware of Aeneas's history before he is. The most important classical allusion in Walcott's *Omeros* is to the following scene in which Dido watches the departure of Aeneas (*Aeneid*, Book IV, ll. 546–565). This is Allen Mandelbaum's translation:

> At this the Teucrians indeed fall to.
> They launch their tall ships all along the beach;
> they set their keels, well-smeared with pitch, afloat.
> The crewmen, keen for flight, haul from the forest
> boughs not yet stripped of leaves to serve as oars
> and timbers still untrimmed. And one could see them
> as, streaming, they rushed down from all the city:
> even as ants, remembering the winter,
> when they attack a giant stack of spelt
> to store it in their homes; the black file swarms
> across the fields; they haul their plunder through
> the grass on narrow tracks; some strain against
> the great grains with their shoulders, heaving hard;
> some keep the columns orderly and chide
> the loiterers; the whole trail boils with work.
>
> What were your feelings, Dido, then? What were
> the sighs you uttered at that sight, when far
> and wide, from your high citadel, you saw
> the beaches boil and turmoil take the waters,
> with such a vast uproar before your eyes?[71]

For Walcott this allusion also has its source in a picture from life. In his 1965 essay "Leaving School," he writes, "Down by the wharf, past the coal dunes near my grandfather's house, I had watched during childhood the crossing friezes of erect, singing women carrying huge panniers of an-thracite coal, each weighing a hundredweight, but the port was no longer a coaling station."[72] Throughout *Omeros*, the poet reworks versions of this scene. In his return to Africa, Achille sees a chain of men captured in a slaving raid: "he watched until the line was a line of ants." Weldon sees "a chain of men / linked by wrists to our cavalry. I watched until / they were a line of red ants." Ma Kilman comes to know the healing plant, grown from the seed of the swift who has brought it from Africa and who is embroidered into Maud Plunkett's tapestry: "she [Ma Kilman] staggered back / from the line of ants at her feet. She saw the course / they had kept behind her, following her from church, signalling a language she could not recognize." By following the ants, she finds this plant and hence delivers the cure for Philoctete's wound. She rubs herself in the dirt and cries out with a cry that goes back to the "black original cave of the Sibyl's mouth." The narrator writes:

> See her there, my mother, my grandmother, my great-great
> grandmother. See the black ants of their sons,
> their coal-carrying mothers. Feel the shame, the self-hate
> draining from all our bodies in the exhausted sleeping
> of a rumshop closed Sunday. There was no difference
> between me and Philoctete. (244–245)

It would be a mistake to say that *Omeros* effects in the end a symbolic erasure of difference or, alternatively, that identification is the point of the poem. In this long work, Walcott seems to have demonstrated every possibility of difference—and "rhyme" as both identification and difference —that can be imagined and has put these possibilities into a temporal relation evocative of constant, yet not random, change. When we examine the broad contour of lyric's transformation of the epic in these works by Brooks and Walcott, we see a historical progression in the recognition, and imaginary inhabitation, of the lived conditions of the existence of others. The seed of that progression lies in the reversals of mock epic, the tragic and tautological circumstances of civil war, the articulation of points of view on the margins of war and at war's deadly center. Following Rorty's claim that in the history of literature we can uncover the traces of a moral evolution, there is here evidence that the form-giving possibilities of *poiēsis* are at odds with the destructive capabilities of war and that this contradiction at the heart of epic making has drawn epic toward extinction. At the same time, lyric has been a development that is only possible given conditions of individuation of persons in culture and a certain breakup of forms of identification available to the audience. Wars themselves hardly seem bound to disappear. But this fact does not negate the continuing struggle between war's erasure of the expression of the historical and individual person of sensuous being and lyric's role as the continuing form of such expression.

AFTERBORN

The first time we see *light*, in Condillac's phrase, we *are* it, rather than see it.

—William James

Sound, voice, touch, motion, extension, and moral recognition: following Condillac, I have, in the successive chapters of this book, animated a figure—the figure made by practices of making themselves. My study as a whole has been concerned with the long historical and material project of anthropomorphization, of the formation of what Blake called "the human countenance" by means of poetic processes. In discussing the *Symposium*, I noted a category mistake that I have furthered throughout this work: the confusion and sympathy Diotima asserts between all kinds of human making. Diotima's ποίησις is the creation of being from nonbeing, the emergence of form out of nothingness. Nevertheless, she explained, the generic term *poetry* is that specific art separated off from the rest of poiēsis and concerned with music and meter.

I have tried to lay a foundation for understanding why, of all made things, poetry should have this place of privilege—the privilege of an exemplary creativity. Made of language, poetry participates both in the generalizations of inherited systems of meaning and in the particularities of expression—at this moment, in this place, with this voice, and so serves as what eighteenth-century aestheticians thought of as a "concrete universal," a form bearing witness to individuation and universality at once. To think of poetry as "individual expression" is both to return to the threshold where individuality becomes intelligible to others and to explore the possible range of qualities characteristic of any individual's subjectivity. The beholding, pointing, hailing, and delineating of those deictic gestures I have emphasized precedes the appearance of the subject. As Wittgenstein explained, the demonstrative cannot be without a bearer; where we find a demonstrative as evidence of being, being can be discerned.

Yet poetry is not made of language as we know it in its ordinary forms: the language of poetry is "concerned with music and meter." The image of human persons brought into being through poems is *aesthetic:* here intelligible meaning is made from sense experiences and generates sense experiences freed from the goals of use and appetite alone. Out of the unformed utterances of laughing and crying out and weeping, a whole decorum of emotional expression develops and merges with conventions of poetic decorum and occasion. Nevertheless, what might seem at first glance to be rule-governed behavior is in fact constantly in tension with the vital and ultimately inarticulate forces of pain and emotion that compel such expression. The fate of pain, the fate of sense impression, the fate of emotional outpouring are the finality of aesthetic form; but, even given this finality, aesthetic form constantly is put under pressure to change and renew itself in order to accommodate what time and experience have brought to it.

I have emphasized that the face-to-face encounter we have with an artwork is deeply embedded in the meanings and conventions we bring to face-to-face encounters with persons. All art is a kind of figuration in this sense, yet specifically this meeting with an artwork that is in itself and for itself is analogous to the free ethical stance in which persons are encountered in themselves and for themselves—without prior determination of outcome or goal. When we apprehend an artwork, considering it as a made thing, it is the intentions and activities of individual persons that we seek to recover and come to know. Anonymous works of art do not serve as exceptions to this meaning hearkening to meetings between persons. Rather, they acquire a particular poignancy, for when works of art are anonymous, they compel an interpretation that moves indeterminately between what might be particular and what might be universal in the presentation of the work, and they underscore our sense that our meetings with artworks and persons in general are always incomplete and unfinished, and so laden with as yet unknowable experiences.

Poetry is encountered with and through our entire sensuous being as we summon our memory and imagination. When we enter by means of reception into the poet's intention, we, too, are involved in making—participating both actively and passively in the process into form. To this extent, I have emphasized the incantatory aspect of poetry throughout this study—incantatory music and meters verge on the shattering of the form and at the same time produce overdetermined and transforming meanings. By means of the incantatory, the poet acknowledges in the work's very being this inevitable paradox of human life: that we actively pursue an *eidos* or fixed image of the human and at the same time passively long for its dissolution. We dream of returning to the sphere of elements from which we have come—even if this means we must imagine ourselves as a kind of thing. Every glimpse of our mortality presses us toward creating some adequate mark in the face of our disappearance. Yet this very aspiration for an immortality of form at the same time is mastered by a demand for the form's erosion; the inevitable limit of any given form undermines its capacity to satisfy the desire that made it. It is the figure of poetic making who most fully and tragically represents the duality of this human desire for representation. On the threshold of the poem, subjectivity emerges and disappears, is fulfilled only as it articulates our unfinished struggle toward fulfillment. The incantatory—that poetry created in a state of possession and therefore by means of a willfulness beyond the will of the speaker, that poetry of compulsive rhythms known not only through the body but through the memory as well—is in this sense not a mere disfigurement of a stable representation. Rather, it provides the most full or "true" account of the fleetingness of the human countenance and the complexity of the human figure subject to time and suffering.

I have considered many implications of the "here and now" of lyric poetry particularly, but all poems—indeed, all works of art—carry over sense experiences, moving their immediacy into discernible forms and providing models of time that are not bound to the exigencies of need and use. In any artwork, the stored time of making is projected into a time of apprehension by another and relieved of its formlessness, its unarticulated privacy. Without this transformation into discernible form, sense experiences are underdeveloped, insignificant, and doomed to disappearance. Hence, we might say they are "merely" forms of suffering, and another kind of suffering ensues from this very ephemerality.

Why not take seriously one of the most unsophisticated questions we can ask of an artist: "How long did it take you to make that?" What did this question mean, or did it even exist, before the alienation of wage labor? If we imagine the time of making as full of the pleasure, struggle, and absorption of sensual engagement with materials, we can rephrase the question: "How much time did you escape in making that?" or "In creating this form, how long were you able to ignore the social grid of abstract time?" The time system that governs industrial and postindustrial society, despite the existence of nostalgia-laden commercial pockets of handicraft production, places more and more emphasis on speed. This relentless emphasis on rapidity contributes to a climate of frustration and delay. Creating an atmosphere of something happening (canned music; recorded messages; advertisements in every interstice of hesitation and pause) is more important than making something happen. Speed is the enemy of difficulty; it tends to absorb or erase every other phenomenal quality.

Artworks apprehended by the pace of a heartbeat, the head's slow turn, steps traced and retraced aimlessly, a hesitant touch or glance, and then perhaps a reversal, in consequence have a powerful value as alternatives to these developments. The incantatory retains the power of ritual: its time and space are distinguished from those states of subjectivity that precede and follow it, and yet by means of such ritual processes subjectivity is dislocated and ultimately changed. Artworks can slow and even stop the frantic activity that characterizes most of the rest of contemporary existence—not in the sense that they help us rest for another onslaught or distract or amuse us but, rather, in that they provide time for the evaluation of intention and consequence. Even more significantly, they provide time for those extensions of memory into the past and imagination into the future by means of which our lives acquire their genuinely intersubjective and moral dimension.

In closing, I want to take up briefly the second quality Diotima ascribes, after the incantatory, to poetry: the quality of the prophetic. While it is true that we have no memories of the future, it is not the case that we cannot envision or project the future. And yet when we do so aesthetically—that is, drawing from the flux of our sense impressions and proceeding without teleology or goal—we encounter a future beyond the limits of our individual wills. We have some intimation of an extension of our notion of the person—either those states of being we can only imagine since they have no ground in our experience or those states of being we can remember or know somatically as prelinguistic or beyond the linguistic. When Keats wrote of "negative capability"—the ability to live among doubts, hesitations, and uncertainties—as among the most important of poetic values, he was responding to a representation of apocalypse, Benjamin West's "Death on a Pale Horse," that he found far too literal in its details.

I mentioned earlier that very few poems are in the future tense—that poetry has rarely been a discourse of social or political utopia. More often, poetry has involved a reconsideration of the past in light of the exigencies of the here and now or a reconsideration of the terms of the here and now once the weight of the past is brought to bear upon them. Yet there is a way in which the future is already embedded in every work of art: each work intends toward the future and is never closed by its reception.[1] All works of art project such situations of reception, and when we encounter artworks, we anticipate their own anticipation of our presence; this is the prophetic aspect of every poem, regardless of its theme. Utopias are often novelistic and particular in that they need to create a social ground for their political or ethical agendas. But the futurity of poetry depends on our sense of the cohesion and ongoingness of persons in general—a cohesion and ongoingness to which we adhere even when we cannot know its ground.

Diotima's distinction between the incantatory and prophetic powers of poetry can be reevaluated, for it is the far-ranging and ultimately untotalizable image of our subjectivity arising from the shattering experiences of the incantatory and vertiginous that gives us an expectation of intelligibility even when we are suspended in uncertainty and there is no frame for anticipating the other. The future, as we saw in the heaven-bent poems of Crashaw, is the ultimate state of "ungroundedness," the ultimate vertiginous ecstasy. Every poem takes a risk into this ungrounded moment of reception, just as every reception retrospectively works to articulate a deictic context in the absence of all determination and in the presence of an infinite range of contingencies that bore upon the making of the poem. There is no limit to the overdetermination and underdetermination of artworks in this sense, but this is not a matter to be regretted: it is because of such pressures against the limits of the form that artworks are endless resources of enduring value. Indeed, all artworks embody the overdetermination of experience and the necessary underdetermination of death. The artwork's finality of form makes it not only intelligible; it also makes such pressures on both creation and reception bearable.

Diotima was concerned with the notion of immortality throughout her discourse on the δαίμων. She drew what is by now a familiar contrast between what she considered to be the time-bound creativity of biological reproduction and the creativity of the poet, whose forms are immortal. Nevertheless, the ways in which poetic forms are immortal is in truth very much like the continuance of human life by physical and social means. The continuity of the self is not merely an effect of the continuity of bodily states of being; it is as well a matter of the continuance of one's actions into the future, of the unending consequences of all actions, including actions in speech, and of the self's capacity to use the imagination to link the past and the future. The projection of the self entails the imagination of its reception from a future perspective—a future perspective that is as untotalizable as the perspective it retrospectively projects back upon the past.

This is why, at the end of the chapter on sound, I emphasized the analogy between the words of a poem and the words of a promise: such a carrying over of significance into the future is a transcendent bond that arises necessarily because of the flux of those pressures working against it and continually forcing the possibility of breaking and erasure. Regardless of actual historical circumstances, of contingency and the decay of materiality, regardless even of the death of those contracted by the promise, the bond of the promise is carried over. The promise as a particular speech act is emblematic of the assumption of connection and intelligibility underlying all linguistic utterance; if one does not speak in good faith, one is not speaking. The difference between the cry of Philoctetes, which has no listener and assumes no listener, and the intersubjective expression of pain is language—this made thing, the mark of human consciousness beyond the individuation of speakers and occasions enabling the individuation of speakers and occasions.

Marx had hoped that over time new human senses would develop; he never seemed to have imagined that entire spheres of sense experience might be lost for many first-world people: a tacit knowledge of tools and forms of dancing or of carrying infants, the disappearance of ways of living with animals or cultivating plant life, along with the smell and feel and sounds and even tastes that accompanied such practices; the sound of wind in uninhabited spaces; the weight of ripe things not yet harvested. These experiences are gone, and even their names will soon be gone. The historical body of poetic forms is more and more an archive of lost sensual experiences; by now an aura of nostalgia accrues around the notion of the poetic itself. It was a mistake of humanism to assume that nature exists for us. But it has been just as serious a mistake to have forgotten that the made world, the world of culture, *is* made by and for us. In time we have diminished our sensuality rather than extended it.

Everywhere we look in contemporary culture, we see evidence of the reification of the traditional Western hierarchy valorizing the most distant senses. A balance, harmony, or interrelation of sense experiences articulated by moments of judgment and reflection is replaced more often than not by bombardments of visual and auditory stimuli that pin and numb the passive observer/hearer as if he or she were a kind of entomological specimen.[2] Herder would hardly be surprised at the two-dimensional world we have created, with its unrelentingly pragmatic emphasis on information rather than meaning. First no one remembered where to find clay in the earth, and then no one remembered how to prepare it, and then it was difficult to make or buy it, even in its manufactured form. A child today can look up endless information about clay or play computer games with "claymation" figures, but it is nearly impossible to have the experience Herder described in his *Plastik* of drawing an image of the three-dimensional depth of persons out of the raw materials of the earth. We no longer allow our children to play god, and a ready animation of all things results in a widespread amnesia regarding death.

What becomes of the poet in this climate of spectacle and auditory novelty? The poet/maker is pressured to become another image, an assemblage on a Web site, a body of work identifiable by a signature that is in truth a brand name, a maker of "personal appearances" that ensure the artifactuality of the reader or presenter and narcissistically project back such aspirations on an audience of poets themselves. And because hearing and seeing are the most mediated senses, poets return again either to the antirhetorical bias of linguistic and geometrical abstraction or to the unintentionally ironic pathos of spectacles of suffering and epiphany. In each instance, distance precludes engagement: the reader or receiver stands like Kant's general watching from a far hillside. Yet meanwhile the entire enduring accomplishment of the history of poetic forms awaits as a vast repertoire for anyone who hopes to enter again into an engagement with the senses. It is that history that has shaped our notion of the first person, and it is that history that will make us intelligible to those who will inhabit the future.

Perhaps I am writing at the end of a world. The insistent, but barely audible, animal scratching sounds of my pen as it crosses the white expanse of the page may be among the last of such sounds. Eventually these marks—idiosyncratic, already in their instability giving evidence of the aging of my body and so signs of my death arising from my own hand—will become those marks you have been reading; uniform, projected onto the surface of the page, a consequence of a series of electronic messages passed from one machine to another once I have transformed these inscriptions, by typing, into their abstract form. For now I can touch what I am making, and smell the must of the ink, and hear the shadowed sounds of the room where I am writing—someone whistling around the corner, the last "cheer-up" of a robin as dusk falls, the rumble and then squeal of the bus stopping at the light, a sudden blast of a song from a car radio, *have you seen her?*, and its equally sudden disappearance as the traffic begins again. And as night falls, the inevitable lengthening of the silences, sirens in the distance, and the human sounds of those lost or left on the street: an occasional moan or cry, a whisper, and then the swift explosion of a curse. What follows the curse is a curse, and what follows the last curse is silence and darkness; after the silence more silence, and after the darkness more darkness.

NOTES

Chapter One

1. Hegel, *Phenomenology of Mind*, 151–152.

2. Aristotle, *De Generatione Animalium*, Book I, chap. 23, 731 B, 56–57.

3. Hegel, "Independence and Dependence of Self-consciousness," in *Phenomenology of Mind*, 229–240.

4. Levinas, "There Is: Existence without Existents," in *The Levinas Reader*, 30. For reasons that will become clear in my chapter 4, I distinguish between absolute conditions of darkness, which necessitate and ground figuration, and the conditions of nocturnal experience, which admit of experience and movement.

5. Denis de Rougement makes a powerful argument that the Western emphasis on the soul's light in darkness stems from the dogma of the Manichean sects contending the soul is imprisoned in the night of terrestrial matter. Especially important is his contention that "the structure of Manichean faith was in essence lyrical. In other words, the nature of this faith made it unamenable to rational, impersonal and 'objective' exposition. Actually, it could only come to be held in being experienced, and the experience of it was one of combined dread and enthusiasm—that is to say, of invasion by the divine—which is essentially poetic" (*Love in the Western World*, 65–66).

6. Hesiod, *Theogony, Works and Days*, 9–10.

7. In his intriguing study of *The Invention of Literary Subjectivity*, Michel Zink explains how medieval writers, especially after the thirteenth century, came to emphasize concepts of truth and fiction: "the problem of truth lay at the heart of courtly poetics, which presupposed an identity between the truth of love and that of poetry and made sincerity the touchstone of amorous and poetic perfection." He continues to explain that "at the end of the thirteenth century the need for universality was no less great in personal poetry than in lyric poetry, since in any case its satisfaction was necessary for the audience to be touched by the fortuitous incidents of a particular subjectivity and to recognize itself in them" (62–63).

8. Homer, *The Iliad*, 211 (Book VI, English ll. 556–565).

9. Book X's theme of the Night Raid has a long ensuing history in epic, including the tale of Nisus and Euryalus in Book IX of the *Aeneid*. A parallel passage in Ariosto's *Orlando Furioso*, the night raid of Medoro and Cloridano, brings out with particular force the night raid's erasure of identity, for Ariosto mentions

that Turpin, Archbishop of Rheims, chronicler of Charlemagne, and the often-acknowledged source of Ariosto's own text, provides no names for the victims:

> And now the Saracen with wary view
> Has pierced his weasand with the pointed sword.
> Four others he, near that Diviner, slew,
> Nor gave the wretches time to say a word.
> Sir Turpin in his story tells not who,
> And Time has of their names effaced record.
> Palidon of Moncalier next he speeds;
> One who securely sleeps between two steeds.
> (Ariosto, Canto XVIII, stanza 175, 187)

10. Childs, *Biblical Theology of the Old and New Testament*, 111.

11. "Creation," in *The Interpreter's Dictionary of the Bible*, I: 725–732.

12. Herder continues by citing Job 4: 12–17 as follows:

> A word stole secretly to me,
> Its whispers caught my ear;
> At the hour of night visions,
> When deep sleep falleth upon man,
> I was seized with fear and shuddering,
> And terrors shook my frame.
> A spirit was passing before me,
> All my hair stood on end.
> He stood still, but I saw not his form,
> A shadowy image was before my eyes;
> It was silently whispered to me,
> How can man, &c.

13. These carols are cited from *The Oxford Book of Carols*, ed. Percy Dearmer, R. Vaughan Williams, and Martin Shaw: "Dark the Night," 11; "Herrick's Carol," 137; "Summer in Winter," 139.

14. Henry Vaughan, "The Night," in *The Complete Poems*, 289–290. The association of Nicodemus with the face of Christ is also key to the legend of the sacred face of Lucca, a wooden crucifix kept in the cathedral at Lucca. The legend tells that Nicodemus began the carving, and while he slept the face of Christ miraculously was completed. See Dante, *Inferno*, Canto XXI, l. 48: "Qui non ha loco il Santo Volta": "Here is not the place to show your sacred face" cry the demons of the Malebranche as they torment the barraters, or sellers of public offices, of Lucca.

15. Milton, "Samson Agonistes," in *John Milton*, 674–675, ll. 80–92.

16. In her study of the classical tradition of erotic lyric, *eros the bittersweet*, Anne Carson discusses triangulation as a form of erotic content: "Where eros is lack, its activation calls for three structural components—lover, beloved, and that which comes between them. They are three points of transformation on a circuit of possible relationship, electrified by desire so that they touch not touching. Conjoined they are held apart, the third component plays a paradoxical role, for it both connects and separates, marking that two are not one, irradiating the presence whose absence is demanded by eros." As the third, interdictory term de-

velops the erotic "plot," so does the third-person viewpoint of the reader of erotic lyrics act as an impediment to the perfect duality of the relation between lovers, as we see in the complications of the private and the public in Eliot's "Dedication." Carson's remarks in this vein conclude her discussion of Sappho's fragment 31, *phainetai moi*, a poem I discuss later in somewhat different, though not contradictory, terms.

17. Vico, *The New Science*, 75–76.

18. Ibid., 75.   19. Ibid., 74.   20. Ibid., 5–6.

21. Schiller, "Twelfth Letter," in *On the Aesthetic Education of Man in a Series of Letters*, 64–65.

22. Ibid., 67.

23. Ibid., 102.

24. Marx, "Economic and Philosophic Manuscripts of 1844," in *Karl Marx and Frederick Engels: Collected Works*, 3:295–297.

25. Kant, "Analytic of the Beautiful," in *Critique of Judgment*, 73–75.

26. Marx, "Economic and Philosophic Manuscripts of 1844," 302.

27. Ibid., 304.

28. Ibid., 301.

29. Vinge, *The Five Senses: Studies in the Literary Tradition*, 37. A brief survey of the topos of the five senses is given as well in Samuel Chew, *The Pilgrimage of the Life of Man*, 192–195.

30. Vinge, *The Five Senses*, 47–70; see especially "The Besieged City," 63–65.

31. *Philo*, VI:74–85.

32. Freud, "Instincts and Their Vicissitudes," in *The Standard Edition of the Complete Psychological Works of Sigmund Freud*, XV:120.

33. Schachtel, *Metamorphosis:* 132–136.

34. Damasio, *The Feeling of What Happens*, 133.

35. Ibid., 26.   36. Ibid., 134.   37. Ibid., 174.

38. Aristotle, "De Anima," in *The Basic Works of Aristotle*, 535–603; see especially 601: "Hence it is that taste also must be a sort of touch, because it is the sense for what is tangible and nutritious." Also: "I call by the name of special object of this or that sense that which cannot be perceived by any other sense than that one and in respect of which no error is possible: in this sense colour is the special object of sight, sound of hearing, flavour of taste. Touch, indeed, discriminates more than one set of different qualities. Each sense has one kind of object which it discerns, and never errs in reporting that what is before it is colour or sound. . . . Such objects are what we propose to call special objects of this or that sense" (567).

39. See Freud's 1909 essay on the Rat Man, "Notes upon a Case of Obsessional Neurosis," in *Standard Edition*, X:247: "the tendency to take pleasure in smell, which has become extinct since childhood, may play a part in the genesis of neurosis." For a discussion of the relation of smell to this case, see Norman Kiell, *Varieties of Sexual Experience*, 158.

40. Aristotle, "De Anima," 572.

41. Ibid., 602–603.

42. Aristotle, "Nicomachean Ethics," in *Basic Works*, 981.

43. Pliny, *Natural History*, Vol. III, Book X, Section LXXXVIII, 415.

44. James, *The Principles of Psychology*, I:326.

45. Elias, *The History of Manners*, I:79. Erasmus is quoted on 55.

46. Stanhope, *Letters of Lord Chesterfield to His Son*, 9.

47. Gibson, "The Mouth as an Organ for Laying Hold on the Environment," in *Symposium on Oral Sensation and Perception*, 135: "In man the mouth remains an organ of sexual-social contact throughout life." There is a "taboo against putting things in the mouth after a certain age, but the mouth retains its tactile capacities."

48. Hardy, *Under the Greenwood Tree*, 65–66.

49. See Bowra, *From Virgil to Milton*, 26: "the later writers of epic (i.e., those of the Reformation and Counter-Reformation) could not and would not laugh at the ideals which they proclaimed. There is no laughter in Tasso, who seems to regard it as particularly pernicious; for when the Knights prepare to rescue Rinaldo from Armida, they are warned against a fountain which makes men laugh." Bowra is thinking of the "Fountain of Laughter" described in Canto XIV, l. 74, and Canto XV, l. 57: "a spring that has waters so pure and inviting that it rouses thirst in those who look upon it: but it conceals within its crystal cold the secret malice of a strange venom, for one little draught of its shining waters straightway intoxicates the soul and makes it giddy; then it moves a man to laughter; and in the end his laughing proceeds so far that he lies dead of it." Tasso, *Jerusalem Delivered*, 317, also 333. The temptress Acrasia, also associated with water, in Book II of *The Faerie Queene* is herself a font of laughter:

> Sometime she laught, that nigh her breth was gone,
> Yet was there not with her else any one,
> That might to her move cause of meriment:
> Matter of merth enough, though there were none,
> She could devise, and thousand waies invent,
> To feede her foolish humour, and vaine jolliment.
> (Spenser, Book II, Canto VI, stanza 3, 94)

See also the discussion of Sir Richard Blackmore's essays against wit—"The Satyr against Wit," "The Nature of Man," and "Essay upon Wit"—in Richard C. Boys, *Sir Richard Blackmore and the Wits*.

50. Shaftesbury, *The Life, Unpublished Letters, and Philosophical Regimen of Anthony, Earl of Shaftesbury*, 228.

51. Ibid., 225.

52. Hogarth, *Analysis of Beauty*, 98–99.

53. Eliot, *Collected Poems, 1909–1962*, 24.

54. Puttenham, *The Arte of English Poesie*, 296–297. Here and elsewhere I have modernized spelling as follows: modern *s* replaces long *s*, and the letters *i*, *j*, *u*, and *v* have been regularized.

55. Feld, *Sound and Sentiment*, 262.

56. Puttenham, *The Arte of English Poesie*, 283.

57. Ibid., 304.

58. See the discussion of smells in poetry in Constance Classen, David Howes, and Anthony Synnott, *Aroma: The Cultural History of Smell*, 74–77. Percy Shelley's "Defense of Poetry" relies on smell as an evaluative metaphor. In writing of the inventors of the pastoral idyll in Alexandria and Sicily, such as Theocritus, Callimachus, and Bion, he says, "their poetry is intensely melodious; like the odour of the tuberose, it overcomes and sickens the spirit with an excess of sweetness; whilst the poetry of the preceding age was a meadow-gale of June which mingles the fragrance of all the flowers of the field, and adds a quickening and harmonizing spirit of its own which endows the sense with a power of sustaining its extreme delight" (in *Shelley's Poetry and Prose*, 492).

59. Spenser, *The Poetical Works of Edmund Spenser*, 573.

60. Donne, *The Complete English Poems*, 103–104.

61. Shakespeare, Sonnets 54 and 69 in *Shakespeare's Sonnets*, 219 and 249, respectively.

62. "Making my mind to smell my fatal day" is clearly the focus as well of many of George Herbert's brief didactic lyrics on the senses in "The Temple." His well-known "Virtue" proceeds from stanza to stanza by means of the refrain of the sense's "closes," the onset of death until the last stanza promises the eternal life of the "sweet and virtuous soul." Herbert, *The English Poems of George Herbert*, 103.

63. Donne, *The Complete English Poems*, 98–100.

64. Ibid., 124–126.

65. Love, *Scribal Publication in Seventeenth-Century England*, 145–147.

66. Ibid., 298.

67. Swift, *The Poems of Jonathan Swift*, II:524–530.

68. Puttenham, *The Arte of English Poesie*, 104–105.

69. Patrides, "Appendix III: Some Secular Poems Parodied by Herbert," in *The English Poems of George Herbert*, 213.

70. Curtius, *European Literature and the Latin Middle Ages*, 284. A helpful survey of the entire issue of the relation between Western and Eastern pattern poems and Puttenham's influences is A. L. Korn, "Puttenham and the Oriental Pattern-Poem." Korn includes a number of photographs of "oriental pattern-poems" in the form of manuscripts and objects.

71. Herbert, *The English Poems of George Herbert*, 47.

72. See Gerald L. Bruns, *Modern Poetry and the Idea of Language*, for the most important exposition of the tension between a Mallarméan poetics and the Orphic tradition I have been emphasizing. For Bruns the two traditions are commensurable, but I would argue that a reified or opaque visual model for language is, like satire's reliance on the lower senses, a reaction against the continuing demands placed on lyric subjectivity. Such visual poetics are useful whenever the lyric tradition exhausts its repertoire. They always involve the prohibitions and supplementations of manifesti, for it is impossible to make language a purely internal system of reference so long as the words being used have a history. And if the poet turns to neologisms, the manifesto must aim to assemble readers and

listeners into an audience for whom such words are intelligible, even at a meta-linguistic level as an indication of their own opacity. Mallarmé's own poetics arise from the exhaustion of lyric resources at the moment of his need for elegiac expression.

73. Quoted in Gage, *In the Arresting Eye*, 14.

74. H[ilda] D[olittle], *Collected Poems 1912–1944*, 25–26.

75. Thomas, *The Collected Poems of Dylan Thomas*, 154–165.

76. Schachtel, *Metamorphosis*, 116.

77. Ibid., 160.

78. Auden, *Collected Shorter Poems, 1927–1957*, 285–288.

79. Marx, "Economic and Philosophic Manuscripts of 1844," 300–302.

80. Ibid., 302.

81. Immanuel Kant, *Critique of Pure Reason*, 33.

82. Coleridge, *Biographia Literaria*, II:33–34.

83. Wordsworth, *Lyrical Ballads and Other Poems, 1797–1800*, 168.

84. Adorno, "On Lyric Poetry and Society," in *Notes to Literature*, I:38.

85. Ibid., 41.

86. Morris, *Writings on the General Theory of Signs*, 116.

87. Adorno, "On Lyric Poetry and Society," 43.

88. Rousseau, *On the Origin of Language*, 1–83. See especially chap. 2, "That the First Invention of Speech Is Due Not to Need but Passion," 12: "Whence then this origin? From moral needs, passions. All the passions tend to bring people back together again, but the necessity of seeking a livelihood forces them apart. It is neither hunger nor thirst but love, hatred, pity, anger, which drew from them the first words . . . the first languages were singable and passionate before they became simple and methodical."

89. Coleridge, *Biographia Literaria*, 50.

90. See the discussion of Anaxagoras and other classical philosophers on pain in Hamlyn, *Sensation and Perception*.

91. Aristotle, "The Poetics," in *Aristotle on the Art of Fiction*, 29: "though a thing itself is disagreeable to look at, we enjoy contemplating the most accurate representations of it—for instance, figures of the most despicable animals, or of human corpses." See also Wordsworth, "Preface to Lyrical Ballads and Appendix" (1850 version) in *Collected Poems*, 296.

92. Coleridge, *Biographia Literaria*, 2:49–50.

93. Jakobson, "Shifters, Verbal Categories, and the Russian Verb," in *Selected Writings* II:131–132. See also Benveniste, "The Nature of Pronouns," in *Problems in General Linguistics*, 217–222. I take up the discussion of shifters and deixis more specifically in chaps. 4 and 5.

94. Agamben, *Language and Death*, 25. Agamben discusses deixis on 19–25.

95. Eliot, *Collected Poems 1909–1962*, 221.

96. Snell, *The Discovery of the Mind in Greek Philosophy and Literature*; see therein "The Rise of the Individual in Early Greek Lyric," 53–54.

97. Ibid., 65.

98. Johnson, *The Idea of Lyric*, 25. See Prins, *Victorian Sappho*, for an account of how Victorian scholarship and literary culture made Sappho into a figure of "exemplary" lyric subjectivity.

99. Sappho, Powell trans., 23–24. Excerpt from *Sappho: A Garland*, by Jim Powell. Copyright © 1993 by Jim Powell. Reprinted by permission of Farrar, Straus and Giroux, LLC.

100. Longinus, *On the Sublime*, Section X.

101. Powell in Sappho, 58.

102. For an argument that Wordsworth most likely borrowed this idea from Schiller's "aus der sanftern und fernenden Erinnerung mag er dichten," see L. A. Willoughby, "Wordsworth and Germany," in *German Studies Presented to H. G. Fiedler*, 444.

103. Boas, "Mythology and Folk-tales of the North American Indian," 400.

104. Swanton, *Tlingit Myths and Texts*, 405–406.

105. Aristotle, "The Poetics," 19.

106. Dauenhauer and Dauenhauer, "Notes on Swanton Numbers 80 and 81." The Dauenhauers see these songs as "highly contextualized in the social structures and genealogies [of the Tlingit]. They report that "many songs use texts from other languages" and think that Among-the-brant's song is "likely to be a mourning song" or elegy (personal correspondence, 2 February 1999).

107. Two important studies of Elizabethan sonnets as eidetic projects are J. B. Leishman, *Themes and Variations in Shakespeare's Sonnets*, which emphasizes particularly the sonnets as poems preserving the friend's image from Time, or a project of "immortalization" (27–91), and Joel Fineman, *Shakespeare's Perjured Eye*, which sees the sonnets as developing the tension between a traditional idealizing Petrarchan language of vision and the voice Shakespeare assumes in praising particular subjects at a moment when such a language is already exhausted. Fineman's study, with its very careful analysis of the particulars of Shakespeare's rhetoric and its interest in the aesthetic dimensions of ambiguity, is a useful book to read against contemporary work on "disfiguration" in Romanticism. In his 1984 work, *The Rhetoric of Romanticism*, Paul de Man sees *prosopopoeia*, or the giving of a face or voice, as both a central function of Romantic texts and a key to symbolization in general. But de Man's project was also to point to the ways in which the linguistic basis of this form of anthropomorphization is always a kind of *defacement*, inadequate to its object (see especially "Autobiography as Defacement," 67–81, and Cynthia Chase's extensive discussion of this aspect of de Man's writing in her *Decomposing Figures: Rhetorical Readings in the Romantic Tradition*, 13–30 and 82–112). I would argue that this approach constantly reinscribes the very allegory it seeks to discover. The mutability of facial expression, the incommensurability between the Romantic poet's apostrophe to nature and nature's response, are not "problems" or "indeterminancies" limiting Romantic texts but are rather the very basis of their emergence to expression. There is an insistence in this school of deconstructive criticism on a static representation of the person. Anything less than reification seems like disfigurement, but disfigurement can also be considered as alteration, difficulty, complexity. My argument

follows those aspects of the thought of Vico, Hegel, Marx, and Levinas that emphasize the human image as a consequence of representational practices rather than a prior referent. Only in this way can human subjectivity be viewed in historical terms. There is a strange form of petrification in the deconstructionist reading of the Romantic figure, most evident when such readings focus on images of the (often female) corpse. For a useful critique of Romantic strategies of affirming subjectivity, see John Koethe, *Poetry at One Remove*, 89–107. The "Epilogue" to Charles Altieri's *Self and Sensibility in Contemporary American Poetry* is an important summary of Altieri's program for a first-person lyric self-consciousness that might both transcend irony and establish cultural values: "strong poets provide, at least implicitly, structures and valuations." He cites Wallace Stevens's model that "the measure of poets is a capacity to involve the lives of other people in their work" (200).

108. Pound, *Personae: Collected Shorter Poems of Ezra Pound:* "On His Own Face in a Glass," 49; "Coda," 113. It is intriguing that each poem is followed by a poem on seeing itself: "On His Own Face" is followed by "The Eyes," and "Coda" by "The Seeing Eye."

109. Pound's rather antiquarian use of *ye* might be considered in light of Shelley's preference for the antiquated second-person singular familiar form, "Spirit of Beauty, that dost consecrate," in "Hymn to Intellectual Beauty." Donald H. Reiman and Sharon B. Powers write in a note to this line, "[S]ee parallel usages in the Collects of the *Book of Common Prayer . . .* and in Milton's sonnets, many of which are modeled on the Collects of the prayer book" (*Shelley's Poetry and Prose*, 93, n. 2).

110. See Peter Marler and Christopher Evans, "Animal Sounds and Human Faces: Do They Have Anything in Common?" in *The Psychology of Facial Expression.*

111. See Nicole Chovil, "Facing Others: A Social Communicative Perspective on Facial Display," in *The Psychology of Facial Expression*, 99–120; and Ray L. Birdwhistell, *Kinesics and Context: Essays on Body Motion Communication*, 163–168. Birdwhistell pioneered the study of the relation of human facial displays to language use in the 1960s.

112. Collingwood, *The Principles of Art*, 152 and 112–113.

113. Lucas, *The Greek Tragic Poets*, 26.

114. Mauss, *Sociology and Psychology*, 68–69.

115. Boas, *The Social Organization and the Secret Societies of the Kwakiutl Indians.*

CHAPTER TWO

1. Herder, "Essay on the Origin of Language," 126.

2. Mauss, *Sociology and Psychology*, 78.

3. Ibid., 90.

4. Ovid, *The Metamorphoses of Ovid.* For the story of Io, see 44–48; for Phaethon's sisters, 59–60; for Ocyrhoe, 67–68; and for Actaeon, 77–80. In his *Les Cinq Sens*, Michel Serres makes the important point that our usual assumption is

that noise always precedes language, and therefore the opposite of these myths: "Avant d'avoir du sens, le langage fait du bruit: celui-ci peut se passer de celui-là, mais non l'inverse" (127).

5. Dennett, "Conditions of Personhood," 177–178.

6. Freud, *Beyond the Pleasure Principle*, 10.

7. See the discussion of the invocatory drive in Lacan's *The Four Fundamental Concepts of Psycho-Analysis*, 118 and 180. Didier-Weill's *Invocations: Dionysos, Moïse, Saint Paul et Freud* argues that the invocatory drive in Lacan's sense is at the root of all music and dance forms.

8. Grossman, *Summa Lyrica*, 362.

9. Kristeva, "Revolution in Poetic Language," 94.

10. Grossman, *Summa Lyrica*, 373.

11. Bolton, *The Counting Out Rhymes of Children*, 100.

12. Peele, *George Peele*, 93–94.

13. Lacan, *The Four Fundamental Concepts of Psycho-Analysis*, 200.

14. Hölderlin, *Essays and Letters on Theory*, 102 and 109. See also n. 52, below, for Hopkins's writing on caesuras. Hopkins emphasized that when caesuras are an expected part of the rhythmic pattern, they contribute to a sense of the poem's organic wholeness.

15. It is suggestive that two contemporary poems that bear an elegiac relation to the AIDS crisis employ caesuras and enjambment in complex ways. John Ashbery's "Finnish Rhapsody," part of his *April Galleons*, uses the middle caesura and restatement technique of the Finnish epic the *Kalevala* to show a voice hesitating and reconsidering itself, as in these lines:

> As moments, then years; minutes, afterwards ages
> Suck up the common strength, absorb the everyday power
> And afterwards live on, satisfied; persist, later to be a source of
> gratification,
> But perhaps only to oneself, haply to one's sole identity. (16)

In contrast, Bob Perelman's elegy, "Chronic Meanings [for Lee Hickman]" in *Ten to One*, 166–169, uses a form of aposiopesis, or what might be called an end-line caesura—the end stops are made absolute by periods, but the syntax is simply broken off, refusing enjambment and refusing semantic closure at once, like the abraded walls of a ruin:

> The coffee sounds intriguing but.
> She put her cards on.
> What had been comfortable subjectivity.
> The lesson we can each. (166)

15. Milton, from *Paradise Lost*, Book III, in *John Milton*, 403, ll. 40–48.

16. Hegel, *The Philosophy of Fine Art*, 333–334.

17. Henri Meschonnic argues for differences of degree, rather than genres or kinds, between prose and verse forms. He considers rhythm to be a significant organizing feature of many kinds of prose discourse and envisions a continuum of more or less stringent rhythmic organization in all verbal forms. See *Critique du rythme*.

18. The most important study of closure in lyric remains Barbara Herrnstein Smith, *Poetic Closure.*

19. See James William Johnson, "Lyric," in *Princeton Encyclopedia of Poetry and Poetics*, 460.

20. Francis Berry, in *Poetry and the Physical Voice*, argues against Susanne K. Langer's contention in *Feeling and Form*, 277–279, that "the treatment of poetry as physical sound comparable to music" rests on an "utter misconception" and that "'the voice of a speaker tends to intrude on the created world'" (7). But Berry writes an entire book on "poetic voice" that largely considers voice in metaphorical terms, making arguments about duration, for example, that are unsustainable with regard to written text. We cannot credibly say that "it takes less time to say Marvell's 'Had we but World enough, and Time . . .' than to say Crashaw's 'Love, thou art Absolute sole Lord'" (9; the example is borrowed by Berry from Eliot's essay on the metaphysicals), for we have world enough and time to read or remember the phrases at any speed we like. Berry's suggestion in conclusion that "the best we can hope for, when the poem is said aloud, is a voice which approaches [in this instance, Thomas] Gray's as nearly as possible," when we have no access to the voice of Gray and it is not clear what it would mean to have such access in the first place, dissolves the reception of poetry into an absurd exercise in mimicry.

21. For a distinction between structural and performative accounts of prosody, see John Hollander, "The Music of Poetry," 232–244.

22. Derek Attridge's *Poetic Rhythm*, 2, does not consider this possibility. Instead, Attridge believes that readers of poems are always more or less "sounding out" a poem, even when reading silently: "it is still possible to shape the words in silence and to feel the rhythm coursing through the lines as we do so. (We manage this by means of minute muscular movements that are enough to suggest the larger movements that take place in actual speech.)"

23. Rimbaud, *Rimbaud*, 120–122.

24. Tsur, *What Makes Sound Patterns Expressive*, 111–135.

25. García Lorca, *The Selected Poems of Federico García Lorca*, 64.

26. Alberti, "Rojo," 173.

27. See [Gino Bonichi] Scipione, *La Terra è secca, ha sete*, trans. Brunella Antomarini and Susan Stewart:

> I hear the shrieks of the seraphim
> clamoring for my salvation
> but the saliva is sweet
> and the blood rushes in to sin
>
> the air is still
> everything is as rosy as the flesh
> if it flows through, then it is a blessing
> it's necessary to break and fall
>
> The sun pierces my chest
> as if it were a basket
>   and I feel emptied

the hand breaks loose from the earth
and touches the air, the light, the flesh
. . . .
. . . .
the spear plunges deep into the bowels
of the mare who runs—and hurls
her head against the sky. (26)

28. Kant, "Analytic of the Sublime," in *The Critique of Judgment,* 196–198.

29. Hegel, *The Philosophy of Fine Art,* I:120.

30. Masson points out that the commonest rhyme vowel in English was and is *a/ai* and that Pope "seems especially addicted to it," using it for 25 percent of the perfect rhymes in *Windsor Forest* (788).

31. Ball, *Flight Out of Time: A Dada Diary,* 70–71. This passage is also discussed in Richard Huelsenbeck, *Memoirs of a Dada Drummer,* 60–61, although the translations differ in several minor respects. (I have provided the Raimes version here.) Huelsenbeck himself critiques the sound poem by saying "the dissection of words into sounds is contrary to the purpose of language and applies musical principles to an independent realm whose symbolism is aimed at a logical comprehension of one's environment. . . . Language, more than any other form of art, hinges on a comprehension of life- and reality-contents . . . the value of language depends on comprehensibility rather than musicality" (62). The transcription of this poem in various texts is inexact, for as Ball describes his "performance" (he wore a special costume of a huge coat collar that permitted winglike movements of his arms and a high blue and white striped "witch doctor's hat"), he "began" with these syllables but then proceeded between separate "texts" on three music stands, with "Labadas Gesang an die Wolken" [Labada's Song to the Clouds] on the right and the "Elefantenkarawane" [Elephant Caravan] on the left, and then improvised a kind of liturgical singing for his conclusion. Hans Richter, in *Dada: Art and Anti-Art,* transcribes the opening sound poem as

gadjiberi bimba glandridi laula lonni cadori
gadjaina gramma berida bimbala glandri galassassa laulitalomini
gadji beri bin glassa glassala laula lonni cadorsi sassala bim
Gadjama tuffm i zimzalla binban gligia wowolimai bin beri ban. (42)

32. There are, however, concrete variations in sound production that can be seen along a spectrum of differences from individual utterance to particular languages at particular historical moments. James Deese, in *Psycholinguistics,* writes of vowels:

Vowels are . . . difficult to characterize in terms of their physical characteristics . . . vowels are traditionally identified by their formants. Formants are narrow bands of frequencies, narrow enough to sound something like musical sounds. They are produced by the shape of the mouth/throat cavity. That cavity provides a resonating chamber for the output of the vocal cords . . . as we change the shape of the mouth we change the frequency of the harmonics that resonate to the output of vocal cords. In general, vowels for particular speakers can be identified with particular formant frequencies. But among different speakers—children, women, as well as different men—it is impossible to characterize any given vowel by the formants that compose it, or by any relation among these formants. (10)

33. Ibid., 117.

34. Skelton, *The Complete Poems of John Skelton*, 260.

35. Raymond Chapman, *Linguistics and Literature*, 86. For a concrete example of how the bias against emphasizing structural words affects English metrics, note the argument George Saintsbury makes for a trochaic reading of Browning's epilogue to *Asolando:* "At the midnight, in the silent of the sleep-time": "Perhaps those who propose this [an English Ionic reading] have been a little bribed by conscious or unconscious desire to prevent 'accenting' *in* and *of;* but no more need be said on this point. The trochees, or their sufficient equivalents, will run very well without any violent INN or OVV." In Saintsbury, *Historical Manual of English Prosody*, 285, n. 1. Saintsbury's book remains invaluable for its historical perspective on issues of meter.

36. Grossman, *Summa Lyrica*, 373.

37. See de Saussure in *Course in General Linguistics:* "Spelling always lags behind pronunciation. The *l* in French is today changing to *y;* speakers say *éveyer, mouyer* just as they say *essuyer* 'wipe,' *nettoyer*, 'clean'; but the written forms of these words are still *éveiller* 'awaken,' *mouiller*, 'soak.' Another reason for discrepancy between spelling and pronunciation is this: if an alphabet is borrowed from another language, its resources may not be appropriate for their new function; expedients will have to be found (e.g. the use of two letters to designate a single sound). . . . During the Middle Ages English had a closed *e* (e.g. *sed*) and an open *e* (e.g. *led*); since the alphabet failed to provide distinct symbols for the two sounds, the spellings *seed* and *lead* were devised" (28). Following de Saussure's argument we can conclude that written versions of lyric will often inscribe an earlier pronunciation than that in operation at the moment of the lyric's production.

38. Fussell, *Theory of Prosody in Eighteenth-Century England*, 156.

39. Zuckerkandl, *Sound and Symbol*, 157–158.

40. Ibid., 158–159.   41. Ibid., 181.   42. Ibid., 169–170.

43. Masson, "Sound," in *Princeton Encyclopedia of Poetry and Poetics*, 785–786.

44. See Riding and Graves, *A Survey of Modernist Poetry*, 37. Another problem with their example is that they have not employed the stress patterns of the grammar in the same fashion as Tennyson did. All the sound pattern words in the Tennyson lines (moan-doves-immemorial elms / murmuring-innumerable bees) are stressed form words, with the connectives remaining unstressed. Riding and Graves make some of the sound pattern words stressed and others unstressed and disperse the sound pattern over connective and form words.

45. Roger D. Abrahams and George Foss, *Anglo-American Folksong Style*, 167.

46. Hardy, *The Collected Poems of Thomas Hardy*, 465–466.

47. For a thoughtful and extensive discussion of this poem and the temporality of refrains in general, see John Hollander, "Breaking into Song: Some Notes on

Refrain," 73–89; see especially Hollander's discussion of Hardy's revisions of his original refrain text, 86–87.

48. See Abrahams and Foss, *Anglo-American Folksong Style:* "Burdens do not always contribute to the meaning of a song; they often simply function as an additional incantatory device This is especially evident in the songs which use flower and herb burdens like 'Savory sage, rosemary and thyme' and ones in which the repeated lines are nonsensical, introduced mainly for the sound patterns which they establish. . . . Burdens . . . consequently often crop up in places in which their effect is nullified by a nonsequitur feeling or by one of lack of appropriateness. 'Twa Sisters'—a horrifying story—has the usual burden in North America of 'Bow and balance to me'" (66).

49. When songs move from oral to written form, changes also ensue. Consider the case of "The Gypsy Laddie" (Child Ballad 200). In version C the Scottish word *glaumerie* or deception of sight by means of a charm is still extant:

> She came tripping down the stair,
> And all her maids before her;
> As soon as they saw her weel-faurd face
> They coost their glamourye owre her.

In version G, the language becomes:

> The Earl of Castle's lady came down,
> With the waiting-maid beside her;
> As soon as her fair face they saw,
> They called their grandmother over.

See discussion and further examples in W. Edson Richmond, "Some Effects of Scribal and Typographical Error on Oral Tradition," 225–235.

50. Wimsatt, *The Verbal Icon*, 153.

51. Lowell, "The Muses Won't Help Twice," 319. See also Pound, *The ABC of Reading.*

52. Thompson, *The Founding of English Meter*, 35, n. 1. Hopkins's writings on meter provide the following catalog of ways in which "monotony in rhythm is prevented":

> (i) by the mere change of the words, like fresh water flowing through a fountain or over a waterfall, each gallon taking on the same shape as those before it—
> (ii) by caesura, the breaking of the feet, or in other words the breaking up of the rhythm into sense-words of different lengths from the sound-words. When the caesura is fixed by rule we have rhythmic counterpoint. By counterpoint I mean the carrying on of two figures at once, especially if they are alike in kind but very unlike or opposite in species.
> (iii) by the tonic accent of the words, esp. in French
> (iv) by the emphatic accent of the words
> (v) smoothness or break of vowel sound
> (vi) all intermittent elements of verse, as alliteration, rhyme. It should be understood that these various means of breaking the sameness of rhythm and especially caesura do not break the unity of the

verse but the contrary; they make it organic and what is organic is one.

From "Lecture Notes: Rhythm and the Other Structural Parts of Rhetoric— Verse," 280. Hopkins also mentions issues of singing without words, whistling, or humming, which he explains is in Greek, τερετίζειν *(teretizein)* "to go la la or ta ra" (223).

53. If in the West reason is associated with the logic of prose and emotion with poetry, we remember that in Kaluli culture men have the most irrational weeping style, yet at the same time they hold rights to song performance, more valued than weeping performance. Steven Feld, *Sound and Sentiment*, 88.

54. Lacan, *The Four Fundamental Concepts of Psycho-Analysis*, 180 and 200.

55. Stevens, *Collected Poems*, 20. The poem was published by Faber and Faber Ltd., and is reproduced from *The Collected Poems of Wallace Stevens*, by Wallace Stevens, copyright 1954 by Wallace Stevens. Used by permission of Alfred A. Knopf, a division of Random House, Inc.

56. Ibid., "Peter Quince at the Clavier," 89–92; "To the Roaring Wind," 113; "Earthy Anecdote," 3.

57. Ibid., "A High-Toned Old Christian Woman," 59.

58. In *Sacred Art of East and West*, Titus Burckhart writes of plowing, "The art of ploughing is often considered as having a divine origin. Physically the act of ploughing the ground has the effect of opening it to the air, thus promoting the fermentation that is indispensable for the assimilation of the soil by vegetation. Symbolically the soil is opened up to the influences of Heaven, and the plough is the active agent or generative organ" (74, n. 14).

59. Coleridge, *The Table Talk*, 253.

60. Burke, "On Musicality in Verse," in *The Philosophy of Literary Form*, 369–378; and Tsur, *What Makes Sound Patterns Expressive*.

61. See table 7.1, in the discussion of "Primitive Stages in Language Development," in Eric H. Lenneberg, *Biological Foundations of Language*, 280.

62. Stevens, "Certain Phenomena of Sound," in *Collected Poems*, 286–287.

63. Ibid., "The Creations of Sound," 310–311.

64. Boas, "Mythology and Folk-tales," 399–400. See also Edward Sapir, "Song Recitative in Paiute Mythology," 456–457.

65. Anyone who has read *Dombey and Sons*, for example, knows that the following sentences—"Your Toxes and your Chickses may draw out my two front double teeth, Mrs. Richards, but that's no reason why I need off 'em the whole set" (a hypothetical clause followed by a qualifying negation) and "I'm very well indeed. Very well indeed, I am. I don't remember that I was ever better, thank you" (a constant renegotiation of the onset of the utterance)—could only be spoken by Susan Nipper and Mr. Toots, respectively.

66. Hopkins, *The Journals and Papers of Gerard Manley Hopkins*, 267.

67. Ibid., 268–269.   68. Ibid., 289.

69. Ibid., 130.   70. Ibid., 204–205.

71. See the discussion of these terms in Catherine Phillips's introduction to Hopkins, *Gerard Manley Hopkins*, xx.

72. J. Hillis Miller pays particular attention to the themes of likeness and un-likeness linking the philosophy of Parmenides, the theology of Duns Scotus, and Hopkins's rhyming practices. He suggests that as a Platonist or realist Hopkins "proposes the existence of inalterable types at definite intervals, intervals which have a mathematical relation providing for a grand system of harmony" ("The Univocal Chiming," 91).

73. Hopkins, *The Journals and Papers of Gerard Manley Hopkins*, 211.

74. Ibid., 267.   75. Ibid., "Early Diaries," 1–11.

76. Ibid., 283–284.   77. Ibid., 270.

78. Hopkins, *The Letters of Gerard Manley Hopkins to Robert Bridges*, 203.

79. Ibid., 212.

80. Hopkins, *The Journals and Papers of Gerard Manley Hopkins*, 269–270.

81. Hopkins, "Spelt from Sibyl's Leaves," in *Gerard Manley Hopkins*, 175. (This volume was prepared directly from Hopkins's manuscripts, so I have used its accentuation for all poems reproduced here.)

82. As a priest, Hopkins was under particular strictures in this regard. As he wrote to Robert Bridges in 1884, "all that we Jesuits publish (even anonymously) must be seen by censors and this is a barrier which I do not know how anything of mine on a large scale would ever pass" (12 November postscript to 11 November letter in *The Letters of Gerard Manley Hopkins to Robert Bridges*, 200). In 1876, he had gone through a difficult time as *The Wreck of the Deutschland* was first accepted, and then rejected, by his friend Henry Coleridge, the editor of the Jesuit journal *The Month*. Coleridge had asked Hopkins to take out the accents and Hopkins complied, but the poem never appeared (Norman White, *Hopkins*, 258–259). Bridges became the archivist of his work; Hopkins sent his work to Bridges frequently, and Bridges's careful attention to the manuscripts and tran-scripts of them enabled editions of Hopkins's work to appear posthumously. In a letter on 1 September 1885 (*The Letters of Gerard Manley Hopkins to Robert Bridges*, 221), Hopkins wrote, "I shall shortly have some sonnets to send you, five or more. Four [written above 'Three,' canceled] of these came like inspirations un-bidden and against my will," but he never actually sent the poems to Bridges or any other correspondent. See also Paul Mariani, *A Commentary on the Complete Poems of Gerard Manley Hopkins*, 210. Mariani suggests, following Jean-Georges Ritz, a logical order to the poems following "the classical descent and ascent of the Ignatian exercises": "To seem the stranger," "I wake and feel the fell of dark," "No worst there is none," "Carrion Comfort," "Patience, hard thing."

83. Hopkins, *The Journals and Papers of Gerard Manley Hopkins*, 236. Nor-man White's biography cites Hopkins's contemporaries as countering his picture of himself as overworked. Hopkins described the terrible headaches he suffered during this time as "accompanied by the visual images of blocks which had to be fitted together," apparently an allegory of his struggle with poetry (386).

84. Here Hopkins is continuing a long preoccupation of Jesuit theology with sound, from the open-plan churches designed to make the preaching voice avail-able all at once to a vast crowd to the work of his predecessor, the seventeenth-century Jesuit Athanasius Kirchner. Kirchner invented a number of speaking and hearing devices and wrote aphoristic poems, including this Latin echo verse,

which cleverly and economically sets forth the terms of Jesuit "clamor" and response: "Tibi vero gratias agam quo clamore? Amore more ore re." For a recent overview of the Jesuit interest in an architecture of sound, see the discussion in R. Po-Chia Hsia, *The World of Catholic Renewal*: "New liturgical and sacramental needs required churches to have innovative features: a more spacious, hall-like and uninterrupted nave to accommodate larger crowds to hear sermons; flat or wooden roofs for better acoustics . . . the Baroque church, exemplified by the Gesu, focussed space and light in a central realm where sermons were preached, mass celebrated and communion dispensed" (161).

85. White, *Hopkins*, 179–180.

86. "Meditation on Hell," in *Gerard Manley Hopkins*, 292–295. See also Daniel A. Harris's discussion of the role of the senses in the 1885 sonnets in *Inspirations Unbidden*. Harris links the sonnets to a crisis in Hopkins's theology regarding the Incarnation and provides an astute reading of the role of the senses in many of the poems.

87. Hopkins, "I wake and feel," in *Gerard Manley Hopkins*, 166.

88. Hopkins, *Sermons and Devotional Writings*, 175. Discussed as well in Daniel A. Harris, *Inspirations Unbidden*, 62.

89. Hopkins, *Sermons and Devotional Writings*, 137.

90. See Tsur's discussion of Jakobson and Waugh, who are themselves responding to an argument about synaesthesia made by E. H. Gombrich, on this parallel between the back–front continuum in vowel production in relation to the dark–light continuum in visual perception (*What Makes Sound Patterns Expressive*, 20).

91. Hopkins, *The Letters of Gerard Manley Hopkins to Robert Bridges*, 219.

92. Hopkins, "No worst," in *Gerard Manley Hopkins*, 167.

93. See Tsur, *What Makes Sound Patterns Expressive*, 32 and 46.

94. Hopkins, "Carrion Comfort," in *Gerard Manley Hopkins*, 168.

95. From Hopkins's sermons, in *Gerard Manley Hopkins*, 282; see also 283–287 for a discussion of "pitch" and free will.

96. Geoffrey Hartman describes the "vocative" aspect of Hopkins's style: "This holds for sound, grammar, figures of speech, and actual performance. Tell and toll become cognates. . . . We find cries within cries as in: 'Not / I'll not / carrion comfort, / Despair / not feast on thee.'" He adds "[language's] end as its origin is to move, persuade, possess. Hopkins leads us back to an aural situation (or its simulacrum) where meaning and invocation coincide. Everything depends on the right 'pitch,' or verbal cast" (*Hopkins*, 6–8). Although Hartman uses one of the 1885 sonnets as an example of this point, it is the facility for the vocative in the majority of Hopkins's work that makes the breakdown of the vocative in these late sonnets so tragic and immediate. See "Introduction: Poetry and Justification," 1–15. See also Hartman's reading of "The Windover," in "The Dialectic of Sense-Perception," in the same volume, 117–130.

97. See Tsur, *What Makes Sound Patterns Expressive*, 109.

98. See R. Murray Schafer, "Acoustic Space"; and G. N. A. Vesey, "Sound," 500–501. "Sound, to our ears, is diffuse, like smell, or relatively massive, imping-

ing without any precise spatial articulation. Such detail as it may convey is temporal. The crash of dishes sliding off an unbalanced tray, or the rustling of a mouse fleeing through dry leaves, has certainly more audible structure than an explosion, but it is the progress of an event through time that it conveys, not spatial form" (Susanne K. Langer, *Mind*, 134).

99. Herder, "Essay on the Origin of Language," 141.

100. Ibid., 143–147.

101. Tsur, *What Makes Sound Patterns Expressive*, 101–102.

102. See Max Picard, *The World of Silence*, 17–44.

103. Herder, "Essay on the Origin of Language," 87.

104. Homer, *The Iliad*, Book II, ll. 819–826, 122.

105. Austin, *How to Do Things with Words*, 157.

Chapter Three

1. I have been greatly informed by Roland Barthes's two essays, "Listening" (245–260) and "The Grain of the Voice" (267–277). Barthes, however, contends that the voice "bears an image of the body" (255).

2. Proust, *In Search of Lost Time*, III:176.

3. Ibid., 175.

4. See Maurice Merleau-Ponty's working notes on this issue in *The Visible and the Invisible*, 254.

5. Freud, *Civilization and Its Discontents*, 50 *passim*.

6. Hegel, *Philosophy of Fine Art*, 170.

7. Murray, *A History of Ancient Greek Literature*, 79.

8. Marjorie Perloff: "the poetry establishment (especially the official verse-culture of the university writing programs) still posits a situation in which the aspiring poet can—indeed must—discover his or her own unique *voice*, a voice that somehow differs from all others. But in what exactly does this uniqueness consist, given the ongoing commodification of language in our culture? How much more 'sensitive-than-thou' can the individual artist be?" (*Wittgenstein's Ladder*, 187).

9. Plato, *Symposium*, 331–332.

10. Ibid., 335–343.

11. Ibid., 339–340.

12. Ibid., 342.

13. Plato, "Phaedrus," 402.

14. Passage numbers come from *Plato's Republic*, trans. and ed. G. M. A. Grube.

15. Plato, "Ion," 289–290.

16. Plato, "Theaetetus," 201–202.

17. Schiller, "Twelfth Letter," in *On the Aesthetic Education of Man in a Series of Letters*, 65 and note cited on 65.

18. Plato, *Symposium*, 332.

19. See the useful discussion of Plato's rhetoric regarding poetry and philosophy in Judovitz, "Philosophy and Poetry: The Difference between them in Plato and Descartes."

20. Beardsley and Wimsatt, "The Intentional Fallacy," in Wimsatt, *The Verbal Icon*, 3–18.

21. Ibid., 6.

22. Abraham, "Notes on the Phantom," 291–292. See also Abraham and Torok, *The Wolf Man's Magic Word:* of particular relevance for this study is Nicholas Rand's discussion of the issue of "readability" in his "Translator's Introduction," li–lxix, and the fuller context of Abraham and Torok's thought now available in Rand's translation of many of their essays in *The Shell and the Kernel.* Avital Ronell, in her work *Dictations: On Haunted Writing,* uses the metaphor of ventriloquism to describe Goethe's "haunting" of Johann Peter Eckermann, Sigmund Freud, and others. For a general discussion of the continuance of features of orality and "corporeal" aspects of cognition in written poetry, see Brunella Antomarini, "Il Fenomeno poetico," 24–26.

23. Abraham, "Notes on the Phantom," 289–290.

24. See Damasio, "Aphasia," 535.

25. It will be useful here to bear in mind that "somatic" in psychoanalytic usage is not coterminous with "the body." Abraham writes:

> The *somatic* must be something quite different from the body proper, which derives from the psychic as one of its functions, the psychic having been described by Freud as an exterior layer, an envelope. The *somatic* is what I cannot touch directly, either as my integument and its internal prolongations or as my psyche, the latter given to the consciousness of self; the somatic is that of which I would know nothing if its representative, my fantasy, were not there to send me back to it, its source as it were and ultimate justifications. The *Somatic* must therefore reign in a radical nonpresence *behind* the Envelope where all phenomena accessible to us unfold. It is the Somatic which dispatches its messengers to the Envelope, exciting it from the very place the latter conceals. (*The Shell and the Kernel*, 87)

26. Abraham, *Rythmes.* Amittai Aviram's *Telling Rhythm: Body and Meaning in Poetry* includes a helpful and critical introduction to Abraham's work on rhythm, discussing its emphasis on the alternations of desire and satisfaction stemming from infantile experience in nursing (153–169).

27. Abraham, "Notes on the Phantom," 290.

28. This kind of "survival" is best described as a form of archaism. See Owen Barfield, "Archaism," in *Poetic Diction*, 152–167. In her comparative quantitative studies of the vocabulary of poetry from the 1540s to the 1940s by century, Josephine Miles discovered considerable continuity across the entire period, with "ten major verbs" and "eight major nouns" carried forward. She concludes "the great change in the five centuries [of verbs] is the loss of *find, tell, think* and the gain of *hear, fall, lie* from the eighteenth and nineteenth centuries. The verbs have become more passive and receptive" (*Continuity of Poetic Language*, 497).

29. Annie Finch's *The Ghost of Meter* is a useful introduction to some of these issues, paying particular attention to the relationship between free verse and iambic pentameter. However, her notion of meter as a kind of "code" (see 3–30) seems to be at once too narrow, for the associations of meter are not in a

one-on-one relation as are the terms of a code, and too broad, for she writes that "the word *code* implies that meter in a metrically organic poem can function like a language, carrying different information at different points within a poem" (12). Languages cannot be mere codes that work by means of one-on-one relations between signs and referents. Meter could function like a language in the traditional structural sense that it could have both a metaphorical dimension (it could point, e.g., to other works in the same meter) and a metonymic dimension (it could be contiguous with other forms of meter). Here we would be saying something like what Lacan says when he says that the unconscious is structured like a language, but that is not the direction Finch pursues.

30. I am indebted to John Szwed for this broad use of the term *creolization,* stemming from his seminar on the creolization of cultural forms at the University of Pennsylvania, Department of Folklore and Folklife Studies, in 1977.

31. Rabaté, *The Ghosts of Modernity,* 115.

32. Thompson, *The Founding of English Meter,* 37 and 47–48.

33. See *Encyclopedia of Poetry and Poetics,* 498.

34. Thompson, 2 and 16.

35. Dickinson, "Safe in Their Alabaster Chambers," in *The Poems of Emily Dickinson,* I:151. All quotations from this collection are reprinted by permission of the publishers and the Trustees of Amherst College from *The Poems of Emily Dickinson,* ed. Thomas H. Johnson, Cambridge, Mass., The Belknap Press of Harvard University Press, copyright © 1951, 1955, 1979 by the President and Fellows of Harvard College.

36. These formal features of the ballad are described in Roger D. Abrahams and George Foss, *Anglo-American Folksong Style.*

37. In *The Ballad as Song,* Bertrand Bronson argues on the basis of internal evidence that "Edward," as it has been passed down from Thomas Percy's version, has probably been amended by literary, rather than folk, culture. See "'Edward, Edward': A Scottish Ballad and a Footnote" (1–17).

38. Reprinted in MacEdward Leach, *The Ballad Book,* 86–87.

39. See ibid., 111–113.

40. Keats, "La Belle Dame sans Merci," in *The Letters of John Keats,* I:73.

41. See Robert Gittings, *John Keats,* 150, 160.

42. Keats, *The Letters of John Keats,* II:356–357.

43. See discussions of the poem's sources in Gittings, *John Keats,* 298–304; Walter Jackson Bate, *John Keats,* 278–281; Jack Stillinger, *The Texts of Keats's Poems,* 232–234 (Stillinger notes that Brown and Woodhouse both added "A Ballad" under the main title of the poem, but Keats's draft in the journal letter does not have this subtitle); Walter H. Evert, *Aesthetic and Myth in the Poetry of Keats,* 249–255; and Marjorie Levinson, *Keats's Life of Allegory,* 45–95.

44. Levinson writes, "Most of the narrative content [of 'La Belle Dame sans Merci']—I refer to forms, not functions—derives from two slightly earlier works [than Chartier's], the Scottish True Thomas and Thomas Rymer ballads which Keats had read 'Englished,' or in translation in Jamieson's and Scott's editions" (*Keats's Life of Allegory,* 53). Levinson does not provide evidence for Keats's read-

ings but lists the contemporary editions—Jamieson's of 1806 and Scott's of 1812. Neither of these books were named in the list of Keats's books made by Charles Brown at the time of the poet's death. See Hyder Edward Rollins, *The Keats Circle*, I:253–261. Yet, as Phyllis Mann wrote in a 1962 essay on "Keats's Reading," "[N]or can Charles Brown's published list of books in Keats's possession or on loan at his death be taken as anything but a small section of his reading" (38–47). Earl Wasserman suggests that the Jamieson text, and perhaps Scott's, were important influences but also provides no direct evidence of Keats's reading:

> Whatever the specific source may have been, the narrative clearly belongs to a folk legend best known in the form of the mediaeval ballad, "Thomas Rymer." In the version available to Keats in Robert Jamieson's *Popular Ballads* 1806 (the variant in Scott's *Minstrelsy* differs in a few important details), Thomas encounters a beautiful lady whom he thinks to be the Queen of Heaven, but who identifies herself as "the queen of fair Elfland." She takes him upon her milk-white steed, for he must serve her for seven years; and for forty days and nights they ride through blood while Thomas sees neither sun nor moon. Forbidden to touch the fruit of this strange country lest he suffer the plagues of hell, Thomas eats the loaf and drinks the claret that the elf-queen has brought. At length they rest before a hill, and the elf-queen, placing his head on her knee, shows him three wonders—the roads to wickedness, to righteousness, and to fair Elfland. It is the last of these that they are to follow, and for seven years "True Thomas on earth was never seen." (*The Finer Tone*, 68–69)

Wasserman thereby provides a useful account of the traditional ballad of True Thomas/Thomas Rymer, but, like Levinson, he does not consider the variations to be found between the traditional ballad and the metrical romances provided by Jamieson and Scott. Aileen Ward's *John Keats: The Making of a Poet* does not mention the ballad as a source of "La Belle Dame," but it does see the poem as having "sprang from" the Wells–Amena correspondence (272). Both Elizabeth McLaughlin ("'The Mermaid of Galloway' and 'La Belle Dame sans Merci'") and Bernice Slote ("The Climate of Keats's 'La Belle Dame sans Merci,'" 195–207), cite Keats's interest in ballads recorded in his letters from his walking tour in the summer of 1818, from his knowledge of Hazlitt's 1818 lecture on Robert Burns, Thomas Chatterton, and ballads and other more general cultural influences. Their essays emphasize thematic connections between "La Belle Dame" and a ballad recorded in R. H. Cromek's 1810 volume *Remains of Nithsdale and Galloway Song*, "The Mermaid of Galloway." It is likely that Keats knew of this volume, for in a letter of 10–14 July 1818 to Tom, he wrote some lines he referred to as a generic "Galloway song." The poem tells the story of Keats's encounter with a wedding party near Ballantrae; he refers to the bridegroom as "Young Tam" who has a "reddened cheek," is "daffed like a chick—He could na speak." "The Mermaid," on the basis of textual evidence alone, obviously has been either created or doctored by Allan Cunningham. Cunningham told his biographer David Hogg that he contributed all but "two little scraps" to the prose and poetry in Cromek's volume. (See the comments on the flyleaf of Maurice Buxton Forman's copy of Cromek, now in the collection at Keats House in Hampstead. My thanks to the curator Christina M. Gee for her help with this issue.) And Keats is using his poem to evoke the picturesque qualities of the landscape, speech, and characters he has discovered on his journey; to work in a blatantly, even comically, imitative style—for he makes each of his "fourteener" lines here one syllable short at thirteen; and to both tease his brother and at the same time express some of his own anxieties about marriage. Neither work could be mistaken for a traditional ballad or metrical romance, but "La Belle Dame"'s *structure* is quite close to that of the traditional ballad and romance; its marked departures from that form are of interest because of their relation to those forms. Finally, further evidence that Keats would have known of the Thomas Rhymer legend is its mention in Thomas Warton's *The History of English Poetry* where Thomas is described as an important figure in the early history of English poetry (56). Grant T. Webster argues in "Keats's 'La Belle Dame sans Merci': A New Source" that Keats used Dante as a source for the poem yet that his knowledge of Dante stemmed from the selection presented in Warton. Even so, there is no definitive proof that Keats read Warton. The picture is complicated even further when we consider that Keats told Benjamin Bailey, in letters of 10 June and 18–22 July 1818 that he was going to take and has taken along the "three little volumes" of Henry Francis Cary's 1814 translation of *The Divine Comedy*. Carol Kyros Walker suggests in *Walking North with Keats*, "Keats gives no evidence of reading or thinking about Dante in his letters and journal. . . . He is perhaps only being polite in telling Bailey that Dante is the only reading material he took with him" (193, n. 15).

45. See Leach, *The Ballad Book*, 131.

46. Wasserman describes the ballad as "a dialogue between the knight and the stranger" (*The Finer Tone*, 66).

47. See Keats, *The Letters of John Keats*, letter 114, II:317–370.

48. Ibid., 344.

49. Ibid., 347–349.

50. I follow here Bate, *John Keats*, 471, and Gittings, *John Keats*, 300.

51. Keats, *The Letters of John Keats*, II:351–352.

52. I will focus on the structural connections between the works. We might note, however, more tangential connections that could have appealed to Keats: the fairy queen's interdiction to Thomas not to speak during their sojourn in Elfland is analogous to the interdiction Keats was under from Isabella Jones at the time. Gittings writes that Isabella Jones asked Keats that they "should be acquainted without any of our common acquaintance knowing it. . . . [Keats] accepted her request as part of the 'enigma' he had always felt her to be" (*John Keats*, 257). We might also note the romance's allusion to claret wine, about which Keats earlier in the journal letter had composed some celebratory prose, describing the wine as walking about the "cerebral apartments" "like Aladin about his enchanted palace so gently that you do not feel his step" (Keats, *The Letters of John Keats*, II:324).

53. Robert Jamieson, "True Thomas and the Queen of Elfland," in *Popular Ballads and Songs*, II:11–12.

54. Sir Walter Scott, *Minstrelsy of the Scottish Border*, IV:79–137. As in the Jamieson text, the choice of birds is suggestive, for, even granting the fluctuations we find in early English bird names, the birds chosen represent variations in bird

song and habit: the "throstell" probably means a blackbird, rather than a thrush, for the mavis or song thrush is listed on its own. Thus, the jay and the blackbird can be yoked (and in the Scott version more accurately "seen" than "heard") as birds that talk rather than sing and that habitually steal the nests of other birds or place their eggs in the nests of other birds; the wodewale is likely here a golden oriole with its flutelike whistle and so the second yoking is of true song birds. See also the more general discussion of singing birds and enchantment in Paton. Paton's work and other studies of fairy lore are linked to "La Belle Dame" in Stuart M. Sperry, *Keats the Poet*, 234–241.

55. See Bate, *John Keats*, 478. Keats could also have had in mind Dante's description in the *Paradiso* of the lark's song and the silence after its descent (Canto XX, l. 73) or Milton's lines from *Paradise Lost* regarding the nightingale's song, "Silence was pleased" (Book IV, l. 604).

56. Jamieson, *Popular Ballads and Songs*, 16–17.

57. Scott, *Minstrelsy of the Scottish Border*, 93–94.

58. This is a central argument of Levinson's reading of the two versions of the poem, claiming that the "self-consciousness" of the *Indicator* version establishes the Brown version as the ur-form. See *Keats's Life of Allegory*, 66.

59. See Lowry Charles Wimberly, *Folklore in the English and Scottish Ballads*, 281 and 282, and Francis B. Gummere, *Old English Ballads*, 362, n. 17. Gummere mentions the use of Latin in fairy encounters. I have taken Mrs. Brown's text from Gummere, 290–292. For a discussion of the use of a dead language as the expression of words "no longer mere sound, but not yet a signification," see Giorgio Agamben, "Pascoli and the Thought of the Voice," 64.

60. Of course, this also seems a conflation of the stricken Scottish subjects and pale warriors of *Macbeth*. In a letter to Tom Keats of 23–26 July 1818, during his walking tour of Scotland, Keats mentions having seen the grave of Macbeth at Iona: "We were shown a spot in the Churchyard where they say 61 kings are buried 48 Scotch from Fergus 2nd to Macbeth." See *The Letters of John Keats*, I:217.

61. For useful discussions of the series in relation to Hardy's poetry in general, see James Granville Southworth, *The Poetry of Thomas Hardy*, and Donald Davie, *Thomas Hardy and British Poetry*. Among specific studies of the series, Robert Cirasa, "Thomas Hardy's Poems of 1912–1913," and Richard A. Sylvia, "Thomas Hardy's 'The Voice,'" are particularly helpful.

62. Hardy, "The Phantom Horsewoman," in *Collected Poems*, 354.

63. See B. E. Maidment, "Hardy's Fiction and English Traditional Music"; Simon Gatrell, "Thomas Hardy and the Dance"; Ruth A. Firor, *Folkways in Thomas Hardy*; and J. Vera Mardon, *Thomas Hardy as a Musician*.

64. Hardy, "The Dead Quire," in *Collected Poems*, 257–258.

65. Noted in Gatrell, "Thomas Hardy and the Dance," 43.

66. Hardy, *The Life and Work*, 28. This biography itself brings up suggestive issues of ventriloquism and ghost writing, as "an authorized biography written by the subject himself but intended for publication after his death over a collaborator's name." See Michael Millgate's introduction to this edition—described as an

edition on new principles of the materials previously drawn on for *The Early Life of Thomas Hardy 1840–1891* and *The Later Years of Thomas Hardy 1892–1928*, published over the name of Florence Emily Hardy (xii).

67. Hardy, *The Life and Work*, 19. See also Gatrell, "Thomas Hardy and the Dance," 46.

68. Martin Seymour-Smith claims in his more recent biography that Hardy's process of self-analysis regarding his marriage, begun in the 1912–1913 poems, is resolved in "Surview," the final poem of *Late Lyrics and Earlier*, which presents a confrontation with self-ventriloquism. The chorus of this poem is "my own voice talking to me," and the final stanza dissolves that voice: *"You taught not that which you set about,* / Said my own voice talking to me; / *That the greatest of things is Charity* / And the sticks burnt low, and the fire went out, / And my voice ceased talking to me." See Seymour-Smith, *Hardy*, 802–803.

69. Hardy, "The Voice," in *Collected Poems*, 325–326.

70. Sharp, *The Country Dance Book*, 60–61. For an opportunity to examine this text and the Baring–Gould book, I am grateful for the generosity of the librarians at the Folklore Society Library, University of London.

71. See, for example, F. B. Pinion, *A Commentary on the Poems of Thomas Hardy*, 105. *The Life and Work of Thomas Hardy*, ed. Millgate, mentions many incidences of visitors' critical comments on Emma's childish and fanciful clothing and records her in old age dressed in "her usual girlish outfit of white dress and blue sash" (483).

72. See the discussion and text in Mardon, *Thomas Hardy as a Musician*, 13.

73. See Baring-Gould and Sheppard. This transcription has minor discrepancies between the text printed with the music and the text printed solely as lyrics. I have followed the lyric text in each case.

74. For Hardy's relation to hymnals, see Dennis Taylor, *Hardy's Metres and Victorian Prosody*, 209–210.

75. Mardon, *Thomas Hardy as a Musician*, 13.

76. Bishop, "At the Fishhouses," in *The Complete Poems 1927–1979*, 64–66.

77. Field, "Wynken, Blynken, and Nod," in *Poems of Childhood*, stanza 1, 38. Although Bishop often discusses her long-standing affection for hymns, I can find no evidence of Bishop mentioning this poem. But it is suggestive to find her friend and Vassar classmate Mary McCarthy citing the poem as a childhood favorite in her autobiography, *How I Grew*, 3 and 4.

78. Moore, "A Grave," in *Collected Poems*, 56–57. Bishop herself once referred to Cape Sable, where her great-grandfather Hutchinson had died, as this "graveyard of the Atlantic," which she would either drown in or write about as means of fulfilling her destiny. Recorded in Brett C. Millier, *Elizabeth Bishop*, 2.

79. The allusion to Moore is specifically marked in the 1955 volume *A Cold Spring*, in which "At the Fishhouses" first appeared in book form by its being followed ten poems later by "Invitation to Miss Marianne Moore."

80. Bishop, "In the Village," in *The Collected Prose*, 251.

81. Whitman, "Vocalism," in *Complete Poetry and Collected Prose*, 509–510.

Chapter Four

1. Merleau-Ponty, *The Phenomenology of Perception:* "movement and time are not only an objective condition of knowing touch, but a phenomenal component of tactile data. They bring about the patterning of tactile phenomena. . . . Smoothness is not a collection of similar pressures, but the way in which a surface utilizes the time occupied by our tactile exploration or modulates the movement of our hand" (315).

2. William Irwin Thompson, *The Time Falling Bodies Take to Light,* 72, 74, and 146. Thompson bases his conclusions on the work of Hockett and Ascher: "At some point during the slow morphological shift to efficient upright posture, the frontal approach for copulation must have first become anatomically possible, and it was doubtless immediately exploited. . . . Just how this change may have affected hominid lifeways is not clear. Our guess is that it changed, for the adult female, the relative roles of the adult male and of the infant, since after the innovation there is a much closer similarity for her between the reception of an infant and of a lover. This may have helped to spread the 'tender emotions' of mammalian mother-infant relations to other interpersonal relationships within the band" (324).

3. Stanley B. Greenfield, *A Critical History of Old English Literature,* 168–169.

4. "Cædmon's Hymn" in *The Anglo-Saxon Minor Poems,* 105. There are seventeen extant manuscripts of the poem, dating from 737 to the late fifteenth century. See Greenfield, *A Critical History of Old English Literature,* 169–170. Elliott Van Kirk Dobbie also includes the Tanner Mss. of the poem, which is in West Saxon dialect (*The Anglo-Saxon Minor Poems,* 106).

5. Greenfield, *A Critical History of Old English Literature,* 170.

6. Ibid., 172.

7. See Grossman's moving essay about his own relation as a poet to Cædmon's calling, "My Cædmon: Thinking about Poetic Vocation," in *The Long Schoolroom,* 1–17.

8. Sidney, *An Apology for Poetry,* 14–15. See also Jeffrey C. Robinson's discussion in *The Walk: Notes on a Romantic Image* of this passage in relation to *A Midsummer Night's Dream,* act 5, scene 1, 12–17:

> The poet's eye, in a fine frenzy rolling,
> doth glance from heaven to earth, from earth to heaven;
> And as imagination bodies forth
> The forms of things unknown, the poet's pen
> Turns them to shapes, and gives to airy nothing
> A local habitation and a name.

Fineman also gives particular attention to epideictic poetry in *Shakespeare's Perjured Eye,* 1–48 and 86–129.

9. "112: Sennuccio, i' vo' che sapi in qual manera." Reprinted by permission of the publisher from *Petrarch's Lyric Poems,* pp. 220–221, trans. and ed. by Robert M. Durling, Cambridge, Mass.: Harvard University Press, copyright © 1976 by Robert M. Durling.

10. Harrison, *The Body of Beatrice,* 101.

11. In an essay on "Petrarch's Song 126," Giuseppe Mazzotta writes, "The symmetrical coupling of contradictory experiences is, in one sense, the emblem of Petrarch's split, the steady play of attraction and repulsion for Laura that has come to be identified as the distinctive trait of his morality and of his voice. In rhetorical terms this oscillation of moods has other implications. The convention of the lyric, for instance, rests on the assumption of immediate and spontaneous emotions, while time is viewed as not a constitutive category of the lyrical expression. The movement between contrasting poles of moods implies, however, that each poem's autonomy is unreal, that the origin of each lyrical experience lies always outside of itself, that each reverses and implicates others in a steady movement of repetition" (124). Harrison's discussion of Petrarch in *The Body of Beatrice* augments the discussion of those features Mazzotta emphasizes—the spontaneity of lyric emotion and the nonconstitutive function of time. He shows that, rather than being caught in an endless repetition of oscillating positions, "the Petrarchan alternative consists in constituting lyric presence through the relentless poetic lament of absence" (100). Harrison distinguishes the epideictic poetry of love from other forms of epideictic poetry, such as those celebrating heroes in contests and war, for "the love poem's subject is defined or constituted by virtue of the mode in which it articulates its subjection to the other" (35). He concludes that Petrarch's struggle against the "temporal predicament," the on-goingness of diachronic time in tension with the rhetorical self-presence of the poem's deixis, is "the constitutive drama" of his work in the *Canzoniere* (105).

12. Grossman, *The Long Schoolroom,* 9.

13. See Richard M. Gale, "Indexical Signs, Egocentric Particulars, and Token-Reflective Words," 151–155. Russell's argument about egocentric particulars is critiqued by Gale, who contends that, in his emphasis on private sense data, Russell necessarily ends up rendering "communication impossible not only between different persons, but in respect to a single person at different moments in his history" (152).

14. Bergson, *Matter and Memory,* 33.

15. Cowper, "Hatred and vengeance, my eternal portion," in *The Poems of William Cowper,* I:209–210; the notes from which I have drawn my discussion appear on 489–490.

16. Bakhtin, *Speech Genres,* 126.

17. A passage from James King, *William Cowper: A Biography,* provides a further gloss on this aspect of the poem's utter despair: "When Cowper returned to Orchard Side in 1774, his nightmares were so frightening that Mrs. Unwin remained in his room throughout the night in order to comfort him. The arrangement continued at least until 1786 when he told Harriet Hesketh about it. . . . Cowper had the conviction of having committed the unforgivable sin of despair, and January and February remained times of great anguish. From January 2, 1773, until his death, certain of being the castaway, he never again attended public worship. After 1774, he did not even wish to enter the Vicarage: 'When I am banished from the House of God, where I have known so much of his presence, I cannot bear to sit down in the house of a friend'" (89).

18. Carson, *eros the bittersweet*, 117–122.

19. Fillmore, *Lectures on Deixis*, 61. Fineman's *Shakespeare's Perjured Eye* also provides a useful discussion of deixis, emphasizing pointing modes, pronominal shifts, and temporal/spatial markers (5). Following his main interest in epideixis, he provides an important discussion throughout of the relations between idealism and visuality. See especially 12.

20. Fillmore, *Lectures on Deixis*, 32–36.

21. Benveniste, "Relationships of Person in the Verb," 195–204; "The Nature of Pronouns," 217–222; "Subjectivity in Language," 223–230, in *Problems in General Linguistics*. Benveniste emphasizes the place of "shifters" or pronouns dependent on the point of view of users in establishing subjectivity in language—the place of the first, second, or third person shifting between the reciprocal situations of the I and you (the you as temporarily "not-I") and the third person as the "not-a-person" (i.e., not someone situated within the reciprocal shift of the situation at hand).

22. Fillmore, *Lectures on Deixis*, 36.

23. Ibid., 48.

24. Jonson, "Song—To Celia," in *The Complete Poetry of Ben Jonson*, 86–87.

25. Herrick, "To the Virgins, to make much of Time," *The Complete Poetry of Robert Herrick*, 117–118. In a discussion of Horace's odes as the classical antecedent to this kind of poem, Ronnie Ancona points out that what is ignored in such poems is often the perspective of the beloved: "the 'season' or 'now' of eroticism [is] the time to get what we can from the beloved regardless of her interests" (*Time and the Erotic in Horace's Odes*, 69). Ancona argues cogently that the poem is an attempt to "dominate" the time of the other. Yet as this tradition develops, we can also see the imploring words of the speaker, his or her "selfish" absorption in the urgency of the now, as fated to disappearance in its very articulation; for the now is always passing and will soon have passed—and it has passed in words, not actions, erotic or otherwise.

26. Wilmot, "Love and Life," in *The Complete Poems of John Wilmot, Earl of Rochester*, 90.

27. Heidegger, *Poetry, Language, Thought*, 177.

28. Quoted from "Prologomena zu einer Psychologie der Architektur," in *Kleine Schriften*, 13–47, in Michael Podro, *The Critical Historians of Art*, 100.

29. Ortega y Gasset, "On Point of View in the Arts," in *The Dehumanization of Art and Other Essays on Art, Culture, and Literature*, 111.

30. Ibid., 28.

31. Dickinson, "Split the Lark—and you'll find the Music—," in *The Poems of Emily Dickinson*, 2:644. Reprinted by permission.

32. Wordsworth, "The Tables Turned," in *Poems*, I:356–357.

33. J. A. V. Bates: "The most primitive representational drawing makes clear that the hand with fingers fully extended was some sort of communication symbol. There are hundreds of such hands in prehistoric cave paintings and one of the earliest representations in Egypt shows each ray from the sun ending in a hand. Metal hands, possibly as lucky charms, have been found in Etruscan graves"

("The Communicative Hand," 176). Jean-Luc Nancy writes in *The Muses* that "to show, *montrer*, is nothing other than to set aside, to set at a distance of presentation, to exit from pure presence, to make absent and thus to absolutize" (70). He describes the traced hands at Cosquer Cave that appear next to animals and various signs as "nothing other than the presentation itself, its open gesture, its displaying, its asperity, its patefaction—and its stupefaction. The hand posed, pressed against the wall grasps nothing. It is no longer a prehensile hand, but is offered like the form of an impossible or abandoned grasp. A grasp that could as well let go. The grasp of a letting go: the letting go of form" (72). We might note that these writings linking two-dimensional forms to touch are in conflict with the basic distinction Herder made in his 1778 *Plastik* between the visual sense of painting and the *Gefühl* or touch of sculpture. Herder's distinction ignores the place of tactility in the making and reception of paintings, but his study is a vital analysis of how the sense of touch, especially in childhood experiences, allows us to figure the human, the third dimension of the bodily form, and hence to realize the image of the body.

34. Merleau-Ponty, *Phenomenology of Perception*, 315. Drew Leder discusses this example as a distinction between subjective agency (the touching hand) and thematic object (the touched hand) in *The Absent Body*, 14.

35. Keats, "This Living Hand," *The Complete Poems*, 459.

36. Harry Berger has helpfully termed this the "shuttle of perception": "Like optical painting, textural painting activates the observer shuttle. It constructs a viewer who is invited to move up close, touch the surface, run fingers over it, make manual contact with the work of the painter's hand (a museum guard's nightmare)—but who is then invited to move back and recompose the texture within the image. The observer is set in motion on a perpendicular shuttle, moving forward and backward before the painting" ("The System of Early Modern Painting," 43).

37. Horace, *Satires, Epistles, Ars Poetica*, 472 and 473.

38. For discussion of Wyatt's titles in Tottel, see Anne Ferry, *The Title to the Poem*, 12–14, and the chapters "Who Gives the Title" and "Who Has the Title" more generally, 11–49.

39. See Howe, *My Emily Dickinson*. Howe's study throughout is based on an appreciation of the materiality and tactility of the fascicles themselves.

40. Quoted in George Deacon, *John Clare and the Folk Tradition*, 51, from Clare's "Northampton Ms. 15, 41. See also *John Clare by Himself*, 78 and 99–101.

41. Clare, *A Midsummer Cushion*. Clare first made the collection in 1832 but never had enough subscribers to publish it. It was not published until 1979.

42. This returns us to those traditions claiming all perception involves pain and linking the sensation of aesthesis to perceptible pain. See D. M. Hamlyn, *Sensation and Perception*, 1–7. Gabriel Josipovici's *Touch* emphasizes the connections between touch (touché) and the transgression of boundaries.

43. Gibson, "The Mouth as an Organ," 113. Lawrence Frank writes in an essay on "Tactile Communication," "It seems probable that the newborn infant, with its undeveloped, inadequate capacity for homeostasis, requires these experiences for maintenance of his internal equilibrium" (7). Erasmus Darwin states in

his 1794 *Zoonomia*, "the figures of small bodies seem to be learnt by children by their lips as much as by their fingers; on which account they put every new object to their mouths." He also notes the importance of movement to knowledge acquired by touch, claiming that our memories of tangible objects are slower than our visual memories because we must conceive ourselves as passing our fingers over such objects. Quoted in Ashley Montagu, *Touching: The Human Significance of the Skin*, 201.

44. Merleau-Ponty, *Phenomenology of Perception*, 315.

45. On tactual after-images, see William Schiff and Emerson Foulke, *Tactual Perception*, 19; and Drew Leder, *The Absent Body*, 41. For a broad discussion of intransitivity and transitivity in bodily sensations, see D. M. Armstrong, *Bodily Sensations*.

46. Gibson, "The Mouth as an Organ," 113 and 125.

47. See Richard Shiff's discussion in *Willem de Kooning's Paintings* of kissing and touching ("lipstick, water, slipping hands") in de Kooning's work.

48. Emil Nolde in Herschel Chipp, *Theories of Modern Art*, 146.

49. See chap. 1, n. 39, earlier. Aristotle emphasizes throughout the argument in Books II and III of *De Anima* (see especially 577–578) that "Whatever can be said of what is tangible, can be said of touch, and vice versa; if touch is not a single sense but a group of senses, there must be several kinds of what is tangible" (577). See also the discussion of this point in Jean Starobinski, "The Natural and Literary History of Bodily Sensation," 354.

50. David Michael Levin, *The Body's Recollection of Being*, 153.

51. See the story of Battus and the origin of touchstone in Ovid, *The Metamorphoses of Ovid*, 68–69.

52. Melville, "Fragments of a Lost Gnostic Poem of the 12th Century," in *Collected Poems of Herman Melville*, 234.

53. Marvell, "The Nymph Complaining for the Death of Her Faun," in *The Poems and Letters of Andrew Marvell*, I:24.

54. Verlaine, "Il pleut doucement sur la ville," in *Oeuvres complètes*, I:155–156.

55. Dickinson, "It sifts from leaden sieves," in *The Poems of Emily Dickinson*, I:231.

56. Levinas, "There Is," 51. See also Edith Wyschograd, "Doing before Hearing," 179–203. Similarly, Michael Argyle argues "bodily contact . . . is different from other bodily signals, in that it doesn't stand for anything else, but is the ultimate behaviour associated with various interpersonal relations—sexual, aggressive, nurturant, dependent and to some extent affiliative. . . . Touching also occurs in many rituals and ceremonies . . . though the reason for this is not known" ("The System of Bodily Communication," 157).

57. Fineman discusses this issue of the speaking subject's relation to the person "bespoken" in *Shakespeare's Perjured Eye*, 311, n. 6.

58. Rilke, "Handinneres," in *The Selected Poetry of Rainer Maria Rilke*, 268–269.

59. John 20:14–18.

60. See Ricoeur, *Conflict*, 249.

61. Ovid, *The Metamorphoses of Ovid*, 232.

62. Gross, *The Dream of the Moving Statue*, 84–85.

63. Bonnot, Book II, "A Treatise on the Sensations,"155–339.

64. Summers, *The Judgment of Sense*, 81 and 102. Vives is cited on 81.

65. Mandrou, *Introduction to Modern France, 1500–1640*, 53.

66. Diderot, "Letter on the Blind," 106–107.

67. Transcribed from the text of "In Praise of Theodore the Great Martyr" on the Gregory of Nyssa home page (www.ucc.uconn.edu/~das93006/nyssa.html).

68. Bann, "Shrines, Curiosities, and the Rhetoric of Display," 21.

69. *Canons and Decrees of the Council of Trent*, 215–216.

70. Wrigley, "Sculpture and the Language of Criticism in Eighteenth-Century France," n.p. I am grateful to Malcolm Baker for providing me with a copy of this paper.

71. Von la Roche, *Sophie in London*, 107–108. The full text of von la Roche's travel diary is available in a reprint of the 1788 edition, *Sophie von la Roche, Tagebuch einer Reiser durch Holland und England*. For the passage cited, see 243–244 of the German edition. This diary first came to my attention through Marcia Pointon's work on mourning jewelry: "Materializing Mourning," 41–42.

72. Focillon, *The Life of Forms of Art*, 46. For Focillon, touch is one of the "processes whereby the life of forms in the mind propagates a prodigious animism" (55).

73. Buonarotti, "Non ha l'ottimo artista alcun concetto," in *Michelangelo, the Poems*, 138–140.

74. Ovid, *The Metamorphoses of Ovid*, 39–40.

75. Goethe, "Elegy VII," in *Roman Elegies and The Diary*, 48–49. See 4–5 of the introduction for a discussion of the Latin precursors of Goethe's elegies. Also 127, the note for Elegy VII. I have also consulted *Roman Elegies and Other Poems*, trans. Michael Hamburger. Hamburger numbers the early poems in the series differently and so lists this elegy as number V (50).

76. Propertius, *Elegies*, I.16, "The door's complaint," 80–85.

77. Propertius, *Elegies*, IV.7, "Cynthia's ghost," 356–364, ll. 2–12; and *Elegies*, IV.11, "Cornelia from the grave," 383–391, l. 14.

78. Michael E. Glasscock III, Robert A. Cueva, and Brett A. Thedinger, eds., *Handbook of Vertigo*, 1–5, 36.

79. Dickinson, "I would not paint—a picture—," in *The Poems of Emily Dickinson*, II:387–388. Reprinted by permission.

80. Dickinson, "Wild Nights!" in ibid., I:179.

81. Dickinson, "I felt a funeral in my brain," in ibid., I:199–200.

82. Teresa of Avila, *The Life of Teresa of Jesus*, 274–275. The full array of Teresa's teachings and writings is available in *The Complete Works*. Of particular interest in relation to Crashaw's idea of the "well-meaning reader" is this passage from Vol. III, Chap. VIII: "Gives certain advice concerning revelations and visions." Here Teresa discusses an opinion of Fray Domingo Bañez, a Dominican:

"Whenever we see a representation of Our Lord it is right for us to reverence it, even if it has been painted by the devil himself; for he is a skilful painter and, though, trying to harm us, he is doing us a kindness if he paints us a crucifix or any other picture in so lifelike a way as to leave a deep impression upon our hearts. This argument seemed to me excellent; for, when we see a very fine picture, we always value it even if we know it has been painted by a wicked man, and we should never allow the identity of the painter to hinder our devotion" (41).

83. I will be citing Crashaw, "The Flaming Heart," 274–277, "A Hymn to the Name and Honor of the Admirable Sancte Teresa," 266–271, and "An Apologie for the fore-going Hym[ne]," 272–273, Carmen deo Nostro, reprinted from the Paris, 1652 edition, in Steps to the Temple, Delights of the Muses, and Other Poems, 185–298.

84. Deleuze, The Fold: Leibniz and the Baroque, 11–12.

85. A. B. Chambers in "Crooked Crosses in Donne and Crashaw" discusses the placement of chiastic terms in other poems by Crashaw, 157–173.

86. Austin Warren, Richard Crashaw: A Study in Baroque Sensibility, 119–120. (Reprinted from the 1939 version, this remains the most important single critical work on Crashaw.)

87. Crashaw, A Concordance to the English Poetry of Richard Crashaw, 254.

88. Gosse, "Richard Crashaw," 433.

89. Winters, "John Crowe Ransom or Thunder without God," 210.

90. Cardella, Memorie storiche, 294–295. This "solemn procession" is also mentioned in the Dizionario di erudizione storico-ecclesiastica, Vol. LI, under the entry for "Pallotta." The text is cited here from editions in the Archivio Segreto Vaticano.

91. For another aspect of Crashaw's relation to existing religious imagery, see Francis E. Barker, "The Religious Poetry of Richard Crashaw," which mentions that the first two verses of the hymn in the breviary for vespers and lauds for Teresa's feast day are an influence on the language of the "Hymn." This article has come to my attention through John R. Roberts's invaluable Richard Crashaw: An Annotated Bibliography of Criticism 1632–1980. Another possible source for "The Flaming Heart" is a painting of Teresa by Gerhard Seghers that was displayed in the Church of the Discalced Carmelites in Antwerp in the 1640s, although there is no evidence that Crashaw actually saw it. See Martz, The Wit of Love, 113–147. Thomas Healy examines the theological context of much of Crashaw's "supposed poetic excess" in his "Crashaw and the Sense of History."

92. Crashaw, A Concordance. For discussions of images of flying in medieval, Renaissance, and Baroque art, see Clive Hart, Images of Flight, and Peter Greenaway, Flying Out of This World. Jeannot Simmon's Vertigo argues that vertigo is of particular importance for modern art. Paul Schilder discusses the coincidence of vestibular irritation and flying dreams: "one experiences especially a change in the weight of the body, but the shape of the body may also be distorted" (The Image and Appearance of the Human Body, 112–113).

93. The foot as the point of contact with the ground, the literal pediment of the orientation enabling us to stabilize our vision and position, plays a similar stranded role in Honoré de Balzac's "Le Chef d'oeuvre inconnu" (Études philoso-

phiques). In this tale, Frenhofer, an imaginary Northern painter of the early seventeenth century, is driven mad by his endless search for a perfect pictorial translation of reality. He finally destroys all his works, including his master work. This painting, accrued from the touches of innumerable applications of paint until it is a formless daub, has only one intelligible image—a perfectly rendered bare foot in the corner of the canvas. Michel Serres presents an elliptical discussion of this work in relation to the concept of "noise" in his chapter "La Belle Noiseuse," in *Genesis*, 9–26.

94. Coleridge, *Table Talk*, 321–322. Coleridge cites the 1646, not the 1652, edition of Crashaw's poetry.

95. Coleridge, *The Complete Poems*, note on 505.

96. All quotations are from "Christabel" in *The Complete Poems*, 187–205.

97. "Kubla Khan," ibid., 249–252.

Chapter Five

1. Barfield, *Poetic Diction*, 182 and 189.

2. Plato, *Plato's Timaeus*, 16–18.

3. Milton, "On Time," in *John Milton*, 15–16. I disagree with E. M. Tillyard's reading of the poem as "two paragraphs, lines 1–8 and 9–22." His division has the merit of showing an imbalance between time and eternity but ignores the shape and focus provided by considering the turn at 11–12. See Tillyard, *Milton*, 55.

4. Carnap is quoted, and these ideas are discussed, in Ilya Prigogine and Isabelle Stengers, *Order Out of Chaos* 214. My thanks to Joseph Perloff for bringing this book to my attention. See also Bergson, *Matter and Memory*.

5. See the discussion of the infinite in Aristotle, "Physics," *The Basic Works of Aristotle*, 259–269, and the discussion of movement in "On the Soul" [De Anima], 543–546 especially.

6. Ovid, *The Metamorphoses of Ovid*, 340–345.

7. This is the text of "Now goþ sonne vnder wod," from *English Lyrics of the XIIIth Century*, 1. Brown has taken the text from the Bodl[eian]. Ms. Arch. Selden.

8. Augustine, *Confessions*, 177–178.

9. Ibid., 202.

10. Ibid., 277–278.

11. Lenneberg, *Biological Foundations of Language*, 108.

12. Descartes, *Meditations on First Philosophy*, 100. See also Dalia Judovitz's discussion of Descartes's general aversion to memory practices in *Subjectivity and Representation in Descartes*, 72–73 and 41, 59–60.

13. Wordsworth, *Lyrical Ballads and Other Poems, 1797–1800*, 164.

14. It is intriguing that Hölderlin, who was Wordsworth's contemporary, noted his conscious use of such inversions of clauses: "It is common practice to have inversions of word order within the period," he wrote, "but clearly much greater effects can be obtained by the inversion of the periods themselves. The logical order of periods, in which the basis (the basic period) is followed by its de-

velopment, the development by its culmination, the culmination by its purpose, and subsiding clauses are merely appended to the main clauses to which they primarily apply—all this can only rarely serve the poet's ends." Cited in the preface of Hölderlin, *Poems and Fragments*, xiii.

15. In her journal entry for 29 April 1802, Dorothy Wordsworth recorded how on a visit to "Johns grave": "William lay, & I lay in the trench under the fence— he with his eyes shut & listening to the waterfalls & the Birds. There was no one waterfall above another—it was a sound of waters in the air—the voice of the air. William heard me breathing & rustling now & then but we both lay still & unseen by one another—he thought that it would be as sweet thus to lie so in the grave, to hear the *peaceful* sounds of the earth & just to know that ones dear friends were near." Wordsworth, *The Grasmere Journals*, 92. Woof's editorial apparatus records that in stanza 8 of the 1814 draft of the "Intimations" ode, Wordsworth had described the young child: "To whom the grave / Is but a lonely bed without the sense or sight / of day or the warm light, / A place of thought where we in waiting lie."

16. See Mark Jones, *The Lucy Poems*, for a comprehensive, if rather disheartening, assemblage of the history of criticism of this poem, especially 87–93 and 207–220.

17. For a discussion of how the deictic present in lyric became the basis for Leopardi's poetics, for example, see Margaret Brose, "Remembrance and the Rhetorical Sublime in Leopardi's Lyric": "The structural principle uniting [Leopardi's] various linguistic, psychological and philosophical inquiries is that of a presupposed opposition between the seriality of time and a hypostatized, atemporal origin recuperable by rhetorical refiguration. The contrast is between the *contractive* experience of every 'present' moment of time and the *expansive* powers of poetic remembrance or Imagination" (115). In a more recent essay, "Leopardi and the Feminine Sublime," Brose connects this process of contraction and expansion to Leopardi's association of the visual with the present and the auditory with remembrance and imagination. Leopardi, who became blind in 1819, wrote that sight is the most material of the senses: "La vista è il più materiale di tutti i sensi, e il meno atto a tutto ciò che sa di astratto" (7).

18. Smart, "Time," 126–134.

19. Daniel Defoe, *Robinson Crusoe*, 121.

20. Petrarch, *Rime sparse*, 26.

21. Merleau-Ponty, *Phenomenology of Perception*, 413.

22. For Valéry's impressions of the relations between walking and dancing, see Valéry, "Poetry and Abstract Thought," 70–72.

23. Wordsworth, *The Prelude*, 480.

24. Wordsworth, *The Grasmere Journals*, 17–18.

25. Hazlitt, *Selected Essays of William Hazlitt 1728–1830*, 517.

26. Wordsworth, *The Grasmere Journals*, 109.

27. See the discussion of related issues linking Wordsworth and Godwin in Langan, *Romantic Vagrancy*, 181, as well as the stimulating analysis of the patterns of breathing, speaking, and walking in Wordsworth's work, 170*ff*. An earlier

and more general study of some connections between walking and Romanticism is Robinson, *The Walk.*

28. Spenser, "Amoretti LXXV," in *The Poetical Works of Edmund Spenser,* 575.

29. Sonnet 55 in *Shakespeare's Sonnets,* ed. Katherine Duncan-Jones, 221. Fineman writes of this sonnet, "[S]uch eternizing claims are extremely common in the poetry of praise, just as the elegy is a central epideictic form. . . . It is not my purpose, therefore, to suggest that there is something necrophiliac in the way the young man's poet regularly looks forward to the time in which 'your monument shall be my gentle verse (which eyes not yet created shall o'er read).' Yet, once we have said this, it becomes possible also to recognize that the young man's poet's epitaphic praise is something the poet characteristically seems in this quite complicated way to *see* as marking something dead" (*Shakespeare's Perjured Eye,* 157).

30. Shelley, "Ode to the West Wind," in *Shelley's Poetry and Prose,* 223.

31. Ammons, "The Pieces of My Voice," in *The Selected Poems,* 3.

32. An exception might be seen in the various forms of the georgic. Although the georgic is often written in the past and present tenses, its entire orientation is toward the future; what it records is meant to be taken up by future generations. I will briefly discuss the ways poetry addresses the future in my last chapter, "Afterborn."

33. The most considered reading of Ammons's work in light of issues of inscription is Harrison, "Tombstones." For an earlier survey of the tension between inscription and natural forces in Romanticism, see Hartman, "Wordsworth, Inscriptions, and Romantic Nature Poetry" in *Beyond Formalism,* 206–230.

34. Vaughan, "They are all gone into the world of light!" in *Complete Poems,* 246–247.

35. Fortunatas Venantius, "Tempora lapsa volant," in *Mediaeval Latin Lyrics,* 66–67 and nn. 300–302. Reprinted by permission of the Trustees of Stanbrook Abbey.

36. "Uuere beþ þey biforen vs weren," in Carleton Brown, ed. *English Lyrics of the Thirteenth Century,* 85–87. For discussion of the manuscript sources, see 202–203.

37. Hayden, "Elegies for Paradise Valley," in *Collected Poems,* 167. For discussion of the elegy in more general terms, see especially Peter Sacks, *The English Elegy,* and Jahan Ramazani, *The Poetry of Mourning.* Ramazani mentions Hayden's "Paradise Valley" elegies on 218 as work that "democratizes, urbanizes, and personalizes the *ubi sunt* tradition."

38. Curtius, *European Literature in the Latin Middle Ages,* 92. Elizabeth Barrett Browning made a particularly affecting translation of this poem: "riverfountains in pity / Weep soft in the hills; and the flowers on thy blood / Redden outward with sorrow." See Bion, Idyl 1, "Lament for Adonis," trans. Mrs. [Elizabeth Barrett] Browning in *Greek Poets in English Verse,* 290.

39. O'Hara, "The Day Lady Died," in *Selected Poems,* 146.

40. Wordsworth, "Surprised by Joy," in *Poems,* I:863.

41. Wittgenstein, *Philosophical Investigations*, #45, 21.

42. Lyons, "Deixis and Subjectivity," 103–104.

43. Ibid., 117–119.

44. Merleau-Ponty, *The Phenomenology of Perception*, 100.

45. See Charles Altieri's insightful discussion of Lyons's approach in relation to this tense and the ways in which such an experiential model provides a valuable critique of Cartesianism: "Descartes's argument [I think, therefore I am] confuses a substantial present tense allowing clear identity statements for entities (It is I who think) with the progressive present (I am thinking), then turns to draw a conclusion which relies on the second to demonstrate the first—that is, that there is a stable identity in thinking. But in fact the 'I think' only makes sense as a progressive present, and thus warrants only the conclusion that 'As I think, that I am'" (*Subjective Agency*, 36). The discussion of Lyons on deixis extends throughout 35–37.

46. Merleau-Ponty, "Temporality," in *The Phenomenology of Perception*, 410–433.

47. Elias, *Time*, 36.   48. Ibid., 129.   49. Ibid., 152–153.

50. Shelley, *Shelley's Poetry and Prose*, 311.

51. See Chandler, *England in 1819*. Chandler's book painstakingly examines the myriad aspects of the poem's relation to historical method in literary scholarship and provides a full account of previous scholarship on the poem, on Shelley's work in general, and the historical period.

52. Ibid., 30.

53. Shelley, *Letters of Percy Bysshe Shelley*, II:166–167.

54. Campion, *Works*, 46, 310, and 147, respectively.

55. Plato, *Timaeus*, 29–30.

56. Aristotle, "Physics," in *Basic Works*, Book IV, chap. 12:221a, 294–295.

57. Curtius, *European Literature and the Latin Middle Ages*, 501–509, surveys practices of "numerical composition."

58. See, for example, Alastair Fowler, *Spenser and the Numbers of Time*, 237–257; Frances Yates, *The Occult Philosophy in the Elizabethan Age*; Curtius, *European Literature and the Latin Middle Ages*; Joseph Leon Blau, *The Christian Interpretation of Cabala in the Renaissance*.

59. Thomas Crump, *The Anthropology of Numbers*, has been helpful to me throughout the construction of this chapter.

60. Perhaps the most vivid study of this aspect of thought is the 1977 film *Powers of Ten* by the office of the architects and designers Charles and Ray Eames. In this film of nine and one-half minutes, the time frame shows forty-two powers of ten, from celestial to human scale to the remotest spaces of particle physics—all structured by the modular taxonomy of the one hundred chemical elements.

61. Augustine, *De Musica:* "All is due to the supreme eternal presidency of numerical rhythm, similitude, equality, and order. If this presidency of mathematical structure is taken from earth, nothing remains. . . . The specific appear-

ance of earth, which distinguishes it from the other elements, shows a kind of unity in so far as so base an element is capable of it" (123–124).

62. David Summers, *The Judgment of Sense*, 134–135.

63. Crump, *The Anthropology of Numbers*, 8. Crump takes this concept of the "nombre marginal" from L. Gerschel, "La Conquête du nombre."

64. Angus Fletcher, *Colors of the Mind*, 174.

65. Curtius, *European Literature and the Latin Middle Ages*, note on 59.

66. S. K. Heninger Jr., *The Cosmographical Glass*, 94, citing Henry Cornelius Agrippa, *Three Books of Occult Philosophy*, trans. [J]ohn F[rench?] (London: 1651), 232.

67. Curtius, *European Literature and the Latin Middle Ages*, 503.

68. Heninger, *The Cosmographical Glass*, 92.

69. Alastair Fowler, *Spenser and the Numbers of Time*, note on 38. "Thus, 1000 is the cube of 10, and itself a cosmic number relating to the firmament of fixed stars."

70. Of particular relevance are these models in relation to the structure of the Dobell manuscript of Traherne's centuries. John Malcolm Wallace, in "Thomas Traherne and the Structure of Meditation," 79–89, claims an Ignatian structure for the *Centuries*. His argument is based on his reading of Louis Martz's 1954 book on *The Poetry of Meditation*. Yet Martz himself in his authoritative work, *The Paradise Within*, traces the influence of Augustine, especially his *De Trinitate*, on Traherne (and of the Platonic and neo-Platonic influences on both of them) and goes on to claim that Traherne's *Centuries* "seem to accord in general" with the method of contemplation found in Saint Bonaventure's *Itinerarium Mentis in Deum*, 35–102. Clements claims a number of influences on Traherne, including the Bible, Plato, Plotinus, Augustine, Dionysius the pseudo-Areopagite, Pico della Mirandola and Marsilio Ficino, Richard of St. Victor, St. Bonaventura, Meister Eckhart, Henry Suso, John Rysbroeck, Julian of Norwich, and Jacob Boehme. Much of this is just speculation (as is his claim, refuted by the *Commentaries of Heaven*, that Traherne was more sympathetic to Aristotle than to Plato in his view of form and matter [14]). Elsewhere Clements turns to a broader analogy that leads him to conclude that the overall pattern of the *Centuries* follows the standard Christian model of Creation-Fall-Redemption. Seelig suggests that Traherne's "ecstasy" does not much resemble any of the logical patterns of Christian meditation (105–115). And DeNeef claims that the structure of the Dobell sequence fits all four patterns: Bonaventura's, the conventional stages of Christian mysticism, Ignatius's stages, and the Christian soul's movement from innocence to fall to redemption (139). All references to *Select Meditations* are from Osborn ms. b.308, Beinecke Library, Yale University. (Because this manuscript was numbered consecutively on each side of the page and several pages were consequently ripped, damaged, or torn out of the binding, I have referred to meditation number and designated page numbers, throughout.)

71. Malcolm Day argues for this connection between the structure of Hall's *Centuries* and the short extemporal meditations of David in the Psalms (*Traherne*, 106–107).

72. See Martin Zeiler, *Centuria Variarum* and *Centuria III*, and Alexander Ross, *A Centurie of Divine Meditations*, for examples.

73. For background to Traherne, see the following editions of his work: the early editions edited by Bertram Dobell are *The Poetical Works of Thomas Traherne*, 1903, and *Centuries of Meditations by Thomas Traherne*, 1908. Standard editions are Thomas Traherne, *Centuries, Poems, and Thanksgivings; Christian Ethicks;* and *Poems, Centuries and Three Thanksgivings.* For secondary texts, see Day, *Thomas Traherne;* Sharon Cadman Seelig, *The Shadow of Eternity;* A. Leigh DeNeef, *Traherne in Dialogue;* A. L. Clements, *The Mystical Poetry of Thomas Traherne;* Louis Martz, *The Paradise Within;* and Wallace, "Thomas Traherne and the Structure of Meditation"; as well as the following: Stanley Stewart, *The Expanded Voice;* Kenneth John Ames, *The Religious Language of Thomas Traherne's Centuries;* A. M. Allchin, Anne Ridler, and Julia Smith, *Profitable Wonders;* Slawomir Wacior, *Strategies of Literary Communication in the Poetry of Thomas Traherne;* Franz K. Wohrer, *Thomas Traherne;* Queenie Iredale, *Thomas Traherne;* Alison Sherrington, *Mystical Symbolism;* Richard Douglas Jordan, *The Temple of Eternity;* Barbara Kiefer Lewalski, *Protestant Poetics and the Seventeenth-Century Lyric;* and Joan Webber, *The Eloquent "I."*

74. *Commentaries of Heaven,* British Library ADD MS. 63054. This manuscript is numbered in the upper right-hand corner of each leaf. In citing the manuscript, I have provided the page number and signified recto (r) or verso (v) in each instance. The most important accounts of the *Commentaries* can be found in Allan Pritchard, "Traherne's *Commentaries of Heaven,*" and Julia Smith, "Susanna Hopton." Smith is now working on an edition of the *Commentaries.* I am grateful for our conversation regarding Traherne in October 1993. I would also like to acknowledge the assistance of the manuscripts librarians at the British Library and the gracious help of the Rev. George Usher of St. Mary's Rectory, Credenhill, who shared his knowledge of Traherne's church and its history with me, opening St. Mary's under difficult circumstances in June 1993, for the church had been recently damaged by an arsonist and was officially closed.

75. See *A Collection of Meditations and Devotions in Three Parts by the First Reformer of the Devotions in the Ancient Way of Offices* (Susanna Hopton); afterward reviewed and set forth by the late Learned Dr. Hickes. For further background on Hopton, see Smith, "Susanna Hopton."

76. See James J. Balakier, "Thomas Traherne's Dobell Series."

77. The Ficino Notebook is British Library ms. Burney 126. Carol L. Marks (Sicherman) has described Traherne's unpublished works and the influences of his studies on his writings in the following important articles: Sicherman, "Traherne's Ficino Notebook"; Sicherman, "Thomas Traherne's Commonplace Book"; Carol L. Marks, "Traherne's Church's Year-Book"; Marks, "Thomas Traherne's Early Studies"; Marks, "Thomas Traherne and Hermes Trismegistus"; Marks, "Thomas Traherne and Cambridge Platonism."

78. Numerical composition in Ficino is discussed in Josephine L. Burroughs's translation of Ficino's "Five Questions Concerning the Mind." In that edition, Burroughs's introduction is 185–192, the translation, 193–212. See also Ficino, *Ficino: The Philebus Commentary,* and Pico della Mirandola, *Heptaplus,* in *On*

the Dignity of Man; On Being and the One; Heptaplus, 85–174. Traherne quotes from Pico's *De dignitate hominis* in the fourth century of the Dobell mss. (74–78), and many aspects of Pico's thought are relevant to his writings, including the Heptaplus as a narration on the six days of creation, Pico's three chief zones of cosmology: the intelligences or angels, the heavenly bodies, and the corruptible earthly bodies; and Pico's transposition and recombination of Hebrew letters in his study of the cabalistic method. In the *Commentaries of Heaven,* Traherne presents "A Comparison of Aristotle and Plato" and argues that Plato was superior to Aristotle: "And the reason is apparent for Plato delighting much in *Jewish traditions* (which he had imbibed partly from the Pythagorean philosophie, partly from his personal conversations with Jews and Egyptians in the Oriental parts) he thereby obtained great notices of *Divine Mysteries* especially such as related to the origins of the universe, the Spiritual Nature and Perfection of God, the Immortalitie of the Soul, etc." (f. 129 v). In the earlier *Select Meditations,* however, Traherne shows some contempt for Plato. He praises Plato for asking the "marvellous question," "Whether Things were Holy because they were commanded or therefore commanded because they were Holy" (Meditation 49) but then goes on to say that "The Heathen answered not his own question: for it was too deep for his Intelligence" (Meditation 50).

79. See Osborn. There are references to "Soften the Kings heart, Teach our Senators Wisdom" in I.82 and "The Government of A Church Established by Laws" in III.24. Other more sketchy autobiographical evidence in the *Select Meditations* dates the manuscript to the period of Traherne's appointment at Credenhill: "nor ever am I happy till I return home" (III.30); "when I see a little Church environed with Trees, how many Things are there which mine Eye discerneth not. . . . Especially I who have been nourished at universities in Beautifull Streets and famous Colledges and am sent thither from God almighty the aer of Heaven and Earth to teach Immortal Souls the way to Heaven" (III.83).

80. It is perhaps not far-fetched to suggest as well that Traherne had a model for breaking off his writing at the fifth section in Ficino. See editor Michael Allen in Ficino, *Marsilio Ficino:* "Ficino had given public lectures on his translation [of the *Philebus*], praised by Alberti. Alberti and Landino asked him to elucidate the theories he had developed in the *Philebus* commentary. After Ficino had announced to his listeners that the *Philebus* is divided into twelve sections, without any warning he interrupts his exposition after the fifth section; and although subsequently—twice in fact—he showed his regret at not having been able to complete his exposition, we see him contenting himself with illustrating it with apologues, an odd conclusion for the treatise" (10).

81. Quoted in Theodor E. Mommsen, "St. Augustine and the Christian Idea of Progress," 295. For Augustine's concept of the "six ages," dividing world history according to the six days of Creation wherein the Christian era is an age of senility and decay leading to a seventh age when time would come to an end, see G. J. Whitrow, *Time in History,* 80.

82. Stephen Toulmin and June Goodfield, *The Discovery of Time,* 60–61. J. J. Scaliger in *De emendatione temporum* (1583) had calculated the system of Julian days as beginning at noon on 1 January 4713 B.C.—his estimation of the date of creation. See Whitrow, *Time in History* 137. Plato had claimed in the *Timaeus*

that the battle between the Athenians and Atlantans had occurred eight thousand years before.

83. In his *Christian Ethicks,* Traherne gives a similar account of the history of the world in Chapter XV: "Of Faith." He says that there can be no "certain knowledge" of the "actions of free agents" except by "history and tradition":

> That the World was made so many years ago, that Man was created in an estate of Innocency, that he fell into Sin, that GOD appeared, and promised the seed of the Woman to break the Serpents Head, that there was a Flood, that Sodom and Gomorrah was burnt by fire, that all the World spake one Language till the Confusion at Babel, that there were such men as Julius Caesar, or Alexander the Great, or such as Abraham, and Moses, and David; that the children of Israel were in Egypt, and were delivered from thence by Miracles; that they received the Law in the Wilderness, and were afterwards settled in the Land of Canaan, that they had such and such Prophets, and Priests and Kings; that Jesus Christ was born of the Virgin Mary, that he was GOD and Man, that he died and rose again, that he ascended into Heaven, and sent the Holy Ghost down upon his Apostles. Nay that there is such a City as Jerusalem. (107–108)

Traherne goes on to say that the histories of peoples; the determination of the Gospels; the accounts of miracles; the existence of emperors, church fathers, and places such as Judea, Rome, and Constantinople are revealed "by the Light of History and received upon Trust from the Testimony of others" to be as clear as "mathematical demonstration, or [what] had been seen with our Eys" because of faith and the reliability of Christian typology. He concludes, "AMONG other Objects of Felicity to be enjoyed, the Ways of GOD in all Ages are not the least considerable and illustrious. . . . Ages are as long and as Wide as Kingdoms" (111).

84. It is worth noting that the *Select Meditations* manuscript, which from all evidence seems to be a fair copy, is written so that there are thirty-three lines of text on each page.

85. Unfortunately, there is a dearth of reliable documents regarding the facts of Traherne's life. Furthermore, much of Traherne's writing on infancy and childhood should be framed in Christian and neo-Platonic, rather than strictly autobiographical, terms. A current project to systematize the archives of the city of Hereford should be of help. Although Wade's biography of Traherne is not always reliable, it does set forth a picture of the violent circumstances of Traherne's childhood in Hereford in light of the general religious and political circumstances of the town in the seventeenth century.

86. It is suggestive of his later interest in cabala that the flyleaf of one of Traherne's early notebooks from Brasenose College has two simple codes (387). One code covers only the vowels, using a kind of tailed Greek as a base. One stroke across the tail corresponds to a, two strokes to b, and so on. The second code on 387 involves a correspondence between letters and numbers ($a = 1, e = 2, i = 3, o = 4, u = 5, m = 6, n = 7, r = 8, c = 9$)—Traherne wrote "1627" or "amen." (Recounted in Marks, "Thomas Traherne's Early Studies," 514.)

87. See Michael Ponsford, "Men after God's Own Heart," 3–11. Ponsford es-

pecially focuses on Traherne's "Thanksgivings," in which Traherne explicitly desires "that I were as David" (many of the "Thanksgivings" are pastiches of the Psalms) and the ways in which the third century links Traherne to a poetics of imitation in the seventeenth century.

88. On the poetics of the Psalms, see Pius Drijvers, *The Psalms;* Robert Alter, "Psalms"; Douglas K. Stuart, *Studies in Early Hebrew Meter;* and Leopold Sabourin, *The Psalms.* Sabourin explains that "the alphabetic psalms are 9–10, 25, 34, 37, 111, 112, 119, and 145. They follow a literary device in which half-lines, lines, verses, or stanzas begin successively with a different letter of the Hebrew alphabet. In Psalm 119, the letter is repeated eight times throughout the 22 alphabetical stanzas. Psalm 9–10 originally formed a single alphabetical poem in which every second, third, or fourth verse began with a successive letter of the alphabet" (26–27). Crump, *The Anthropology of Numbers,* 110–111, also discusses Psalm 119, emphasizing that the Hebrew letters are also used as numbers here and that psalm tradition will play a part in the development of cabala.

89. James M. Osmond, "A New Traherne MS.": "Traherne is lavish in the use of the first person singular, a device which on a careless reader may leave an impression of monstrous conceit; but it should be noted that, in a section where the self-revelation becomes especially intimate, he adopts the third person" (243). This technique is especially complicated in the *Select Meditations* manuscript where Traherne sometimes does write in the first person about himself, as he does in the passage I have quoted in n. 27. He refers as well to his "brother" and "SH" (Susanna Hopton) and writes in Meditation 93 of the first century, "know lady of our Happiness in being Redeemed," thereby perhaps addressing these centuries as well to Hopton. Yet there is also a recurring metaphor in the *Select Meditations* of Traherne himself as "the bride of Christ." In these passages of poetry and prose, Traherne, in a remarkable poem making up Meditation 17 of the second century, concludes, "I on Thy Turtle [Dove] shall with joy Behold / Angelique Life / Throughout her Skin / Shall clad thy wife and make her Shine within." Meditation 18, which follows, makes a direct appeal to God: "O my God would She See thy Goodness! How should her soul be ravished! Thy goodness and thy wisdom seen, would make thy Bride of Heaven and Earth a Queen!"

90. For an introduction to issues of aesthetic form in poetic collections, see Neil Fraistat, *Poems in Their Place* and Roland Greene, *Post Petrarchism.*

91. For a helpful overview of such practices in Modernist and postmodern poetry, see Marjorie Perloff, "The Return of the (Numerical) Repressed: From Free Verse to Procedural Play," in *Radical Artifice,* 134–170.

92. See, for example, the entry on "lyric" in *Encyclopedia of Poetry and Poetics,* 460–470. The authors begin by saying lyric is not narrative or dramatic, then speak of the "musical" qualities of lyric, going on to qualify this as a criterion, adding brevity, expression, and other qualities to the list of defining features. "Most of the confusion in the modern (i.e., 1550 to the present) critical use of the term 'l,' is due to an overextension of the phrase to cover a body of poetic writing that has drastically altered its nature in the centuries of its development" (460). An argument in favor of the usefulness of generic categories and in refutation of the frequent materialist assumption that the only alternative to local modes of explanation is a transcendent model can be found in Norman Bryson,

Looking at the Overlooked: "I strongly sympathise with this materialist objection [to a higher Platonic realm]. . . . But the objection brings with it an exceedingly drastic consequence, if the only way forward would seem to be to abandon and disown the concept of generic series even though such series exist objectively and historically. Whenever a series is *dis*continuous, and jumps from one specific cultural milieu to another, it would seem that materialist analysis must close its eyes, or issue an automatic accusation of idealism to anyone who thinks it is still a series. But it may be that the analysis is not being materialist *enough*" (12; Bryson's emphasis).

93. We are reminded here of Althusser's distinction between ideology in general, which has no history, and particular ideologies, subject to history, and of his claim that the concept of history is itself not historical. See "Ideology and Ideological State Apparatuses" in *Lenin and Philosophy*, 121–173. Althusser's attempt to find a metahistorical term under which historical critique might proceed constantly appears as a gesture of transcendence under which all limits to transcendence are articulated.

94. Aristotle, *De Poetica*, in *Basic Works*, 1464. Aristotle goes on to say that narrative poetry requires its maker to be "more of the poet" than "verses," for narrative works necessitate the imitation of actions: "And if he should come to take a subject from actual history, he is none the less a poet for that; since some historical occurrences may very well be in the probable and possible order of things" (ibid.).

95. Sidney, *An Apology for Poetry*, 31–42. For an important discussion of the psychology of "the defense" as a genre, see Ferguson, *Trials of Desire*. Paul Fry's recent *A Defense of Poetry* makes the case for poetry's value on the basis of its semantic indeterminancy.

96. See Hegel's discussion of romantic art in *The Philosophy of Fine Art*, cited in chap. 2, "Sound." Osmaston has a note to this passage saying that Hegel underestimates the sonorous quality of poetry. A similar criticism is made by Charles Taylor, *Hegel*, 478 and 479. Yet Hegel would find it impossible to allow any sonorous aspect of the lyric to remain *unworked*—that is, not subjected to the cognitive transformation whereby every material element transcends itself.

97. Vico, *The New Science*, 79.

98. Ibid., 257 and Sidney, *An Apology for Poetry*, 9.

99. Vico, *The New Science*, 260.

100. Benjamin, *Illuminations*, 263.

101. Benedetto Croce, *Theory and History of Historiography*, 108–110: "There is no fear of going astray in history, because, as we have seen, the problem is in every case prepared by life, and in every case the problem is solved by thought, which passes from the confusion of life to the distinctness of consciousness" (110).

102. Ibid., 113.   103. Ibid., 115.

104. Contrast, for example, Bruno Snell's argument for lyric subjectivity as an invention of Greek culture and Michel Zink's argument that lyric subjectivity was an invention of medieval French tradition discussed in our first chapter with the position of the authors of *A History of Private Life*, who emphasize the six-

teenth century: "Ronsard, and with him the group of poets known as La Pléiade, can be credited with originating lyric poetry as the Romantics would later define it: poetry that expresses private feelings and experiences," in Roger Chartier, ed., Vol. III, *Passions of the Renaissance*, 368. In yet another account, Stopford A. Brooke singles out the poetry of the early eighth century as the origin of such personal lyric in English: "These poems are concerned with personal fates, and with the emotions these fates awaken; with the personal relation of the soul to God and its eternal state; and many of them are written with the eye of the writer fixed on his own heart and its imagination. Baeda's death-lay is a short piece . . . steeped in personal feeling. This subjective drift of poetry is especially marked in Cynewulf" (*The History of Early English Literature*, 352). He sees such work as a significant departure from the absence of self-consciousness in Cædmon.

105. For a discussion of archaism, as mentioned in the previous chapter on "Voice and Possession," see Barfield, *Poetic Diction*, 152–167.

106. Hölderlin, "Heimkunft," in *Poems and Fragments*, 261.

107. Hölderlin, "Dichterberuf," in ibid., 176–177.

108. See, for example, Taylor, *Sources of the Self*, 199–207; and Baxandall, *Painting and Experience*.

109. Johnson, *The Idea of Lyric*, 123–126.

110. Milton, *John Milton*, 359. In lines 185–191, the next instance of end rhyme, Milton uses an abcadea structure.

111. Ibid., 355.

112. Hollander, *Vision and Resonance*, 172–173. See also in this volume the discussion of quantitative meter (59–70) and of Campion's attempts to adapt English meters to musical systems (71–90). Hollander's work is an important guide to issues of formal transformation. See also his position on aurality, emphasizing the tension between repetition and time, in *The Figure of Echo*.

113. For example, the discussion of "time as a means of structure" in Lowry Nelson, *Baroque Lyric Poetry*, 19–84.

114. See David Perkins, *Is Literary History Possible?* for a critique of "historical contextualism."

CHAPTER SIX

1. Ovid, *The Metamorphoses of Ovid*, 225–227 and 246–247.

2. Henry, *Orpheus with His Lute*, 73. This study is an engaging introduction to the history of the Orpheus myth in Western literature.

3. The night is often the secret site of initiation, purification, and other threshold activities bridging the relation between what is human and what is not human and providing a context for changed roles and states of being. See, for example, Ono no Komachi and Izumi Shikubu, *The Ink Dark Moon*. Another tradition is the well-known Navaho *yerbichai*, or "night chants" sung during "Night Way" rituals, described in Clyde Kluckhohn and Dorothea Leighton, *The Navaho*, 304–305 and 310–311, and Harold E. Driver, *Indians of North America*, 412–413.

4. See Judovitz, *Subjectivity and Representation in Descartes*, 63.

5. Athanassakis, "Hymn to Night," in *The Orphic Hymns*, 6–9.

6. Athanassakis, *The Orphic Hymns*, note on 131.

7. Finch, "A Nocturnal Reverie," in *Miscellany Poems*, 291–293.

8. Wordsworth, "Essay," in *Prose Works*, III:73 and *The Later Years*, 5: pt. 2 of *The Letters*, 236–239 and 259–260. There are indeed a number of similarities between the two poems, both of which were published in 1713. Pope's poem was begun in 1704 and is part of his larger pastoral project. His "waving groves" with their similarly "chequer'd scene," unlike Finch's, are inhabited by nymphs. But Pope's polemical attack on hunting is analogous to Finch's discussion of "unmolested kine" and his first-person nature descriptions are dramatically vivid, as in these lines (111–114) on the shooting of a pheasant:

> See! from the brake the whirring pheasant springs,
> And mounts exulting on triumphant wings:
> Short is his joy; he feels the fiery wound,
> Flutters in blood, and panting beats the ground.

See "Windsor Forest," 41.

9. See, for example, Jean Mallinson, "Anne Finch"; Charles H. Hinnant, *The Poetry of Anne Finch*; Ann Messenger, "Selected Nightingales"; Ruth Salvaggio, *Enlightened Absence*; Barbara McGovern, *Anne Finch and Her Poetry*; Norman Callan, "Augustan Reflective Poetry"; and Jean M. D'Alessandro *When in the Shade. . . .*

10. Reynolds, "Introduction," in *The Poems of Anne, Countess of Winchelsea*, xvii–cxxxiv; Rogers, *Selected Poems of Anne Finch*, ix–xxiv; Hinnant, *The Poetry of Anne Finch*; Reuben Brower, "Lady Winchelsea and the Poetic Tradition of the Seventeenth Century"; and D'Alessandro, *When in the Shade . . .*, ix–xl.

11. John Middleton Murry, in his 1928 edition of Finch's work, *Poems by Anne Finch, Countess of Winchelsea 1661–1720*, seems to have been the first person to note this connection, but he mistakenly cites the Shakespeare as "On such a night" (16). Mallinson writes that the poem "looks back to Shakespeare, from whom Anne Finch took the refrain 'In such a night.'" She goes on to mention the poem's links to "Il Penseroso . . . Young and Coleridge and the genre of Night Thoughts" ("Anne Finch," 61). McGovern notes the poem "recalls . . . act V . . . in which Lorenzo and Jessica exchange a series of imaginative musings on the beauty of nature, each beginning with the phrase 'In such a night'" (*Anne Finch and Her Poetry*, 80). She writes, "From her arrival at court in 1682 until she and her husband left six years later, over forty English plays were performed at the court theater. . . . Particularly popular were Shakespeare and Beaumont and Fletcher" (53–54).

12. All quotations are from *The Merchant of Venice*, Arden edition.

13. Ibid., xxii.

14. Chapman, "Hymnus in Noctem," Pt. I of *The Shadow of Night*, 23 (ll. 139–144).

15. Ibid., 25 (ll. 223–232).

16. Athanassakis, "Hymn to Hekatē," 5–7.

17. Raymond Waddington explains that Chapman had in mind the Orphic hymns in writing his poems and, more particularly, was concerned with the function of Orphic music: "The true harmony of the soul is symbolized by chastity or

by the moon, which marks the boundary between the orders of nature, and the symbols coalesce in the figure of the chaste moon goddess, Cynthia, Diana, Luna. The poet or musician reproduces in audible form that cosmic harmony which Pythagoras once heard and so through art becomes an instrument of reform or regeneration, providing fallen man with a pattern of that larger lost harmony" (94). There was a continuing tradition of Orpheus himself addressing hymns to the night, to the moon, and to Diana, which Chapman had known and followed. See Waddington, *The Mind's Empire*, 95.

18. In *Anne Finch and Her Poetry*, McGovern discusses Finch's use of contemporary conventions of melancholy and mentions Burton in her chapter on "The Spleen," 159–178. McGovern sees Finch as using "The Spleen" to attack the Puritan affinity for melancholy in particular: "From Speech restrain'd, by thy Deceits abus'd, / To Deserts banish'd, or in Cells reclus'd, / Mistaken Vot'ries to the Pow'rs Divine, / Whilst they a purer Sacrifice design, / Do but the Spleen obey, and worship at thy Shrine" (176). Given this hypothesis, it is interesting that Finch takes up Milton's gesture of the *banishment* of Melancholy itself to a cave safe-confined.

19. See Waddington, *The Mind's Empire*, 96–97; Frances Yates, *The Art of Memory*; Klibansky, Panofsky, and Saxl, *Saturn and Melancholy*. Of additional relevance is the larger context of the relation Chapman had to the "School of Night," the intellectual circle that also included Raleigh and Marlowe, parodied by Shakespeare in *Love's Labour Lost*. For background, see M. C. Bradbrook, *The School of Night*, and Yates, *A Study of* Love's Labour Lost.

20. Finch, "The Spleen," in *Miscellany Poems*, 88–96.

21. Finch, "Ardelia to Melancholy," in *The Poems of Anne, Countess of Winchelsea*, 15. In other poems she also discusses this theme of melancholy and sleeplessness. "An Invocation to Sleep" begins:

> How shall I wooe thee gentle rest,
> To a sad Mind, with cares opress'd?

and ends bleakly:

> For, if thou wilt not hear my Pray'rs,
> Till I have vanguish'd all my cares,
> Thou'llt stay, 'till kinder Death supplys thy place,
> The surer Friend, tho' with the harsher face.

See Finch, "An Invocation to Sleep," in *The Poems of Anne, Countess of Winchelsea*, 16–17.

22. Finch, "To the Right Honorable the Countess of Hartford with her Volume of Poems," in ibid., 61.

23. All quotes are from "L'Allegro" (22–25) and "Il Penseroso" (25–30), in *John Milton*, ed. Orgel and Goldberg.

24. See *John Milton*, note on 744.

25. See Gibson, "The Mouth as an Organ"; the "haptic" system is discussed on 111–121. Following our discussion of metrics and walking in the last chapter, it is intriguing to read Perloff's analysis of the metrics of Goethe's "Wandres Nachtlied" (Wanderer's Nightsong) in *Poetry on and off the Page*, 119–123. Perloff argues that the poem approaches the simple repetitions of a folk song and then

carefully "defamiliarizes" its own structures of recurrence. Although her analysis shows the particular role of such relation between the "natural" and "the poetic" in Goethe's thought, it also speaks to the more general poetic quality that is associated with the nocturnal wanderer's journey—the sensation of being lost, of losing direction, or surprising and circling returns.

26. Lorus J. Milne and Margery J. Milne, *The World of Night,* 43–49 and 63–64. This beautiful little study in natural history has been useful throughout this chapter. See also Pierre Charles Dominique, *Ecology and Behaviour of Nocturnal Primates,* vii–4, for introductory remarks on nocturnal primate behavior.

27. "Hymnus in Cynthiam," Pt. II of *The Shadow of Night,* ed. Phyllis Brooks Bartlett, 31–45.

28. Lines 157–162, ibid., 34.

29. See *Three Books of Occult Philosophy or Magic by Henry Cornelius Agrippa von Nettesheim,* Book I, *Natural Magic,* 145 and 96. The passages are also discussed in Waddington, *The Mind's Empire,* 100.

30. Athanassakis, "Hymn to the Moon," 14–17.

31. Hesiod, *Works and Days,* ll. 795 and 798, "the moon is waning, middle, and standing." Cited in ibid., 116, n. 9.

32. Wordsworth, *Prose Works,* 3:63.

33. John Dixon Hunt, "Picturesque Mirrors," draws a suggestive connection among mirrors, the eighteenth-century "Claude glass," and reversed images in water: "Claude mirrors held in the hand went out of fashion [by the early years of the nineteenth century], but they surrendered their primacy to reversed images in real water—Wordsworth's 'bosom of the steady lake,' Constable's Stour or Turner's Venetian lagoon—and to the mind's reflections" (268).

34. Milne and Milne, *The World of Night,* 27–28.

35. Ibid., 8.

36. Ibid., 10.

37. *Eastwell Blue Book,* quoted in *The Poems of Anne, Countess of Winchelsea,* xxxiii.

38. "An Invitation to Dafnis" in ibid., 28.

39. We might also note that Keats seems to have made similar careful use of *A Midsummer Night's Dream*'s flower imagery in the "Ode to a Nightingale" with its hawthorne, eglantine (sweet briar), fading violets, and "coming musk-rose," the latter the characteristic flower of midsummer.

40. This account is from Arthur Thompson. The trivial beauties "watch" in Finch's lines on the glow-worm reminds us of the corollary of night wandering: νυκτοφυλακέω *(nuktophylakeō),* "keeping watch or guarding a gate or opening by night." This is the theme of Piero's fresco of the attendants to the dream of Constantine and of Shakespeare's drunken porters on the threshold. The night watch guards the interior and so becomes vulnerable; standing in the light and looking into the darkness, he or she is more visible than seeing. The audience for such a theme is in the dark and yet knows more than the watcher—just the situation that will be exploited in the development of horror film and film noir more generally.

41. See Hinnant, *The Poetry of Anne Finch*, 154: "Wordsworth's desire that these and the preceding two lines be expunged from the poem may not have been misplaced." In an article on Finch in *Poetry Nation Review* published in 1982 ("Anne Finch," 8, no. 6: 35–38), Denys Thompson claims to quote "in full" the "Nocturnal Reverie" *[sic]*, but omits these lines, going from ". . . shine" to "When odours. . . ." An exception to the neglect of the lines can be found in Germaine Greer's claim that the presence of Salisbury adds to a thematic that "females are unmolested only when man sleeps." See Greer, "Wordsworth and Winchelsea," 11. Also see McGovern, *Anne Finch and Her Poetry*, 82–83. McGovern considers the lines to be central in that the poem is a kind of "compliment" to a "female friend" and discusses Finch's friendship with Lady Thanet and her two oldest daughters, Catharine and Anne, on 110–111. Of particular interest is her analysis of two other poems by Finch to Anne Tufton: a playful satire asking to be Salisbury's "captive,": "The white mouse's petition to Lamira the Right Hon:^ble the Lady Ann Tufton now Countess of Salisbury" and an elegy, "On the Death of the Queen," in which "Lamira" comforts the speaker.

42. See *The Poems of Anne, Countess of Winchelsea*, xxxviii.

43. Chapman's n. 13, in *The Poems of George Chapman*, 44. Explicit allusions to Elizabeth as a Virgin Queen/Cynthia figure of course appear frequently in Renaissance imagery. See, for example, Chapman, "Hymnus in Cynthiam," Pt. II of *The Shadow of Night*, 38, ll. 328–348; and 42, ll. 507–508. Waddington gives an example (*The Mind's Empire*, note on 79) of the ways in which virginity, moonlight, water, and chastity make up such a constellated image: "It seems unlikely that at Elizabeth's 1566 Oxford visit the choice of topic, whether the moon controls the ebb and flow of the sea—on which Edmund Campion delivered the affirmative position—was purely accidental. . . . And when Alencon's party inspected the fleet at Rochester, they confessed 'that of good right the Queene of England was reported to be Ladie of the seas.'" Waddington also cites the discussion of the theme in Spenser and Raleigh's "Cynthia, the Ladie of the Sea" provided in Wilson.

44. I have taken all references from *The Owl and the Nightingale*, ed. Stanley. D'Alessandro discusses the influence of "The Owl and the Nightingale"; however, she sees the Owl's presence as "a warning to mankind as to the shortness of life" (*When in the Shade . . .*, 186). Such a reading seems to neglect the agonistic, playful, and erotic dimensions of the medieval poem. Hinnant and Messenger both have suggested a relation between Finch's poem "The Nightingale" and Richard Crashaw's "Musicks Duell," including Crashaw's own borrowings from Famianus Strada's *Prolusiones*, with its duel between a nightingale and a lute player. In Finch's poem the sweetness of the nightingale is derided at the poem's closure: "Let division shake thy Throat. / Hark! Division now she tries.; Yet as far the Muse outflies." See Hinnant, *The Poetry of Anne Finch*, 101–134; and Messenger, "Selected Nightingales," 75. Hollander has extensively discussed the relation between Crashaw and Strada and the nightingale's duel in *The Untuning of the Sky*, 226–238. See also Praz's seminal study, *The Flaming Heart*. It seems useful to consider Finch's use of the nightingale's duel as including the medieval poem, for the latter is certainly more clearly connected to the notion of two types of *female* singers.

45. *The Owl and the Nightingale*, 24.

46. Milne and Milne, *The World of Night*, 13.

47. Ibid., 22.

48. At least since the Renaissance, the terms *mode* and *mood* were synonymous, at the time pronounced identically as well. Poussin, a direct influence on Turner, early on appreciated the possibilities of adapting classical poetic modes, with their roots in emotional states, to other art forms. The most important discussion of this connection remains the chapter "What Passions Cannot Music Raise and Quell?" in Hollander's *The Untuning of the Sky*, 162–244, especially 206–220. Hollander explains the connections between "mood and mode" and discusses Poussin's extension of musical modes into the art of painting.

49. Although many studies, as cited earlier, and even the *Norton Anthology*, mention the relation of the poem to Lady Salisbury, I have found no reference in the Finch scholarship to the Stonehenge connection. D'Alessandro singularly emphasizes the symbolism of Salisbury cathedral in a discussion of the religious implications of the poem (*When in the Shade . . .* , 191–193, 203), but she does not seem to locate the action of the poem itself in any particular location.

50. See Piggott, *The Life and Music of John Field*, 27–135.

51. Jones, *The Most Notable Antiquity of Great Britain*. This edition was assembled by John Webb, Jones's son-in-law; the quote is from 108.

52. Gilpin, *Observations on the Western Parts of England*, 78.

53. Keysler, *Antiquatates Selectae*, 3.

54. The use of playful pseudonyms by this group, which included a number of aristocratic women scholars, suggestively follows the use of such "play" names in Finch's poetry and circle. The Roman Knights had names related to their homes or country seats: Lord Winchelsea's name was "Cingetorix, a Belgic prince of Eastern England" (Piggott, *William Stukeley*, 54). Unfortunately, the measurements taken by Stukeley and Finch turned out to be inaccurate.

55. Quoted in Piggot, *William Stukeley*, 107.

56. See also the translation from Thomas Taylor, *Thomas Taylor, the Platonist*, 200.

57. Quoted in Roberto Calasso, *The Marriage of Cadmus and Harmony*, 309. Taken from Aristophanes, *Ranae*, 1032; transcription from http://www.perseus.tufts.edu/cgi-bin/ptext?doc=Perseus.

58. See "Owling," in *The Encyclopaedia Britannica*, 11th ed.

59. See "Night," in *Standard Dictionary of Folklore*, ed. Leach; and Francesca Greenoak, *All the Birds of the Air*, 133–135. These traditions play a role of course in the "Walpurgis Night" section of Goethe's *Faust* and, in a transformed sense, in the "Nighttown" section of Joyce's *Ulysses*.

60. Greenoak, *All the Birds of the Air*, 107–108.

61. Hinnant discusses Vaughan's "The Night" in relation to Finch's reverie. He sees Vaughan's poem as expressing day and night "as polar opposites" and so contrasting to Finch's "temporalizing process in which morning will bring an inevitable and necessary renewal of the day's 'Cares,' 'Toils,' and 'Clamours'" (*The Poetry of Anne Finch*, 157). Although I would agree that Finch's poem is not in

the metaphysical tradition of Vaughan's in any overall sense, I think Hinnant underestimates the relation Finch has to this tradition, especially in the turn to meditative language in the closing lines.

62. See also Vaughan's "Midnight," in *Complete Poems*, 174–175, also dating to 1655.

63. Lines 400–409, in *The Shadow of Night*, 39–40.

64. Taylor, *Thomas Taylor, the Platonist*, 221.

65. Milne and Milne, *The World of Night*, 25.

66. These lines in Finch also anticipate rather remarkably the opening passage of the second of Novalis's *Hymns to the Night:* "Muß immer der Morgen wiederkommen? Endet nie des Irdischen Gewalt? unselige Geschäftigkeit verzehrt den himmlischen Anflug der Nacht" (Must the morning always return? Will earthly force never end? Unholy busyness devours the Night's heavenward approach) (14–15).

67. The typicality of the poem in its mixed approaches might be considered in light of Dixon Hunt's claim that the early eighteenth century was a time when horticulture, agriculture, and other empirical pursuits were seen as antidotes to excessive religious enthusiasm (*Figure in the Landscape*, 25–26) and when there was an "eventual triumph of expressive over emblematic design" (73). Josephine Miles's work on adjectives in English poetry drew conclusions regarding a similar shift from abstractions to sense impressions: "In terms of aesthetic versus ethic, therefore, we are able to discern three stages of poetic vocabulary: the sixteenth–seventeenth-century quantitative emphasis on good and bad primarily and true and false secondarily, with bright-dark a very weak third type, a proportion kept also by Pope, Tennyson, Browning; second, the equally strong line from Milton to Housman through Cowper and Wordsworth by which bright-dark was made close second to good; and, third, the extreme aesthetic emphasis, shared in by the five intense lyricists, Collins and Gray, Shelley and Keats, and Poe, by which sense terms as represented by bright-dark were made the prime movers of the poetic form" (*Wordsworth and the Vocabulary of Emotion*, 414).

68. Pope, Book IV, *The Dunciad*, in *Pope: Poetical Works*, ed. Herbert Davis, 547–584.

69. Young, "Night Thoughts," in *The Poetical Works of Edward Young*, 5–344; "Night IX," 343.

70. A recurring pastoral motif of the critique of court and centralized power runs throughout the night poems. This is the theme offered in Lorenzo's speech, and we find it, of course, in the complex historical and political situation underlying Finch's reverie and in Warton as well: "What are the splendors of the gaudy court, / It's [sic] tinsel trappings, and it's [sic] pageant pomps? / To me far happier seems the banish'd Lord / Amid Siberia's unrejoycing wilds" (Warton, *Pleasures of Melancholy*, 18). The first quote in the text is from 21; the second, from 14.

71. Coleridge, "Frost at Midnight," in *The Complete Poems*, 231–233.

72. Keats, *The Complete Poems:* "Ode On Melancholy," 348–349; "Ode to a Nightingale," 346–348.

73. See James Thomson, *The Poetical Works*, I:122–172. Bertram Dobell's memoir, ix–xciii, introducing this edition, is a helpful survey to the reception of

Thomson. Among Thomson's many other night poems is his long work, "Insomnia," II:31–43, in which he describes night as a cavern:

I let my lids fall, sick of thought and sense,
    But felt that Shadow heavy on my heart;
And saw the night before me an immense
    Black waste of ridge-walls, hour by hour apart,
Dividing deep ravines: from ridge to ridge
Sleep's flying hour was an aerial bridge;
    But I, whose hours stood fast,
Must climb down painfully each steep side hither,
And climb more painfully each steep side thither,
And so make one hour's span for years of travail last. (35)

This poem turns to wandering as well: he "paced the silent and deserted streets." Pausing "against a bridge's stony parapet," "some stray workman, half-asleep but lusty, / Passed urgent through the rainpour wild and gusty, / I felt a ghost already, planted watching there" (41).

74. See Clare A. Culleton, "James Thomson and the Influence of *The City of Dreadful Night* on T. S. Eliot," 85–89. Culleton notes the obvious links to "The Waste Land" but also draws connections to "Little Gidding" and, following Elizabeth Schneider, to "Rhapsody on a Windy Night" (*T. S. Eliot*, 17). For discussions of the social and political regulation of night in the city, see A. Alvarez, *Night*, 217–256, and the following essays from a special edition, "La Notte: Ordine, sicurezza e disciplinamento in eta moderna," of *Laboratorio di storia* (vol. 3) (Florence: Ponte alle Grazie, 1991): Crouzet-Pavan, Cajani, Saba, Lacche, and Corrain. I am grateful to Randolph Starn for drawing my attention to this journal. Two recent important works by contemporary American poets also take up the theme of nocturnal meditation: see Grossman's romance, "The Philosopher's Window," and the two series Frank Bidart uses to frame his *Collected Poems*, "In the Western Night" and "The First Hour of the Night."

75. Thomson, *The City of Dreadful Night*, III:130.

76. See Peter C. Noel-Bentley, "'Fronting the Dreadful Mysteries of Time,'" 193. For further discussions of the poem, see also Raymond Williams, *The Country and the City*, and William Sharpe, "Learning to Read *The City*." Dominique Millet-Gerard, in "Une Réécriture 'fin de siècle' de l'*Enfer* dantesque," draws many useful comparisons to Dante's *Inferno*, Poe, and Melville, emphasizing the fantastic and dreamlike elements of the poem.

77. Thomson, *The City of Dreadful Night*, 172.

78. "The Extraordinary Tale of the City of Brass," in *The Book of the Thousand Nights and One Night*, trans. Powys Mathers, II:285–303.

79. Piggott, *The Life and Music of John Field*. See also the nationalistic pamphlet on Field published by Grattan Flood. Field spent most of his life in Russia, living in St. Petersburg and Moscow at various times. He had first traveled there in 1802 with his teacher, Muzio Clementi. Field gave performances and also served as a salesman of Clementi pianos. When Clementi returned to Europe in 1803, Field stayed behind. He augmented his composing with an active performance career, teaching, and continuing work on innovative piano technology.

80. See Kallberg, "The Rhetoric of Genre," 238.

81. Kallberg, "The Harmony of the Tea Table," 102–133. The quotation from the review is on 103. In "Understanding Genre," Kallberg suggests that it is anachronistic to call Field's piano compositions "nocturnes," since reviewers did not develop a vocabulary for the genre until the 1820s.

82. I am indebted to Charles Baxter for bringing these and other examples of musical nocturnes to my attention and for his many valuable insights into the nocturne form, correspondence January–April 1995.

83. For a discussion of the relation between night and miracles, see Jean-Claude Maire Viguer, "valenze della notte," 23–29. Regarding light and the nocturnal in painting, see Lucia Corrain, "Raffigurare la notte." Corrain argues that Uccello's "nocturnal" hunting scene in fact occurs just at dawn (147). She discusses further issues of representing the night in "Chiara di luna e pittura di luce."

84. Hinks, *Michelangelo Merisi da Caravaggio*, 51.

85. See Benedetti, "Caravaggio's *Taking of Christ*" (Letter), 37–38, which identifies the figure. The letter is consequent to the discussion in Benedetti, "Caravaggio's *Taking of Christ*: A Masterpiece Rediscovered." Caravaggio's relation to sound is briefly discussed in René Jullian, *Caravage*, 128–129. Hibbard's biographical study *Caravaggio* cites Brandi recording that X rays of Caravaggio's paintings show that, in his direct approach to the canvas, Caravaggio painted "heads that almost always begin with an ear." See the note on 29.

86. John Gage, *Color in Turner*, 186.

87. Ronald Paulson, "Turner's Graffiti."

88. Quoted in Ann Lapraik Livermore, "Turner and Music," 47.

89. Andrew Wilton, *Turner and the Sublime*, 155–164.

90. Burke, *A Philosophical Enquiry*, 80–82 and 144–147.

91. Coleridge, *Biographia Literaria*, 2:5.

92. Whistler, *Notes, Harmonies, and Nocturnes*, 53.

93. Linda Merrill, *A Pot of Paint*, 31.

94. E. R. Pennell and J. Pennell, *The Life of James McNeill Whistler*, 113. Quoted in Stephen Hackney, "Colour and Tone," 695. Hackney points out that Whistler's nocturnes are small canvases because he wanted to have the image be the same size it would be when viewed from whatever prospect he had chosen.

95. See Hackney, "Colour and Tone," 698.

96. Merrill, *A Pot of Paint*, 144.

97. Ibid., 235.

98. Hazlitt, *Collected Works*, I: note on 76.

CHAPTER SEVEN

1. Marx, *Economic and Philosophic Manuscripts of 1844*, 302.

2. Ibid., 310.

3. Kant, "Analytic of the Sublime," 122.

4. Ibid., 120.

5. Rorty, *Contingency, Irony, and Solidarity*, 192.

6. See Margot Norris, "The [Lethal] Turn of the Twentieth Century," 151–159.

7. Eliot, *Essays of George Eliot*, 270. First printed in *Westminster Review* 66 (July 1856): 51–79.

8. Rorty, *Contingency, Irony, and Solidarity*, 94.

9. Homer, *Iliad*, 263.

10. Bakhtin, *Dialogic Imagination*, 31.

11. Vico, *The New Science*, 257. Vico did not think there was one historical Homer but rather that the epic was passed down through a succession of rhapsodes.

12. Bowra, *From Virgil to Milton*, 10.

13. Horkheimer and Adorno, *Dialectic of Enlightenment*, 45.

14. Bakhtin, *The Dialogic Imagination*, 16.

15. See Horkheimer and Adorno's description of "the Homeric gift as halfway between barter and offering" and how in the *Odyssey* "the inner organization of individuality in the form of time is still so weak that the external unity and sequence of adventures remains a spatial change of scenery, of the spots sacred to the local deities by whose virtue the storm drives and tosses" (*Dialectic of Enlightenment*, 48–49).

16. Bakhtin, *The Dialogic Imagination*, 15.

17. I have discussed these works with more specificity in *Crimes of Writing: Problems in the Containment of Representation*, 76–78.

18. Barlow cited in Curran, *Poetic Form and British Romanticism*, 170.

19. Bond, *English Burlesque Poetry*, 30–31, note on 31.

20. Quotations from Tennyson are taken from *The Poems*, ed. Ricks.

21. Tennyson, "Ulysses," 560–566.

22. Tennyson, "The Epic," 582–584.

23. Tennyson, "Maud," 1037–1093.

24. Quotations from Whitman are taken from *Complete Poetry and Collected Prose*.

25. Ibid., 437.

26. Ibid., 453–454.

27. Owen, "Conscious," in *Collected Poems*, 63.

28. Rosenberg, "In War," in *Collected Poems*, 105–107.

29. Sassoon, *War Poems*: "Suicide in the Trenches," 119; "The Fathers," 93. See also the discussion of "Suicide in the Trenches" in Paul Fussell Jr., *The Great War and Modern Memory*, 283 and 304.

30. See Fussell's chapter on pastoral, "Arcadian Resources," in *The Great War and Modern Memory*, 231–269.

31. See Tillyard, *Milton*, 23–24 *passim*.

32. All quotations from Moore's work are taken from *Collected Poems*.

33. Moore, "The Hero," 16.

34. Moore, "What Are Years," 99.

35. Moore, "Nevertheless," 127–128.

36. Moore, "The Mind Is an Enchanting Thing," 133–134.

37. See Kimon Friar and John Malcolm Brinnin, eds., *Modern Poetry: American and British*, 523. The work is also quoted in "The Other Voice," a chapter particularly focusing on Moore's poetry from this period and its relation to World War II, in George W. Nitchie, *Marianne Moore*, 109–146.

38. Moore, "Interview with Donald Hall," 261.

39. Moore, "In Distrust of Merits," 135–137.

40. Moore, *Complete Prose*, 271.

41. Moore, "'Keeping Their World Large,'" 144–145.

42. In *A Gulf So Deeply Cut*, Susan Schweik discusses fully many of the other pressures on Moore as she struggled to represent her feelings about the war. Schweik particularly focuses on the way a legacy of "authenticity" from the soldier-poets of World War I made it difficult for Moore and other women to be considered as valued interpreters of the war. Yet Schweik also clarifies how Moore's sophisticated use of poetic resources had an impact on poets of World War II like Randall Jarrell who in fact were soldier-poets. As such soldier-poets criticized "bystander" poetry, they often borrowed from it as well. See especially "Writing War Poetry 'Like a Woman': Moore (and Jarrell)," 31–58. Perloff's "Poetry in Time of War" in *Poetry on and off the Page* is an important analysis of a later conflict over how the poet speaks in a time of war—here in the context of the war in Vietnam. Robert Duncan and Denise Levertov both were involved in the antiwar movement, but Levertov felt called to write an abstract and rhetorical poetry against the war, whereas Duncan argued that such rhetoric was only a supplement to the very ideology that fueled the war. For Duncan, "THERE HAS BEEN NO TIME IN HUMAN HISTORY THAT WAS NOT A TIME OF WAR" (cited by Perloff from a letter of 4 October 1971 [212]), and the task of the poet is to particularize language to enough of a degree that moral abstraction has a grounding in life.

43. All quotations from Stevens's poems are from *Collected Poems*.

44. Stevens, "Examination of the Hero in a Time of War," 273–281; passages quoted are from 273, 276, and 279, respectively. Bloom discusses Stevens's identification of the poet with the hero; see also his discussion of references in the opening lines to earlier poems, particularly "Adagia" and "The Sun This March," 158–159. Bloom does not mention the prose statement. See also A. Walton Litz, *Introspective Voyager*, 264–265, but Litz's claim that Stevens became a "successful war poet" jars with the ethos of Stevens's discussion of war: what would it mean to be a "successful war poet" if war established conditions under which the pressure to produce ideology-driven "fact" overwhelmed the critical and creative function of the imagination? The most extensive and detailed discussion of Stevens's relation to the war can be found in Alan Filreis, *Wallace Stevens and the Actual World*, especially chapter 2, "Formalists under Fire," 29–147.

45. Holly Stevens later reprinted the work in her selected edition, *Wallace Stevens: The Palm at the End of the Mind*, 206.

46. Stevens, "Examination of the Hero in a Time of War," 278.

47. All quotations from Brooks are taken from *Selected Poems*. Significant

analyses of "The Anniad" can be found in the following: D. H. Melhem, *Gwendolyn Brooks*, 61–70; Claudia Tate, "Anger So Flat," 140–152; Harry B. Shaw, "Perceptions of Men," 136–159; and Mary Helen Washington, "'Taming All That Anger Down,'" 460–461.

48. Extensive commentaries on *Omeros*, aside from specific citations in the discussion later here, appear in the following: Robert D. Hamner, *Derek Walcott*, 1–14; Sidney Burris, "An Empire of Poetry"; and Rei Terada, *Derek Walcott's Poetry*, 187–198.

49. Cited in Ann Folwell Stanford, "Like Narrow Banners for Some Gathering War," 180, n. 2.

50. Miller, "'Define . . . the Whirlwind,'" 160.

51. Brooks, *Report from Part One*, 17.

52. See also Shaw, "Perceptions of Men," 137–139.

53. Stanford, "Like Narrow Banners for Some Gathering War," 172. See also John Hope Franklin, *From Slavery to Freedom*.

54. Brooks, *Report from Part One*, 158.

55. George E. Kent, *A Life of Gwendolyn Brooks*, 76.

56. Bond, *English Burlesque Poetry*, 67.

57. In this passage, Brooks also seems to be calling on the "master" usage of Emily Dickinson. In the line "narrow master master-calls," following on the earlier imagery of green springtime, readers of Dickinson will associate this narrow master both with Dickinson's "master" and her "narrow fellow in the grass" —a snake.

58. Hamner, *Derek Walcott*, 144, quoting the review by Leithauser.

59. The mystery is resolved on 86. For a discussion of epic conventions, see also Hamner, *Derek Walcott*, 11.

60. Patricia Ismond, "Self-portrait of an Island," 61–65.

61. Walcott, "The Caribbean," 57.

62. Ibid., 53.

63. Walcott, *Another Life*, 41.

64. Walcott, "The Sea Is History," in *The Star-Apple Kingdom*, 25–28, 25, and 28.

65. Walcott, "Homecoming: Anse la Raye," in *The Gulf*, 84.

66. "An Interview with Derek Walcott," 24.

67. Cited in Hamner, *Derek Walcott*, 143.

68. Walcott, "Iona: Mabouya Valley," in *Sea Grapes*, 40. This poem is written in Creole on the verso pages and English on the recto pages. Walcott notes, "Saint Lucian *conte*, or narrative Creole song, heard on the back of an open truck travelling to Vieuxfort, some years ago."

69. Quoted in Benjamin, *Illuminations*, 108.

70. David Humphreys Miller, *Ghost Dance*, 133.

71. Virgil, *Aeneid*, 96–97.

72. Reprinted in Hamner, *Derek Walcott*, 27.

AFTERBORN

1. My thinking here is much influenced by the arguments of Derek Parfit. See particularly "Personal Identity and Morality" (chap. 15:321–350) and all of Pt. Four: "Future Generations," 351–456. I have found Mary Warnock's critical discussion of Parfit's work and other issues of aesthetics and temporality in her *Imagination and Time* equally useful.

2. Georg Simmel anticipated some of this contemporary development toward abstraction in a 1907 essay, "Soziologie der Sinne," in *Simmel on Culture*, 109–119. There he writes, "[T]he perceptual acuity of all the senses evidently sinks as culture becomes more refined, whereas its emphasis upon liking and disliking rises. Indeed, I believe that the heightened sensibility in this direction generally brings much more suffering and repulsion than joys and attractions in its wake. The modern person is shocked by innumerable things, and innumerable things appear intolerable to their senses which less differentiated, more robust modes of feeling would tolerate without any such reaction" (118).

Poems Cited

Alberti, Rafael. "Rojo." In *Selected Poems,* ed. Ben Belitt. Berkeley: University of California Press, 1966, 172.

Ambrose. "Evening Hymn" In Saint Augustine, *Confessions,* trans. R. S. Pine-Coffin. London: Penguin, 1961, 202.

Among-the-brant. "To me is very hard this my mind." In *Tlingit Myths and Text,* ed. John R. Swanton. Bulletin 39, Bureau of American Ethnology. Washington, D.C.: Smithsonian Institution, 1919, 405.

Ammons, A. R. "The Pieces of My Voice." In *The Selected Poems.* New York: Norton, 1986, 3.

Anonymous. "Dark the Night." In *The Oxford Book of Carols,* ed. Percy Dearmer, R. Vaughan Williams, and Martin Shaw. London: Oxford University Press, 1928, 11.

———. "Edward." In *The Ballad Book,* ed. MacEdward Leach. New York: Barnes, 1955, 86–87.

———. "The Gypsy Laddie." In *The Ballad Book,* ed. MacEdward Leach. New York: Barnes, 1955, 539–544.

———. "The Mermaid of Galloway." In R. H. Cromek, *Remains of Nithsdale and Galloway Song.* London: Cadell & Davies, 1810.

———. "Nou goþ sonne vnder wod." In *English Lyrics of the XIIIth Century,* ed. Carleton Brown. Oxford: Clarendon, 1932, 1.

———. "Thomas the Rymer." In Walter Scott, *Minstrelsy of the Scottish Border,* ed. T. F. Henderson, 4 vols. Edinburgh: Oliver & Boyd, 1932, 4:92.

———. "The Three Ravens" (variant "The Twa Corbies"). In *The Ballad Book,* ed. MacEdward Leach. New York: Barnes, 1955, 111–113.

———. "True Thomas and the Queen of Elfland." In *Popular Ballads and Songs: From Tradition, Manuscripts, and Scarce Editions,* ed. Robert Jamieson. 2 vols. Edinburgh: Constable, 1806, Vol. II:3–43.

———. "Uuere beþ þey biforen vs weren." In *English Lyrics of the Thirteenth Century,* ed. Carleton Brown. 85–87.

———. "The Wife Wrapt in Wether's Skin." In *Anglo-American Folksong Style,* ed. Roger D. Abrahams and George Foss. Englewood Cliffs, N.J.: Prentice Hall, 1968, 167–169.

Ariosto, Ludovico. *Orlando Furioso*, trans. William Stewart Rose; ed. Stewart A. Baker and A. Bartlett Giamatti. Indianapolis: Bobbs-Merrill, 1968.

Ashbery, John. "Finnish Rhapsody." In *April Galleons*. New York: Viking, 1987, 14.

Athanassakis, Apostolos N., trans. "Hymn to Hekatē." In *The Orphic Hymns: Text, Translation and Notes*. Missoula, Mont.: Scholars, 1977.

———. "Hymn to the Moon." In *The Orphic Hymns: Text, Translation and Notes*. Missoula, Mont.: Scholars, 1977.

———. "Hymn to Night." In *The Orphic Hymns: Text, Translation and Notes*. Missoula, Mont.: Scholars, 1977.

Auden, W. H. "As I walked out one Evening." In *Collected Shorter Poems, 1927–1957*. New York: Vintage, 1975, 85.

———. "Precious Five." In *Collected Shorter Poems, 1927–1957*. New York: Vintage, 1975, 285–288.

Ball, Hugo. "Gadji beri bimba." In *Flight Out of Time: A Dada Diary*, ed. John Elderfield; trans. Ann Raimes. New York: Viking, 1974, 70–71.

Bidart, Frank. *Collected Poems 1965–90: In the Western Night*. New York: Farrar, Straus, & Giroux, 1990.

Bion. Idyl 1, "Lament for Adonis," trans. Mrs. [Elizabeth Barrett] Browning. In *Greek Poets in English Verse*, ed. W. H. Appleton. Boston: Houghton Mifflin, 1893, 288–293.

Bishop, Elizabeth. "Arrival at Santos." In *The Complete Poems 1927–1979*. New York: Farrar, Straus, & Giroux, 1983, 89–90.

———. "At the Fishhouses." In *The Complete Poems 1927–1979*. New York: Farrar, Straus, & Giroux, 1983, 64–66.

———. "The Burglar of Babylon." In *The Complete Poems 1927–1979*. New York: Farrar, Straus, & Giroux, 1983, 112–118.

———. "One Art." In *The Complete Poems 1927–1979*. New York: Farrar, Straus, & Giroux, 1983, 178.

———. "The Riverman." In *The Complete Poems 1927–1979*. New York: Farrar, Straus, & Giroux, 1983, 105–109.

———. "Visits to St. Elizabeths." In *The Complete Poems 1927–1979*. New York: Farrar, Straus, & Giroux, 1983, 133–135.

Brooks, Gwendolyn. "The Anniad." In *Selected Poems*. New York: Harper & Row, 1963, 38–49.

———. "Appendix to the Anniad." In *Selected Poems*. New York: Harper & Row, 1963, 50–51.

———. "Gay Chaps at the Bar." In *Selected Poems*. New York: Harper & Row, 1963, 22.

———. "love notes." In *Selected Poems*. New York: Harper & Row, 1963, 27–29.

———. "Negro Hero." In *Selected Poems*. New York: Harper & Row, 1963, 19–21.

———. "piano after war." In *Selected Poems*. New York: Harper & Row, 1963, 24–25.

———. "the white troops had their orders but the Negroes looked like men." In *Selected Poems*. New York: Harper & Row, 1963, 25–26.

Browning, Robert. "Epilogue," *Asolando*. In *The Complete Poetic and Dramatic Works of Robert Browning*. Boston: Houghton Mifflin, 1895, 1007.

Cædmon. "Cædmon's Hymn." In *The Anglo-Saxon Minor Poems*, ed. Elliott Van Kirk Dobbie. New York: Columbia University Press, 1942, 105.

Campion, Thomas. "Now winter nights enlarge." In *The Works of Thomas Campion*, ed. Walter R. Davis. New York: Norton, 1969, 147.

———. "Rose-cheeked Laura." In *The Works of Thomas Campion*, ed. Walter R. Davis. New York: Norton, 1969, 310.

———. "When thou must home." In *The Works of Thomas Campion*, ed. Walter R. Davis. New York: Norton, 1969, 46.

Carroll, Lewis [Charles Dodgson]. "Jabberwocky." In *The Annotated Alice*, ed. Martin Gardner. New York: Clarkson Potter, 1960, 270.

Chapman, George. *The Shadow of Night*. In *The Poems of George Chapman*, ed. Phyllis Brooks Bartlett. New York: Modern Language Association; London: Oxford University Press, 1941, 17–45.

Clare, John. *A Midsummer Cushion*. Ed. Kelsey Thornton and Anne Tibble. Ashington, Eng.: Carcanet, 1990.

Coleridge, Samuel Taylor. "Christabel." In *The Complete Poems*, ed. William Keach. London: Penguin, 187–205.

———. "Frost at Midnight." In *The Complete Poems*, ed. William Keach. London: Penguin, 231–233.

———. "Kubla Khan." In *The Complete Poems*, ed. William Keach. London: Penguin, 249–252.

Cowper, William. "Hatred and vengeance, my eternal portion." In *The Poems of William Cowper: Vol. I. 1748–1782*, ed. John D. Baird and Charles Ryskamp. Oxford: Clarendon, 1980, 209–210.

Crashaw, Richard. "An Apologie for the fore-going Hym[ne]." In *Carmen deo Nostro*, 272–273. Reprinted from the Paris, 1652 edition, in *Steps to the Temple, Delights of the Muses, and Other Poems*, ed. A. R. Waller. Cambridge: Cambridge University Press, 1904, 185–298.

———. "The Flaming Heart." In *Steps to the Temple, Delights of the Muses, and Other Poems*, ed. A. R. Waller. Cambridge: Cambridge University Press, 1904, 274–277.

———. "A Hymn to the Name and Honor of the Admirable Sancte Teresa." In *Steps to the Temple, Delights of the Muses, and Other Poems*, ed. A. R. Waller. Cambridge: Cambridge University Press, 1904, 266–271.

———. "Summer in Winter." In *The Oxford Book of Carols*, ed. Percy Dearmer, R. Vaughan Williams, and Martin Shaw. London: Oxford University Press, 1928, 139.

———. "The Weeper." In *Steps to the Temple, Delights of the Muses, and Other Poems*, ed. A. R. Waller. Cambridge: Cambridge University Press, 1904, 258–265.

Creeley, Robert. "The Rain." *The Collected Poems of Robert Creeley 1945–1975.* Berkeley: University of California Press, 1982, 207.

Dickinson, Emily. "I felt a Funeral in my Brain." In *The Poems of Emily Dickinson.* 3 vols. Cambridge, Mass.: Harvard University Press, 1979, I:199–200.

———. "I would not paint—a picture—," In *The Poems of Emily Dickinson.* 3 vols. Cambridge, Mass.: Harvard University Press, 1979, II:387–388.

———. "It sifts from Leaden Sieves." In *The Poems of Emily Dickinson.* 3 vols. Cambridge, Mass.: Harvard University Press, 1979, I:231–232.

———. "It was not Death, for I stood up." In *The Poems of Emily Dickinson.* 3 vols. Cambridge, Mass.: Harvard University Press, 1979, II:391.

———. "Publication is the Auction." In *The Poems of Emily Dickinson.* 3 vols. Cambridge, Mass.: Harvard University Press, 1979, II:544.

———. "Safe in their Alabaster Chambers." In *The Poems of Emily Dickinson.* 3 vols. Cambridge, Mass.: Harvard University Press, 1979, I:151.

———. "Split the Lark—and you'll find the Music—," In *The Poems of Emily Dickinson.* 3 vols. Cambridge, Mass.: Harvard University Press, 1979, II:644.

———. "Wild Nights—Wild Nights!" In *The Poems of Emily Dickinson.* 3 vols. Cambridge, Mass.: Harvard University Press, 1979, I:179.

Dolittle, Hilda. [H.D.] "Sea Violet." In *Collected Poems 1912–1944,* ed. Louis L. Martz. New York: New Directions, 1983, 25–26.

Donne, John. "Elegy 8, The Comparison." In *The Complete English Poems,* ed. A. J. Smith. London: Penguin, 1976, 103–104.

———. "The Canonization." In *The Complete English Poems,* ed. A. J. Smith. London: Penguin, 1976, 47–48.

———. "Elegy 19, To his Mistress Going to Bed." In *The Complete English Poems,* ed. A. J. Smith. London: Penguin, 1976, 124–126.

———. "Elegy 4, The Perfume." In *The Complete English Poems,* ed. A. J. Smith. London: Penguin, 1976, 98–100.

———. "A Nocturnal upon S. Lucy's Day, being the shortest day." In *The Complete English Poems,* ed. A. J. Smith. London: Penguin, 1976, 72–73.

Durling, Robert, trans. and ed. "112: Sennuccio, i' vo' che sapi in qual manera." In *Petrarch's Lyric Poems: The Rime Sparse and Other Lyrics.* Cambridge, Mass.: Harvard University Press, 1976.

———, trans. and ed. Francesco Petrarca, "#125," *Rime sparse.* In *Petrarch's Lyric Poems: The Rime Sparse and Other Lyrics.* Cambridge, Mass.: Harvard University Press, 1976.

Eliot, T. S. "A Dedication to My Wife." In *Collected Poems 1909–1962,* New York: Harcourt, Brace & World, 1970, 221.

———. "Hysteria." In *Collected Poems 1909–1962.* New York: Harcourt, Brace & World, 1970, 24.

Field, Eugene. "Wynken, Blynken, and Nod." In *Poems of Childhood.* New York: Scribner's, 1920, 44–46.

Finch, Anne. "Ardelia to Melancholy." In *The Poems of Anne, Countess of Winchelsea,* ed. Myra Reynolds. Chicago: University of Chicago Press, 1903, 15–16.

——. "An Invitation to Dafnis." In *The Poems of Anne, Countess of Winchelsea*, ed. Myra Reynolds. Chicago: University of Chicago Press, 1903, 28–30.

——. "An Invocation to Sleep." In *The Poems of Anne, Countess of Winchelsea*, ed. Myra Reynolds. Chicago: University of Chicago Press, 1903, 16–17.

——. "A Nocturnal Reverie." In *Miscellany Poems on Several Occasions*. London: printed for J.B. and sold by Benj. Tooke, 1713, 291–293.

——. "The Spleen." In *Miscellany Poems on Several Occasions*. London: printed for J.B. and sold by Benj. Tooke, 1713, 88–96.

——. "To the Right Honorable the Countess of Hartford with her Volume of Poems." In *The Poems of Anne, Countess of Winchelsea*, ed. Myra Reynolds. Chicago: University of Chicago Press, 1903, 61.

Fortunatus, Venantius. "Tempora lapsa volant." In *Mediaeval Latin Lyrics*, ed. and trans. Helen Waddell. New York: Holt, 1933, 66–67.

Frost, Robert. "The Oven Bird." In *The Poetry of Robert Frost.* ed. Edward Connery Lathem. New York: Holt, Rinehart, & Winston, 1969, 119–120.

García Lorca, Federico. "Romance Sonambulo." In *The Selected Poems of Federico García Lorca.* ed. Francisco García Lorca and Donald M. Allen. New York: New Directions, 1955, 64–68.

Goethe, Johann Wolfgang von. "Elegy VII." In *Roman Elegies and The Diary*, verse translation by David Luke; introduction by Hans Rudolf Vaget. London: Libris, 1988, 48–49.

Gray, Thomas. "Elegy Written in a Country Churchyard." In *The Complete Poems of Thomas Gray*, ed. H. W. Starr and J. R. Hendrickson. Oxford: Clarendon, 1966, 37–43.

Grossman, Allen. *The Philosopher's Window.* New York: New Directions, 1995.

Guildford [John or Nicholas of?]. *The Owl and the Nightingale.* Ed. Eric G. Stanley. London: Nelson, 1960.

Hardy, Thomas. "The Dead Quire." In *The Collected Poems of Thomas Hardy.* London: Macmillan, 1952, 257–258.

——. "During Wind and Rain." In *The Collected Poems of Thomas Hardy.* London: Macmillan, 1952, 465–466.

——. "The Paphian Bull." In *The Collected Poems of Thomas Hardy.* London: Macmillan, 1952, 774–777.

——. "The Phantom Horsewoman." In *The Collected Poems of Thomas Hardy.* London: Macmillan, 1952, 354.

——. "The Rash Bride." In *The Collected Poems of Thomas Hardy.* London: Macmillan, 1952, 236–239.

——. "Seen by the Waits." In *The Collected Poems of Thomas Hardy.* London: Macmillan, 1952, 370.

——. "The Voice." In *The Collected Poems of Thomas Hardy.* London: Macmillan, 1952, 325–326.

Hayden, Robert. "Elegies for Paradise Valley." In *Collected Poems*, ed. Frederick Glaysher. New York: Liveright, 163–170.

Herbert, George. "The Altar." In *The English Poems of George Herbert*, ed. C. A. Patrides, London: Dent, 1974, 47.

————. "Virtue." In *The English Poems of George Herbert*, ed. C. A. Patrides, London: Dent, 1974, 103.

Herrick, Robert. "Herrick's Carol." In *The Oxford Book of Carols*, ed. Percy Dearmer, R. Vaughan Williams, and Martin Shaw. London: Oxford University Press, 1928, 137.

————. "The Night-piece, to Julia." In *The Complete Poetry of Robert Herrick*. New York: New York University Press, 287–288.

————. "To the Virgins, to make much of Time." *The Complete Poetry of Robert Herrick*. New York: New York University Press, 1963, 117–118.

Hesiod. *Theogony, Works and Days*. Trans. M. L. West. Oxford: Oxford University Press, 1988.

Hölderlin, Friedrich. "Dichterberuf." In *Poems and Fragments*, trans. Michael Hamburger. London: Routledge & Kegan Paul, 1966, 176–177.

————. "Heimkunft." In *Poems and Fragments*, trans. Michael Hamburger. London: Routledge & Kegan Paul, 1966, 254–261.

————. "Der Spaziergang." In *Poems and Fragments*, trans. Michael Hamburger. London: Routledge & Kegan Paul, 1966, 576–577.

Homer. *The Iliad*. Trans. Robert Fagles; introduction by Bernard Knox. London: Penguin, 1990.

Hopkins, Gerard Manley. "Carrion Comfort." In *Gerard Manley Hopkins*, ed. Catherine Phillips. Oxford: Oxford University Press, 1986, 168.

————. "I wake and feel." In *Gerard Manley Hopkins*, ed. Catherine Phillips. Oxford: Oxford University Press, 1986, 166.

————. "No worst." In *Gerard Manley Hopkins*, ed. Catherine Phillips. Oxford: Oxford University Press, 1986, 167.

————. "Patience, hard thing." In *Gerard Manley Hopkins*, ed. Catherine Phillips. Oxford: Oxford University Press, 1986, 170.

————. "Spelt from Sibyl's Leaves." In *Gerard Manley Hopkins*, ed. Catherine Phillips. Oxford: Oxford University Press, 1986, 175.

————. "The Wreck of the Deutschland." In *Gerard Manley Hopkins*, ed. Catherine Phillips. Oxford: Oxford University Press, 1986, 110–119.

Jonson, Ben. "Song: To Celia." In *The Complete Poetry of Ben Jonson*, ed. William B. Hunter. New York: New York University Press, 1963.

Keats, John. "La Belle Dame sans Merci." In *The Letters of John Keats*, ed. Maurice Buxton Forman. Oxford: Oxford University Press, 1931, 2:356–357.

————. "Hyperion: A Fragment." In *The Complete Poems*, ed. John Barnard, London: Penguin, 1988, 283–307.

————. "Ode on Melancholy." In *The Complete Poems*, ed. John Barnard, London: Penguin, 1988, 348–349.

————. "Ode to a Nightingale." In *The Complete Poems*, ed. John Barnard, London: Penguin, 1988, 346–348.

————. "This Living Hand." In *The Complete Poems*, ed. John Barnard. London: Penguin, 1988, 459.

Marvell, Andrew. "The Nymph Complaining for the Death of Her Faun." In *The*

Poems and Letters of Andrew Marvell: Vol. I. Poems. Ed. H. M. Margoliouth. Oxford: Clarendon, 1927, 22–24.

Melville, Herman. "Fragments of a Lost Gnostic Poem of the 12th Century." In *Collected Poems of Herman Melville,* ed. Howard Vincent. Chicago: Packard, 1947, 234.

Michelangelo [Buonarroti]. "Non ha l'ottimo artista alcun concetto." In *Michelangelo, the Poems,* ed. and trans. Christopher Ryan. London: Dent, 1996, 138–140.

Milton, John. "L'Allegro." In *John Milton.* ed. Stephen Orgel and Jonathan Goldberg. Oxford: Oxford University Press, The Oxford Authors, 1991, 22–25.

———. "On Time." In *John Milton.* ed. Stephen Orgel and Jonathan Goldberg. Oxford: Oxford University Press, The Oxford Authors, 1991, 15–16.

———. *Paradise Lost.* In *John Milton,* ed. Stephen Orgel and Jonathan Goldberg. Oxford: Oxford University Press, The Oxford Authors, 1991, III:401–420.

———. "Il Penseroso." In *John Milton.* ed. Stephen Orgel and Jonathan Goldberg. Oxford: Oxford University Press, The Oxford Authors, 1991, 25–30.

———. "Samson Agonistes." In *John Milton.* ed. Stephen Orgel and Jonathan Goldberg. Oxford: Oxford University Press, The Oxford Authors, 1991, 671–715.

Moore, Marianne. "A Grave." In *Collected Poems.* New York: Macmillan, 1951, 56–57.

———. "The Hero." In *Collected Poems.* New York: Macmillan, 1951, 15–16.

———. "In Distrust of Merits." In *Collected Poems.* New York: Macmillan, 1951, 135–137.

———. "'Keeping Their World Large.'" In *Collected Poems.* New York: Macmillan, 1951, 144–145.

———. "Nevertheless." In *Collected Poems.* New York: Macmillan, 1951, 127–128.

———. "The Mind Is an Enchanting Thing." In *Collected Poems.* New York: Macmillan, 1951, 133–134.

———. "What Are Years?" In *Collected Poems.* New York: Macmillan, 1951, 99.

Novalis. *Hymns to the Night.* Trans. Dick Higgins. Kingston, N.Y.: McPherson, 1988.

O'Hara, Frank. "The Day Lady Died." In *The Selected Poems of Frank O'Hara,* ed. Donald Allen. New York: Vintage, 1974, 146.

Owen, Wilfred. "Conscious." In *The Collected Poems of Wilfred Owen,* ed. C. Day Lewis. New York: New Directions, 1963 (reprint of 1920 edition), 63.

Peele, George. "Bethsabe's Song." In *George Peele,* ed. Sally Purcell. Salisbury, Eng.: Fyfield, 1972 (reprint of Oxford: Carcanet, 1972), 93–94.

Perelman, Bob. "Chronic Meanings [for Lee Hickman]." In *Ten to One.* Middletown, Conn.: Wesleyan University Press, 1999, 166–169.

Petrarch, Francesco. *Petrarch's Lyric Poems: The Rime Sparse and Other Lyrics,* trans. and ed. by Robert Durling. Cambridge, Mass.: Harvard University Press, 1976.

Plath, Sylvia. "Lady Lazarus." In *The Collected Poems,* ed. Ted Hughes. New York: Harper & Row, 1981, 244–247.

Pope, Alexander. *The Dunciad.* In *Pope: Poetical Works,* ed. Herbert Davis. New York: Oxford University Press, 1983, 547–584.

———. "The Rape of the Lock." In *Pope: Poetical Works,* ed. Herbert Davis. New York: Oxford University Press, 1983, 86–109.

———. "Windsor Forest." In *Pope: Poetical Works,* ed. Herbert Davis. New York: Oxford University Press, 1983, 37–50.

Pound, Ezra. *The Cantos of Ezra Pound.* New York: New Directions, 1975.

———. "Coda." In *Personae: Collected Shorter Poems of Ezra Pound.* London: Faber & Faber, 1952, 113.

———. "On His Own Face in a Glass." *Personae,* 49.

Propertius. *Elegies.* I.16, "The door's complaint." Ed. and trans. G. Goold. Cambridge, Mass.: Harvard University Press, Loeb Classical Library, 1990, 80–85.

———. *Elegies.* IV.11, "Cornelia from the grave." Ed. and trans. G. Goold. Cambridge, Mass.: Harvard University Press, Loeb Classical Library, 1990, 383–391.

———. *Elegies.* IV.7, "Cynthia's ghost." Ed. and trans. G. Goold. Cambridge, Mass.: Harvard University Press, Loeb Classical Library, 1990, 356–363.

Rilke, Rainer Maria. "Handinneres." In *The Selected Poetry of Rainer Maria Rilke,* ed. and trans. Stephen Mitchell. New York: Random House, 1984, 268–269.

Rimbaud, Arthur. "Voyelles." In *Rimbaud: Complete Works and Selected Letters,* trans. Wallace Fowlie. Chicago: University of Chicago Press, 1966, 120–122.

Rosenberg, Isaac. "In War." In *Collected Poems,* with a foreword by Siegfried Sassoon, ed. Ian Parsons. London: Chatto & Windus, 1979, 105–107.

Sappho. "Peer of the Gods." In *Sappho: A Garland,* trans. Jim Powell. New York: Farrar, Straus, & Giroux, 1993, 23–24.

Sassoon, Siegfried. "The Fathers." In *The War Poems of Siegfried Sassoon,* ed. Rupert Hart-Davis. London: Faber & Faber, 1983, 93.

———. "Suicide in the Trenches." In *The War Poems of Siegfried Sassoon,* ed. Rupert Hart-Davis. London: Faber & Faber, 1983, 119.

Sáxá. "Already you have seen going up to the spirit world." In *Tlingit Myths and Texts,* ed. John R. Swanton. Bulletin 39, Bureau of American Ethnology. Washington, D.C.: Smithsonian Institution, 1919, 406.

Scipione [Gino Bonichi]. "Sento gli strilli degli angioli." In *La Terra è secca, ha sete.* Trans. Brunella Antomarini and Susan Stewart. Milan: Charta, 2001, 27.

Shakespeare, William. *The Merchant of Venice.* In *Arden Edition of the Works of William Shakespeare,* ed. John Russell Brown. Cambridge, Mass.: Harvard University Press, 1959.

———. *A Midsummer Night's Dream.* Ed. Arthur Quiller-Couch and John Dover Wilson. Cambridge: Cambridge University Press, 1968.

———. Sonnet 54. In *Shakespeare's Sonnets,* ed. Katherine Duncan-Jones. London: Nelson, The Arden Shakespeare, 1997, 219.

————. Sonnet 55. In *Shakespeare's Sonnets*, ed. Katherine Duncan-Jones. London: Nelson, The Arden Shakespeare, 1997, 221.

————. Sonnet 69. In *Shakespeare's Sonnets*, ed. Katherine Duncan-Jones. London: Nelson, The Arden Shakespeare, 1997, 249.

————. *The Tragedy of Hamlet, Prince of Denmark*. Ed. George Lyman Kittredge; rev. Irving Ribner. Waltham, Mass.: Blaisdell, 1967.

Shelley, Percy. "England in 1819." In *Shelley's Poetry and Prose*, ed. Donald Reiman and Sharon Powers. New York: Norton, 1977, 311.

————. "Ode to the West Wind." In *Shelley's Poetry and Prose*, ed. Donald Reiman and Sharon Powers. New York: Norton, 1977, 221–223.

Skelton, John. "Speak Parrot." In *The Complete Poems of John Skelton*, ed. Philip Henderson. London: Dent, 1931, 259–281.

Smith, Charlotte. "Beachy Head." In *The Poems of Charlotte Smith*, ed. Stuart Curran. New York: Oxford, 1993, 217–247.

Spenser, Edmund. "Amoretti LXIV" [follows LXIII as "LXIIII" in this edition]. In *The Poetical Works of Edmund Spenser*, ed. J. C. Smith and E. De Selincourt. London: Oxford University Press, 1960, 573.

————. "Amoretti LXXV." In *The Poetical Works of Edmund Spenser*, ed. J. C. Smith and E. De Selincourt. London: Oxford University Press, 1960, 575.

————. *The Faerie Queene*. In *The Poetical Works of Edmund Spenser*, ed. J. C. Smith and E. De Selincourt. London: Oxford University Press, 1960, 1–406.

Stevens, Wallace. "Certain Phenomena of Sound." In *The Collected Poems of Wallace Stevens*. New York: Knopf, 1969, 286–287.

————. "The Creations of Sound." In *The Collected Poems of Wallace Stevens*. New York: Knopf, 1969, 310–311.

————. "Depression Before Spring." In *The Collected Poems of Wallace Stevens*. New York: Knopf, 1969, 63.

————. "Earthy Anecdote." In *The Collected Poems of Wallace Stevens*. New York: Knopf, 1969, 3.

————. "Examination of the Hero in a Time of War." In *The Collected Poems of Wallace Stevens*. New York: Knopf, 1969, 278.

————. "A High-Toned Old Christian Woman." In *The Collected Poems of Wallace Stevens*. New York: Knopf, 1969, 59.

————. "Peter Quince at the Clavier." In *The Collected Poems of Wallace Stevens*. New York: Knopf, 1969, 89–92.

————. "Ploughing on Sunday." In *The Collected Poems of Wallace Stevens*. New York: Knopf, 1969, 20.

————. "To the Roaring Wind." In *The Collected Poems of Wallace Stevens*. New York: Knopf, 1969, 113.

Swift, Jonathan. "The Lady's Dressing Room." In *The Poems of Jonathan Swift*, 3 vols., ed. Harold Williams. Oxford: Clarendon, 1937, II:524–530.

Tasso, Torquato. *Jerusalem Delivered*, Trans. and Ed. Ralph Nash. Detroit: Wayne State University Press, 1987.

Tennyson, Alfred, Lord. "The Charge of the Light Brigade." In *The Poems of*

Tennyson, ed. Christopher Ricks. New York: Norton; London: Longman, 1969, 1034–1036.

———. "The Epic." In *The Poems of Tennyson*, ed. Christopher Ricks. New York: Norton; London: Longman, 1969, 582–584.

———. "Maud." In *The Poems of Tennyson*, ed. Christopher Ricks. New York: Norton; London: Longman, 1969, 1037–1093.

———. "The Princess." In *The Poems of Tennyson*, ed. Christopher Ricks. New York: Norton; London: Longman, 1969, 741–844.

———. "Ulysses." In *The Poems of Tennyson*, ed. Christopher Ricks. New York: Norton; London: Longman, 1969, 560–566.

Thomas, Dylan. "Vision and Prayer." In *The Collected Poems of Dylan Thomas*. New York: New Directions, 1957, 154–165.

Thomson, James. *The City of Dreadful Night*. In *The Poetical Works of James Thomson; The City of Dreadful Night*, 2 vols., ed. Bertram Dobell with a memoir of the author. London: Reeves & Turner, 1895, I:122–172.

———. "Insomnia." In *The Poetical Works of James Thomson; The City of Dreadful Night*, 2 vols., ed. Bertram Dobell with a memoir of the author. London: Reeves & Turner, 1895, II:31–43.

Traherne, Thomas. *Centuries of Meditations by Thomas Traherne*. Ed. Bertram Dobell. London: Dobell, 1908.

———. *Centuries, Poems, and Thanksgivings*. 2 vols. Ed. H. M. Margoliouth. Oxford: Clarendon, 1958.

———. *Commentaries of Heaven*. ADD MS. 63054, British Library, London.

———. *Poems, Centuries and Three Thanksgivings*. Ed. Anne Ridler. London: Oxford University Press, 1966.

———. *The Poetical Works of Thomas Traherne*. Ed. Bertram Dobell. London: Dobell, 1903.

———. *Select Meditations*. Osborn ms. b.308, Beinecke Library, Yale University, New Haven, Conn.

Vaughan, Henry. "Midnight." In *Complete Poems*, ed. Alan Rudrum. London: Penguin, 1976, 174–175.

———. "The Night." In *Complete Poems*, ed. Alan Rudrum. London: Penguin, 1976, 289–290.

———. "They are all gone into the world of light!" In *Complete Poems*, ed. Alan Rudrum. London: Penguin, 1976, 246–247.

Verlaine, Paul. "Il pleut doucement sur la ville." In *Oeuvres complètes de Paul Verlaine*, 2 vols. Paris: Messein, 1919, I:155–156.

Virgil. *The Aeneid of Virgil*. Trans. Allen Mandelbaum. Berkeley: University of California Press, 1981.

Walcott, Derek. *Another Life*. New York: Farrar, Straus, 1973.

———. "Homecoming: Anse la Raye." In *The Gulf*. New York: Farrar, Straus, & Giroux, 1970, 84–86.

———. "Iona: Mabouya Valley." In *Sea Grapes*. New York: Farrar, Straus, & Giroux, 1976, 40–45.

———. *Omeros.* New York: Farrar, Straus, & Giroux, 1990.

———. "The Sea Is History." In *The Star-Apple Kingdom.* New York: Farrar, Straus, & Giroux, 1979, 25–28.

Warton, Joseph. *The Pleasures of Melancholy.* London: Dodsley, 1747.

Watson, Thomas. *The Hekatompathia or Passionate Centurie of Love* (1582). Facsimile reproduction and introduction by S. K. Heninger Jr. Gainesville, Fla.: Scholars' Facsimiles and Reprints, 1964.

Whitman, Walt. "Come Up from the Fields Father." In *Complete Poetry and Collected Prose.* New York: Library of America, 1982, 436–438.

———. "How Solemn as One by One." In *Complete Poetry and Collected Prose.* New York: Library of America, 1982, 453–454.

———. "Reconciliation." In *Complete Poetry and Collected Prose.* New York: Library of America, 1982, 453.

———. "Vocalism." In *Complete Poetry and Collected Prose.* New York: Library of America, 1982, 509–510.

Williams, William Carlos. "Asphodel, That Greeny Flower." In *Selected Poems.* New York: New Directions, 1968, 142–155.

Wilmot, John, Earl of Rochester. "Love and Life." In *The Complete Poems of John Wilmot, Earl of Rochester,* ed. David M. Vieth. New Haven, Conn.: Yale University Press, 1968, 90.

Wordsworth, William. *The Prelude 1799, 1805, 1850.* Ed. Jonathan Wordsworth, M. H. Abrams, and Stephen Gill. New York: Norton, 1979.

———. "A Slumber Did Her Spirit Seal." In *Lyrical Ballads and Other Poems, 1797–1800,* ed. James Butler and Karen Green. Ithaca, N.Y.: Cornell University Press, The Cornell Wordsworth, 164.

———. "Surprised by Joy." In *Poems,* 2 vols., ed. John O. Hayden. London: Penguin, 1977, I:863.

———. "The Tables Turned." In *Poems,* ed. John O. Hayden. London: Penguin, 1977, 356–357.

Wyatt, Sir Thomas. *The Complete Poems.* Ed. R. A. Rebholz. London: Penguin, 1988.

Yeats, William Butler. "The Lake Isle of Innisfree." In *The Collected Poems of W. B. Yeats.* New York: Macmillan, 1974, 39.

Young, Edward. "Night Thoughts." In *The Poetical Works of Edward Young, with a Memoir by Rev. J. Mitford.* Boston: Houghton Mifflin, 1880, 5–344.

OTHER WORKS CITED

Abraham, Nicolas. "Notes on the Phantom: A Complement to Freud's Metapsychology," trans. Nicholas Rand. *Critical Inquiry* 13, no. 2 (Winter 1987): 287–292.

———. *Rythmes: de l'oeuvre, de la traduction, et de la psychanalyse.* Ed. Nicholas T. Rand and Maria Torok. Paris: Flammarion, 1985.

Abraham, Nicolas, and Maria Torok. *The Shell and the Kernel: Renewals of Psychoanalysis.* Vol. I. Chicago: University of Chicago Press, 1994.

———. *The Wolf Man's Magic Word.* Trans. Nicholas Rand. Minneapolis: University of Minnesota Press, 1986.

Abrahams, Roger D. and George Foss. *Anglo-American Folksong Style.* Englewood Cliffs, N.J.: Prentice Hall, 1968.

Adorno, Theodor W. "On Lyric Poetry and Society." In *Notes to Literature,* 2 vols., ed. Rolf Tiedemann; trans. Shierry Weber Nicholsen. New York: Columbia University Press, 1991–1992, I:37–54.

Agamben, Giorgio. *Language and Death: The Place of Negativity.* Trans. Karen Pinkus. Minneapolis: University of Minnesota Press, 1991.

———. "Pascoli and the Thought of the Voice." In *The End of the Poem: Studies in Poetics,* trans. Daniel Heller-Roazen. Stanford, Calif.: Stanford University Press, 1999, 62–75.

Agrippa, Henry Cornelius. *Three Books of Occult Philosophy.* Trans. [J]ohn F[rench?]. London: Printed by R.W. for Gregory Moule, 1651.

———. *Three Books of Occult Philosophy or Magic by Henry Cornelius Agrippa von Nettesheim: Book I. Natural Magic,* ed. Willis Whitehead. Chicago: Halan & Whitehead, 1898.

Alberti, Rafael. *Selected Poems.* Ed. Ben Belitt. Berkeley: University of California Press, 1966.

Allchin, A. M., Anne Ridler, and Julia Smith. *Profitable Wonders: Aspects of Thomas Traherne.* Oxford: Amate, 1989.

Alter, Robert. "Psalms." In *The Literary Guide to the Bible,* ed. Robert Alter and Frank Kermode. Cambridge, Mass.: Harvard University Press, 1987, 244–262.

Althusser, Louis. *Lenin and Philosophy.* Trans. Ben Brewster. New York: Monthly Review Press, 1971.

Altieri, Charles. *Self and Sensibility in Contemporary American Poetry.* Cambridge: Cambridge University Press, 1984.

———. *Subjective Agency: A Theory of First-Person Expressivity and Its Social Implications.* Oxford: Blackwell, 1994.

Alvarez, A. *Night: Night Life, Night Language, Sleep, and Dreams.* New York: Norton, 1995.

Ames, Kenneth John. *The Religious Language of Thomas Traherne's Centuries.* New York: Revisionist, 1978.

Ammons, A. R. *The Selected Poems.* New York: Norton, 1986.

Ancona, Ronnie. *Time and the Erotic in Horace's Odes.* Durham, N.C.: Duke University Press, 1994.

Antomarini, Brunella. "Il Fenomeno poetico come ereditá della cognizione corporea." *Pagine* (Autumn 1999): 24–26.

Argyle, Michael. "The System of Bodily Communication." In *The Body as a Medium of Expression,* ed. Jonathan Benthall and Ted Polhemus. New York: Dutton, 1975, 143–161.

Ariosto, Ludovico. *Orlando Furioso.* Trans. William Stewart Rose; ed. Stewart A. Baker and A. Bartlett Giamatti. Indianapolis: Bobbs-Merrill, 1968.

Aristotle. *Aristotle on the Art of Fiction: "The Poetics."* Trans. and ed. L. J. Potts. Cambridge: Cambridge University Press, 1968.

———. "De Anima." Trans. J. A. Smith. In *The Basic Works of Aristotle*, ed. Richard McKeon. New York: Random House, 1941, 535–603.

———. *De Generatione Animalium.* Trans. D. M. Balme. Oxford: Clarendon, 1992.

———. *De Poetica.* Trans. Ingram Bywater. In *The Basic Works of Aristotle*, ed. Richard McKeon. New York: Random House, 1941, 1453–1487.

———. "Nicomachean Ethics." Trans. W. D. Ross. In *The Basic Works of Aristotle*, ed. Richard McKeon. New York: Random House, 1941, 927–1112.

———. "Physics." In *The Basic Works of Aristotle*, ed. Richard McKeon. New York: Random House, 1941, 259–269.

Armstrong, D. M. *Bodily Sensations*, London: Routledge & Kegan Paul, 1962.

Ashbery, John. *April Galleons.* New York: Viking, 1987.

Athanassakis, Apostolos N., trans. *The Orphic Hymns: Text, Translation and Notes.* Missoula, Mont.: Scholars, 1977.

Attridge, Derek. *Poetic Rhythm: An Introduction.* Cambridge: Cambridge University Press, 1995.

Auden, W. H. *Collected Shorter Poems, 1927–1957.* New York: Vintage, 1975.

Augustine. *Confessions.* Trans. R. S. Pine-Coffin. London: Penguin, 1961.

———. *De Musica.* Trans. W. F. Jackson Knight. London: Orthological Institute, 1949.

Austin, J. L. *How to Do Things with Words.* Ed. J. O. Urmson. New York: Oxford University Press, 1962.

Aviram, Amittai. *Telling Rhythm: Body and Meaning in Poetry.* Ann Arbor: University of Michigan Press, 1994.

Babees Book and A Booke of Precedence. Ed. F. J. Furnivall. Extra series, No. 8. London: Early English Text Society, 1869.

Bakhtin, M. M. *The Dialogic Imagination: Four Essays by M. M. Bakhtin.* Ed. Michael Holquist; trans. Caryl Emerson and Michael Holquist. Austin: University of Texas Press, 1981.

———. *Speech Genres and Other Late Essays.* Trans. Vern W. McGee; ed. Caryl Emerson and Michael Holquist. Austin: University of Texas Press, 1986.

Balakier, James J. "Thomas Traherne's Dobell Series and the Baconian Model of Experience." *English Studies* 70, no. 3 (June 1989): 233–247.

Ball, Hugo. *Flight Out of Time: A Dada Diary.* Ed. John Elderfield; trans. Ann Raimes. New York: Viking, 1974.

Balzac, Honoré de. *The Unknown Masterpiece.* Trans. Michael Neff. Berkeley, Calif.: Creative Arts, 1984.

Bann, Stephen. "Shrines, Curiosities, and the Rhetoric of Display. In *Visual Display*, ed. Lynne Cooke and Peter Wollen. Seattle: Bay, 1995, 14–29.

Barfield, Owen. *Poetic Diction: A Study in Meaning.* Hanover, N.H.: University Press of New England, 1987.

Baring-Gould, Rev. S., and Rev. H. Fleetwood Sheppard, eds. *Songs and Ballads of the West: A Collection Made from the Mouths of the People.* London: Methuen, 1892.

Barker, Francis E. "The Religious Poetry of Richard Crashaw." *Church Quarterly Review* 96 (1923): 39–65.

Barthes, Roland. *The Responsibilities of Forms.* Trans. Richard Howard. New York: Hill & Wang, 1985.

Bate, Walter Jackson. *John Keats.* Cambridge, Mass.: Harvard University Press, 1963.

Bates, J. A. V. "The Communicative Hand." In *The Body as a Medium of Expression,* ed. Jonathan Benthall and Ted Polhemus. New York: Dutton, 1975, 175–194.

Baxandall, Michael. *Painting and Experience in Fifteenth Century Italy.* Oxford: Oxford University Press, 1972.

Beardsley, Monroe C., and W. K. Wimsatt. "The Intentional Fallacy." In *The Verbal Icon,* ed. W. K. Wimsatt. Louisville: University of Kentucky Press, 1982, 3–18.

Benedetti, Sergio. "Caravaggio's *Taking of Christ*" (Letter). *Burlington Magazine* 137, no. 1102 (January 1995): 37–38.

———. "Caravaggio's *Taking of Christ:* A Masterpiece Rediscovered." *Burlington Magazine* 135, no. 1088 (November 1993): 731–741.

Benjamin, Walter. *Illuminations.* Ed. Hannah Arendt; trans. Harry Zohn. New York: Schocken, 1969.

Benveniste, Emile. *Problems in General Linguistics.* Trans. Mary Elizabeth Meek. Coral Gables, Fla.: University of Miami Press, 1971.

Berger, Harry. "The System of Early Modern Painting," *Representations* 62 (Spring 1998): 31–52.

Bergson, Henri. *Matter and Memory.* New York: Zone, 1988.

Berry, Francis. *Poetry and the Physical Voice.* London: Routledge & Kegan Paul, 1962.

Bidart, Frank. *Collected Poems 1965–90: In the Western Night.* New York: Farrar, Straus, & Giroux, 1990.

Bion. Idyl 1, "Lament for Adonis." Trans. Mrs. [Elizabeth Barrett] Browning. In *Greek Poets in English Verse,* ed. W. H. Appleton. Boston: Houghton Mifflin, 1893, 288–293.

Birdwhistell, Ray L. *Kinesics and Context: Essays on Body Motion Communication.* Philadelphia: University of Pennsylvania Press, 1970.

Bishop, Elizabeth. *The Complete Poems 1927–1979.* New York: Farrar, Straus, & Giroux, 1983.

———. "In the Village." In *The Collected Prose,* ed. Robert Giroux. New York: Farrar, Straus, 1984, 251-274.

Blau, Joseph Leon. *The Christian Interpretation of Cabala in the Renaissance.* New York: Columbia University Press, 1944.

Bloom, Harold. *Wallace Stevens: The Poems of Our Climate.* Ithaca, N.Y.: Cornell University Press, 1973.

Boas, Franz. "Mythology and Folk-tales of the North American Indian." *Journal of American Folklore* 27, no. 106 (October–December 1914): 374–410.

———. *The Social Organization and the Secret Societies of the Kwakiutl Indians*. Report of the National Museum. Washington, D.C.: Smithsonian Institution, 1895.

Bolton, Henry Carrington. *The Counting Out Rhymes of Children: Their Antiquity, Origin, and Wide Distribution. A Study in Folk-Lore*. New York: Appleton, 1888.

Bond, Richmond *English Burlesque Poetry 1700–1750*. Cambridge, Mass.: Harvard University Press, 1932.

Bonnot, Étienne, Abbé de Condillac. "A Treatise on the Sensations." Trans. Franklin Phip in collaboration with Harlan Lane. In *Philosophical Writings*. Hillsdale, N.J.: Erlbaum, 1982, II:155–339.

Bowra, C. M. *From Virgil to Milton*. London: Macmillan, 1948.

Boys, Richard C. *Sir Richard Blackmore and the Wits*. New York: Octagon, 1969 (first published by the University of Michigan Press, 1949).

Bradbrook, M. C. *The School of Night: A Study in the Literary Relationships of Sir Walter Ralegh*. Cambridge: Cambridge University Press, 1936.

Brandi, Cesare. "L'Epistemé caravaggesca." *Colloquio* (1974): 9–17.

Brathwayt, Richard. *Essaies upon the Five Senses with a pithie one upon Detraction continued with sundry Christian Resolues, full of passion and devotion, purposely composed for the zealously-disposed*. 2d ed. London: Whittaker, 1620.

Bronson, Bertrand. *The Ballad as Song*. Berkeley: University of California Press, 1969.

Brooke, Stopford A. *The History of Early English Literature*. New York: Macmillan, 1892.

Brooks, Gwendolyn. *Report from Part One*. Detroit: Broadside, 1972.

———. *Selected Poems*. New York: Harper & Row, 1963.

Brose, Margaret. "Leopardi and the Feminine Sublime." Unpublished manuscript, Modern Language Association Meetings, 28 December 1998, San Francisco.

———. "Remembrance and the Rhetorical Sublime in Leopardi's Lyric." *Stanford Literature Review* 6 (Spring 1989): 115–133.

Brower, Reuben. "Lady Winchelsea and the Poetic Tradition of the Seventeenth Century." *Studies in Philology* 42, no.1 (1945): 61–80.

Brown, Carleton, ed. *English Lyrics of the XIIIth Century*. Oxford: Clarendon, 1932.

Bruns, Gerald L. *Modern Poetry and the Idea of Language*. New Haven, Conn.: Yale University Press, 1974.

Bryson, Norman. *Looking at the Overlooked: Four Essays on Still Life Painting*. Cambridge, Mass.: Harvard University Press, 1990.

Burckhardt, Titus. *Sacred Art of East and West: Its Principles and Methods*. London: Perennial, 1967.

Burke, Edmund. *A Philosophical Enquiry into the Origin of Our Ideas of the Sublime and Beautiful*. Ed. J. T. Boulton. London: Routledge & Kegan Paul; New York: Columbia University Press, 1958.

Burke, Kenneth. "On Musicality in Verse." In *The Philosophy of Literary Form: Studies in Symbolic Action*. Berkeley: University of California Press, 1967, 369–378.

Burris, Sidney. "An Empire of Poetry." *Southern Review* 27, no. 3 (1991): 558–574.

Cajani, Luigi. and Silvia Saba. "Potere politico e spazio sociale: il controllo della notte a Venezia nei secoli XIII–XV." *Laboratorio di storia* 3 (1991): 46–66. Florence: Ponte alle Grazie.

Calasso, Roberto. *The Marriage of Cadmus and Harmony*. Trans. Tim Parks. New York: Knopf, 1993.

Callan, Norman. "Augustan Reflective Poetry." In *From Dryden to Johnson*, ed. Boris Ford. Harmondsworth, Eng.: Penguin, 1957, 357–362.

Campion, Thomas. *The Works of Thomas Campion*. Ed. Walter R. Davis. New York: Norton, 1969.

Canons and Decrees of the Council of Trent. Trans. Rev. H. J. Schroeder. Rockford, Ill.: Tan, 1978 (first published by Herder Books, 1941).

Cardella, Lorenzo. *Memorie storiche de'Cardinali della santa romana chiesa*. Rome: Pagliarini, 1792–1797.

Carroll, Lewis [Charles Dodgson]. *The Annotated Alice*. Ed. Martin Gardner. New York: Clarkson Potter, 1960.

Carson, Anne. *eros the bittersweet*. Normal, Ill.: Dalkey Archive Press, 1998 (first published by Princeton University Press, 1986).

Chambers, A. B. "Crooked Crosses in Donne and Crashaw." In *New Perspectives on the Life and Art of Richard Crashaw*, ed. John R. Roberts. Columbia: University of Missouri Press, 1990, 157–173.

Chandler, James. *England in 1819: The Politics of Literary Culture and the Case of Romantic Historicism*. Chicago: University of Chicago Press, 1998.

Chapman, George. *The Poems of George Chapman*. Ed. Phyllis Brooks Bartlett. New York: Modern Language Association; London: Oxford University Press, 1941.

———. *Linguistics and Literature*. Totowa, NJ.: Littlefield, Adams, 1973.

Chartier, Roger, ed. *A History of Private Life: Vol. III. Passions of the Renaissance*, ed. Roger Chartier; trans. Arthur Goldhammer. Cambridge, Mass.: Harvard University Press, Belknap, 1989.

Chase, Cynthia. *Decomposing Figures: Rhetorical Readings in the Romantic Tradition*. Baltimore: Johns Hopkins University Press, 1986.

Chew, Samuel. *The Pilgrimage of the Life of Man*. New Haven, Conn.: Yale University Press, 1962.

Childs, Brevard S. *Biblical Theology of the Old and New Testament*. Minneapolis: Fortress, 1993.

Chipp, Herschel. *Theories of Modern Art*. Berkeley: University of California Press, 1968.

Chovil, Nicole. "Facing Others: A Social Communicative Perspective on Facial Displays." In *The Psychology of Facial Expression*, ed. James A. Russell and José-Miguel Fernández-Dols. Cambridge: Cambridge University Press, 1997, 321–333.

Cirasa, Robert. "Thomas Hardy's Poems of 1912–1913: The Engagement of Loss." *Thomas Hardy Year Book* 17 (1988): 20–27.

Clare, John. *John Clare By Himself.* Ed. Eric Robinson and David Powell, Manchester, Carcanet, 1996.

———. *A Midsummer Cushion.* ed. Kelsey Thornton and Anne Tibble. Ashington, Eng.: Carcanet, 1990.

Classen, Constance, David Howes, and Anthony Synnott. *Aroma: The Cultural History of Smell,* New York: Routledge, 1994.

Clements, A. L. *The Mystical Poetry of Thomas Traherne.* Cambridge, Mass.: Harvard University Press, 1969.

Coleridge, Samuel Taylor. *Biographia Literaria.* 2 vols. Ed. John Shawcross. Oxford: Clarendon, 1907.

———. *The Complete Poems.* Ed. William Keach. London: Penguin.

———. *The Table Talk and Omniana of Samuel Taylor Coleridge.* Ed. T. Ashe. London: Bell, 1923.

Collingwood, R. G. *The Principles of Art.* London: Oxford University Press, 1958.

Corrain, Lucia. "Chiara di luna e pittura di luce." *Laboratorio di storia* 3 (1991): 165–169. Florence: Ponte alle Grazie.

———. "Loca occulta, dimensioni notturne e legittima difesa: per un paradigma del diritto di punire." *Laboratorio di storia* 3 (1991): 127–140. Florence: Ponte alle Grazie.

———. "Raffigurare la notte" *Laboratorio di storia* 3 (1991): 141–161. Florence: Ponte alle Grazie.

Cowper, William. *The Poems of William Cowper.* 2 vols. Ed. John D. Baird and Charles Ryskamp. Oxford: Clarendon, 1980.

Crashaw, Richard. *A Concordance to the English Poetry of Richard Crashaw.* Comp. Robert M. Cooper. Troy, N.Y.: Whitson, 1981.

———. *Steps to the Temple, Delights of the Muses, and Other Poems,* ed. A. R. Waller. Cambridge: Cambridge University Press, 1904 (reprinted from the Paris, 1652, edition).

Croce, Benedetto. *Theory and History of Historiography.* Trans. Douglas Ainslie. London: Harrap, 1921.

Cromek, R. H. *Remains of Nithsdale and Galloway Song.* London: Cadell & Davies, 1810.

Crouzet-Pavan, Elizabeth. "Notte in città, notte in campagna tra Medioevo ed Età moderna." *Laboratorio di storia* 3 (1991): 30–45. Florence: Ponte alle Grazie.

Crump, Thomas. *The Anthropology of Numbers.* Cambridge: Cambridge University Press, 1990.

Culleton, Claire A. "James Thomson and the Influence of *The City of Dreadful Night* on T. S. Eliot." *Yeats Eliot Review* 11, no. 4 (Fall 1992): 85–89.

Curran, Stuart. *Poetic Form and British Romanticism.* New York: Oxford University Press, 1986.

Curtius, Ernst Robert. *European Literature and the Latin Middle Ages.* Trans. Willard Trask. New York: Harper,1953.

D'Alessandro, Jean M. Ellis. *When in the Shade . . . : Imaginal Equivalents in Anne the Countess of Winchelsea's Poetry.* Studi di Anglistica. Verona: Del Bianco, 1989.

Damasio, Antonio R. "Aphasia." *New England Journal of Medicine* 326, no. 8 (20 February 1992): 531–539.

———. *The Feeling of What Happens: Body and Emotion in the Making of Consciousness.* New York: Harcourt Brace, 1999.

Dauenhauer, Richard. "Notes on Swanton Numbers 80 and 81," *Journal of American Folklore* 94, no. 3 (July–September 1981): 358–364.

Davie, Donald. *Thomas Hardy and British Poetry.* New York: Oxford University Press, 1972.

Day, Malcolm. *Thomas Traherne.* Boston: Twayne, 1982.

De Man, Paul. *The Rhetoric of Romanticism.* New York: Columbia University Press, 1984.

De Rougement, Denis. *Love in the Western World.* Trans. Montgomery Belgion. Princeton, N.J.: Princeton University Press, 1983.

de Saussure, Ferdinand. *Course in General Linguistics.* Ed. Charles Bally and Albert Sechehaye in collaboration with Albert Riedlinger; trans. Wade Baskin. New York: McGraw-Hill, 1959.

Deacon, George. *John Clare and the Folk Tradition.* London: Sinclair Browne, 1983.

Deese, James. *Psycholinguistics.* Boston: Allyn & Bacon, 1970.

Defoe, Daniel. *Robinson Crusoe.* Ed. Michael Shinagel. New York: Norton, 1975.

Deleuze, Gilles. *The Fold. Leibniz and the Baroque.* Trans. Tom Conley. Minneapolis: University of Minnesota Press, 1993, 11–12.

DeNeef, A. Leigh. *Traherne in Dialogue: Heidegger, Lacan and Derrida.* Durham, N.C.: Duke University Press, 1988.

Dennett, Daniel. "Conditions of Personhood." In *The Identities of Persons,* ed. Amelie Oksenberg Rorty. Berkeley: University of California Press, 1976, 175–196.

Descartes, René. *Meditations on First Philosophy.* Trans. Elizabeth S. Haldane and G. R. T. Ross; ed. Stanley Tweyman. London: Routledge, 1993.

Dickinson, Emily. *The Poems of Emily Dickinson.* 3 vols. Cambridge, Mass.: Harvard University Press, 1979.

Diderot, Denis. *Diderot's Early Philosophical Works.* Trans. Margaret Jourdain. Chicago: Open Court, 1916.

Didier-Weill, Alain. *Invocations: Dionysos, Moïse, Saint Paul et Freud.* Paris: Calmann-Lévy, 1998.

Dixon Hunt, John. *The Figure in the Landscape: Poetry, Painting and Gardening during the Eighteenth Century.* Baltimore: Johns Hopkins University Press, 1976.

————. "Picturesque Mirrors and the Ruins of the Past." *Art History* 4, no. 3 (September 1981): 264–270.

Dizionario di erudizione storico-ecclesiastica. Vol. LI. Comp. Gaetano Morori Romano. Venice: Emiliana, 1851.

Dobbie, Elliott Van Kirk, ed. *The Anglo-Saxon Minor Poems.* New York: Columbia University Press, 1942.

Dolittle, Hilda. [H.D.] *Collected Poems 1912–1944.* Ed. Louis L. Martz. New York: New Directions, 1983.

Dominique, Pierre Charles. *Ecology and Behaviour of Nocturnal Primates.* Trans. R. D. Martin. New York: Columbia University Press, 1977.

Donne, John. *The Complete English Poems.* Ed. A. J. Smith. London: Penguin, 1976.

Drijvers, Pius. *The Psalms: Their Structure and Meaning.* New York: Herder & Herder, 1964.

Driver, Harold E. *Indians of North America.* Chicago: University of Chicago Press, 1961.

Elias, Norbert. *The History of Manners: The Civilizing Process.* Vol. I, trans. Edmund Jephcott. New York: Pantheon, 1978.

————. *Time: An Essay.* Trans. Edmund Jephcott. Oxford: Blackwell, 1992.

Eliot, George. *Essays of George Eliot.* Ed. Thomas Pinney. New York: Columbia University Press, 1963.

Eliot, T. S. *Collected Poems 1909–1962.* New York: Harcourt, Brace & World, 1970.

Encyclopaedia Britannica. 11th ed. Cambridge: Cambridge University Press, 1910.

Encyclopedia of Poetry and Poetics. Ed. Alex Preminger, Frank J. Warnke, and O. B. Hardison Jr. Princeton, N.J.: Princeton University Press, 1965.

Evert, Walter H. *Aesthetic and Myth in the Poetry of Keats.* Princeton, N.J.: Princeton University Press, 1965.

Feld, Steven. *Sound and Sentiment: Birds, Weeping, Poetics and Song in Kaluli Expression.* Philadelphia: University of Pennsylvania Press, 1990.

Ferguson, Margaret W. *Trials of Desire: Renaissance Defenses of Poetry.* New Haven, Conn.: Yale University Press, 1983.

Ferry, Anne. *The Title to the Poem.* Stanford, Calif.: Stanford University Press, 1996.

Ficino, Marsilio. "Five Questions Concerning the Mind." Trans. Josephine L. Burroughs. In *The Renaissance Philosophy of Man,* ed. Ernst Cassirer, Paul Oskar Kristeller, and John Herman Randall. Chicago: University of Chicago Press, 1956, 185–212.

————. *Marsilio Ficino: The Philebus Commentary.* Trans. and ed. Michael J. B. Allen. Berkeley: University of California Press, 1975.

Field, Eugene. *Poems of Childhood.* New York: Scribner's, 1920.

Fillmore, Charles. *Lectures on Deixis.* Center for the Study of Language and Information. Stanford, Calif.: Stanford University Press, 1997.

Filreis, Alan. *Wallace Stevens and the Actual World*. Princeton, N.J.: Princeton University Press, 1991.

Finch, Anne. *Miscellany Poems on Several Occasions*. London: Printed for J.B. and sold by Benj. Tooke, 1713.

——. *Poems by Anne Finch, Countess of Winchelsea 1661–1720*. Ed. John Middleton Murry. New York: Cape, 1928.

——. *The Poems of Anne, Countess of Winchelsea*, ed. Myra Reynolds. Chicago: University of Chicago Press, 1903.

——. *Selected Poems of Anne Finch, Countess of Winchelsea*. Ed. Katherine M. Rogers. New York: Ungar, 1979.

Finch, Annie. *The Ghost of Meter: Culture and Prosody in American Free Verse*. Ann Arbor: University of Michigan Press, 1993.

Fineman, Joel. *Shakespeare's Perjured Eye: The Invention of Poetic Subjectivity in the Sonnets*. Berkeley: University of California Press, 1986.

Firor, Ruth A. *Folkways in Thomas Hardy*. New York: Russell & Russell, 1931.

Fletcher, Angus. *Colors of the Mind: Conjectures on Thinking in Literature*. Cambridge, Mass.: Harvard University Press, 1991.

Focillon, Henri. *The Life of Forms in Art*. Trans. Charles Beecher Hogan and George Kubler. New Haven, Conn.: Yale University Press, 1942.

Fowler, Alastair. *Spenser and the Numbers of Time*. London: Routledge, 1964.

Fraistat, Neil, ed. *Poems in Their Place*. Chapel Hill: University of North Carolina Press, 1986.

Frank, Lawrence. "Tactile Communication." In *Explorations in Communication: An Anthology*, ed. Edward Carpenter and Marshall McLuhan. Boston: Beacon, 1960, 4–11.

Franklin, John Hope. *From Slavery to Freedom: A History of African Americans*. 7th ed. New York: Knopf, 1994.

Freud, Sigmund. *Beyond the Pleasure Principle*. Trans. and ed. James Strachey. New York: Norton, 1961.

——. *Civilization and Its Discontents*. Trans. and ed. James Strachey. New York: Norton, 1961.

——. "Instincts and Their Vicissitudes." In *The Standard Edition of the Complete Psychological Works of Sigmund Freud*, trans. James Strachey. London: Hogarth, 1955, XIV:117–140.

——. "Notes upon a Case of Obsessional Neurosis." In *The Standard Edition of the Complete Psychological Works of Sigmund Freud*, trans. James Strachey. London: Hogarth, 1955, X:153–318.

Friar, Kimon, and John Malcolm Brinnin, eds. *Modern Poetry: American and British*. New York: Appleton-Century-Crofts, 1951.

Frost, Robert. *The Poetry of Robert Frost*. Ed. Edward Connery Lathem. New York: Holt, Rinehart & Winston, 1969.

Fry, Paul. *A Defense of Poetry*. Stanford: Stanford University Press, 1995.

Fussell, Paul, Jr. *The Great War and Modern Memory*. London: Oxford University Press, 1977.

————. *Theory of Prosody in Eighteenth-Century England*. New London: Connecticut College, 1954.

Gage, John. *Color in Turner: Poetry and Truth*, New York: Praeger, 1969.

Gage, John T. *In the Arresting Eye: The Rhetoric of Imagism*. Baton Rouge: Louisiana State University Press, 1981.

Gale, Richard M. "Indexical Signs, Egocentric Particulars, and Token-Reflexive Words." In *The Encyclopedia of Philosophy*, ed. Paul Edwards. New York: Macmillan, 1972, IV:151–155.

García Lorca, Federico. *The Selected Poems of Federico García Lorca*, ed. Francisco García Lorca and Donald M. Allen. New York: New Directions, 1955.

Gatrell, Simon. "Thomas Hardy and the Dance." *Thomas Hardy Year Book* 5 (1975): 42–47.

Gerschel, L. "La Conquête du nombre: des modalités du compte aux structures de la pensée." *Annales Économies, Sociétés, Civilisations* 17 (1962): 691–714.

Gibson, James J. "The Mouth as an Organ for Laying Hold on the Environment." In *Symposium on Oral Sensation and Perception*, ed. James F. Bosma. Springfield, Ill.: Thomas, 1967, 111–136.

Gilpin, William. *Observations on the Western Parts of England*. London: Cadell & Davies, 1798.

Gittings, Robert. *John Keats*. Boston: Atlantic, Little Brown, 1968.

Glasscock, Michael E., III, Robert A. Cueva, Brett A. Thedinger, eds. *Handbook of Vertigo*. New York: Raven, 1990.

Goethe, Johann Wolfgang von. *Roman Elegies and The Diary*. Verse translation by David Luke; introduction by Hans Rudolf Vaget. London: Libris, 1988.

————. *Roman Elegies and Other Poems*. Trans. Michael Hamburger, London: Anvil, 1996.

Gosse, Edmund. "Richard Crashaw." *Cornhill Magazine* 47 (1883): 424–438.

Grattan Flood, W. H. *John Field of Dublin: The Inventor of the Nocturne*. Dublin: O'Loughlin, Murphy, & Boland, 1920.

Gray, Thomas. *The Complete Poems of Thomas Gray*. Ed. H. W. Starr and J. R. Hendrickson. Oxford: Clarendon, 1966.

Greenaway, Peter. *Flying Out of This World*. Chicago: University of Chicago Press, 1994.

Greene, Roland. *Post Petrarchism: Origins and Innovations of the Western Lyric Sequence*. Princeton: Princeton University Press, 1991.

Greenfield, Stanley B. *A Critical History of Old English Literature*. New York: New York University Press, 1965.

Greenoak, Francesca. *All the Birds of the Air: The Names, Lore and Literature of British Birds*. London: Deutsch, 1979.

Greer, Germaine. "Wordsworth and Winchelsea: The Progress of an Error." In *The Nature of Identity: Essays Presented to Donald E. Haydon by the Graduate Faculty in Modern Letters, the University of Tulsa*. Tulsa, Okla.: University of Tulsa Press, 1981, 1–13.

Gregory of Nyssa. "In Praise of Theodore the Great Martyr." On the Gregory of

Nyssa home page, ed. and trans. David A. Salomon and Richard McCambly (http://www.ucc.uconn.edu/~das93006/nyssa.html).

Gross, Kenneth. *The Dream of the Moving Statue.* Ithaca, N.Y.: Cornell University Press, 1992.

Grossman, Allen. *The Long Schoolroom: Lessons in the Bitter Logic of the Poetic Principle.* Ann Arbor: University of Michigan Press, 1997.

———. *The Philosopher's Window.* New York: New Directions, 1995.

———. "Summa Lyrica: A Primer of the Commonplaces in Speculative Poetics." In Allen Grossman with Mark Halliday, *The Sighted Singer: Two Works on Poetry for Readers and Writers.* Baltimore: Johns Hopkins University Press, 1992, 205–383.

Gummere, Francis B. *Old English Ballads.* Boston: Ginn, 1904.

Hackney, Stephen. "Colour and Tone in Whistler's 'Nocturnes' and 'Harmonies' 1871–1872." *Burlington Magazine* 136, no. 1099 (October 1994): 695–699.

Hamlyn, D. M. *Sensation and Perception: A History of the Philosophy of Perception.* London: Routledge, 1961.

Hamner, Robert D. *Derek Walcott.* New York: Twayne, 1993.

———, ed. *Critical Perspectives on Derek Walcott.* Washington, D.C.: Three Continents Press, 1993.

Hardy, Thomas. *The Collected Poems of Thomas Hardy.* London: Macmillan, 1952.

———. *The Life and Work of Thomas Hardy by Thomas Hardy.* Ed. Michael Millgate. Athens: University of Georgia Press, 1985.

———. *Under the Greenwood Tree.* London: Penguin, 1994.

Harris, Daniel A. *Inspirations Unbidden: The 'Terrible Sonnets' of Gerard Manley Hopkins.* Berkeley: University of California Press, 1982.

Harrison, Robert Pogue. *The Body of Beatrice.* Baltimore: Johns Hopkins University Press, 1988.

———. "Tombstones." In *Complexities of Motion: New Essays on A. R. Ammons's Long Poems,* ed. Steven Schneider. Madison, Wisc.: Fairleigh Dickinson University Press, 1999, 167–180.

Hart, Clive. *Images of Flight.* Berkeley: University of California Press, 1988.

Hartman, Geoffrey. *Beyond Formalism: Literary Essays 1958–1970.* New Haven, Conn.: Yale University Press, 1970.

———, ed. *Hopkins: A Collection of Critical Essays.* Englewood Cliffs, N.J.: Prentice Hall, 1966.

Hayden, Robert. *Collected Poems.* Ed. Frederick Glaysher. New York: Liveright, 1985.

Hazlitt, William. "My First Acquaintance with Poets." In *Selected Essays of William Hazlitt 1778–1830,* ed. Geoffrey Keynes. New York: Random House, 1948, 500–502.

———. *The Collected Works of William Hazlitt.* Ed. A. R. Waller and Arnold Glover. 12 vols. London: Dent, 1902.

Healy, Thomas. "Crashaw and the Sense of History." In *New Perspectives on the*

Life and Art of Richard Crashaw, ed. John R. Roberts. Columbia: University of Missouri Press, 1990, 49–65.

Hegel, G. W. F. *Phenomenology of Mind*. Trans. J. B. Baillie. New York: Harper, 1967.

———. *The Philosophy of Fine Art*. Trans. F. B. Osmaston. New York: Hacker Art, 1975 (reprint of 1920 edition).

Heidegger, Martin. *Poetry, Language, Thought*. Trans. Albert Hofstader. New York: Harper Colophon, 1971.

Heninger, S. K., Jr. *The Cosmographical Glass: Renaissance Diagrams of the Universe*. San Marino, Calif.: Huntingdon Library, 1977.

Henry, Elizabeth. *Orpheus with His Lute: Poetry and the Renewal of Life*. Carbondale: Southern Illinois University Press, 1992.

Herbert, George. *The English Poems of George Herbert*. Ed. C. A. Patrides. London: Dent, 1974.

Herder, Johann Gottfried. "Essay on the Origin of Language," trans. Alexander Gode. In *On the Origin of Language: Jean-Jacques Rousseau, "Essay on the Origin of Languages" and Johann Gottfried Herder, "Essay on the Origin of Language,"* trans. John H. Moran and Alexander Gode. Chicago: University of Chicago Press, 1966, 87–176.

———. *Plastik: Einige Wahrnehmungen über Form und Gestalt aus Pygmalions Bildendem Traume*. Cologne: Hegner, 1969.

———. *The Spirit of Hebrew Poetry*. 2 vols. Trans. James Marsh. Burlington, Vt.: Smith, 1833.

Herrick, Robert. *The Complete Poetry of Robert Herrick*. Ed. J. Max Patrick. New York: New York University Press, 1963.

Hesiod, *Theogony, Works and Days*. Trans. M. L. West. Oxford: Oxford University Press, 1988.

Hibbard, Howard. *Caravaggio*. New York: Harper & Row, 1983.

Hinks, Roger. *Michelangelo Merisi da Caravaggio*. London: Faber & Faber, 1953.

Hinnant, Charles H. *The Poetry of Anne Finch: An Essay in Interpretation*. Newark: University of Delaware Press, 1994.

Hockett, Charles F., and Robert Ascher. "The Human Revolution." In *Man in Adaptation*, ed. Yehudi Cohen. Chicago: Aldine, 1968, 315–332.

Hogarth, William. *Analysis of Beauty*. Ed. Ronald Paulson. New Haven, Conn.: Yale University Press. Paul Mellon Centre for British Art, 1997.

Hölderlin, Friedrich. *Essays and Letters on Theory*. Trans. and ed. Thomas Pfau. Albany: State University of New York Press, 1988.

———. *Poems and Fragments*. Trans. Michael Hamburger. London: Routledge & Kegan Paul, 1966.

Hollander, John. "Breaking into Song: Some Notes on Refrain." In *Lyric Poetry: Beyond New Criticism*. Ed. Chaviva Hošek and Patricia Parker. Ithaca, N.Y.: Cornell University Press, 1985, 73–89.

———. *The Figure of Echo: A Mode of Allusion in Milton and After*. Berkeley: University of California Press, 1981.

——. "The Music of Poetry." *Journal of Aesthetics and Art Criticism* 15, no. 2 (December 1956): 232–244.

——. *The Untuning of the Sky: Ideas of Music in English Poetry 1500–1700.* Princeton, N.J.: Princeton University Press, 1961.

——. *Vision and Resonance: Two Senses of Poetic Form.* New Haven, Conn.: Yale University Press, 1985.

Homer. *The Iliad.* Trans. Robert Fagles, introduction by Bernard Knox. London: Penguin, 1990.

Hopkins, Gerard Manley. *Gerard Manley Hopkins,* ed. Catherine Phillips. Oxford: Oxford University Press, The Oxford Authors, 1986.

——. *The Journals and Papers of Gerard Manley Hopkins.* Ed. Humphry House, completed by Graham Storey. London: Oxford University Press, 1959.

——. *The Letters of Gerard Manley Hopkins to Robert Bridges.* Ed. Claude Colleer Abbott. London: Oxford University Press, 1955.

——. *The Sermons and Devotional Writings of Gerard Manley Hopkins,* ed. Christopher Devlin SJ. London: Oxford University Press, 1959.

Hopton, Susanna. *A Collection of Meditations and Devotions in Three Parts by the First Reformer of the Devotions in the Ancient Way of Offices (Susanna Hopton); afterwards reviewed and set forth by the late Learned Dr. Hickes.* London: Spinckes, 1717.

Horace. *Satires, Epistles, Ars Poetica,* trans. H. Rushton Fairclough. Cambridge, Mass.: Harvard University Press, 1991 (reprint of 1926 edition, Loeb Classical Library).

Horkheimer, Max, and Theodor W. Adorno. *Dialectic of Enlightenment.* Trans. John Cumming. New York: Continuum, 1990.

Howe, Susan. *My Emily Dickinson.* Berkeley, Calif.: North Atlantic Books, 1985.

Hsia, R. Po-Chia. *The World of Catholic Renewal.* Cambridge: Cambridge University Press, 1998.

Huelsenbeck, Richard. *Memoirs of a Dada Drummer.* Ed. Hans J. Kleinschmidt; trans. Joachim Neugroschel. New York: Viking, 1969.

Interpreter's Dictionary of the Bible. 4 vols. New York: Abingdon, 1962.

Iredale, Queenie. *Thomas Traherne.* Oxford: Blackwell, 1935.

Ismond, Patricia. "Self-portrait of an Island: St. Lucia through the Eyes of Its Writers." *Journal of West Indian Literature* 1, no. 1 (October 1986): 61–65.

Jakobson, Roman. "Shifters, Verbal Categories, and the Russian Verb." In *Selected Writings: Vol. II. Word and Language.* The Hague: Mouton, 1971, 130–147.

James, William. *The Principles of Psychology.* 2 vols. New York: Dover, 1950.

Jamieson, Robert. *Popular Ballads and Songs.* 2 vols. Edinburgh: n.p., 1806.

Johnson, James William. "Lyric." In *Princeton Encyclopedia of Poetry and Poetics,* ed. Alex Preminger. Princeton, N.J.: Princeton University Press, 1965, 460–470.

Johnson, W. R. *The Idea of Lyric: Lyric Modes in Ancient and Modern Poetry.* Berkeley: University of California Press, 1982.

Jones, Inigo. *The Most Notable Antiquity of Great Britain Vulgarly Called Stone-*

Henge on Salisbury Plain. Restored by Inigo Jones, Esquire, Architect General to the Late King. London: James Flesher for Daniel Pakeman and Laurence Chapman, 1655.

Jones, Mark. *The Lucy Poems: A Case Study in Literary Knowledge.* Toronto: University of Toronto Press, 1995.

Jonson, Ben. *The Complete Poetry of Ben Jonson.* Ed. William B. Hunter. New York: New York University Press, 1963.

Jordan, Richard Douglas. *The Temple of Eternity: Thomas Traherne's Philosophy of Time.* Port Washington, N.Y.: Kennikat, 1972.

Josipovici, Gabriel. *Touch.* New Haven, Conn.: Yale University Press, 1996.

Judovitz, Dalia. "Philosophy and Poetry: The Difference between Them in Plato and Descartes." In *Literature and the Question of Philosophy,* ed. Anthony J. Cascardi. Baltimore: Johns Hopkins University Press, 1987, 26–51.

———. *Subjectivity and Representation in Descartes: The Origins of Modernity.* Cambridge: Cambridge University Press, 1988.

Jullian, René. *Caravage.* Paris: IAC, 1961.

Kallberg, Jeffrey. "The Harmony of the Tea Table: Gender and Ideology in the Piano Nocturne," *Representations* 39 (Summer 1992): 102–133.

———. "The Rhetoric of Genre: Chopin's Nocturne in G Minor." *19th-Century Music* 11, no. 3 (Spring 1988): 238–261.

———. "Understanding Genre: A Reinterpretation of the Early Piano Nocturne." In *Atti del XIV Congresso della Società Internazionale di Musicologia: Trasmissione e recezione delle forme di cultura musicale.* Bologna, 1987. Torino: EDT, 1990, Papers III: 775–779.

Kant, Immanuel. *Critique of Judgment.* Trans. Werner S. Pluhar. Indianapolis: Hackett, 1987.

———. *Critique of Pure Reason.* Trans. F. Max Müller. Garden City, N.Y.: Doubleday/Anchor, 1966.

Keats, John. *The Complete Poems.* Ed. John Barnard. London: Penguin, 1988.

———. *Keats: The Poetical Works.* Ed. H. W. Garrod. Oxford: Oxford University Press, 1982.

———. *The Letters of John Keats.* 2 vols. Ed. Maurice Buxton Forman. Oxford: Oxford University Press, 1931.

Kent, George E. *A Life of Gwendolyn Brooks.* Lexington: University Press of Kentucky, 1990.

Keysler, Johann Georg. *Antiquitates Selectae Septentrionales et Celticae.* Hanover: Foersteri, 1720.

Kiell, Norman. *Varieties of Sexual Experience: Psychosexuality in Literature.* New York: International Universities Press, 1976.

King, James. *William Cowper: A Biography.* Durham, N.C.: Duke University Press, 1986.

Klibansky, Raymond, Erwin Panofsky, and Fritz Saxl. *Saturn and Melancholy: Studies in the History of Natural Philosophy, Religion and Art.* London: Nelson, 1964.

Kluckhohn, Clyde, and Dorothea Leighton. *The Navaho.* New York: Anchor, 1962.

Koethe, John. *Poetry at One Remove: Essays.* Ann Arbor: University of Michigan Press, 2000.

Komachi, Ono no, and Izumi Shikibu. *The Ink Dark Moon: Love Poems by Ono no Komachi and Izumi Shikibu, Women of the Ancient Court of Japan.* Trans. Jane Hirshfield, with Mariko Aratani. New York: Vintage, 1990.

Korn, A. L. "Puttenham and the Oriental Pattern-Poem." *Comparative Literature* 6, no. 4 (Fall 1954): 289–303.

Kristeva, Julia. "Revolution in Poetic Language." In *The Kristeva Reader,* ed. Toril Moi. New York: Columbia University Press, 1986, 90–136.

Lacan, Jacques. *The Four Fundamental Concepts of Psycho-Analysis.* Ed. Jacques-Alain Miller; trans. Alan Sheridan. New York: Norton, 1973.

Lacche, Luigi. "'Le Notti malinconiche': Esecuzioni capitali e disciplinamento nell'Italia del XVII secoli." *Laboratorio di storia* 3 (1991): 94–126. Florence: Ponte alle Grazie.

Langan, Celeste. *Romantic Vagrancy: Wordsworth and the Simulation of Freedom.* Cambridge: Cambridge University Press, 1995.

Langer, Susanne K. *Feeling and Form.* London: Routledge & Kegan Paul, 1953.

———. *Mind: An Essay on Human Feeling.* 2 vols. Baltimore: Johns Hopkins University Press, 1972.

Leach, MacEdward, ed. *The Ballad Book.* New York: Barnes, 1955.

Leach, Maria, ed., and Jerome Fried, associate ed. *Standard Dictionary of Folklore, Mythology and Legend.* New York: Funk & Wagnalls, 1949.

Leder, Drew. *The Absent Body.* Chicago: University of Chicago Press, 1998.

Leishman, J. B. *Themes and Variations in Shakespeare's Sonnets.* London: Hutchinson, 1961.

Leithauser, Brad. "Ancestral Rhyme." *New Yorker* 60, no. 52 (11 February 1990): 91–95.

Lenneberg, Eric H. *Biological Foundations of Language,* with appendices by Noam Chomsky and Otto Marx. New York: Wiley, 1967.

Levin, David Michael. *The Body's Recollection of Being: Phenomenological Psychology and the Deconstruction of Nihilism.* London: Routledge & Kegan Paul, 1985.

Levinas, Emmanuel. "There Is: Existence without Existents." In *The Levinas Reader,* ed. Seán Hand. London: Blackwell, 1989, 29–36.

Levinson, Marjorie. *Keats's Life of Allegory: The Origins of a Style.* Oxford: Blackwell, 1988.

Lewalski, Barbara Kiefer. *Protestant Poetics and the Seventeenth-Century Lyric.* Princeton, N.J.: Princeton University Press, 1979.

Litz, A. Walton. *Introspective Voyager: The Poetic Development of Wallace Stevens.* New York: Oxford University Press, 1972.

Livermore, Ann Lapraik. "Turner and Music." In *Turner Studies* 3, no. 1 (Summer 1983): 45–48.

Longinus, *On the Sublime*. Trans. W. R. Roberts. Cambridge: Cambridge University Press, 1899.

Love, Harold. *Scribal Publication in Seventeenth-Century England*. Oxford: Clarendon, 1993.

Lowell, Robert. "The Muses Won't Help Twice." *Kenyon Review* 17 (Spring 1955): 317–324.

Lucas, D. W. *The Greek Tragic Poets*. New York: Norton, 1964.

Luck, George. *The Latin Love Elegy*. New York: Barnes & Noble, 1959.

Lyons, John. "Deixis and Subjectivity: *Loquor, ergo sum?*" In *Speech, Place and Action*, ed. R. J. Jarvella and W. Klein. New York: Wiley, 1982, 101–124.

Maidment, B. E. "Hardy's Fiction and English Traditional Music." In *Thomas Hardy Annual* 4, ed. Norman Page (1986): 3–18. Hampshire, Eng.: Macmillan, 1986.

Mallinson, Jean. "Anne Finch: A Woman Poet and the Tradition." In *Gender at Work: Four Women Writers of the Eighteenth Century*, ed. Ann Messenger. Detroit: Wayne State, 1990.

Mandrou, Robert. *Introduction to Modern France, 1500–1640*. Trans. R. G. Hallmark. New York: Holmes & Meier, 1976.

Mann, Phyllis. "Keats's Reading." *Keats Shelley Memorial Bulletin* 13 (1962): 38–47.

Mardon, J. Vera, as told to J. Stevens Cox. *Thomas Hardy as a Musician*. Monographs on the Life of Thomas Hardy, No. 15. Beaminster, Eng.: Toucan, 1964.

Mariani, Paul. *A Commentary on the Complete Poems of Gerard Manley Hopkins*. Ithaca, N.Y.: Cornell University Press, 1970.

Marks, Carol. "Thomas Traherne and Cambridge Platonism." *PMLA* 81 (1966): 521–534.

———. "Thomas Traherne and Hermes Trismegistus." *Renaissance News* 19 (1966): 118–131.

———. "Thomas Traherne's Early Studies." *Papers of the Bibliographical Society of America* 62 (1968): 511–536.

———. "Traherne's Church's Year-Book." *Papers of the Bibliographical Society of America* 60 (1966): 31–72.

Marler, Peter, and Christopher Evans, "Animal Sounds and Human Faces: Do They Have Anything in Common?" In *The Psychology of Facial Expression*, ed. James A. Russell and José-Miguel Fernández-Dols. Cambridge: Cambridge University Press, 1997, 133–157.

Martz, Louis. *The Paradise Within: Studies in Vaughan, Traherne, and Milton*. New Haven, Conn.: Yale University Press, 1964.

———. *The Wit of Love: Donne, Carew, Crashaw, Marvell*. Notre Dame, Ind.: University of Notre Dame Press, 1969.

Marvell, Andrew. *The Poems and Letters of Andrew Marvell: Vol. I. Poems*. Ed. H. M. Margoliouth. Oxford: Clarendon, 1927.

Marx, Karl. *Economic and Philosophic Manuscripts of 1844*. In *Karl Marx, Frederick Engels, Collected Works*, ed. James Allen, Philip S. Foner, Howard Selsam, Dirk J. Struick, and William Weinstone; trans. Clemens Dutt. New York: International, 1975, 3:229–346.

Masson, David I. "Sound." In *Encyclopedia of Poetry and Poetics*. Ed. Alex Preminger, Frank J. Warnke, and O. B. Hardison Jr. Princeton, N.J.: Princeton University Press, 1965, 784–790.

Mathers, Powys, trans. *The Book of the Thousand Nights and One Night*. 4 vols. New York: St. Martin's, 1972.

Mauss, Marcel. *Sociology and Psychology: Essays*. London: Routledge, 1979.

Mazzotta, Giuseppe. "Petrarch's Song 126." In *Textual Analysis: Some Readers Reading*. New York: Modern Language Association, 1986, 121–131.

McCarthy, Mary. *How I Grew*. San Diego, Calif.: Harcourt, Brace, 1986.

McGovern, Barbara. *Anne Finch and Her Poetry: A Critical Biography*. Athens: University of Georgia Press, 1992.

McLaughlin, Elizabeth. "'The Mermaid of Galloway' and 'La Belle Dame Sans Merci.'" *Philological Quarterly* 28 (1949): 471–476.

Melhem, D. H. *Gwendolyn Brooks: Poetry and the Heroic Voice*. Lexington: University Press of Kentucky, 1987.

Melville, Herman. *Collected Poems of Herman Melville*. Ed. Howard Vincent. Chicago: Packard, 1947.

Merleau-Ponty, Maurice. *The Phenomenology of Perception*. Trans. Colin Smith. London: Routledge, 1989.

———. *The Visible and the Invisible*. Ed. Claude Lefort; trans. Alphonso Lingis. Evanston, Ill.: Northwestern University Press, 1968.

Merrill, Linda. *A Pot of Paint: Aesthetics on Trial in "Whistler v Ruskin."* Washington, D.C.: Smithsonian Institution Press, 1992.

Meschonnic, Henri. *Critique du rythme: Anthropologie historique du langage*. Lagrasse: Verdier, 1982.

Messenger, Ann. "Selected Nightingales: Anne Finch, Countess of Winchelsea, et al." In *His and Hers: Essays in Restoration and Eighteenth-Century English Literature*. Lexington: University Press of Kentucky, 1986, 71–83.

Michelangelo [Buonarroti]. *Michelangelo, the Poems*. Ed. and trans. Christopher Ryan. London: Dent, 1996.

Miles, Josephine. *The Continuity of Poetic Language: Studies in English Poetry from the 1540's to the 1940's*. Berkeley: University of California Press, 1951.

———. *Wordsworth and the Vocabulary of Emotion*. Berkeley: University of California Press, 1942.

Miller, David Humphreys. *Ghost Dance*. Lincoln: University of Nebraska Press, 1985.

Miller, J. Hillis. "The Univocal Chiming." In *Hopkins: A Collection of Critical Essays*, ed. Geoffrey H. Hartman. Englewood Cliffs, N.J.: Prentice Hall, 1966, 89–116.

Miller, R. Baxter. "'Define . . . the Whirlwind': Gwendolyn Brooks's Epic Sign for a Generation." In *Black American Poets between Worlds, 1940–1960*, ed. R. Baxter Miller. Knoxville: University of Tennessee Press, 1986, 160–173.

Millet-Gerard, Dominique. "Une Réécriture 'fin de siècle' de l'*Enfer* dantesque: *The City of Dreadful Night* de James Thomson." *Revue de Litterature Comparée* 61, no. 2 (April–June 1987): 143–166.

Millier, Brett C. *Elizabeth Bishop: Life and the Memory of It.* Berkeley: University of California Press, 1993.

Milne, Lorus J., and Margery J. Milne. *The World of Night.* New York: Harper, 1956.

Milton, John. *John Milton.* Ed. Stephen Orgel and Jonathan Goldberg. Oxford: Oxford University Press, The Oxford Authors, 1991.

Mommsen, Theodor E. "St. Augustine and the Christian Idea of Progress: The Background of *The City of God.*" In *Medieval and Renaissance Studies*, ed. Eugene F. Rice. Ithaca, N.Y.: Cornell University Press, 1959, 265–298.

Montagu, Ashley. *Touching: The Human Significance of the Skin.* New York: Columbia University Press, 1971.

Moore, Marianne. *Collected Poems.* New York: Macmillan, 1951.

———. *The Complete Prose of Marianne Moore.* Ed. Patricia C. Willis. New York: Penguin, 1986.

———. *A Marianne Moore Reader.* New York: Viking, 1961.

Morris, Charles. *Writings on the General Theory of Signs.* The Hague: Mouton, 1971.

Murray, Gilbert. *A History of Ancient Greek Literature.* New York: Unger, 1966.

Nancy, Jean-Luc. *The Muses.* Trans. Peggy Kamuf. Stanford, Calif.: Stanford University Press, 1996.

Nelson, Lowry. *Baroque Lyric Poetry.* New Haven, Conn.: Yale University Press, 1964.

Nitchie, George W. *Marianne Moore: An Introduction to the Poetry.* New York: Columbia University Press, 1969.

Noel-Bentley, Peter C. "'Fronting the Dreadful Mysteries of Time': Dürer's *Melencolia* in Thomson's *City of Dreadful Night.*" *Victorian Poetry* 12, no. 3 (Autumn 1974): 193–204.

Norris, Margot. "The [Lethal] Turn of the Twentieth Century: War and Population Control." In *Centuries' Ends, Narrative Means*, ed. Robert Newman. Stanford, Calif.: Stanford University Press, 1996, 151–159.

Novalis. *Hymns to the Night.* Trans. Dick Higgins. Kingston, N.Y.: McPherson, 1988.

O'Hara, Frank. *The Selected Poems of Frank O'Hara.* Ed. Donald Allen. New York: Vintage, 1974.

Ortega y Gasset, José. *The Dehumanization of Art and Other Essays on Art, Culture, and Literature.* Trans. Willard R. Trask. Princeton, N.J.: Princeton University Press, 1968.

Osborn, James M. "A New Traherne MS." (London) *Times Literary Supplement* (6 October 1964).

Osmond, Percy. *The Mystical Poets of the English Church.* London: Society for Promoting Christian Knowledge; New York: Macmillan, 1919.

Ovid. *The Metamorphoses of Ovid.* Trans. Mary M. Innes. London: Penguin, 1955.

Owen, Wilfred. *The Collected Poems of Wilfred Owen.* Ed. C. Day Lewis. New York: New Directions, 1963 (reprint of 1920 edition).

The Owl and the Nightingale. Ed. Eric G. Stanley. London: Nelson, 1960.

The Oxford Book of Carols. Ed. Percy Dearmer, R. Vaughan Williams, and Martin Shaw. London: Oxford University Press, 1928.

Parfit, Derek. *Reasons and Persons.* Oxford: Clarendon, 1984.

Paton, Lucy. *Studies in the Fairy Mythology of Arthurian Romance.* New York: Franklin, 1960.

Patrides, C. A. "Appendix III: Some Secular Poems Parodied by Herbert." In *The English Poems of George Herbert.* London: Dent, 1974, 209–213.

Paulson, Ronald. "Turner's Graffiti: The Sun and Its Glosses." In *Literary Landscape: Turner and Constable.* New Haven, Conn.: Yale University Press, 1982, 63–103.

Peele, George. *George Peele.* Ed. Sally Purcell. Salisbury, Eng.: Fyfield, 1972 (reprint of Oxford: Carcanet, 1972).

Pennell, E. R., and J. Pennell. *The Life of James McNeill Whistler.* 5th rev. ed. London: Heinemann, 1911.

Perelman, Bob. *Ten to One.* Middletown, Conn.: Wesleyan University Press, 1999.

Perkins, David. *Is Literary History Possible?* Baltimore: Johns Hopkins University Press, 1992.

Perloff, Marjorie. *Poetry on and off the Page: Essays for Emergent Occasions.* Evanston, Ill.: Northwestern University Press, 1998.

———. *Radical Artifice: Poetry in the Age of Media.* Chicago: University of Chicago Press, 1991.

———. *Wittgenstein's Ladder: Poetic Language and the Strangeness of the Ordinary.* Chicago: University of Chicago Press, 1996.

Petrarca, Francesco. *Petrarch's Lyric Poems: The Rime Sparse and Other Lyrics.* Ed. Robert Durling. Cambridge, Mass.: Harvard University Press, 1976.

Philo. Trans. F. H. Colson and G. H. Whittaker. 10 vols. and supplement. London: Loeb Classical Library, 1981.

Picard, Max. *The World of Silence.* Trans. Stanley Goodman, Washington, D.C.: Regnery Gateway, 1988 (first published 1948).

Pico della Mirandola. *Heptaplus.* Trans. Douglas Carmichael. In *On the Dignity of Man; On Being and the One; Heptaplus,* introduction by Paul J. W. Miller. Indianapolis: Bobbs-Merrill, 1940, 85–174.

Piggott, Patrick. *The Life and Music of John Field, 1782–1837, Creator of the Nocturne.* Berkeley: University of California Press, 1973.

Piggott, Stuart. *William Stukeley: An Eighteenth-Century Antiquary.* Oxford: Clarendon, 1950.

Pinion, F. B. *A Commentary on the Poems of Thomas Hardy.* New York: Harper & Row, 1977.

Plath, Sylvia. *The Collected Poems.* Ed. Ted Hughes. New York: Harper & Row, 1981.

Plato. "Ion." In *The Works of Plato*, 4 vols.; trans. and ed. B. Jowett. New York: Tudor, 1936, IV:277–298.

———. "Phaedrus." In *The Works of Plato*, 4 vols.; trans. and ed. B. Jowett. New York: Tudor, 1936. III:359–449.

———. *Plato's Republic*. Trans. and ed. G. M. A. Grube. Indianapolis: Hackett, 1974.

———. *Plato's Timaeus*. Trans. Frances Cornford; ed. Oskar Priest. New York: Macmillan, 1959.

———. "The Symposium." In *The Works of Plato*, 4 vols.; trans. and ed. B. Jowett. New York: Tudor, 1936, III:275–358.

———. "Theaetetus." In *The Dialogues of Plato*, 2 vols.; trans. B. Jowett. New York: Random House, 1937, II:143–217.

Pliny. *Natural History*. 10 vols. Trans. H. Rackham. Cambridge, Mass.: Harvard University Press, Loeb Library, 1967, Vol. III, Book X, Section LXXXVIII.

Podro, Michael. *The Critical Historians of Art*. New Haven, Conn.: Yale University Press, 1982, 100.

Pointon, Marcia. "Materializing Mourning: Hair, Jewellery and the Body." In *Material Memories*, ed. Marius Kwint, Christopher Breward, and Jeremy Aynsley. Oxford: Berg, 1999, 39–57.

Ponsford, Michael. "Men after God's Own Heart: The Context of Thomas Traherne's Emulation of David." *Studia Mystica* 9, no. 4 (Winter 1986): 3–11.

Pope, Alexander. *Pope: Poetical Works*, ed. Herbert Davis. New York: Oxford University Press, 1983.

Pound, Ezra. *The ABC of Reading*, New York: New Directions, n.d.

———. *Personae: Collected Shorter Poems of Ezra Pound*. London: Faber & Faber, 1952.

Praz, Mario. *The Flaming Heart*, Gloucester, Mass.: Smith, reprint 1966.

Prigogine, Ilya, and Isabelle Stengers. *Order Out of Chaos*. New York: Bantam, 1984.

Prins, Yopie. *Victorian Sappho*. Princeton, N.J.: Princeton University Press, 1999.

Pritchard, Allan. "Traherne's *Commentaries of Heaven* (with Selections from the Manuscript)," *University of Toronto Quarterly* 53, no. 1 (Fall 1983): 1–35.

Propertius. *Elegies*. Ed. and trans. G. Goold. Cambridge, Mass.: Harvard University Press, Loeb Classical Library, 1990.

Proust, Marcel. *In Search of Lost Time: Vol. III. The Guermantes Way*. Trans. C. K. Scott Moncrieff and Terence Kilmartin; rev. D. J. Enright. New York: Modern Library, 1993.

Puttenham, George. *The Arte of English Poesie*. Ed. Edward Arber. London: English Reprints, 1869.

Rabaté, Jean-Michel. *The Ghosts of Modernity*. Gainesville: University Press of Florida, 1996.

Ramazani, Jahan. *Poetry of Mourning: The Modern Elegy from Hardy to Heaney*. Chicago: University of Chicago Press, 1994.

Reynolds, Myra. "Introduction." In *The Poems of Anne Countess of Winchilsea.* Chicago: University of Chicago Press, 1903, xvii–cxxxiv.

Richmond, W. Edson. "Some Effects of Scribal and Typographical Error on Oral Tradition." In *The Critics and the Ballad,* ed. MacEdward Leach and Tristram Coffin. Carbondale: Southern Illinois University Press, 1961, 225–235.

Richter, Hans. *Dada: Art and Anti-Art.* New York: McGraw-Hill, 1965.

Ricoeur, Paul. *The Conflict of Interpretations.* Evanston, Ill.: Northwestern University Press, 1974.

Riding, Laura, and Robert Graves, *A Survey of Modernist Poetry.* Edinburgh: Clark, 1928; Folcraft Library reprint, 1971.

Rilke, Rainer Maria. *The Selected Poetry of Rainer Maria Rilke.* Ed. and trans. Stephen Mitchell. New York: Random House, 1984.

Rimbaud, Arthur. *Rimbaud: Complete Works and Selected Letters.* Trans. Wallace Fowlie. Chicago: University of Chicago Press, 1966.

Roberts, John R., ed. *New Perspectives on the Life and Art of Richard Crashaw.* Columbia: University of Missouri Press, 1990.

———, ed. *Richard Crashaw: An Annotated Bibliography of Criticism 1632– 1980.* Columbia: University of Missouri Press, 1985.

Robinson, Jeffrey C. *The Walk: Notes on a Romantic Image.* Norman: University of Oklahoma Press, 1989.

Rollins, Hyder Edward, ed. *The Keats Circle.* 2 vols. Cambridge, Mass.: Harvard University Press, 1965.

Ronell, Avital. *Dictations: On Haunted Writing.* Lincoln: University of Nebraska Press, 1986.

Rorty, Richard. *Contingency, Irony, and Solidarity.* Cambridge: Cambridge University Press, 1989.

Rosenberg, Isaac. *Collected Poems.* Foreword by Siegfried Sassoon; ed. Ian Parsons. London: Chatto & Windus, 1979.

Ross, Alexander. *A Centurie of Divine Meditations upon Predestination and Its Adjuncts wherein Are Shewed the Comfortable Uses of This Doctrine; to Which Are Annexed Sixteen Meditations upon God's Justice and Mercy.* London: Young, 1646.

Rousseau, Jean-Jacques. "Essay on the Origin of Languages." Trans. Alexander Gode. In *On the Origin of Language: Jean-Jacques Rousseau, "Essay on the Origin of Languages" and Johann Gottfried Herder, "Essay on the Origin of Language,"* trans. John H. Moran and Alexander Gode. Chicago: University of Chicago Press, 1966, 1–83.

Russell, Bertrand. *Introduction to Mathematics.* New York: Macmillan, 1920.

Sabourin, Leopold. *The Psalms: Their Origin and Meaning.* 2 vols. New York: Society of St. Paul, 1969.

Sacks, Peter. *The English Elegy: Readings in the Genre from Spenser to Yeats.* Baltimore: Johns Hopkins University Press, 1985.

Saintsbury, George. *Historical Manual of English Prosody.* London: Macmillan, 1914.

Salvaggio, Ruth. *Enlightened Absence: Neo-classical Configurations of the Feminine.* Urbana: University of Illinois Press, 1988.

Sapir, Edward. "Song Recitative in Paiute Mythology." *Journal of American Folklore* 23 (1910): 456–457.

Sappho. *Sappho: A Garland.* Trans. Jim Powell. New York: Farrar, Straus, & Giroux, 1993.

Sassoon, Siegfried. *The War Poems of Siegfried Sassoon.* Ed. Rupert Hart-Davis. London: Faber & Faber, 1983.

Schachtel, Ernest G. *Metamorphosis: On the Development of Affect, Perception, Attention, and Memory.* New York: Basic Books, 1959.

Schafer, R. Murray. "Acoustic Space." In *Dwelling, Place, and Environment: Towards a Phenomenology of Person and World,* ed. David Seamon and Robert Mugerauer. Dordrecht: Martinus Nijhoff, 1985.

Schiff, William, and Emerson Foulke. *Tactual Perception: A Sourcebook.* Cambridge: Cambridge University Press, 1985.

Schilder, Paul. *The Image and Appearance of the Human Body.* New York: International Universities Press, 1950.

Schiller, Friedrich. *On the Aesthetic Education of Man in a Series of Letters.* Trans. Reginald Snell. New Haven, Conn.: Yale University Press, 1954.

Schneider, Elizabeth. *T. S. Eliot: The Pattern in the Carpet.* Berkeley: University of California Press, 1975.

Schweik, Susan. *A Gulf So Deeply Cut: American Women Poets and the Second World War.* Madison: University of Wisconsin Press, 1991.

Scipione [Gino Bonichi]. *La Terra è secca, ha sete.* Trans. Brunella Antomarini and Susan Stewart. Milan: Charta, 2001.

Scott, Sir Walter. *Minstrelsy of the Scottish Border.* 4 vols. Ed. T. F. Henderson. Edinburgh: Oliver & Boyd, 1932.

Seelig, Sharon Cadman. *The Shadow of Eternity. Belief and Structure in Herbert, Vaughan and Traherne.* Louisville: University Press of Kentucky, 1981.

Serres, Michel. *Genesis.* Trans. Genevieve James and James Nielson. Ann Arbor: University of Michigan Press, 1995.

———. *Les Cinq Sens.* Paris: Grasset, 1985.

Seymour-Smith, Martin. *Hardy.* London: Bloomsbury, 1974.

Shaftesbury, Anthony, Earl of. *The Life, Unpublished Letters, and Philosophical Regimen of Anthony, Earl of Shaftesbury.* Ed. Benjamin Rand. London: Swan Sonnenschein, 1900.

Shakespeare, William. *The Merchant of Venice.* In *Arden Edition of the Works of William Shakespeare,* ed. John Russell Brown. Cambridge, Mass.: Harvard University Press, 1959.

———. *A Midsummer Night's Dream.* Ed. Arthur Quiller-Couch and John Dover Wilson. Cambridge: Cambridge University Press, 1968.

———. *Shakespeare's Sonnets.* Ed. Katherine Duncan-Jones. London: Nelson, The Arden Shakespeare, 1997.

————. *The Tragedy of Hamlet, Prince of Denmark.* Ed. George Lyman Kittredge; rev. Irving Ribner. Waltham, Mass.: Blaisdell, 1967.

Sharp, Cecil J. *The Country Dance Book: Containing a Description of Eighteen Traditional Dances Collected in Country Villages.* London: Novello, 1909.

Sharpe, William. "Learning to Read *The City.*" *Victorian Poetry* 22, no. 1 (Spring 1984): 65–84.

Shaw, Harry B. "Perceptions of Men in the Early Works of Gwendolyn Brooks." In *Black American Poets between Worlds,* ed. R. Baxter Miller. Knoxville: University of Tennessee Press, 1986, 136–159.

Shelley, Percy. *Letters of Percy Bysshe Shelley.* 2 vols. Ed. Frederick L. Jones. Oxford: Clarendon, 1964.

————. *Shelley's Poetry and Prose.* Ed. Donald Reiman and Sharon Powers. New York: Norton, 1977.

Sherrington, Alison. *Mystical Symbolism in the Poetry of Thomas Traherne.* Queensland: University of Queensland Press, 1970.

Shiff, Richard, and David Sylvester. *Willem de Kooning's Paintings: Essays by David Sylvester and Richard Shiff.* Washington, D.C.: National Gallery of Art; New Haven, Conn.: Yale University Press, 1994.

Sicherman, Carol Marks. "Thomas Traherne's Commonplace Book." *Papers of the Bibliographical Society of America* 58 (1964): 458–465.

————. "Traherne's Ficino Notebook." *Papers of the Bibliographical Society of America* 63 (1969): 73–81.

Sidney, Sir Philip. *An Apology for Poetry.* Ed. Forrest G. Robinson. Indianapolis: Bobbs-Merrill, 1970.

Simmel, Georg. *Simmel on Culture.* Ed. David Frisby and Mike Featherstone. London: Sage, 1997.

Simmon, Jeannot. *Vertigo: Schwindet der modernen Kunst.* Munich: Klinkhardt & Biermann, 1990.

Skelton, John. *The Complete Poems of John Skelton.* Ed. Philip Henderson. London: Dent, 1931.

Slote, Bernice. "The Climate of Keats's 'La Belle Dame sans Merci.'" *Modern Language Quarterly* 21 (1961): 195–207.

Smart, J. J. C. "Time." In *The Encyclopedia of Philosophy,* ed. Paul Edwards. New York: Macmillan, 7: 126–134.

Smith, Barbara Herrnstein. *Poetic Closure: A Study of How Poems End.* Chicago: University of Chicago Press, 1968.

Smith, Julia. "Susanna Hopton: A Biographical Account." *Notes and Queries* 38, no. 2 (June 1991): 165–172.

Snell, Bruno. *The Discovery of the Mind in Greek Philosophy and Literature.* New York: Dover, 1982 (reprint of 1953 ed.: *The Discovery of the Mind: The Greek Origins of European Thought,* trans. T. G. Rosenmeyer).

Southworth, James Granville. *The Poetry of Thomas Hardy.* New York: Russell & Russell, 1962.

Spenser, Edmund. *The Poetical Works of Edmund Spenser.* Ed. J. C. Smith and E. De Selincourt. London: Oxford, 1960.

Sperry, Stuart M. *Keats the Poet.* Princeton, N.J.: Princeton University Press, 1994 (reprint of 1973 edition).

Stanford, Ann Folwell. "Like Narrow Banners for Some Gathering War: Readers, Aesthetics, and Gwendolyn Brooks's 'The Sundays of Satin-Legs Smith.'" *College Literature* 17, nos. 2–3 (1990): 162–182.

Stanhope, Philip Dormer, Lord Chesterfield. *Letters of Lord Chesterfield to His Son.* Ed. Ernest Rhys. London: Dent, 1929.

Starobinski, Jean. "The Natural and Literary History of Bodily Sensation." *Zone* 4 (1989): 350–393.

Stevens, Wallace. *The Collected Poems of Wallace Stevens.* New York: Knopf, 1969.

———. *Wallace Stevens: The Palm at the End of the Mind.* Ed. Holly Stevens. New York: Knopf, 1971.

Stewart, Stanley. *The Expanded Voice: The Art of Thomas Traherne.* San Marino, Calif.: Huntington Library, 1970.

Stewart, Susan. *Crimes of Writing: Problems in the Containment of Representation.* Oxford: Oxford University Press, 1991.

Stillinger, Jack. *The Texts of Keats's Poems.* Cambridge, Mass.: Harvard University Press, 1974.

Stuart, Douglas K. *Studies in Early Hebrew Meter.* Missoula, Mont.: Scholars Press for the Harvard Semitic Museum, 1976.

Summers, David. *The Judgment of Sense: Renaissance Naturalism and the Rise of Aesthetics.* Cambridge: Cambridge University Press, 1987.

Swanton, John. ed. *Tlingit Myths and Texts.* Bulletin 39, Bureau of American Ethnology. Washington, D.C.: Smithsonian Institution, 1919.

Swift, Jonathan. *The Poems of Jonathan Swift.* 3 vols. Ed. Harold Williams. Oxford: Clarendon, 1958.

Sylvia, Richard A. "Thomas Hardy's 'The Voice' in the Context of Poems of 1912–1913." *Thomas Hardy Year Book* 17 (1988): 20–33.

Tasso, Torquato. *Jerusalem Delivered.* Trans. and ed. Ralph Nash. Detroit: Wayne State University Press, 1987.

Tate, Claudia. "Anger So Flat: Gwendolyn Brooks's 'Annie Allen.'" In *A Life Distilled: Gwendolyn Brooks, Her Poetry and Fiction,* ed. Maria K. Mootry and Gary Smith. Urbana: University of Illinois Press, 1987, 140–152.

Taylor, Charles. *Hegel.* Cambridge: Cambridge University Press, 1975.

———. *Sources of the Self: The Making of the Modern Identity.* Cambridge, Mass.: Harvard University Press, 1989.

Taylor, Dennis. *Hardy's Metres and Victorian Prosody.* Oxford: Clarendon, 1982.

Taylor, Thomas. *Thomas Taylor, the Platonist. Selected Writings.* Ed. Kathleen Raine and George Mills. London: Harper, Routledge & Kegan Paul, 1969.

Tennyson, Alfred, Lord. *The Poems of Tennyson.* Ed. Christopher Ricks. New York: Norton; London: Longman, 1969.

Terada, Rei. *Derek Walcott's Poetry: American Mimicry.* Boston: Northeastern University Press, 1992.

Teresa of Avila. *The Complete Works of Saint Teresa of Jesus.* Trans. and ed. E. Allison Peers. London: Sheed & Ward, 1946.

———. *The Life of Teresa of Jesus.* Trans. E. Allison Peers. New York: Doubleday, 1991.

Thomas, Dylan. *The Collected Poems of Dylan Thomas.* New York: New Directions, 1957.

Thompson, Arthur R. *Nature by Night.* London: Nicholson & Watson, 1931.

Thompson, Denys. "Anne Finch." *Poetry Nation Review* 8, no. 6 (1982): 35–38.

Thompson, John. *The Founding of English Meter.* New York: Columbia University Press, 1989.

Thompson, William Irwin. *The Time Falling Bodies Take to Light.* New York: St. Martin's, 1981.

Thomson, James. *The Poetical Works of James Thomson; The City of Dreadful Night.* Ed. Bertram Dobell with a memoir of the author. 2 vols. London: Reeves & Turner, 1895.

Tillyard, E. M. W. *The English Epic and Its Background.* New York: Oxford University Press, 1966.

———. *Milton.* New York: Collier, 1967.

Toulmin, Stephen, and June Goodfield. *The Discovery of Time.* New York: Harper & Row, 1965.

Traherne, Thomas. *Centuries of Meditations by Thomas Traherne.* Ed. Bertram Dobell. London: Dobell, 1908.

———. *Centuries, Poems, and Thanksgivings.* 2 vols. Ed. H. M. Margoliouth. Oxford: Clarendon, 1958.

———. *Christian Ethicks.* Ed. Carol L. Marks and George R. Guffey Ithaca, N.Y.: Cornell University Press, 1968.

———. *Commentaries of Heaven.* ADD MS. 63054, British Library, London.

———. *Poems, Centuries and Three Thanksgivings.* Ed. Anne Ridler London: Oxford University Press, 1966.

———. "The Ficino Notebook." MS. Burney 126, British Library, London.

———. *The Poetical Works of Thomas Traherne.* Ed. Bertram Dobell. London: Dobell, 1903.

———. *Select Meditations.* Osborn ms. b.308, Beinecke Library, Yale University, New Haven, Conn.

Tsur, Reuven. *What Makes Sound Patterns Expressive: The Poetic Mode of Speech Perception.* Durham, N.C.: Duke University Press, 1992.

Valéry, Paul. "Poetry and Abstract Thought." In *The Art of Poetry,* trans. Denise Folliot. New York: Vintage, 1961, 52–81.

Vaughan, Henry. *Complete Poems.* Ed. Alan Rudrum. London: Penguin, 1976.

Venantius Fortunatas. "Tempora lapsa volant." In *Mediaeval Latin Lyrics*, ed. and trans. Helen Waddell. New York: Holt, 1933, 66–67.

Verlaine, Paul. *Oeuvres complètes de Paul Verlaine*. 2 vols. Paris: Messein, 1919.

Vesey, G. N. A. "Sound." In *The Encyclopedia of Philosophy*, ed. Paul Edwards. New York: Macmillan, VII:500–501.

Vico, Giambattista. *The New Science*. Trans. Thomas Goddard and Max Harold Fisch. Ithaca, N.Y.: Cornell University Press, 1970.

Viguer, Jean-Claude Maire. "Valenze della notte in alcune esperienze religiose medievali (Italia centrale, XIII–XIV secolo)." *Laboratorio di storia* 3 (1991): 23–29. Florence: Ponte alle Grazie.

Vinge, Louise. *The Five Senses: Studies in a Literary Tradition*. Lund: Gleerup, 1975.

Virgil. *The Aeneid of Virgil*. Trans. Allen Mandelbaum. Berkeley: University of California Press, 1981.

von la Roche, Sophie. *Sophie in London 1786, Being the Diary of Sophia v. la Roche*. Trans. Clare Williams. London: Cape, 1933, 107–108.

———. *Sophie von la Roche, Tagebuch einer Reiser durch Holland und England*. Nachdruck der Ausgabe von 1788. Karben: Wald, 1997.

Wacior, Slawomir. *Strategies of Literary Communication in the Poetry of Thomas Traherne*. Lublin: Redakcja Wydawnictw Kul, 1990.

Waddell, Helen, ed. *Mediaeval Latin Lyrics*. New York: Holt, 1933.

Waddington, Raymond B. *The Mind's Empire: Myth and Form in George Chapman's Narrative Poems*. Baltimore: Johns Hopkins University Press, 1974.

Wade, Gladys. *Thomas Traherne*. Princeton, N.J.: Princeton University Press, 1944.

Walcott, Derek. *Another Life*. New York: Farrar, Straus, 1973.

———. "The Caribbean: Culture or Mimicry?" [1974]. Reprinted in *Critical Perspectives on Derek Walcott*, ed. Robert Hamner. Washington, D.C.: Three Continents, 1993, 51–57.

———. *The Gulf*. New York: Farrar, Straus, & Giroux, 1970.

———. "An Interview with Derek Walcott," with J. P. White. *Green Mountains Review* 4 (1990): 16–35.

———. *Omeros*. New York: Farrar, Straus, & Giroux, 1990.

———. *Sea Grapes*. New York: Farrar, Straus, & Giroux, 1976.

———. *The Star-Apple Kingdom*. New York: Farrar, Straus, & Giroux, 1979.

Walker, Carol Kyros. *Walking North With Keats*. New Haven, Conn.: Yale University Press, 1992.

Wallace, John Malcolm. "Thomas Traherne and the Structure of Meditation." *English Literary History* 25, no. 2 (June 1958): 79–89.

Ward, Aileen. *John Keats: The Making of a Poet*. New York: Viking, 1963.

Warnock, Mary. *Imagination and Time*. Oxford: Blackwell, 1994.

Warren, Austin. *Richard Crashaw: A Study in Baroque Sensibility*. Ann Arbor: University of Michigan Press, 1957.

Warton, Joseph. *The Pleasures of Melancholy.* London: Dodsley, 1747.

Warton, Thomas. *The History of English Poetry.* London: Alexander Murray, 1870; reprint of London edition of 1778.

Washington, Mary Helen. "'Taming All That Anger Down': Rage and Silence in Gwendolyn Brooks's *Maud Martha.*" *Massachusetts Review* 24, no. 2 (Summer 1983): 453–466.

Wasserman, Earl. *The Finer Tone: Keats' Major Poems.* Baltimore: Johns Hopkins University Press, 1967.

Watson, Thomas. *The Hekatompathia or Passionate Centurie of Love* [1582]. Facsimile reproduction and introduction by S. K. Heninger Jr. Gainesville, Fla.: Scholars' Facsimiles and Reprints, 1964.

Webber, Joan. *The Eloquent "I": Style and Self in Seventeenth-Century Prose.* Madison: University of Wisconsin Press, 1968.

Webster, Grant T. "Keats's 'La Belle Dame sans Merci': A New Source." *English Language Notes* 3 (September 1965): 42–47.

Whistler, James McNeill. *Notes, Harmonies, and Nocturnes. Small Works by James McNeill Whistler.* Introduction by Margaret F. MacDonald. New York: Knoedler, 1984.

White, Norman. *Hopkins: A Literary Biography.* Oxford: Clarendon, 1992.

Whitman, Walt. *Complete Poetry and Collected Prose.* New York: Library of America, 1982.

Whitrow, G. J. *Time in History: The Evolution of Our General Awareness of Time and Temporal Perspective.* Oxford: Oxford University Press, 1988.

Williams, Raymond. *The Country and the City.* Oxford: Oxford University Press, 1973.

Williams, William Carlos. *Selected Poems.* New York: New Directions, 1968.

Willoughby, L. A. "Wordsworth and Germany." *German Studies Presented to H. G. Fiedler.* Oxford: Clarendon, 1932, 432–458.

Wilmot, John, Earl of Rochester. *The Complete Poems of John Wilmot, Earl of Rochester.* Ed. David M. Vieth. New Haven, Conn.: Yale University Press, 1968.

Wilson, E. C. *England's Eliza.* Harvard Studies in English 20. Cambridge, Mass.: Harvard University Press, 1930.

Wilton, Andrew. *Turner and the Sublime.* London: British Museum Publications, 1980.

Wimberly, Lowry Charles. *Folklore in the English and Scottish Ballads.* New York: Dover, 1965.

Wimsatt, W. K. *The Verbal Icon.* Lexington: University Press of Kentucky, 1954.

Winters, Yvor. "John Crowe Ransom or Thunder without God." In *The Anatomy of Nonsense.* Norfolk, Conn.: New Directions, 1943, 168–228.

Wittgenstein, Ludwig. *Philosophical Investigations.* Trans. G. E. M. Anscombe. New York: Macmillan, 1968.

Wohrer, Franz K. *Thomas Traherne: The Growth of a Mystic's Mind.* Salzburg

Studies in English Literature. Salzburg: Institut for Anglistik und Amerikanistik; University of Salzburg, 1982.

Wordsworth, Dorothy. *The Grasmere Journals*. Ed. Pamela Woof. Oxford: Clarendon, 1991.

Wordsworth, William. *The Letters of William Wordsworth and Dorothy Wordsworth, Arranged and Selected by the Late Ernest de Selincourt*. Ed. Alan G. Hill. Oxford: Oxford University Press, 1979.

———. *Lyrical Ballads*. Ed. W. J. B. Owen. Oxford: Oxford University Press, 1969 (1798 reprint).

———. *Lyrical Ballads and Other Poems, 1797–1800*. Ed. James Butler and Karen Green. Ithaca, N.Y.: Cornell University Press, The Cornell Wordsworth, 1992.

———. *Poems*. 2 vols. Ed. John O. Hayden. London: Penguin, 1977.

———. *The Prelude 1799, 1805, 1850*. Ed. Jonathan Wordsworth, M. H. Abrams, and Stephen Gill. New York: Norton, 1979.

———. *The Prose Works of William Wordsworth*. Ed. W. J. B. Owen and Jane Worthington Smyser. Oxford: Clarendon, 1974.

———. *Selected Prose*. Ed. John O. Hayden. London: Penguin, 1988.

Wrigley, Richard. "Sculpture and the Language of Criticism in Eighteenth-Century France." Unpublished manuscript, presented at the conference "Augustin Pajou 1730–1809," The Louvre, Paris, November 1997.

Wyatt, Sir Thomas. *The Complete Poems*. Ed. R. A. Rebholz. London: Penguin, 1988.

Wyschograd, Edith. "Doing before Hearing: On the Primacy of Touch." In *Textes pour Emmanuel Levinas*, ed. Maurice Blanchot. Paris: Place, 1980, 179–203.

Yates, Frances. *The Art of Memory*. Chicago: University of Chicago Press, 1966.

———. *The Occult Philosophy in the Elizabethan Age*. London: Routledge, 1979.

———. *A Study of* Love's Labour Lost. Cambridge: Cambridge University Press, 1936.

Yeats, William Butler. *The Collected Poems of W. B. Yeats*. New York: Macmillan, 1974.

Young, Edward. *The Poetical Works of Edward Young, with a Memoir by Rev. J. Mitford*. Boston: Houghton Mifflin, 1880.

Zeiler, Martin. *Centuria III. Variarum Quaestionum, Oder, das Dritte Hundert Fragen von allerley Materien und Sachen*. Ulm: Wildeysen, 1659.

———. *Centuria Variarum Quaestionum, Oder Ein Hundert Fragen, von allerley Materien und Sachen*. Samt Unvorgreifflicher Antwort. Ulm: Wildeysen, 1658.

Zink, Michel. *The Invention of Literary Subjectivity*. Trans. David Sices. Baltimore: Johns Hopkins University Press, 1999.

Zuckerkandl, Victor. *Sound and Symbol: Music and the External World*. Trans. Willard R. Trask. Bollingen Series XLIV. New York: Pantheon, 1956.

INDEX OF POEMS

GENERAL INDEX

For titles of works, see under authors' names.